THE CLASSICAL BODY IN ROMANTIC BRITAIN

*

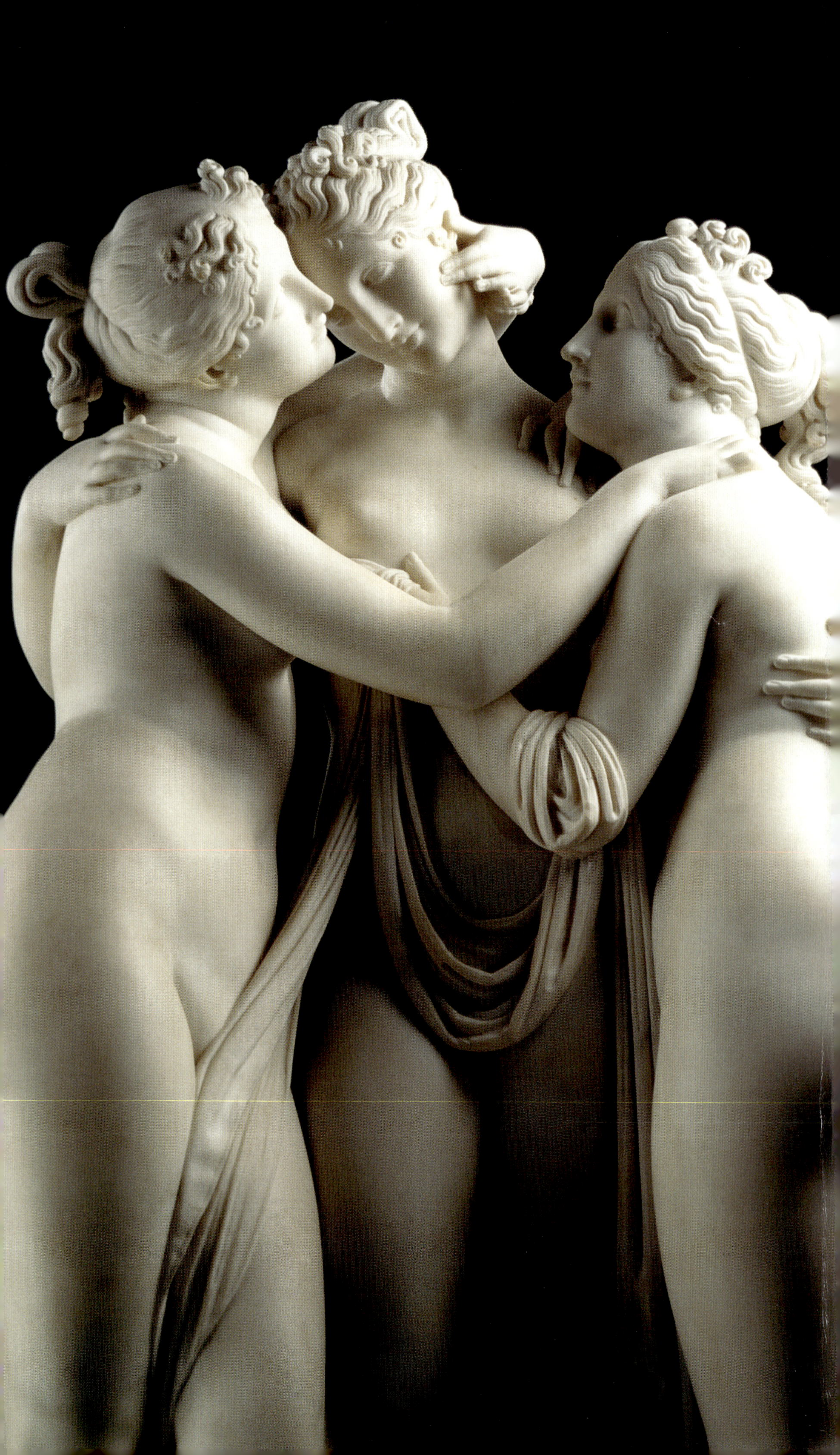

CORA GILROY-WARE

THE CLASSICAL BODY IN ROMANTIC BRITAIN

PAUL MELLON CENTRE
FOR STUDIES IN BRITISH ART

Distributed by Yale University Press
New Haven and London

First published in 2020 by the
Paul Mellon Centre for Studies in British Art
16 Bedford Square · London WC1B 3JA

paul-mellon-centre.ac.uk

ISBN 978-1-913107-06-2 HB

Library of Congress Control Number: 2019947772

British Library Cataloguing-in-Publication Data
A catalogue record for this book is available from the British Library

Designed by Dalrymple
Typeset in Robert Slimbach's Adobe Text
Origination by DL Imaging
Printed in China through World Print Ltd

FSC www.fsc.org MIX Paper from responsible sources FSC® C014688

Frontispiece:
Antonio Canova, *Three Graces*, 1813–16, marble.
Victoria and Albert Museum, London,
and National Gallery of Scotland, Edinburgh,
(detail of fig. 2).

CONTENTS

ACKNOWLEDGMENTS

THIS BOOK WAS written in London, Naples, New York, New Haven, and Los Angeles. In each of these places I was supported by people who, in various ways, contributed to the painstaking yet infinitely rewarding process of finding my voice. First, I must thank Martin Myrone and Elizabeth Prettejohn, both of whom were model supervisors during my doctoral studies. Their intellectual openness gave me a way into a world I would otherwise have glimpsed from a distance, and I am grateful for their unwavering encouragement over the years. I would not have reached them were it not for the curiosity and dedication of those who taught me during my undergraduate and masters degrees: Adriana Bontea, Matthew Bradley, Matthew Dimmock, Stefano Evangelista, Lara Fiegel, Nicholas Halmi, Ankhi Mukherjee, Stephanie Newell, Lindsay Smith, and William Spurlin. Kathryn Barush and Louise Bernard provided advice at exactly the right time.

Mark Hallett's commitment to creative scholarship is inspiring. I am humbled by his faith in me and want to thank him, Sarah Turner, Emily Lees, and others at the Paul Mellon Centre for actively nurturing the work of young scholars. Two fellowships at the Huntington Library gave me time to research, reflect, and write in a stimulating and beautiful environment. The generosity of Steve Hindle made those months productive as well as pleasurable, as did the support of Juan Gomez, Catherine Hess, Melinda McCurdy, and Catherine Wehry. Conversations with Kevin Gilmartin at the California Institute of Technology were invaluable. On the west side, Leslie Dick took me under her wing and shaped my thinking about objects. Back in London, the book was much refined by the guidance of Tamar Garb during a fellowship at the Institute of Advanced Studies, University College London. I have greatly benefitted from the company of Jason Edwards and Richard Johns. At crucial moments, Stephen Bann shared his precious time and deep knowledge. Thanks, too, to the Yale Center for British Art for awarding me a predoctoral fellowship that ended up being even more pivotal than I had anticipated.

Lidia Curti and Iain Chambers are fearless creativity personified. I am so grateful to be a part of their intellectual and artistic community, a group that includes my dear friends Alessandro Buffa, Silvana Carotenuto, and Alessandra Cianelli, who supported me while I was researching and writing in Naples. Esther Chadwick and Brigid von Preussen are my sisters, my intellectual comrades who have had more of a direct impact on the actual content of the book than perhaps anyone else. Lucia Trimbur is another adopted sister, someone who has helped me in so many ways and made the completion of this book possible.

My perspective on art and history has been contoured by communication with Giorgio Agamben, Anna Arabindan-Kesson, Thomas Ardill, Caroline Arscott, Malcolm Baker, Tim Barringer, Tim Batchelor, David Bindman, Elleke Boehmer, Grace Brockington, Luisa Calè, Stephen Cheeke, John Chu, Caroline Corbeau-Parsons, Matthew Craske, Penelope Curtis, William Fitzgerald, Hayley Flynn, Dehn Gilmore, James Glisson, Simon Goldhill, Dena Goodman, Darcy Grimaldo Grigsby, John Griswold, Catherine Hall, Catherine Hess, Daniel Immerwahr, Lars Kokkonen, Petra Lange-Berndt, Kwai Lau, Ed Lilley, Charles Martindale, Fiontán Moran, Molly Murray, Temi Odumosu, Tawny Paul, Veronica Peselmann, Carla Pestana, Ingrid Pollard, Mark Pomeroy, Alex Potts, Hector Reyes, Cecily Robinson, Shirley Samuels, Phillip Sargeant, Asif Siddiqi, Helen Small, Alison Smith, Jada Snow, David Solkin, Paris Spies-Gans, Greg Sullivan, Brandon Taylor, Tiziana Terranova, Claudia Tobin, Sarah Turner, Joris van Gastel, and Marina Warner. Inevitably, there are many more.

My friends Karen Alexander, Sonia Boyce, Hannah Donovan, Isaac Julien, Cora Kaplan, Theo Leanse, Oli Marshall, Mark Nash, Alondra Nelson, Luciana Parisi, Flemming Røgilds, Mandy Rose, Sivamohan Valluvan, Ed Vulliamy, and Nadira Wallace all expressed sincere interest in my work and gave me courage. Other friends and family left their mark on this book by providing much needed diversion: Sarah Aranda, Chloe Aridjis, Holly Arnold, Rachel Bolle, Maggie Boyd, Dan Canetti, Hazel Carby, Jamie Castell, Ingrid Chen, Adam Coghlan, Antonia Dawes, Lloyd de Beer, Michael Denning, Antonio Diaz, Paul Elliman, Craig Gilmore, Ruthie Gilmore, Darla Jane Gilroy, Matthew Gilroy, Hannah Goldfield, Cleo Parisi Gordon, Hannah Hammond, Dan Hancox, Hermione Harris, Harriet Hedden, Edd Humphries, Ellis Humphries, Vjosa Isein, Rebecca May Johnson, Maria Juur, Carole Latham, Claire Latham, Holly Latham, John Latham, Rachel Levine, Jill Lewis, Asma Maroof, Manal Massalha, Achille Mbembe, Robyn Mirams, Sarah Nuttall, Blake Pearlstein, Emmanuel Raymundo, Cath Ritchins, Ezra Rubin, Ruth Samuels, Marianne Sangster, Marieke Schut, Carlie Steadman, Alba Sunderland, James Sunderland, Catherine Trimbur, Catie Trimbur, Rahul Vanjani, Caroline Ware, Eleanor Ware, Elizabeth Ware, Honor Ware, Joanna Ware, Mikey Wood, and Maggie Yolen.

A generous grant from the Marc Fitch Fund provided support for this book's illustrations. Fran Ware's photographic talents were indispensable, and I must thank him for accompanying me on trips to acquire fresh images. Thanks also to Andrew Loukes and Simon Carter for letting us take pictures at Petworth and St. Paul's respectively.

It feels futile to try and distill my gratitude to Jack Latham into a few sentences. For the past decade we have been inseparable even when apart, and it is not an exaggeration to say that I continue to learn from him and laugh with him every day. He is my best friend, collaborator, and partner, someone who has an immeasurable effect on the quality of my life and work. To him I say "cheers."

Somehow I have not one but two kindred spirits for parents. I am fortunate to have been brought up by two such fun, kind, and intelligent individuals. Marcus, my brilliant brother, has picked up the pieces countless times. Until now, I've not had the chance to convey to him how much his patience and understanding, let alone his own intellectual and artistic prowess, mean to me. Together, the four of us have withstood so much and remain closer than ever. Infinite thanks go out to them, not least because their dreams made space for my poetry.

— IN MEMORY OF LIVIA CANETTI AND CLAYTON JANER —

PREFACE

FIRST PUBLISHED IN 1848, the *Life, Letters and Literary Remains of John Keats* by Richard Monkton Milnes contains an articulate error. Recounting the final months of the poet's life, Milnes states that Keats had been given a letter introducing him to Antonio Canova, the foremost sculptor of the age. Canova lived in Rome, where Keats had travelled to convalesce, if not to die, from tuberculosis. Sadly, writes Milnes, Keats's declining health meant that the letter could not be put to use: "the time was gone by when even Art could please, and his shattered nerves refused to convey to his intelligence the impressions by which a few months before he would have been rapt into ecstasy."[1] Subsequent biographers deduced that it was not Keats but his friend, the painter Joseph Severn, who possessed the letter. Yet in 1848, the thought of Keats and Canova wandering through the latter's studio – smooth, candlelit limbs looming from every corner – made perfect sense. It was an image that brought together two architects of a sweet, sensual classicism that had a tremendous impact on visual culture in its wake. To this day the smooth forms that obsessed both Canova and Keats are everywhere.

Sweet, sensual, smooth: such adjectives threaten to become clichés or empty abstractions when confined to the page. They are qualities that are tasted, seen and felt rather than grasped through written description. Diverse spectators have used them in response to sculptures by Canova, while generations of critics rhapsodize on Keats's peculiar sweetness, a quality associated with the feminine that goes hand in hand with the poet's tendency toward ornamental language. In Keats's *oeuvre* textures as smooth as Canova's figures abound, from the "smooth and lavender'd" sheets in "The Eve of St. Agnes" to Scylla the sea nymph's "smooth arms and lips" in *Endymion*, not to mention the poet's own references to the materiality of marble: the "smooth-sculptured stone."[2] But as compelling as it would be to zero in on this aesthetic, charting its afterlife in advertising, confectionery or cosmetics perhaps, this book is not based on Canova and Keats alone. My aim is to navigate the process by which the sweet, sensual kind of classicism with which they came to be associated during and, especially in Keats's case, beyond their overlapping lifetimes came to replace other strains of engagement with Greco-Roman art. It is my contention that the rise of this aesthetic in Britain during the first half of the nineteenth century was dependent on the fall of politicized appropriations of Greco-Roman antiquity. In the context of France, scholars have been thinking through the entanglement of classical art and contemporary politics for decades. It is well established that, in the years around the French Revolution, the naked human form – idealized according to the proportions of the most revered Greco-Roman statues – was bound up with the pursuit of a society unmoored from monarchy, its excessive tastes and religious traditions. Jacques-Louis David is the artist predominantly associated with this weaponized aesthetic. The situation in Britain is harder to discern, the politicized artists more obscure, the elite art education system comparatively nascent and therefore all the more vulnerable to subtle deviations from its official agenda. A counterpart revolution did not erupt in London, although many hoped, or feared, that it would. Numerous hitherto neglected artworks manifest these hopes and fears, the classical body being amenable, at this time, to harbouring them. One outcome of this entanglement of art and politics, I argue, is the ascendance of the sweet, sensual classicism crafted by Canova – a great celebrity and taste-maker in Britain – as well as Keats and a host of contemporaneous British artists in the aftermath of the Napoleonic Wars including William Etty, Edward Hodges Baily and John Gibson. Behind these artists' honeyed style is the failure of the previous generation's efforts to reconcile classicizing art and current events, attempts that Canova himself, and some of the others I discuss, witnessed first hand. The self-imposed remoteness of the likes of Etty, Baily and Gibson from partisan concerns and their capacity to be upheld by sculpture and painting betrays the desire to foster an alternative way of experiencing art objects: a way of seeing, and feeling, in direct opposition to utopian conceptions of Greece, the body, and the future, that had seized classicizing art at the close of the previous century.

This may read as one way to restage the all too familiar argument that, as the nineteenth century progresses, fine art is yoked to a bourgeois milieu impervious to the historical dynamics that conditioned painting and sculpture in earlier times. Without question, this is a period in which the audience for art in Britain was in a process of becoming rather than being, a time in which the seeds were sown for sculpture and painting as we know them today: rarefied commodities designed, by and large, to bring pleasure while providing a space outside and alternative to the "clamour of politics," to use Etty's phrase.[3] The triumph of sweet, sensual classicism over politicized classicism does reflect the wider cultural evolution taking place during this phase. But it also provides a way of thinking beyond the assumptions and stigmas that render this process not only a simplistic one, but a closed chapter from which we have nothing left to learn. This book is about the subjectivities of artists and the classical bodies – marble, plaster, clay, painted and flesh – that take us to the battleground between interested and obstinately disinterested attitudes toward beauty and form.

Broadly, this book demonstrates that, rather than derivative, the classical body was protean: volatile, active, and alive. The decision to designate the period "Romantic" Britain was motivated by the word's capacity to capture this sense of flux. Rather than just specify an era, "Romantic" implies the tide of anti-idealizing sentiment that grew during these years, one of the factors demanding that the classical body be updated according to the priorities of a fiercely nationalistic post-Napoleonic War culture. It is a word readily applied to poetry, often to landscape and genre painting, but with more difficulty to visual art focused on the exposed human form. Both "Classical" and "Romantic" appear in my title in order to highlight, from the outset, not the platitudinous passage from one to the other, but the coexistence and interaction between radical and reactionary, inanimate and living, idealized and naturalistic, fanatical and fantastical, as well as the gradations in between. Conveniently, the word also conjures the twilight of Revolutionary dreams, intergenerational transmission, the ascendance of industrialism and the effects of war, all of which are relevant to the following chapters. But first I offer a new vocabulary for talking about the image of the human form in British art of the period, a set of terms that I will deploy throughout the book. Indebted to Keats, whose name is virtually synonymous with the word "Romantic," these terms have helped me make sense of what, when I began to work on classicizing sculpture and painting in Britain of the period, felt like an intimidatingly eclectic array of material that refused the sweeping categories "Neoclassicism" and "Romanticism." My hope is that it does the same for others.

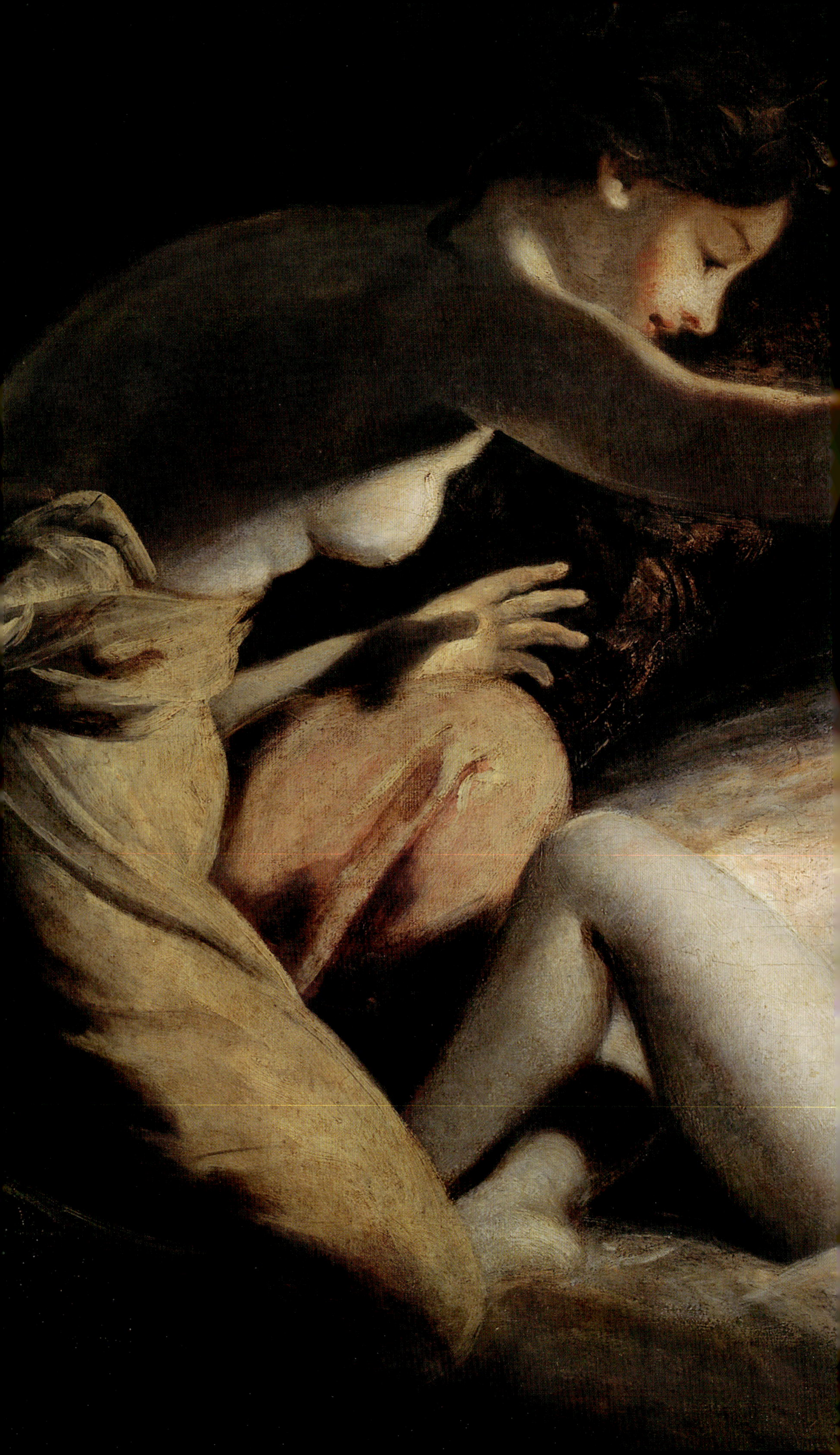

PSYCHE'S TRIUMPH
Toward a New Vocabulary

I have a dream, today …
Martin Luther King, Jr.

WHAT IS THE CLASSICAL BODY? Surely the answer is straightforward. In the context of artistic practice, the classical body is the embodiment of an aesthetic convention rooted in the figurative sculpture of Greco-Roman antiquity. The classical body can be realized through the imitation of this sculpture, through the imitation of works that imitate this sculpture – such as paintings and drawings by the most revered Renaissance masters – or through the artist's mind, which, after adequate training, can acquire the ability to select the "scattered beauties of Nature," to use a phrase found in eighteenth-century art theory, and fuse them into a more "perfect" whole than nature could produce.[1] Already this dense, multilayered and outdated definition suggests that the classical body is anything but straightforward.

The first hurdle is that figurative sculpture of Greco-Roman antiquity refuses to be seen as a monolithic body of work. Contained within it is a plethora of styles and temporalities that, due to enduring mysteries surrounding the precise attribution of objects, resists compression into a single formal exemplar. During the heyday of the classical body – the late eighteenth century – when the index of an artist's ambition was her dedication to perpetuating it, its metonym "the antique" was referred to as a stable notion immune from changes in taste and fashion. Yet after the import of authentically fifth-century Greek works – the Parthenon Marbles – to British shores toward the end of the Napoleonic Wars, the received notion of "the antique" was splintered, eventually leaving formerly supreme incarnations of the classical body like the *Apollo Belvedere* tainted by allegations of inferiority. On the one hand, this is an index of the historical and archaeological consciousness that rose as the nineteenth century progressed. It also exemplifies how the definition of the classical body was especially sensitive to historicizing tendencies, that it readily lay open to revisions at any minute. Long before the Marbles' arrival, anxieties surrounding the modern restoration of ancient objects had already ruffled the classical body's composure.

Second, the art of classicizing old masters is equally pluralistic. In Michelangelo's red chalk drawings, the classical body appears very different than in the

1 Detail of Joshua Reynolds, *Cupid and Psyche*, 1789 (fig.3).

trompe l'oeil niches of Correggio's Camera di San Paolo in Parma, for instance, or in Titian's Ovidian paintings for Philip II of Spain. Although complex, the contact between these artists and Greco-Roman sculpture has long preoccupied historians. My point is that while traditional academic art theory is concerned with harmonizing the perceived strengths of the canonized masters (Michelangelesque or Raphaelesque design, Venetian color, Lombardian softness of light) to forge a composite style, each of these artists/schools produced images of the body that, in Britain by the late eighteenth century, could fall under the umbrella of the classical.[2] Following the foundation of the Royal Academy in 1768, the institution's president Joshua Reynolds took it upon himself to condense both "the antique" and the established set of Italian masters into a single, consistent methodology. To inaugurate a new tradition in the mould of multiple extant traditions from bygone times and distant places was a paradoxical, even proto postmodern task that was bound to cause dissent. Reynolds's eventual successor as Royal Academy president, the Pre-Raphaelite painter John Everett Millais, made light of it when he quipped that his predecessor sought to make "the stem of a rose as big as the butt-end of a fishing-rod."[3] The outcome of Reynolds's model and, more generally, the relatively late establishment of the Royal Academy was a national school that, for the first sixty-odd years of its existence, is characterized by uncommon diversity. Even among those wedded to classicizing aesthetics and the so-called higher genres, there are stark differences from artist to artist, as critics pointed out at the time.[4] This is to say that, especially in relation to British art of the late eighteenth and early nineteenth centuries, the classical body does not mean just one thing.

Lastly and most importantly for my purposes, this variable entity I refer to as the classical body could, as an idealized image of the human form, be conceived of in vastly different ways. I do not mean in terms of technique, although this is true as per my previous point, but in terms of its power to signify, or not to signify, ideas beyond its form, ideas attached to a collective vision of how society ought to be. Despite nuanced studies such as Martin Myrone's *Bodybuilding: Reforming Masculinities in British Art*, in the context of Britain we are still accustomed to thinking of visual classicism before 1800 as an aristocratic field, one tied to the ruling classes and their patronage.[5] This is supported by scholarship that avoids the overwhelming diversity of contemporary classicizing art in favor of Grand Tourism and the more cohesive culture of collecting antiquities.[6] In the late eighteenth century, however, one of the many contrapuntal engagements with art of the past was the politicization of Greco-Roman sculpture – most of its prized indices then, thanks to the writings of Johann Joachim Winckelmann, assumed to be "pure" Greek – by artists and writers devoted to challenging the existing hegemony.[7] The artist most committed to this egalitarian classicism was the sculptor Thomas Banks. From a family that can be designated working class, his father a labourer on an estate in Gloucestershire, Banks was committed to bringing about social change through classicizing art and radical activism. Just these few details instantly destabilize prevailing assumptions about the nature of classical reception in Britain of the period.

As well as an activist, Banks was the most innovative sculptor of his day. This is not my own value judgment. Another common assumption about classicizing art is that it represents a set of constraints that only the avant-garde will loosen. But while his corpus of surviving marble figures struggles to be read as anticipating the avant-garde on a formal level, Banks made it a priority to overcome the constraints that had long been imposed upon sculptural practice. Usually it is Antonio Canova who is credited with updating contemporary European sculpture by taking the basic corporeal template provided by what were then most revered ancient statues, including the *Apollo Belvedere* and *Venus de' Medici*, and producing novel figures cast in original situations. Evidence suggests that Banks was actually first out of the two to venture in this direction and that Canova possibly followed his example. In 1817, Canova reflected on his time in Rome as a young artist recently arrived from rural Veneto. Back in 1779, he recalls, the careers of living sculptors were determined by the two things then desirable among patrons: restorations and copies of antiquities.[8] He goes on to list some of the notable practitioners in Rome at that time. One name on his inventory is that of "Bench," cited as one of several otherwise unnamed English sculptors. Although he left that year, Banks was in fact there when Canova arrived, having been based in Rome with his wife Elizabeth since 1772. I am not the first to deduce that "Bench" is Banks.[9] Yet the connection between the two sculptors is more significant than has previously been allowed. Canova implies that Banks was one of the sculptors who blindly went along with the demand for restorations and copies rather than create his own original designs. As Julius Bryant has acknowledged in a number of essays, this was not the case.[10] Rather than appeasing the mainstream of Grand Tourists able to afford such works, Banks designed sculptures that, while formally based on ancient relics, were of entirely his own invention. Once settled in Rome, Canova set out to do the same and, like Banks, initially found it hard to secure patronage.[11] Writing of Canova's early years in Rome, Hugh Honour ascribes the sculptor's refusal to play the game, as it were, and churn out restorations and copies to the influence of northern European artists based in the Eternal City, particularly the Scottish history painter Gavin Hamilton, who, according to Honour, stimulated Canova's pathbreaking "empirical approach to the antique."[12] Hamilton did take Canova under his wing and there is much to affirm that the painter's influence was seminal. Yet Canova's citation of Banks in the 1817 letter is enough to prove that there was a marked awareness of, even interest in, the British sculptor on his part. As Myrone acknowledges, the community of artists in Rome was teeming during these years.[13] It meant a lot to be singled out from the crowd, even more to be remembered forty years later, despite the fact that the letter suggests that prior to Canova's arrival, all living sculptors, including "Bench," were stuck in a rut which Canova's genius would guide them out of.

Crucial to this book are not the similarities between the sculptural innovations of Banks and Canova, but the momentous differences between their roughly contemporaneous "empirical approach[es]" to the antique. For Banks, the practice of making "the antique" his own formed part of a radical political vision. In his hands, the classical body became a vessel for utopian ideas tied to a particular image of ancient Greece that intersected with the wider pursuit of liberty permeating European culture over the course of the late eighteenth century, a movement reaching its climax during the Revolution in France. For him and others with equal faith in the possibility of a more equal society, the classical body was not necessarily an emblem of freedom and attendant virtues prized by radical activists. To me, the word "emblem" implies an image whose form and content are essentially immutable yet able to be transposed into different contexts while keeping meaning intact. Competing claims over Greco-Roman culture – especially the aristocratic – thwarted this kind of direct signification. Instead, it was the very dynamism of the classical body – the capacity of Greco-Roman forms to be refreshed and energized by the "empirical approach" – that rendered it a vessel that could be filled with convictions held by radicals. This idea of the classical body as a vessel, a container that can be loaded or emptied of notions that have nothing to do with the body as a somatic entity, is central to my argument. Often, the contents of a vessel are not visible on the outside of a container: that is, they are only known to those who imbibe. Meaning is not inscribed upon the surface of the form but contained within it and, as a result, is able to conceal itself when necessary. Hence the artist who deploys the classical body as a vessel for a political vision is able to uphold and circulate that vision while keeping their work within the bounds of the status quo.

The connection between radical politics and Greco-Roman sculpture, or rather classical Greek sculpture as represented in both its perceived "originals" and what we know now to be its Hellenistic or Roman works, was established largely through an oral tradition stemming from Winckelmann. As well as positing the Greeks as the most noble of all ancient civilizations, his *Geschichte der Kunst des Alterthums*, first published in 1764, claims that the freedom of the Greeks was a key ingredient in bringing forth their supremely beautiful art and supremely beautiful people.[14] The zenith of Greek freedom is held to be the democratic political system of fifth-century Athens, when the "high" style developed by Phidias, Polykleitos and Myron took shape, creating space for the emergence of the "beautiful" style cultivated by Praxiteles and others in the fourth century.[15] Winckelmann argues that art in Greece was nurtured by a lack of constraints in the minds of individuals and among the civic community at large: a way of life which, in his view, resounds beyond the fifth century in either direction.[16] For the artists who were Winckelmann's contemporaries, one implication of this idea was the possibility that art would improve if their social order was less hierarchical. Built on numerous precedents including Pausanias's reflections on Hellenic civilization, Pliny's *Natural History* and Whig theories of liberty, this causal relationship between freedom and aesthetics via the classical body proved influential.[17] Scholars have assessed its afterlife during the French Revolution, when the movement to dislodge the monarchy was anchored by references to classical art.[18] Whitney Davis observes that by the end of the century, Winckelmann's theory "became a cliché among political activists who echoed Winckelmann but lacked his learning."[19]

What for Davis is a mere cliché lacking erudition is for me a point of fascination. Following studies by Michael Baxandall and later David Bindman on the "vulgar" adoption of learned texts in artistic criticism and, in turn, in works of art, Banks can be seen as a proponent of a "vulgar Winckelmannianism" on the level of practice.[20] From the strictly connoisseurial to the queer, the scholar's output has multiple dimensions. The Winckelmann passed down to Banks was the author who identified a vital connection between classical body and self-determination. An English translation of the *Geschichte*, or the *History of the Art of Antiquity*, did not appear until well into the nineteenth century, long after Banks's death.[21] The sculptor would have gained familiarity with the text's most controversial passages through verbal discussion as opposed to reading. In Rome, Banks was involved with artist-activist groups that would have viewed Winckelmann's writings as a point of departure.[22] One of his close colleagues was the Anglo-Swiss painter Henry Fuseli, a cosmopolitan intellectual who had translated Winckelmann's *Gedanken über die Nachahmung der griechischen Werke* of 1754 into English as *Reflections on the Painting and Sculpture of the Greeks*.[23] In this earlier treatise, Athenian democracy is not credited with nurturing art and beauty. Rather, it is proclaimed that, in addition to Greece's temperate climate, the physical freedom enjoyed by every Greek citizen from birth nurtured their pre-eminent beauty and taste. Babies born in various parts of Greece, states the text's opening pages, were not wrapped in swaddling, hence their limbs were allowed to grow without obstruction in the open air.[24] This idea in particular inspired Banks and those in his circle, a network that included William Godwin and Mary Wollstonecraft. A common thread running through the literary and artistic output of this group is the invocation of Greece as the absolute antithesis of eighteenth-century Britain, where from a tender age the body was bound by corsetry and other restrictive garments. Arguments about the Greeks' bodily freedom threw into relief the barbarity of eighteenth-century custom, tied, as it was, to a hierarchical social order. Banks's "empirical approach to the antique" – that is, the adaptation of Greco-Roman sculptural exemplars into fresh, original designs – materialized the otherwise ethereal discourse on ancient Greece and freedom. This discourse was born from a fusion of two texts by Winckelmann, their oral reception and reapplication to champion a live cause. By 1790, this cause had very little to do with Winckelmann and his own agenda, yet drew from his claims nonetheless.

That Canova took up the "empirical approach" after arriving in Rome and, as the 1817 letter suggests, coming into contact with Banks's work connects politically charged sculpture to the kind practiced by the far better known artist. It forces these two engagements with the classical body into the same conversation, with one side deeply and consciously political, the other side forcibly removed from the prescribed set of ideological, social, and civic concerns that were dear to activists like Banks. Scholarship has tended to view Canova as a "gentle apolitical" or "escapist" artist, one who had no interest in the effusion of anti-establishment ideas that flourished during his early to mid-career.[25] Certainly, his activities during the Revolution and after the Napoleonic Wars,

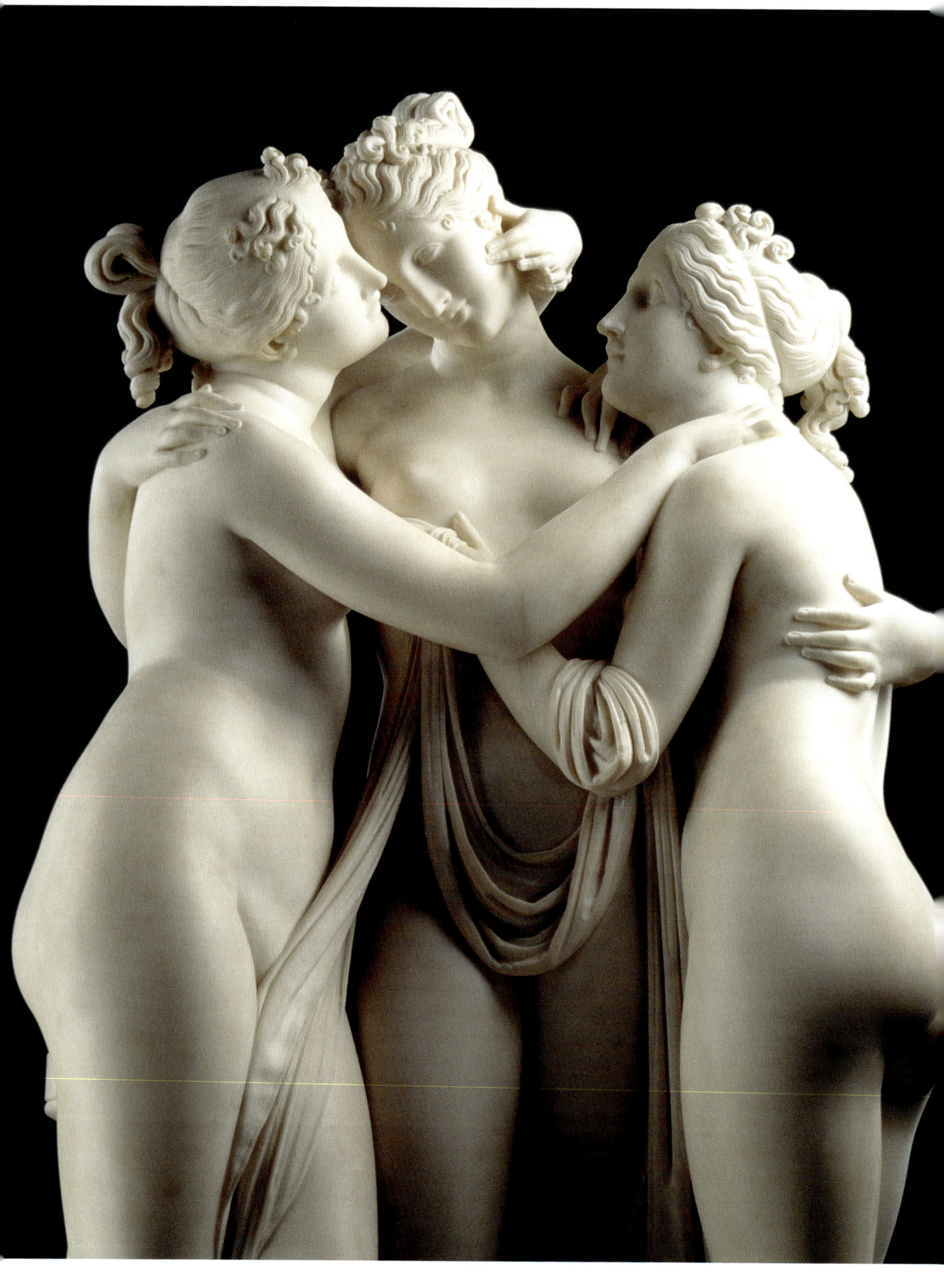

2 Antonio Canova, *Three Graces*, 1813–16, marble.
Victoria and Albert Museum, London, and National Gallery of Scotland, Edinburgh.

not to mention the tone of his intermedial artistic output, support the assertion that for him beauty and political liberty were different topoi, moreover topoi that needed to be cleaved apart. While the classical body-as-vessel is concerned with the notions that fill the container – the logocentric political discourse to which form and surface are subordinate – Canova's take on the human figure empties the body of all non-somatic contents. Accordingly, the exterior of the art object takes precedence. The image of the classical body is prized for the sensuality of its surface and capacity to conjure living matter. When the artist overrides the status of the body-as-vessel, a process I call "re-corporealization" occurs. Designed in 1810, a work like Canova's immensely popular *Three Graces* represents this incarnation; the softly yearning gazes, the play of interwoven limbs, the kinaesthetic emphasis on skin pressing against skin, all function to empty the classical body of any excrescent implications and turn it back into a somatic being, complete with all the mysteries and irrational desires that accompany bodies of flesh (fig. 2).

The act of unmooring the classical body from political discourse shifts weight to the ocular, superficial, and somatic qualities of the represented form. This book makes the claim that these two visual classicisms are not only intricately connected, but that they are also at war with one another. Chronologically speaking, this war parallels the French Revolutionary Wars, and although one side has won by the time of the Peace of Amiens in 1802, its conflict smoulders throughout the Napoleonic Wars and into the Victorian period. Of course, it is Canova's remote and sensual kind of classical body that triumphs over politicized classicism, or the classical body-as-vessel. Although Canova is rarely seen as a forerunner of aesthetes like Walter Pater and Edward Burne-Jones, the winning of this conflict by the side guided to victory by the Veneto-born sculptor had an unacknowledged influence on the character of classicizing imagery produced in Britain over the course of the nineteenth century and beyond, a point to which I will return later in this chapter. For now I want to emphasize that my argument is intended to apply exclusively to the history of art in Britain, where the binary of these two visual classicisms was especially fixed.[26] From a continental perspective, British artists of Banks's generation were perceived to be bastions of an interested classicism that threatened the sensuality of the represented body. The high-minded French aesthete Quatremère de Quincy warned Canova to stay away from English artists because their "rigid and cold" taste "lacks antique warmth, that truth, that profound expression which inspired the Greeks."[27] For de Quincy and others, the spirit with which antiquity was emulated was the crucial factor in determining the nature of an art object, and British practitioners like Banks were prone to draining the sensuality from the classical body and replacing it with prescribed, "cold," that is, non-somatic values.

In my account of this war there is a mediating figure, someone who, although not a visual artist like Banks and Canova, picked up on the conflict between politicized classicism and its sensual counterpart. A child of the period, John Keats was well aware of the changing orientation of art, particularly classicizing art, during his lifetime. Sculpture obsessed him. Carved matter suffuses his verse in terms of both content and form, causing literary scholars to call his poems "dream sculpture," "death sculpture," their heroes seen to inhabit "a threshold space somewhere between life and statuary."[28] From his reading of mythological dictionaries as a schoolboy to his encounter with the Parthenon Marbles to his imagined Grecian Urn, the impact of Greco-Roman objects on his formation has been thoroughly explored. Arguably more significant in relation to gauging the evolving priorities of British culture during his lifetime, Keats's response to contemporary art is relatively uncharted territory. Born in London in 1795, he would unquestionably have known of Canova. The sculptor's celebrity status in Britain meant that Keats would have grown up hearing that pleasing name even before he met his mentor Leigh Hunt, who knew Canova's *oeuvre* well. Mentioned in my preface, Keats's own sweet, sensual classicism has led scholars of both Keats and Canova to acknowledge their affinity.[29] Although there are no explicit allusions to Canova in his poetry, *Psyche Revived by a Kiss*, one of Canova's best known works then as now, designed in 1793, is widely accepted as a source for Keats's 1819 "Ode to Psyche." For both sculptor and poet, Psyche was a mythological figure who encapsulated the kind of art that shirked the burden of political concerns. Although technically goddess of the soul, Psyche was conceived of during the period as a tactile and erotic figure, one whose unparalleled beauty was all the more precious because it existed for no other reason than to be consumed and enjoyed. Later on I will return to Psyche and her hold over British artists during the period. The point I want to make here is that Keats and Canova are brought together by a shared investment in sensual surfaces and beauty purged of responsibility, for which Psyche provided an icon.

At the same time, however, there is significant common ground between Keats and Banks. Although his poetry is not as explicitly radical as, say, Shelley's, the poet voiced agreement with the project of the French Revolution, which Banks supported as it unfolded.[30] Keats was also derided as a "cockney" poet whose middling background rendered his engagements with Greco-Roman culture a travesty.[31] Born in London into a humbler family than Keats's, Banks can be seen as a proto-cockney classicist, one who confidently adapted ancient models into innovative works in spite of his class background. Unlike the genteel Canova, Banks made few attempts to be deferential to the elite, much to the chagrin of his colleagues at the Royal Academy. His adaptation of Winckelmann's learned claims into original works of art, the laborious manual art of sculpture no less, indicates the depth and extent of his belief in the importance of self-determination. Reynolds is said to have rhapsodized that Banks's "mind was ever dwelling on subjects worthy of an ancient Greek," a description foreshadowing posthumous appraisals of Keats as a natural Hellenist, an upholder of "the pure Greek ideal, because he had its essence in his soul."[32] Banks did not face the same degree of class-based derision that Keats received from conservative critics. On the whole, the physical nature of sculptural practice insulated him from allegations that, by opting to be a classicizing artist, he had ideas above his station. In 1802, however, a group of aristocratic men was gathered to keep in check the design of the second war monument Banks was commissioned to make for

St. Paul's Cathedral. These men, some of whom were part of the band of titled antiquarians, the Society of Dilettanti, saw themselves as the chief guardians of classical culture and expressed scathing opinions about the potential of the recently established Academy. They would not necessarily have been aware of Banks's activism, or at least the passion behind it; while he remained active until his death, his great skill as a sculptor could minimize his radical reputation. But the supervising body, later referred to as the "Committee of Taste," saw their claim over Greco-Roman antiquity as authoritative in relation to the sculptor's, anticipating the reaction against Keats's bottom-up classicism decades later.

Given the correlations between Keats and both of these sculptors, it is no wonder that his poetry becomes useful in navigating the conflict between their respective approaches. For the rest of this introduction, Keats will be an illuminating presence as I delve deeper into the war between representations of the classical body in art made during and beyond the poet's lifetime, a split spearheaded by Canova and Banks respectively. While not technically a British artist, the Canova that concerns me is the Canova that Keats would have grown up hearing of: Canova the celebrity who influenced from afar, and later taught directly, several of the artists that feature in this book.[33] After looking closely at both sides of this war, I will arrive at the set of terms that I will use in each of the chapters that follow. Lifted from Keats, these terms answer what I consider an urgent need for a new vocabulary with which to describe the classical body in British art of the period.

— RE-ENCHANTING THE CLASSICAL BODY —

It is 2018 and I am in a "Vinyasa Flow" yoga class. The teacher instructs us to make each pose "feel sensual"; "make it look sensual," she continues, "I want to see slow, dancer-like movements." While I think I understand what it means to make the poses feel sensual, what does it mean to make an action look sensual? Luckily, the specification "dancer-like" hints that for a form to look sensual, it ought to have, in the teacher's eyes, a balletic grace. The rigid angles of a pose like "warrior 2" are softened and smoothed, allowing the fleshier parts of the body to release. I am distracted. In my mind, the instruction underscores the fact that, in the Anglophone world at least, most modern yoga practices are a bastardization of an ancient tradition. Another teacher once told the class that the "warrior" poses were performed by Indian soldiers before going into battle, but it is clear that no one in the class is concerned with finding out more. Yoga's antiquity has itself become a myth. Sanskrit names for poses are used interchangeably with English words that may or may not be valid translations, while the philosophical tenets that were once essential to the practice are contradicted by the acrobatic, competitive mood of the class. Top 40 pop music chimes in the background. Although rooted in antiquity, yoga exists outside of time. It is ripe for the reinterpretation, the embellishment, the feminization that this teacher tells us to perform. Yoga's atemporality has allowed it to survive and to thrive.

Over two centuries earlier, a similar process began to catch on among sculptors and painters. Known collectively as "the antique," Greco-Roman sculptural exemplars were reinterpreted, embellished, and feminized, producing works of contemporary art so divorced from the relics of Greece and Rome that they evolved into something quite different. In Britain, this process began to be perceptible just after another type of art had achieved visibility: appropriations of "the antique" motivated by the belief that the way of life that allegedly gave birth to classical sculpture – freedom – can be recovered in the present day. These two practical engagements with the classical body are opposed. While they both update "the antique" by recasting it into new poses and characters, one stays truer to the "ideal Text of Antiquity," the other departs from it.[34] With its fixation on Greek freedom, one keeps itself simple. In order for the classical body to harbour a certain vision of how society ought to be, it must appear legible; paint is thin, color muted, marble left untreated or washed with coffee to render it more evocative of the relics of ancient Athens.[35] Conversely, the other kind of art is focused on the exterior. It softens and smoothens "the antique"; painted textures are made slick and buttery – the modern-day term "moisturized" is useful – while colors are rich and often changeable over time as a result of their layered, wet-in-wet application. Marble is carefully selected, prized for its quality, excessively polished and sometimes tinted with wax and pigment. As such, the second category loses its footing in Greece and Rome, bringing forth objects with a complex material construction as well as temporality. Consequently, these objects become more relevant to contemporary experience and, aided by the doomed fate of the political discourse around Greece and freedom, will eventually displace the other kind of art.

The sensual type of classicizing art is open about its eroticism. Material richness serves to mystify, to make seductively opaque, the bodies it showcases. Beyond either homosexual or heterosexual desire, the sensuality of such objects works to preserve art's eroticism in the face of delibidinizing politics, specifically what Edmund Burke, in reference to the French Revolution, describes as "that new, conquering empire of light and reason" that aims to sanitize social relations as it makes them more equal.[36] Closely linked to the experience of sensuality in art and in life, the imagination was an indispensable notion among artists committed to making this kind of object. Giorgio Agamben identifies a sea change that took place regarding the status of the imagination in relation to perception.[37] In Greco-Roman antiquity and in the medieval and early modern worlds, the imagination stood as a mediation between the intellect and sensible objects.[38] Rather than simply an unreality, fantasy – the fruit of the imagination – possessed the same primacy that post-Cartesian culture grants to experience. Fantasy was the lens through which objects were known, appreciated, loved. With the spread of Enlightenment rationality, fantasy was denigrated and the imagination theorized in such a way that it lost its mediating role.[39] Imagination and fantasy re-emerged as the murky ground on which the ego cogito was destabilized; in time, they came to be seen as little more than agents of "superstition," the *bête noire* of Enlightenment thought, or sexual perversion.[40] According to Agamben, this had an effect on representations of the body and of desire. Without the imagination as mediating force, the subject looks directly upon the object – whether the work of art or the living human form – and finds only a thing rid of the qualities that might have made it a vivid thought. The imagination's cancellation in the equation of desire results in needs that are perpetually frustrated, never satisfied, unable to live up to expectations. Viewed in this light, the ennui experienced by present-day gallery visitors before great works of art, or hard-core pornography and its proven effects on the quantity of gray matter in the brain, could be traced back to the imagination's rationalization and loss of authority.

In the context of the visual arts, Roberto Calasso writes of a similar development, ascribing it not directly to Cartesian rationality but to a later chapter in the history of Enlightenment thought: the French Revolution. Calasso argues that the impact of the Revolution on contemporary art is prefigured in the 1760s by the harsh turn against the art of Giovanni Battista Tiepolo and the corresponding rise of history painter Anton Raphael Mengs, a friend of Winckelmann. The author sees the swirling, supernatural energy of Tiepolo's painted schemes as representative of an "all-embracing air no longer present in painting after the French Revolution."[41] Hyperbolic as this statement is, the reaction against Tiepolo does relay something significant about wider changes in artistic theory and practice during these years. Tiepolo's deteriorating reputation comes to fruition in Salon criticism of the 1780s which, according to Calasso, is marked by "a certain barren, jaded character, a certain meanness of soul" allergic to art that still speaks, first and foremost, to the imagination.[42] With its humanist morality – amplified not only by the rigid contour describing the classical body but by encyclopaedically researched costumes – Mengs's painting is a prime example of the variety of classicizing art that upholds the Enlightenment's rationalizing mission. Although more of a royal favorite than radical, Mengs conceived of ancient Greece as a utopia and was invested in the claim that in Athens liberty had stimulated great art.[43] He was a direct influence on the early work of Jacques-Louis David, the French Revolutionary classicist par excellence.

In Britain, a congruent shift was perceived by Joshua Reynolds. Scholarship mentioning Reynolds in passing tends to misunderstand him as a proponent of austere and rational classicism, a painter whose certainty in the ascendancy of "the antique" was, for all intents and purposes, indistinguishable from the likes of Mengs or even David.[44] But Reynolds came to loathe this strain of art and, not coincidentally, was a collector of works by Tiepolo.[45] By the end of the century, as rationalist ideology was acquiring firmer ties to radical politics and, in turn, radical politics to the classical body, we find Reynolds attempting to salvage the mystifying powers of the imagination in relation to the making and appreciation of art. Delivered late in 1786, his thirteenth Discourse instructs artists to let "imagination and its sensibility" be the engine driving their practices.[46] Whereas before, in his seventh Discourse, for instance, delivered nine years earlier, Reynolds had insisted upon a universal standard of beauty to be achieved through a strict set of guidelines, the individual artist's imagination was now named the starting point for guaranteeing a work's success. Rules are to come into the picture only after the imagination has been allowed free rein.

From this point on, proclaims the painter, the imagination ought to be the force that converts the "gross state of nature" into something potentially "Divine."[47] Agamben's case is supported by Reynolds's conspicuous reinstatement of the imagination as a mediation between subject and object. Reynolds's valorization of "feeling" over "reason" is anticipated in his eighth Discourse, in which – possibly as a corrective to his previous lecture – he attacks the notion of "simplicity."[48] A Winckelmannian ideal, the simplicity of classicizing art, meaning its crystalline delineation, emotive calm, and unexaggerated materiality, usually hints that the work in question – provided that it post-dates Winckelmann – is touched by the trope of Greek freedom.[49]

Reynolds's revision betrays a political anxiety. An intimate friend and adherent of Burke, he was terrified of radical politics infringing on his beloved classical body. His "Ironical Discourse," an unpublished satirical text composed in 1791, betrays his awareness that radical ideology had embraced Greco-Roman sculpture and, what is more, filled it with insurrectionary meaning.[50] Embracing the imagination at this juncture was an effort to re-enchant the classical body as a means of curtailing the impact of "that new conquering empire of light and reason" on contemporary art. Reynolds died in 1791, just as politicized classicism was in its prime. One of his last exhibited subject pictures was a *Cupid and Psyche*, a subject treasured by Canova (fig. 3). Full of creamy flesh and firelight, this is a boldly imaginative and highly sensual work. A teenage Psyche raises a flame over the half-folded form of a younger Cupid sleeping in a bower. One breast is shown in profile, its naked curve a pocket in the tight space between the two figures: a gap only the imagination can close. This was no arbitrary choice of subject. For an artist averse to revolution yet wedded to the classical body, Psyche was the perfect muse.

Neglected in literature on the artist, Reynolds's *Cupid and Psyche* and his other late subject pictures are important documents of the sensual, richly rendered classicism that would eventually displace the other variety of classicizing art.[51] The painter's renewed emphasis on the role of the imagination in his lectures signals a concern that becomes visible in his paintings: that engagement with ancient models needs to be re-enchanted, that the classical body needs to be re-enveloped in fantasy after rationalist ideology and its political offshoots have demystified it and brought it down to earth. In both the Platonic and Christian traditions, sensuality is conceived of as an animalistic quality in opposition to the celestial. Although Reynolds too cites the "danger" of indulging "sensual gratification," the reverse becomes true in British classicizing painting and sculpture.[52] The sensualization of art repositions the classical body in a remote realm untroubled by base instincts and quotidian affairs. By contrast, the absence of sensuality indicates the work's connection to the earthly, mortal terrain of political values. The will to re-enchant the classical body is articulated, therefore, in the materiality, the sensuality, of the finished artwork. On canvas and marble respectively, both Reynolds and Canova are known for their layering of additional substances to boost the ocular impact of their figures.[53] Although both had assistants, the painter and the sculptor are each said to have sequestered themselves in private

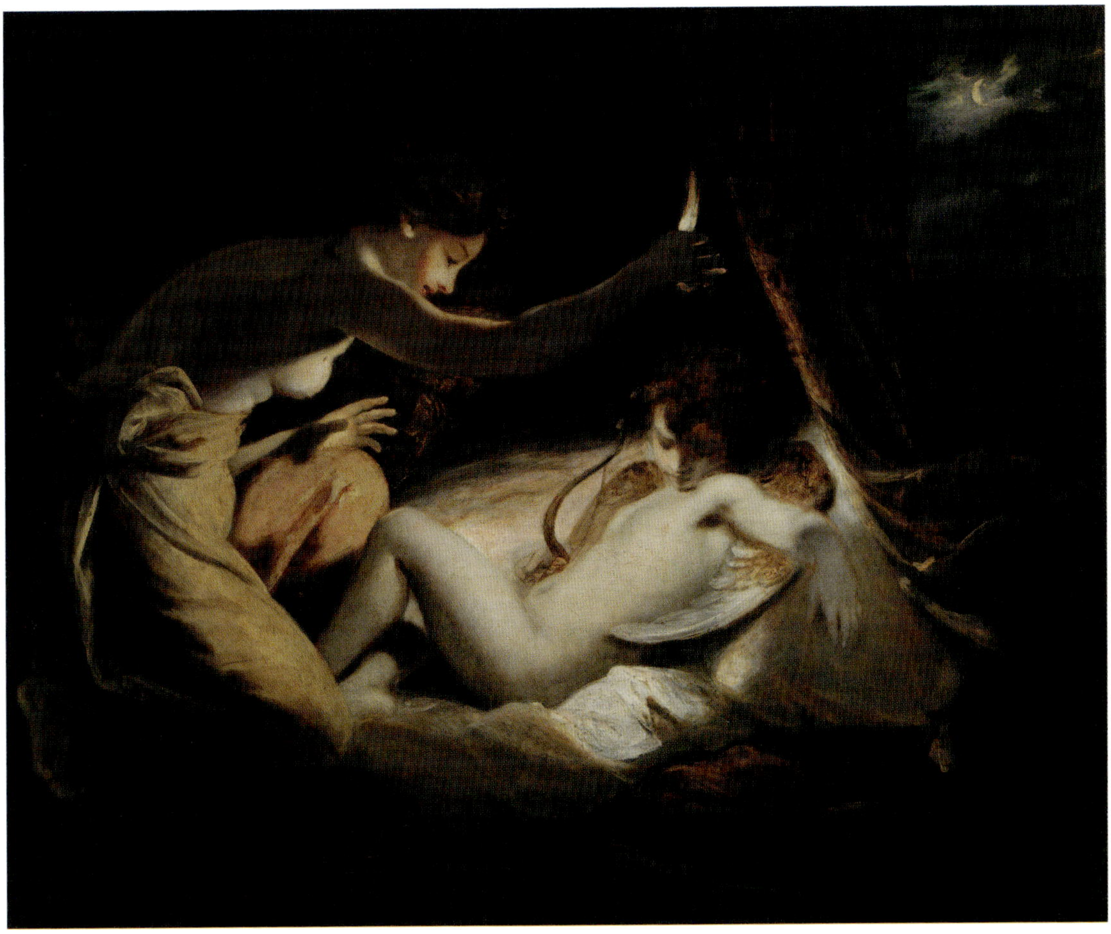

3 Joshua Reynolds, *Cupid and Psyche*, 1789, oil on canvas.
Courtauld Institute, London.

rooms so that they could carry out these embellishments in secret. To enhance their works, the two are even said to have used some of the same substances: litharge (lead oxide) in addition to wax. So damaged was Reynolds's *Cupid and Psyche* by his layering of substances that, like so many of his paintings, it had to undergo painstaking restoration. This overlap between the practices of Reynolds and Canova betrays a shared conviction that, if the imagination is to regain its mediating position, it needs to be lubricated by the artist. One of the characters in Thomas Love Peacock's 1816 novella *Headlong Hall* suggests this sort of technique when he offers to "wave the wand of enchantment" over the grounds of a country estate, adding "a new tint to the complexion of nature."[54] Late works by Reynolds and much of Canova's *oeuvre* wave this wand over the classical body.

Surely, then, the resulting figures appear very artificial and hence nothing like the living human form. Surprisingly, this is not the case. The embellishment of the work of art through additional materials brings the classical body closer to the living body, eroticizing the figure in the process. By living body I do not mean the naturalistically wrought corporeality of flesh and blood that becomes understood through scientific observation. Rather, in these works by Reynolds and Canova, the represented human form takes on the life of a living, breathing person because it is designed to be desirable, and the enhancement of the paint or marble intended to cultivate such a response. Upon visiting Canova's studio after the end of the Napoleonic Wars, a British major was transfixed by one of the sculptor's life-size marble dancers: "The extreme beauty of the leg and foot," he wrote in his journal, "the pulpiness of the arms, the expressive sweetness of the face, and the resemblance of the marble to wax in the point of mellowness, gives to this beautiful statue the appearance of a living female brunette."[55] Here we get a sense of the way that the heightened materiality of such works remystifies the object by bringing it away from antiquity and into the present moment. This is the process I call recorporealization at work. Waxen – that is, artificially enhanced – marble conjures radiant flesh, which in turn makes the dancer sexually desirable, alive, and mysterious in the imagination of the spectator. Under his gaze, grayish white marble hair deepens all the way to brown. Typical of the more positive reactions to works by Canova, this response outpaces Pygmalion's fabrication of Galatea. Rather than brought into being by the hands of the desiring male subject, the dancer is glimpsed but never touched, becoming all the more spectacular because of the frisson of unattainability. In this sense, the major's description of the dancer foreshadows the postmodern image of the supermodel more than it rehearses the formula of the statue come to life.[56]

Literary scholars have been troubled by how, in certain poems by Keats, there is an abundance of ornamental language that achieves effects not dissimilar to those pursued by Reynolds and Canova in painting and sculpture. Ian Jack writes that there is "something artificial and *voulu* about" the "Ode to Psyche" – the poem whose subject links Keats to these artists – which adds to "the problem of exactly what it is about."[57] In the "Ode," everything is intensified and added to, enhanced and embellished so that all prescriptive meaning is occluded. Toward the end, the speaker promises to construct an imaginative shrine to Psyche by decorating a "rosy sanctuary" with "the wreath'd trellis of a working brain … buds, and bells, and stars without a name," and "all the gardener Fancy e'er could feign."[58] According to Martin Aske, Keats's propensity toward metaphysical ornament "discloses a psychic need, a desire to leave a final embellishment or signature on the ideal Text of Antiquity, given the impossibility of the modern poet ever recovering that Text in its original plenitude."[59] Rather than simply making a virtue, as Keats did, of the immeasurable gap between the modern practitioner and "perfect" antiquity, Reynolds, Canova, and other artists with kindred techniques were actively at odds with the notion that ancient Greece and its liberated way of life could ever be recovered. So they did not hesitate to augment and reimagine the classical body. An erotic poem, Keats's "Ode" implies that such interventions may salvage, if not the ontological freedom, then at least the heady sensuality of the ancients, a sensuality epitomized in the figure of Psyche.

I have observed that politicized classicism is marked by a comparatively barren materiality that sanitizes the classical body, drawing the image of the human form away from the imagination and its irrational desires. By sensualizing their materials (paint, marble, language), Reynolds, Canova, and Keats idealize these irrational desires to create wilfully enchanting works. The classical body re-emerges as a mysterious and erotically charged object.

But do works of politicized classicism not possess an erotic charge? Winckelmann's utopian conception of Greece is itself dripping with desire, and the author is now accepted as a queer figure whose love of the male body drove his fascination with classical sculpture. Writing of Fuseli and other outsider artists in late eighteenth-century Rome, Myrone observes that the link between Greece and freedom was often a codification of sexual nonconformity.[60] Alex Potts has navigated the uneasy negotiation of politics and sexual desire that, through the filter of Winckelmann's writings, is performed in French Revolutionary history painting, works by David in particular.[61] Satish Padiyar hones in on the dormant sexual charge of David's later work.[62] Still, apart from the pornographic images made by Fuseli and his circle, eroticism is always veiled in such engagements with the classical body. Kenneth Clark was critical of images of the undraped human form that keep sexual desire at bay; if a painting or sculpture showcasing such an exposed body does not arouse a "vestige of erotic feeling," he writes, it is "bad art and false morals."[63] It makes sense, then, that Clark was, in his own words, a "stick in the mud," a self-styled conservative who had no time for politicized representations of the classical body, especially those containing an insurrectionary vision.[64] While he was equally dismissive of the "fashion plate" classicism of Canova, his total rejection of anerotic nakedness alludes to French Revolutionary art. The fact that, in his history of the nude, he hardly mentions David hints at his distaste for the once-regicide painter.[65]

In British art, Clark has an even more conspicuous target. Here, the homoeroticism of the classically idealized naked male body – a body, as Whitney Davis explores, rooted in the culture of Hellenic pederasty – tended to be suffocated, especially once that form was inserted into works with directive or subtly directive codes relating to ideological concerns.[66] The suffocation of the classical body's entrenched eroticism was facilitated, in part, by the Protestant aversion toward the sensual potential of all visual images.[67] Together with the deployment of the body as a vessel for a political vision, Protestant asceticism informs the way the art object is rendered. When Banks's portrayal of a dead naval captain as a classically idealized naked figure was placed in St. Paul's Cathedral in 1803 – his first monument for the space – its aloof pose, sinewy but still generalized musculature and relatively bland surface treatment allowed it to go unquestioned throughout the ensuing decade as a modish figuration of state-sanctioned heroism honouring the nation's military prowess (fig. 4). For Banks, the work was a covert radical statement grounded in the bond between the classical body and freedom: a vessel for his "vulgar Winckelmannianism." The next chapter dwells at length on this sculpture. For now my point is that the potential erotic charge

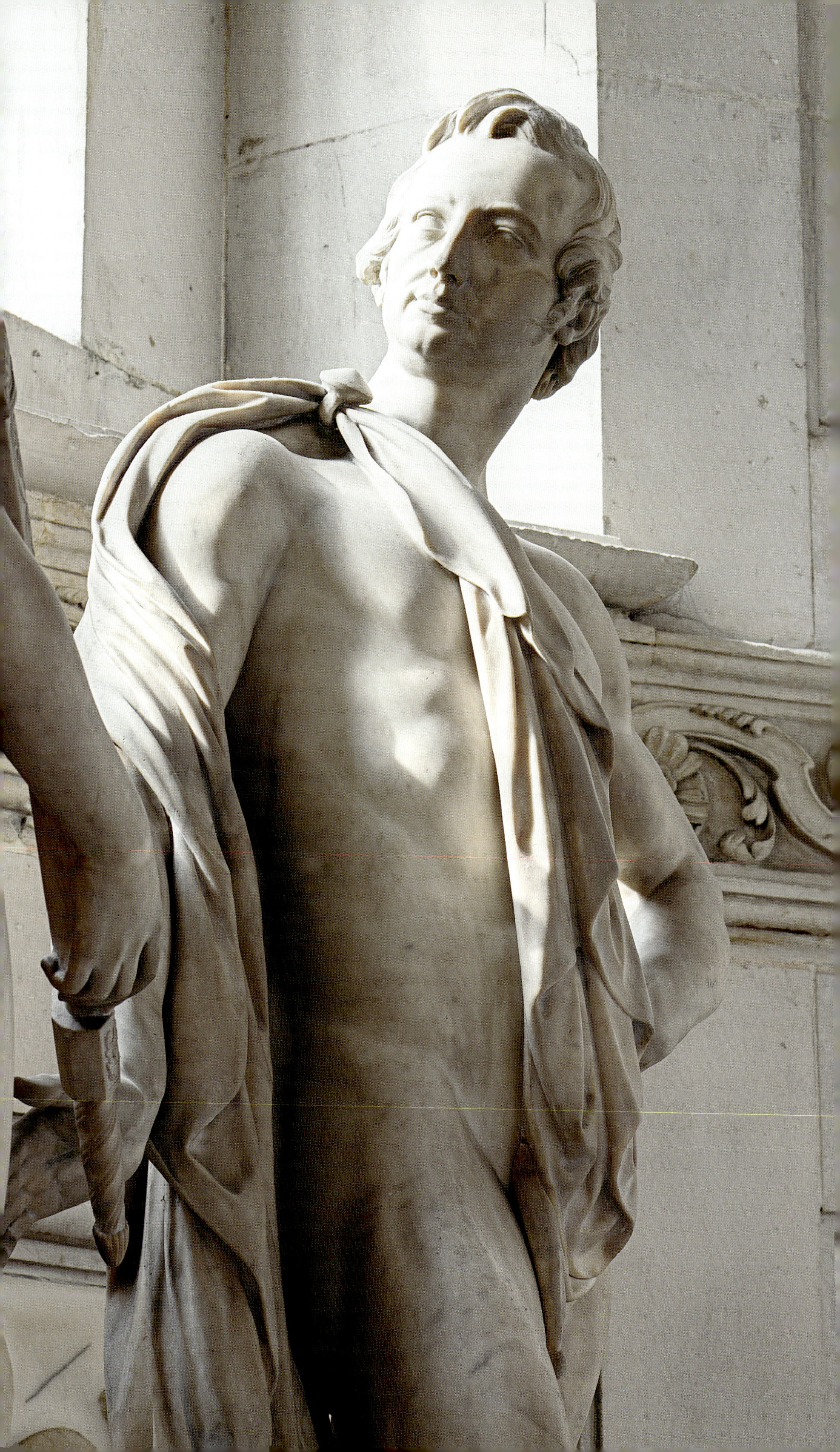

of this particular exposed male body did not present an issue until well into the nineteenth century. Michael Hatt and Jason Edwards have explored the ways in which, by the end of the nineteenth century, images of conventionally beautiful male forms were incorporated into homoerotic and homophobic narratives.[68] But the years around Banks's St. Paul's monument were a distinct window in time in which a naked, classically idealized male body could stand at a firm distance from its genealogy in ancient Greece and well within the bounds of Anglican propriety. A trip to St. Paul's affirms how oddly mundane the naked body of a man appears in this case.

In addition to Protestantism, another factor insulating the naked male body from erotic interpretations was the conception of the Greeks as "the human universal" during the years around the making of this monument.[69] Emulative of Greco-Roman sculpture considered representative of classical Greece, the naked male body had come to represent a bipartisan image of humanity at large, one that proved useful for honorific and radical purposes alike. Having begun as cutting-edge, this view of the Greeks became the height of fashion in the early 1790s and by 1798 had become mainstream in Britain, so much so that George III, who feared universalist ideology, could glance over the design of Banks's monument and authorize its facture for St. Paul's. For Banks, the wider acceptance of Greek nakedness presented an opportunity. He could now place a work of art that reinforced his outsider politics in one of the nation's most important sites. All the while, the classical body remained a vessel within his circle.

Banks's monument is trapped in time. It is trapped in the time of its creation, when the taste of the British state intersected with imagery prized by radical activists. It is also fixed to a conception of Greece particular to this moment. As the wars against France continued, the bipartisan admiration for the Greeks that had flourished during this phase was altered by the ever more inflexible sense of the British national character. Nakedness evolved from a figurative idea to a literal one. Toward the end of the Napoleonic Wars, the incompatibility between British national identity and the figures of Greco-Roman sculpture emerges as a recurring theme within art criticism. At roughly the same time, the arrival of the Parthenon Marbles threatened the integrity of the image of Hellenic form received by Banks and his contemporaries. Winckelmann had not been to Greece and was therefore unfamiliar with the Parthenon Marbles. Now there was tangible document of the "High" Style sitting in a shed on Park Lane. Banks had been dead for several years by the time the fragments arrived. In comparison to the broad musculature, flexible skin, and prominent subdermal structures of what was then identified as the figure of Theseus from the Parthenon (now thought to be a Dionysus), his naked captain – elbow cocked and hand on hip – now seemed delicate and affected, a far cry from the citizens of fifth-century Athens. In short, Banks's sculpture and other documents of politicized classicism from the same period rely on an image of Greece that quickly became outmoded. Shelley's declaration, in 1821, that "We are all Greeks" reveals the

4 Detail from Thomas Banks, *Captain Richard Rundle Burges* (fig. 17).

extent to which, by the post-war period, Hellenic civilization could no longer unproblematically be thought of as a universal ideal. Shelley's point was now strictly a counter-cultural badge of allegiance.[70]

How did this affect what Davis calls the "spatio-temporal principle" of later works of art that reproduce the classical body?[71] Although it was forced to relinquish ties to a universalist image of Greece, the pre-Elgin image of the ideal human form did not disappear. Attempts to make sense of its de-authenticated status crop up in art criticism. Appraising a sculpture by John Gibson in 1837, a critic considered it necessary to specify that the work represented the "petty-classic or Roman-Greek style," that is, "the later period of Greek art, after it had become corrupted by the Roman effeminacy."[72] Likewise, a few years later a critic writing of another sculpture by the same artist wrote that the "style of the group is Roman, or that kind of sculpture which the Greeks practiced under the Romans."[73] Such efforts to provide a historically accurate lexicon for appraising the classical body do not just reveal the impact of the Parthenon Marbles on artistic discourse or a rising historicism. Their vagueness and self-conscious grasp of hybridity – "petty-classic," "Roman-Greek" – indicates that the kind of form reproduced by Gibson was outside of time and, what is more, that there was value in this indeterminacy. As it became increasingly probable that Winckelmann's definition of the "Beautiful" style depended on works that were not "pure" Greek but Hellenistic and Roman, the allure of these bodies was such that it did not matter. More than their synchronicity, it was their atemporality – in other words, their "anachronic" status (a concept recently probed by Elizabeth Prettejohn) – that allowed them to persist as exemplars long after their outing, as it were, as not necessarily Greek.[74] In spite of critics' attempts to mark these bodies as indices of "Roman effeminacy," such works were still being cast, carved, and consumed. This fact troubles the view of the nineteenth century as a phase characterized by a "stringent concern for cognitive values" over affective responses.[75] Atemporality had a purchase of its own. Desirable, the atemporality of the pre-Elgin body protected it from falling short of the rubric of authenticity, allowing it to persist as a model in contemporary art for decades to come. In turn, atemporality permitted artists to take risks with their materials. First exhibited in 1862, Gibson's *Venus* took the practice of re-enchanting the classical body with wax and other substances – a Reynoldsian and Canovian method – to unprecedented heights (fig. 5).

Although Reynolds, Canova, and Gibson all made representations of Venus, it was not the goddess of love who served as the icon of the kind of classical body that exists outside of time. Psyche, the mortal beauty turned goddess of the soul, is at the center of the common ground shared by these artists. Belatedly accepted into the society of Olympian deities, Psyche is the most accessible of all Greek mythological figures. In the only full-length ancient telling of her myth, written in Latin by the North African author Lucius Apuleius, Psyche must earn her seat at the gods' table through a series of tasks.[76] Born into an ordinary family, she is chosen by Cupid to be the god's own wife but is kept in the dark about his identity. The marriage is consummated nonetheless, the pair meeting nightly. After

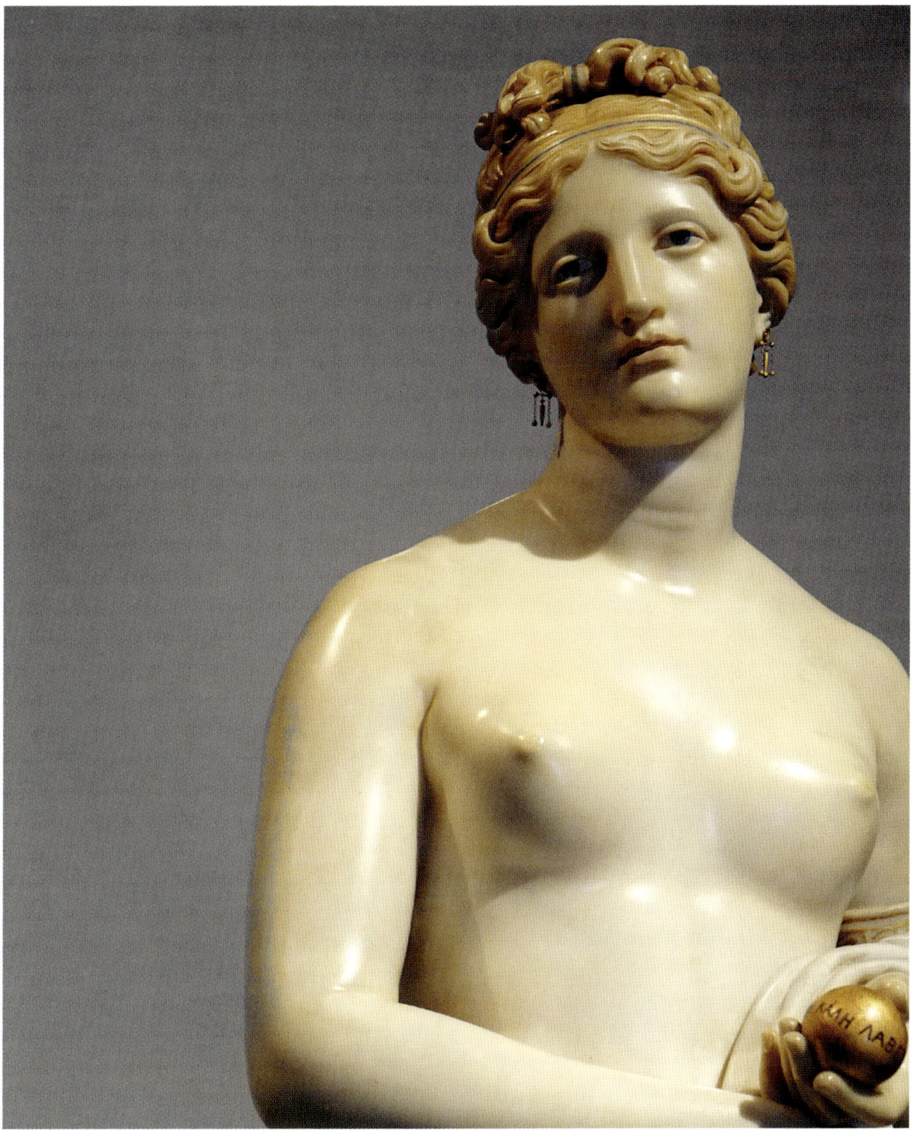

5 John Gibson, *Venus*, 1862, marble with polychromy. Walker Art Gallery, Liverpool.

her all-too-earthly sisters urge her to discover his identity, Psyche breaks the god's trust by lighting a lamp to inspect him while he sleeps: the moment chosen by Reynolds. Hot oil burns his wings and Cupid leaves her. Only after attempting four arduous missions set by Cupid's mother, Venus, jealous of Psyche's beauty, does she regain his trust. Psyche is consequently made immortal at a ceremony on Mount Olympus. When, in his "Ode to Psyche," Keats invokes the goddess as the "latest born ... Of all Olympus' faded hierarchy," the poet acknowledges not only that her deification was hard won. He also highlights Apuleius's status as a latter-day author, active during the second century AD in a Roman colony.[77] Antiquarian literature from Keats's lifetime suggests that, prior to Apulieus, Psyche was predominantly represented in the form of a butterfly. Yet the poet remained convinced that "Psyche was not a goddess before the time of Apuleius and consequently … was never worshipped or sacrificed to with any of the ancient fervour – and perhaps never thought of in the old religion."[78] Ancient representations of the figure such as the "Marlborough Gem," an onyx cameo depicting Cupid and Psyche's marriage procession, generated more than the usual amount of debate around their provenance. Instead of lessening the figure's appeal, Psyche's belatedness made her less distant, more relatable.[79]

As a modern goddess, Psyche was an atemporal subject for art, a categorically hybrid and pliable figure shaped and continually remade by the different periods of her reception. Winckelmann saw the Romans as fundamentally inferior to the Greeks, but Psyche, a figure associated with a distanced, imperial Roman author, resisted being marginalized even during the heyday of "vulgar Winckelmannianism." In fact, Psyche benefitted from her ties to a supposedly impure phase of ancient history. For those averse to politicized appropriations of Greco-Roman antiquity – the utopian image of Greece in particular – Psyche offered an alternative route through which antiquity could be revered. In spite of the vogue for universal Greece in the years around the making of Banks's monument, some discerning critics of radical politics, including artists, were from the beginning suspicious of the cult of "the antique" or "the ancients."[80] Then there were those seduced by the cult who had no interest in the version of Greece that appealed to the state and to radicals. Located on the opposite end of the spectrum to democratic Athens, Psyche stood as an alternative locus for the channelling of interest in classical antiquity. Thomas Taylor, the translator whose widely read English version of *Cupid and Psyche* would have been known to both Keats and Gibson, condemned and even produced a pamphlet making fun of Banks's circle.[81] It was Psyche's atemporality that allowed her to compete with the fixation on Greece that was prevalent in Britain during the final decade of the eighteenth century. The chronologically more recent, exotic world of Apuleius may not have possessed the same aura of authenticity as the idea of Phidias's Greece. Yet its aura was still potent: perfumed and sensual. As an idealized figuration of irrational desire in late eighteenth-century Britain, Psyche was a formidable opponent to the trope of Greek freedom.

Atemporality and eroticism are closely interlinked. Considered in relation to the sexlessness of Banks's naval hero, Apuleius's story verges on the obscene.[82] Even the most spiritual adaptations cannot avoid the heroine's nightly encounters with Cupid. Positioned outside the bounds of the historical record, Psyche embodies what Michel Maffesoli describes as "a poetic and erotic time, a time of the amorous body."[83] Both in Apuleius and in her subsequent reception, the zone inhabited by Psyche is in opposition to theories of cyclical or linear development deployed in typological discourse on art objects. Her eroticism is at odds with stable identities (desire turns her from mortal to immortal), political activism (in the modern world to this day, sexual desire possesses an uneasy status within the political arena because of such desire's capacity to cloud judgment), and morality (a story featuring a girl having sex with the god of love does not present a version of ancient myth from which a virtuous subtext can easily be recovered).

Psyche's femininity allowed her to challenge the Enlightenment rationality that forms the bedrock of politicized classicism. As a doubly female figure – a mortal girl turned goddess – she evades humanist ideology. But hers is no abject femininity bound to flesh. Her sexuality has an adolescent quality, the innocence of which lends her a palatability that renders her a more dignified rival to rationalizing theories than, for example, the more mature figure of Venus or the robust personification of Pleasure in depictions of the Choice of Hercules, the recurring Enlightenment subject that scapegoats a disorderly feminine Other.[84] At once passive and active, subjective and objectified, irreverent and chaste, Psyche's distinctly feminine beauty gives her strength. Keats expressed the idea that beauty was a force that, in and of itself, could surpass extant – Enlightenment – models of heroism, having the Titan Oceanus proclaim in "Hyperion" that "first in beauty should be first in might."[85] Alan J. Bewell writes that such faith in beauty works to "[rewrite] political revolution in non-violent, aesthetic terms."[86] Political revolution does not erupt in the streets but takes place within Psyche's dominion: the soul. As revolution moves from the exterior world to inside the body, it turns into a sensual, rather than political, revolution.

With the idea of a sensual revolution we come full circle back to Winckelmann. For the scholar, Greek freedom was a condition of consciousness and therefore not confined to a particular political vision, something that "vulgar Winckelmannianism" conveniently overlooks.[87] Indeed, after the fall of politicized classicism, Winckelmann's theories came to be appreciated on fresh terms, leading ultimately to the pursuit of a sensual revolution in the form of the Aesthetic movement that arose later on in the nineteenth century. Decades after the Napoleonic Wars we see the atemporal kind of classicism fructify not only in the imaginative prose of Walter Pater but in paintings by Edward Burne-Jones and certain works by Frederic Leighton, each of whom produced versions of Psyche's story.[88] The brilliant collection of essays, *Pater the Classicist*, edited by Elizabeth Prettejohn, Charles Martindale, and Stefano Evangelista, shows how the intellectually sophisticated Pater, inspired by the erotic and emotive dimension of Winckelmann's writings, made a virtue out of favoring a sensual rather than exclusively scientific view of ancient art.[89] In Pater's essay on the scholar, the political implications of Winckelmann's theories on beauty and freedom fade altogether from view, the significance of fifth-century democracy eclipsed by intrigue around his private life. Pater also detaches Winckelmann from the Enlightenment milieu by positing him as the last vestige of the Renaissance. Despite these significant connections, however, I want to emphasize that I am not charting a process of aestheticization that reaches its apogee in the Aesthetic movement. Instead, I seek to do the opposite: to de-aestheticize objects by bringing to light their lost connection to politicized art.

And one does not have to look far to discover concrete links between the agenda of these late nineteenth-century authors and the artists under consideration in this book. One of the first instances, in English, of art being described as for its own "sake" is in Elizabeth Eastlake's biography of Gibson, published in 1870.[90] Out of all the representations of Psyche made by Gibson, and there are many, his most ambitious is *Psyche Borne Aloft by the Zephyrs*, a sculpture first exhibited at the Royal Academy in 1827 (fig. 6). Although not one of his tinted creations, this just smaller than life-size group conjures a sense of smooth, adolescent flesh both in the rendering of Psyche's form and the ephebic bodies of her two male companions. Although any three-figured sculpture from the period is likely to be indebted to Canova's landmark *Three Graces*, Gibson's composition plays equally on conventions of British war monuments made during his infancy, works belonging to a class of art Gibson considered to be tainted by interestedness, by an dearth of sensuality and fixedness in a bygone time.[91] In several of these monuments, the subject is propped up by supernatural beings, either gods or allegorical personifications of concepts such as Valor.[92] Hoisted on the shoulders of the wind gods, Psyche occupies the space between divine and earthly realms conventionally reserved for the male hero. Maybe this is, as Eastlake writes, "Art for her own sake only"; simultaneously, however, it is art that subverts the conventions adhered to by the previous generation of practitioners. Although Banks, as far as I know, was the only monument maker to participate in activism, several sculptors commissioned to execute works for St. Paul's in the decade after his death reproduced his radical appropriation of the classical body even after it lost its relevance to the contemporary political situation. This is why, from the end of the Napoleonic Wars, the monuments in St. Paul's steadily began to be viewed as a national embarrassment.

In *Psyche Borne Aloft by the Zephyrs*, monumental conventions are subverted by the erotic, atemporal figure of Psyche. An earlier work demonstrates how actual monumental sculpture could be inflected by the same counterforce. Canova's portrayal of Napoleon as a smooth, ideally naked Mars – transfigured into "the peacemaker" (Marte pacificatore) – is less of a god, hero, or emperor than a feminized monument, or Ode, to sensuality (fig. 7). Although his fame and high regard meant that he was summoned to work for the Bonapartes, Canova's consistent severance from the political arena is consolidated in this, the work ostensibly most informed by an interested conception of the classical body. The array of temporalities at work in this sculpture is overwhelming. It is, first and foremost, a statue of Napoleon. Stripped of temporalizing dress, the portrait is refracted through the prism of Greek form and Roman mythology, so that it is simultaneously a representation of Mars. Only this is Mars not in the god's regular guise as god of war, but presented as peacemaker: a modern conceit. The work is part monument, part portrait mythology, part contemporary art, part provocative satire of the subject only possible from an artist as untouchable as Canova. Most strikingly of all, the sculptor has transformed the figure into a mysterious and sexually desirable object. The modelling of the limbs and description of the muscles are oblique not rigid, and the consul's chin is tucked, as with Gibson's Psyche, to imply the negation of ego. The figure does not gaze outwardly like the *Apollo Belvedere*, the ancient figure with a similar

6 John Gibson, *Psyche Borne Aloft by the Zephyrs*, 1827, marble. Galleria Corsini, Rome.

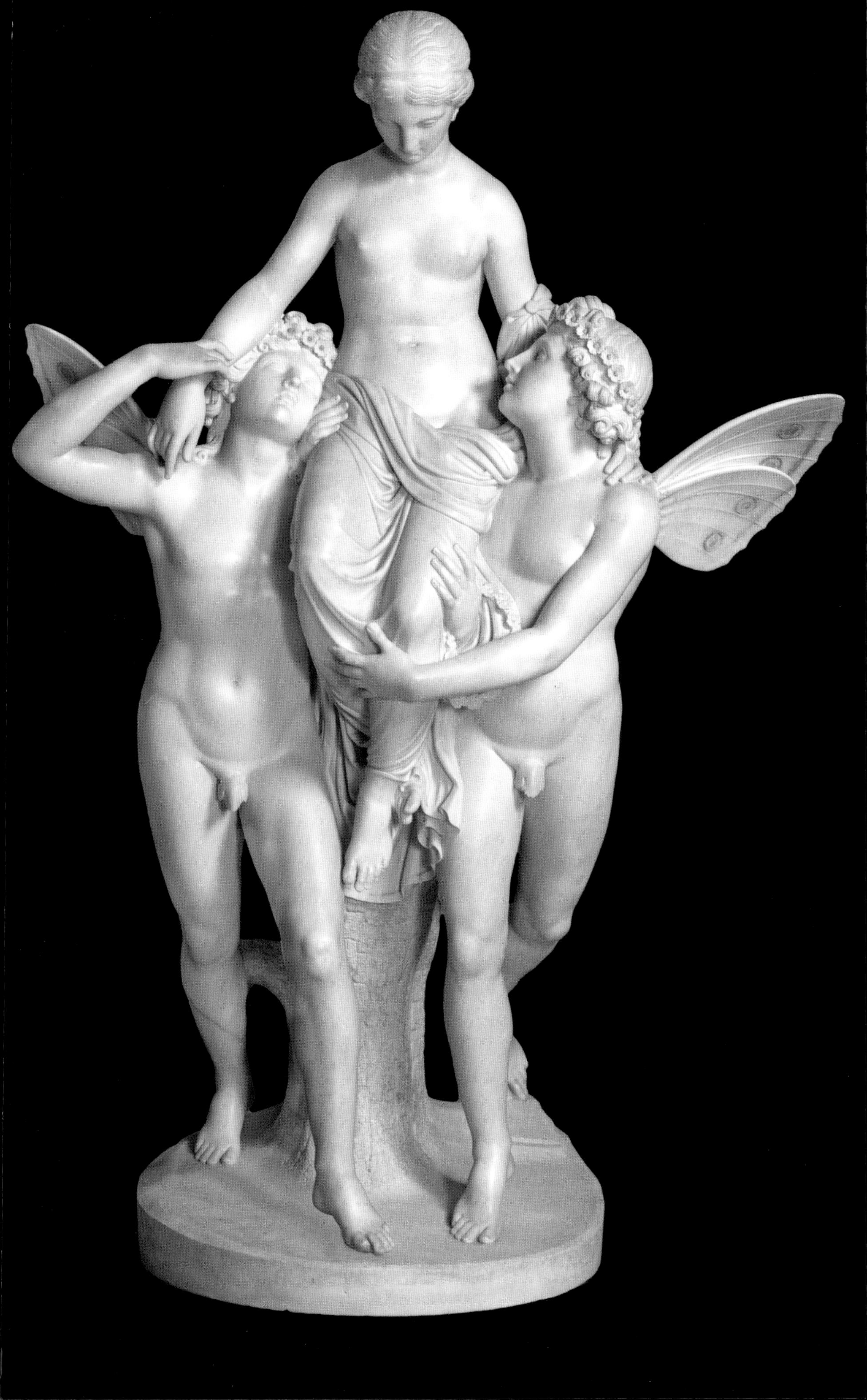

contrapposto, but slightly down toward the ground, away from the world and the labor of war. Relaxed almost to the point of languor, the would-be dictatorial pose becomes the stance of surrender. The golden orb surmounted by a statuette of Victory is offered with acquiescence. Finished by the hand of Canova, the flesh is tender, feeding the desire to caress. At eleven feet, only the height of the work retrieves it from the limits of heroic convention. Napoleon's rejection of the sculpture and its subsequent hiding until its ironic postwar purchase for the Duke of Wellington confirms Canova's success in overthrowing the politicization of the classical body. Rather than glorifying the subject and the upheaval that made him leader of France, the statue destabilizes the "conquering empire of light and reason," like Psyche does too.

— DREAMS AND POEMS —

The material and temporal discrepancies between these two kinds of classicizing art find expression in Keats's poetry. In 1819, months after he wrote the "Ode to Psyche," Keats composed a work that invokes an artist opposed, as Reynolds, Canova, Gibson, and others were, to the capacity of art to challenge the extant social order. "The Fall of Hyperion" opens with an indictment of "fanatics" whose "dreams" of a new world – a "paradise" – promise freedom only for "a sect." Like an ignorant "savage," the fanatic "Guesses at Heaven," hubristically attempting to unsettle the order of things in their attempt to revolutionize. These fanatics merely "live, dream and die," leaving nothing of lasting significance behind. After falling asleep, Keats's speaker wakes to find himself in a temple. Ascending a series of marble steps he is confronted by Moneta, mother of the Muses and Roman equivalent of Mnemosyne, Greek goddess of memory. Jaded by what, over centuries, she has witnessed, Moneta warns the speaker of the ultimate impotence of mortals striving to make the world anew. The "dreamer venoms all his days, bearing more woe than all his sins deserve," in the end, for nothing. By contrast, those who truly "labour for mortal good" are content to "seek no wonder but the human face, no music but a happy noted voice." Through Moneta, Keats constructs a binary between two subjectivities and, implicitly, two types of artist: "the dreamer," on the one hand, and their "sheer opposite": "the poet." How do they differ? The poet "pours out a balm upon the world," the dreamer "vexes it."[93]

Scholars have disagreed on the meaning of Keats's distinction between "the poet" and "the dreamer."[94] This, I would argue, has to do with the semantics of dreaming. "To dream" can be synonymous with "to hope for": a heartfelt aspiration often deployed in political rhetoric. Martin Luther King, Jr.'s "I Have a Dream" speech is the quintessential example of this usage. King dreams "today," while awake. At the same time, "to dream" has its oneiric significance. To dream is to yield to the imagination and/or the unconscious mind. In defining the fanatical "dreamer" against the "poet," Keats suggests the former usage. By

7 Antonio Canova, *Napoleon as Mars the Peacemaker*, 1802–6, marble. Apsley House, London.

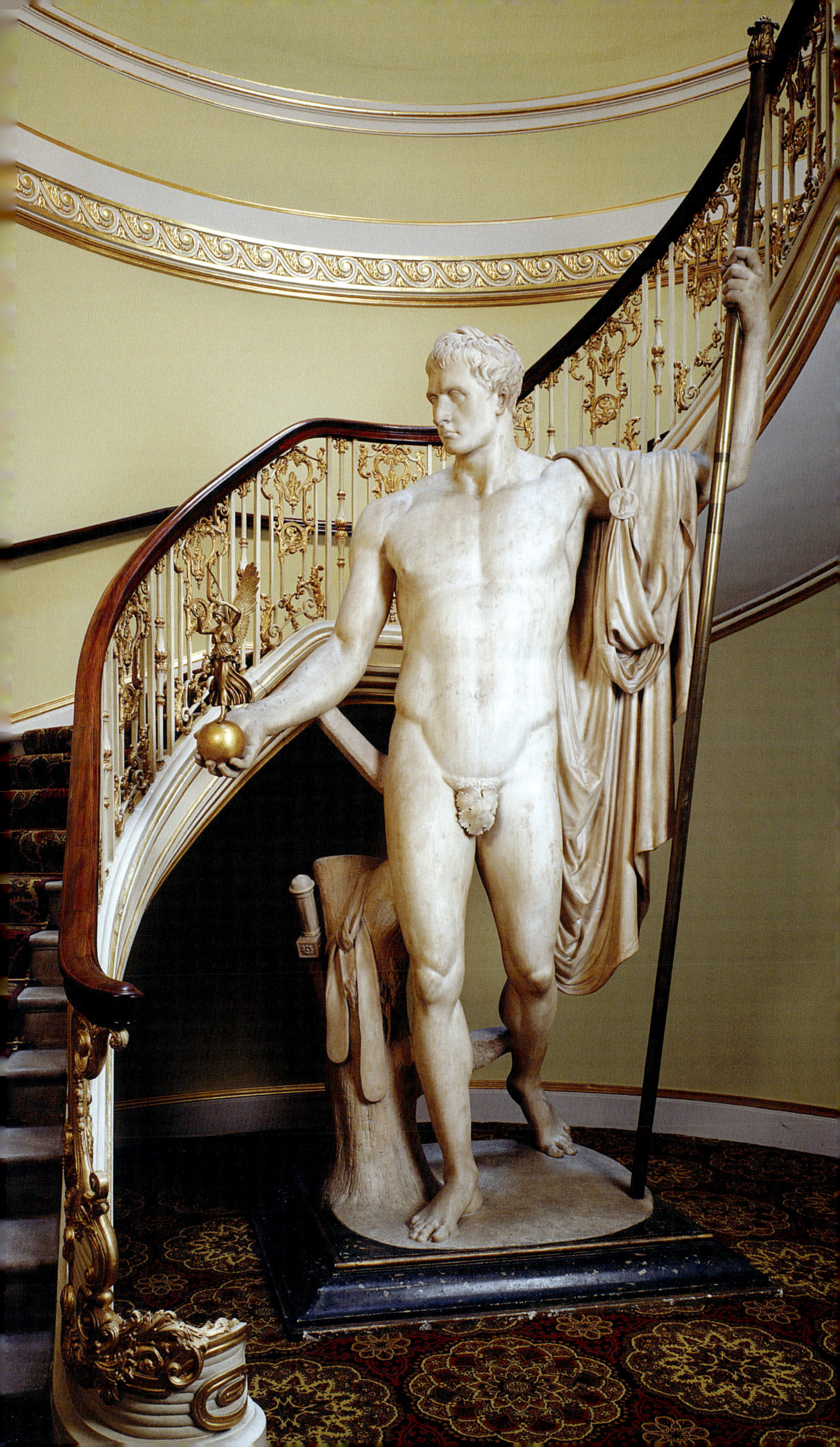

"vexing" the world, "the dreamer" uses art as a tool of political intervention. The "dreamer" is an activist. Their counterpart, "the poet," accepts the limits of human agency and instead uses art to "pour out a balm.".

The materiality of certain works by Reynolds, Gibson, and Canova elucidates this dialectic. Made by Keatsian "poets" par excellence, these works are, to use another phrase of Edmund Burke's, "pleasing illusions" addressed, first and foremost, to the viewer's imagination.[95] Canova's marble figures appear to be lathered in a balm, quite literally smoothened by a healing salve. "Sweetened" was the word used to describe this effect by the Italian critic Melchiore Missirini, the words "dolce" and "dolcezza" becoming part of the standard language for appraising Canova's sculpture.[96] Keats's figure of the "poet," then, suggests that to embrace the sensuality of the material – the balm – was to disavow politicized art. Etymologically speaking, the word "poet" bears associations with the material rather than immaterial aspects of creation, originally meaning maker or shaper. And it is the materiality of the object that bolsters what, in Davis's words, is the "transhistorical vitality" of the classical body, allowing it to endure while continually being reimagined.[97]

In "The Fall of Hyperion," Keats does not take sides in the conflict between the "poet" and the "dreamer." The speaker leaves it up to posterity to determine whether or not the work is itself a "dream" or a "poem." Only when "this warm scribe," the hand of the author, is "in the grave" will its allegiance become clear. Further in, Moneta accuses the speaker of being a "dreaming thing," a member of the "dreamer tribe," an indictment that urges us to remember Keats's sympathy with the French Revolutionaries. But it was the "sweet" Keats that was canonized in the nineteenth century, the Keats that embellished and adorned, smoothened and sensualized. Until only relatively recently, posterity saw the more polemical aspects of his life eclipsed, saw the "poet" triumph over the "dreamer." This was Psyche's triumph too.

If not already clear, Thomas Banks was a quintessential "dreamer," an artist who fought to change the world through art and activism, in Keats's words, "a slave ... to poor humanity." He and his activist circle saw the classical body as "vexing": a vessel carrying a radical "dream." But the dreaming cut both ways. Before looking at Banks and his fellow radicals, Chapter 1 examines how the politicization of Greece gave the sculptor John Bacon senior, a staunch Methodist and opponent of radical thought, motive to engage with the classical body in such a way as to undermine the association between Greece and freedom. Classicizing in a different style to Banks's, Bacon's art is the vessel for an equally "vexing" vision: a passionate combination of royalism and evangelicalism. Chapter 2 centers on John Flaxman, an artist whom I posit as a "poet." A friend, admirer, and in some ways protégé of Banks, Flaxman smoothened, feminized, and sensualized the version of "the antique" he inherited from his radical forbear, thereby depoliticizing the classical body. Chapter 3 looks at Henry Howard, an artist virtually unknown in the present day. Howard's paintings carried the designs of Banks and Flaxman, whom he knew and worked alongside, into the age of industrial capitalism. Considering Howard's art as a precursor to the display of classical bodies at the Great Exhibition of 1851, I argue that it was the artist's status as both "dreamer" and "poet" that led to the rejection of his work both during his lifetime and after his death. Comparing his work to that of his more successful contemporary, the fiercely anti-radical William Etty, provides insight into the reintegration of eroticism into representations of the classical body during the post-Napoleonic War period. Because of the intersecting practices of Banks, Flaxman, and Howard, these three chapters work as a unit, forming Part I of this book, entitled "Earth and Air."

As the chapters unfold, the question of gender becomes all the more integral. Sticking with Keats's distinction between the "dreamer" and the "poet," Part II, "Stone and Flesh," centers on the proximity of the living body to classicizing British art of the post-Napoleonic period. Chapter 4 looks at certain real-life individuals employed as living approximations of "the antique," including Emma Hamilton, Saartjie Baartman, and, in particular, Wilson, a sailor from Boston employed as a model by the painter Benjamin Robert Haydon. I gauge the ways in which the arrival of the Parthenon Marbles reignited the political utility of classicizing art. Martin Bernal's case that Hellenic civilization was essentially bleached, as it were, to become the preserve of an ethnically northern European heritage finds support in British artistic practice during these years. At this time, a new strain of politicized classicism emerges, one divorced from egalitarian ideology and wedded to a racial hierarchy. As the justification for the supremacy of white Europeans, this was another manifestation of a Keatsian dream: "a paradise" but only "for a sect." Centering on Gibson and other post-Napoleonic sculptors, Chapter 5 examines the triumph of "poetic" art, particularly sculpture in the decade following the cessation of the Napoleonic Wars and the acquisition of the Parthenon Marbles. I look at how works by practitioners such as Richard Westmacott, John Graham Lough, Edward Hodges Baily, Richard James Wyatt, and John Gibson signal, through emphatically gendered forms designed to conjure the allure of the actual human body, the defeat of the kind of art that turned the classical body into a vessel. Each of these artists engage in processes of what I call recorporealization.

The terms "dreamer" and "poet" will operate as an alternative vocabulary for describing the tension between these two types of classicizing art. To avoid confusion I will distinguish these terms with a capital letter, referring to Dreams and Poems, as well as Dreaming and Poetic works/artists throughout. I am grateful to the scholars whose more traditional methodologies have paved the way for my somewhat unconventional take on the period, a phase in history that, as Thomas Crow points out, "has eluded more straightforward approaches."[98] The vast majority of objects discussed in the following chapters have been neglected and maligned. Keats helped me to see this art on the period's own terms and avoid altogether the trappings of the modernist gaze. I have let my senses guide me. As someone who did not have the option of learning Greek or Latin at school, who grew to love classical and classicizing art without a sense of its chronologies, above all as a Londoner, I am happy to continue the "cockney" and "vulgar" tradition.

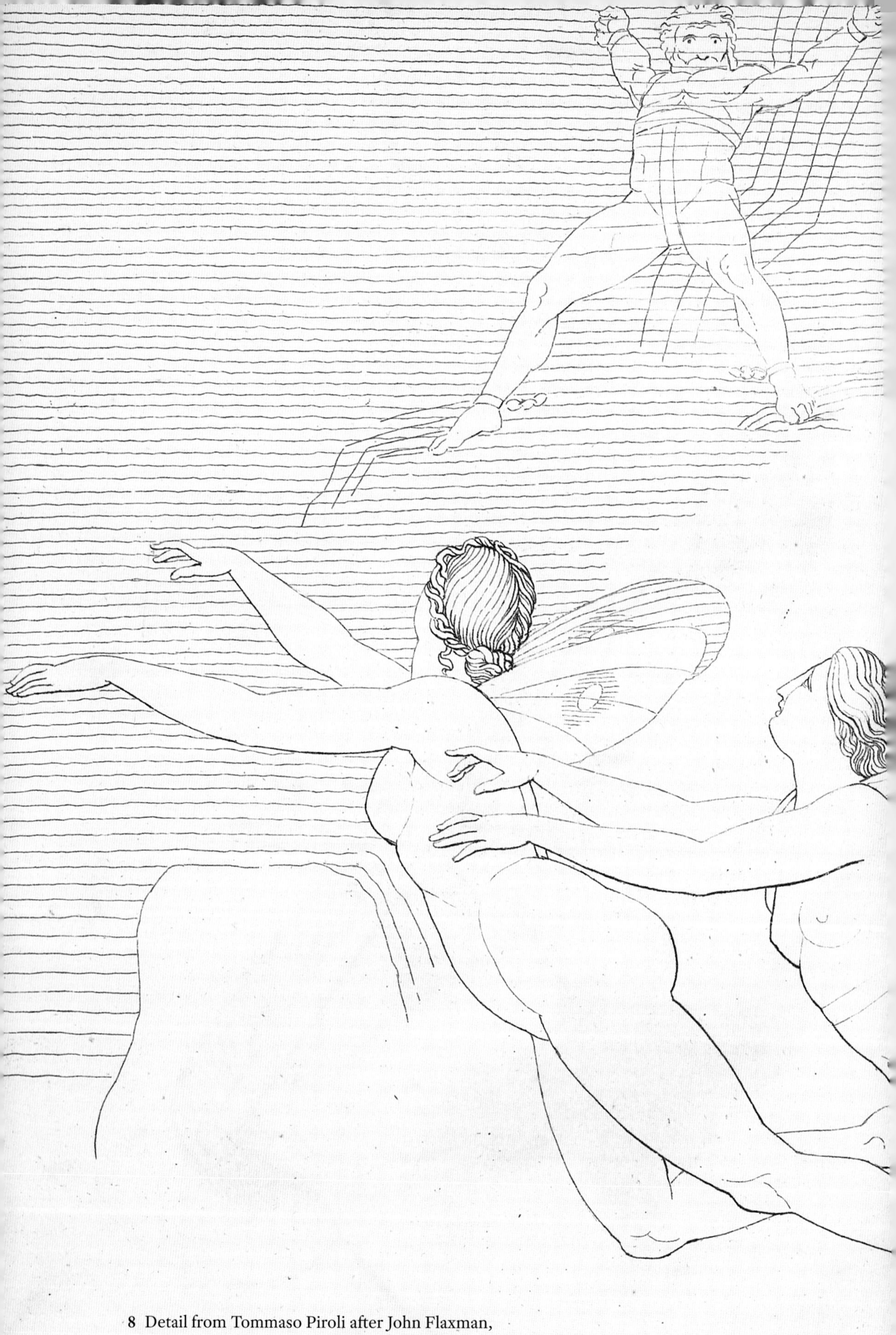

8 Detail from Tommaso Piroli after John Flaxman, *Nymphs of the Ocean Visit Prometheus* (fig. 44).

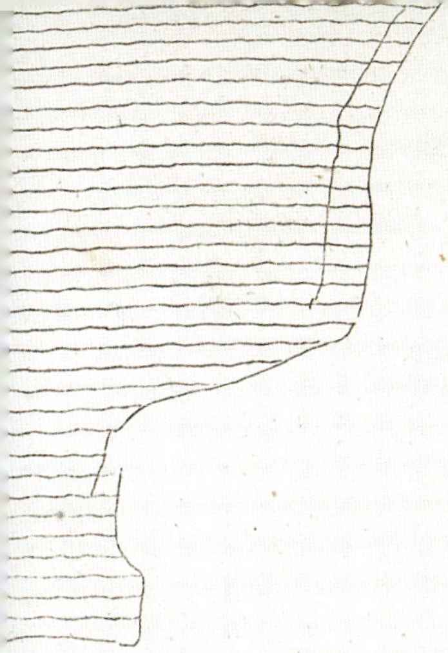

PART I

EARTH AND AIR

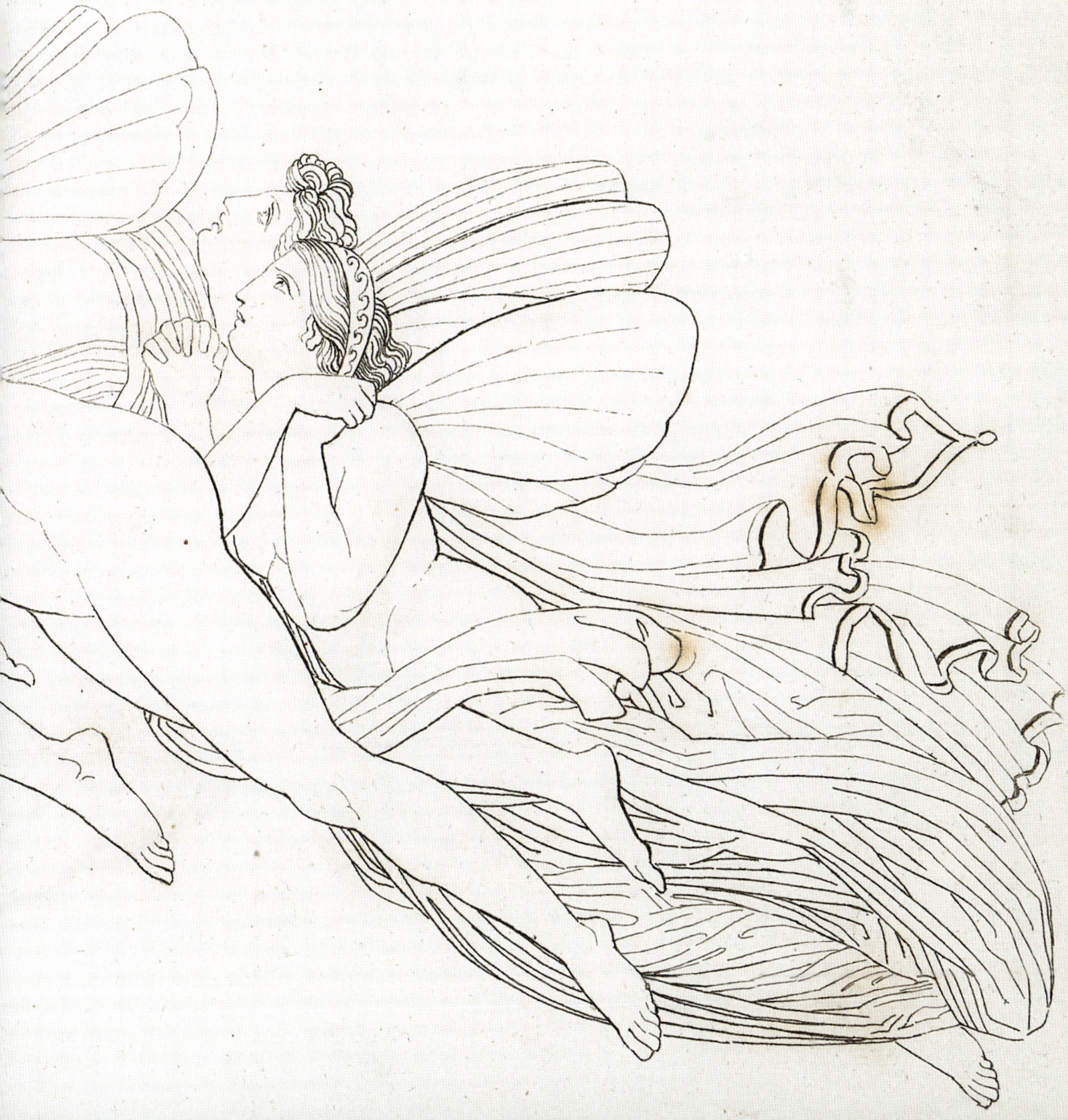

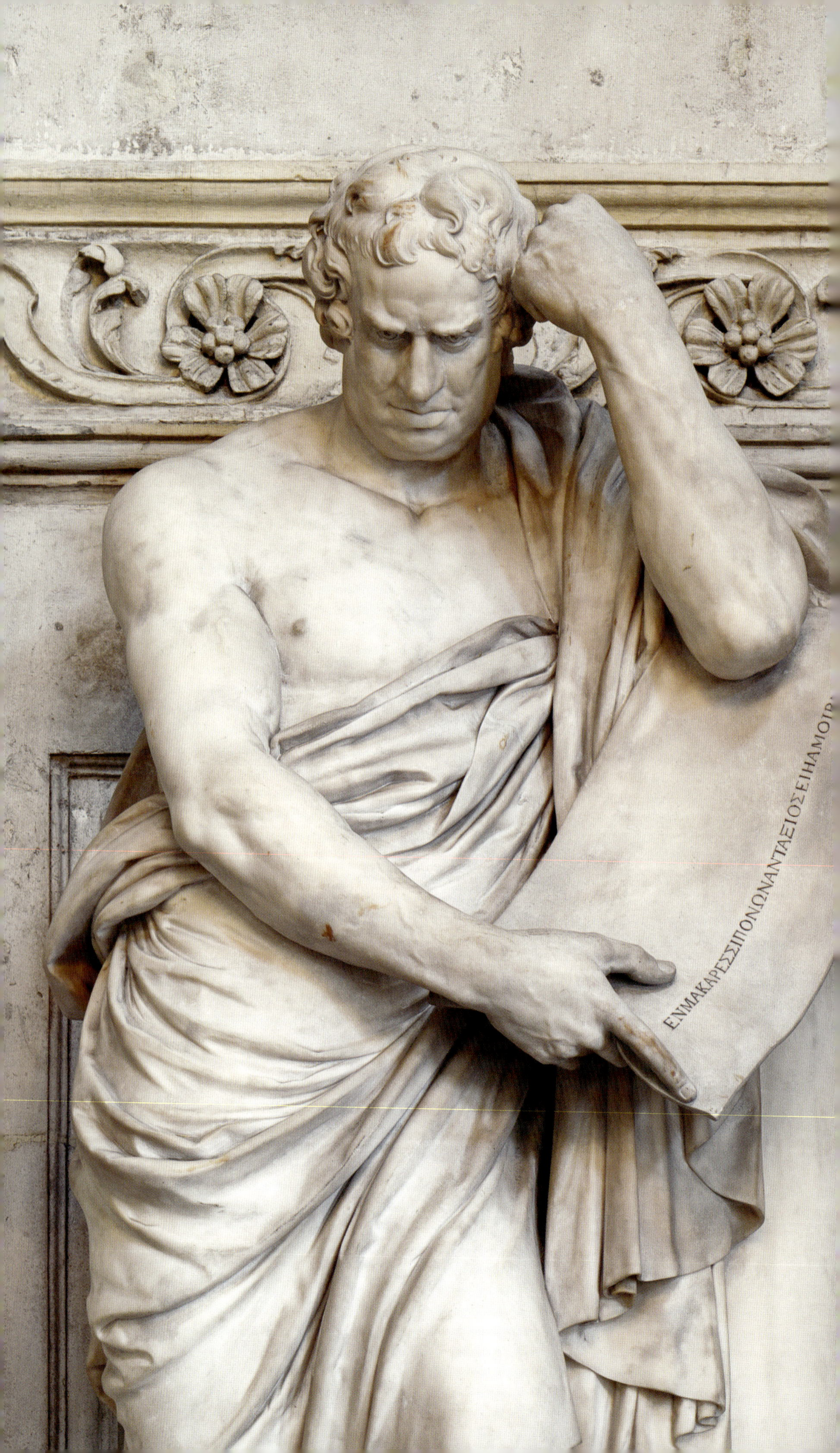
ΕΝΜΑΚΑΡΕΣΣΙΠΟΝΩΝΑΝΤΑΞΙΟΣΕΙΗΑΜΟΙ

CHAPTER ONE

HIDDEN DREAMS

Inside St. Paul's Cathedral there are many monuments. Resurrected soldiers perch on the back of stiff-eyed horses, their bayonets pointing to an absent sky. Bloated infants surface from crypt walls to comfort a desolate Britannia. Corpses are held by gentle bearded men, personifications of the rivers and seas that turn blood into clear water. Angel-bodied girls are not angels but winged Victories that congratulate the dead. Beneath them all lies Nelson, or rather a wooden coffin encased in a shiny black sarcophagus intended for another but that now bears his name. Although not all of the monuments in St. Paul's are remnants of war, it is the war monuments that dominate each corner, wall, aisle, and transept. Boer, Indian, Crimean, First and Second Burmese, Napoleonic, French Revolutionary – not to mention all the sub-battles that escorted the world's entrance into the twentieth century – are rendered equal in this vast mausoleum. Today the sculptures are forgotten. While their silhouettes remain intact, apart from a chipped laurel wreath or two, their once-eloquent allegories have not aged well. Lonely and neglected, this marble tribe seem unsuited to eternal life. Whether reclining in the round or standing in relief, they seem to mourn not those many lives lost, but the fact that they themselves are still here, fixed in a material that refuses to decay.

Even when larger-than-life bodies re-enact scenes of battlefield suffering, pathos is difficult to recover in these sculptures. Over time, each has been subsumed into the cathedral's interior architecture, overshadowed by the sparkling gilt and multicolored mosaics that in 1891 were installed into the spandrels, or the baroque ironwork on the south side of the quire. That such enormous and laborious art should suffer this fate is not uncharacteristic of monuments. In her classic study on allegory and the female form Marina Warner invokes the Austrian novelist Robert Musil, who in his 1936 *Nachlass zu Lebzeiten* reflected on the oddly inconspicuous nature of public statuary: "The most striking feature of monuments is that you do not notice them. There is nothing in the world as invisible as monuments. Doubtless they have been erected to be seen – even to attract attention; yet at the same time something has impregnated them against attention."[1] Large and heavy in imported marble, the St. Paul's monuments honoring men who fought in the Revolutionary and Napoleonic Wars are especially unassuming. By the 1920s, these sculptures had evolved into cumbersome relics of distant conflicts: battles now eclipsed by rings of red poppies on the

9 Detail of John Bacon, *Samuel Johnson*, 1791–5 (fig.11).

Cenotaph's Portland stone. Most of them are installed near the main entrance of the cathedral. Today streams of tourists pass by, glancing in their direction before letting them dissolve, undigested, into the recesses of their minds. Not even mindless cameras point in their direction. Photography is strictly forbidden inside St. Paul's.

What is it about these sculptures that has allowed them to become so mute and moribund? Was there ever a time in which they were alive, so to speak, a time in which they pulsated with relevance to contemporary life? The answer is yes, and this is part of the reason why they have become so easy to ignore. The current impotence of these sculptures stems from the fact that they are inexorably tied to the years of their design. With these works in mind, Whitney Davis's notion of the "spatio-temporal principle of an artwork" can be expanded to incorporate not just the moment depicted or the temporality of the classical bodies they reproduce, but the entrapment of an object in a limited set of years, the passing of which evacuates the work of its former significance.[2] Such is the "spatio-temporal principle" of these monuments: they are trapped in time.

Two monuments in particular present extreme cases of this self-contained temporality. The scheme to fill the cathedral with war monuments was inaugurated in 1798 when three contracts for three new sculptures honoring distinguished men who died on duty during the French Revolutionary Wars were issued by the government to three different sculptors, all of whom were members of the Royal Academy. The king checked and signed off on their designs. While one of the works does its job and simply commemorates – in a style that reconciles the conventions of earlier eighteenth-century British war monuments with the image of "the antique" then fashionable – a naval officer killed by the French in 1794, the other two are more daring.[3] These two works actively address the contemporary political situation in Britain at the time, taking opposing sides in the great ideological divide that gripped the country in the wake of the Revolution itself. Both give access, therefore, to a window in British history when it was possible for practitioners to translate their political visions into highly visible, state-funded works of art – art rendered in the "eternal" material of marble no less. Quintessential manifestations of an approach I have identified as Dreams, these visions are articulated most forcefully in the artists' treatment of the classical body.

Recovering these Dreams means removing the cloak of invisibility that conceals these works and looking closely at their content and the specifics of the styles in which they are designed. In order to bring them back to life, it is necessary to examine the networks of which the artists were a part, their pursuits beyond sculpture, and their responses to seismic events of the day. But, first, why are these sculptures even in St. Paul's? A Protestant church seems a strange place for secular memorials, let alone works suffused with earthly politics. Prior to the 1790s the cathedral possessed few works of art, almost all having been destroyed during the Great Fire of 1666 when most of the original structure was razed. Consecrated in 1697, Christopher Wren's cathedral – the St. Paul's that stands today – remained largely empty for most of its early life. For decades, wariness toward anything ostensibly Catholic prevented artists from decorating the space with devotional painting and sculpture in the vein of the Italian basilicas that inspired Wren's design.[4] Executed by the workshop of the Anglo-Dutch craftsman Grinling Gibbons, the stone fruit and floral festoons and winged heads between the fluted Corinthian pilasters, and the bronze cherubim sprawling over the organ, provided much of the interior decoration until the final decade of the eighteenth century, when new monuments began to arrive. With most of its contents made in the nineteenth century, the cathedral contrasts with its elder cousin down the Thames, Westminster Abbey, in which every surface throbs with memorials dating back to the time of William the Conqueror. But the relative emptiness of St. Paul's worked in its favor. It was this emptiness, this lack of clutter and material residue, that allowed the space to be transformed into a gallery of modern sculpture. Although the St. Paul's monuments now appear lifeless, they once represented the cutting edge of British art. The most feted practitioners of the day were called upon to bring forth, as an anonymous poet would describe it in 1830, a "church that's almost like a town," where "on either hand White monuments of marble stand," each with its own distinct purpose.[5] Sarah Burnage rightly calls the project "a bold sculptural experiment."[6]

The earliest monuments to arrive in the cathedral were not war memorials but tributes to recently deceased men of other kinds of fame. Installed in February 1796, the first was a standing effigy of John Howard, a Hackney-born prison reformer and philanthropist who died from typhus in 1790 (fig. 10). With one hand clutching a scroll with the words "Hospitals" and "Plan for the Improvement of Prisons," the other a key, Howard is portrayed in a knee-length tunic, his eyes cast down and introspection rasped into his brow. Before long another sculpture entered the building, this time in honor of Samuel Johnson (fig. 11). This is also a standing effigy, a thick-set and brooding figure portrayed like a middle-aged actor playing Hercules as he pauses for breath during a soliloquy. These two sculptures were the first works to break through the fiercely guarded Anglicanism that had banned all art for a century.[7] Although they were not commissioned by the government, they paved the way for the stream of state-funded sculptures that, commissioned from 1798, would start to trickle in around five years later. The sculptor behind both of these effigies is John Bacon senior, a Dreamer.

— THE DRAPED DREAM —

John Bacon senior was a self-taught craftsman turned Royal Academician and favorite of the Georgian court. His rise to become the most sought-after sculptor in late eighteenth-century Britain, and one of the nation's wealthiest artists, was in a large part due to his close relationship with George III, to whom he was introduced in 1770 by the king's former chaplain. It is Bacon, or rather his numerous workmen, who were responsible for the group known as *George III and the River Thames*, the set of bronze figures in the quadrangle of Somerset House. Matthew Craske notes that during his lifetime Bacon was thought of as a "monopoliser" among his fellow sculptors, an artist that used his ties to the

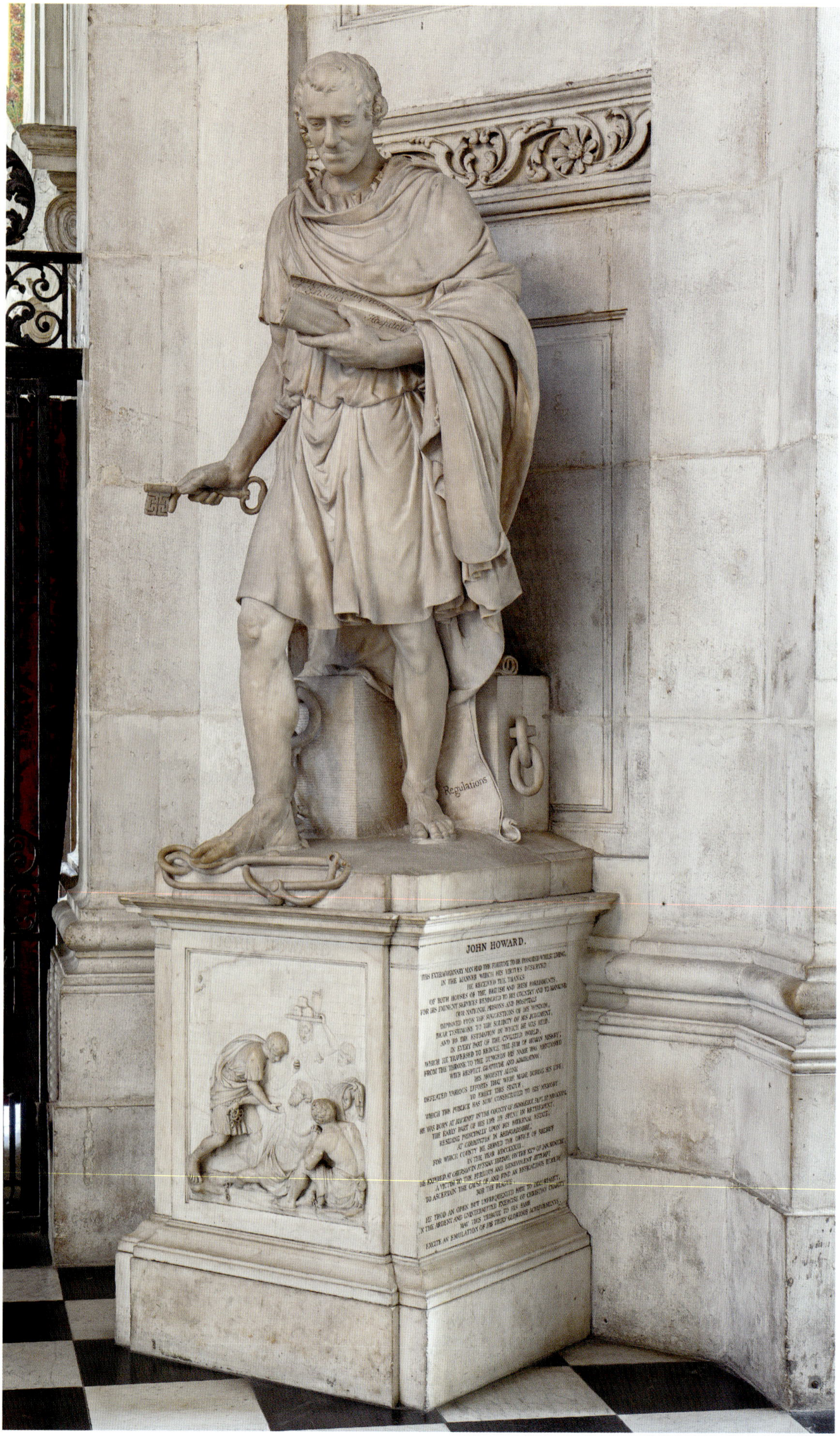

10 John Bacon, *John Howard*, 1791–5, marble.
St. Paul's Cathedral, London.

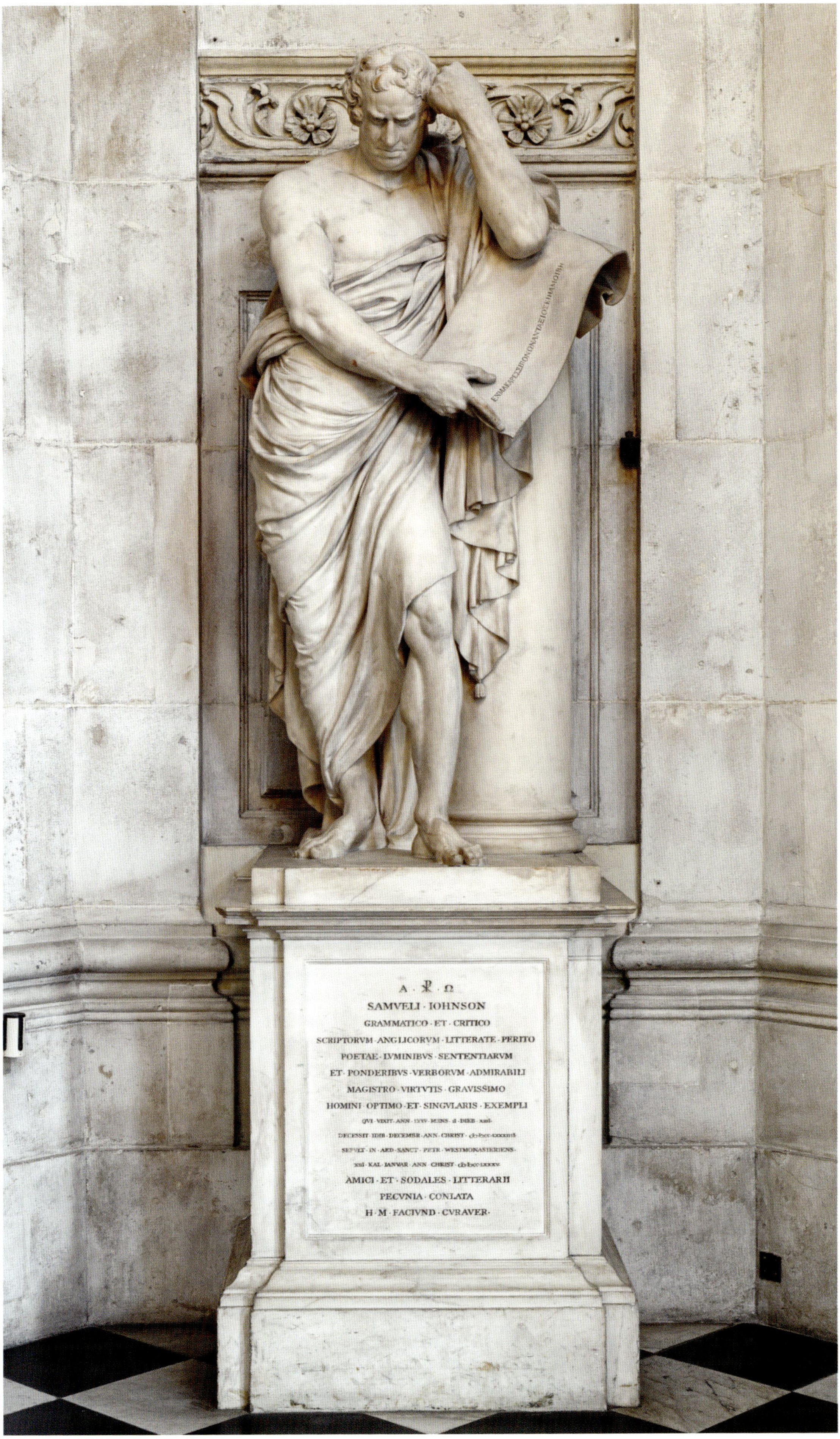

11 John Bacon, *Samuel Johnson*, 1791–5, marble.
St. Paul's Cathedral, London.

monarchy to "strangle competition" from less influential names.[8] It was reported that as soon as plans for the new St. Paul's war monuments had been circulated, Bacon went straight to the king to voice his desire that his workshop alone be given contracts to execute all three sculptures. Granting him control over all the impending monuments, Bacon apparently argued, would foster a sense of continuity with his statues of Howard and Johnson installed a few years earlier. His request was denied, opening up space for sculptors with less privileged positions and, as I will explore, one with an opposing world view.

Bacon's royalism is essential to understanding his Dream. Still more important than his devotion to the king was his Methodism. The first and only full-length biography of the sculptor, written by his friend, the pro-Methodist Evangelical priest Richard Cecil, is at pains to state that religion was the driving force behind every aspect of Bacon's life.[9] Likewise, his obituary in the *Gentleman's Magazine* ends with a lengthy account of Bacon's religious activism, his "practical Christianity"; for him religion was a lifelong preoccupation, and he spent money and time promoting causes like the preservation of the Sabbath.[10] Although his denomination lay outside the bounds of the Church of England, it did not interfere with his royal favor. Rather, it appears to have enhanced it. George III was known for his tolerance of non-Anglican Christians, particularly Methodists. The king is even said to have declared that if he himself could choose a new denomination, it would be Methodism.[11] As politically radical ideas were rising to the surface of European culture, the king would have appreciated an artist like Bacon. Clearly, the sculptor was seen to possess an unwavering faith in God that meant he perceived all earthly pursuits to be a gateway to heavenly salvation. Scholars have long attempted to come to terms with a potential link between political conservatism and Methodism in the context of the years around the French Revolution. Writing at the start of the twentieth century, French historian Élie Halévy went as far as to claim that the rise of Methodism during this period prevented a counterpart uprising from occurring in Britain.[12] Without question, it was a strain of Christianity that appealed predominantly to the working classes, both those with aspirations to transcend their lot and those obdurately limited by it. Born in Southwark, his father a clothworker, and beginning his career an apprentice to the ceramicist Nicholas Crispe at the Bow porcelain factory, Bacon fell into the former camp. Long after he found fame he was active in London's Methodist community, playing a role in the movement to set up Sunday schools.[13] E. P. Thompson makes the case that the Methodist Sunday schools were part of a broader political agenda, in that they sought to exert control over the poor.[14] Bacon had an unusually pastoral relationship to his workmen – labourers who were less socially mobile than him – and is said to have delivered sermons at their bedside while they were sick.[15] After war broke out in 1793 he practiced military drills with these men and even armed them in case the French managed to reach British shores. He also donated money to local anti-Revolutionary militias.[16]

The central tenet of Methodism is that all of humankind are sinners from birth, and that only those who adhere to the gospel have the chance of salvation in the afterlife. In practice, it is characterized by a dramatic, emotional preaching style designed to arouse new devotees. The idea of "work discipline" figures strongly in the Methodist belief system, as idleness leads one astray from the path toward salvation.[17] Cecil hints at Bacon's take on the Gordon Riots of 1780 when he relays that the sculptor composed a tract "to correct and allay the political ferment that prevailed a few years ago among the common people. To say something popular to this class was the principal ambition he seemed to have in using his pen."[18] Methodism promised to quieten disaffection with the monarchy, government, and dominant religious institutions by stressing the transience of mortal existence; in heaven, all would be put right.

For the king, then, Bacon was a safe artist, moreover one who might actively quell the outcome he so feared: a British revolution. But while Bacon's faith brought him closer to the monarchy, it appears to have cast him as an outsider in other respects. Among the sceptical, Methodism was seen a "new fangled doctrine," "experimental" at best, "ignorant" at worst.[19] Many during the late eighteenth century appeared to have had "no other notion of Methodism than that it was an eccentricity."[20] Hence Bacon's life did not neatly coincide with the status quo. He went against the grain, accepting, according to Cecil, that "vital godliness must bear those Stigmas with which the thoughtless ... brand every man who dares to differ themselves."[21] The fact that he was seen as a "monopoliser" among his fellow practitioners, some of whom held radical, democratic beliefs, further distanced him from those of a similar social background.[22] A later account of his life by Edmund Gosse states that other sculptors referred to him as "the presumptuous potter" because of his constant proselytizing; he composed hymns, writes Gosse, "he preached sermons, he distributed epitaphs and parables and admonitions."[23] Taking his own words as evidence, it becomes clear that Bacon saw himself as an agent to try and change the world, "to vex it": "What a blessed thing it is to fight for the *Truth*," he wrote in a letter to his daughter included in Cecil's biography, "for the honour of God – for everlasting Life – to strive for the noblest Prize – to wear celestial Armour ... to fight with the Captain at our side, and to be *sure* of the victory at last!"[24] In monumental works, Bacon had the opportunity to preach. While sculpture intended for ornamental purposes was, in the end, inconsequential, in his words mere "toys" and he the "toyman," public statuary could "be employed to an important moral purpose."[25]

One of the characteristics of Dreaming art is that, in order for its utopian ideas to be upheld, the material must be left in a simple state. That Bacon saw himself as a spreader of God's word first, a sculptor second, is confirmed by his distance from the superficial appearance of his finished creations: namely, the process of carving and finishing marble. Although commissioned for numerous important marble monuments, Bacon had little skill in carving the stone. His training among potters and ceramicists gave him an aptitude for modelling small figures in clay, yet he was out of his depth when it came to the execution of larger schemes, hence the reliance on the discipline of his workmen.[26] Yet this did not inhibit his success because the crux of his art was not the dazzling surface but the will to intervene, to instill belief.

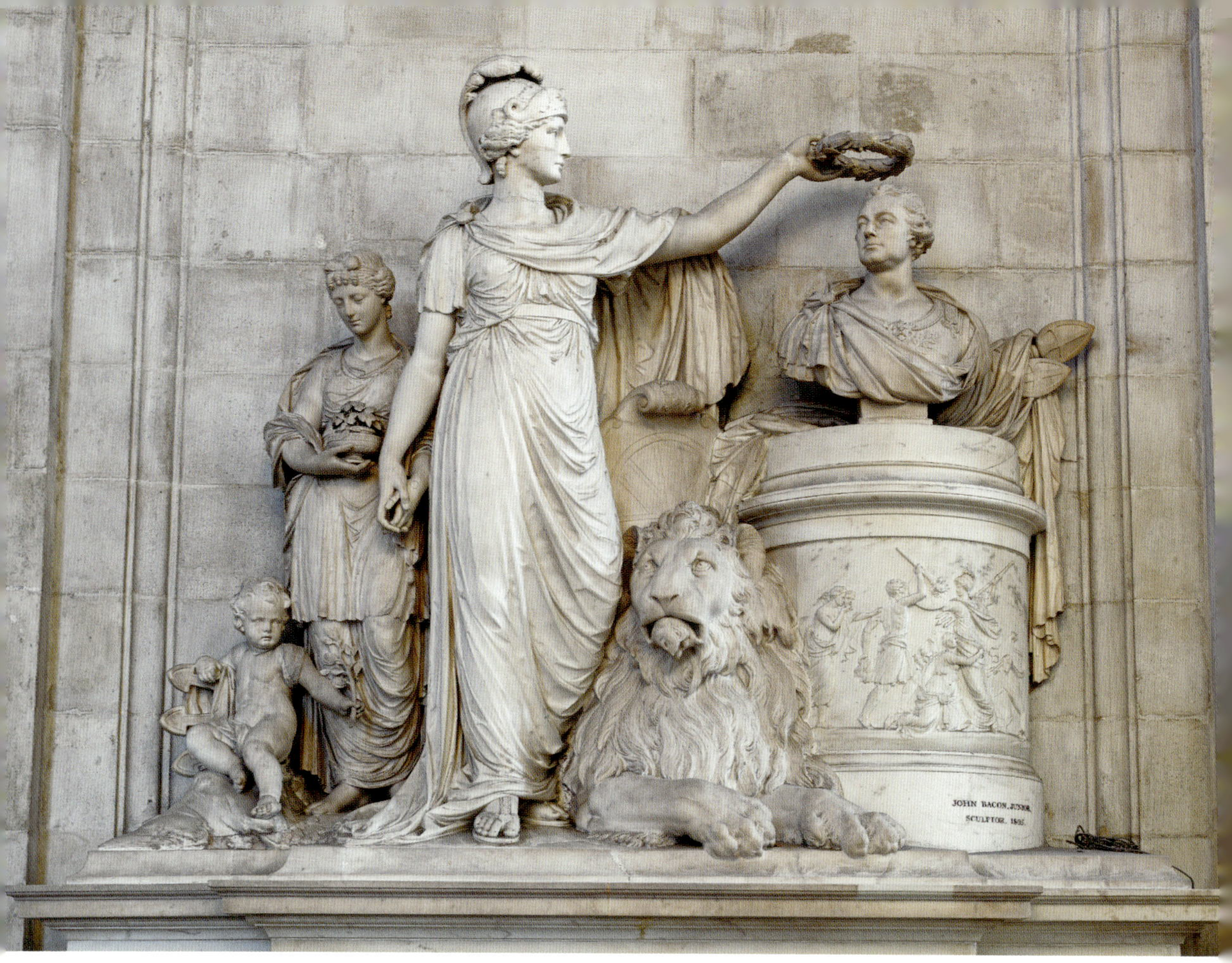

12 & 13 John Bacon, *Major General Thomas Dundas*, 1798–1805, marble, and detail. St. Paul's Cathedral, London.

Preaching through sculpture was possible even in subtle ways. His monument to the *Earl of Chatham* at the Guildhall pays tribute to a Whig politician who sympathized with the rebels in the years leading up to the American War of Independence. Craske explores how Bacon essentially hijacked the commission from a rival sculptor with an anti-monarchy agenda, turning the monument into an anodyne affirmation of the subject's commitment to commercial and maritime interests.[27] In the context of the St. Paul's war monuments, Bacon could go several steps further, as his Methodist, royalist Dream corresponded neatly with the ideological orientation of the commission itself. These were sculptures that were not only to glorify king and country, but that, housed in a Christian edifice, could defend religion in the face of French Revolutionary atheism. Most significantly, they were to pay tribute to men that had died fighting against such forces, men who carried out the task for which Bacon himself was preparing his workmen. In 1798, he was granted a contract for a large monumental group, a monument to *Major General Thomas Dundas*. In this work, the sculptor's Dream is consolidated in three dimensions (fig. 12).

Look first at the relief on the columnar plinth on which the portrait bust of Major Dundas is placed (fig. 13). Here a personification of Liberty, the estranged sister of French Revolutionary allegories of Liberty, falls at Britannia's feet, wrapping her arms around Britannia's lower body in a bid for protection. Britannia, meanwhile, is battling a male Anarchy, distinguished by the severed head clutched in his free hand. As Britannia wields her trident, Anarchy raises his torch: a symbol of democratic enlightenment now cast as sinister and capable of bodily harm. Behind Anarchy is Hypocrisy wearing a mask. This is an explicitly anti-Revolutionary scene. The subject of the monument was no regular war hero, and Bacon's design reflects his distinct fate. Having caught yellow fever after helping to secure the British seizure of Guadalupe, Dundas was killed on duty but not in battle. After the French won back the island, Dundas's body was dug up and his remains crudely disposed of.[28] When word of his exhumation reached England, Dundas was made a major general, a verified war hero and a martyr to French cruelty. The significance of his gruesome fate in granting him heroic status presented a challenge in terms of how it could be alluded to in monumental form. Bacon's preliminary drawing for the sculpture verges on the Gothic, with Dundas's feet protruding from within a cracked sarcophagus, the original location for the anti-French relief (fig. 14). The broken tomb articulates the perversion of Dundas's humiliation in the hands of the French, for which Britannia seeks revenge. This macabre detail, and the small group of unidentifiable male figures on top of a column at the left, did not find their way onto the finished sculpture. Given that Bacon died the year after producing the design,

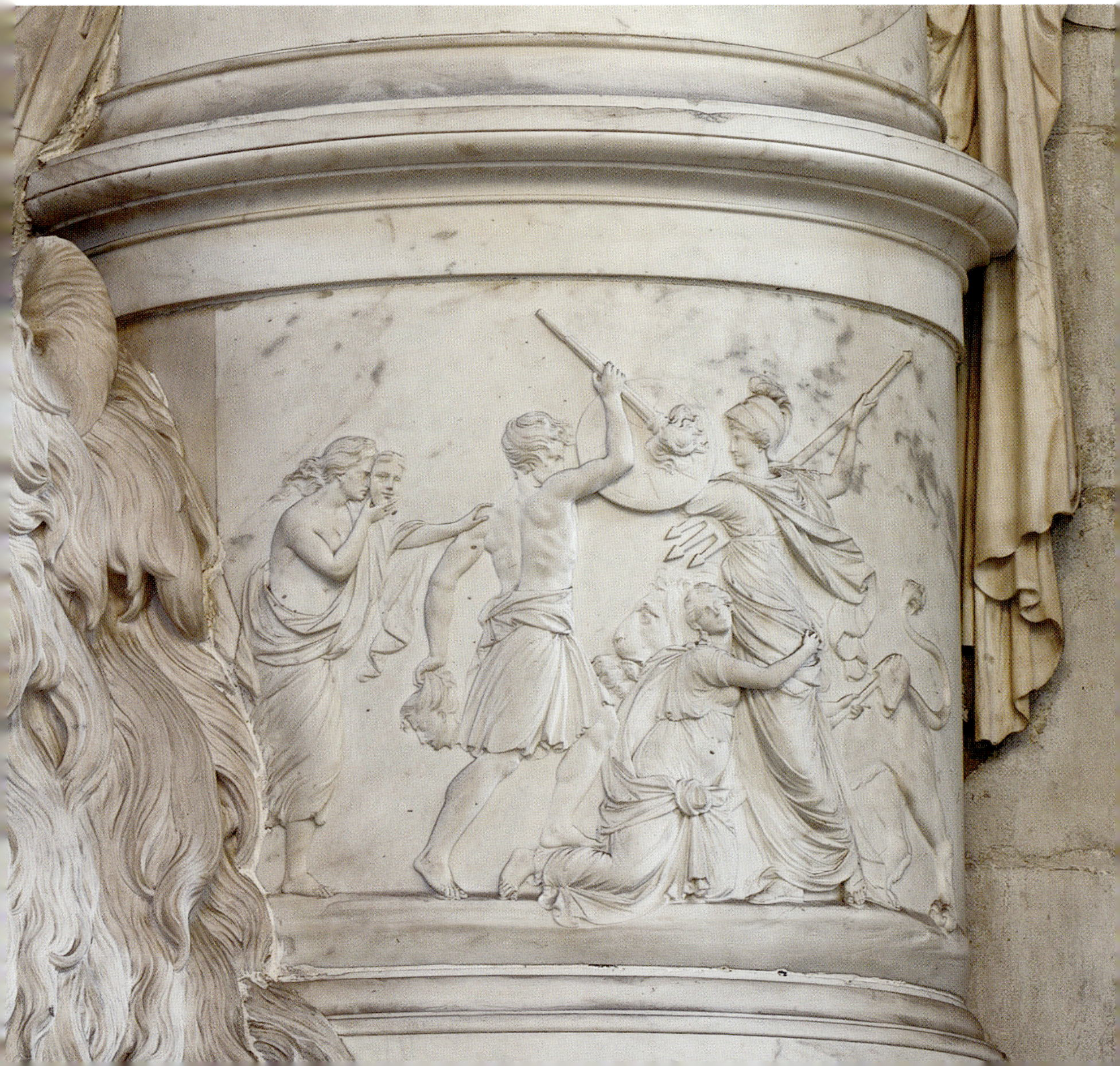

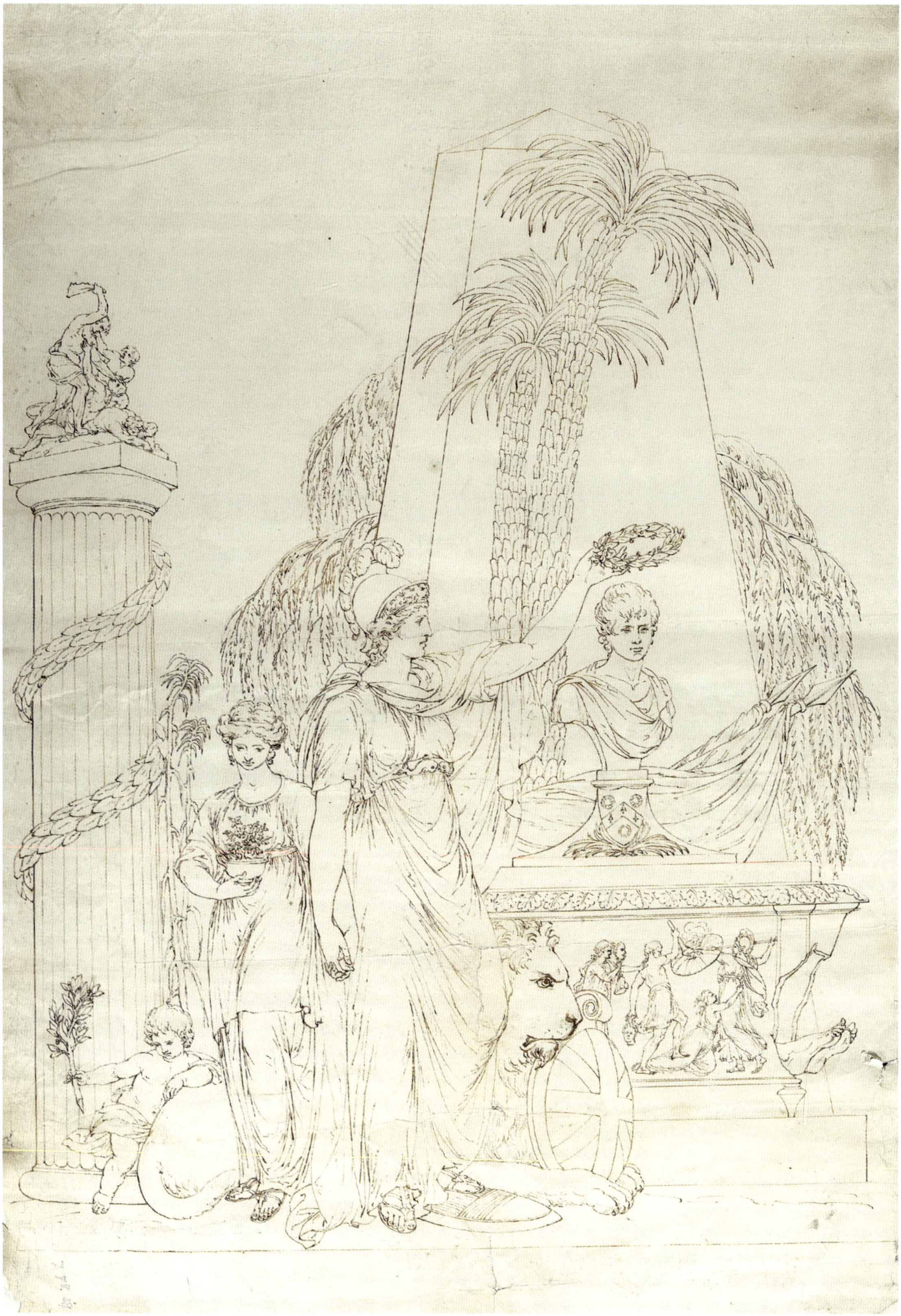

14 John Bacon, design for monument to *Major General Thomas Dundas*, 1798, pen on paper. National Archives, Kew.

it could be that his son, who oversaw the facture of the work, chose to omit these elements.

In both the design and the finished monument, Major General Dundas appears in the form of a portrait bust (fig. 15). Due to the subject's posthumous dishonor, a life-size figure, such as was customary in marble war monuments on this scale, would have been inappropriate.[29] In disembodied form, Dundas is clad in a vaguely ancient armor partly covered by drapery and clinched with a fibula. A lion, one of three that feature in the sculpture, appears as a cameo

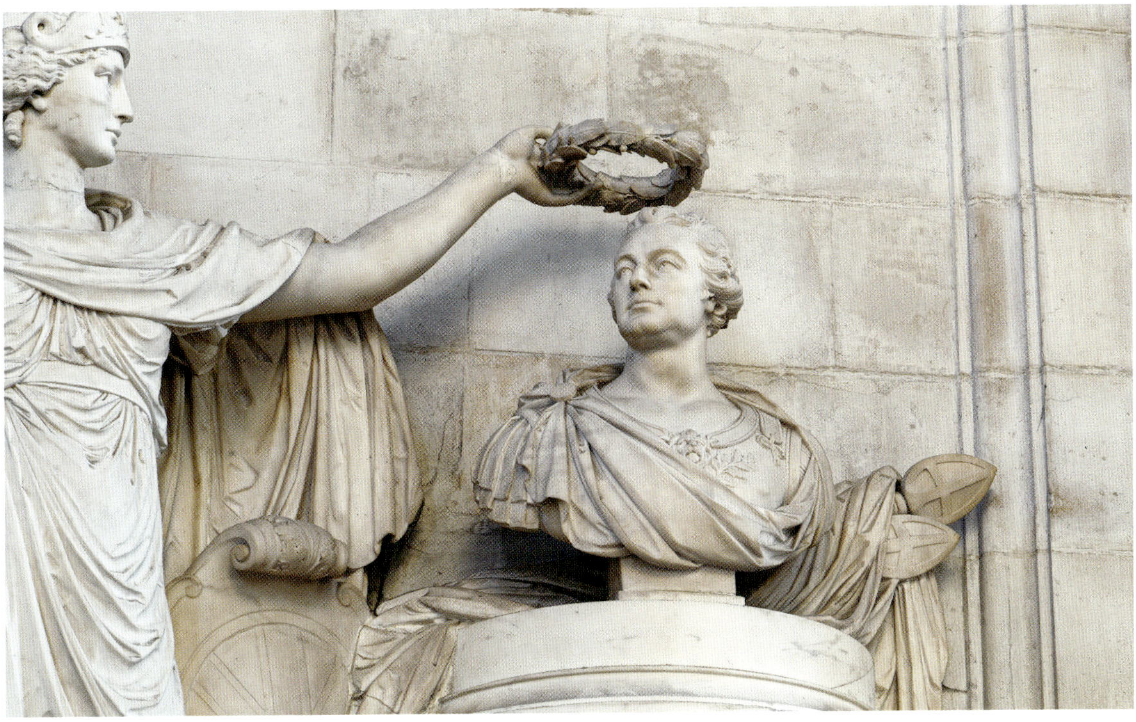

15 Detail from John Bacon, *Major General Thomas Dundas* (fig. 12).

affixed to the neck of the breastplate. Armor has a special place in Methodist thought. I observed that Bacon himself, writing to his daughter, referred to his own "celestial Armour"; in the Epistle to the Ephesians, the book of the New Testament cited often by Methodist priests, St. Paul instructs: "put on the whole armour of God ... put on the breast plate of righteousness."[30] A Methodist magazine published in London months after the work was designed features a sermon entitled "The Whole Armour of God" in which the author proclaims, "We wrestle not against flesh and blood only, but against principalities, against powers, against the rulers of the darkness of this world, against wicked spirits in high places."[31] Dundas wears this godly armor: a form of impenetrable protection with a special resonance in relation to the notion of the ruler who apes God's power. In a treatise entitled "Short Hints to a Soldier," Bacon's friend Cecil yokes this trope of celestial armor explicitly to the fight against Revolutionary France.

Addressing the average lower-ranking member of the English armed forces, Cecil begins by defining a good soldier as one who "fears God and the King, and meddles not with them that are given to change ... While bad men will always be murmuring and complaining, he knows his privileges as an Englishman. He is firmly attached to his King and Country. He feels bound, in honour and conscience, to defend both."[32] The priest goes on to suggest that although the French "mean to do here, as they have done wherever they came ... to strip us of our property, to ravish our wives and daughters, to make slaves of us, and then to tell us we are free," they are not the real enemy. The real enemy is the world of sin, the flesh and the Devil. Hence the most loyal friend to the English solider is the "Government under which you live, and all who strive to promote rule and order under it ... by them, we all enjoy that liberty and tranquillity of which no other nation can boast."[33] Christ, the "Captain of our Salvation," makes soldiers invincible by "putting upon them the whole armour of God."[34] Cecil would have written this political-religious pamphlet in the years leading up to his friend's design for the monument. Indeed, the wars were evidently in an early stage when it was composed. Cecil writes that if the Jacobins do succeed by taking control of a few English villages, their victory will be short lived. Only victories led by faith in God are guaranteed to last. Cecil also pays homage to the piety of Bacon's patron, George III.[35]

Considered in conjunction with Methodist theology, the armor worn by Dundas expresses something significant about religious culture in Britain at the time the monument was made. Evangelical thought – utopian in the sense that it holds out the promise of a more perfect life after death – was targeted toward impressionable young soldiers. To allude to Evangelical ideas in a monument honoring a dead military official was to secure a bond already forged between the conduct of the soldier and the prize of redemption. Only at this, pre-Napoleonic phase of the wars could the demonization of the French provide such a concrete method of encouraging submission to the gospel. Legible only when we unpack the ephemera generated during the years around its design, Dundas's "armour of God" is one of the details that traps the sculpture in time.

As I stated at the start of this chapter, it is in Bacon's treatment of the classical body that his Dream is most forcefully expressed. Look now at the life-size female statues that accompany the subject's bust. The larger of the two is an amplification of the miniature Britannia battling Anarchy on the plinth only more peaceful, crowning the bust with laurels. With her left hand she holds that of an attendant figure caught in her shadow. When the monument was installed in 1806, this girlish attendant was revealed to be a personification of Sensibility, an allegory not only unusual for a monument but, according to the sculptor, one not previously represented in marble. As there was no iconographic tradition for the figure, Bacon invented his own, giving the girl a "sensitive plant" – a vessel brimming with thin, petal-like leaves – to imply the need for careful cultivation.[36] Sensibility is there to idealize the rightful response to the brutality of Dundas's fate, valorizing "the general feeling which took place at the savage treatment that hero's remains received."[37] While Bacon did not embrace the fashion for evocations of Hellenic art like some of his contemporaries did, the novelty of Sensibility suggests that he was more open than we might assume to the practices of his more overtly classicizing colleagues. To invent a new icon with her own attributes ought to be seen as an instance of the "empirical approach to the antique" with which Banks and Canova are associated, even if "the antique" as a particular style ends up being transcended in the process. Indeed, I want to emphasize that Bacon's sculpture, and this monument, are fundamentally classicizing in spite of the artist's expression of distrust of "the antique," an important point to which I will return.

The most striking feature of Bacon's original icon is the extra drapery the figure wears: garments that hide all of what would be her marble flesh. Floor length, Sensibility's drapery has three layers leaving only her neck, feet, and forearms exposed. At first it may seem inevitable that the human body, especially that of a female figure, be concealed in an English Protestant church. Looking at the other monuments commissioned the same year, however, it becomes clear that the fixation on Greece prevalent in 1798 permitted works containing female figures that are lightly draped and males that are covered only at the loins. Rather than simply a question of propriety, the shrouding of Sensibility has a distinct meaning of its own. Earlier I observed that Methodism was characterized by the passionate oratory style in which the gospel was spread and new members recruited. Phyllis Mack writes that Methodists saw emotion not as a weakness, but as "the basis of a positive, disciplined moral energy."[38] But for feeling to be moralized, it had to be purged of all traces of sensuality: that is, the physical, somatic feelings that are in some way pleasurable. Both sensibility and sensuality were conditions associated with the archetypal female body. Although one of the more radical aspects of Methodism was the encouragement of female priests, the dangers of sensuality and feminine temptation are a recurring refrain in their sermons.[39] Of course, it was a woman that had sealed the fate of all mankind to exist in a state of perpetual sin: the Methodist point of departure. While in Bacon's monument the icon of Britannia is, as usual, modelled on the sexless Greco-Roman goddess Minerva/Athena, Sensibility had no safe, concrete mooring. From antiquity through to Bacon's lifetime, idealized representations of more girlish female figures in sculpture – Psyche, for instance – tend to be infused with an unavoidable eroticism linked to their straddling of youth, associated with virginal purity, and sexual desirability, associated with attractiveness. Hence Bacon's Sensibility is a representation of feeling, but on restricted terms. From her head to her ankles she must be covered up so that the "victory over sensuality" so dear to Methodists can be guaranteed.[40] With Sensibility, the charge of the undraped human form becomes visible through its emphatic covering up.

The heavy draping of Sensibility is also a register of Bacon's aversion to political radicalism. In his invective against the French Revolution published only a few years earlier, Edmund Burke had claimed that placing value on emotion is intrinsic to the upper-class way of life, now under threat from the cold rationalism of radicals; the "true lawgiver," he declares, "ought to have a heart full of sensibility."[41] Bacon's Sensibility not only embodies the feelings of compassion ideally caused by Dundas's story. She also stands for the strata of society now in need of defence from the French Revolutionaries and their British supporters, from Burke's "new conquering empire of light and reason."[42] This movement seeks to strip Sensibility of her copious layers, her "coat of prejudice," in Burke's words, humiliating her by exposing her "naked shivering nature" to the unfeeling world.[43] Like Bacon, Burke deviated from the Hellenic view of nakedness, viewing the unclothed body through a Christian lens of irrecoverable sin. Intended as an emblem of "the genius of Britain," the naked putto at the base of the sculpture does not disturb the monument's correspondence with Burke's metaphysical drapery. The representation of cherubim and seraphim in a similar corporeal form, as well as the infant Christ and John the Baptist, gave the male child's nakedness an exceptional status.

In addition to betraying attitudes toward emotion peculiar to his denomination while adhering to Burke's conception of the aristocratic order as a kind of drapery, the figure of Sensibility presents the complexities of Bacon's sculptural aesthetic. In contrast to his fellow sculptors with connections to the Royal Academy, he claimed to be uninterested in the ancient world and archaeological relics. He did not tour Rome, confining himself to Britain and never even visiting Paris (although he did have dealings with Jean-Antoine Houdon, a fellow sculptor with royal allegiances), and did not subscribe to the vogue for Greece that took hold of contemporary sculpture of the 1790s.[44] Instead, he remained committed to perpetuating the "modern" classical style associated with the émigré sculptors active in his youth including John Michael Rysbrack, Peter Scheemakers and especially Louis-François Roubiliac, artists responsible for much of the monumental sculpture made in Britain before Bacon's rise. On the whole, these practitioners favored a realistic style characterized by varied, illusionistic textures, theatrical gestures, and fluttering drapery. Although they hang gravitationally to conceal most of the body, the creased layers shrouding Sensibility conform to this tradition. Rather than simply reactionary in relation to the Hellenic turn, this style persisted, in Bacon's late designs, as provocatively modern, acquiring an edge it had not possessed when it was standard. Traceable back to Gian Lorenzo Bernini in baroque Rome, the style had originally emerged as a competitive approach to the emulation of Greco-Roman exemplars. But by taking on the ancients and attempting to vie with the legacy of Greek sculptors, such works remain a kind of classicizing art. Although he was openly averse to the blind worship of "the antique" among his contemporaries, Bacon produced numerous classical gods and goddesses that would not look out of place in the piazzas of Rome, and his contemporaries even drew comparisons between his sculpture and Bernini's.[45]

There is a sensuality about this modern style that seems to chafe against Bacon's Methodist renunciation of the flesh. Perhaps this is why the sculptor apparently distanced himself from those who upheld it before him, even Roubiliac, the artist who most directly influenced his own practice. Cecil relays an anecdote that, after having been told a story about Roubiliac's undying passion for his craft, Bacon replied that he himself felt such fervor for God rather than art. Sculpted figures were destined to remain "but dead forms," and artists "were too often found talking so coolly and indifferently about" religious matters.[46] A Catholic by birth who married a Huguenot, Roubiliac was a godless man compared to Bacon.

The earlier monuments to Howard and Johnson are equally representative of the modern style that rediscovers its competitive edge in Bacon's hands. While they are clad in a more strictly ancient drapery than the sleeved, three-layered shroud Bacon designed for his Sensibility, the statues of Howard and Johnson contend with the influence of Greco-Roman art on a formal level. With their intense, individualized facial expressions, they too conform to the tradition that ties Bernini to eighteenth-century London; this would have been even more obvious had Bacon's initial design – reportedly much more florid – been realized.[47] At the same time, these figures have the air of a Roman orator and Greek philosopher respectively, creating a tension between body and dress, form and content. Although, as Sarah Burnage points out, the Academy was not officially involved in the commission for these sculptures, the nation's leading artists were, under the guidance of the Academy's president Reynolds, able to steer the design of these two important sculptures toward, if not an overtly Hellenic aesthetic, a simpler, less Roubiliac-esque style more in tune with current taste.[48] Like the monument to Dundas, these works are trapped in the moment of their creation not because they draw on the prevailing aesthetic inclinations of the day, but because they manifest stylistic tensions and compromises that are particular to this moment. Reynolds was scathing about the modern style of sculpture, railing against Bernini and his wizard-like ability to make "stone sport and flutter in the air."[49] The painter did not live to see the introduction of war monuments into St. Paul's. As a vestige of the sculptural style he condemned, the figure of Sensibility signals a total retreat from the principles he puts forth in the Discourse; although she does not technically wear modern dress, her layers purposefully hide the "beauty of form alone" that Reynolds considered the essence of all good sculpture.[50] Yet bearing in mind the painter's concerns about the encroachment of radical ideology on classicizing art discussed in the introductory chapter, he likely would have come to tolerate this kind of figure and her Burkean shroud. The fact that Reynolds acquired Bernini's restored *Neptune and Triton* six years after he delivered the Discourse blasting the sculptor points to the flimsiness of his unequivocal condemnation of the more ornate modern style.[51]

The provocative aspect of Bacon's aesthetic is represented in his striking bust of *Sickness* submitted to the Academy as his diploma piece (fig. 16). Here, Bacon expands on a figure in his contemporaneous monument to *Thomas Guy* in a niche in the crypt of Guy's Hospital chapel. In the monument, a life-size representation of the hospital's founder takes the hand of a seated, half-naked invalid, gesturing in the direction of salvation. In the bust, Bacon extracts and disembodies the invalid, elevating the figure to autotelic subject rather than foil to honor Guy's charity. Crippling thirst is expressed by the parted lips and exposed, animalistic teeth of the figure. His wide eyes sink into their sockets, hollow as the cavities in his cheeks. A vertical line plunges down the center of his chest, crossed by smaller rivulets. In the Greco-Roman tradition, busts were reserved for gods and goddesses, semi-divine beings or living people of some note. To elevate a myth-less personification to such a high status was to

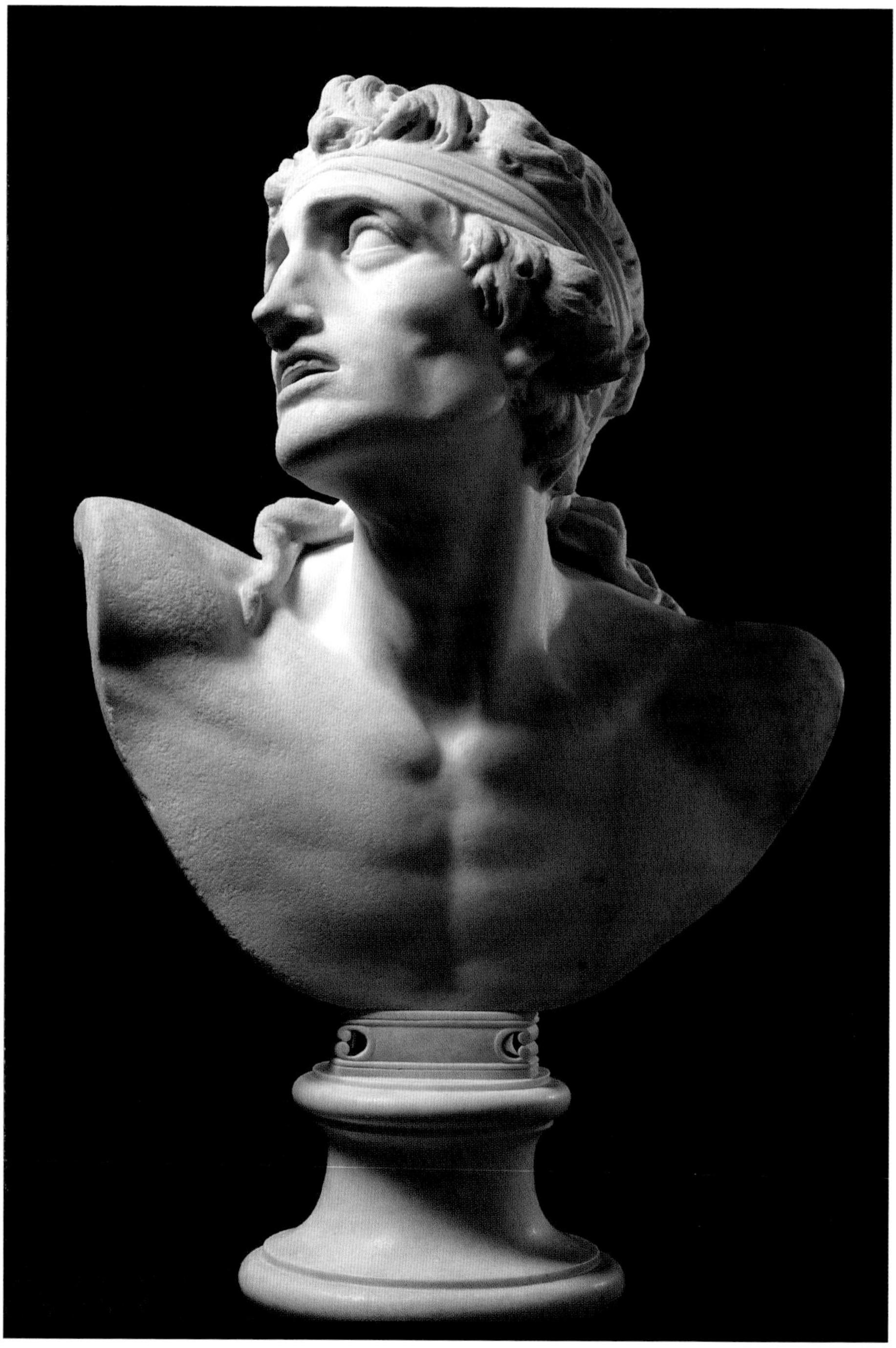

16 John Bacon, *Sickness*, 1778, marble. Royal Academy of Arts, London.

challenge the legacy of classical antiquity while simultaneously adhering to it. In a sense, the work betrays somewhat of a kinship with the more visceral northern European tradition of novel figurines than it does to the Bernini-esque: for example, the open-mouthed *Allegory of Sickness* carved in boxwood by Ulm-based sculptor David Heschler a century before.[52] However, Bacon's sculpture is not a statuette but a bold statement in stone. Like Sensibility, the figure of Sickness had never before been rendered in marble and presented before the public. While his peers were imbibing Winckelmann, who, as well as stimulating a discourse around political liberty that Bacon abhorred, argued that the beauty of Greek sculpture stemmed from its very lack of intensive expression, Bacon zoomed in on the meticulous details of suffering: an emotion with little sensuality. The crude quality of the sculpture's surface hints that this, too, is a Dreaming work of art. As I pointed out earlier, Bacon was not adept at carving and finishing marble. With this bust, which, as his Academy diploma piece, would not have been produced by his workmen, Bacon appears to turn a shortcoming into a means of making art to conform to his world view. Left in a grainy state, the marble does not give pleasure to the beholder but throws the grotesque features of Sickness further into relief. We are not meant to enjoy looking at this work of art. Rough stone does not conjure flesh, but rather frustrates the sculpture's capacity to give the sense of an actual head. Indeed, the object is not anthropomorphic. Incrementally smaller than life, it does not conjure an actual man but operates as a vessel for the artist's Dream. Bacon's Sickness is the archetypal Methodist subject: a vulnerable soul ripe for conversion, desperate to be saved. Recall that Bacon is said to have read sermons to his workmen when they themselves were sick.

If Bacon had been allowed to procure contracts for all of the new St. Paul's monuments, perhaps the cathedral would have been filled with numerous marble works that materialize his Methodist, anti-Revolutionary Dream: "a paradise for a sect." But the sculptor died in 1799, the year after he received the commission, leaving his son John Bacon junior to oversee the completion of the monument. From the age of twelve, the younger Bacon had trained at the Academy and was a competent practitioner. Critics, however, could accuse him of possessing no originality of his own.[53] Yet while the younger Bacon struggled to mark himself apart from his father, there was also a vast gulf between their practices that speaks to an exceptional aspect of the elder's lifetime. The religious fervor instilled in the younger Bacon by his father grew to be incompatible with artistic practice. According to an account given by a family member, Bacon junior came strongly to believe that religious piety was totally at odds with the life of an artist.[54] This is a generational shift that aligns with the conflict between Dreaming and Poetic art. In his father's time, religion and classicizing art could be reconciled even for the most avid of Methodists, but this was not the case later on in the nineteenth century.[55] Antje Matthews has identified other instances of this shift among artists raised into religious families at this time.[56] This tension shaped the life of the younger Bacon. By the time he acquired a degree of success in his own right, Dreams had been purged from the classical body.

In order to introduce the second Dreamer I want to jump briefly back to the present day where this chapter began. A 2012 edition of the *Rough Guide to London* features a passage on the war monuments of St. Paul's.[57] But the guide mentions the sculptures only to dismiss them as the least interesting feature of the cathedral. In the author's view they are nothing more than "overblown" monstrosities one passes on the way to the mosaics or up into the whispering gallery. One monument is especially repulsive. Thomas Banks's monument to *Captain Richard Rundle Burges* is pronounced "simply ludicrous" because it represents the subject – a naval captain who perished at sea in 1797 during the Battle of Camperdown – naked, covered only by a swathe of drapery that hangs vertically to conceal the pubic area (fig. 17).[58] Standing resurrected, not only is the naval captain without clothes; the figure is portrayed "holding hands with an angel," a lightly draped female figure with wings. What the author interprets as an angel is actually Victory, an allegorical figure whose iconography is intertwined with that of Christian angels. And Victory does not hold the captain's hand but rather bestows upon him her sword. Yet the guide's reaction to the sculpture stems from the proud, standing nakedness of the naval captain. Given their obscurity, it is surprising that a popular guidebook even mentions these sculptures, if only to dismiss them. It is testament to the power of this particular sculpture that it repelled the author with such force.

When the author of the guidebook wrote his response he had no idea of the significance of the monument to *Captain Burges*. In this he is not alone. The few historians who mention the work have dismissed it entirely. Scholarship unanimously sees it as bad art, "naïve," little more than an index of an unfortunate "Neoclassical" taste.[59] One historian describes the captain as a "strange naked man" before moving swiftly on.[60] Another proclaims that, because of its "practically nude but be-whiskered" protagonist, the sculpture is "neither successful nor moving."[61] Elsewhere, the work is described as "near to the ridiculous."[62] They all imply that by the time it was placed inside the cathedral – early in the year 1803 – it was seen as an embarrassment. But one does not have to look far to see that this was not actually the case. For the most part, the sculpture was praised by Banks's contemporaries and admired throughout the wars with France, with two very different engravings of it appearing in a literary and a military magazine respectively (see figs. 29, 30). Only in the post-Napoleonic period did its resonance begin to fade, an articulate shift in fortune to which I shall refer in each chapter of this book. Changing responses to the work over time indicate that the sculpture only made sense within a limited set of years. Again, this is a work that is trapped in time.

What scholars misread as no more than the re-creation of a classical paradigm is infinitely more complex. Indeed, the sculpture tricks the viewer, luring them into a false sense of security that what they are looking at is purely derivative. From the *Rough Guide* to academic attacks on the work, the trick has been fallen for time and again. But while it purports to be an evocation of "the antique" akin to relics like the work erroneously known as the *Belvedere Antinous*

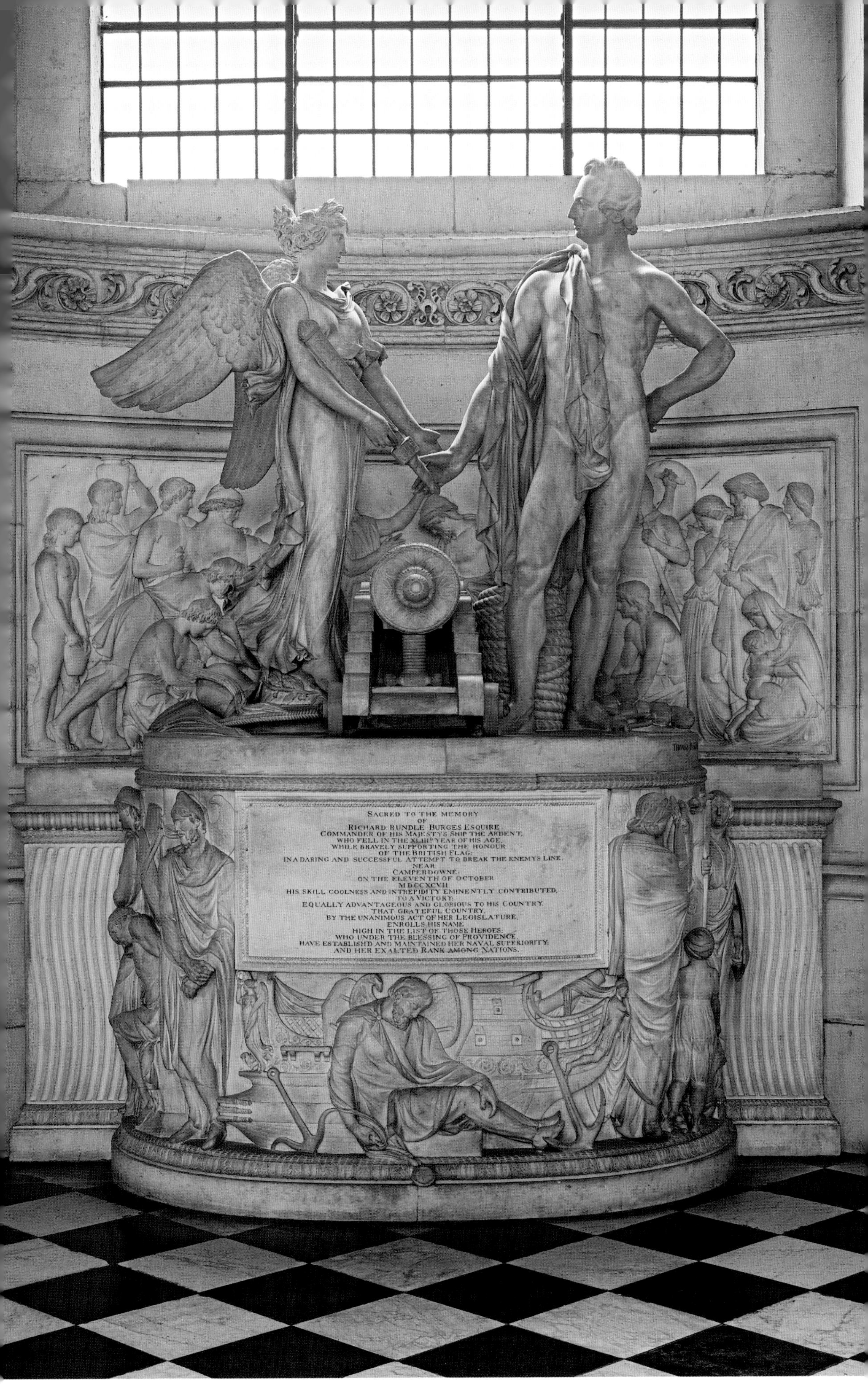

17 Thomas Banks, *Captain Richard Rundle Burges*, 1798–1802, marble.
St. Paul's Cathedral, London.

(contemporaries did describe the work as "Antinous-like"), Banks's work is born out of a polemical political vision, a Dream shared by numerous others during the period.[63]

While it readily lends itself to the interpretation that it is a straightforward nod to ancient Greece, the very idea of Greece was highly charged in the mind of the sculptor and his fellow London-based activists. Having trained in Rome in the 1770s where he was taught by Italian practitioners to cut marble, Banks became fluent in Greco-Roman relics from a practical point of view. This is how he rose to become one of the nation's most in-demand sculptors in spite of his involvement in outsider politics, an association that led to his questioning by the Privy Council during the Treason Trials of 1794, during which he was forced to lie to absolve himself.[64] While Bacon's confinement to Britain and rejection of archaeological studies could work in his favor, Banks's time on the Continent gave him an aura of legitimacy that was equally desirable in an era in which Greece was in vogue, especially for a high-profile monumental project such as this one. The complexity of Banks and his contested legacy as Britain's "first modern sculptor" stems from the simultaneous tensions and deep connection between his art and his activism.[65] On the one hand, as an artist committed to Hellenic form during years in which the Greeks were widely conceived as "the human universal," Banks is the prototypical representative of the late eighteenth-century turn to archaeological-sculptural classicism. It was in this capacity that he was commissioned in 1798 to design one of the prestigious war monuments for St. Paul's, even afforded the most expensive contract out of the three issued that year. In the introductory chapter, I argued that his refusal to restore and copy antiquities and produce original designs in the Greco-Roman mold – the "empirical approach to the antique" – was a radical political practice rooted in the "vulgar" reception of Winckelmann's writings on Greek freedom. That Banks could be at once mainstream and countercultural has led scholars to neglect the radicalism of both his mythological and monumental works. Writing of Banks's political pursuits, Julius Bryant focuses primarily on how the broader classical idea of liberty appealed to some of Banks's Whig patrons and hence is discernible in certain works; John Barrell claims that the only politicized works Banks created after 1789 had to have been uncommissioned projects or portraits of his radical friends and associates.[66] Neither scholar looks at the mobilization of Greece among Banks's fellow activists during the years around the Treason Trials and the making of this monument. Both Bryant and Barrell overlook the adaptation of Winckelmann's ideas on beauty and freedom to suit radical political ends.

There is an extra dimension to Banks's politics, one that is especially relevant to the monument to *Captain Burges*. Unlike some of the country's leading political reformers, such as Major John Cartwright, founder of the Society for Constitutional Information, the radical organization of which Banks was an active member, the sculptor did not consider military action a path to bringing about change. While he supported the French Revolution to the extent that in 1802 he could reflect with admiration on the achievements of "the first republicans in France," there is much affirming that the sculptor was against all forms of war.[67] Hence his Dream was that of a committed radical – a supporter of the egalitarian ideology behind the French Revolution – and that of an ardent pacifist opposed to war. Extraordinarily, he was able to express this composite Dream in a state-funded war monument, moreover one dedicated to a man who had died fighting against Revolutionary France. In the rest of this chapter, I will make the case that this work deserves to be seen less as a monument to a particular individual than a political manifesto in marble. The nakedness of the figure turns the effigy of Burges into an icon of humanity at large as opposed to a specific naval captain who died during the Battle of Camperdown.

When in May 1798 Banks first heard of the plan to fill St. Paul's with war monuments, his response could not have been more different to Bacon's when he received the same news. Rather than trying to procure all the contracts for his own workshop, the sculptor wrote to his close friend George Cumberland, another radical classicist and activist, expressing his opinion that the forthcoming sculptures would only glorify unnecessary loss of life. Reflecting on the death that facilitated the plan, the letter states that the monuments are to honor "some of our Naval Heroes who have been kill'd in attempting to kill Others."[68] The sculptor's emphasis on the indiscriminate nature of death on the battlefield shows an uncommon sensitivity to the realities of warfare. In her work on the Napoleonic Wars, Mary Favret observes that in "the work of war, the necessity of killing means killing must not be pathologized. That a soldier kills himself can have nothing to do with the fact he has been trained to kill."[69] Opposed to the work of war, Banks saw death and military action as one and the same. His letter to Cumberland renders the death of the soldier at once murderous and suicidal, a far cry from Richard Cecil's attempt to convert young soldiers. In 1801, when Banks received a second contract to execute a group for St. Paul's, he described the men who would be honored by the next round of sculptures as those "who have carried the National Glory to the greatest height in destroying the greatest Numbers of Mankind."[70] He conveyed these words after he had already produced a monument for the same project.

Looking again at the monument with Banks's anti-war convictions in mind, his Dream begins to emerge. Notice that the cannon between Victory and the naked captain faces backwards, pointing away from us toward the cathedral wall. Adorned by a simple decorative motif of leaves and petals, the knob at the butt of the weapon – officially termed a cascabel – faces us head-on. The sculptor could have placed the cannon the conventional way around, gesturing toward peace by capping it with a muzzle to signify the end of conflict for the memorialized hero. Instead, he reversed the instrument, nullifying its catastrophic function and rendering it useless. As a result, the war monument is pacified, its virility denied. That the sculpture is castrated by this detail is supported by the testicular cluster of cannon balls discarded on the ground behind the naked captain. When the Treasury approved the design, they evidently thought little of the backwards cannon. Access to the sculptor's confession of disdain for the commission charges this detail with significance.

I want to emphasize that the idea of Greece that legitimized Banks's portrayal of a British naval captain in such a guise was not, nor did it purport to be, an accurate account of life in ancient Greece. As architects of democracy, the Athenians offered an image of unbridled human potential that, in this limited window in time, could be projected onto the present and onto Britain. While there is much in Winckelmann's writings suggesting that the re-creation of Greek beauty and freedom is categorically impossible, let alone in modern Britain, the very essence of "vulgar Winckelmannianism" is its generalized, interested appropriation of only select claims made by the scholar.[71] In British radical discourse, Greek nakedness is a central preoccupation, one that is applied to the present situation with hopes that it might actually bring about change. Of course, clothing was then the primary marker of class. To imagine a world where it was not an absolute necessity was to question the fabric, literally, of social difference. Worn by men, women, and sometimes even children of the period, stockings, stays, and corsets denied the human form the freedom of movement that was its inherent right. With all such clothing removed, Banks's naked captain represents humanity returned to a lost state of bodily freedom. This may sound like a rehashing of the Genesis myth, but the Hellenic form of the work, and the swathe of drapery that covers the figure's pubic area, underscore that this is not Edenic but Periclean nakedness.

Taking up the connection between beauty, art, and freedom to suit their own agenda, British radicals posited Greek nakedness not simply as an index of how far humanity had fallen in their own country, but how, potentially, humanity might rise up and assert itself anew. In addition to Banks's sculpture, a striking instance of "vulgar Winckelmannianism" appears in Mary Wollstonecraft's *Vindication of the Rights of Woman*. Banks knew Wollstonecraft through mutual friends and, following her death in 1797, produced an impression of her face.[72] Like Banks, Wollstonecraft would have discussed ideas around Greece and freedom with her friend Henry Fuseli.[73] In an almost exact quotation from Fuseli's translation of Winckelmann's *Gedanken*, the *Vindication* declares that in ancient Greece, "the human form must have been far more beautiful than it is at present" in "our luxurious society" precisely because "barbarous ligatures" did not retard the body's "expansion, or render it deformed."[74] Whereas Winckelmann's reverence for Hellenic form stems from his fascination with the male body, Wollstonecraft removes all traces of homoerotic awe and eroticism more broadly from his ideas. In order to project Winckelmannian theories onto the female body which she herself identifies with, she must drain all sexuality from the idea of the beautiful body. It is a characteristic of Dreaming art that sensuality is purged from its forms. As I noted in the introduction, the sexlessness of Banks's naked figure is a remarkable achievement, one whose banality is worth seeing in person. It seems that the total absence of eroticism is one of the factors that has caused the unanimous censure of the monument among more recent commentators. Elsewhere we find Banks draining the eroticism from ancient art objects whose sensuality was otherwise perceived to be the source of their appeal. In a memorandum on classical sculpture, he praises the *Venus de' Medici*, the sculpture widely considered during the period to be the supreme embodiment of female beauty, not for its alluring qualities but for the figure's status as a human body unbound by tight clothing (fig. 18). "Some connoisseurs have also thought this elegant figure round-shouldered," he writes with a detachment unusual in the period's responses to this sculpture, "because the back from the nape of the neck is rounder than where that beautiful part is distorted into a straight line by unnatural bandages."[75]

Wollstonecraft's "vulgar Winckelmannianism" cites outdoor exercise as a way to nurture the intellects as well as bodies of women and girls, echoing the German scholar's investment in the athletic prowess of the Greeks. She celebrates the physical and the cerebral, suggesting that the ideal female subject is a woman who manifests intellectual and corporeal beauty in a balanced measure. For her, this balance is epitomized in "the relics of antiquity," especially the "Grecian statues," in other words, in sculptures like the *Venus de' Medici*.[76] Of course, it was not important to her argument that the life of the average ancient Greek woman was hardly free, and that, certainly in Athens, the display of the naked female body was not encouraged.[77] For her, the Greek body was a vessel, a non-somatic entity.

Produced the year before he designed the monument, Banks's mask of Wollstonecraft's face provides a tangible link between two figures otherwise brought together by their "vulgar Winckelmannianism" and their mutual friends. When designing the St. Paul's monument under a year later, it is inevitable that her writings on the subject would remain relevant, especially as her *Posthumous Works*, edited by another of Banks's associates, her widower William Godwin, had recently been published.[78] The sculptor's daughter Lavinia was eighteen when *Vindication* first appeared, and it is not spurious to suggest Banks may have shared it with her. Lavinia and her father were close, and as a young woman in 1805 she felt able to defend her father's reputation after his death when detractors of his politics attempted to prevent the celebration of his life.[79] Lavinia Banks came to be known as highly articulate: a kind of new, post-Wollstonecraft woman.[80]

Godwin's "vulgar Winckelmannianism" – his version of Greek nakedness as a radical figuration of freedom – can be found in the textbook he wrote on Greco-Roman mythology under the pseudonym Edward Baldwin. Like the earlier *Pantheon* by Andrew Tooke, Joseph Spence's *Polymetis* and John Lemprière's *Classical Dictionary*, the volume presents itself as an accessible manual for those untutored in Latin.[81] But Godwin's is an interested text. The opening section includes a digression on the bodily freedoms enjoyed by the Greeks. Echoing the opening pages of the *Gedanken*, the manual soon morphs into an outraged commentary on modern custom, dress, and the implicit disregard for the human form:

> *One of the reasons why the Greeks excelled all other nations in their representations of the human figure is that they were probably the finest race of men that ever existed ... the garments that they wore had no ligatures to compress and destroy the strength and grace and free play of the muscles: while modern nations, by garters,*

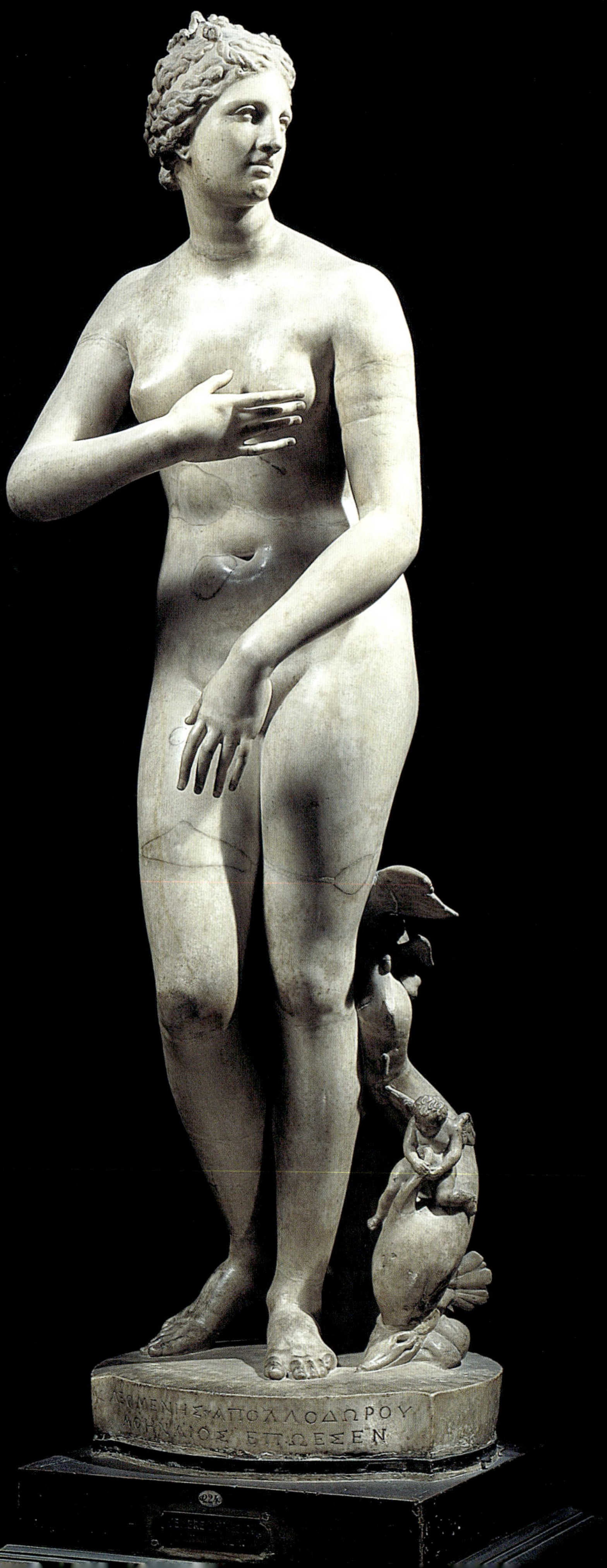
ΑΠΟΛΛΟΔΩΡΟΥ

> *and buckles, and waistbands, and kneebands, and wristbands, and collars, and fifty barbarous contrivances, are continually spoiling the flowing and active forms with which nature has endowed us: it is not a hundred years ago, since a child, as soon as it came into the world, was swaddled and swathed and pinched with I know not how many yards of broad, strong binding, so that he could scarcely move a limb or a muscle of his whole body.*[82]

In his *Enquiry Concerning Political Justice*, first published in 1793, Godwin had repeatedly politicized the idea of nakedness not in relation to sculpture but in its more metaphorical sense as a condition of truth. Describing his case against the aristocracy as a "scheme of naked truth," he indicts indices of systemic inequality such as hereditary titles.[83] Until society is capable of acting upon "the naked statement of what they really perceive" instead of blindly accepting the supremacy of the ruling class, citizens will continue to be terrified into obedience. Via Godwin we see how the rhetoric of "naked truth" and Greek sculpture came to overlap. The very month Banks received a summons to St. Paul's to discuss the new war monuments, Godwin recorded dining with the sculptor at the house of John Horne Tooke, the radical politician and Banks's close comrade. Between 1793 and 1804, Godwin and Banks met regularly through friends.

Although it is true that nakedness had long been deployed as a metaphorical trope in eighteenth-century poetry and prose, during the years around the design of the monument the word "nakedness" acquired a fresh significance thanks to its recurring presence in this kind of radical discourse. Reactionaries were quick to respond. In the summer of 1792, a satirical adaptation of Thomas Paine's *Rights of Man* was printed in London, penned by an anonymous author.[84] Entitled *Buff, or a dissertation on nakedness*, the pamphlet mocks Paine's recent manifesto by replacing certain words and passages so that the argument no longer reads as a condemnation of the present political system but as a treatise on man's right not to wear clothes. Paine's justification of "a revolution in the system of governments" becomes a call for "a revolution in the system of *dress; or rather by a total annihilation of it.*"[85] Where Paine had stated that the "origin of monarchy and kings" is arbitrary, the anonymous author questions the true "origin of Coats" (calling to mind Burke's "coat of prejudice"). So the pamphlet continues, ridiculing the ideas that were so dear to Banks, Godwin, and Wollstonecraft, who in the *Vindication* declares that the "drapery of situation hides the man."[86] In the preface to the satire, the author writes that the topic of nakedness was selected at random for its amusing irrelevance to political discourse. Clearly, the choice was not so capricious.

During these years, nakedness was being radicalized by another familiar figure, one on the fringes of Banks's network. In the catalog to his self-curated solo exhibition in 1809, William Blake rails against the necessity of clothing. Fantasizing about life in a Britain during a vague "ancient happy period," he pictures human flesh "exposed to the open air, nourished by the spirits of the

18 *Venus de' Medici*, first century BC copy of lost Greek sculpture, marble. Uffizi Gallery, Florence.

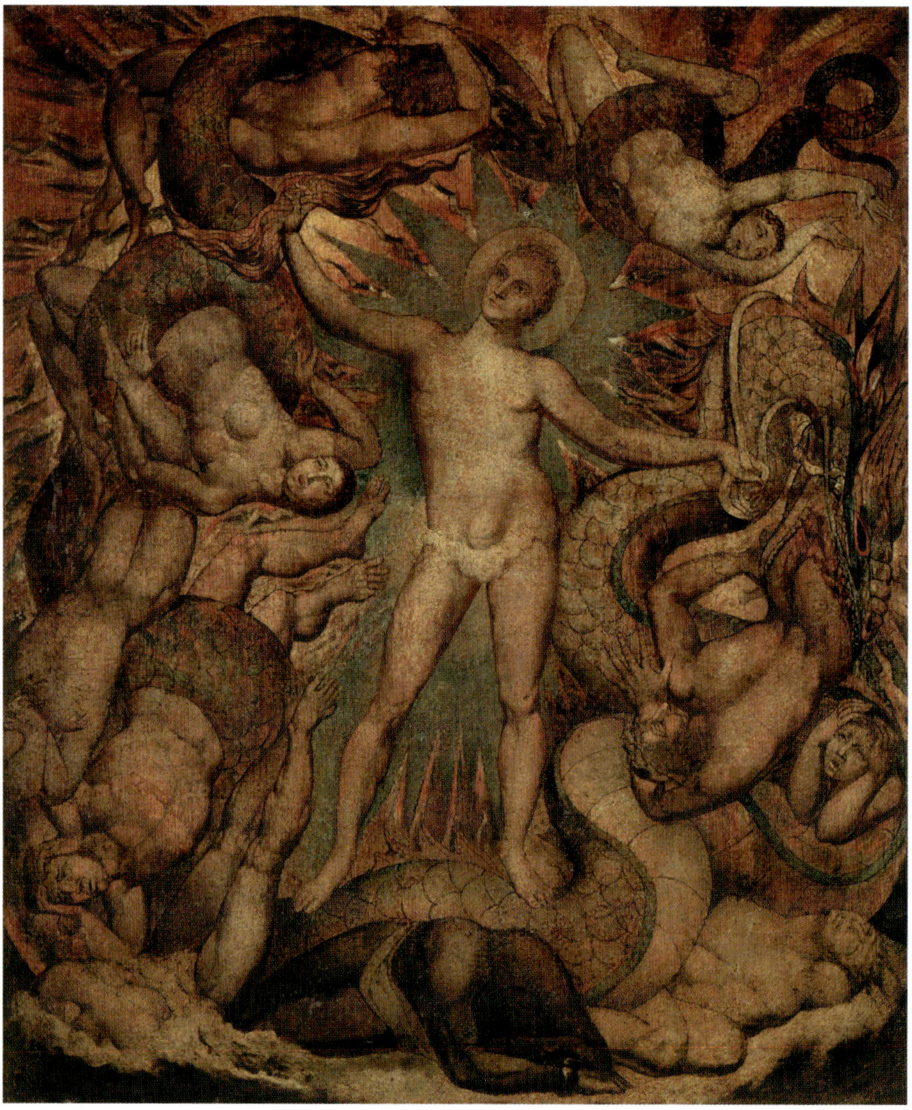

19 William Blake, *Spiritual Form of Nelson Guiding Leviathan*, 1805–9, tempera on canvas. Tate Gallery, London.

forests and floods."[87] Strip "modern Man" of his copious layers and one finds his pale, weak physicality quivering "like a dead corpse."[88] In the same exhibition Blake displayed *Spiritual Form of Nelson Guiding Leviathan*, a tempera painting representing the English admiral as a haloed figure wearing only a tiny loincloth (fig. 19). Surrounded by floating legs and torsos representing those defeated by the British during the wars, Nelson's spirit basks in victory. It is an image, claimed the artist, just as indebted to "Persian, Hindoo, and Egyptian antiquity" as Greek sculpture. In the exhibition catalog, he put forth the controversial case that the period's most cherished classical bodies, such as the *Venus de' Medici*, are faint imprints of Asian and Egyptian monuments.[89] Even more complex and multilayered than Banks's naked figure, Blake's tempera also demands to be seen as an anti-war work. While Nelson is portrayed sympathetically, luminous and almost Christ-like as he shows off his effortless strength, the leviathan he wields in his right hand – a symbol of marine warfare – destroys everything in its path, its tentacles strangling civilian men and women. Nelson's naked spirit remains impervious to death while others suffer as a result of his actions.

Banks would have known of Blake through George Cumberland, the friend with whom he first discussed the war monuments. Cumberland described Blake as a "true son of freedom" and, aware of his originality and skill, tried to convince John Horne Tooke to employ him to execute the frontispiece of a forthcoming edition of the latter's radical treatise on the English language, *Diversions of Purley*.[90] Engraved by William Sharp, another politically radical artist, the frontispiece for the previous edition was, according to one source, designed by Banks (fig. 20).[91] The image depicts a seated naked male figure – easily identifiable as the god Mercury by the winged accessories that surround him – in the act of taking off his sandals. The design encapsulates the argument of the book itself, which is that the English language in its present state is filled with words, "winged words," that are inessential. What happens, Tooke asks, when we remove all decoration from language? Seeking to "strip [Mercury] of

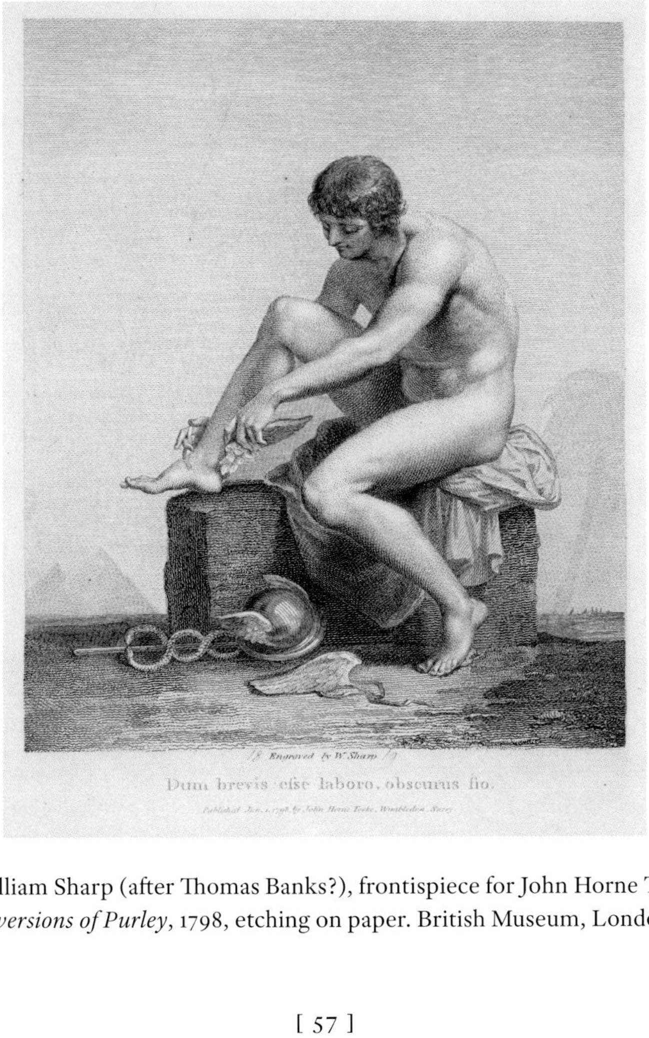

20 William Sharp (after Thomas Banks?), frontispiece for John Horne Tooke's *Diversions of Purley*, 1798, etching on paper. British Museum, London.

his wings" and "see what sort of figure he will make without them," *Diversions of Purley* defends the "man of plain common sense" against the bombastic courtier.[92] The frontispiece presents yet another embodiment of radical discourse in the form of an idealized naked body.

As Blake was exalting the sacred art of other parts of the world, Cumberland too was picturing images of ideal nakedness beyond the classical paradigm. His first novel, *The Captive of the Castle of Sennaar*, was finished the same month that Banks signed the contract for the monument. Set in a prison cell, the story is told from the perspective of one inmate, a Greek named Lyco, who recounts his time among a democratic, love-worshipping civilization called the Sophians, inhabitants of a fictional island on a lake in central Africa. Lyco describes the Sophians' attitude toward the naked body:

> *Soon the whole hall was filled with groups of naked figures, very few of which might not have formed a model for the heroes of former times ... Like the ancient statues, which still remain, they appeared to glory in the form the Creator had assigned them; and would have spurned at the unnatural depravity that affixed ideas of shame to the most necessary, wonderful and noble organs of the human superstructure.*[93]

In Cumberland's book, the beautiful body regains the eroticism it loses in the work of Banks and Wollstonecraft. Indeed, the private form of the novel permits Cumberland to mention the sexual customs of the Sophians, reconciling a politicized conception of nakedness with a sensual one. Yet there is a practicality, even an Apollonian quality, to the novel's eroticism. Sophians are open about the fact that women chose their sexual partners. Marriage does not exist, but there is order.[94] Beautiful bodies have sex, but they remain vessels of a certain world view.

Due to its implicit critique of the state, Cumberland's novel was suppressed not long after it was published. At precisely the same point in time, Banks got to work on bringing forth the monument to *Captain Burges*. The sculptor and Cumberland were in continual contact during these years.[95] The correlation between the nakedness within the sculpture and the nakedness within his friend's censored novel – both documents of a "vulgar Winckelmannianism" – is another element trapping the sculpture in time.

— FRENCH CONNECTIONS —

After his interrogation by the Privy Council in 1794 sealed his ties to radical politics, Banks remained somewhat of a controversial figure when the monument was commissioned. Ever since his training in Rome, some of his colleagues at the Royal Academy noticed that he missed out on opportunities because of his political leanings. After Banks's death in 1805, the landscape painter Joseph Farington went as far as to refer to the sculptor as a "violent democrat," a term that, in the period's parlance, did not suggest physical violence as much as ideological zeal.[96] Yet in 1798, the government needed Banks. He now stood as one of the few practitioners capable of designing a monument that could reproduce the fashionable lineaments of Hellenic sculpture and, moreover, rival monuments in Revolutionary France. Holger Hoock has observed that the project to fill St. Paul's – described as a "Temple of British Fame" – was, in the early stages of its development, thought of as London's equivalent to the Panthéon in Paris.[97] Founded in 1791 on the site of a Catholic basilica, this space had recently been repurposed to house statues of Revolutionary martyrs in drapery or naked.[98] Aesthetically, the implications of the rivalrous relationship between the St. Paul's monuments and the Panthéon presented a paradox. If they were to rival the French, the British sculptures would need to represent the latest in contemporary monumental design, which, as I mentioned earlier, had broken from Bacon's modern style to the extent that Bacon could now stand as an outlier. As the king's personal favorite, it was inevitable that Bacon be involved in the scheme; yet Bernini-esque pomp was not the aesthetic of the people and would not do to commemorate the non-aristocratic men who fought on their behalf. Linda Colley identifies the kernel of this paradox: "The prime opponent of the French Revolution had itself to employ revolutionary methods in order to stand a chance of succeeding"; she continues, to "beat the French, the British had been required to imitate the French."[99]

But for French Revolutionary artists, the appropriation of Greco-Roman sculpture was not just a question of style. As the guillotine loomed large over Paris, the very notion of antiquity was increasingly coextensive with the abolition of the old regime. Karl Marx summed this up when, in 1852, he wrote that the French Revolution had draped "itself alternately as the Roman republic and the Roman empire ... in Roman costume and with Roman phrases."[100] While the classicism of the French Revolutionaries may have seemed, from Marx's vantage point, to have functioned as a veil for bourgeois aspiration, at the time it signalled the precise opposite: the casting off of layers to reveal a new body politic: a political candour, a "naked truth" consolidated in the image of the beautiful, unclothed human body more relevant to Greece than to Rome. Bolstered by the writings of Winckelmann, this French adaptation of antiquity unfolded alongside the mobilization of Greek nakedness among British radicals. In non-Revolutionary Britain, however, the allure of Greece remained bipartisan. The demand for monuments in the Hellenic style, moreover of a comparable quality to those planned for Paris, was greater than concerns, or knowledge, that such appropriations might carry a harmful political subtext, even if the sculptor behind them was known for his connections to radical troublemakers. The British state was invested in its own utopian image of Greek freedom that chimed with Parliament's hard-won independence from monarchic rule a century earlier. In an essay republished in 1792, the influential eighteenth-century painter and art theorist Jonathan Richardson foreshadowed the vogue for universalized Greece in Britain during this era: "No nation under heaven so nearby resembles the ancient Greeks, and Romans as we. There is a haughty courage, an elevation of thought, a greatness of taste, a love of liberty, a simplicity and honesty amongst us."[101] For a long while, British collectors had been pioneers in their appreciation and acquisition of copies or restorations of allegedly Greek

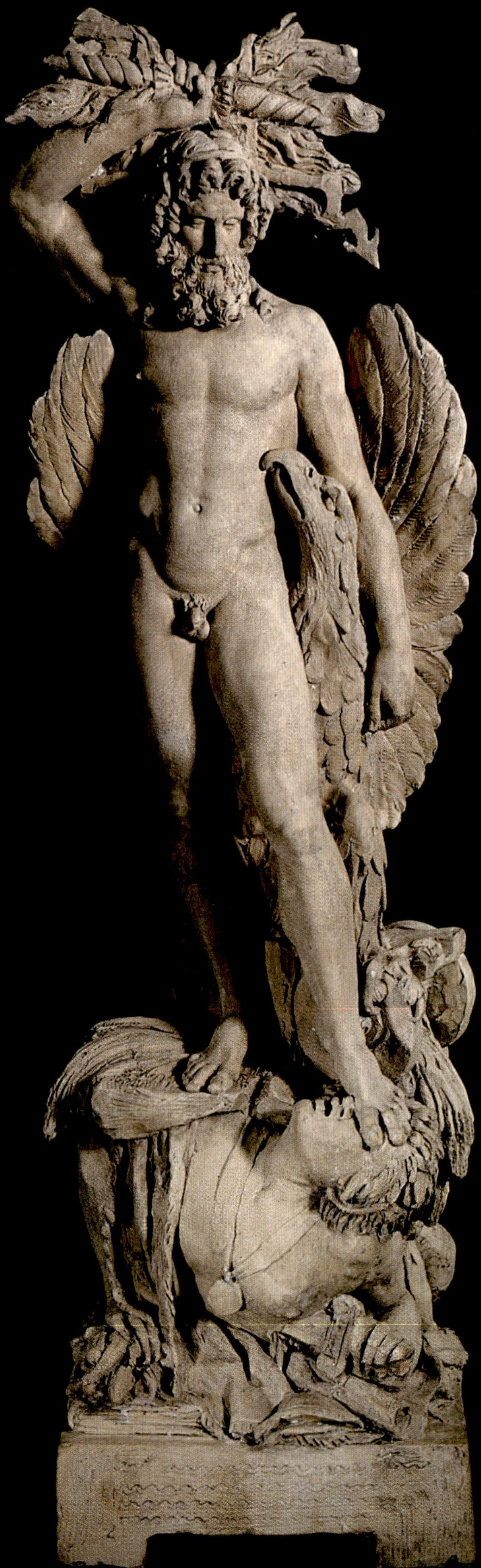

21 Joseph Chinard, *Jupiter Treading Aristocracy Underfoot*, 1792, terracotta. Musée Carnavalet, Paris.

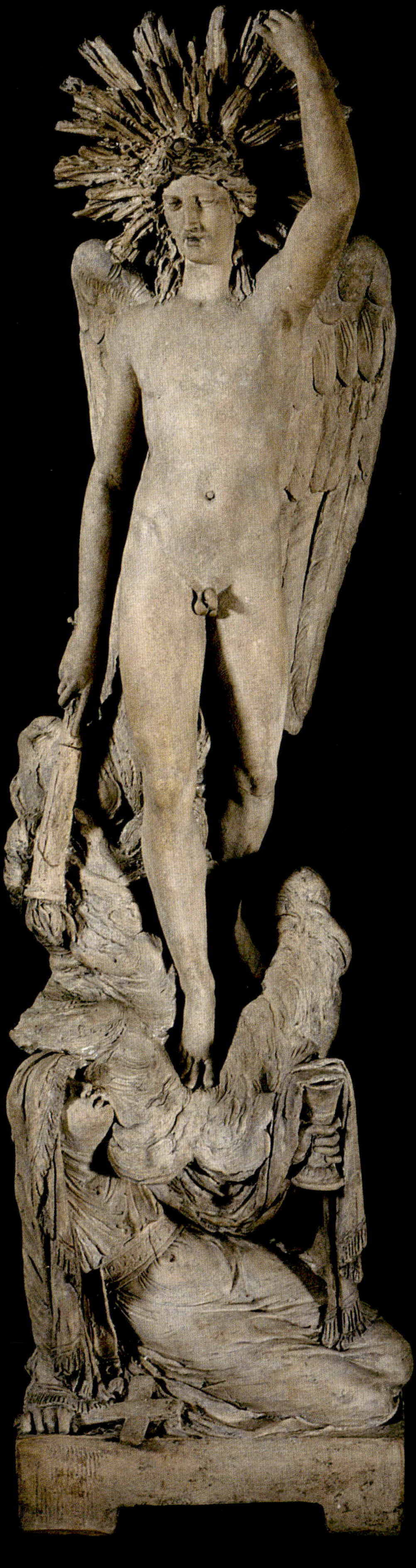

22 Joseph Chinard, *Apollo Treading Superstition Underfoot*, 1792, terracotta. Musée Carnavalet, Paris.

works.[102] When cast in the image of Hellenic sculpture, nakedness was tolerated by aristocratic connoisseurs who were the nation's authorities on art. Banks's figure, therefore, had a network already in place to support it. So it was that his Dream – the vessel filled with illicit contents – slipped past the guards, so to speak, and into the cathedral.

Naked bodies were also prevalent in paintings exhibited at the annual Royal Academy exhibitions. James Barry, an ardent classical idealist, had long produced representations of the naked human form that strove to be virtuous and pure: that is, with their sensuality kept at bay. Although they were not friends or professional allies, Banks acknowledged that he and Barry shared some of the same aesthetic convictions.[103] By the time contracts for the first war monuments had been drafted, Barry – once Professor of Painting – disgraced himself by disseminating a belligerent critique of the Academy. To add insult to injury he conveyed his admiration for Jacques-Louis David, the leading light of French history painting turned regicide and designer of Revolutionary spectacles.[104] As a chief proponent of politicized reworkings of the classical body, David is a key figure in the unpacking of Banks's sculpture. With his consummate ability to translate Greco-Roman forms into wanly tinted figures on canvas, David's history paintings from the Revolutionary years are trapped in time in that their value consists primarily in their status as registers of the link between ancient past and radical future particular to their date and place: what Lynn Hunt calls "the mythic present."[105] From his *Death of Young Bara*, begun in 1794 to mark the death of a young republican in royalist hands, to his epic *Intervention of the Sabine Women* of 1798, Hellenic nakedness functions as an tool to aggrandize the recent total upheaval. While there is no evidence of them ever having met, Banks's time in Rome overlapped with David's own stay.

Despite the plans to fill the Panthéon with Revolutionary monuments, the scheme was not carried out. In Paris, materials were scarce and allegiances fluctuating far quicker than the laborious practice of finishing a marble group. Small in scale but rife with significance are the works of Joseph Chinard, a Lyonnais sculptor who trained in Rome in the years after Winckelmann, Fuseli, Banks, and David had all been based there. Executed in 1792, two of his terracotta statuettes document the integration of antiquity and radical futurity during the final decade of the century: *Jupiter Treading Aristocracy Underfoot* and *Apollo Treading Superstition Underfoot* (figs. 21, 22). Both consist of pagan gods defeating personifications of the *ancien régime*.[106] The first portrays Jupiter trampling a personification of the nobility, the god's smooth unadorned skin contrasting with the scrambled, Gothic pile of limbs beneath him. The god's contrapposto is incorporated into the sculpture's narrative: his leading foot blinds Aristocracy, his toes spreading across the monster's eyes. The second statuette has a similar composition only with Apollo in the role of usurper and a female allegory of Religion crushed as he strides, her hand clutching a crucifix. Commissioned by a Jacobin merchant, these two groups represent the collision of the classical body and the ideal image of the post-Revolutionary order. The fact they were originally conceived as candelabra lends credence to Marx's claim of the bourgeois agenda driving the upheaval in France. Bacon and Cecil would have seen them as the definition of blasphemy.

I am grateful to Julius Bryant for dicovering a source that connects Banks's monument directly to the French Revolution, a connection neglected by Barrell when he claims that only in uncommissioned works could Banks articulate his political convictions.[107] At some point before 1798, the sculptor acquired a contentious work for his own collection: a print by French engraver Louis Charles Ruotte after a drawing by Guillaume Guillon-Lethière, one of David's fellow propagandists. Made in 1793 in the months leading up to the Terror, the print, entitled *L'Union* or *Liberty and Equality United by Nature*, marks the Festival of Reunion, a celebration that took place on August 10 that year not long before the execution of the king (fig. 23). Exhibited at the Salon of 1795, the engraving was risky for someone like Banks to own let alone reuse for a state-funded war monument. But with the print defiantly in hand Banks got to work on a preliminary design, using the French figures as models for the composition of his sculpture (fig. 24). He reconfigured the French original by turning its Revolutionary icons into the principal pair we see in the monument. Liberty, the goddess of the republic, morphs into Victory, while Equality changes sex to become the naked captain. In the print, Liberty holds a scale emblematic of justice, her remaining hand gripping Equality's over a stele. Banks replaced this action with the sword offered by Victory to the naked captain. Equality wears the Phrygian cap thought to have been worn by liberated slaves in the ancient world. In the form of the velvet *bonnet rouge* with its tricolor rosette, French republicans had recently resuscitated this accessory. On the base of the monument is a frieze featuring reliefs with prisoners of war, some of whom wear the Phrygian cap. Unlike Victory and the captain, these adjunct figures are neither celebratory nor serene. Their weary, crushed silhouettes convey little more than the brutality of armed conflict, their caps suggesting that the war commemorated in the sculpture is a war on freedom itself.

Out of this complex web of French and British, Greek, Greco-Roman, and generalized antiquity, the monument to *Captain Burges* was born. From Wollstonecraft to Ruotte, Banks's monument to *Captain Burges* amalgamates an array of discourses and sources bound together by their faith in the possibility of a more equal world. For a brief period in time, this faith, thanks to the "vulgar" reception of Winckelmann's writings, found expression in the image of the classical body. Banks's captain is the antithesis to Blake's corpse disfigured by the ligatures condemned by Wollstonecraft. He is Chinard's Apollo without the crushing violence. He is not a "strange naked man" nor an index of outmoded convention, but the naked truth as Banks perceived it.

— THE SYMMETRY OF DREAMS —

In his account of British sculpture from the period, Edmund Gosse writes, "There could be no greater contrast than between Bacon and Banks. The one was a realist in his art, a fanatic in religion; the other an idealist and a pagan, always dreaming about beauty, always aspiring towards an impossible altitude

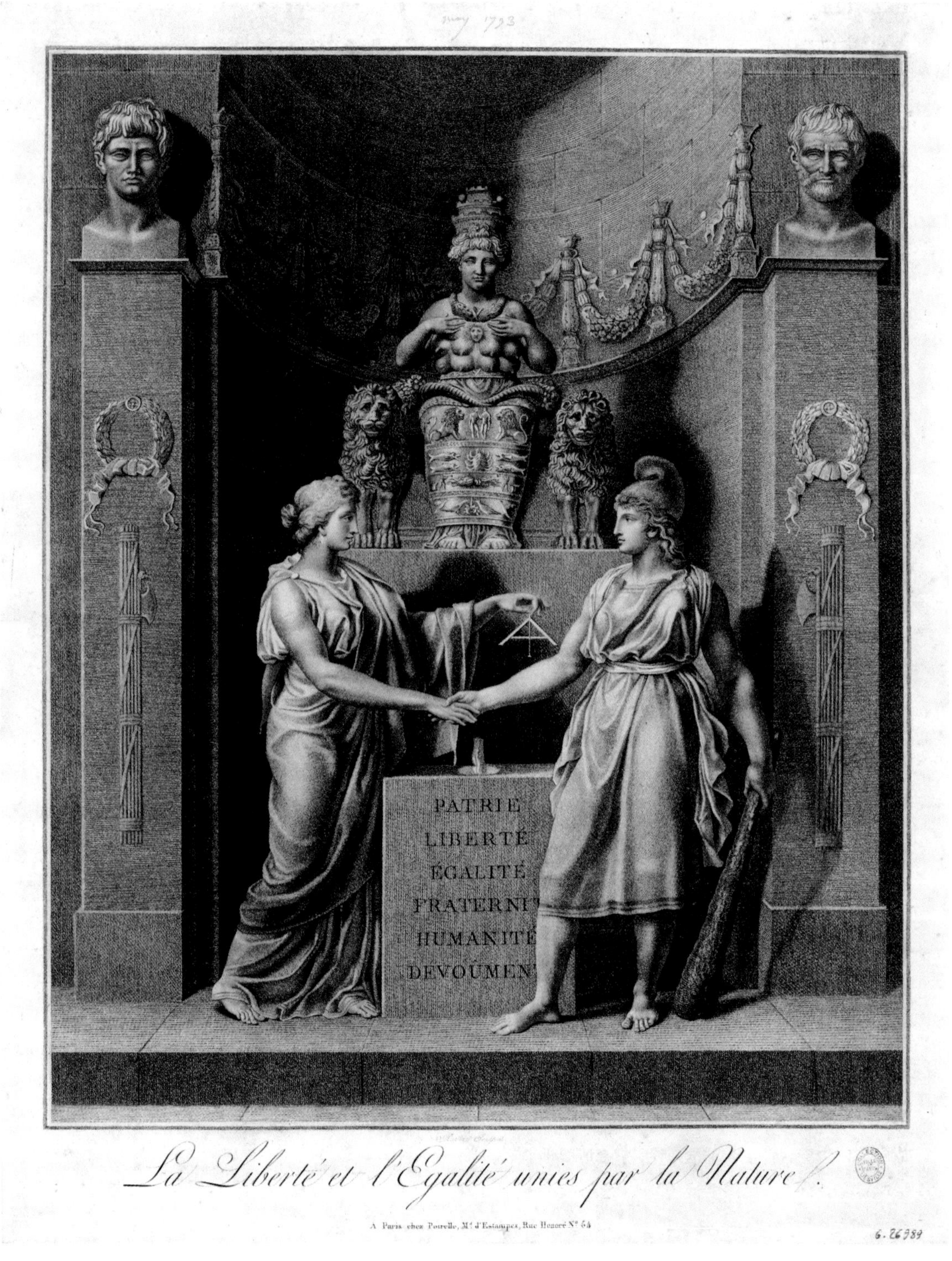

23 L. C. Ruotte after Guillaume Guillon-Lethière, *L'Union* or *Liberty and Equality United by Nature*, 1793, engraving. Musée Carnavalet, Paris.

24 Thomas Banks, Design for monument to *Captain Richard Rundle Burges*, 1798, pen on paper. National Archives, Kew.

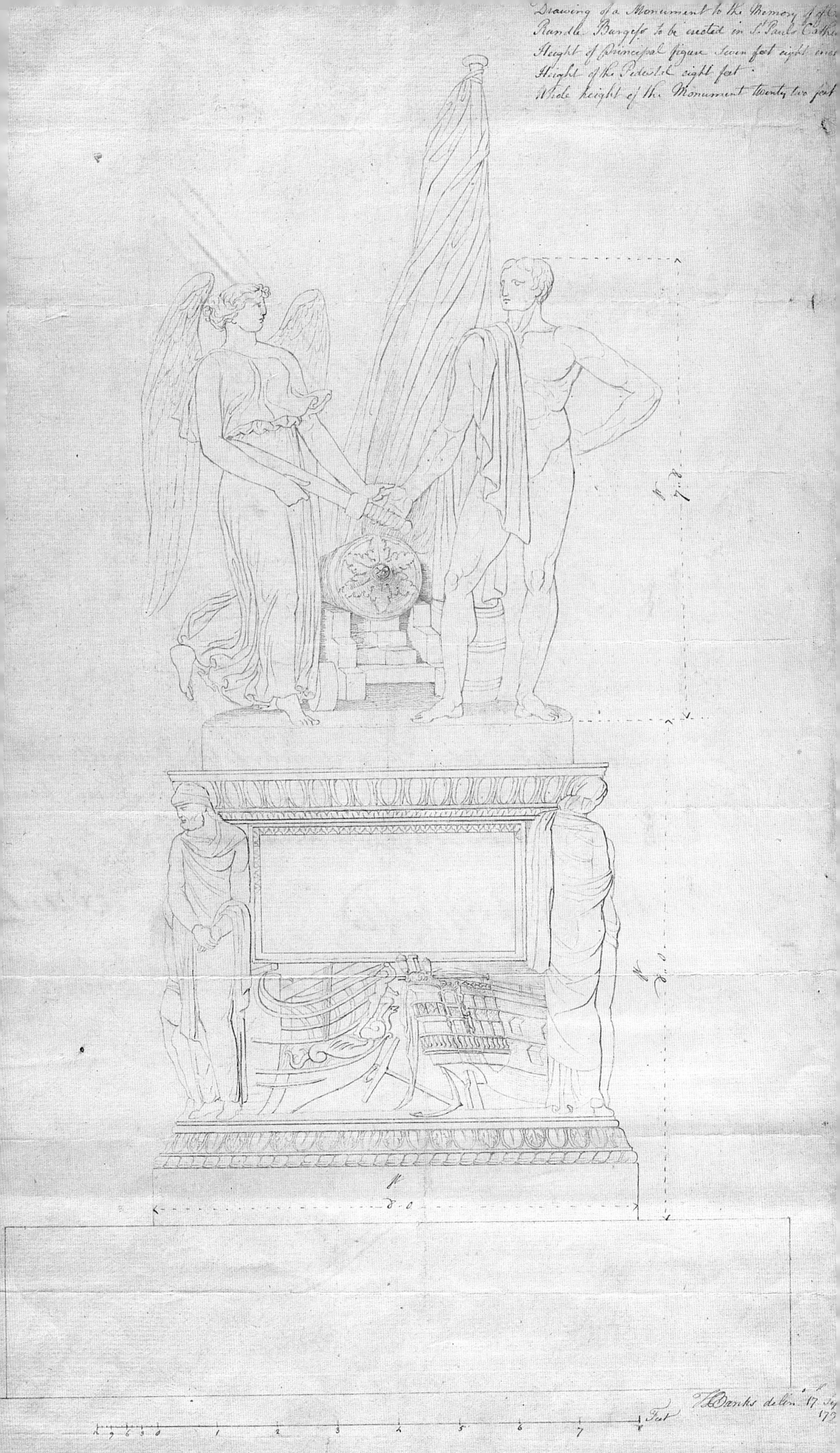
Drawing of a Monument to the Memory of Capt
Randle Burgess to be erected in St Pauls Cathe
Height of Principal figure seven feet eight inc
Height of the Pedestal eight feet
Whole height of the Monument twenty two feet
Feet
T. Banks delin. 17
179

of delicacy and distinction."[108] Although he attempts to distinguish these artists, Gosse inadvertently ends up acknowledging the similarity between them. Keats opens "The Fall of Hyperion" with the assertion that "Fanatics have their dreams wherewith they weave a paradise for a sect"; Bacon was a "fanatic," writes Gosse, while Banks was an artist "always dreaming ... always aspiring" to materialize an "impossible," that is, utopian, image of humankind. Gosse sees Banks just as the subsequent detractors of the monument to *Captain Burges* view its naked protagonist: nothing more than a bastion of a misguided yet essentially disinterested classical aesthetic. But Gosse does not have to recover the artist's radical activism to convey the profundity of Banks's belief in Greece and Greek form. Without politicizing Banks, Gosse still manages to touch on the symmetry of these sculptors and their respective approaches.

One would not expect the ideological rift that fractured Europe in the wake of the French Revolution to find its way into St. Paul's Cathedral: a site of Anglicanism and, after the decision to allow secular sculptures into its guarded interior, state-sanctioned nationalism.[109] But the first round of commissions for war monuments to be placed in the site brought forth two works that reflect the extremes of the moment in which they were designed. Bacon's bond with the king, his Methodism, and support of military action against the French are unified in the monument to *Major General Dundas*. Banks designed a group that ingeniously masks its subversive form and content in the bipartisan thirst for evocations of Greece. Bacon's war hero is covered up, clad in "celestial Armour." Banks resurrects the war hero, presenting him fully formed. Unlike other war monuments made both immediately before and after, Banks's captain is represented not in the throes of death but standing up, unscathed. The figure is an idealized representation of humanity at large, a body liberated from the restraints, physical and metaphysical, that cause injustice and lead to the murder/suicide of the soldier.

For one sculptor nakedness was a condition of sin, the other a condition of truth. And while Bacon shrouded his figures to hide their bodies, Banks conceived nakedness as something that could characterize the representation of the captain's head as well as form. One of the factors contributing to the scholarly consensus that this is a bad sculpture is the way in which Banks combines idealized limbs with a realistic portrait head. Why did the sculptor not portray both head and body, face and limbs, in the same classicizing guise? A precedent had been Roman sculptors who grafted portrait heads onto prototypic ideal bodies. But with Banks there is another justification for this decision. The head reminds us that, while Hellenic form may carry freedom, radical activism is in the name of the common people. Those slightly sagging cheeks, wrinkles, and receding hairline bring the ethereal association between Greek beauty and freedom down to earth and into late eighteenth-century Britain. The features offer a different kind of nakedness, one that is not normatively beautiful but wilfully authentic, like the famous statue of Voltaire by Jean-Baptiste Pigalle with its matchstick arms, veins, sinews, and signs of advanced age.[110] So while the head and the body of Banks's captain appear disparate, they operate on the same register, bringing universalism and particularity into the same political vision. To recreate the captain's likeness, Banks referred to a stipple engraving of Burges's portrait miniature by John Smart, originally painted on ivory. The military uniform worn by Burges in this image would be stripped off for his classicizing resurrection, but we can see from Smart's portrait that the face of Banks's captain is not at all idealized (fig. 25).

It was this kind of nakedness that Banks himself put into practice in his daily life. Affectionately observed by his friends and family, his personality – rough around the edges – went hand in hand with his contempt for all pretence.[111] In turn, his distance from upper-class mores was reflected in his sculptural aesthetic, his rejection of the florid "modern" style practiced by Bacon. Even after his election to Royal Academician he refused to wear the powdered wig typical for gentlemen of the period, choosing instead to reveal his natural hair, which was cropped to his head. Worn also by Charles James Fox, the Whig politician who supported events in France, this hairstyle was a declaration of democratic allegiance. Banks's refusal to adopt an urbane persona could not be more different to Bacon's status as, in Gosse's words, a "born courtier."[112]

In spite of these stark differences, the overlap between these artists positions them both in opposition to classicizing art made in the wake of their deaths. As a Methodist activist and a radical activist, both lived outside of convention. Born south of the river, both were from humble backgrounds and learned, in separate ways, to bend the classical body to their will. By the post-Napoleonic period their symmetry was set in stone. Visitors to St. Paul's found it hard to distinguish between their achievements.[113] Already, the charge of both was spent, and the marble figures – draped and naked – trapped in a bygone time.

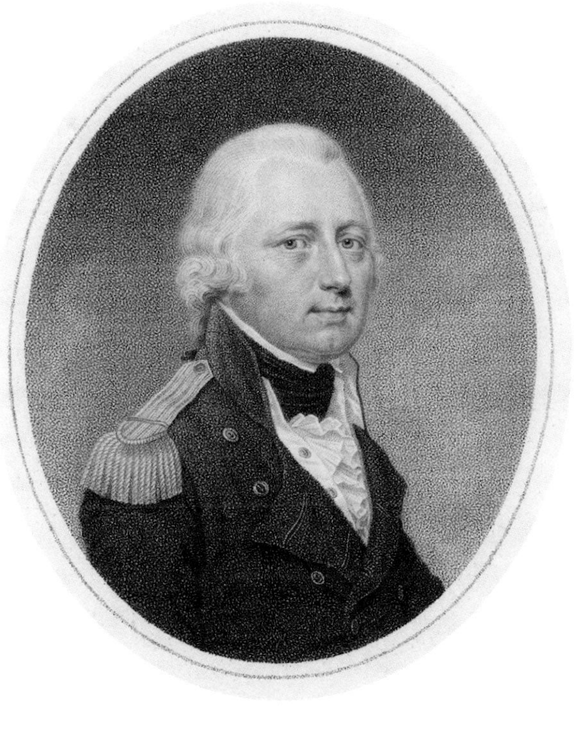

25 Unknown engraver after John Smart, *Captain Richard Rundle Burges*, 1797, stipple engraving on paper. National Portrait Gallery, London.

MORNING.

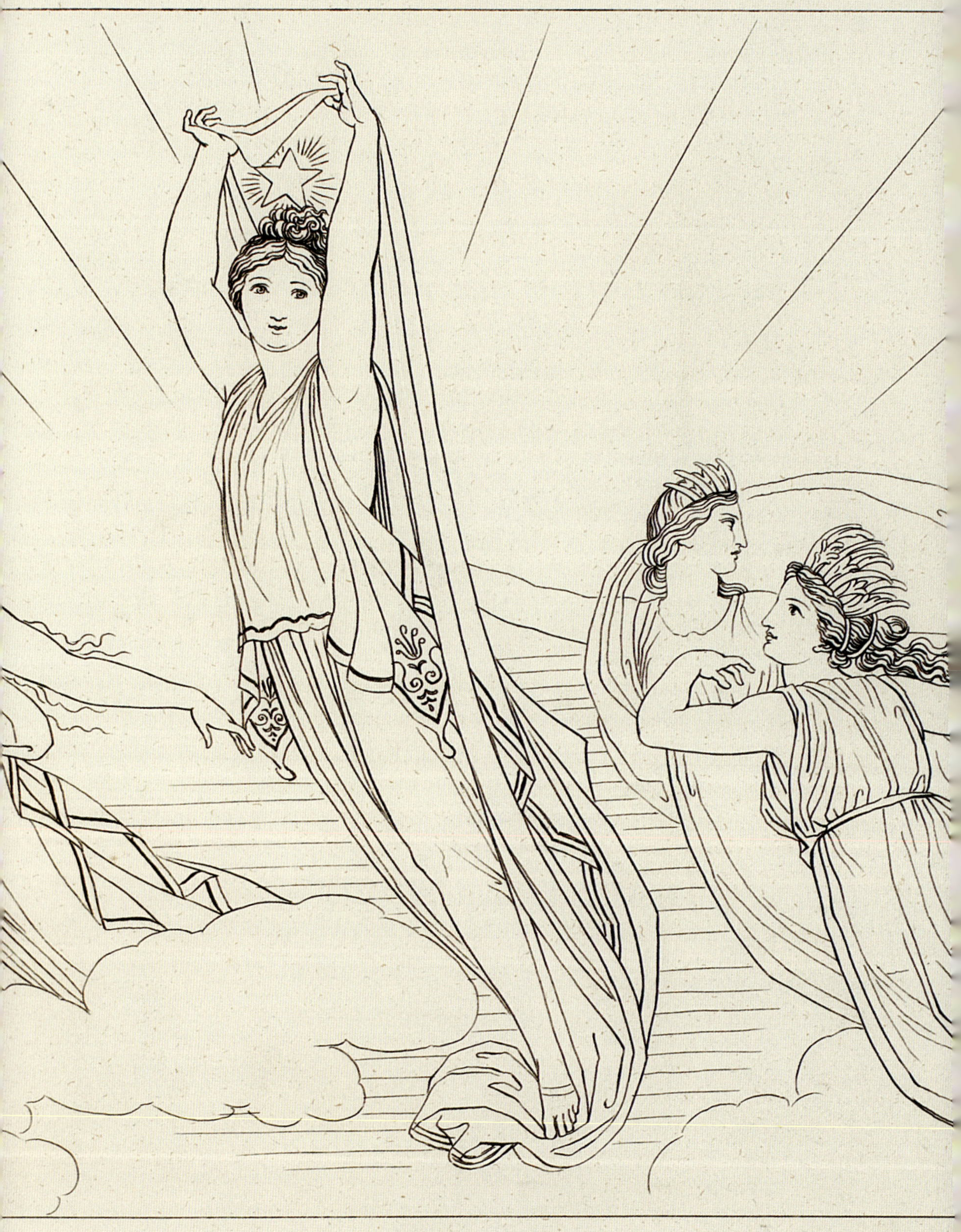

HERE THE GAY MORN RESIDES IN RADIENT BOWRS,
HERE KEEPS HER REVELS WITH THE DANCING HOURS.

Pope's Homer's Odyssey B. 12. Line 2.

CHAPTER TWO

POETIC DEPARTURES

THE MOST FORTHRIGHT declaration of Banks's radical, anti-war Dream came after the installation of the monument to *Captain Burges* in St. Paul's. On the morning of Sunday January 9, 1803, the sculpture was unveiled. Out of the three large-scale war monuments commissioned in 1798, Banks's contribution was the first to be erected. In the months leading up to its completion, the cathedral had been closed for renovations. Eager to see the fresh interior and inspect the inaugural monument designed for the space, a crowd gathered to witness the sculpture's debut. Following the signing of the Treaty of Amiens in March the previous year, Britain and France were now in the midst of a period of peace, the first in a decade. One would think, then, that Banks would have celebrated the cessation of the conflict he had been so vocal in criticizing. Yet in a letter to George Cumberland dated not long after the agreement had been reached, Banks made it clear that he was unimpressed by the treaty. The same letter informing Cumberland that the monument is to be placed in the "very best light" of the cathedral contains the following passage, so passionate that it demands to be quoted at length:

> *I rejoice with you that an end is put to the Warhoop of European savages ... but I differ from you that any feelings of humanity Actuated our rulers to induce them to give repose to 30 Millions of their innocent Neighbours – No their end in carrying on the war was answer'd, which was that of rendering themselves despotic over their own people, which they have most Completely & effectually done by this War – They have effected that which in the beginning of their Career they declar'd they wou'd not effect which was to give their Neighbours either a dictator or President or Protector or Consul or any thing else that bears some resemblance to a King however distant & may hereafter without much difficulty be turn'd into one – this is what they have for these Nine years past been shedding the blood of some Millions of their innocent Neighbours about – however as peace is come to us we must rejoice & I do rejoice at the peace but sorrow for the Oppres'd African; for I rather doubt whether the time for his deliverance is yet come – as Mr. Buonaparte is become a Governor & his Government a regular one like all others, he will have the Assistance of all the regular Governments in this quarter of the Globe, shou'd he not be able to Compleat the enslaving the blacks himself – this is my Opinion of the Matter & if you reflect a little I believe you'll find reason to be something of the same yourself*

26 Detail of James Neagle after John Flaxman, *Morning*, 1805 (fig. 39).

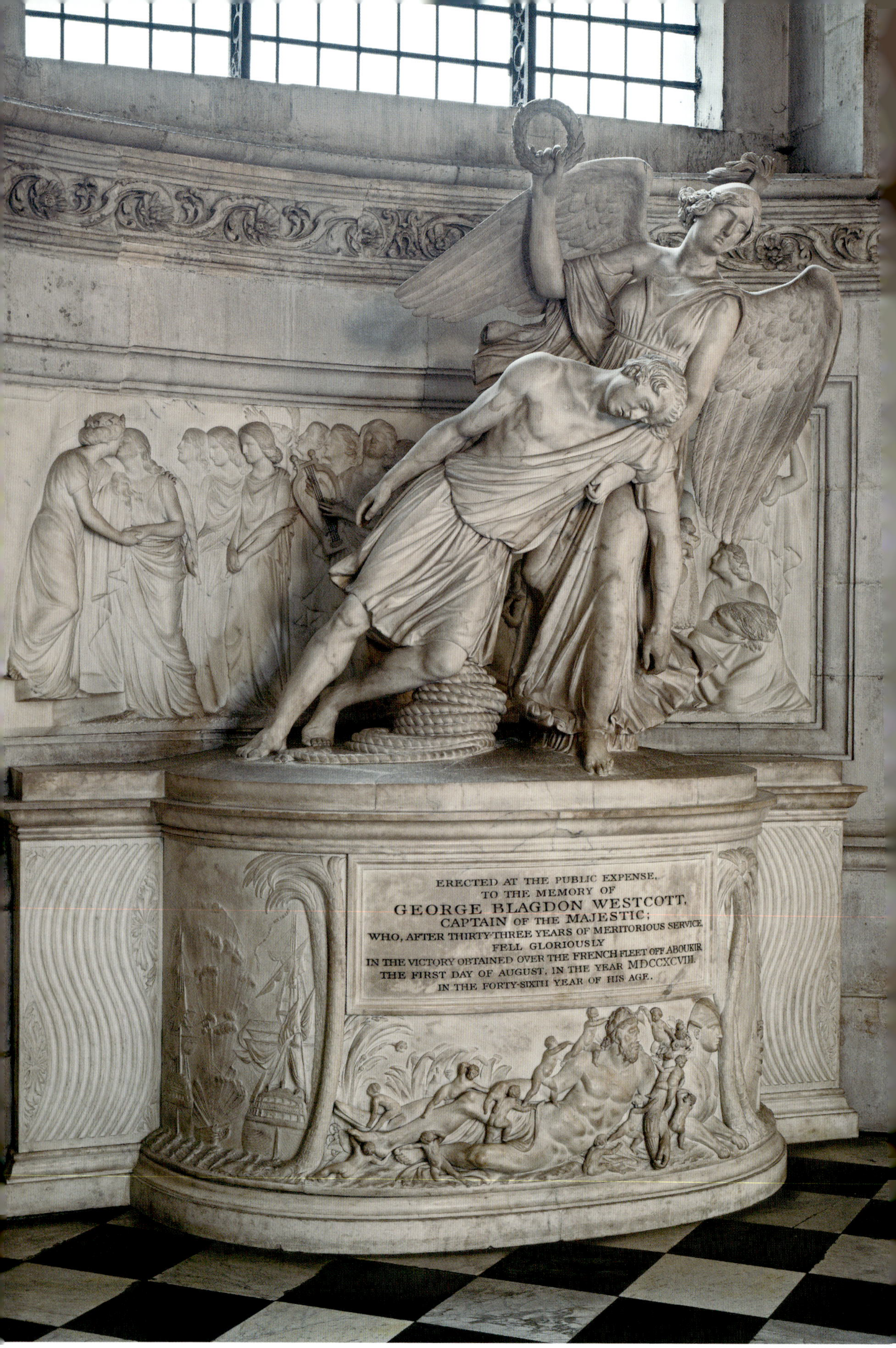

27 Thomas Banks, *Captain George Blagdon Westcott*, 1802–05, marble. St. Paul's Cathedral, London.

28 Unknown artist after Raphael, *Dead Christ Carried to the Tomb*, date unknown, pencil on paper. British Museum, London.

– if Mr. Buonaparte was a well wisher to humanity he ought to give the Blacks their liberty (as the first republicans in France were doing) instead of endeavouring to rivet their chains the closer in order to continue them in their enslaved State.[1]

While Banks had been at work on the sculpture, Napoleon had taken over France. After a decade of faith in a potential neo-Athenian democracy, it seemed as if the queenless, kingless nation was being plunged back into absolutism. The Treaty of Amiens seemed to announce the apotheosis of totalitarian rule: precisely what the "first republicans" sought to dismantle a decade earlier. For years Banks had looked to France as a site of possibility. By 1802, he was disillusioned. His second monument for St. Paul's, dedicated to the naval officer George Blagdon Westcott, is a less hopeful sculpture. The subject slumps onto Victory's lap as she drags him off the battlefield, his body limp with imminent death (fig. 27). Commissioned in 1802, the design was overseen by the group of affluent, mostly aristocratic gentlemen gathered by the government to exert greater control over the public sculptures that followed the inaugural round, later dubbed "the Committee of Taste." Despite his disillusionment, Banks evidently remained invested in the practice of forging polemical sculptural statements and simultaneously masking them. Eleanor Hughes makes a convincing case that, even with the added supervision of the committee, his second St. Paul's monument manages to harbor a subversive counter-significance.[2] This time, however, the monument's covertly critical content was not harbored within the classical

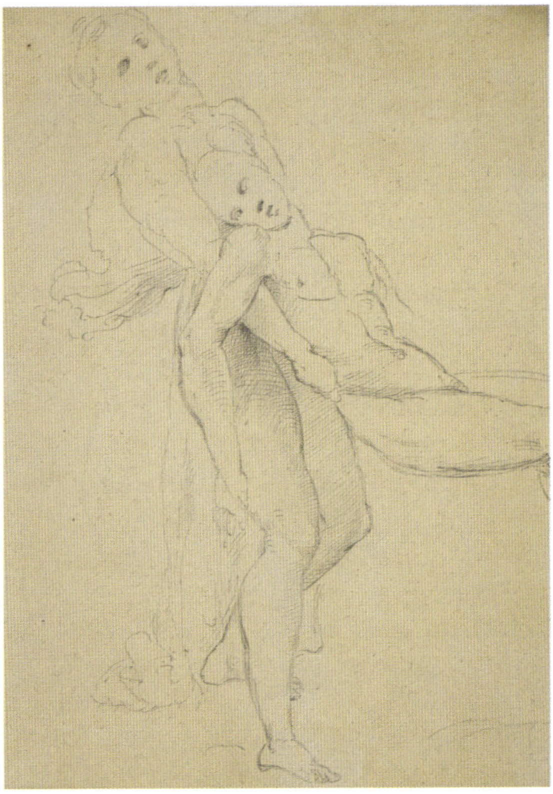

body. Rather, the group as a whole dramatizes the brutality of warfare, from the reliefs on the pedestal depicting violent battle scenes to the sensitive portrayal of the subject's loss of life. For the composition of the work, Banks turned to a drawing after Raphael from his personal collection (fig. 28). This politically neutral source was guaranteed to resonate with the committee, who were effusive admirers of the cinquecento masters. It is telling that, in the image after Raphael, the limp figure that Banks converts into Westcott is naked, yet in the monument Westcott wears a toga. During the interval between the Burges and Westcott monuments, the naked male body relinquished the political charge it possessed when the Revolutionary spirit was still sentient. By 1802, the countercultural capacity of the classical body optimistically to evoke radical meaning had diminished, just as Napoleon's retrogressive attitude toward slavery crystallized the failure of the Revolution to stay true to its original promises.

Classical sculpture, however, remained an object of desire among an expanding audience for art. The Treaty of Amiens opened the border to France, and in the autumn of 1802, British artists flocked to the Louvre – soon to be known as the Musée Napoléon – where they encountered the *Apollo Belvedere* among numerous other sculptures wrenched from the Papal States and paraded in the utopian environment that was the public museum. In contrast to the Vatican's Pio Clementino or even the Uffizi in Florence, Greco-Roman relics in Napoleon's Louvre were disconnected from any claims of geographic, cultural, or ethnic continuity with classical antiquity. In Paris, the display of ancient art was itself the achievement of a revolutionary Dream. Bathed in daylight, the sculptures lost some of the mystery, and the sensuality, that they possessed in their original locations.[3] The looting had begun the year before Banks designed his monument to *Captain Burges* when the Treaty of Tolentino ceded papal power to the French. Eyewitness accounts report Napoleon eyeing up the *Venus de' Medici* in Florence six years before he was able to get his hands on the sculpture.[4] His infatuation caused the Venus to be sent to Sicily for protection. In September 1802, the sculpture was handed over from a hideout in Palermo and acquired as the museum's crown jewel. Banks's detached description of the Venus's unbound shoulders anticipates the oddly practical terms of Napoleon's seizure of the sculpture. Rather than seeing the figure as others had before him – as an icon of pagan sensuality upon which the contemporary viewer could gaze with longing – Napoleon is said to have invoked the sculpture as a "bride" for the *Apollo*, which was already in Paris on a smart new red granite plinth by the time the *Venus* arrived.[5] Crowds took to the streets as the *Venus* entered the city, crowned by flowers and allegedly accompanied by wild animals in cages as well as, on a separate float, some of Winckelmann's manuscripts.[6] At that moment the Revolutionary fusion of ancient past and democratic future – the "mythic present" – lost its insurrectionary vitality.[7] Greece was no longer an idea that could be easily manipulated to champion the cause Banks and his fellow activists fought for. At the consul's whim, the two principal exemplars of "the antique" re-emerged as the most famous married couple in Paris: certified representatives of the entitlement to cultures, land and bodies, stone and flesh.

Antonio Canova did not approve of the looting. Following the defeat of the French in 1814, he worked tirelessly to restore many of the pillaged objects back to their former sites. In 1802, he began his statue of *Napoleon as Mars the Peacemaker* (see fig. 7). Considering this sculpture alongside Banks's monument to *Captain Burges* underscores that for Canova nakedness was not a condition of truth. Far more idealized than the head of Banks's figure, Napoleon's portrait is a flattering likeness. The cheeks have the illusion of being smooth-shaved, the head of hair full, and the lips slightly pursed, adding to their volume and heightening the comeliness of the face. These qualities lend Canova's sculpture an air of intimacy entirely absent from Banks's sexless figure. As I discussed in the introduction, although it is a naked male figure born out of the same "empirical approach to the antique" shared by Canova and arch-Dreamer Banks, Canova's is not a Dreaming work of art. For Canova, Greek nakedness possessed no ulterior significance beyond its disinterested capacity as a paradigm of beauty: hence how readily it accommodated the "vulgar Kantianism" David Bindman identifies as a thread running through international criticism of the sculptor's works.[8] The norm set by "the antique" did not offer a figuration of the naked truth so much as its opposite: a kind of veil that elevates humanity above the irregularity of animate nature.

Dismissed as "too athletic" (in other words too untrue) by the consul himself, Canova's statue of Napoleon was hidden away after its completion.[9] Despite the fact that the work was not known in Britain until later on, it was the aesthetic conventions that legitimized the appearance of a monument such as this one, and the congruent, contemporaneous claim by the French over classical relics, that helped hide the once radical charge of Banks's monument during the decade or so after is erection. Accompanied by flattering descriptions, two prints after the sculpture appeared as frontispieces to popular journals: first the *European Magazine and London Review* and later the *Naval Chronicle* (figs. 29 and 30). Fashioning himself as Britain's heir to Vasari, the Scottish critic, poet, and historian Allan Cunningham is responsible for disseminating a tale about the monument that caused subsequent scholars to overlook the popularity of the work and these engravings. In his biographical vignette on Banks published in 1830, he scoffed at "those perilous days, when 'revolution' and 'liberty and equality' were putting wise men mad".[10] Conscious that the dead sculptor's art was couched in an ever more remote political agenda, Cunningham, a nationalist and reactionary, goes out of his way to describe the nakedness of Captain Burges as literal rather than figurative: "Only think of Victory, a modest well dressed lady, presenting a sword to a naked gentleman!" he quips, "historical truth and national delicacy are alike wounded." The author claims that the captain caused so great a scandal when first unveiled that the bishops of St. Paul's were forced to order Banks to extend the swathe of drapery that covers the captain's pubic area. Not only is there no seam indicating such an alteration nor any evidence of scandal in Banks's correspondence, the drapery in the finished monument is identical to how it appears in Banks's preliminary drawing of 1798. Historians, however, have taken Cunningham at his word that the work was met by outraged clergy

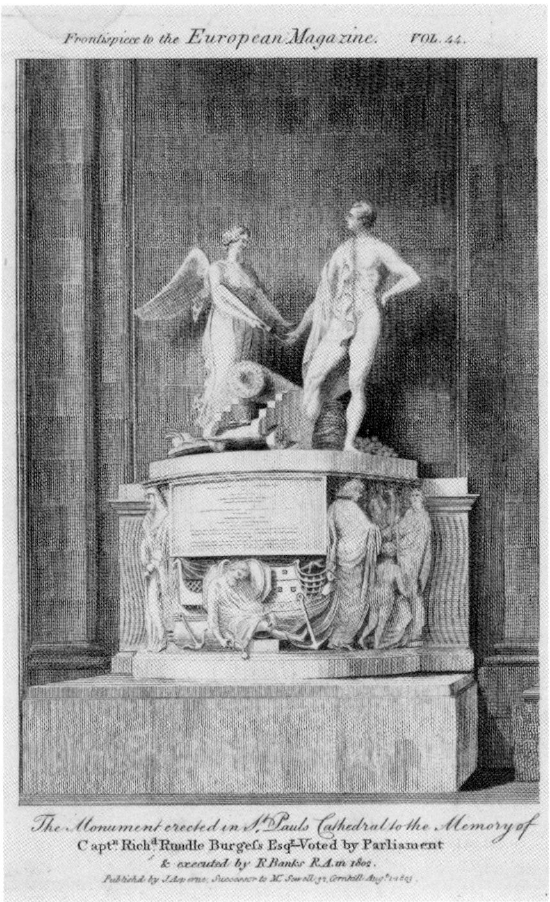

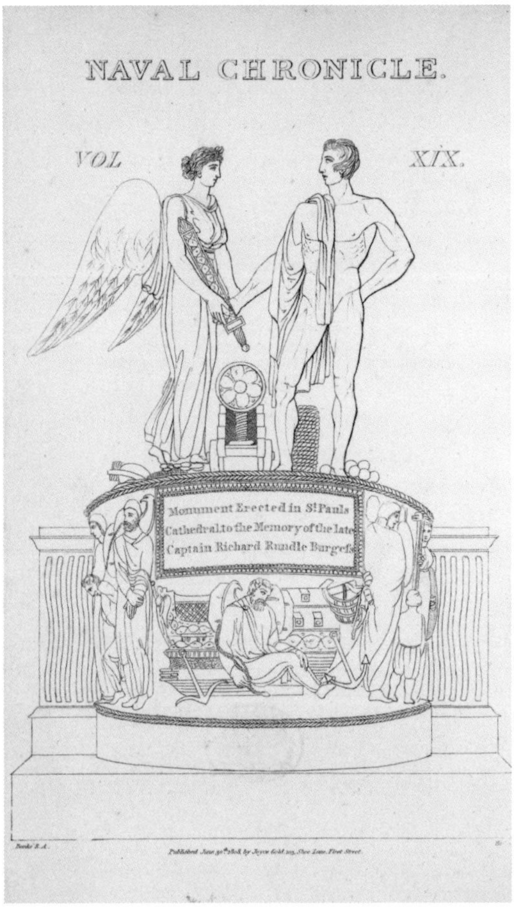

29 Unknown engraver, *Captain Richard Rundle Burges*, 1803, line engraving on paper. National Portrait Gallery, London.

30 Unknown engraver, *Captain Richard Rundle Burges*, 1808, line engraving on paper. Frontispiece to the *Naval Chronicle*, vol. 19 (1808).

and ladies blushing into "the flutter of fans."[11] The fiction has been repeated in several accounts of the sculptor's life and work. In actual fact, the nakedness of the figure was not the source of any controversy until over a decade after 1803. One article marking its installation praises Banks's portrait of Burges, stating that the likeness has been approved by the captain's family and friends. Of the corporeal nakedness it is enough to point out that "the Artist has attentively studied antique sculpture."[12] For the duration of the wars, the naked captain in St. Paul's continued to be received as an appropriate tribute to a military hero.

Throughout the years in which Greek nakedness could still harbor radical ideas, as well as be an aesthetic expression of state-sanctioned nationalism and a paradigm of disinterested beauty, there was one artist who was forced to exercise caution when representing the naked male body precisely because of its capacity to serve as a vessel. While the critique of war and the valorization of universal humankind represented in the monument to *Captain Burges* went largely undetected, John Flaxman was all too aware of the interplay between radicalism and Hellenic form latent within the work. Regarding Banks's group he was ambivalent. On the one hand, it possessed some "beams of light," he remarked to Joseph Farington.[13] Yet any glimmer of genius was overshadowed by "much imbecility," and the work, in the end, was deemed a failure. "Imbecility" is a revealing choice of word. It suggests that Flaxman's problem with the sculpture did not stem so much from its stylistic characteristics, its Hellenic form, but rather something more cerebral: namely, the political vision contained within that form. Flaxman would have been especially sensitive both to the polysemic nature of Greek nakedness and Banks's tendency to integrate art and activism. As a practitioner who had followed Banks's path by favoring the same classicizing aesthetic over the "modern" style that preceded it, Flaxman had a vested interest in distancing himself from Banks's politics, which he did not share.

This chapter will look at instances in which Flaxman drained Banks's Dream from the classical body. Like Canova, Flaxman sought to position his work at a distance from politicized mobilizations of the human form. Yet he continued to emulate Banks's art, looking up to him as the most significant contributor to modern sculpture during his lifetime. Elizabeth Prettejohn opens her *Modern Painters, Old Masters* by asking: "when an artist (consciously or unconsciously) imitates a visual form, how far does he or she also import into their own work meanings and contexts associated with that form in its previous incarnation? How far can an artist change those meanings and contexts?"[14] In relation to Banks and Flaxman, such a question has a different kind of urgency because their relationship was so close. They were not separated, as were the artists Prettejohn examines, by centuries, languages, and national borders, but by a twenty-year age gap. This generational divide exacerbated the friction between their attitudes toward the political situation in Britain, and in France, during the years leading up to the design of Banks's monument to *Captain Burges*. So while they shared the same aesthetic convictions, their visions were otherwise at odds.

Flaxman's debt to the elder sculptor is nowhere more apparent than in his emulation of a particular visual form designed by Banks during his time in Rome: a group of female figures – nymphs – of which Flaxman produced numerous reworkings throughout his career. Indeed, Flaxman's fixation on this one particular group verges on obsession. Each of his own designs, including the ones patently indebted to Banks, were extremely influential not just among British artists of his own generation but among subsequent generations of painters, sculptors, decorative and even performing artists across Europe until well into the twentieth century. Flaxman, therefore, was able to release Banks's art from its "spatio-temporal" confinement, untrapping his work from the narrow set of years in which it not only Dreamed, but was praised as the ultimate resuscitation of the classical body. Flaxman achieved this by smoothing and sensualizing Banks's art and removing the elements, particularly the naked male body, that had been used as a vessel. Although a utopian thinker, Banks was an artist who viewed his art as an agent of his quest to help bring about tangible social and political change in modern Britain. Flaxman was the opposite: an artist concerned not with visible reality but with the play of the imagination, with fantastical phenomena whose representation could enchant and delight the spectator. Flaxman is thus a Poet in the Keatsian sense, an artist who sought to "pour out a balm upon the world" rather than "vex it," as Banks and Bacon senior had done before him. In Flaxman's emulation of Banks, we see Dreaming and Poetic art collide, and the war between the two play out before our eyes.

— FROM DREAMS TO POEMS —

Since Flaxman's days as a Royal Academy student, Banks had been a kind of guru to him. As the sculptor credited with introducing the clean lines of "the antique" into contemporary British sculpture and, what is more, breaking away from the expectation that practitioners were supposed to churn out restorations and copies rather than produce their own original designs, Banks was someone for Flaxman to admire above all other living artists. But Flaxman did not approve of his mentor's activism, all the more so because it threatened to politicize the aesthetic he saw as the only acceptable style for sculpture. His fears were not unfounded; Flaxman could risk guilt by association. In 1798, a group of gentlemen employed by the government to oversee designs for new silver coinage – a precursor to the 1802 "Committee of Taste" – suspected that Flaxman's "new and curious" appropriations of Greco-Roman models might be tinged by a political motive intended to critique "the present times and circumstances."[15] Given that suspicion of Flaxman was aroused the very year Banks submitted his design, it is remarkable that the monument to *Captain Burges* seems not to have generated similar concerns.

Flaxman's father was a cast-maker for some of the leading sculptors of the mid-eighteenth century, so from an early age he would have encountered representations of mythological figures in three dimensions. Despite the familiarity he would have had with classical imagery from childhood, however, antiquity remained for him a heavenly rather than terrestrial idea. Throughout his life he remained religious but, unlike Bacon junior and senior, did not find that his Christian piety jarred with his art. This is due to the fact that at some point in the 1780s he discovered a theosophy that could complement images of the classical body: that of Emmanuel Swedenborg, the Nordic visionary whose mystical interpretation of the Bible was the basis for the foundation of London's New Church in 1787. As with the Neoplatonists before him, the standard of beauty represented in Greco-Roman sculpture could, for a Swedenborgian artist like Flaxman, be interpreted as a manifestation of God's work.[16]

Delivered after his election to Professor of Sculpture at the Royal Academy in 1810 – the first ever holder of the position – Flaxman's *Lectures on Sculpture* return frequently to the question of the reconciliation of pagan and Christian imagery. While classical sculpture provides invaluable formal exemplars for the living artist, it was Christian painters and sculptors in the fifteenth century who imbued the received image of the beautiful body with a morality that purifies, while still preserving, its beauty. Although the *Lectures* make clear that Flaxman was well versed in Winckelmann's theory of the development and decline of art in the ancient world, Flaxman was not a proponent of "vulgar Winckelmannianism." In his lecture on modern sculpture he states that, although the Athenians fought to defend their democracy from "foreign invaders," they had more slaves than free citizens and "tolerated the most frightful offenses."[17] Greek freedom has a value in the history of art, yet its value, Flaxman implies, has been overstated by artists and writers of the generation before him. Instead of fixating on the Greeks, living artists should content themselves with the "Perfect Dispensation" that is Christianity, a way of life allowing for just enough "political freedom" to keep society in order, while instilling "duties and charities ... not to be found under any other code."[18] It is evident that Flaxman had a bone to pick with those radical classicists who, emboldened by Winckelmann's musings on Greece, beauty, and freedom, had injected political meaning into the image of the ideal human form. Crucially, Flaxman is not suggesting that artists ought to use their work to impart Christian morality (à la Bacon senior), but rather that Christian morality provides the ideal framework for living artists to experiment with various exemplars of beauty, whether ancient or modern, pagan or Christian, or – and this was Flaxman's way – a combination of both.

During the years around the making of Banks's monument to *Captain Burges* when "vulgar Winckelmannianism" was at its height, Flaxman had been critical of the contamination of classicizing art by something so earthly as political activism. When in Paris in 1802, he is said to have refused to meet Jacques-Louis David because, although he admired the French painter's abilities and commitment to "the antique," he "had an abhorrence" for the service of both to the Revolutionary cause.[19] The contrast between Flaxman and David, and in turn Flaxman and Banks, adheres to Satish Padiyar's distinction, made in relation to French art of the period, between "the 'ancients' as otherworldly and the 'ancients' as politically recuperable."[20] Such stubborn guardedness against radical views, however, did not inhibit Banks and Flaxman's closeness. Drawn before her marriage to the writer Edward Forster in 1799, Flaxman's wispy pencil sketch of Lavinia Banks playing the harp illustrates that they were not merely colleagues or mentor/mentee but family friends (fig. 31). There is also a tender pencil portrait of Banks in profile, drawn by Flaxman in 1804 while the elder sculptor's health was declining.[21]

When Banks died from a stroke a year later, Flaxman composed an essay paying tribute to his life and work written to be read out loud at the Academy. Opening with an account of modern sculpture in Europe before Banks came on the scene, the essay leads with praise of the style the late sculptor favored. As Reynolds had done in his Discourse on sculpture, Flaxman condemns the aesthetic favored by Bacon – the formal tradition growing out of "the bizarre and childish" creations of Bernini – as an infectious disease contracted by generations of practitioners. Banks and his commitment to recovering the lineaments of Hellenic form appeared just in time to rescue sculpture from "the low state of the Arts" that marked his youth. But there was more to Flaxman's essay than the desire to give Banks credit for the aesthetic development that had conditioned the style of his own art: the "cleansing antique vision" more commonly attributed to Canova.[22] Behind the eulogy was a pressing agenda. By invoking Banks as the patriarch of modern British sculpture – even European sculpture more broadly – Flaxman diluted his political past. As Julius Bryant has also suggested, Flaxman sought to cleanse Banks's legacy, to state for posterity that there was nothing radical about his dead friend's art, his investment in Hellenic art, his naked captain in St. Paul's.[23] Clearly, Flaxman had spent enough time with Banks to know that this was not the case. Without doubt, his choice of the word "imbecility" with regard to the monument to *Captain Burges* was motivated by an inner conflict between the aspects of Banks he admired and the aspects it was in his best interest to eclipse.

One of the final works Banks placed before the public during his lifetime had been overtly provocative: a model head of Lord Protector Cromwell.[24]

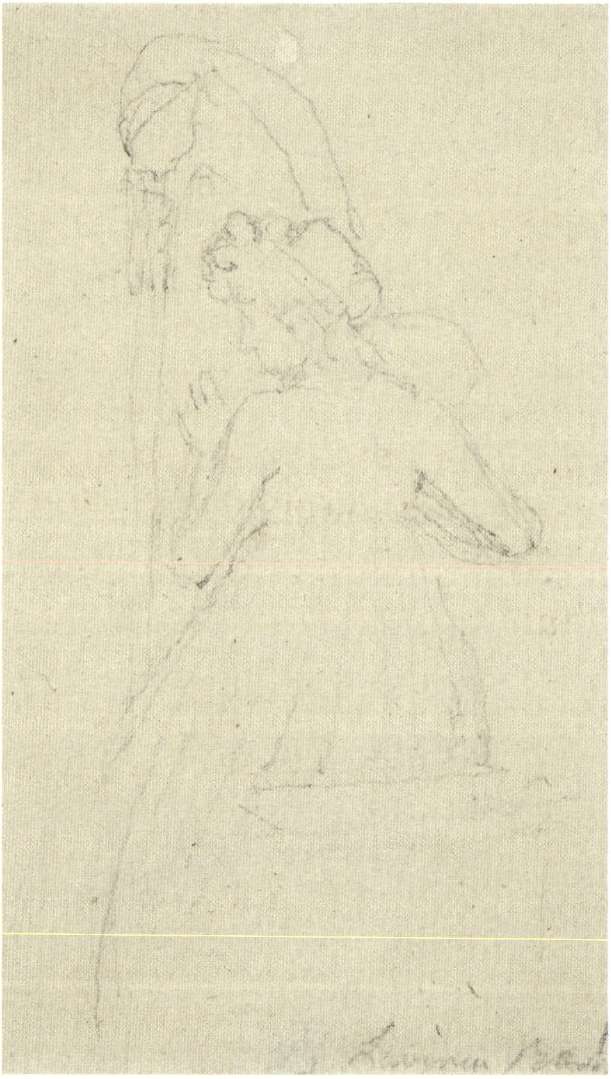

31 John Flaxman, *Lavinia Banks*, before 1799, pencil on paper. British Museum, London.

Following the Royal Academy exhibition of 1803, certain members of the institution had lobbied to remove the model from Somerset House. After shirking suspicion enough to gain commissions for two prestigious war monuments, the sculptor became a divisive figure in the closing years of his life and immediate wake of his death. Due to fear that praise of a contentious member might offend the increasingly paranoid George III, Flaxman's speech was banned from being read in the Academy's lecture room. At the height of her own interest in activism, Lavinia pronounced the artists preventing the tribute "servile wretches."[25] For decades, Flaxman's expression of praise for her father remained unknown. Not until 1838, when she herself was sixty-four, did it appear in the second, posthumous edition of Flaxman's *Lectures*.

Following a long stretch of obscurity, an account of Banks's life appeared exactly a century after the publication of Flaxman's tribute. Put together by Charles Francis Bell, a descendant of the sculptor and Keeper of Fine Art at the Ashmolean Museum, *The Annals of Thomas Banks* makes explicit the wariness toward radicalism that Flaxman's tribute implies. Clearly critical of left-wing politics, Bell is at pains to underplay the activism of his ancestor: "Apart from his attitude towards monarchy, consistency does not appear to have been the sculptor's strongest quality," he writes; "[Banks] competed for commissions for memorials to men who, according to his theories, had been so misguided as to have flung away their lives."[26] With both the public monument and the private letters in front of him, Bell is appalled at Banks's conception of the soldier as both murderous and suicidal. He goes on to condemn the guests at Horne Tooke's table: Banks "openly consorted with people who, like himself, detested the existing government, but were also able, and not merely eager, to embarrass it."[27] To drive a wedge between the sculptural and political endeavors of his subject, Bell turns to none other than Flaxman. Banks's artistic "ideas were so completely in harmony with those of" the younger sculptor, Bell writes, "that it is scarcely paradoxical to think of the two men as if they had been the same artist."[28]

By equating Banks with the younger sculptor, Bell purges the political motivation behind Banks's engagement with the classical body, reducing decades of radical activism to a mere dalliance with no effect on his *oeuvre*. It is as if, like Samuel Taylor Coleridge in his "France: An Ode" – a poem that opens with the famous renouncement, "Forgive me freedom, oh forgive those dreams!" – Banks was transfigured into Flaxman and in the process cast aside his faith in the possibility of a more equal society, adopting a reactionary position instead.[29] Banks's Dream is reduced to a juvenile distraction. Flaxman represents his maturity, his respectable side.

Yet while it is not as fluid as Bell suggests, the author is right to emphasize the continuity between Banks and Flaxman. Scholars tend to contextualize the latter, first and foremost, in terms of either his Swedenborgian spirituality or his antiquarian studies: his understanding of mythic figures and the minutiae of their representation on Egyptian, Greek, Etruscan, and Roman artefacts, as well as early Christian and Renaissance art. Banks's influence has never been fully recognized, despite the fact that traces of his work suffuse Flaxman's *oeuvre* right up until the latter's death in 1826. Throughout his career, Flaxman expressed admiration for one work in particular by Banks: an oval bas-relief completed in plaster while the artist was in Rome, an unfinished marble version brought back with him to London. With the long title *Thetis and her Nymphs Rising from the Sea to Console Achilles for the Loss of Patroclus*, the sculpture depicts the tragic moment in Homer's *Iliad* when the Greek hero Achilles learns that his close companion Patroclus has been killed in a duel against Hector, the Trojan prince (fig. 32). Having lent his own armor to his ill-fated friend, Achilles arrives at the scene stripped of all protection. Banks portrays Achilles naked, his head thrown back in the lap of another Greek soldier, possibly either Menelaus or Ajax, the guardians of Patroclus's corpse. Still figurative, the nakedness of Banks's Achilles is both a representation of universal humanity and an allegorical personification of the ravages of war. Again, the vulnerable exposure of the hero underlines the capacity of the undraped body to aggrandize the naked truth of human experience. In this instance, muscular, ideal limbs express something unexpected: emotional frailty, a state elevated by its grounding in heroic self-sacrifice. While in other artists' hands the homoerotic undertones of the bond between Achilles and Patroclus pervade or are hinted at in representations, Banks creates another sexless work.[30] Patroclus, the object of the hero's desire and his pain, does not appear in the design, making this an anerotic scene in which the sensuality of the narrative is erased. There is sensuality in the sculpture, yes, but it is concentrated in the group of female figures on the other side of the composition, and, still, the fact that the principal member of the attendant female group is the hero's mother neutralizes the erotic charge of her nakedness. The suppression of the classical body's sensuality betrays that this is Dreaming art. The American Revolutionary War was raging during the time of its production, and, thanks to concerned testimony from Flaxman, we know that Banks was involved with radical politics while living in Rome.[31]

The relief was begun toward the end of Banks's time in Rome. As Bryant has noted, the circumstances around its making were extremely fraught.[32] It was commissioned by the Irish aristocrat Frederick Hervey: the Bishop of Derry, Earl of Bristol, and a notoriously unreliable patron. While Bryant's account of their relationship minimizes the impact of Hervey's personality on his dealings with Banks, Hervey was widely known as an erratic man who, although a high-ranking Anglican cleric, had luxurious appetites and was rumored to be an alcoholic and even a non-believer.[33] He rubbed shoulders with Voltaire and vehemently defended the rights of Irish Catholics.[34] His liberalism is important because it puts his investment in an artist like Banks, and the Homeric relief, into perspective. In 1780–81, Hervey's chaplain, the Reverend Martin Sherlock, published his *Letters from an English Traveller*, in which he opines on the superiority of Greek sculpture, distinguishing it from Roman copies and crediting it, Winckelmann-style, as the foundation of all the best artistic achievements.[35] Victim to the same fashion for Hellenic form that became ubiquitous in Britain of the 1790s, Hervey too believed in the superiority and universality of Greece. As a collector of both

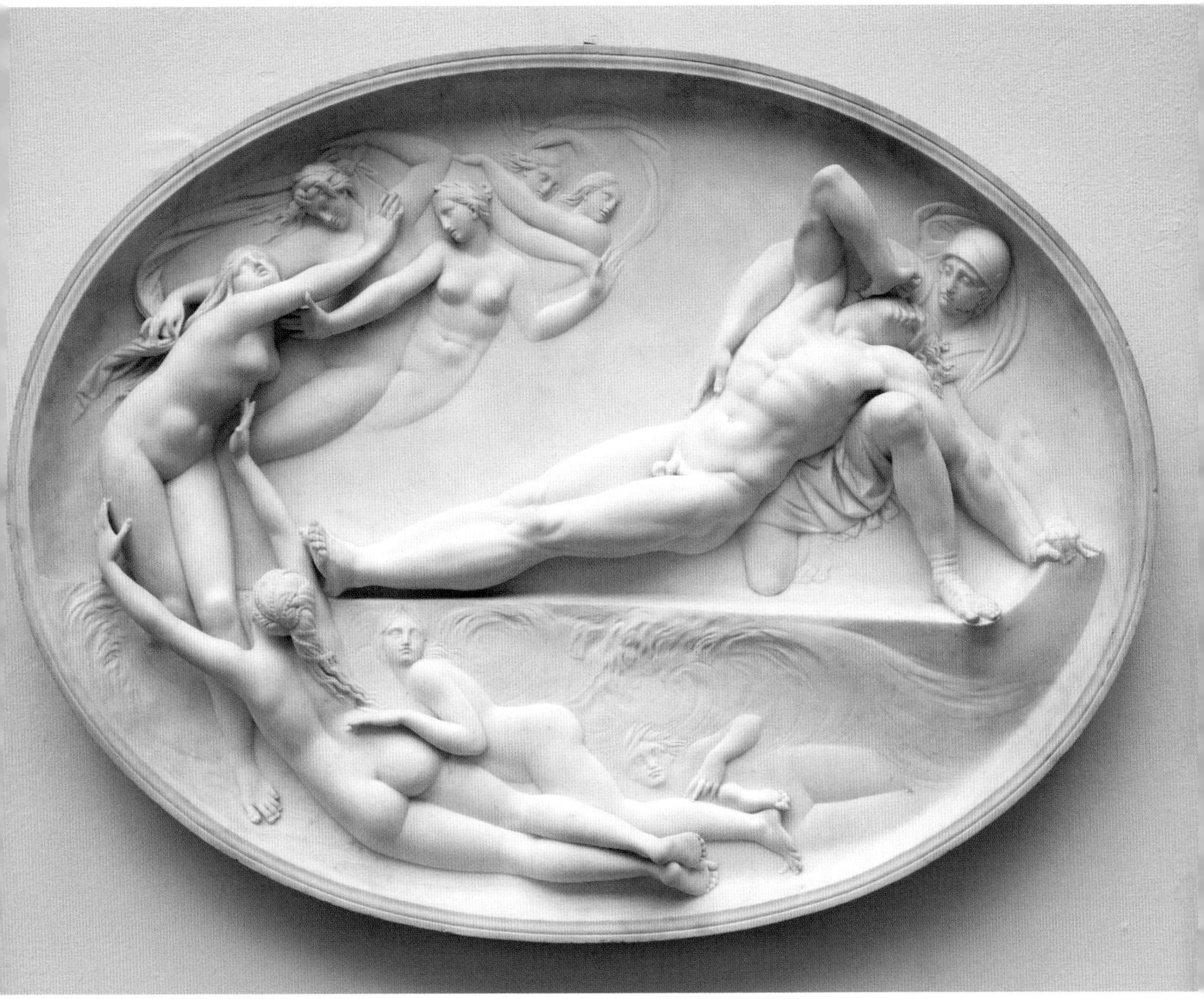

32 Thomas Banks, *Thetis and her Nymphs Rising from the Sea to Console Achilles for the Loss of Patroclus*, c. 1777–78 (plaster, marble finished posthumously, c. 1805), marble. Victoria and Albert Museum, London.

ancient and modern objects in the streamlined "antique" style, Hervey encouraged the rise of Homer as the supreme artistic source material, a source material that matched the veneration of supposedly Greek sculptures. Scholars have long observed that at the beginning of the eighteenth century, Homer was thought of as an important ancient author, but one on an equal footing with Roman Virgil. By the end of the century, Homer "towered above the ancient world" and was heralded as equivalent to Shakespeare and Dante.[36] Winckelmann helped elevate Homer when he proclaimed that the originality of the earlier bard in relation to the derivative "polish of Virgil" was comparable to the superiority of Greek over Roman art.[37] Hervey's commission of Banks's relief is an index of the Homeric turn. A patron with his provocative tendencies would have been especially open to the period's craze for the *Iliad* and the *Odyssey* as subjects for visual art, and

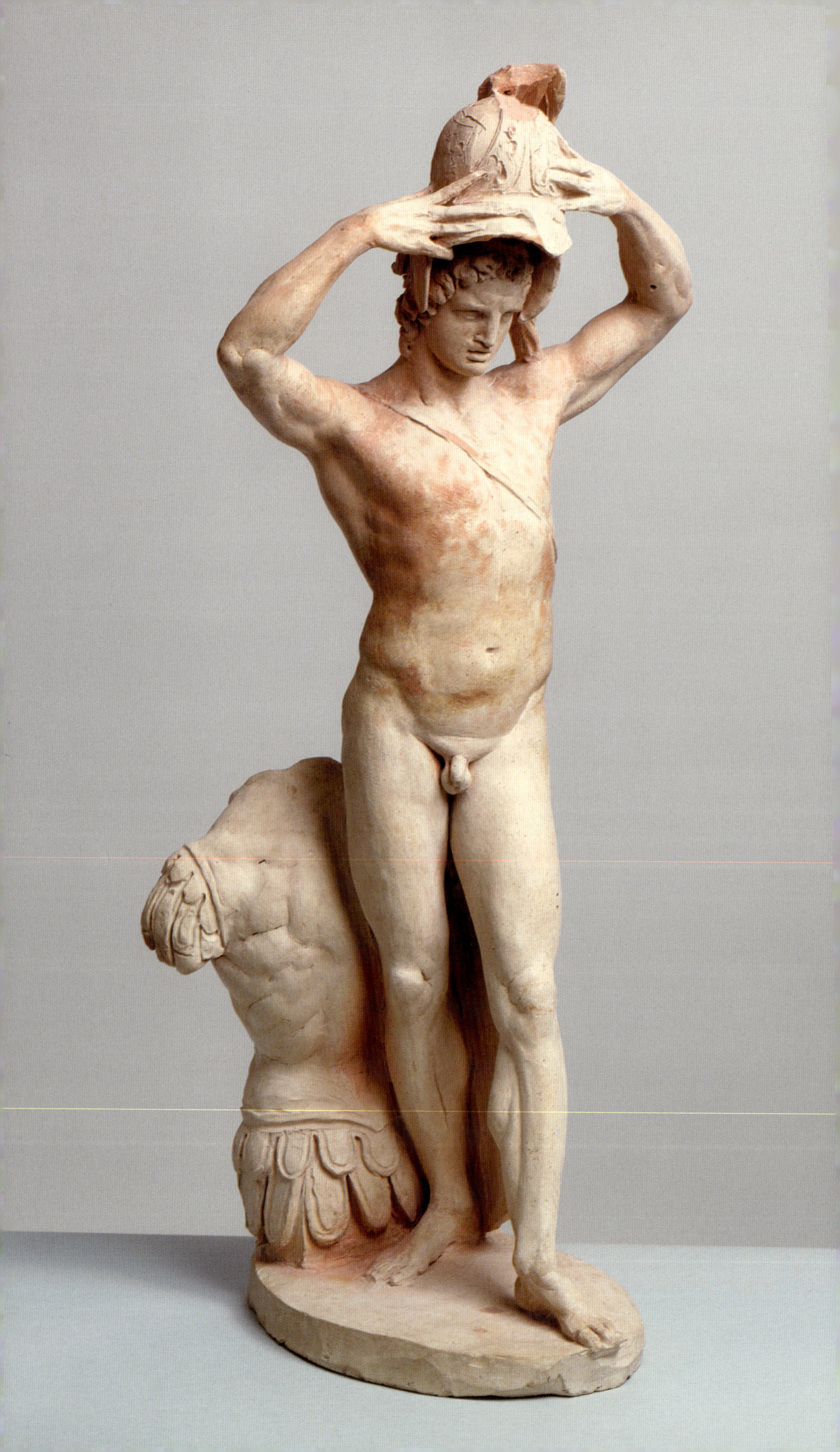

therefore more tolerant of Banks's "empirical approach to the antique" than other potential patrons. For Ickworth, his estate in Suffolk, the same patron ordered a series of Homeric friezes from Flaxman.

But after ordering Banks's work in marble, Hervey abandoned the commission. Having purchased the materials, Banks was furious at the bishop's change of heart. According to his wife, Elizabeth, the sculptor took the rejection personally, falling into a deep depression due to his faltering finances.[38] With only the plaster complete, he returned to London, where the work was feted but not exhibited. After his death, Elizabeth appears to have had the marble finished by workmen.

Despite the genesis of the work in these difficult circumstances, the Dreaming elements of the relief remain intact. Along with Winckelmann's integration of beauty and freedom, the elevation of Homer to godlike status was a factor strengthening the universality of Greece among radical activists. In another representation of Achilles by Banks, we gain more insight into how the *Iliad* provided a particularly useful source for materializing Banks's anti-war convictions. Like Chinard's Revolutionary candelabra, this work is a standing terracotta figure (fig. 33). Although it has come to be known as *Achilles Arming*, the original title remains unknown. Scholars point out that the action – the hero placing a helmet on his head – does not actually occur in the ancient text.[39] Taking into account what I observed, in the previous chapter, about the metaphorical significance of removing external layers in radical discourse, it seems just as likely that this is, in fact, not Achilles putting his armor on but taking it off, just as Mercury removes his sandals on the frontispiece to Tooke's *Diversions of Purley*, an image said to be designed by Banks (see fig. 20). After all, the first to refer to the work as "Achilles arming amidst his Myrmidons" was Allan Cunningham, the author responsible for the sensationalizing fiction around the drapery worn by the naked captain in St. Paul's.[40] In addition to Banks's anti-war beliefs – so vehemently expressed in his letter to Cumberland following the Treaty of Amiens – the proposition that the figure is taking off his armor and therefore renouncing war is supported by details of the work itself. A close inspection suggests a backward motion of Achilles's hands, his tiny fingers taut as if guiding the helmet off. Achilles is naked. Would the first piece of armor one might put on be a helmet, or would a helmet be the last thing one might take off? Either way, in spite of subsequent unilateral interpretations, there is an unquestionable ambiguity about the action. The connection to the engraving of Mercury in *Diversions of Purley* is particularly significant because, in the context of this print, the difference between the act of taking off versus putting on was acknowledged to be unclear. Cumberland worried that in the frontispiece "it was impossible to say whether Mercury was taking off or putting on his Sandals and winged appendages."[41] The statuette of Achilles underscores the anti-war implications of the same figure in the relief. Achilles was, for Banks, the ideal subject for espousing a critique of battlefield

33 Thomas Banks, *Achilles Arming*[?], date unknown, terracotta. Victoria and Albert Museum, London.

bloodshed. Both works can be seen as forerunners to the retelling of the *Iliad* by the poet Alice Oswald, *Memorial*, in which the casualties of the Trojan War are listed one by one. In the sculptures and poem alike, what Banks perceived as the murder-suicide of the soldier is brought home.[42]

What did Flaxman make of the adaptation of Achilles into an anti-war icon? In the numerous works in which he emulated Banks's relief, the younger artist chose to take the figure out. Guarded against the suggestiveness of the naked male body, Flaxman focused not on the combination of the two gendered parts that make up the relief's bipartite composition, but solely on the feminine side. On this half of the relief, Banks identifies Achilles's nymph-mother Thetis by way of higher projection from the background and from the other female figures that surround her, her long hair loose as it mingles with a strip of drapery.[43] Gently twisting away from the oval's edge, she guides a group of fellow nymphs, their bodies rising above and beneath her as they surface in varying levels of relief "from the dark sea like mist," as translations of Homer put it.[44] More bands of unworn drapery flutter about them as they traverse the sculpted waves. One of Flaxman's emulations of Banks's nymphs is his depiction of the same figures from the *Iliad* in his celebrated outline illustrations, executed in Rome and first published in 1793 (fig. 34). Choosing to portray the group descending back into the sea rather than emerging to console Achilles, the nymphs remain bunched as they are in Banks's work. In Flaxman's version, Thetis floats apart from the rest, crowned with a diadem and hair half restrained. A preliminary drawing depicts Thetis with both arms raised as she is in Banks's relief (and in other incarnations of Thetis by Flaxman in this series), but her nymphs facing the opposite direction, although still descending rather than rising (fig. 35). Banks's group has been rearranged, and the body of the hero lifted from the scene.

Significantly, Flaxman depicts a moment in the narrative that follows the one chosen by Banks. After comforting Achilles, Thetis, in the ancient tale, appeals to Hephaestus, god of craftsmanship, for a gleaming new shield to protect her son while he avenges his friend's death. Flaxman's decision to illustrate Thetis and her nymphs returning to their underwater haunt after the hero's strength has been restored dismantles the critique of violence implied by the earlier scene of mourning.

Flaxman saw the relief not only as Banks's master work, but as one of the greatest achievements of post-antique sculpture. In his posthumous tribute to Banks he writes that the interaction between the two gendered parts of the composition – the static naked male form and the vaporous cluster of female bodies – was unprecedented in the history of art: the "composition is so unlike any work ancient or modern that the combination may be considered as the artist's own."[45] Although Flaxman did not acknowledge it in the essay, the relief does bear traces of a work by an earlier artist both he and Banks admired: Lorenzo Ghiberti's *Gates of Paradise*. Executed in bronze between 1425 and 1452 for the doors of Florence's Baptistery of St. John, these square reliefs would probably have been seen by Banks during his trip to Florence in 1772. Long after his return from Rome, he drew from casts of two of the panels that were in the Royal

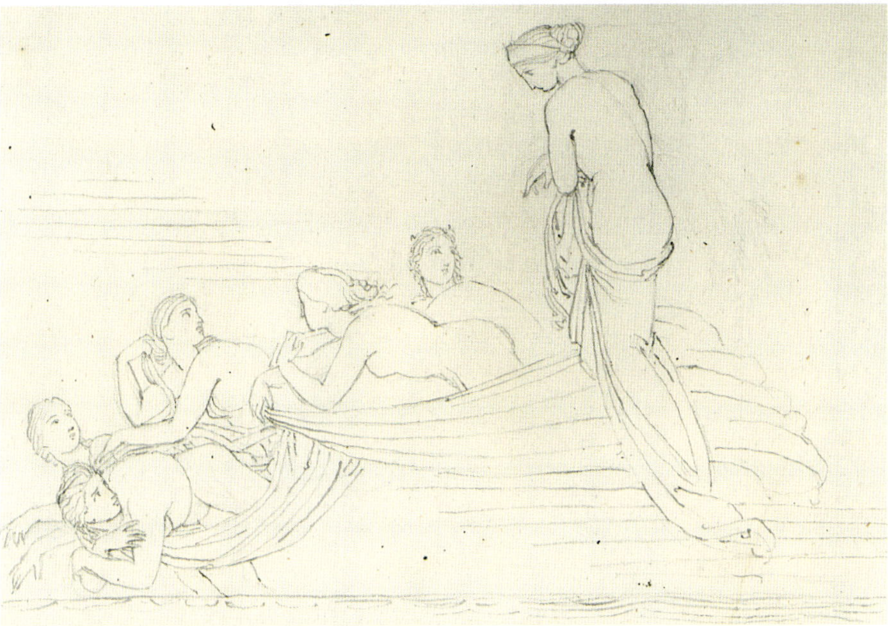

34 John Flaxman, *Thetis Ordering the Nereids to descend into the Sea*, 1792–93, pencil, pen, and ink on paper. Royal Academy of Arts, London.

35 John Flaxman, preliminary study for *Thetis Ordering the Nereids to descend into the Sea*, 1792–93, pencil, pen, and ink on paper. British Museum, London.

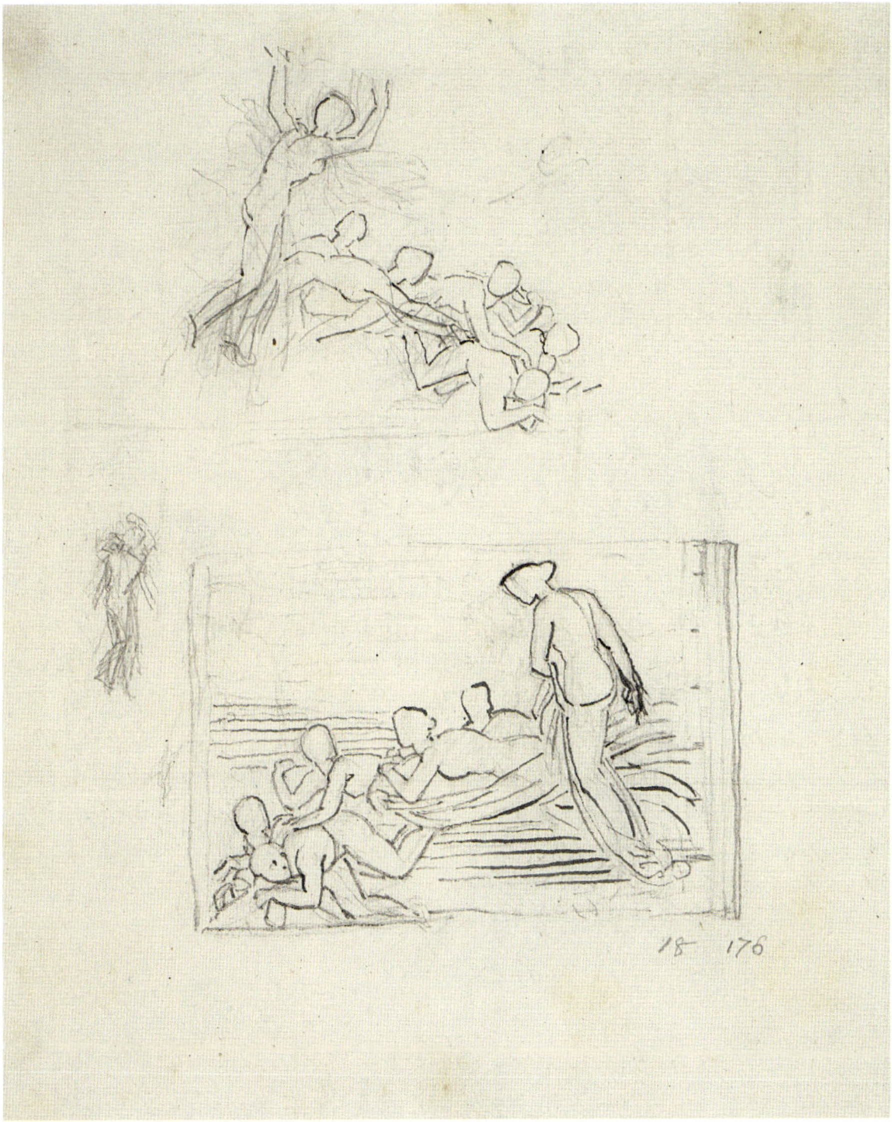

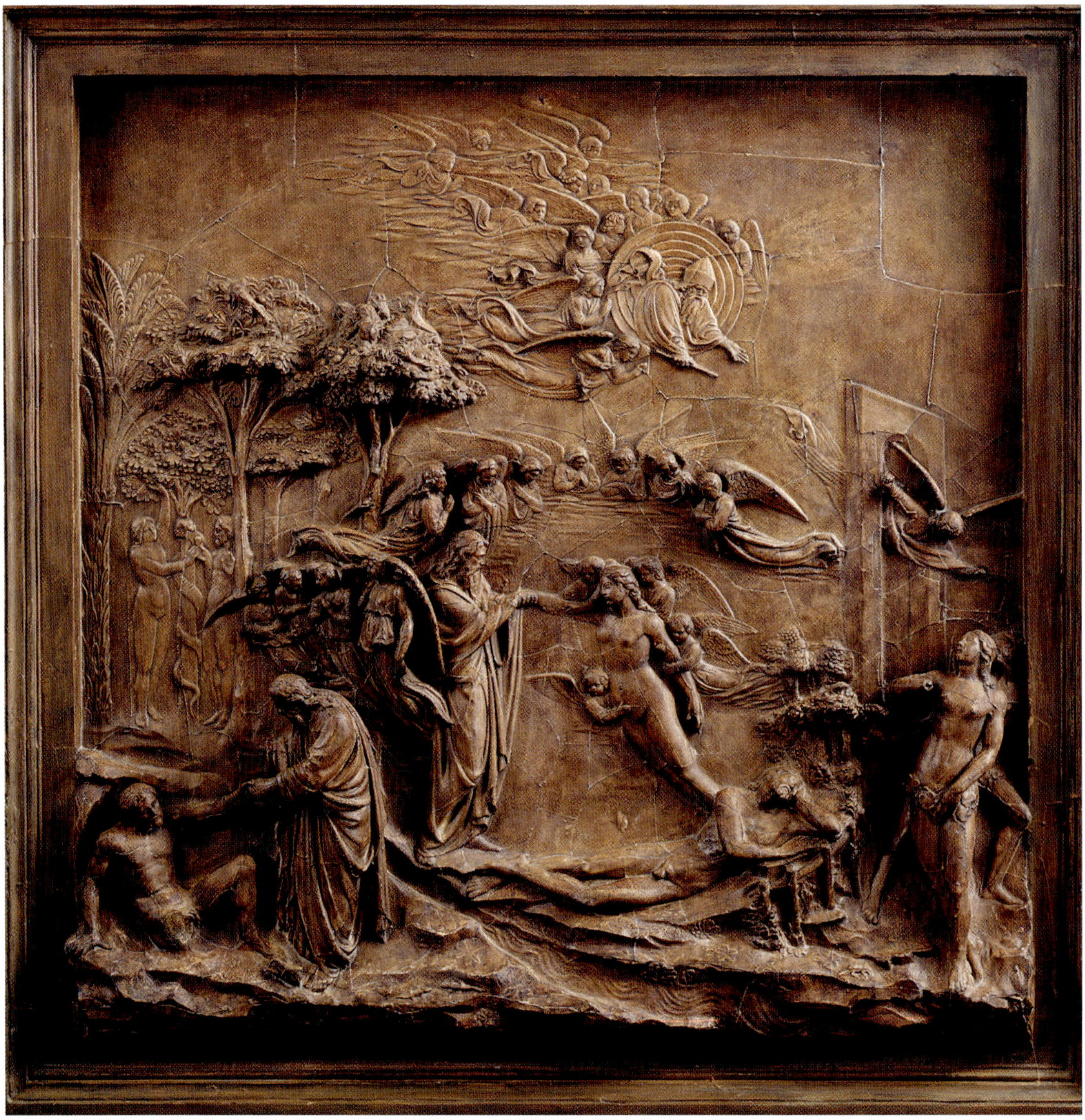

36 After Lorenzo Ghiberti, *Expulsion of Adam and Eve*, late eighteenth century, plaster cast. Royal Academy of Arts, London.

Academy collection.[46] One of these reliefs, the *Adam and Eve* panel, is a precedent for the Homeric relief (fig. 36). On a jagged mount at the base lies a half-awake Adam, head resting on one hand and his naked body facing the viewer. A diagonally upright Eve emerges from behind his shoulder, steered by little angels toward God. More angels populate the sky, hovering in arcs and denser flocks. Not only is Eve's floating motion and sidelong position akin to Banks's Thetis; the juxtaposition of Adam's nakedness and the hovering formations of angels prefigures the contrast between Achilles and his mother's retinue. Like the nymphs, Ghiberti's angels overlap, creating a play of light on the varying elevations of the surface that makes Adam look all the more still. In Banks's design, however, all superfluous space has been eliminated so that the figures are tightly contained within the oval boundary. That Ghiberti allowed too much ambient space, drowning his figures in an excessive backdrop, was a recurring criticism of the *Gates* among later British artists, including Reynolds and Flaxman himself.[47] Nonetheless, this work is significant in relation to Flaxman's reception of Banks because it offers a quintessential example of a Christianized adaptation of the classical body that suited Flaxman's position as a classicizing Christian artist. In the politicized sculpture, Banks had reconfigured Ghiberti's clusters of angels into Greek nymphs whose resemblance to the flocks in the Adam and Eve panel is only faint. Flaxman extracted the nymphs, depoliticized them and, in works to come, turned them back into Christian angels. Whether nymphs, angels, or other feminine spirits, the visual form is altered by Flaxman's renunciation of politically radical art in favor of a celestial version of antiquity. His adaptations proved successful among subsequent artists precisely because of his willingness to let the celestial and the sensual commingle, as Ghiberti, and some of the other fifteenth-century "restorers of art" he considered morally superior to the Greeks, had done before him.[48] This celestial sensuality is the basis of his Poetic status.

— THE SWEET, SENSUAL LINE —

Can Flaxman's art really be called sensual? His best known achievements are the drawings engraved by Tommaso Piroli, such as the plate depicting Thetis and her nymphs. Is this kind of image – executed in pure outline – not the precise opposite of sensual art? Flaxman has been called an artist of "spartan austerity."[49] Erwin and Dora Panofsky are typical in their conception of his aesthetic: "Reduced to pure contours, the visible world ... seemed to assume an unearthly, ethereal character, detached from the 'material' qualities of colour, weight and surface texture."[50] The unearthly character of such a mode conforms to what we know about Flaxman's spirituality. Yet the distinction between line and the "material" – that is, sensual – aspects of the "visible world" is not as cut and dry as the Panofskys suggest. Flaxman's art proves that forms can be sensual even if they possess no color, little weight, and no surface texture. Although they are almost always read in relation to the emergence in the late eighteenth century of outline drawing in both antiquarian literature and contemporary art – a trend also associated with the Rome-based draftsmen Asmus Carstens and Johann Tischbein among others on the Continent – Flaxman's designs shirk many of the defining characteristics of the outline genre as it was practiced during his lifetime.

In the introduction I stated that part of the conundrum of Poetic art is that its sensuality – normally associated with earthly and animalistic drives – places such works in a remote realm untroubled by mortal concerns. Paradoxically, it is the lack of sensuality that brings the object down to earth, implicating it in political affairs. Flaxman is the chief representative of this counterintuitively ethereal sensuality. The sensuality of his works is not achieved, as in a late subject picture by Reynolds or one of Canova's waxen marble dancers, by way of an exaggerated, "moisturized" materiality, but rather through the artist's sensualizing of outline, an otherwise emphatically desensualized aesthetic. By the time he relocated to Rome in 1787, where for six years he lived and worked as Banks had done, outline had become a highly charged approach. On the one hand, it was the most fitting way to capture the essence of Greco-Roman relics on paper. With this kind of drawing, vases, sculptures, and even frescoes could be reproduced in a simple, accessible fashion. At the same time, skeletal delineations offered a mode of representation that readily adhered to the contemporaneous movement that was challenging extant forms of power: the casting off of excess layers to reveal the bare bones of life as well as art. In paintings by David, for which Flaxman's outlines came to offer a spring of ideas for poses and actions, the linear contour articulates the quest to create works aligned with the Revolutionary and post-Revolutionary order. The male protagonists of David's *Intervention of the Sabine Women* – the naked Tatius and Romulus – are direct (but reversed) quotations of Flaxman's plate from the *Iliad*, *The Fight for the Body of Patroclus*.[51] Earlier paintings by James Barry, the Irish Academician banished from the Royal Academy in 1798 for, in part, his praise of the regicide David, are equally representative of the edifying implications of linear description.[52] In historical tableaux by both David and Barry, the privileging of line seals the ideological bent of the depicted subject. Undistracted by showy effects, the spectator has access to the naked truth of the scene. Paint, especially oil paint, was a contradictory medium for art with such prescriptive aims. While neither relied on painterly techniques such as impasto and glazing, the high-minded Dreams of both David and Barry were compromised by the viscosity of their media.

British radical discourse makes explicit the political implications of outline. In 1796, Banks's friend George Cumberland published a volume entitled *Thoughts on Outline*, an eccentric homage to linear description: "there is as much harmony to be produced by lines," he writes, "as by colour, or sound, or figures."[53] The volume concludes with a selection of designs of Cumberland's own invention, all in outline. Some of these are engraved by William Blake, who deemed it a "beautiful book."[54] Like Barry and also Blake, who famously loathed the works and teachings of Reynolds, Cumberland had a tense relationship with the Royal Academy. *Thoughts on Outline* is not just a defence of an artistic approach but a bold critique of the institution's perceived bias toward the taste of the aristocracy: namely, men like those appointed to the "Committee of Taste." The radical author posits outline as a moral corrective for the decadence of art valued by the Academy, particularly oil painting from the sixteenth century onwards. Blake was another vocal advocate of outline and its status as the antidote to the slick painterly surfaces and blurry gradation of light and shade that, in his view, characterized much of the art cherished by experts. For Blake, outline could speak directly to the spectator, allowing the content of the image to resonate among more than a select few. In the catalogue for his 1809 exhibition he attacks major masters such as Titian, Correggio, and Rubens for their "love of soft and even tints without boundaries"; only strong, "wiry" lines can pierce through the haziness valued in the traditional, that is, aristocratic, art theory.[55] As Martin Myrone points out, the opposition of "classical and intellectual line to base painterliness" had been a recurring trope within art criticism for decades before Blake and

Cumberland.[56] These men, however, applied this paragone to the indictment of the ruling class. Cumberland's book is dedicated to Charles James Fox, the Whig politician who supported the French Revolution. It is worth noting that Banks's preliminary design for the monument to *Captain Burges* is also drawn in outline. Outline articulates the capacity of the classical body to serve as a container for ideas.

Then as now, Flaxman is the artist chiefly associated with the outline aesthetic. He is also someone who, in his youth, had grounds to be as suspicious of the Royal Academy as Cumberland and Blake. Although he began his career on the peripheries of the institution, he lost out on their prestigious gold medal and associated Rome scholarship and had to fund his trip by other means. What is more, Flaxman is someone who, as we know, was a close friend and fervent admirer of a known radical activist in whose defence he readily leapt after his death. He was on intimate terms with Blake and knew Cumberland. Yet Flaxman was not interested in the politically radical capacity of the genre he helped popularize. Looking closely at designs such as his Banksian depiction of Thetis and her nymphs, we see that in his drawings the lines that describe the figures are not strong and "wiry" but gentle, alternately thin and slightly thicker, and always a touch uneven, replacing some of what is lost by the absence of tonal value. Piroli stays true to this intentional inconsistency. In other, unpublished drawings, Flaxman frequently introduced washes to give his outlines a volumetric softness that recorporealizes the figure drawn in line. So while he took a radicalized aesthetic and fused it with what we know to be an equally radical practice – Banks's "empirical approach to the antique" – Flaxman produced works that subvert the underlying implications of both.

Benjamin Robert Haydon voiced a common response to Flaxman's group of nymphs and other female figures when he labelled them "sweet," a word that, as I mentioned in the preface, was used in relation to sculptures by Canova and appears frequently in Keats's poetry and its criticism.[57] Otherwise elusive, the meaning of this non-gustatory sweetness becomes intelligible once we note that "dolce" and "dolcemente" are musical terms. Published in 1837, an English musical dictionary states that the instruction "Dolce maniera" requires a "delicate, and finished style of performance," while "Dolcissimo" implies "extremely soft and delicate."[58] Such definitions are helpful in gauging the materiality of a seemingly immaterial aesthetic. Flaxman's reduction of form to "sweet" contour produces lyrical configurations that move across the page like sonic wave-forms or even a musical score. His outlines attain a sensuality in spite of their lack of physical substance, a sensuality that thwarts interested interpretations of the work of art just as music, especially non-vocal music and its refusal to possess a prescribed meaning, does too. Contrasting with the "spatio-temporal" limitations of Banks's art, Flaxman's outlines break with a specific place and time, hence their influence – direct and indirect – on artists right up to the twentieth century.[59] As the philosophers Edmund Husserl and Theodor Adorno have theorized, music has its own temporality – intervals between notes, progressions of chords – that can take us, for a moment, to a similarly unmoored zone.[60]

This zone is protected from happenings outside its bounds, from the historical conditions in which political visions are incubated. Adorno calls these historical conditions "empirical time"; "there is no mistaking time as such in music," he writes, "yet it is so remote from empirical time that, when listening is concentrated, temporal events external to the musical continuum remain external to it and indeed scarcely touch it."[61] Flaxman's outlines are beyond "empirical time" and Banks's art is entrenched in it.

It was Walter Pater who, almost a century after Piroli's engravings were first published, declared that "all art constantly aspires toward the condition of music."[62] By this Pater meant "all art" that could find value according to the Aesthetic gaze. Vocal in his appreciation for art that achieves "sweetness" (which, in Pater's imagination stands for a kind of gentle eroticism traceable in works by Michelangelo and in Venetian painting), Pater posited Keats as a forerunner of this agenda, a prophet of the call, in the conclusion to *The Renaissance*, to give the "highest quality to your moments as they pass."[63] Pater was also an admirer of Blake yet not, as far as I know, of Flaxman. But while it may ostensibly appear less avant-garde and hence amenable to Pater's more modernist leanings, Flaxman's art aligns far more with Pater's philosophy than Blake's. Flaxman's outlines were popular because they were visual arias, translations of myths and modern literature into an idiom that allowed the sensuality of the source to cast off politicized projections.

Flaxman's designs are also "sweet" in the sense that they eliminate all elements that are unpalatable. Always smooth and predominantly curvilinear even when representing a geometric structure, his forms avoid everything that has the potential to be rough or serrated. Even when depicting masculine scenes like *The Fight for the Body of Patroclus* – the plate adapted by David – Flaxman bunches the figures together to produce a lyrical tumble of bodies that is more than the sum of its angular parts. In his *Philosophical Enquiry into the Origin of Our Ideas of the Sublime and Beautiful*, Burke equates sweetness with smoothness: "In the smell and taste, we find all things agreeable to them, and which are commonly called sweet, to be of a smooth nature, and that they all evidently tend to relax their respective sensories."[64] Using Burke as evidence, Byung-Chul Han argues that both sweetness and smoothness are "are phenomena of pure positivity." In art that reproduces these qualities, there "exists no disaster, no injury, no ruptures, also no seams. Everything flows in soft and smooth transitions; everything appears rounded, polished, smoothed out." Images that manifest these qualities have been "emptied of any depth, any shallows, any profound sense."[65] That the sweetness of outlines by Flaxman is a conscious evacuation of negativity is especially evident when we compare his depiction of Thetis and the nymphs with Banks's relief. Without the body of Achilles the nymphs are safe, their pleasing motion untroubled by the presence of the grieving naked man that is the nucleus of the radical sculptor's Dream. As Myrone puts it, Achilles's body is "bizarrely taut"; Banks "gives Achilles's torment full expression" by stretching the figure across the composition "with complete disregard for naturalistic space," his arms and torso straining into a rigid triangle.[66] Originally intended as designs for bas-reliefs, Flaxman's outlines accommodate this same evasion of naturalistic space, manifesting an equally bold move away from mimetic scale. Yet they do not contain figures whose form and action are as disturbing as that of Banks's Achilles. Even in his illustrations of a macabre text like Dante's *Divine Comedy*, we find that Flaxman's forms are perpetually delicate, smooth, relaxed, and ungeometric. In the tenth plate – *Limbo: The Guiltless Throng* – a swarm of babies erupt from the mouth of a skull bathed in clouds with the same gentle overlapping motion as the nymphs in Thetis's train (fig. 37). His portrayal of *Dis, or Lucifer* gives the demonic spirit a feminine tenderness as it shovels the body of a man into its mouth, its muscles resembling rolling hills more than taut anatomy (fig. 38).

The Dante plates were ordered by Thomas Hope, a shrewd collector of classicizing art and heir to a Dutch banking fortune who had been one of the first to capitalize on the fashion for outline. Flaxman completed Hope's Dante drawings and the *Iliad* illustrations during his stay in Rome. While working on the

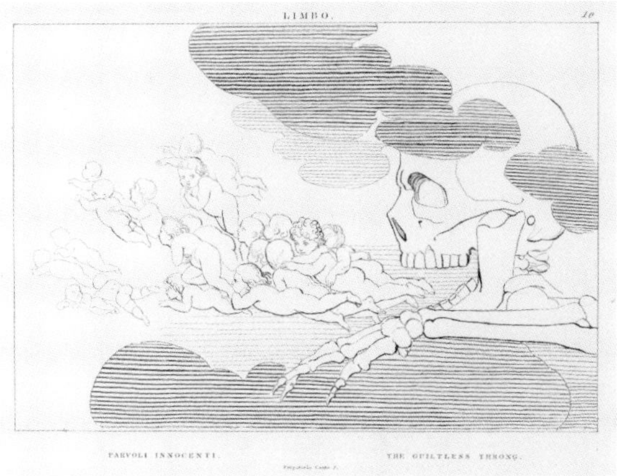

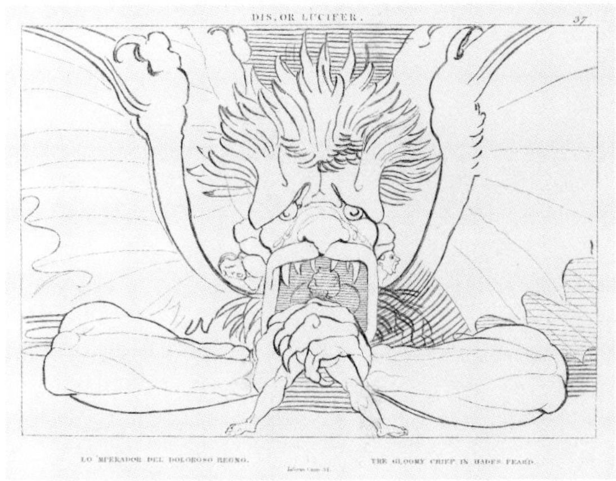

37 Tommaso Piroli after John Flaxman, *Limbo: The Guiltless Throng*, 1807, etching on paper. Royal Academy of Arts, London.

38 Tommaso Piroli after John Flaxman, *Dis, or Lucifer*, 1807, etching on paper. Royal Academy of Arts, London.

latter he produced a set of plates representing Homer's *Odyssey*. His drawing of *Morning* depicts a Banksian group of nymphs basking in celestial isolation. Four girls are led by Aurora, goddess of the dawn, who recalls Banks's Thetis with her raised arms. Her companions encircle her like the nymphs on the relief, their bodies weaving in and out of clouds like the nymphs between the waves. This was the stand-out design from the *Odyssey* plates (fig. 39). Well into the Victorian period it was praised for its "floating clouds embodied in the forms of graceful nymphs, whose fair faces are fresh with dew, and jubilant with the songs of birds."[67] "Graceful," "fair," and "jubilant" are positive adjectives which tap into

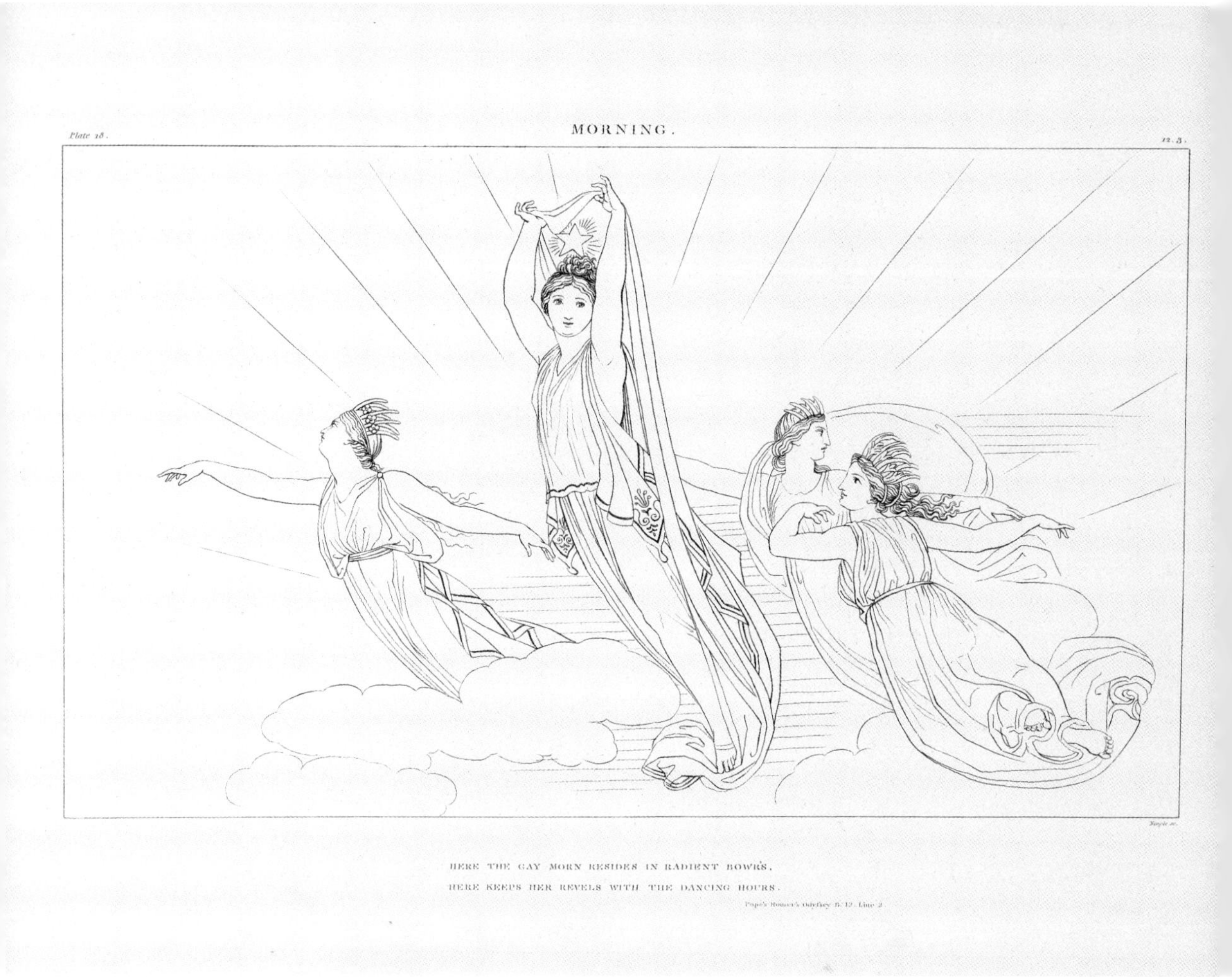

39 James Neagle after John Flaxman, *Morning*, 1805, etching on paper, Royal Academy of Arts, London.

the musicality, the sweetness, of Flaxman's outlines. Once part of a Dreaming composition, Banksian nymphs are converted into a paradigm of the intersensory category that is sweetness.

Flaxman's last set of outlines was published in 1817 as a volume illustrating the *Works and Days* and *Theogony* of Hesiod. Engraved by Blake, this series contained his most overt emulation of Banks to date. Plates 18 and 19 depict the Pleiades, seven stars in the constellation of Taurus known as the seven sisters and traditionally represented as a group of maidens. In the ancient world, the position of these stars was a guide for agricultural and maritime pursuits. Hesiod cites the stars to specify the time of year when it is safe for ships to sail without fear of turbulence and, after their eventual setting, when it is "time to plough."[68] Flaxman's first depiction shows the rising of the Pleiades after the birth of their father Atlas, another Titan, the second their falling away (figs. 40 and 41). Given the rectangular format of the printed page, Flaxman's fidelity to Banks's grouping

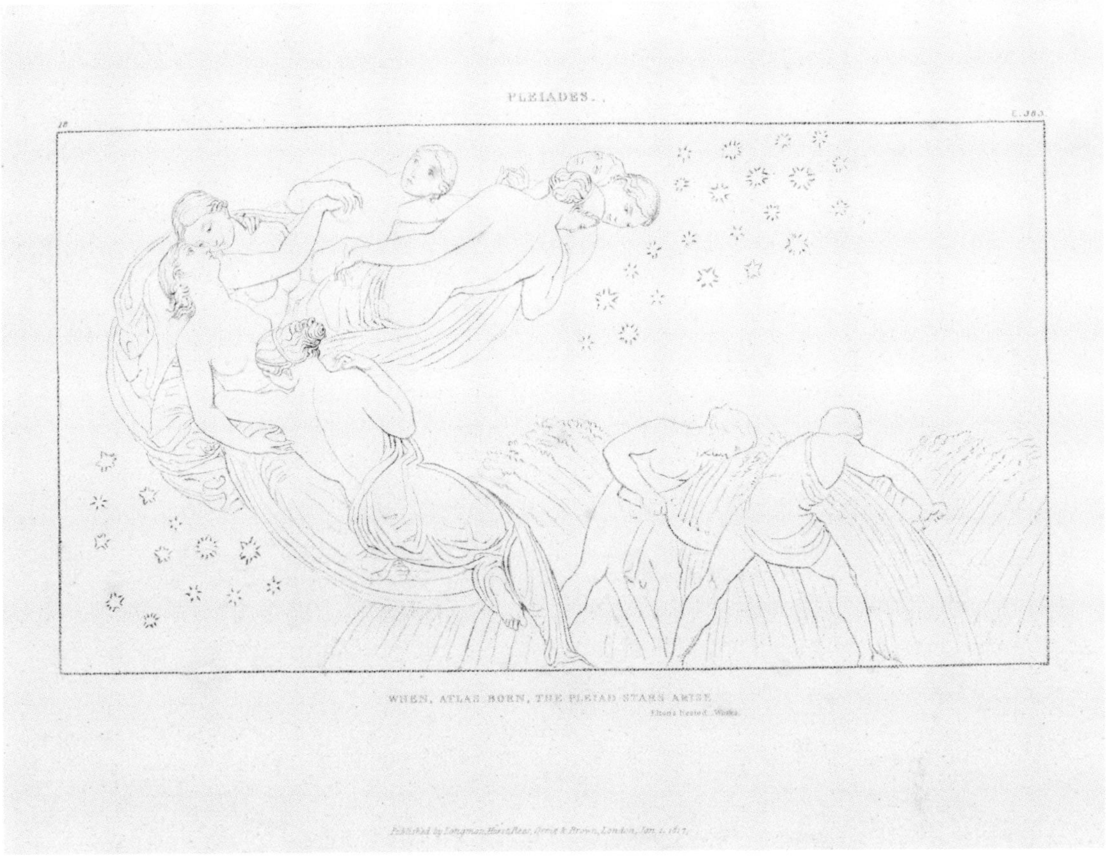

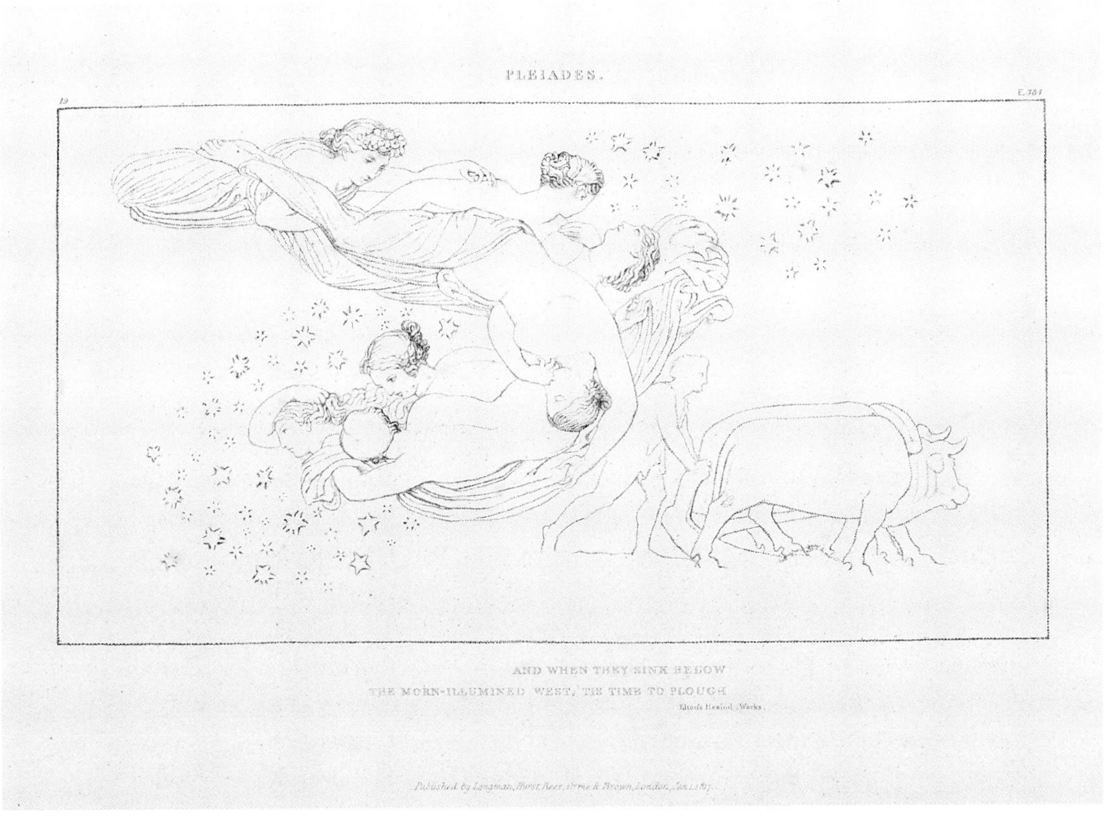

40 William Blake after John Flaxman, *Pleiades*, 1817,
stipple engraving and etching on paper, Royal Academy of Arts, London.

41 William Blake after John Flaxman, *Pleiades*, 1817,
stipple engraving and etching on paper, Royal Academy of Arts, London.

of the nymphs to fit the oval shape of the relief appears stubborn. Rather than conforming to the layout of the actual constellation, Flaxman's stars wrap around the right half of the design in a configuration almost identical to the nymphs in Banks's sculpture. Only now there is no hierarchy and the figures move without a maternal leader. Draped only from the waist they cling to each other, two nuzzling while another buries her head in a sister's torso, the rest gazing into space. The illustration of their descent shows the stars – still arranged into a half-oval – moving in the opposite direction. In mythology, the mother of the Pleiades is Pleione, a sea nymph. With their parents symbolic of water and earth respectively, the daughters embody the space between the two elements. Traversing the waves onto dry land, Banks's nymphs provided an ideal model for Flaxman's interpretation of these half-water, half-land offspring whose own domain is in the sky. In this reworking, the visual form becomes a "phenomen[on] of pure positivity" because it does not make contact with the earth, the land, or the sea, remaining a spectacle whose bearing on mortal life is as a tiny configuration of light glimpsed from a cosmic distance.

— THE POEM AS PATHOSFORMEL —

Flaxman's reworking of Banks's nymphs is a specific kind of emulation. The younger artist does not directly quote from the Homeric relief but rather adapts one of its visual forms to suit alternative ends, ends that consciously break from – and are therefore in conflict with – the political vision that guided his forebear's practice. This simultaneous continuity and discontinuity between Banks and Flaxman matches the dialectic of the Poet and the Dreamer. It also correlates to a tension embedded within the reception of Greco-Roman antiquity more broadly.

In 1917, Aby Warburg wrote that a "classically rarefied version of the ancient gods has been so successfully imposed on us, ever since Winckelmann, as the central symbol of antiquity, that we are apt to forget that it was entirely the creation of humanist scholars: this 'Olympian' aspect of antiquity had first to be wrested from its entrenched, traditional, 'daemonic' aspect."[69] Warburg is not necessarily stating that Winckelmann himself was exclusively concerned with the antique in its "Olympian" guise, but that the cult of the antique spawned by the reception of his writings favored a heroic and masculine classicism. It is certainly true that the "vulgar Winckelmannianism" prevalent among British radicals was oriented toward a "classically rarefied ... symbol of antiquity" consolidated in the male bodies of Greco-Roman sculpture, making Mary Wollstonecraft's feminist allusions to the *Gedanken* all the more provocative. For a limited phase, radical activists and the British state were united in their investment in this selective approximation of Greece, and Greek art. Banks's grieving Achilles, his terracotta statuette of the same Homeric figure, and his naked captain in St. Paul's are all embodiments of the strain of reception Warburg identifies as a distinctly late eighteenth-century phenomenon. Banks stands apart from other arbiters of this approach, however, because of the way he made it his own, recasting it to forge a Dream that is anti-war and therefore not traditionally heroic.

One of Warburg's resounding contributions to the history of art was his effort to recover the dialectical counterpart to this classicism: the "daemonic" aspect of antiquity. The ancient figure he perceived to be most representative of this aspect is the maenad, a class of female figure found on Greek and Roman art, mainly sarcophagi, vases, and gems devoted to the cult of Dionysus or Bacchus, god of wine and ecstatic visions. For Warburg, the maenad's characteristically frenzied motion – hair and drapery tossed by wind and life force energy – is the ultimate representation of a heightened psychic state. He designated this figure the "Ninfa" (the maenad of mythology is in some cases a type of nymph) and traced its appearance in post-antique art, arguing that when similar figures appear, it gives the image an emotional frequency it would not otherwise possess.[70] As such, the "Ninfa" is a paradigmatic example of another Warburgian concept, the *Pathosformel*: a device for the visual representation of intense feeling through gesture. Although Banks was apparently not on Warburg's radar and Flaxman not an artist he appears to have dwelled on in his relatively scant writings, the interplay between these two classicisms does correspond to the relationship between the two British sculptors. Flaxman's art does not appear to manifest a "demonic" side of antiquity, yet the younger artist was oriented toward not only the representation of energetic figures like nymphs and other beings with a female shape, but the capacity of such forms to perform an emotive function. In his monument to *Agnes Cromwell*, a vertical marble tablet installed in Chichester Cathedral in 1800, an idealized representation of the subject – an English girl dead at only eighteen – is carved in relief, carried up by angels who transport the girl's soul to heaven, her hands touching in prayer (fig. 42). Margaret Whinney notes that the key source for this design is precisely the same ancient maenads posited by Warburg as the *Pathosformel* for unbridled emotion.[71] Flaxman's *Lectures* indicate a marked interest in these particular figures, and the second edition, published in 1838 and with the tribute to Banks, contains an illustration of a maenad as part of a passage discussing how to give the illusion of motion.[72] In the Cromwell sculpture, Flaxman takes the maenad and refracts it through the prism of Swedenborg. At the core of the theologian's writings are the guardian angels that carry the souls of the dead – still, according to the doctrine, in human shape – to the world of the spirits. Like nymphs in Greek mythology, the bodies of Swedenborgian angels are barely distinguishable from those of mortals. In the Cromwell monument, the "Ninfa" has been spiritualized. Rather than representing a heightened psychic state, the motion and swelled drapery of the maenad-nymph-angels are intended to generate both sympathy from the viewer and belief in the afterlife. In the monument to *Agnes Cromwell*, the *Pathosformel* has been sweetened, the "demonic" aspect of antiquity made palatable.

But as much as Flaxman's devotion to such female figures signals his distance from the "Olympian" model, his emulation of Banks indicates that things were not so clear-cut. The work of modern sculpture that Flaxman emulated time and again – Banks's Homeric relief – presents not just the heroic and Olympian figure of Achilles, albeit reshaped by grief, but the group of nymphs who themselves possess something of the maenad. Indeed, in this sculpture we find Banks experimenting with what Warburg called the "demonic" aspect of antiquity and, like Flaxman was to do in numerous works, reconfiguring its emotional pitch. According to Bryant, Banks sourced the unbound hair and fluttering drapery of Thetis and her train from ancient representations of the maenad.[73] Instead of frenzied energy, the nymphs on the relief embody a sense of comfort that will ease the hero's distress, much like the angels on the monument to *Agnes Cromwell* are embodiments of sympathy and the soul's safety after death. Banks's

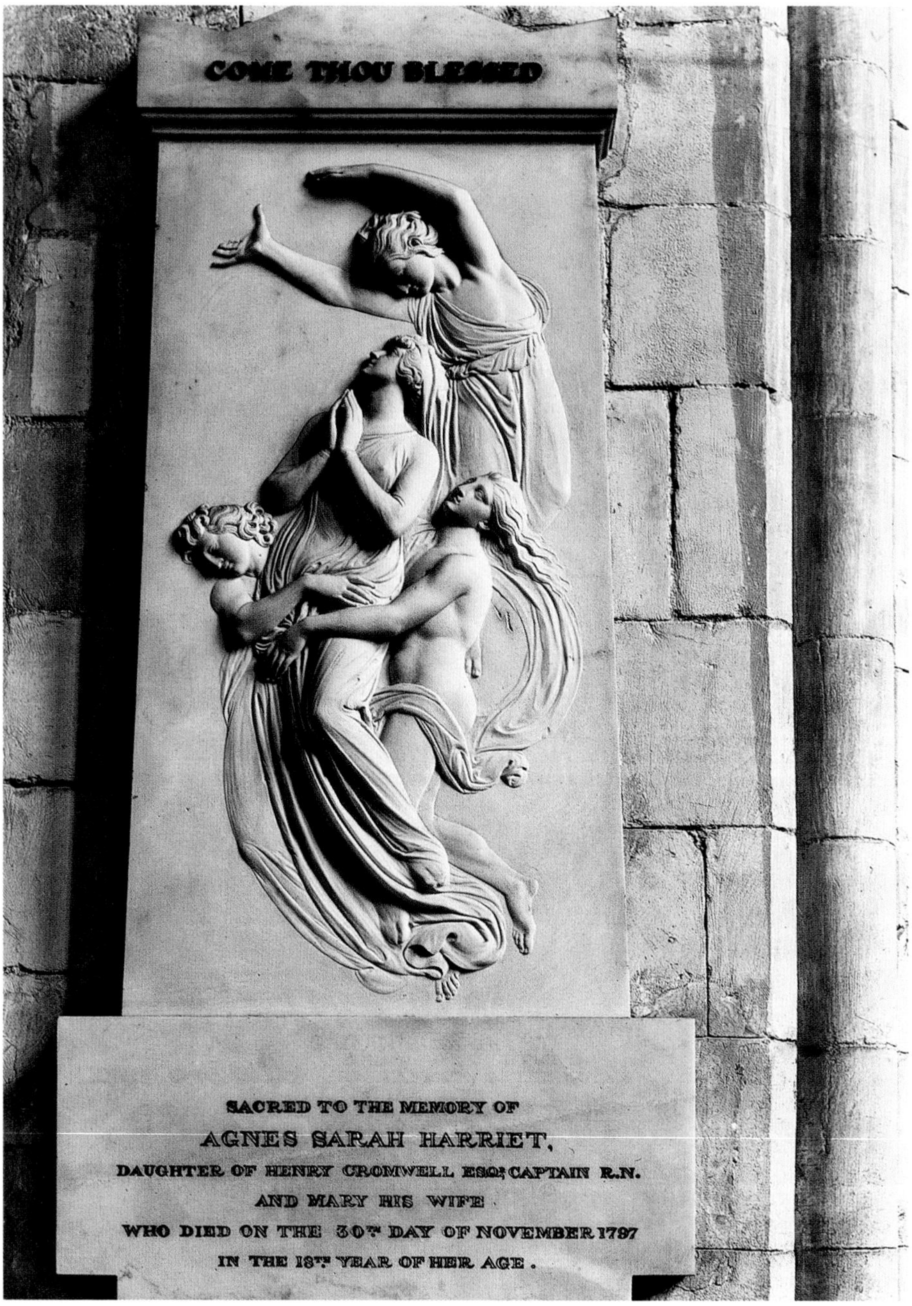

42 John Flaxman, *Agnes Cromwell*, 1799, marble. Chichester Cathedral.

work therefore contains Warburg's dialectic and subverts its logic. Intense feeling is represented not by the Ninfa-esque forms but by the tensely rendered "classically rarefied" male body, described by Myrone in Warburgian terms as a "geometric sign of grief."[74]

In her assessment of Flaxman's monument to *Agnes Cromwell*, Whinney does not acknowledge the connection to Banks's nymphs. While ancient representations of maenads likely did inform the design of the figures on both sculptures, Flaxman's group is another indication of his fixation on Banks's design. Flaxman's half-draped angels move, as Banks's nymphs do, between two elements: in this case earth and air rather than water and earth. One even raises her arms just like Thetis. Exposed in profile, the torso of the angel on the bottom right is naked, her hair and a strip of drapery fluttering behind her form, echoing one of Banks's nymphs. The nakedness of this angel points to the reconciliation of pagan and Christian values that characterizes Flaxman's art, especially his funerary sculpture. The balletic flight of Flaxman's wingless (and therefore all the more nymph-like) angels converts the tragic death of a young girl into the promise of a miracle. In the hands of these guides, her soul is safely chaperoned.

So while it appears to distance Flaxman from Banks, Flaxman's obsession with groups of maenadic figures ties him closer to Banks's relief while revealing, at the same time, the aspect of Banks he wished to perpetuate and the side he wished to leave behind. In other funerary sculpures, including the monument to *Elizabeth Knight* at Milton Church, Cambridgeshire, the monument to *Frances Schutz Drury* in Kingsbridge Cathedral in Devon, and his destroyed monument to *Ann Bowling*, formerly installed in Croydon Parish Church, South London, Flaxman upholds the status of Banks's group of nymphs to operate as a *Pathosformel* for comfort in the context of mourning. Always to female subjects, such monuments are seemingly worlds away from the radical Homeric relief. By isolating and magnifying the group of females, they censor the negativity with which Banks imbued the "classically rarefied" male body.

Another image by Flaxman separates the emotive frequency of Banks's nymphs from the Dreaming subject in which they first appeared. A delicate pen and wash drawing depicts a group of female figures arranged vertically into a column, their forms overlapping and seeming to rise in unison (fig. 43). The figure at the top has both arms raised like Thetis. An inscription reveals that they are the Heliades – Greek nymphs of the sun – together with their mother, Clymene, an ocean nymph. As told by Homer, Aeschylus, Ovid, and other ancient authors, the Heliades are seized with grief after their brother Phaeton is killed in a reckless chariot ride. They are so overcome that, after months of ceaseless grief, the gods convert them into poplar trees, their tears solidifying into beads of amber. Phaeton's friend Cycnus, meanwhile, is converted into a swan. While they do not technically represent a comforting force, their overlapping bodies once again appear in the context of grief. Their fusion into a unit suggests the cathartic nature of collective mourning. Between Cycnus, Clymene, and the Heliades, grief is shared and the tragedy of their shape-shifting fate lessened by their union. Flaxman could have represented Cycnus's body in the midst of its transition as

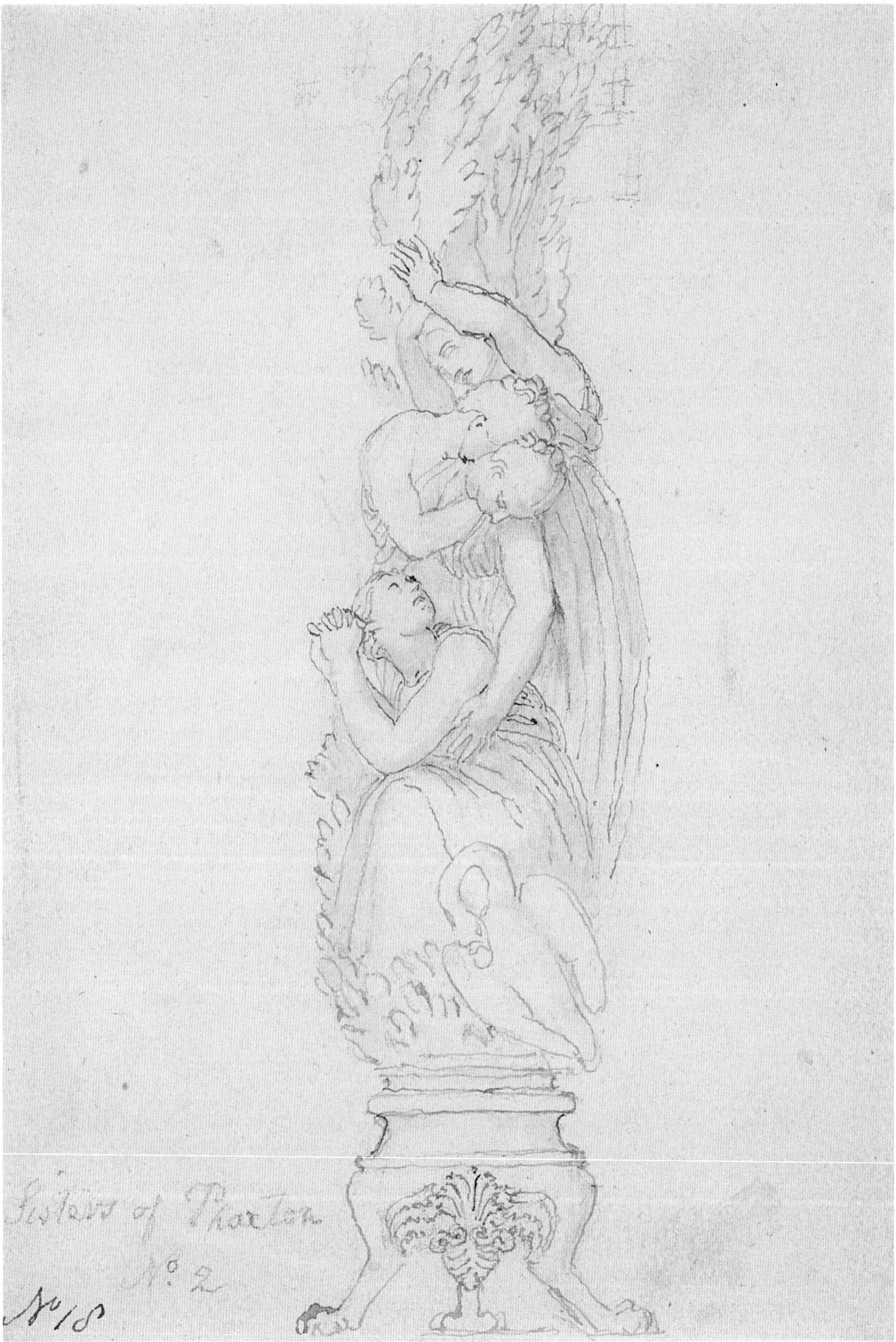
Sisters of Phaeton
No. 2
No 18

he did with the female forms, who still retain most of their human features, or even with his human shape intact and in "classically rarefied" form. But instead he chose to portray the male body fully transformed into a bird. Cycnus is further diminished by his placement at the foot of the sprouting column.

In one of his outline illustrations to the tragedies of Aeschylus, produced in Rome shortly after the *Iliad* plates, Flaxman reintroduces a male figure into an emulation of Banks's nymphs. Just three pages into the plates for *Prometheus Bound* we are reunited with a familiar group of overlapping female forms (fig. 44). Now they appear in the guise of a winged chorus rising from the ocean floor to visit Prometheus. In this incarnation, they flit across the page like butterflies, a caption at the bottom describing "the soft beat of light-moving wings" as it fills the "panting" air.[75] As with Banks's group, each member of the chorus is naked, with bands of drapery fluttering behind them to conjure the sense of ascending motion. A nymph toward the back of the train clasps her hands with compassion for the shackled deity, a gesture that heightens the emotive frequency of the scene. Crucially, the male figure is minimalized in this image. Prometheus appears as a diminutive specter in the distance, his masculine authority diminished by his

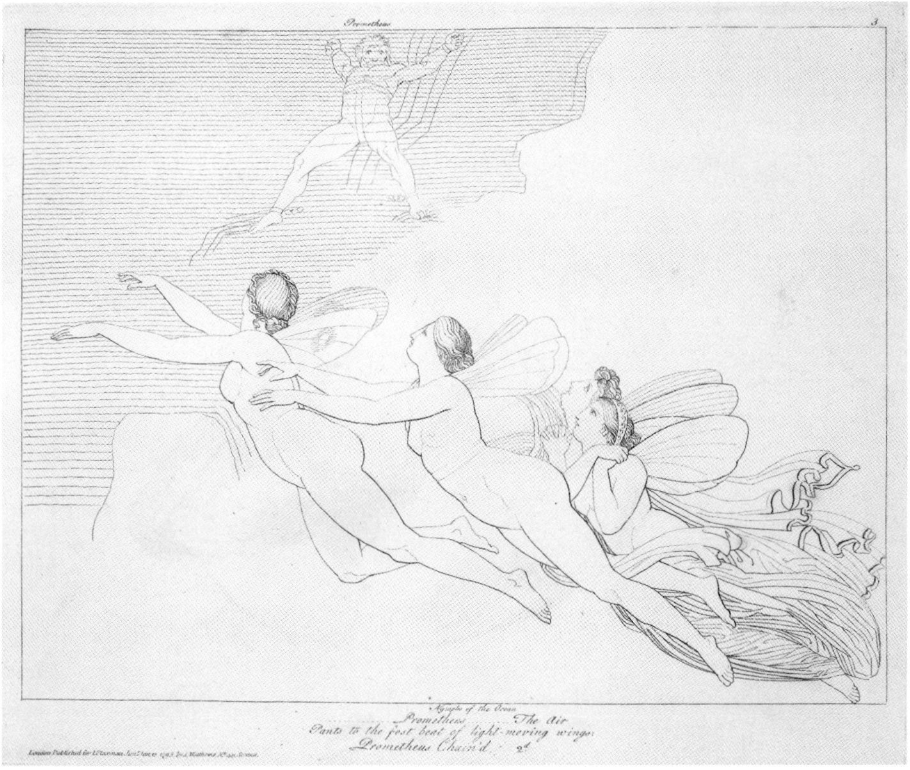

43 John Flaxman, *Sisters and Mother of Phaeton Transformed into Poplars and Cycnus into a Swan*, pen, ink, and graphite on paper, date unknown. British Museum, London.

44 Tommaso Piroli after John Flaxman, *Nymphs of the Ocean Visit Prometheus*, engraving. Printed in John Flaxman, *Compositions of the Tragedies of Aeschylus* (London: J. Matthews, 1795), pl. 3.

size as well as his confinement. The intentionally uneven horizontal lines that appear in many of Flaxman's illustrations work to cancel the Titan out, diminishing his already faint contour. Elsewhere in *Prometheus Bound*, similar female forms provide and express comfort. The next plate centers on Oceanus, the Titan who plots to travel to land to visit Prometheus. In the distance we glimpse the clustered nymphs, now congregating at the captive's feet.[76] The following illustration introduces Io, the mortal maiden whom Flaxman depicts asleep with her head tilted toward the viewer and both breasts bared (fig. 45). Performing the same consolatory function, three female spirits hover above her. The caption at the bottom reads: "Still, when retired to rest, air-bodied forms visit my slumbers nightly soothing me."[77]

An exception to Flaxman's marginalization of the male body in his representation of Banksian female forms subsists in another plate from *Prometheus Bound*. His illustration of *The Storm* shows the nymph chorus gathered at Prometheus's feet (fig. 46). They are earthbound this time, their conciliatory function inhibited by the onslaught of an "impetuous storm" from which they shelter. Each nymph closes in on herself, folding her body away from the others in order to protect her own individual form. This creates space for the male body to take center stage. Uncharacteristically angular for Flaxman, Prometheus's form unfolds, tugging against the chains that hold him captive. The combination of the sheltering chorus and the Titan's thick limbs produces a negative image in which the sweetness typical of Flaxman is replaced by a more conventionally heroic, "classically rarefied" mode. Only the locus of this heroic mode – the naked male body – is kept in shackles. Limits are still placed on its power.

From the Dante illustrations to the plates representing Hesiod, Flaxman's repetition of Banksian forms over several decades points to the expansive "spatio-temporal" condition of his work. In addition to the intermediality of his works – their spanning of sculpture, drawing, and graphic design – they are not limited to the era of their making. This is evidenced not just by the repetition of this one visual form over the course of many years – years that witness the peak of French Revolutionary fervor, the rise of Napoleon, the defeat of the French, and the restoration of the monarchy; the success of his designs among younger artists points to the temporal elasticity of Flaxman's art. Firmly rooted in the narrow set of years in which the artist's Dream was recoverable, Banks's relief has never received the credit it deserves in relation to Flaxman's designs. Yet these very designs went on to be incorporated not only into subsequent painting and sculpture by a plethora of international practitioners, but into the performing arts as late as the Second World War. In 1940, a ballet choreographed by the celebrated Frederick Ashton – set to Franz Liszt's *Dante Sonata* – opened at Sadler's Wells in London. Entitled *Dante Sonata*, the choreography and set design were

45 Tommaso Piroli after John Flaxman, *The Vision of Io*, 1795, etching on paper. Royal Academy of Arts, London.

46 Tommaso Piroli after John Flaxman, *The Storm*, 1795, etching on paper. Royal Academy of Arts, London.

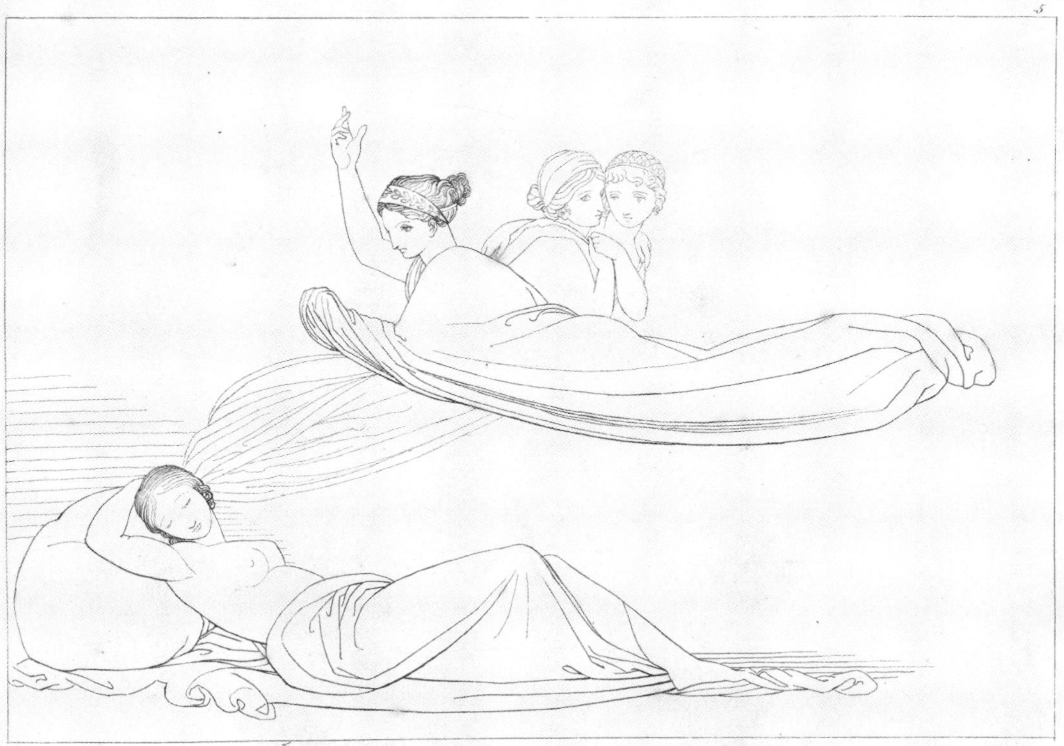

Still, when retired to rest, air-bodied forms
Visit my slumbers nightly soothing me
Prometheus Chain'd 4.

London Published for I. Flaxman Jun.r Jan 17 1795, by J. Matthews, N.o 441 Strand.

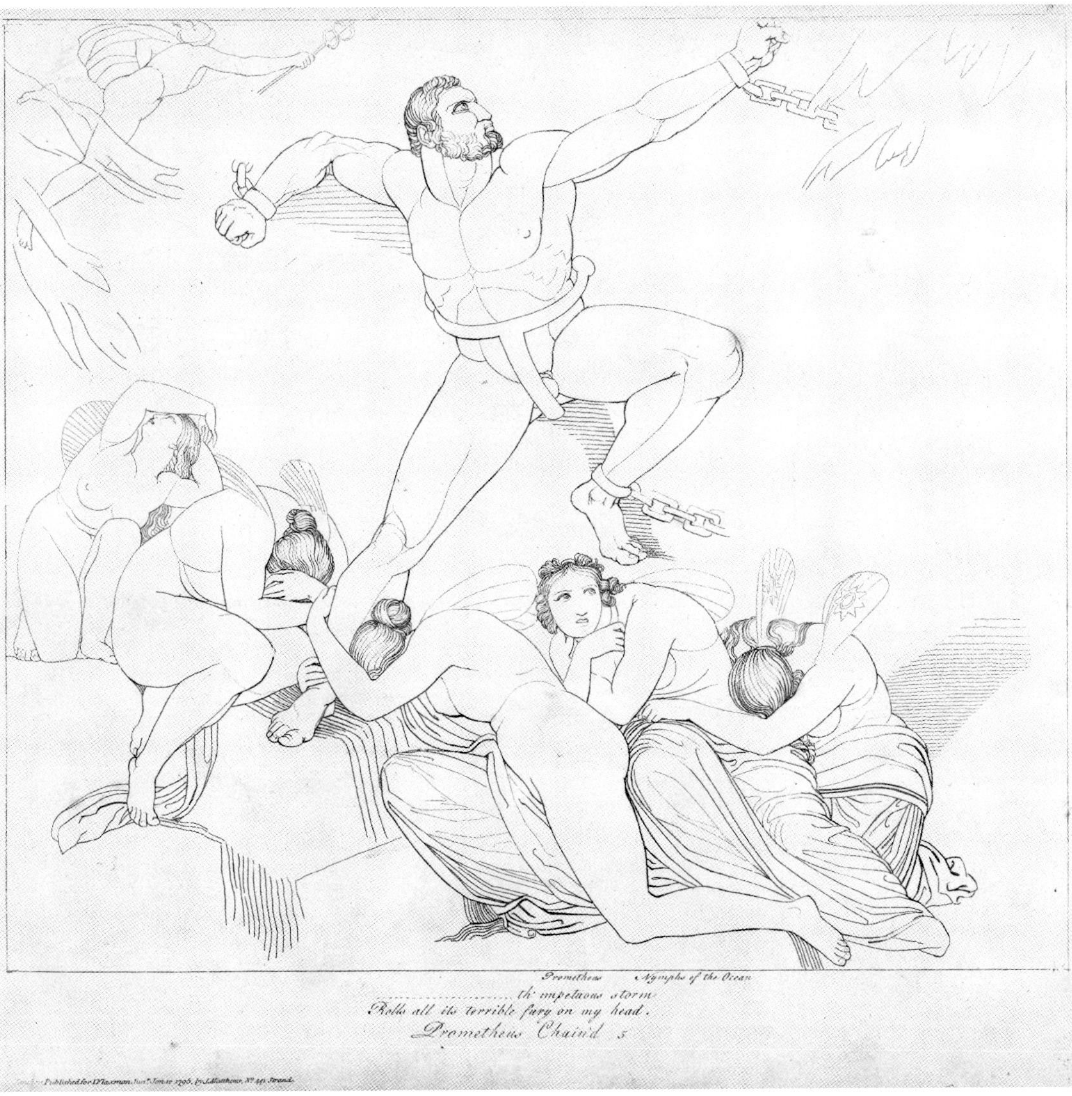

Prometheus Nymphs of the Ocean
.............................th' impetuous storm
Rolls all its terrible fury on my head.
Prometheus Chain'd 5

London Published for I. Flaxman Jun.r Jan 17 1795, by J. Matthews, N.o 441 Strand.

based on Flaxman's outlines of the *Divine Comedy* (fig. 47). Jane E. Everson informs us that, like Flaxman's illustrations, the performance did not offer a scene-by-scene portrayal of the text but rather attempted to convey the psychological sensations experienced when reading the text, as Liszt had strived to do with his musical interpretation.[78] The Dante outlines were brought to rehearsals and, under the direction of Ashton and the designer Sophie Fedorovitch, studied at length by the performers. Made up of a configuration of long, horizontal lines evoking the separation of earthly and celestial realms, the set was indebted to Flaxman's outlines as a unit, which feature such backdrops throughout, as in some of the plates from *Prometheus Bound*. With its two distinct and gendered elements separated by a dividing line, Banks's relief set a precedent for this linear configuration. Yet, significantly for my purposes, the radical sculptor's mediated influence persisted more so in the dance itself. Everson states that the most striking aspect of the *Dante Sonata* was the swirling motion of the performers as they moved in unison "now forming smaller groups, now circling, now piling up into a pyramid of bodies."[79] Against the conventions of classical ballet, the female dancers wore their hair unbound, loose, and flowing to heighten the emotional drama of the show. Everston mentions that they raised their arms up (like Thetis), their limbs intertwining with their hair and fluttering garments. Ashton's wish to capture and preserve the pathos of the text – to represent the otherwise intangible through synchronized limbs – gave the ballet a harrowing power. Partly due to the timing of the performance, the first audience was said to have been completely overcome. Choreographed not long after the German invasion of Poland, the dance was interpreted as an allegory of the futility of armed conflict. Only seventeen minutes long, it consists of a battle between forces of light and darkness, in which ideals of heroism and victory relinquish their traditional values, collapsing into chaotic ambiguity. On the one hand, the ballet's conscious emulation of Flaxman points to the distinct sensuality of the younger sculptor's art, its connection to music and hence straightforward adaptation into choreography. Yet when the connection between Flaxman's designs and Banks is unearthed, we glean that the ballet recovers the negativity that is absent in Flaxman's "sweet" achievements. Drafted for military service, Ashton, like Banks, found subtle ways of critiquing war and set out to indict its ravages in this particular production.[80] The *Dante Sonata*, then, reintegrates the Dream back into the work of art. Its overlapping groups were sourced from Flaxman's Banksian designs and, what is more, the dance mobilized such groups to put forward an anti-war statement. In the process, Flaxman's desire to counteract any polemical interpretation of his designs is overruled. Unlike Flaxman, Banks and Ashton chose to yoke their art to contemporary events and were not afraid to introduce disturbing elements in order to do so. Everson notes the poignant coincidence that the most recent staging of the ballet took place in the immediate aftermath of September 11, 2001.[81]

47 Baron, Pamela May performing in *Dante Sonata*, Sadler's Wells, 1940, photograph. Hulton Archive, London.

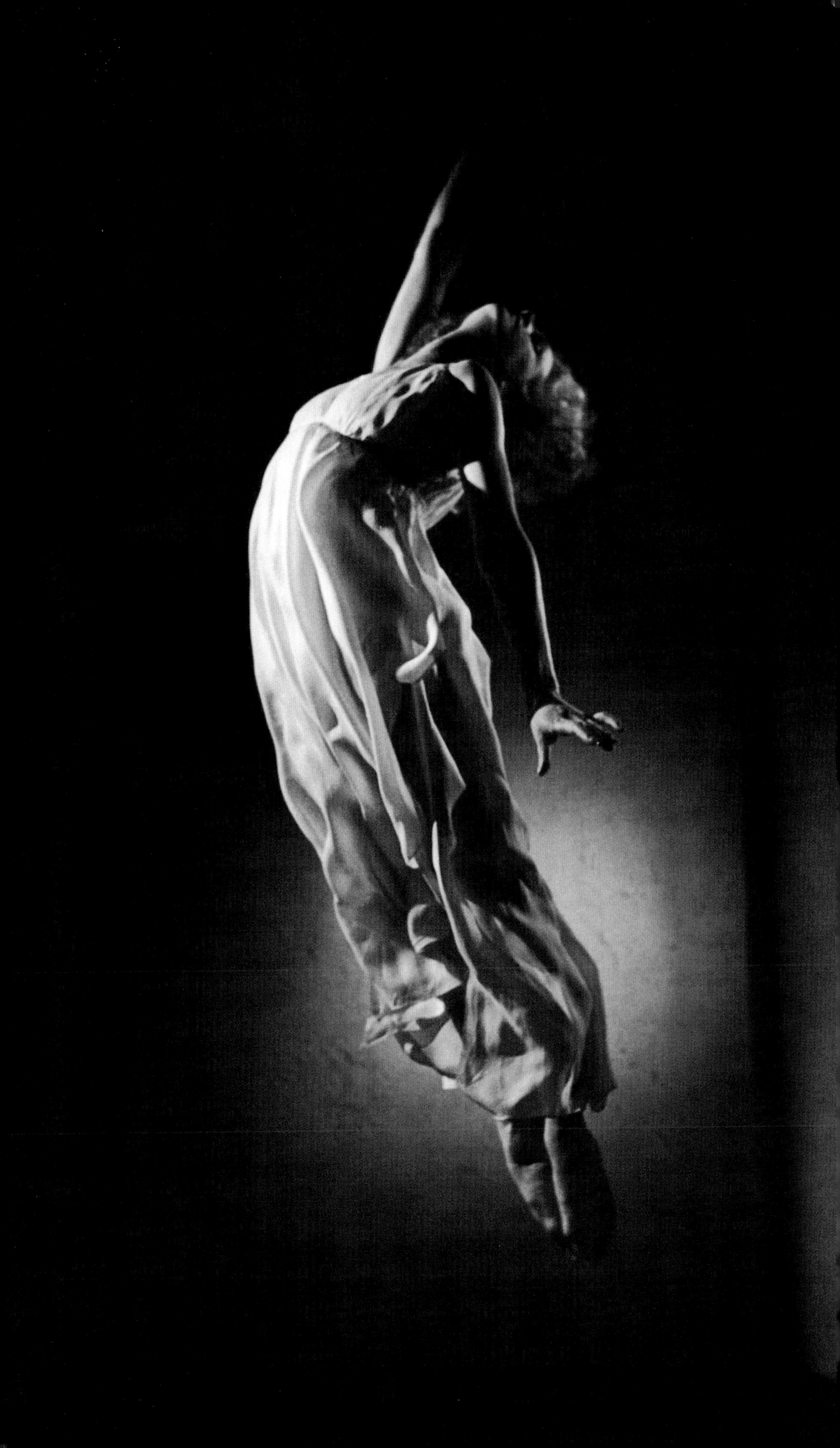

With the *Dante Sonata*, the Dreaming roots of Flaxman's Poetic designs are rediscovered. Yet it was precisely the artist's detachment from political affairs that allowed Flaxman's designs to remain relevant for over a century and eventually deployed as inspiration for modern dance. Sadler's Wells in 1940 was not the first instance of such forms appearing on stage. A century earlier, Lavinia Banks presented the marble version of her father's relief to the National Gallery. In the months after, a new ballet entitled "The Island Nymph" opened at the Drury Lane Theatre. With the celebrated Mademoiselle Maria as prima ballerina, the dance opened with a scene that signals the survival of works by Flaxman via Banks. Dressed in sheer white drapery, a cluster of ballerinas appeared on the stage in the guise of beach-dwelling nymphs, creating an effect that, according to an author in the *Illustrated London News,* "seemed the realisation of an antique basso-relievo."[82] Like "maenads bright" the dancers moved together in an airy whirl, their arms raised above, up, and down in time with the music. Although it called ancient sculpture to mind, the performance was described as "charming and unconventional," essentially denoting the same "empirical approach to the antique" that Flaxman learned from Banks.[83] The article is preceded by a short notice marking the nation's acquisition of Banks's relief, accompanied by a crude line engraving of the object. The post gushes over Banks's nymphs, their "buoyant and elastic elegance," thought to be unparalleled in "any work, either of ancient or modern art."[84] Distinguished from the rest of the composition, the nymphs are officially proclaimed to have an exceptional status that, due to the work's "spatio-temporal" limitation in a specific set of years, the figure of Achilles, and the sculpture as a whole, did not possess.

In addition to identifying a split in the reception of antiquity that is relevant to the divide between these two artists, Warburg is one of the few scholars interested in the complex kind of emulation represented by Flaxman's adaptation of Banks's relief. The overlapping groups of female figures that recur in Flaxman's illustrations, funerary sculptures, and other works may not be direct quotations of the Homeric sculpture. But they are instances of the afterlife of Banks's art in the hands of a younger, better-known artist, one who shunned the world view that gave the original work its charge. Warburg's interest in the afterlife (*Nachleben*) of certain visual forms is consolidated in his *Mnemosyne Atlas*: a series of black canvas panels in which the author placed various reproductions of objects, from engravings to ephemera such as stamps and advertising. Panel 46 is dedicated to the "Ninfa," the figure that, starting her life as a maenad, persisted in visual culture right up to Warburg's own day via detours in paintings by Florentine Renaissance artists Botticelli and Ghirlandaio (fig. 48). Banks's nymphs and their angelic adaptations by Flaxman would be fitting additions to Panel 46, as would the flocks of angels on the Adam and Eve relief by Ghiberti.[85] But between the two British artists there is an additional process at work that distinguishes their figures from the ancient or Florentine precepts. In her work on Warburg, Jill Bennett writes that the interval between the various manifestations of a visual form is "a space for the re-emergence and activation of pictorial forces"; the relatively infinitesimal interval between Banks's relief and Flaxman's

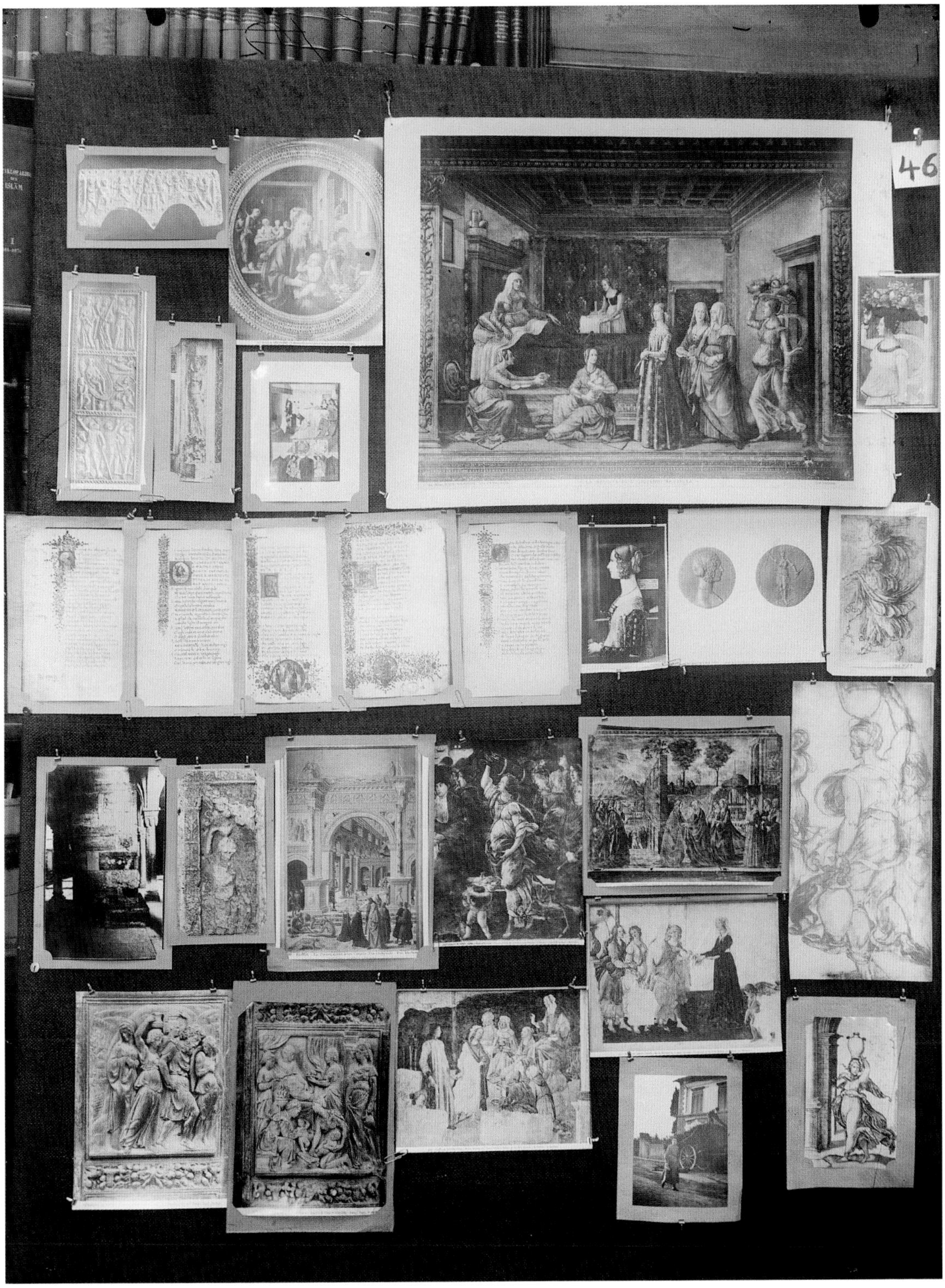

48 Aby Warburg, Panel 46 of the *Mnemosyne Atlas*, photograph. Warburg Institute, London.

numerous emulations generated not so much an activation as a deactivation of the pictorial force of the earlier work.[86] This deactivation allowed the visual form to travel across time, to re-emerge again and again in various guises.

— THE MONUMENTAL POEM? —

Banks filled the classical body with a radical political vision. Flaxman saw the celestial and sensual potential in his forebear's aesthetic, particularly the group of nymphs featured on the elder's Homeric relief. When the speaker of Coleridge's "Ode to Freedom" addresses the heavens – "Ye Clouds! that far above me float and pause, Whose pathless march no mortal may control!" – the poet taps into precisely the reaction that steered Flaxman's aesthetic away from the radicalism of Banks and other proponents of outline. As humanity strives in vain (that is, "dreams," in Coleridge's own words) for a more equal society, the floating clouds above – the seat of angels, the Pleiades, and also Psyche after her removal to Cupid's realm – remain unchanged, immune to humanity's attempts to alter the world. Impervious to human activity, the "pathless march" of clouds is a foil for the alleged vanity of activists. Flaxman valued divine authority over human intervention.[87] His figures navigate the skies but he himself, as an artist, never attempted to claim God's authority. His spirituality is bottom-up as opposed to top-down and hence differs from Bacon's Methodist sermons in stone. A Dreamer, Bacon saw religion as a way to bring about social and political change: a means of remaking society through the publication of tracts dedicated to working-class readers, the preservation of the Sabbath, and Sunday schools. By contrast, Flaxman's more passive Christianity conforms to Marx's famous pronouncement that religion functions as "the opium of the people."[88] This is not to belittle Flaxman's faith, only to observe that both opium and artistic "balm" – the mark of the Keatsian Poet – ameliorate pain. Flaxman's works strive to do exactly that. Nowhere is this more visible than in his recurring groups of "sweet" female forms.

Allan Cunningham, the author who belittled Banks's radicalism and made up the story about the drapery of Banks's naval captain, writes that in Flaxman's angelic funerary monuments, "the abstract coldness of allegory gives way and glows with benevolence."[89] Cunningham sees Flaxman as a transitional practitioner, one that softened and sentimentalized the prescriptive codes, both covert and overt, deployed by his predecessors. Both during his lifetime and in his later reception among scholars, Flaxman is situated on the fault line between art marked by its entanglement in contemporary events and art removed to a distant realm. He is at once a leading figure in aesthetic reform, carrying the style pioneered by Banks into a new age and translating it into a variety of formats, and one who actively went to war with subversive interpretations of this very style. Although I posit him as an archetypal Poet, his connection to Banks implicates him in Dreaming art. In the war between these two approaches, he is

49 John Flaxman, *St. Michael Overcoming Satan*, 1817, plaster. Victoria and Albert Museum, London.

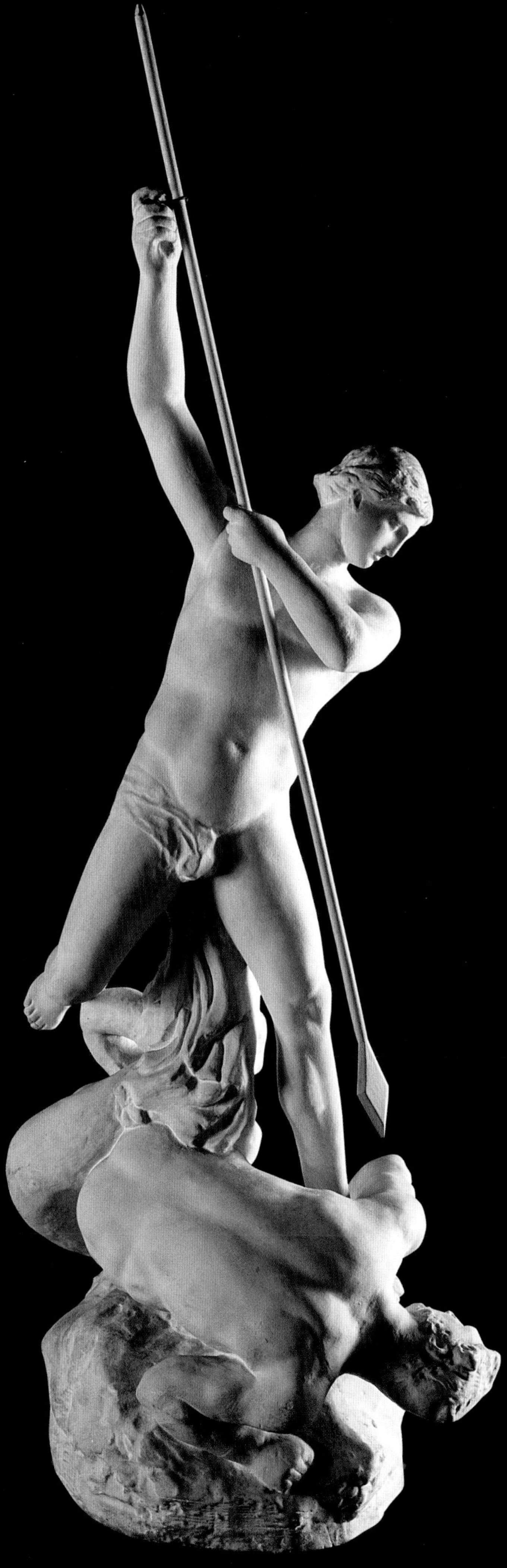

the fighter with brothers on the opposing side. Or, in Winckelmannian terms, he might be seen as an upholder of a style that is "beautiful" in relation to Banks's "high" style. Arguably, Banks's pursuit of both aesthetic and political freedom created space for Flaxman's wilfully disinterested art, and the genealogical relationship between the two sculptors might be conceived as one of fulfillment as well as conflict. As Alex Potts states in his analysis of Winckelmann's theories: "Freedom marks the prelude to an artistic flowering for which it prepares the way, but with which it can never be identical."[90] This captures something of the simultaneous continuity and rupture between the art of Banks and Flaxman.

Flaxman is never utopian. Even his large-scale monumental works are anathema to the achievements of his Dreaming friends and admirers, from Blake and Banks to David. His two biggest groups, the *Fury of Athamas* and *St. Michael Overcoming Satan*, were designed for contemplation inside the confines of the private gallery.[91] While the first was commissioned by the same erratic bishop who cancelled the order for Banks's Homeric relief, the second was not only ordered but co-designed by George Wyndham, Earl of Egremont, for the purpose-built sculpture chamber at Petworth House in Sussex. As the representation of a violent biblical scene, *St. Michael Overcoming Satan* appears as a forthright expression of Flaxman's religious faith and therefore potentially a kind of Dream suffused with a negativity that is absent from his other works (fig. 49). Yet, as Philip McEvansoneya has explored, the patron guided Flaxman on every aspect of the group's appearance, ultimately considering himself "a contributor to the creative process."[92] Forced to heed advice from Wyndham at every turn, Flaxman was essentially reduced to the role of assistant or manual laborer. From 1806, this same patron sat on the so-called "Committee of Taste," the group responsible for keeping sculptors in check regarding their designs for public art. Like others belonging to the committee, Wyndham had a penchant for old master painting. When it came to Flaxman's group, he urged the sculptor to produce a work that faithfully adapted Raphael's beloved *St. Michael Vanquishing Satan* into three dimensions. Thus, in a work ostensibly infused with the sculptor's fear of God, we find an absence. Rather than uphold a Dream, *St. Michael Overcoming Satan* testifies to the duty to satisfy an employer and the visitors to his home.

Even when, in 1799, he lobbied to erect a colossal statue of Britannia on Greenwich Hill, Flaxman did not design a Dream. Instead, the sculptor envisaged a monument that would give the population reason to come together, to grieve and be comforted as the wars raged on, staying fixed, eternally, after the eventual cessation of conflict. Casting her shadow over mortal inhabitants of the city, Britannia could be the people's angel. In the vein of the giant figure of Victory proposed by modernist sculptor Mickaël Bigot in 1931 for the Rond-point de la Défense in Paris, Flaxman's Britannia was designed to supervise the people down below, emphasizing humanity's "childlike dependence on forces greater than itself, given the cosmic scale of world events and the destinies of nations."[93] A sketch of the proposed colossus presents it head on (fig. 50). On the land surrounding the sculpture, minute human forms and a carriage

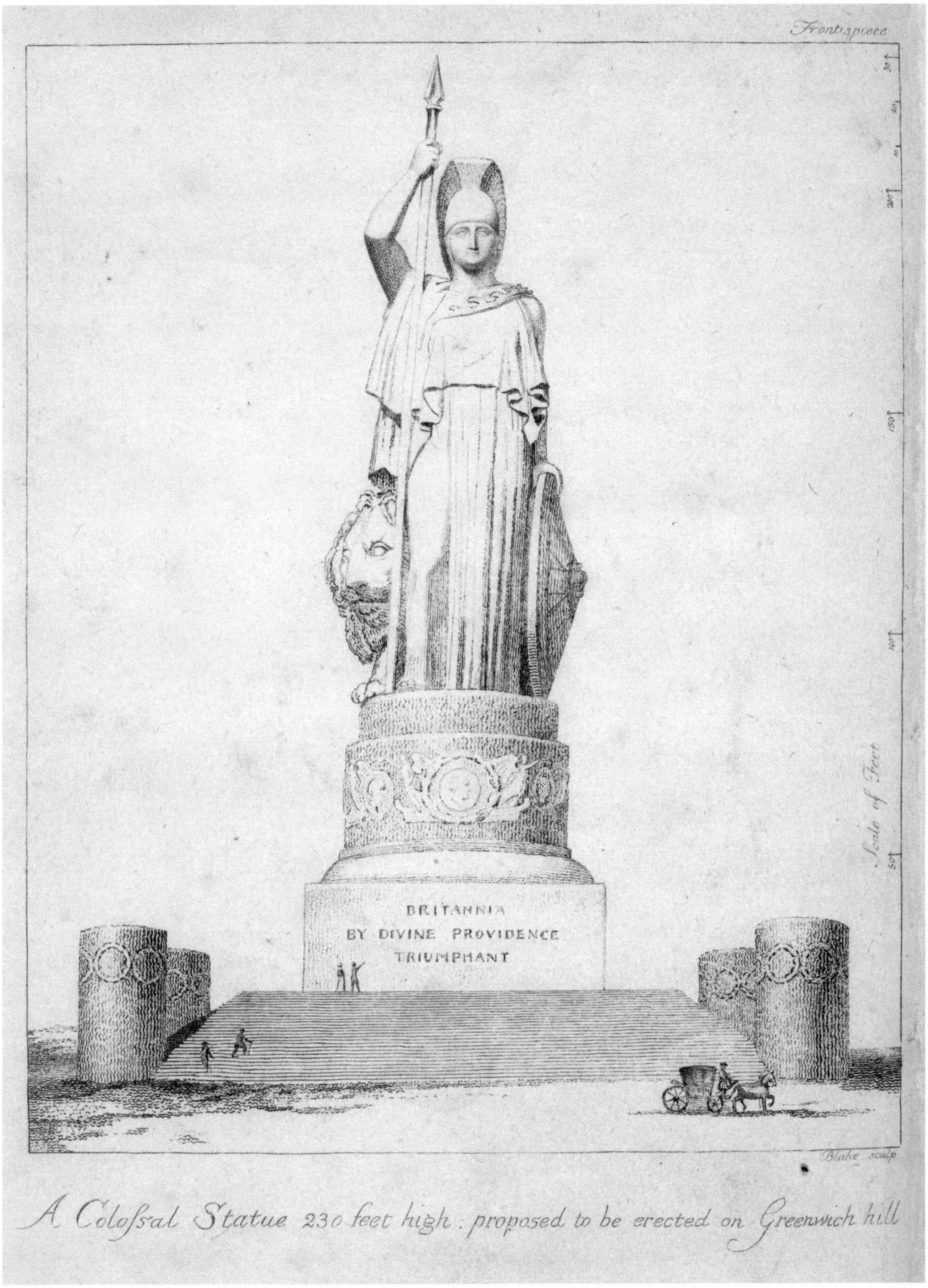

50 William Blake after John Flaxman, *A Colossal Statue 230 Feet High, Proposed to be erected on Greenwich Hill*, 1799, etching and engraving on paper. British Museum, London.

can be made out, some individuals pointing up toward the statue in awe of its towering grandeur. An inscription on the base reads: "Britannia: by Divine Providence Triumphant."

The giant Britannia was never realized. Flaxman did, however, design two large-scale monuments for St. Paul's Cathedral dedicated to men who died fighting in the Napoleonic Wars. Nestled among the groups by Banks and Bacon, these works register the extent to which Flaxman rejected the Dreams of his predecessors. Commissioned in 1803, his monument to *Earl Howe* does not contain any traces of the artist's distinct perspective as Bacon's tribute to Dundas and Banks's to Burges both do; there are no allusions to Swedenborg or to any kind of spirituality (fig. 51). Nor does Flaxman soften, sensualize, and sweeten monumental conventions as Canova did with his effigy of Napoleon. Anathema to Banks's naked captain on a corporeal level, his burly effigy of Earl Howe stands in full uniform, his cocked elbow echoed by the prow of a ship behind him. Figures of Fame and apparently Victory, though she possesses no wings, gather to the left. There are no allusions to the soul or the afterlife. The gravitational weight of the earl and the grave Britannia at the apex deny any sense that the subject's efforts were worth the trouble. Even the sisterly touch of Victory on Fame's shoulder is neutralized by Howe's distracted air as he glances outward away from his female companions, apparently still preoccupied with the war.

Unveiled in 1818, Flaxman's second group for St. Paul's, the monument to *Admiral Nelson*, is a more dynamic design, perhaps due to the higher status of the subject (fig. 52). The hero of all British war heroes is placed atop a columnar plinth decorated with reliefs representing the Battle of the Nile, the Battle of Trafalgar, and the Battle of Copenhagen, each of which is represented in the form of a bearded man based on the Hellenistic sculpture of the Nile in the Pio Clementino. The life-size lion at the base is represented mid-growl, ready to pounce on any foes of the empire. Britannia too is less staid than usual, her right arm gently reaching round the heads of two young naval cadets as they gaze respectfully up at Nelson, their small feet propped up on the outer ring of the plinth. Still, despite the atypical action of Britannia and the inclusion of novel characters, the sculpture shows the artist sabotaging his own voice. So eager was he to produce a work that did not Dream, Flaxman says nothing at all. Wishing to repress the "vexing" ventures of Bacon and Banks, the sculptor produced two voids that reveal nothing about the time of their making but the most routine wartime nationalism.

David Bindman is right when he states that Banks has been "overshadowed" by Flaxman, something that Charles Francis Bell inadvertently encouraged when he equated the two artists. Bindman points out that although it was Flaxman who took up the mantle of the most influential British sculptor of the period, Banks's "contemporaries had no doubts of [the elder's] greatness."[94] It is certainly true that, by and large, expressions of admiration for Banks's art are confined to the sculptor's lifetime. But it is all too easy to use this fact as an excuse to criticize Banks's Dreaming works: works so intimately bound up with the years in which they were made. Bindman concludes that Banks was able to

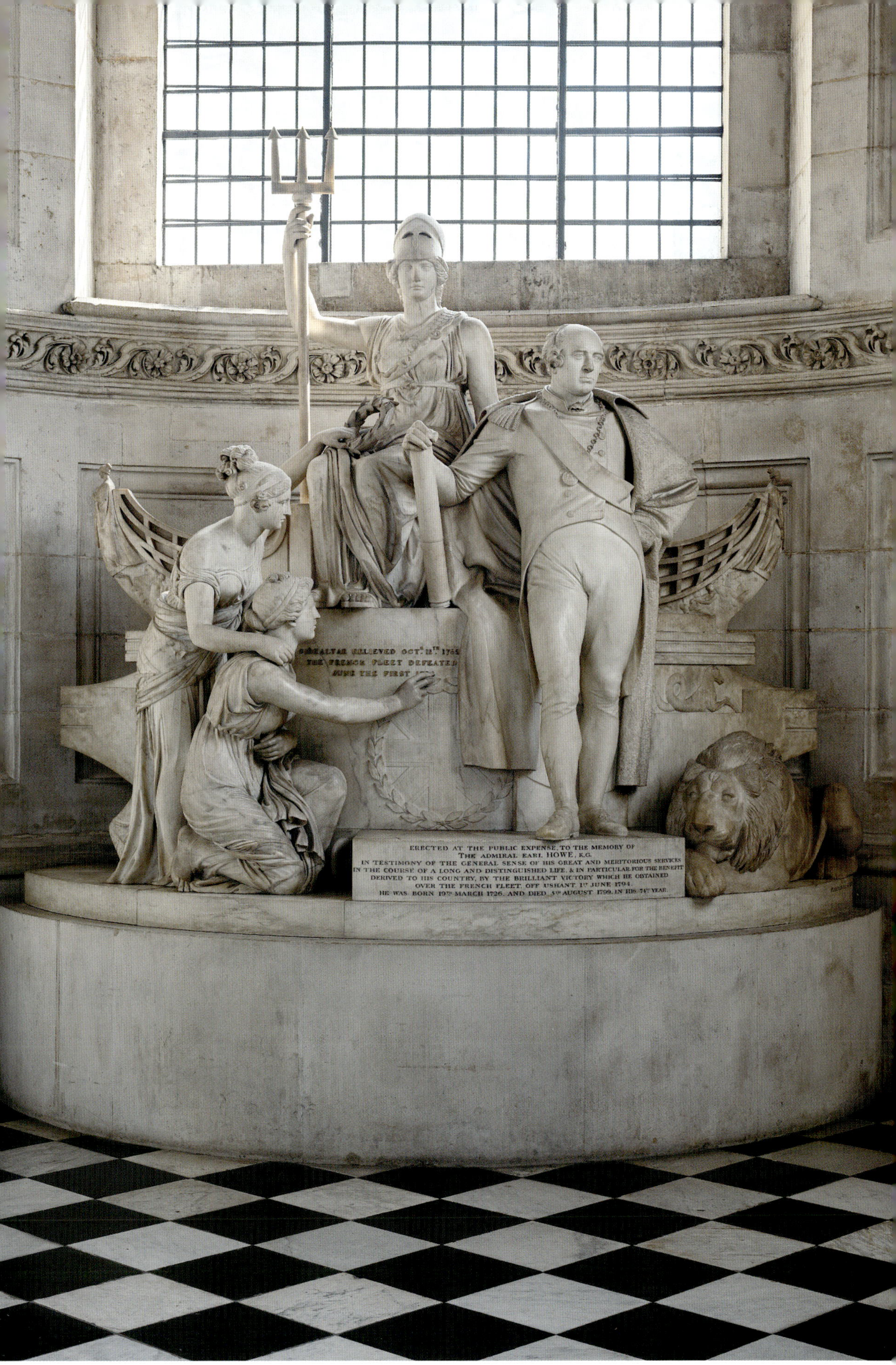

51 John Flaxman, *Earl Howe*, 1803–11, marble. St. Paul's Cathedral, London.

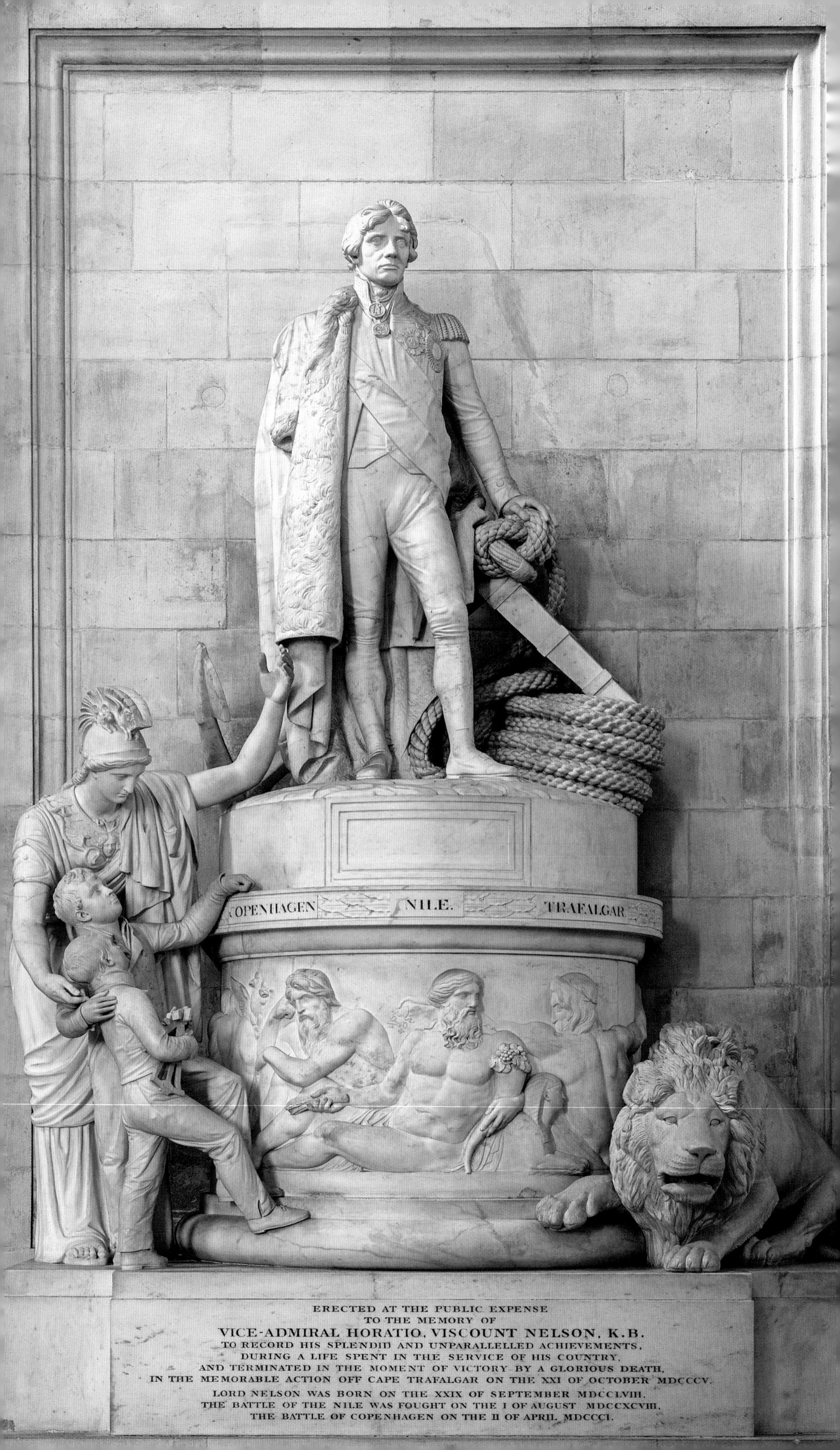
COPENHAGEN
NILE.
TRAFALGAR
ERECTED AT THE PUBLIC EXPENSE
TO THE MEMORY OF
VICE-ADMIRAL HORATIO, VISCOUNT NELSON, K.B.
TO RECORD HIS SPLENDID AND UNPARALLELLED ACHIEVEMENTS,
DURING A LIFE SPENT IN THE SERVICE OF HIS COUNTRY,
AND TERMINATED IN THE MOMENT OF VICTORY BY A GLORIOUS DEATH,
IN THE MEMORABLE ACTION OFF CAPE TRAFALGAR ON THE XXI OF OCTOBER MDCCCV.
LORD NELSON WAS BORN ON THE XXIX OF SEPTEMBER MDCCLVIII,
THE BATTLE OF THE NILE WAS FOUGHT ON THE I OF AUGUST MDCCXCVIII,
THE BATTLE OF COPENHAGEN ON THE II OF APRIL MDCCCI.

capture the interest of his contemporaries not in spite of his radical politics (as one might assume given the furore at the Royal Academy after his death), but in spite of the fact that he had "little gift for the monumental." With this value judgment, Bindman falls victim to his own position as a scholar writing in the late twentieth century, a subject position situated outside the temporal framework that cradles Banks's art. From this vantage point, works like the monument to *Captain Burges* are readily dismissed as bad and empty. The Howe and Nelson monuments reveal that it was Flaxman who struggled far more to take risks in order to integrate his convictions into monumental sculpture, his monument to *Agnes Cromwell* and other feminine funerary works being exceptions. If it is true, as one Victorian commentator put it, that "a monument requiring an explanation is a truly English one," then we can see why Flaxman was not suited for the glorification of lives sacrificed to a political divide.[95] His art could not be weighed down by Dreams. Emptied, his classical bodies float above us.

52 John Flaxman, *Admiral Nelson*, 1807–18, marble. St. Paul's Cathedral, London.

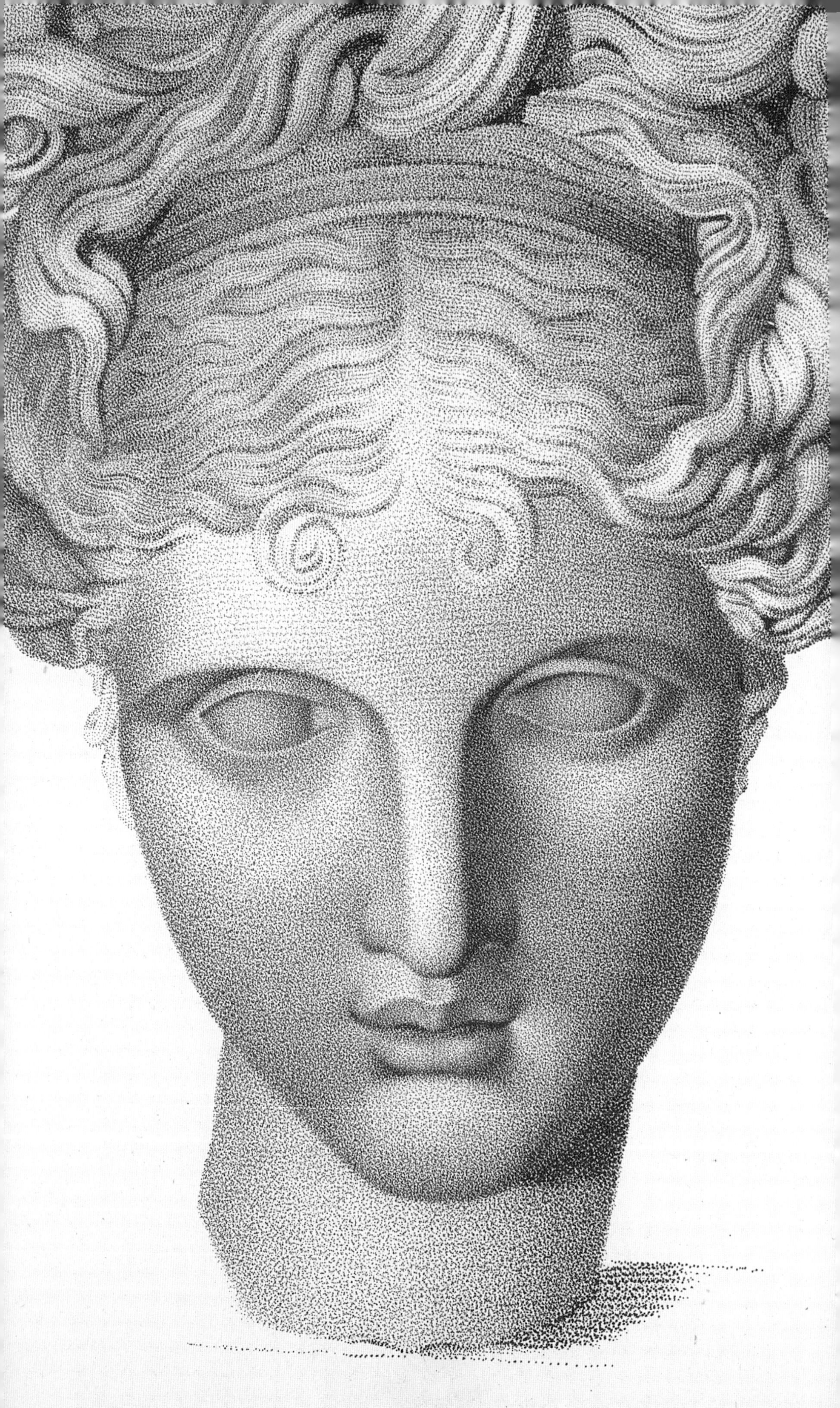

CHAPTER THREE

INDUSTRIAL DREAMS, CONSUMER POEMS

THE PECULIAR SENSUALITY that characterizes Flaxman's achievements found expression not just in illustration, funerary sculpture, painting, and dance but in the numerous decorative art objects featuring his designs. Over the course of his career he worked consistently for this industry, most notably for Wedgwood & Co. and the luxury metalsmiths Rundell & Bridge. In the introduction, I identified the will to re-enchant the classical body in the face of earthly politics as a characteristic of Poetic art. As industrialism began to alter all aspects of life in Britain, functional objects adorned with mythological subjects promised not only to remystify the idea of classical antiquity after Greece's tainting by radical and governmental interests, but to re-enchant everyday life, particularly among the widening middle classes who could now afford to ornament their homes with luxuries formerly the preserve of the elite. Scholars have claimed that Keats himself first experienced classical art filtered through Flaxman's designs for Wedgwood.[1] By the early Victorian period, an art critic could lament the fact that the sculptor had been forced to stoop to designing mass-produced commodities in order to earn a decent living in the burgeoning consumer society that was Romantic Britain: "When foreigners visit us they inquire after the works of Flaxman, but nobody knows whither to refer them. They at length have visited Rundell and Bridge's, and have learned that the poetry of sculpture becomes only respectable among us when it derives its value from gold and silver."[2]

Despite the complaint of the Victorian critic, the mid-nineteenth century saw classical and classicizing art embraced by industrial culture. The re-enchantment of everyday life through material objects came to a head at London's first ever Great Exhibition, held in 1851 – twenty-five years after Flaxman's death – in a glass structure erected in Hyde Park. Here a few of his designs were shown, including a jasper Wedgwood chess set and a walnut *guéridon* table inlaid with a shell, metal, and ivory frieze of Pandora opening the box. Susan Buck-Morss notes that the 1851 Great Exhibition was described by contemporary visitors as resembling a "fairyland."[3] From the alien to the familiar, a disparate range of things was displayed in such a way that visitors felt transported to a mythical realm upon entering. The latest technological innovations glistened like treasure, some moving like unknown creatures. Vegetation opened a central hall filled with fountains and casts of ancient sculpture, which in turn led to corridors

53 Detail of John Samuel Agar after Henry Howard, head of Diana (fig. 60).

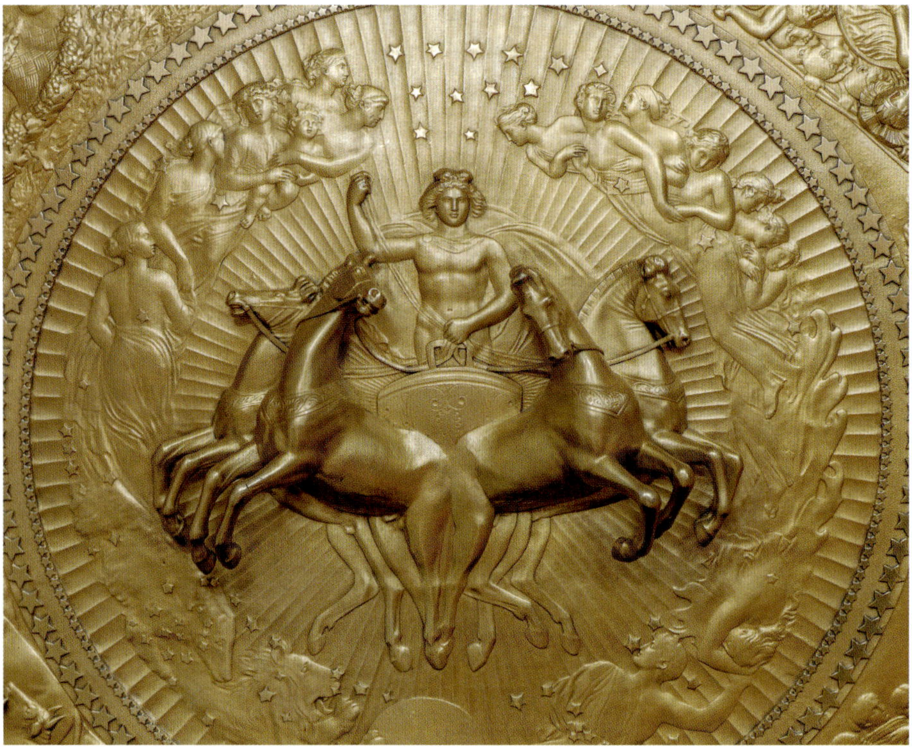

54 Detail from Rundell & Bridge after John Flaxman, *Shield of Achilles*, 1821, silver-gilt. Huntington European Art Gallery, San Marino, California.

lined with tapestries, stained glass, suits of armor, and other marvels. Visitors were instantly transfixed by the exhibition's "phantasmagoric quality, a blend of machine technologies and art galleries, military cannons and fashion costumes, business and pleasure, synthesized into one dazzling visual experience."[4] Up to this point, this kind of collective departure from everyday life had not been possible for such a large volume of people. The Great Exhibition was an adult playground, a manufactured paradise for the masses.

Along with the chess pieces and table, an electrotype version of Flaxman's *Shield of Achilles* was exhibited in 1851. Designed for Rundell & Bridge in 1817, this roundel – conceived originally for rendering in silver-gilt – reconstructs the shield made by Hephaestus for Achilles at the request of his mother, Thetis, in the *Iliad* (fig. 54). The Greek hero is placed at the center of an engraved plaque holding the reins of four rearing horses in high relief. Like halves of a giant laurel wreath, two groups of maidens enclose his chariot, streaming out from a sphere. These overlapping female forms will be all too familiar. Banksian nymphs are once again enlisted to represent stellar constellations as they had been in Flaxman's outlines of the Pleiades, published the same year that the first versions of the plaque were produced. But the orientation of the work is more earthly than cosmic. With the shield, the nymphs are repurposed to serve a militaristic end. Commissioned at the height of the Napoleonic Wars, the *Shield of Achilles* does not merely avoid the anti-war implications of Banks's relief, but subverts the design into a glorious validation of wartime bloodshed. Armed with the shield, Achilles returns to the fray to seek revenge for the death of Patroclus. And to bring this, Flaxman's final emulation of the nymphs, even further away from Banks's beliefs, the silver-gilt version plaque was presented to the infamously prejudiced George IV upon his coronation in 1821. In addition to manufacturing objects that were coveted by the widening middle classes, Rundell & Bridge were official goldsmiths to the Crown. A Latin inscription on the shield broadcasts its royal connection, sealing it to the hierarchical system Banks and his fellow radical activists fought against. Rundell & Bridge owned shares in the General Mining Association: overseers of gold, silver, and gem quarries that, worked by slaves, supplied them with their precious materials. Down to its very fabric, then, Flaxman's *Shield* is an affront to Banks's Dream.

But by 1851, Flaxman's shield had become equally estranged from the conditions that witnessed its design. A method of reproduction reliant on an electric current and wax mold, electrotyping was perceived to be nothing short of a magical process among the majority of the public at the time. At the Great Exhibition, the electrotype shield was displayed not as a rarefied object intended for aesthetic contemplation, a tribute to the nation's martial prowess, nor as an example of a dead monarch's taste. It had become, rather, a novelty: one of thousands nestled within the fairyland. With Banks's Dream long faded into obscurity, Flaxman's Poetic approach had been eclipsed by the wonders of technology. The synthesis of luxury object and cutting-edge method of mechanical reproduction returned Banks's nymphs to where they began: the Dreaming work of art. The electrotype shield did not uphold the political vision – at once anti-war and "vulgar Winckelmannian" – of the sculptor to whom its streams of overlapping female figures can be traced, but another kind of Dream: the construction, in Buck-Morss's words, of a "mass utopia" in which consumer goods were inexhaustible, endlessly and magically reproducible without hours of manual labor, and where art itself was fully democratized. Like the Great Exhibition as a whole, the shield announced the desire for "a social world in alliance with personal happiness, and promised to adults that its realization would be in harmony with the overcoming of scarcity for all."[5] Economic not political freedom was the end of this particular utopian vision. This was a Dream that, unlike the one espoused by Banks, was to endure, for the most part intact, for decades to come.

Just as the Great Exhibition presented the nymphs in a revolutionary new incarnation to the enchanted masses, other representations of the same visual form in more traditional media sat in private collections. Before Banks's death, Henry Fuseli had reconfigured the nymphs for a watercolor entitled *Kriemhild at the Wake of Siegfried*: a scene from the German epic poem *The Song of the Nibelungs* (fig. 55). Reduced to three, the nymphs are fully draped this time, their fingers pointing to a woman, Kriemhild, kneeling over a corpse: her husband Siegfried. Wrapping round the outer edge of the composition, their bodies curve into the same half-oval as in Banks's Homeric relief. While it retains an association with mourning, Fuseli drains the *Pathosformel* of its comforting function. Cast as Gothic apparitions, the figures embody Kriemhild's guilt for

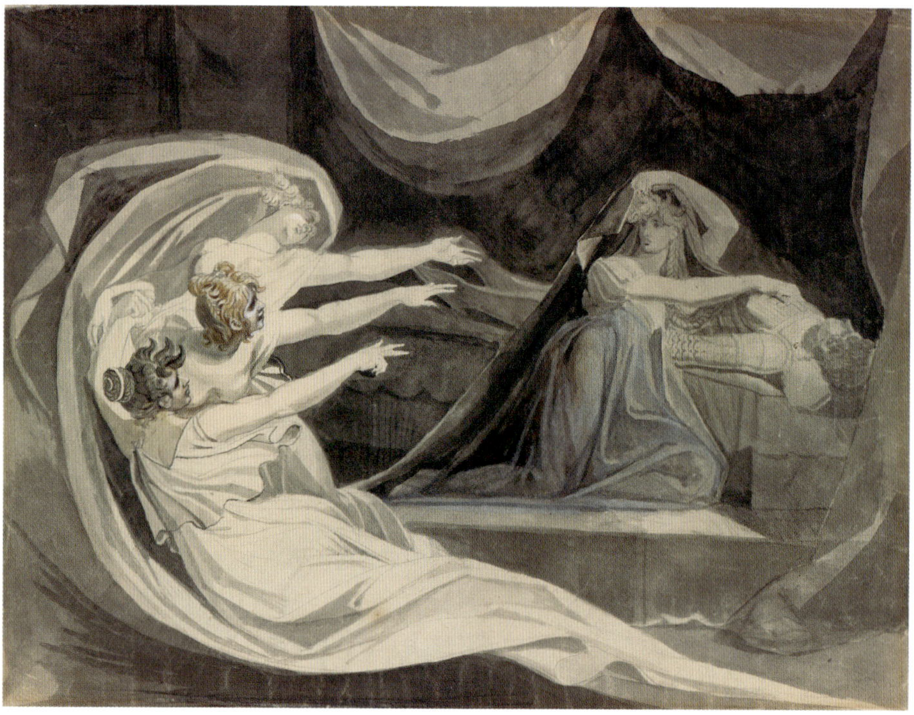

55 Henry Fuseli, *Kriemhild at the Wake of Siegfried*, 1805, pen, wash, pencil, and watercolor on paper. Morgan Library and Museum, New York.

her part in Siegfried's death.[6] The forms now seek to terrify, each face lashed by shadows and their robes billowing in an eerie, auricular arc. Fuseli was in Rome when Banks designed the relief, and it has been argued that the Anglo-Swiss painter was a guiding influence on the more daring aspects of its design, as well as the sculptor's "vulgar Winckelmannianism" through his translation of the *Gedanken*.[7] Fuseli, however, does not perpetuate the radical aspect of the sculpture in *Kriemhild at the Wake of Siegfried*. Long before he produced the watercolor, Fuseli had given up on countercultural politics and the capacity of art, especially the classical body, to serve as a vessel for utopian ideas, becoming increasingly indifferent to the progressive ideology championed by his associates John Horne Tooke, Mary Wollstonecraft, and William Godwin, as well as Banks.[8] In spite of his position at the helm of the dissident community of artists in Rome, by the closing decades of the century we find the orientation of Fuseli's art coinciding more with that of Flaxman. Though he did not justify such a belief on religious grounds, Fuseli accepted that society was subject to "irremovable causes" that rendered human intervention in the injustices of the world entirely futile.[9] Hence, although he associated with Dreamers as did Flaxman, Fuseli too came to stand as a definitively Poetic artist. Along with his history paintings, including the equally Banksian *Vision of Catherine of Aragon*, works like *Kriemhild at the Wake of Siegfried* draw the beholder into an enchanted ground, "a fancy or fantasy for the spectator's pleasure" as Nicola Bown has argued: in other words, quite literally, "a fairyland" (fig. 56).[10] Andrei Pop has explored the theatrical aspect of Fuseli's work, an assessment that chimes with the musicality of Flaxman's art and the translation of his designs into dance.[11] Fuseli is said to have lavished praise on the Dante plates, allegedly declaring that, having once thought of himself "the best composer," he had been forced to "own Flaxman to be the greater man."[12] By identifying as a *composer* of novel subjects in which the classical body is recast, Fuseli positions himself as a proponent of the "empirical approach to the antique" that for Banks remained a politicized mode of representation.

There is a key difference, however, between Fuseli and Flaxman. Whereas, from the start of his career, Flaxman permitted his work to be translated into decorative objects, Fuseli was opposed to the status of art-as-ornament alone.[13] His own compositions never found their way onto chess sets, tables, fruit stands, or tureens intended for middle-class or aristocratic interiors. In 1851, no works with schemes by Fuseli were displayed in the glass structure in Hyde Park, even though his reputation as a fine artist in the Victorian period was more solid than Banks's. Anathema to the man-made phantasmagoria of the Great Exhibition, Fuseli's fairyland was strictly pre-industrial terrain.

The rest of this chapter will focus on an artist who oscillated between these pre-industrial and consumer fairylands, and whose reputation suffered as

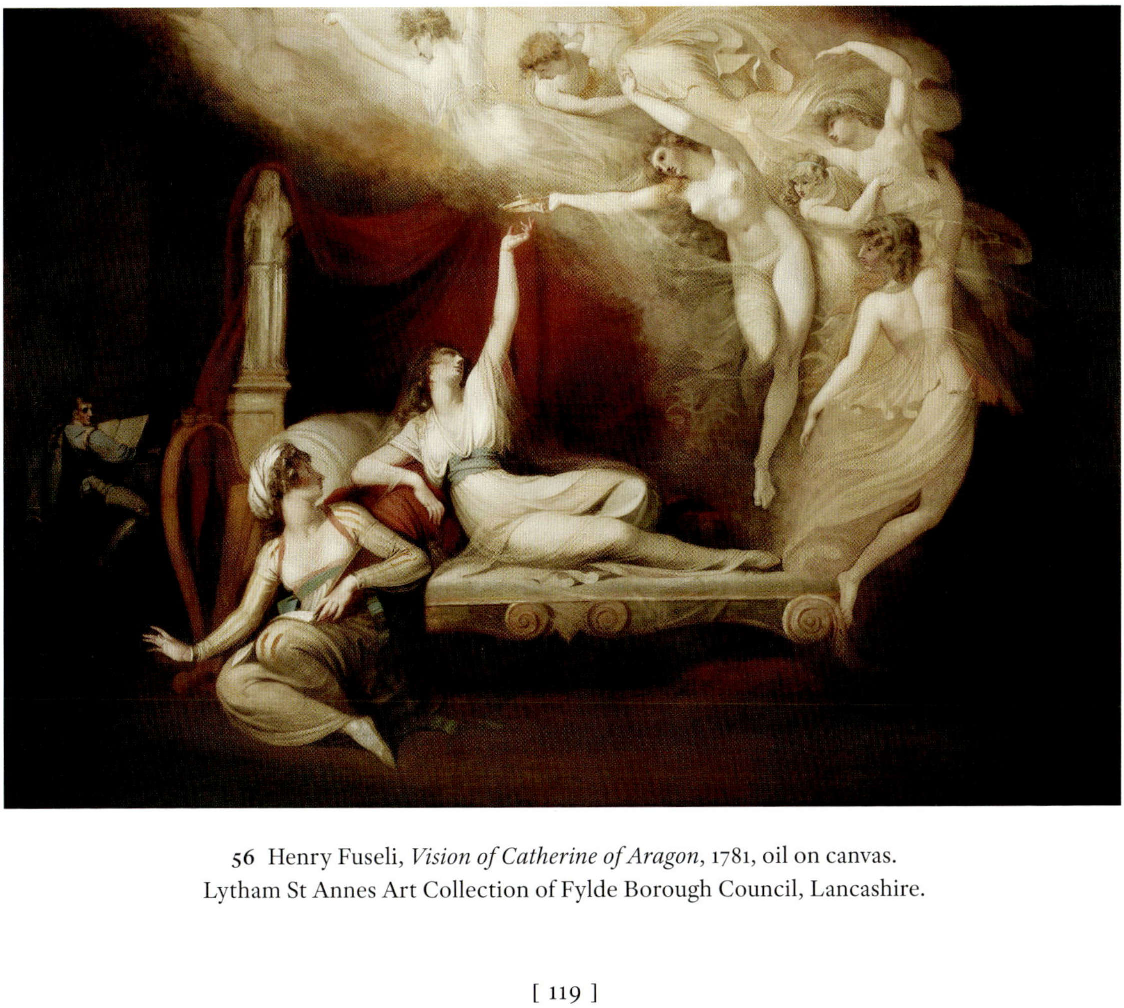

56 Henry Fuseli, *Vision of Catherine of Aragon*, 1781, oil on canvas. Lytham St Annes Art Collection of Fylde Borough Council, Lancashire.

a result of his refusal to make his art conform exclusively to either one. Born in 1769 and trained at the Royal Academy Schools from 1788, Henry Howard belonged to the generation of British artists conditioned by the influence of Fuseli, Banks, and Flaxman.[14] During Fuseli's tenure as Professor of Painting at the Academy, Howard had been one of his students, and after he himself took up the same position in 1833 he relied heavily on Fuseli's lectures, which had been published as a single volume in 1831. But while his pedagogy was informed by the Anglo-Swiss painter, Banks and Flaxman were extremely influential on Howard's own practice. Even though oil paint was his primary medium, he was considered the artistic heir to these sculptors, carrying their simplified Hellenic aesthetic into a new age. Significantly for my purposes, his attachment to Banks and Flaxman becomes visible by way of his own emulation of the very same visual form that, sourced from Banks's Homeric relief, Flaxman reworked over and over again in various formats. Critics concurred that, from around 1815 until his death, Howard's "best and peculiar" manner, "full of buoyancy and spirit," was populated with "bright and radiant figures ... floating in the air."[15] He was "the unrivalled painter of floating female figures and fairy scenes," of "Pleiades, Hyades, Nymphs and Morning Stars."[16] So often was his propensity for "beautiful females in airy and combined motion" pointed out that by the end of his life it had come to be something of a cliché, making numerous critics hostile to his art.[17] Indeed, he claimed the nymphs – usually placing them, as Flaxman had done, in celestial settings – as his signature motif, so much so that the little scholarly literature mentioning his works positions him as a derivative artist who clung onto Flaxmanesque formations (which we know now to have a footing in Banks's art) without adding anything significant of his own.

Regardless of how posterity may have judged Howard, he was once intimately linked with two formidable members of the Royal Academy – Banks and Flaxman – together with whom he formed an artistic dynasty built on shared aesthetic convictions. Flaxman was one of Howard's first patrons, purchasing his *Puck and Ariel* in 1795 and commissioning several drawings from him six years later.[18] Flaxman went on to commission Howard to paint his portrait and that of his wife, Anne, and he himself sculpted Howard's bust (fig. 57).[19] Banks also appears to have requested Howard to paint his daughter Lavinia's portrait together with the sculptor's granddaughter Emma (on whom Banks doted to the extent that he carved her a marble apple and cucumber: two purely Poetic exceptions within the sculptor's predominantly Dreaming *ouevre*).[20] After Banks died in 1805, Howard moved into his home on Newman Street in central London, the attached studio still containing what was left after the posthumous sale of Banks's effects. Crucially, this lot included the plaster cast of the Homeric relief.[21] In his lecture on composition, Howard praised this particular work by Banks, as Flaxman had done in his tribute to the radical sculptor, for its "exquisite harmony of lines, and graceful motion in the females ... so finely contrasted with the rigid, energetic action, and noble style of the Achilles." The artist goes on to proclaim: "In any era of art, this would have been considered a composition of singular felicity."[22] In the lecture Howard refers to Banks as Flaxman's "rival" not to identify a sense of competition between the two artists, but to acknowledge their closeness. His own bond with both was picked up on even at the end of his life, when Banks and Flaxman had been dead for decades. After his death in 1847, one of his obituaries reflects on how the two gave Howard "friendly encouragement in all he did, and suggested ... new subjects for his pencil."[23] The painter's son Frank also engraved some of Flaxman's Aeschylus outlines for an edition published in 1831.[24]

Based on the preceding chapters, one would assume that Howard was a Poet like Flaxman. As with Flaxman's works, the male body – the epicenter of Banks's Dream – tends to be removed from his reworkings of the visual form. As the period's criticism of his works suggests, his nymphs and nymph-like groups of figures are cast in imaginative and fantastical situations that keep them at a distance from earthly concerns. Moreover, as I noted earlier, by 1802 the artistic war I have identified had been won. The classical body could no longer contain a political agenda. Expressed in his lectures, Howard's views appear to conform to the Keatsian notion that art should "pour out a balm upon the world"; in his own words, painting and sculpture ought to provide a "delightful solace."[25]

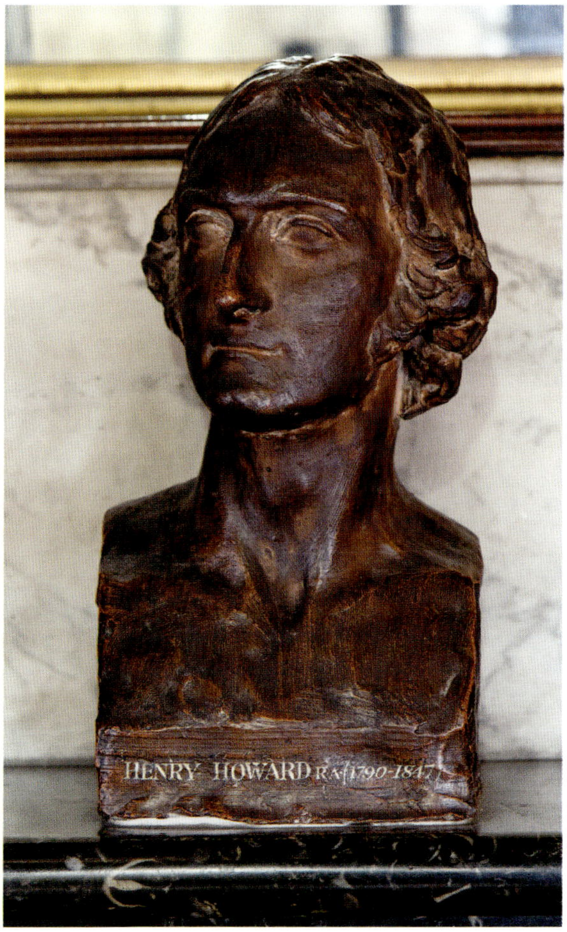

57 John Flaxman, *Henry Howard*, c. 1800, terracotta. Sir John Soane's Museum, London.

Classicizing art specifically, according to his own definition, can be defined by its avoidance of "everything mean, sordid and vulgar" (here he betrays his separation from Fuseli, whose *oeuvre* is marked by a compulsion toward disturbing imagery as in *Kriemhild*).[26] In other words, classicizing aesthetics were, for Howard, a "phenomen[on] of pure positivity" as they had been for Flaxman before him. Howard identified as very much a classicizing artist, one committed to upholding Greco-Roman sculptures as templates for representing the body even as less idealized modes of representation were ousting the antique from its elevated position in artistic theory and practice, a shift to which I will return. Striving "to improve public taste" via the preservation of classical ideals, reflects one of his contemporaries, Howard obstinately believed "that all excellency came from Greek statuary."[27] Adding to this Poetic status, his paintings are wrought with a slick, rich paintwork that unites the sensuality of certain works by Reynolds and Canova with the unearthly "sweetness" of Flaxman's outlines. One of the last items he exhibited at the Academy was *Psyche Wafted over the Mountains by Zephyrus* (untraced), a representation of the subject cherished by Poetic artists.

Yet despite how much he appears to conform to the definition of Poetic art I have put forward so far, Howard's subjectivity evades unequivocal classification. His unwavering faith in the superiority of the antique went against the grain of the period's artistic culture. He was, after all, an oil painter, not a sculptor and a designer like Flaxman. And, after the entanglement of the antique – the idea of Greece specifically – in the political situation unique to the years around the French Revolution, British oil painting struggled to accommodate the classical body in the way that it previously had. Indeed, Reynolds's anxiety toward the end of his life – that classicizing art was being threatened by contemporary concerns – was, in a sense, justified. For the subsequent generation of Royal Academic oil painters, Howard among them, the classical body was a contentious notion, one that lay open to derision because of its associations with revolution, regicide, and French art.[28] There is a Dreaming element to Howard's persistence in holding onto the idea, long after Greece lost its universality, that classicizing art was the only mode of representation. His own son credited the painter's fixation on ancient sculpture to the time he spent in Paris as a youth in the 1780s when the city was in the midst of a "classic furore" coextensive with the lead-up to the Revolution.[29] In addition to stating that art ought to provide solace, Howard declared that painting and sculpture ought never to relinquish their "Great moral advantage"; in order to do so, their figures needed to remain "universal, – intelligible to the learned and the unlearned, subject to no change."[30] In this instance, his perspective puts him at a distance from Reynolds, who in his *Discourses* claims that taste must be cultivated even as he extolls the primacy of the artist's imagination.

But just when it begins to be graspable, Howard's status as a Dreamer is thwarted by the fact that there was no ideological movement with which his faith in the classical body could align. He was not a Keatsian "fanatic" who inserted himself and his practice into the process to bring about political change. At the same time, his works were readily embraced by industrial culture, which as we know had its own, more durable Dream. Rather than being viewed in their primary incarnations as oil paintings, his works were consumed primarily as affordable, mass-produced engravings that, as illustrations to sumptuously bound periodicals featuring stories and snippets of poetry, found their way into homes across the country. In print form, his emulations of the nymphs were subsumed into the wider desire to re-enchant everyday life through industrially produced objects, the same desire that saw the continued popularity of Flaxman's decorative designs and their display at the Great Exhibition. The Dreaming side of Howard's art consists of the way in which his achievements were oriented toward mass circulation. With his commitment to the antique expressed through clear linear draftsmanship, Howard pursued not the democratization of society at large but the democratization of classical and classicizing art, which, with his unmatched skills in drawing from sculpture, he was able to achieve to an extent by circulating such works among a much broader audience than they had previously been capable of reaching. Although his exclusion of the male body from his most popular works appears to cast him as a Poet, for Howard the image of the female body retained a universal quality even after attitudes toward Greece in Britain had changed. In Howard's art, the female body Dreams.

Howard is both, in between, intersubjective. Before looking at his take on the gendered body and how it complements industrial culture, I want to examine the ways in which he himself operated as a bridge between worlds: pre-industrial and consumer, painting, sculpture, and drawing, the fine, graphic, and decorative arts. It is this flexibility that allowed the visual forms cultivated by Banks and Flaxman to find new audiences by way of their emulation in his paintings: works of art, in the words of Walter Benjamin, "designed for reproducibility"; it is also the factor making him one of the most spectacularly forgotten names in the history of British art.[31] Howard is worth returning to precisely because he was so central to the fortunes of the classical body during a period in which its image underwent significant revisions. In the limited set of years in which the universalized image of Greece was in vogue and the classical body still serving as a vessel for politically radical ideas, Howard began his career as a prodigy, one whose art was appreciated by Dreamers and Poets alike. Although a reaction against his art would soon eclipse the memory of his early successes, this strong foundation set him up for a long career and regular employment at the Academy, first as its secretary from 1811 and then as Professor of Painting. Starting out at the height of the desire for Greece, his capacity to move between worlds was considered a great advantage.

— THE SCULPTOR'S PAINTER —

As Banks and Flaxman had before him, Howard spent several years living in Rome. After travelling down central Europe, sketching and making notes in various collections as he went, the twenty-two-year-old painter reached his apartment on the Via Gregoriana during the winter of 1791, where he would remain for the duration of his three-year stay. Based on the nearby Via Felice, now the Via Sistina, Flaxman was there when Howard arrived. The two artists made each other's acquaintance and discovered their shared interests. Howard arrived in time to see the Homeric illustrations before Piroli engraved them. It was not long before he began his own set of outlines representing specific works of ancient statuary including the soon-to-be pillaged *Apollo Belvedere* and *Venus de' Medici*.[32] Although he had already trained as a painter at the Royal Academy Schools, in Rome he appears to have focused almost exclusively on sculpture. In addition to his outlines and other drawings after marbles, he reimagined an untraced group of sea nymphs by the Greek sculptor Skopas as described in Pliny's *Natural History*.[33] Along with Flaxman, Howard worked side by side with the Liverpool-born sculptor John Deare. According to the short biography of the painter written by his son, Flaxman, Deare, and Howard "corrected the other's sketches, until they had, like Apelles and Protogenes, made the nearest approach to perfection."[34] This reference to ancient Greek painters, all of whose works are lost to time, articulates something profound about the kind of artist Howard was. This painter was at home among the sculptors, so much so that, by 1848, the year the biography was published as an introduction to his *Lectures*, his own works had been buried by the divide between painting and sculpture that intensified during his lifetime.

This was not Howard's first time on the Continent. Having left school at the age of thirteen, he lived for periods in Paris with his father, a coachbuilder. When settled back in London he took up an apprenticeship with the painter Philip Reinagle before joining the Royal Academy Schools as a student in 1788. From the start his abilities were noticed. Two years in he won a silver medal for a life drawing and a gold for a painting from English poetry. So taken was the aging Reynolds with his work that he pronounced it "the best that had been presented to the Academy ever since its establishment."[35] After winning the prizes he headed to Rome, where Flaxman had been based for four years.

Rooted in Rome and their complementary interests, the bond between Howard and Flaxman is visible not simply in the latter's direct influence on the former, but by way of Howard's engagement with the work of other artists who admired Flaxman. It was Flaxman who would have introduced Howard to the work of one of the elder artist's French fans, Anne-Louis Girodet, the former pupil of David based in Rome during their shared time there. In 1814, Girodet sent Flaxman an engraving of his moonlit painting of the *Sleep of Endymion*, possibly the etching by Henri Guillaume Chatillion from 1810 (fig. 58).[36] Several years later, Howard mined Girodet's painting for his *House of Morpheus*, a scene from Spenser's *Fairy Queene* (fig. 59). Here Howard directly quotes Girodet's reclining shepherd, placing him largely unchanged in a new setting, recast as Morpheus, god of oneiric dreams, accompanied by Tethys, Cynthia, and a personification of Night. This is a rare instance of an exposed male body taking center stage within one of Howard's paintings. By 1821, the year the *House of Morpheus* was exhibited, the uneasy status of the undraped male form had lost the potential danger it possessed for Flaxman. Still, we can see that in this image the body – draped only at the loins – is presented in such away that it shirks even

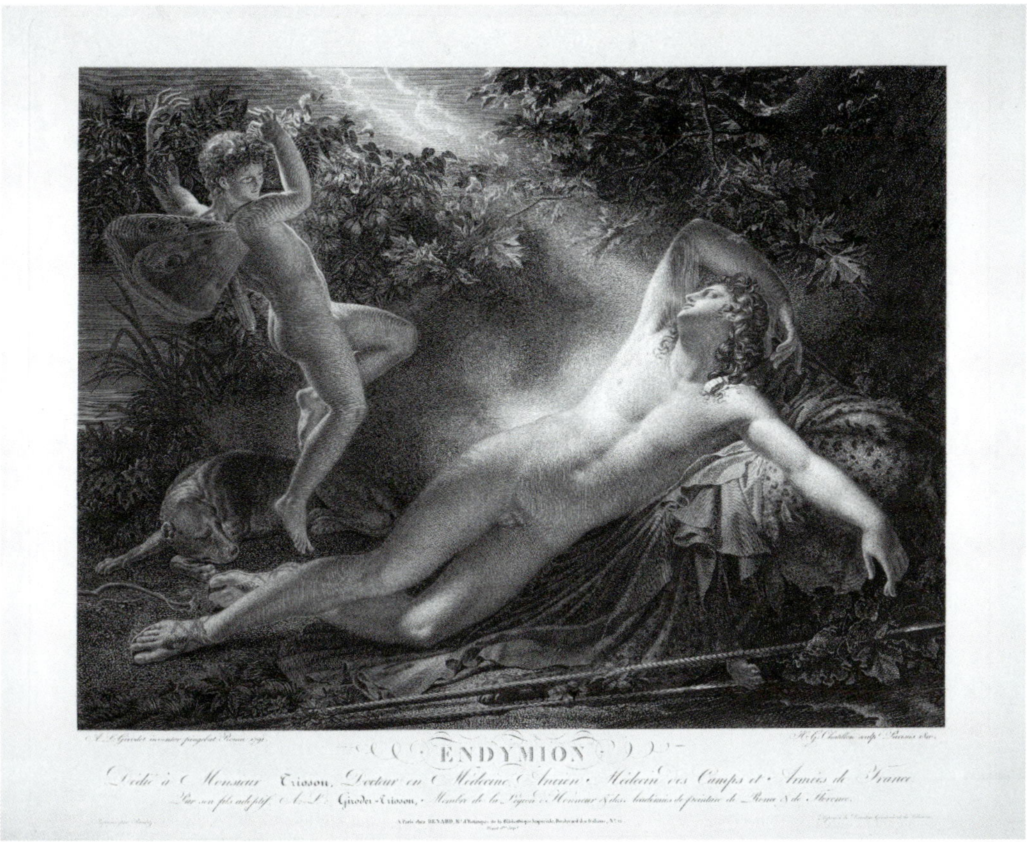

58 Henri Guillaume Chatillion after Anne-Louis Girodet, *Sleep of Endymion*, 1810, etching on paper. British Museum, London.

59 Henry Howard, *House of Morpheus*, 1821, oil on canvas. Petworth House, West Sussex.

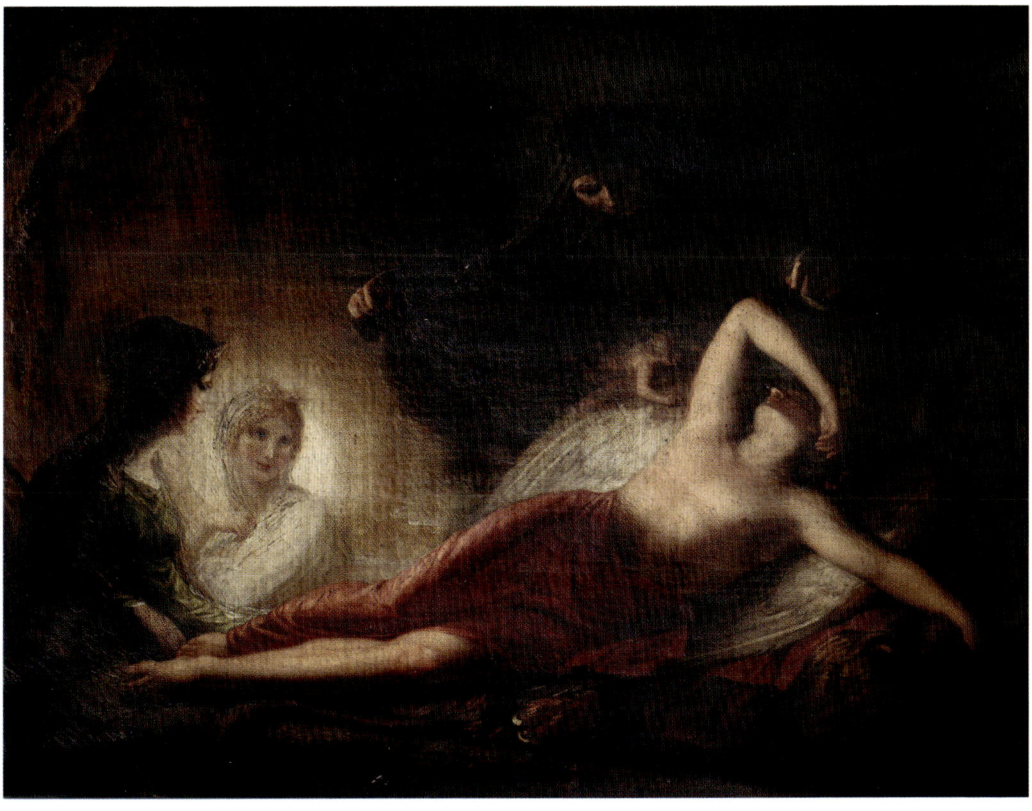

residual connections to the idea of naked truth. Not only is the subject phantasmagorical and therefore harder to yoke to the fortunes of humanity. Both the concealment of the god's face and the figure's passive flesh, softly modelled by the rays emitting from Cynthia (an incarnation of Artemis or Diana, goddess of the moon), quell the capacity of this kind of body to harbor radical significance. An admirer of Canova as well as Flaxman, Girodet was an artist who came to place himself apart from Revolutionary ideology, his *Sleep of Endymion* exemplary of the unearthly yet sensual, rather than "politically recuperable," strain of classicizing art.[37]

After his return from Rome, Howard established a reputation as a consummate draftsman, one whose speciality was capturing ancient marbles on paper. William Hayley, a writer and friend of Flaxman, championed the emerging painter as a much needed boost to the British school; finally, he gushed in a note in his *Essay on Sculpture*, the Royal Academy could boast "an English artist, who has the rare talent of drawing from sculpture" with the utmost "precision and delicacy."[38] Already by this point, Howard stood as a bridge between worlds. So widely acknowledged was his ability to represent sculpture that Charles Townley, one of the leading members of the Society of Dilettanti, employed him as an intermediary draftsman for the first volume of the society's compendium of ancient relics in British collections: *Specimens of Ancient Sculpture*, published in 1809.[39] The plates in this hefty volume are engraved in stipple, the printmaking method thought best to capture the play of light and shade on plastic forms. Each print is accompanied by a description detailing the properties of the relic in question: where it was found, an approximation of its temporal context, its iconography, and its condition. Often these texts include additional commentary on the merits and defects of the print, which may seem odd to present-day readers who take for granted a fundamental harmony between the various contributors to a book no matter their roles. Howard drew only a few plates, most being both copied and engraved by the printmaker John Samuel Agar. Because Howard was rising to become a leading academic oil painter, he is attacked in some of the captions for exercising too much creative autonomy. The society, some of whom belonged to the "Committee of Taste," were scathing about the potential of a modern British school built on ancient precepts.[40] For these connoisseurs, there was a sense in which artists associated with the Royal Academy were acquiring ideas above their station. In the text adjacent to Howard's representation of a marble head of Apollo, the painter is accused of having infused his own stylistic tendencies into what ought to offer an accurate visual record: "The artist has been guilty of a fault, which we have found it difficult to prevent, that of indulging his own taste for the elegant and beautiful at the expense of fidelity of imitation."[41] In his drawing of a marble head of Diana, the relic is indeed afforded an uncannily human quality, somehow managing to stare straight into the eyes of the beholder even though the irises are not drilled (fig. 60). It is as if, rather than looking at carved stone, we confront the goddess as she appears in Milton's *Comus* or Spencer's *Fairy Queene*: dynamic, active, and capable of feeling. Throughout *Specimens of Ancient Sculpture*, Howard is condemned for this "fault," while Agar, who never strove to become a painter or professor, is praised for knowing his rightful place. The year before the compendium was published, thirty-nine-year-old Howard was elected a Royal Academician.

Howard's fellow practitioners appreciated his capacity to bring sculpture to life, and his works were given prominent positions at the Royal Academy exhibitions. Not only did his art appeal to an institutional figurehead like Reynolds; it also struck a chord with the dissidents, including George Cumberland, Banks's radical ally and vocal opponent of the Academy. In his provocative *Thoughts on Outline*, Cumberland pauses in a footnote to cite Howard's contributions to the most recent exhibition as a glimmer of hope on the horizon: the promising "antidote" to the "evil" ways of the institution.[42] The young painter's ability to marry the delineation of classical sculptural forms with the materiality of oil paint made

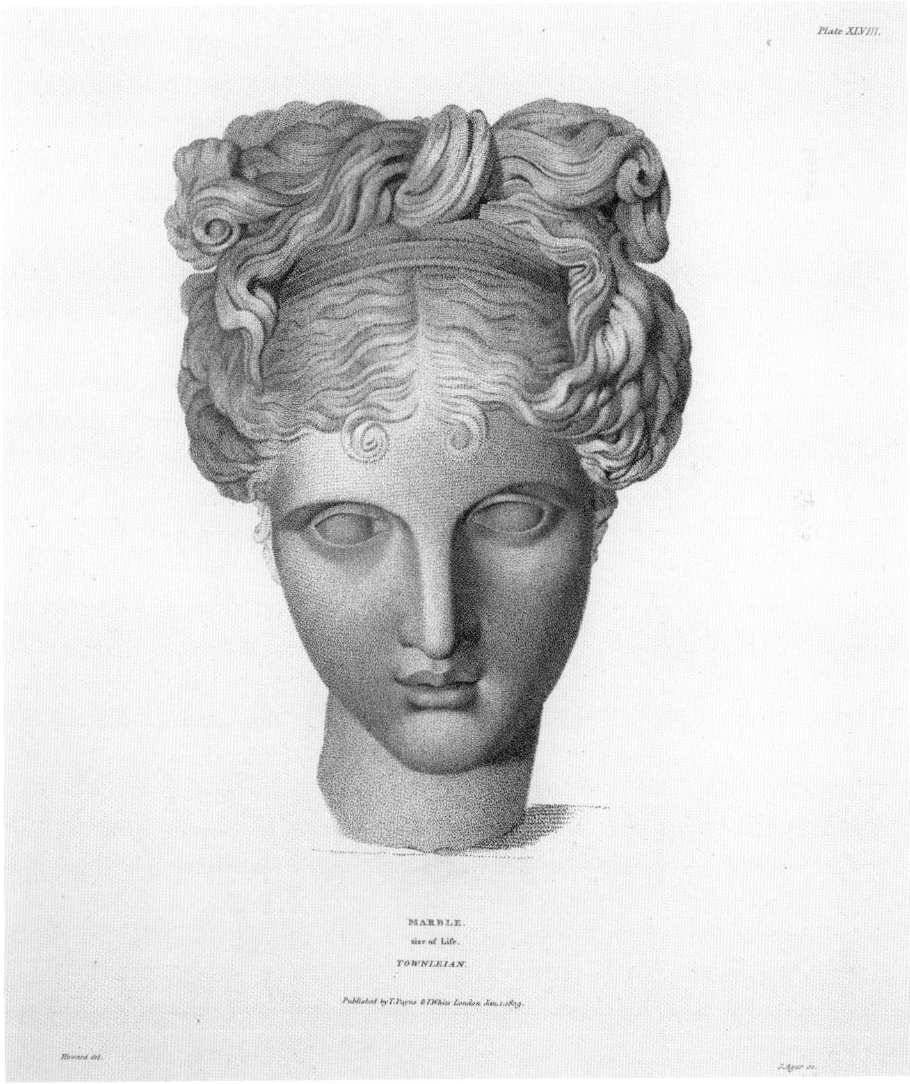

60 John Samuel Agar after Henry Howard, head of Diana. Printed in Richard Payne Knight (ed.), *Specimens of Ancient Sculpture* (London: T. Bensley, 1809), pl. 48.

him attractive to both reactionaries and radicals, Poets and Dreamers. Whereas Cumberland viewed Howard's attention to draftsmanship as a refreshing intervention to the alleged decadence of Royal Academic taste, the Academy placed a premium on the fact that, in committing to sculptural forms, Howard did not sacrifice color, visual effect, and other painterly qualities. He was no David or Barry seeking to curb the viscosity of oils in favor of a moralized linear disegno, but rather a sculptor's painter who, at the same time as prioritizing the lines of classical statuary, did not shy away from the glittering and textural potential of paint. The Academy's investment in Howard also pertains to the way in which his works seemed to realize the composite style of painting valued in continental art theory since the Carracci. Although to contemporary eyes the simultaneous presence of marmoreal contour, Venetian-esque coloring and a touch of Lombardian softness of light may appear, in William Vaughan's words, to "cancel (each other) out," in the early years of Howard's career this amalgamation was satisfactory to the gatekeepers of the Academy.[43] For Reynolds at the end of his life, an artist like Howard would have appeared, as he did for Cumberland in a completely different way, like a glimmer of hope: a painter who did not wish to strip and simplify the classical body and claim it as icon of the "new conquering empire of light and reason," but rather dress it up in the accoutrements of old-masterly effect.

Begun in 1805, Howard's *Sabrina* is an example of his composite style. The work has a rich, multilayered surface that would have dazzled beholders when the coloring was fresh (fig. 61). Yet the figures remain carefully, even coldly described, their contours in intense relief against the darker woodland background, softened only by a few consummately placed shadows along certain limbs. Seven maidens dance in front of the painting's namesake, the Celtic water nymph revived by Milton, who sits sorceress-like, cross-legged on a throne at the left of the scene. Currently in storage at the Victoria and Albert Museum, *Sabrina* is marred by a type of decay known as alligatoring for its scaly pattern, indicating that Howard used additional substances to alter the behavior of his paint. An acquaintance of the artist informs us that he mixed his own megilp "by pouring oil on litharge" (lead oxide).[44] A variable blend usually composed of boiled linseed oil, mastic varnish, and lead acetate, megilp is what is known as a "thrixotropic medium modifier" employed by painters for the buttery texture it gives to pigment and binding mediums. Known as "nostrums" during the period, such substances were used by Reynolds with abandon along with numerous other artists until the end of the nineteenth century.[45] I observed in the introduction that the eagerness to use this kind of extra substance to heighten the sensuality of art objects is a unifying characteristic of Poetic subjectivity. This tendency was usually held asunder from the perceived purity of "the antique," hence the reason why Barry, a didactic and linear artist, was disapproving about their deployment.[46] Myrone cites the connoisseur Benjamin Bates, who was typical in contrasting outline drawing and classical sculpture against the "Plump-Round-Flowing dimpled Rosey-Peachey-Transparent-Simpering" figures populating works by Reynolds.[47] In the previous chapter, I suggested that Flaxman's

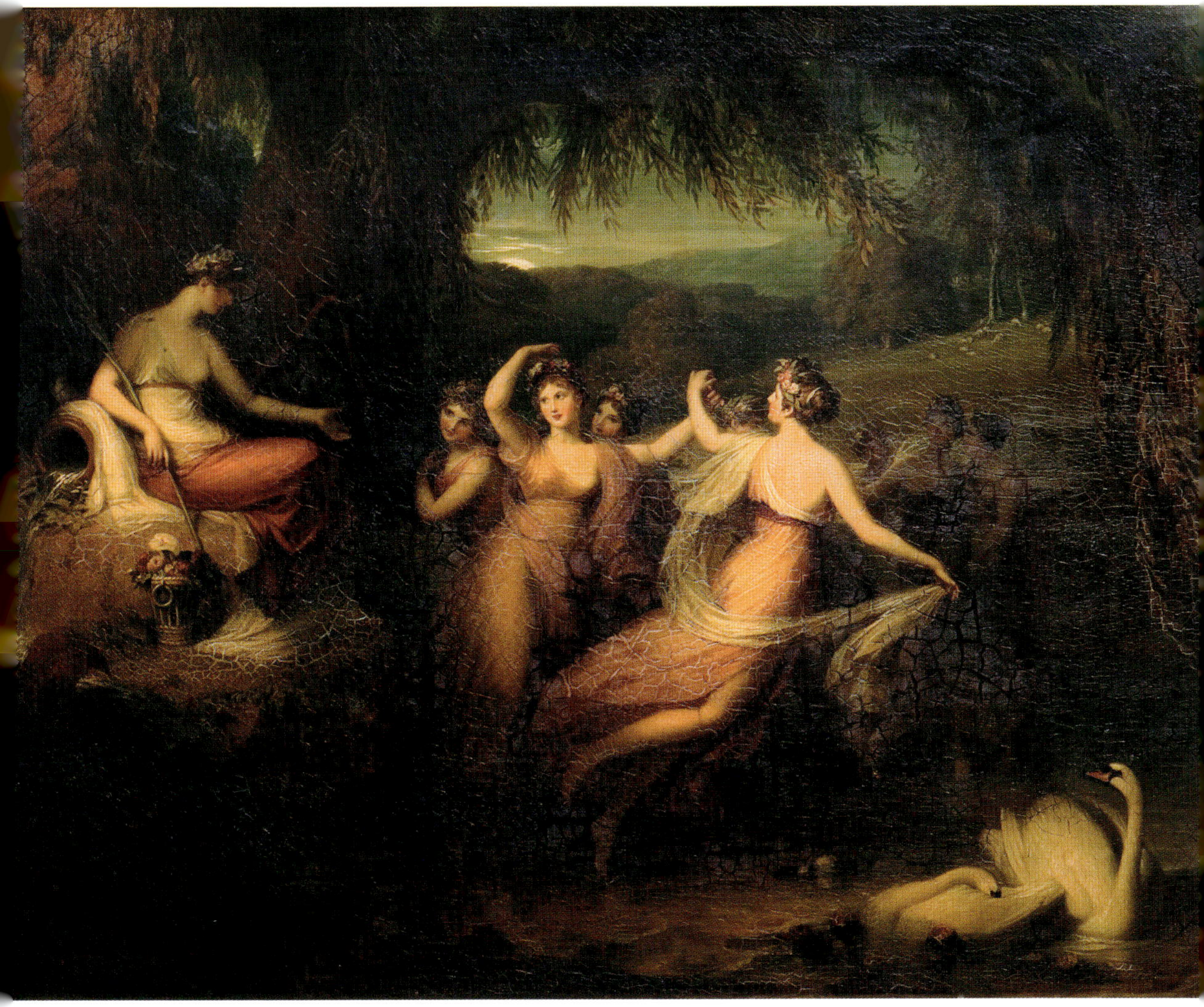

61 Henry Howard, *Sabrina*, 1805–15, oil on canvas.
Victoria and Albert Museum, London.

outlines possess a sensuality that renders them more akin to this aspect of Reynolds's painting than has been assumed. By uniting the two, Howard's art exposes the common ground between these seemingly constrasting aesthetics.

As time went on, Howard's painting became less and less appealing precisely because of its attention to drawing. By the early Victorian period there was a general consensus that he was an uninspired artist, moreover that his paintings were too akin to industrially produced commodities to be considered great works of fine art. In 1839, a critic ridiculed his painting of the *Rising of the Pleiades*, currently untraced, on the grounds that it resembled a functional household object: "this picture is a design for a tea-tray, and not for a Royal Academy ... it is only fit for purchase by some tin or papier mache merchant who comes to a gallery, as a cotton printer to a kaleidoscope, in search of new patterns."[48] While it could happily be placed in a middle-class interior, it was not a fitting object to be worked up in rich pigments and placed on the walls of a gallery. This critic betrays the fact that Howard's career was coterminous with the democratization of classicizing art. While they had once been heralded as an index of his success as a Royal Academic painter, his marmoreal figures were now received as fodder for a tea tray. In the context of fine art they appeared utilitarian, empty, stencil-like. Only in the confines of the home did they have the potential to enchant.

The *Rising of the Pleiades* is one of Howard's numerous emulations of Banks's nymphs refracted through Flaxman's designs, particularly the representation of the Pleiades in the Hesiod plates. It had been acceptable for Flaxman to be employed simultaneously as a sculptor, illustrator, and designer. The enthusiastic reception of his outlines – themselves originally conceived of as designs for sculpted reliefs – among painters such as David and Girodet posed a challenge to the hierarchical interplay between genres that saw the applied arts at the bottom, history painting at the top. But, as Napoleonic battles raged and victory was eventually achieved by the British, Howard's paintings no longer found value within this international nexus of intersecting practices. His dual embracing of oils and sculpture was totally out of step with the ever more crystalline sense of British identity that arose during the wars. While the desire to compete with French artists was a factor in allowing a work like Banks's monument to *Captain Burges* to enter St. Paul's Cathedral, British painting was less and less amenable to French connections. Classicizing draftsmanship had long been perceived as a particularly French point of excellence, which, as the Royal Academy strove to distinguish itself, caused its art-theoretical opposite – color and painterly effect – to be claimed as a specialism of the British.[49] Academic painting was moving away from the universality of Greece – an idea that, for a limited time, had united the orientation of French and British art – in favor of modes of representation more in line with the perceived particularities of British national identity, artistic and otherwise. The fact that Girodet had been successful in amalgamating sensual coloring and ideal design was a factor that worked against Howard, not for him. By choosing to identify as an painter, Howard faced pressure to conform to the identity of the stereotypically *British* painter. His devotion to drawing and to the classical body meant that he consistently fell short of this expectation.

From the founding of the Royal Academy and throughout Howard's lifetime, British oil painters were conditioned to see themselves as superior in relation to decorative artists. As I noted earlier on, Fuseli was as equally invested in the primacy of design as Flaxman, yet saw the reduction of art to ornament as a symptom of decadence. Barry was scornful of connoisseurs who saw painting as a kind of furniture.[50] Thomas Stothard, one of the leading Academicians of the day, was one of the few artists able to operate as both a prominent classicizing painter and a designer of ornamental goods, but his style was much more wayward and expressive and therefore could be read as quintessentially British.[51] Having grown out of architectural ornament, sculpture as a fine art was hard to separate from decorative contexts. While Victorian critics could convey their disdain that some of Flaxman's best-known works were his designs for Rundell

& Bridge, the sculptor's reputation was enhanced rather than tarnished by his employment as a designer. Throughout the era following the foundation of the Royal Academy, a thriving school of sculpture had long been deemed essential for the development of British industry, with modern approximations of the antique recognized as a suitable pattern for industrial manufacture because of their attention to contour.[52] At the same time, classical sculpture possessed pedagogical status as the root of all art; while painting had always been prioritized by the institution, to even gain entry to the Academy prospective students had to produce drawings after casts, which is why the young Howard had been so successful. As a sculptor's painter, in time he came to be caught out by these associations. He had been derided by the Society of Dilettanti because of his ambition to become a leading oil painter, but this ambition was curtailed by his commitment to a certain kind of drawing, precisely the skill that had made him an attractive employee for the society in the first place. As well as delineating antiquities for volumes like *Specimens of Ancient Sculpture*, Howard also worked for Wedgwood, an opportunity likely gained for him by Flaxman. In 1797, he had been commissioned to produce a set of drawings for the company and to paint directly onto their pottery. In 1801, alongside some oil paintings, he exhibited a transparency he had produced for Wedgwood at the Academy, thereby publically proclaiming his status as both oil painter and decorative designer. Toward the end of the Napoleonic Wars, he produced another transparency and an ornamental plaque for Rundell & Bridge. It was at this time that Flaxman was commissioned to design the *Shield of Achilles*. In his lecture on composition, Howard describes the shield as Flaxman's best work and the "glory of modern sculpture"; he goes on to lavish praise on Banks's Homeric relief to which the shield's streams of overlapping female figures are indebted. The nymphs are at the core of Howard's notion of what constitutes brilliance in sculpture and indeed in art more broadly. Expressed in oil painting, however, his reverence for such works acquired a decorative aspect seen only to be permissible in sculpture. In addition to industrially produced wares, this aspect bore equally displeasing connotations with French painters of the Revolutionary generation.

During the years between the feting of his art and his critical failure, then, Howard fell victim both to the separation of painting from sculpture and to the separation of Britain from the rest of the world. As the Greeks lost their status as "the human universal," painting began to be increasingly isolated from sculpture, cordoned off and elevated to a realm all of its own.[53] It was during these years that sculpture began to be located in a separate chamber at Royal Academy exhibitions and the post of Professor of Sculpture first established, taken up by Flaxman. This fracture was foreshadowed in one of the few negative reviews of Howard's early work. Two years after his return from Rome, a critic wrote that while it made sense in three dimensions or in outline alone, Howard's style was guaranteed to be "neglected and unprofitable" when forced into paint.[54] The review concludes that, rather than projecting his designs onto canvas, Howard should have "confined himself to drawing."[55] But he did not. Howard continued to paint in oils until his death in 1847.

It was precisely this career-long emphasis on drawing that allowed Howard's paintings to gain traction outside the sphere of the Royal Academy. Although they increasingly failed to find buyers, their linearity made them easily reproducible as engravings. Prints after his works were circulated far and wide, with brightly colored lithographs published in Paris in the years following the July Revolution of 1830.[56] In Britain they were widely consumed through a variety of publications that emerged in the early 1820s when the economy was picking up after the postwar decline. Known as "gift books," these small but sumptuously bound volumes brimmed with the latest in British poetry and prose, all carefully selected and accompanied by monochrome illustrations in octavo or quarto size. With titles like *Forget Me Not*, *The Gem* and *The Keepsake*, their tone tended to be sentimental to the extent that they were dismissed by more high-minded critics for their watered-down, "vapid" approach.[57] Marketed as assets for the perfectly curated middle-class bookshelf, they were targeted mainly toward young women.[58] Their production was facilitated by the invention of steel engraving in 1820 by the printmaker William Say. Using a steel rather than copper plate, this technique allowed works of art to be engraved quickly and in record numbers. Only among the discerning was the lessened quality of the image thought to be an issue.[59] Placing the Society of Dilettanti's *Specimens of Ancient Sculpture* and a typical gift book side by side gives dramatic insight into the shift that steered the course of Howard's art. The former is illustrated by large, high-quality stipple prints engraved on copper, the latter with tiny steel engravings. That Howard played a role in both registers his centrality to the democratization of classical and classicizing forms that occurred in the interval between their publication.

One of the many documents of his paintings being adapted for gift books is Joseph Goodyear's print after one of the versions of Howard's *The Iris*, featured in a volume entitled *Lyrics of the Heart* (fig. 62).[60] In this image, the Greek goddess of the rainbow, here presented in her guise as a character in Milton's *Comus*, is hoisted upwards by a coterie of auxiliary spirits, including, atypically, a male figure. As with Flaxman's monument to *Agnes Cromwell*, the group encircles the central figure, the drapery of each member swelling as they traverse the celestial realm. Although Howard was vocal in his admiration for Banks's relief, he took up Flaxman's propensity to catapult the nymphs into the air. After the exile of this kind of classical body from British oil painting and its congruent adoption by industrial culture, the clouds emerge as a crucial setting.

Indeed, by placing his figures in the clouds, Howard held onto the capacity of "the antique" – that is, the classical body embraced by Banks and Flaxman before him – to function as a universal aesthetic, one that could appeal to the masses. His fixation on otherworldly imagery offered a mode of escapism at one with the distinctly nineteenth-century desire to re-enchant everyday life through material objects: the basis for the Great Exhibition of 1851. So while his paintings did not sell and were perceived to be unoriginal, their "fairyland" qualities allowed them to recover some value. Responding to his *Chaldean Shepherd Contemplating the Heavenly Bodies* at the Academy exhibition of 1833, a journalist

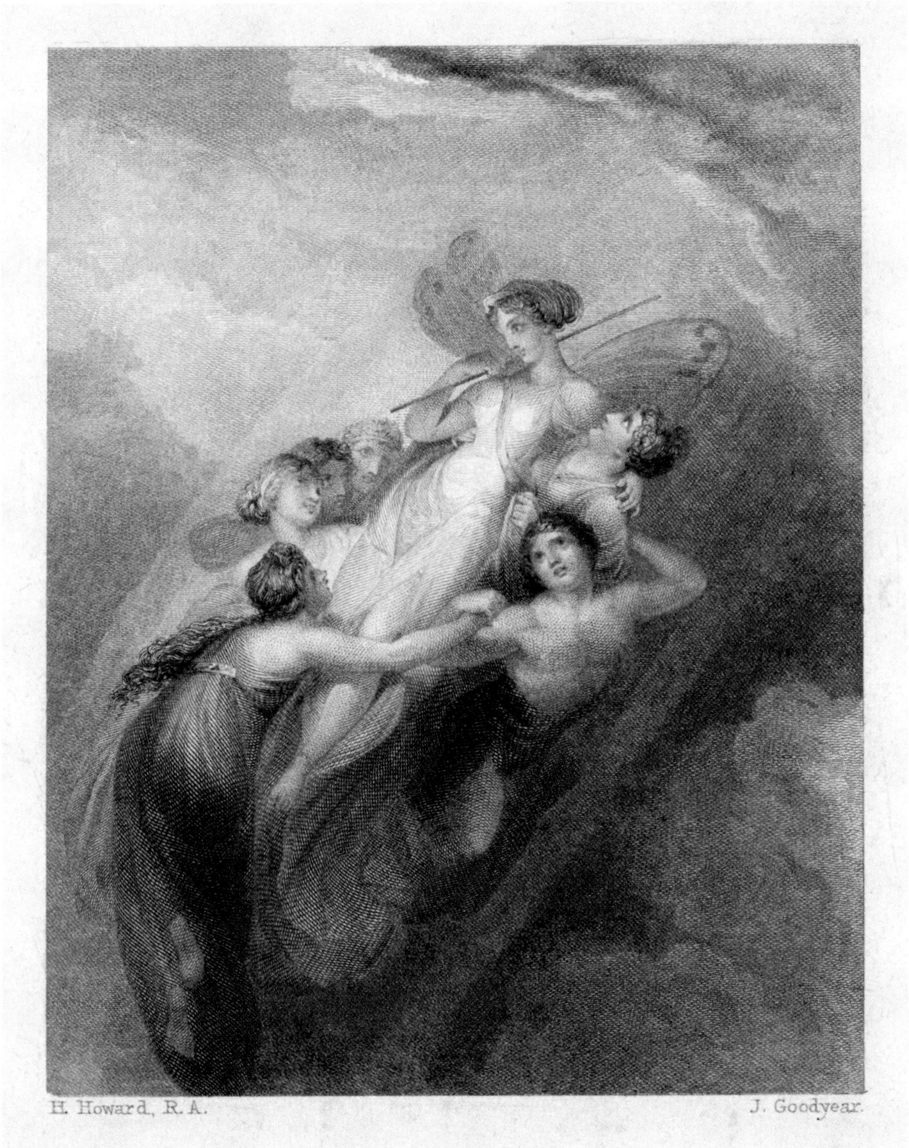

62 Joseph Goodyear after Henry Howard, *The Iris*, 1851, etching and engraving on paper. British Museum, London.

in a popular newspaper declared: "It is good to look upon works like this, and forget for a while the care and clamour with which the every-day's concerns of life are fraught."[61] Unsold during his lifetime, the appeal of this painting in the era of high industrialism is testified by the fact that it fetched the highest price at the posthumous sale of Howard's works in 1849, just two years before the Great Exhibition. Untraced, it survives in a steel engraving by Moseley Isaac Danforth, printed in a gift book from 1836 (fig. 63).[62]

Not long after the display of the *Chaldean Shepherd Contemplating the Heavenly Bodies* and the artist's contemporaneous election to Royal Academician, an article dedicated to Howard appeared in a gift book entitled *The Cabinet of Modern Art and Literary Souvenir*, edited by the prolific middle-class tastemaker Alaric Alexander Watts. Laden with quotations from Milton and Byron, the text elaborates on the retreat from mundane reality promised by Howard's art. The painter seems

> *to breathe a more ethereal atmosphere than that which clogs the aspirations of ordinary mortals in this "gross material world," to have his "mansion"*
>
> *Where those immortal shapes*
> *Of bright aerial spirits live insphered,*
> *In regions mild of calm and serene air,*
> *Above the smoke and stir of this dim spot*
> *Which men call Earth*
>
> *The impersonations of his mind (stored as it is with the most popular fictions of poetical mythology) have a grace and a spirituality about them, which indicate, at a glance, the divinity whence they spring; that they are beings having no sympathy or connexion with the passions and prejudices or ordinary humanity: —*
>
> *Gay creatures of the element,*
> *That in the colours of the rainbow live,*
> *And play in the plighted clouds.*
>
> *We never enter his Studio, from the crowded street, peopled as it is with the loveliest creations of his fancy, without feeling that*
>
> *all Paradise*
> *Can by the single opening of a door,*
> *Let itself in upon us.*
>
> *It is a sort of enchanted ground, – an Arcadia, alive with beings as bright as the "stars" which he worships, and as far removed as they from "earth-born jars" and "human frailties."*[63]

This rhapsodic interpretation of Howard's art overlooks the glaring fact that the escapist potential of his painting was realized thanks to the latest technologies. Illustrated by steel prints after his works, the article was itself contained within a mass-produced commodity whose consumers would be familiar with the painter's works via shrunken mechanical reproductions. Rather than being at odds with "the utilitarian spirit of the present age," Howard's "bright aerial spirits" are born from an integration of forms by Banks and Flaxman with the magic of industrial technology. As the sea was tainted by war, the land broken up, altered, and divided by industrialism, the sky presented a kind of neutral ground. Unlike the earth, air could be seen as infinite and indivisible: the most universal of the elements. Earlier in this chapter I mentioned that in his Academy lectures Howard states that art should resonate among a diverse and expansive audience, no matter their status, training, or education. According to the Reverend Henry Scott Trimmer, who knew both artists well, Howard

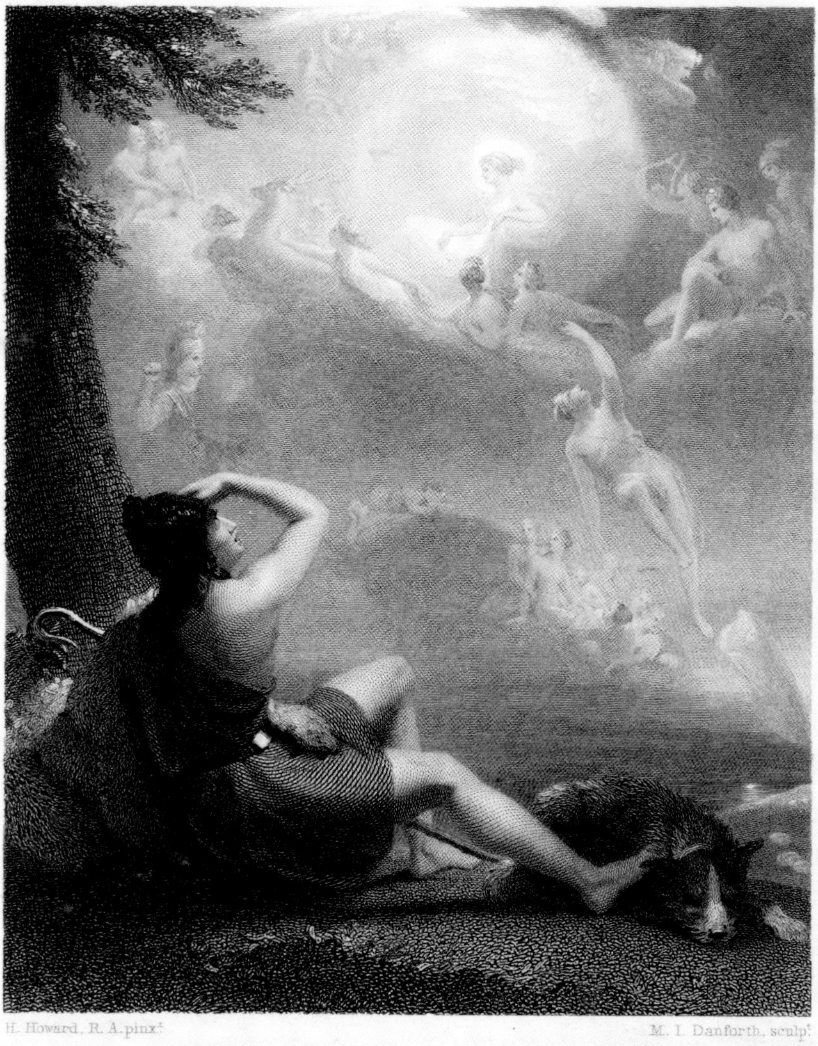

63 Moseley Isaac Danforth after Henry Howard, *Chaldean Shepherd Contemplating the Heavenly Bodies*, 1836, engraving on paper. Royal Academy of Arts, London.

argued with another of his close artist friends – J.M.W. Turner – about precisely who constituted the perfect audience for their art. Turner believed that his works ought only to be judged by the initiated, whereas Howard strove to reach as wide an audience as possible, something that was fulfilled through the reproduction of his paintings in gift books.[64] In this sense, Howard's cosmic classical imagery differs from Flaxman's spiritual take on the skies. In spite of the supernatural beings that populate it, the painter's celestial realm is undergirded by a radical regard for the fundamental equality of all mortals down below. He was by no means an activist, yet his democratic views secure his bond with Banks, whose former studio on Newman Street Howard had converted into "a sort of enchanted ground."

But while Banks had posited the male body as the ultimate figuration of universal humanity, the universality prized by Howard was reliant on female forms. It was the male body that had borne the brunt of evolving conceptions of Greece and the corresponding shift in attitudes toward "the antique" in British art. Changing responses to Banks's monument to *Captain Burges* during Howard's lifetime reveal the marked hostility toward the naked male form that took firm hold after the defeat of France. Now that the British no longer needed to appropriate French aesthetic values in order to vie with the enemy nation, the captain's nakedness came to be seen as culturally specific and literal rather than universal and figurative. Published in 1815, the first postwar edition of the *Encyclopaedia Londinensis* deems the figure of Burges "too naked for an English protestant church."[65] Another author complains: "In historical and monumental sculpture a very questionable taste has been fostered by an ill-directed study of the remains of antiquity."[66] Informed by the nationalist politics of reaction that marks the post-Napoleonic period, more attacks on the captain appeared during these years, a phase in British history characterized by hostility to "foreign" influence.[67] While it had once yoked contemporary art to the fortunes of humanity, the image of the classical body was now blasted for its utter irrelevance to life in Britain. Ironically given Bacon's long-standing reticence toward the cult of antiquity, his effigies of John Howard and Samuel Johnson came to be tarred by the same brush as Banks's Burges, with all three works read by subsequent commentators as little more than symptoms of a stagnant preoccupation with the ancients. Only in the narrow set of years during which these sculptures were commissioned was the obsession with classical antiquity such that it brought forth a marble representation of an English man of letters wearing a "toga and sandals" and placed a British naval captain "stark naked with a sword in his hand to ... break the French line."[68] Since around 1810, reactionary publications like the *Anti-Jacobin Review* and the *Edinburgh Annual Register* had set the tone for widespread reaction against such works with their diatribes against living artists committed to the "beautiful ideal."[69] What was once conceived of as an timeless aesthetic was purged of its immunity. Furthermore, almost all of the radical activists who had believed in the radicalized image of antiquity were now dead or infirm. Only Godwin was left to continue to perpetuate a politically radical image of classical Greece long after the Dream had been defeated.[70]

As the naked male body relinquished its universal implications, we find classicizing imagery protected by the ubiquitous, bipartisan investment in female beauty. Confronting Banks's monument to *Captain Burges* in 1814, the topographer Edward Wedlake Brayley found himself repulsed by the fact that it was the war hero, rather than the winged Victory by his side, that is "almost literally naked ... a state by far more befitting the goddess herself than the representation of a naval officer."[71] The female body thus became an essential tool for Howard's efforts to retain the universality of classicizing art. His painting of the *Chaldean Shepherd Contemplating the Heavenly Bodies* sets a clothed male figure against a plethora of undraped or lightly draped female forms (see fig. 63). In this work,

Artemis rides across the night sky in a stag-drawn chariot, her silhouette haloed by an oversized moon. In the guise of nymph-like maidens, various planets and constellations appear in the air around her. One can make out the Pleiades soaring alongside the chariot while other forms repose on clouds. Toward the right, a personified planet raises just one arm up into the air, evoking the same gesture performed by Banks's Thetis and numerous figures by Flaxman. Gazing up at the sky, the shepherd rests at the base of a tree, his right leg extended across the width of the scene and his foot resting on a dog. As in Banks's relief, the composition is divided into two distinct and gendered parts, only this time they do not make contact, the females remaining at an immeasurable distance from the male gaze. As foil to the maidens' "graceful motion," the shepherd mirrors the viewer's perspective.[72] We can tell from Danforth's engraving that the shepherd's back is darkened by shadows so that his form blends into the foreground, his body grounded and at one with the tree and the earth. His terrestrial rooting highlights his, and our, separation from the cosmic marvel. The figures in the sky do not comfort, console, or soothe him. With the *Pathosformel* no longer active, only the spectacle of female beauty remains.

In a painting rife with undraped and lightly clad female forms, Howard's portrayal of the adult male body proclaims the uneasy status recently acquired by male nakedness in British art.[73] The shepherd is clothed in a cap and belted tunic lest the exposure of his flesh complicate the image by reorienting our gaze toward him rather than the female forms. As goddess of modesty as well as the hunt, Artemis wears full drapery. Yet her silhouette is radiantly bared in profile, the contours of her breasts, slim neck, and gently sloping shoulders operating as the focal point of the composition. Marina Warner has argued that in classicizing works of art male bodies tend to be represented as specific individuals, so that they appear "in command of their own characters and their own identity, to live inside their own skins."[74] Draped and dignified, Howard's shepherd is the characteristic male subject in this respect. Unaware of his presence, the female objects of his voyeuristic captivation unknowingly entertain him.

With Banks's monument to *Captain Burges* in mind, we can assert that, in the context of British art, the tendency identified by Warner only increased as a result of rising nationalism after the Napoleonic Wars. At this time, the consolidation of universalist principles in the image of the naked male body became obsolete. But as the male body was covered up, the female form was expected to be undressed even in the most public of artworks. As an invaluable and eternally precious concept, the beauty of women could bolster Britain's claim to greatness and hence complement the nationalist and reactionary turn. Klaus Theweleit notes that the myth of the Englishwoman's supreme comeliness had been prevalent for almost a century by the time of the French Revolution.[75] When they travelled to Paris during the Peace of Amiens, Royal Academic artists were just as attuned to the comparative beauty of French and British women as they were to painting and sculpture in the Louvre.[76]

Feminist scholars have probed the fact that the universal human subject – the archetypal recipient of human rights, for instance – has long been automatically thought of as male, leaving issues fundamentally attached to the experience of being female by the wayside. Art tells a complementary story. The male body lies at the heart of Enlightenment rationality, of which French Revolutionary ideology and "vulgar Winckelmannianism" are outcrops. But after the dwindling of the kind of radical politics espoused by Banks, the male body loses its capacity to function as an icon of what feminists perceive as the "false universalism" equating humanity with the male body.[77] The denial of the archetypal male body's abstract symbolism, however, only increased the authority of individual masculine subjectivity: the self-possession Warner describes. Destined to be held to an aesthetic standard at odds with a thriving selfhood, female bodies were confined to objecthood, ornamentality, and equation with one another. Amid the pursuit of equality during the years leading up the Revolution, living women were, in the end, granted "beauty instead of freedom."[78] Even Wollstonecraft cannot give up the idea that women should be physically beautiful.[79] Cumberland ends a section of his radical *Thoughts on Outline* with a homage to the beauty of living woman: the only entity capable, in his view, of rivalling Greek art.[80]

The obverse of the authoritative masculinity that Warner identifies is the reduction of female bodies to stock models, figures suspended "between the ideal and the general, the fantasy figure and the collective prototype."[81] Numerous works of art made during the latter half of Howard's career testify to the unwavering tendency to dilute representations of female forms into vague distillations. After the end of the wars, Antonio Canova set to work on a series of ideal heads: marble figurations of abstract beauty that carried no specific identity of their own. While in an earlier age this project might have included a male head or two, it was now expected that beauty be gendered female. In Britain, publications such as *Heath's Book of Beauty* and *Finden's Gallery of the Graces* went on sale: books containing steel prints of prettified female portraits sandwiched between passages of anodyne verse.[82] While some of the portraits in this book are given token identities like "Sophy," "Medora," or "Genevieve," most are distillations of vague notions: "The Enchantress," "Meditation," "Nature's Favourite" (figs. 64, 65).

Probably written by Allan Cunningham, the author who made fun of Banks's radicalism and fabricated the story about the captain's too short drapery, an article from 1822 concludes that "the symbols of the classical age are grounded upon a creed wholly foreign to us, and which has reached us only in disjointed fragments. The alphabet has gone out of use, and the language is a dead language."[83] Here it is made official that Greece no longer enjoys the universal status it once possessed among an earlier generation of British artists. What endured after this tide of reaction was the one visual language that could still viably lay claim to universality: ideal female beauty and the endless possibilities of its reincarnations. One only has to look at the similarities between the smooth, slender female figures in Canova's art and the models in postmodern fashion advertising to see exactly how much traditional notions of female beauty have withstood the test of time. With their waxen, Poetic skins, Canova's life-size marble dancers are especially characteristic of the evacuation of the female form. They do not claim

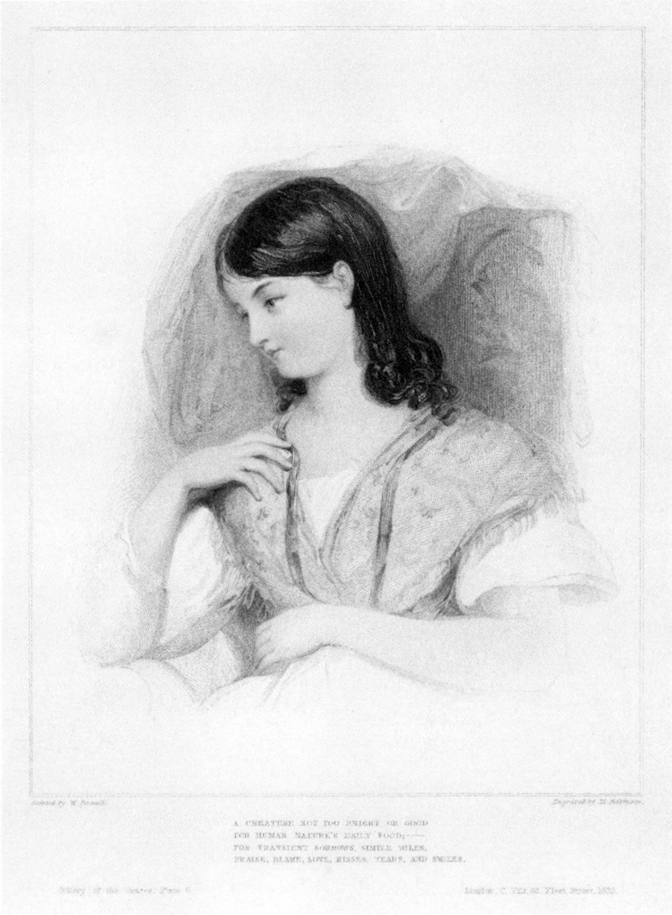

64 Henry Robinson after William Boxall, illustration to *Finden's Gallery of the Graces*, 1834, stipple and etching on paper. British Museum, London.

65 James Hopwood after Henry Corbould, illustration to *Heath's Book of Beauty*, 1833, stipple and etching on paper. British Museum, London.

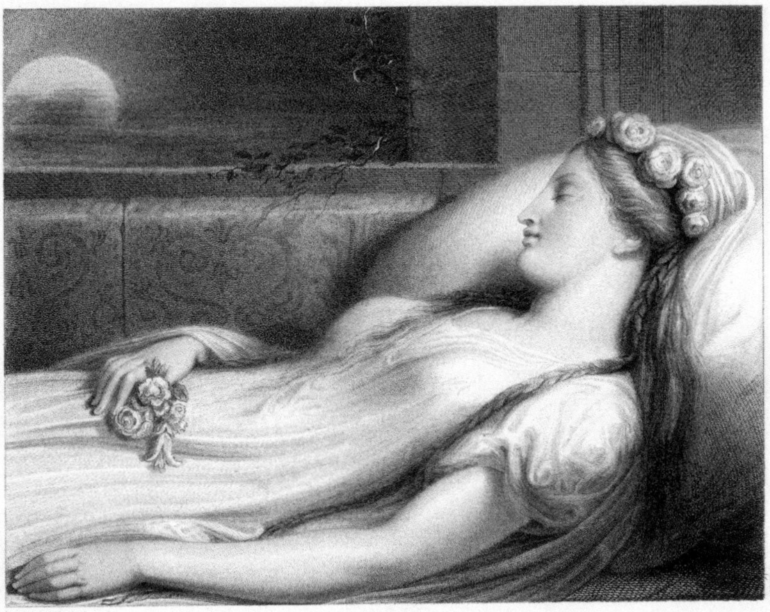

to be specific goddesses or even unnamed nymphs but are representations of mortal women with no identity beyond their appearance (fig. 66).

Dwarfing the female figures in the sky, Howard's Chaldean shepherd embodies the self-possessed masculine character that is the dialectical counterpart to such figurations of the female. Even with his back turned he cuts a commanding figure. His subjectivity itself is depicted in the painting, his physical form operating as a framing device for the objects of his gaze. With its unusual inclusion of a male figure to offset the charm of the female form, this painting encapsulates the way in which Howard fulfilled his ambition of maintaining a universal and democratized classicism even after the cult of the antique had disbanded. Achieved through sculptural delineation, however, the ornamentality of his female figures became a factor in the claim that his paintings were too decorative. In works like the *Pleiades Rising*, his female figures apparently looked too much like they came from a stencil; that is, they lacked the spontaneity and individuality that male figures, provided they were clothed, could more easily manifest. But while his paintings fell short of the criteria for evaluating Royal Academic painting, their escapist bent had an allure of its own, one that could be readily packaged into a commodity because of its linearity and hence reproducibility, on the one hand, and because of its synthesis with the Dreams of industrial culture, on the other.

In addition to its inclusion of a male figure, Howard's *Chaldean Shepherd Contemplating the Heavenly Bodies* is doubly distinct within Howard's *oeuvre* because it portrays the mythical origins of human civilization as opposed to a scene from English literature. As well as placing idealized female forms center stage, Howard compensated for the classical body's increasing incompatibility with British national identity by focusing almost exclusively on English literary scenes as opposed to passages from Greco-Roman mythology. He remained a painter of gods, goddesses, and other classical personae, but almost always mediated by the most cherished early modern English authors who adapted ancient texts. Rather than a visual representation of the stars as described in Hesiod's *Works and Days* as the same subject was for Flaxman, his numerous depictions of the Pleiades, for instance, are presented as characters from *Paradise Lost*. In gift books he could be considered as an heir to Milton himself: "Milton and Howard are kindred spirits in more ways than one," wrote the poet Thomas Kibble Hervey in another edition of *The Cabinet of Modern Art and Literary Souvenir*, "taste ... led the one and the other to engraft the lofty and spiritual fictions of the classical mythology upon the wild, sweet superstitions of our own, and to beautify the streams and hills and glades of green England with the poetry of graceful and immortal thought. Anglo-Greeks are they both."[84] By painting from Spencer, Shakespeare, and Milton, Howard held onto a degree of Englishness that his classicizing draftsmanship otherwise threatened to undermine. As literary frameworks, these authors permitted images of the classical body, especially

66 Antonio Canova, *Dancer with Finger on Chin*, 1809–14, marble. Galleria Pietro Bazzanti e Figlio, Florence.

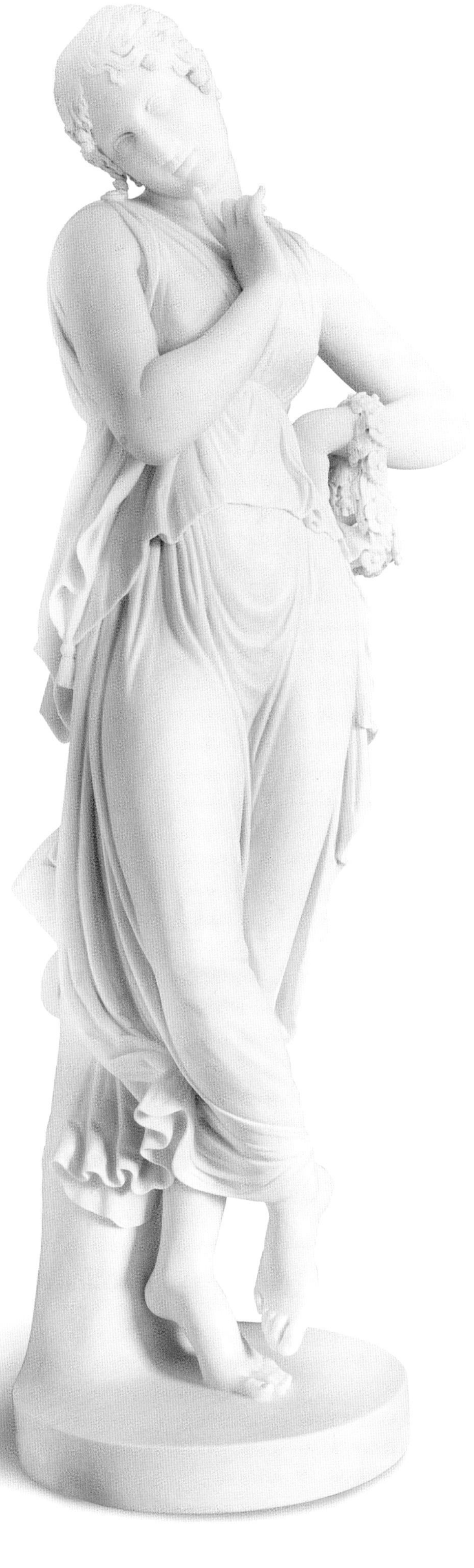

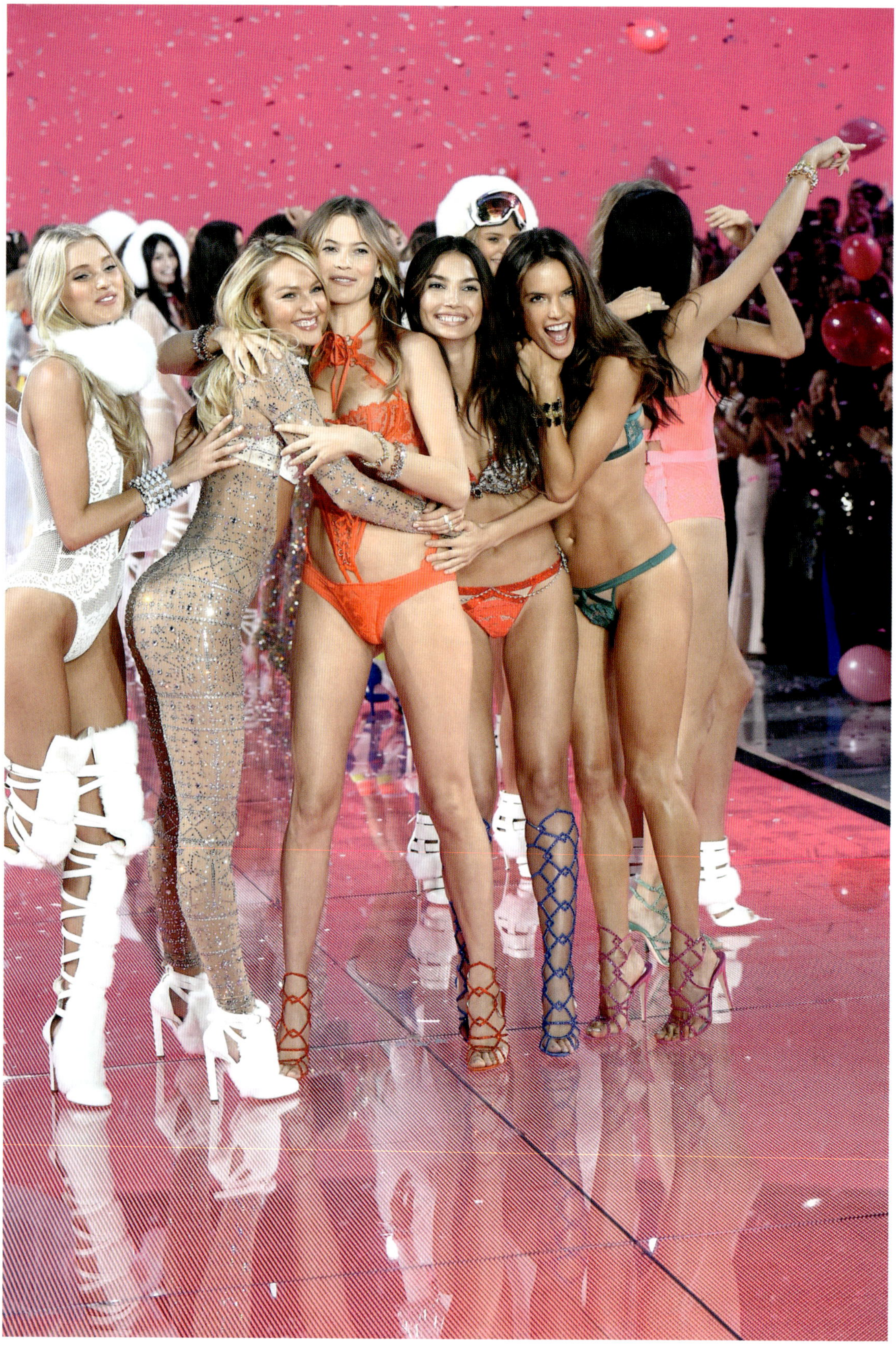

67 Jamie McCarthy, Victoria's Secret fashion show, 2015, photograph.

the naked body, to appear not so fundamentally at odds with the British character. Howard's reliance on these sources also betrays the influence of Fuseli, whose own Miltonic paintings are a paradigm of Anglicized classicism. In spite of his orientation toward domestic authors, however, Howard refused to give up the idea that art ought to be universally accessible across time and place. Although some of his colleagues at the Academy lamented the fact that they were forced, for financial reasons, to have their work reproduced in the form of steel engraving, Howard was happy to have his art consumed in this democratic way. Contained in mass-produced commodities, his images of the female body achieved far more visibility than they did as original works.

Hence his nymphs, angels, spirits, fairies, and stars embody the last vestige of a possible universalism in the guise of the classical body. As such, they ought to be repositioned as the ancestors of the ornamental female forms that suffuse late capitalist culture, from the models – called "Angels" – that have guaranteed the women's lingerie company Victoria's Secret a financial value in the billions, to the successful flaunting of idealized female bodies – living sculptures of a wife and a daughter – during the 2016 U.S. presidential campaign (fig. 67). It is not a hyperbolic assertion that conventional images of female beauty continue to be the one axis around which visual culture, and indeed the world at large, rotates, not necessarily for their desirability (of course, not everyone who consumes such images desires the female body, and, more significantly, not all images are erotic) but for their endurance, adaptability, and power to bring people together.

— THE POETIC NUDE —

In the present day, ideal images of the human form can be achieved through various means, including digital applications such as "Facetune" or "Make Me Thin," which are now freely available to anyone with a smartphone. During Howard's lifetime, normative constructions of female beauty were produced either by abstracting a form according to the proportions of select Greco-Roman sculptures, as in the work of classicizing artists like himself, Banks, Flaxman, and Canova, through the adaptation of some other classicizing type from the post-antique canon, or according to a contemporary, more flexible norm of female beauty that dresses up the classical model while staying true to its duty to refine living nature, as in the smooth, doe-eyed faces in *Heath's Book of Beauty* or *Finden's Gallery of the Graces*. Idealized images of female bodies had the potential to attract consumers of the literate middle classes no matter their age or gender, no matter their political orientation.

Focusing primarily on works by Canova and the French painter Ingres, Carol Ockman has explored the ways in which more sensual incarnations of the ideal female form appealed to women during the period.[85] Uniting the forms of Canova, Ingres, Flaxman, Banks, and Howard is the way in which techniques of idealization delimit the eroticism of the body. We do not look upon Ingres's odalisques, Canova's dancers, Flaxman's nymphs, or Howard's celestial maidens and find profusions of tactile flesh, but rather figures whose streamlined contours control the sensuality of the body, thereby opening up its enjoyment beyond a heterosexist libidinal gaze. Mechanical reproduction allowed such forms to continue to trespass and be appreciated in alternative contexts. In their evolution from paintings to prints, Howard's images of idealized female bodies were rerouted away from the male dominated world of the Royal Academy – its canon, pedagogy, exhibitions, and critical discourse – and made accessible to young women all over the country, most of whom would have viewed this kind of art on entirely different terms.

Not every artist wanted their work to resonate with a more diverse audience. Just as Howard's paintings came to be marginalized from the sphere of fine art and consumed in print form, another artist was rising to become prominent, one whose representations of the female body were targeted toward upper-class male patrons rather than a heterogeneous audience that included women. William Etty was drawn myopically to the representation of living female models, spending hours in the Academy's life drawing room long after his election to Royal Academician in 1828, ten years after Howard's.[86] Although he dabbled in portrait and still life, Etty was a prolific producer of mythological and literary scenes that showcase the undraped female form. Classical in the sense that they rely heavily on evocations of goddesses by old master painters, his forms deviate dramatically from the antique. Because of the period's nationalistic climate, Etty's determination to break with the expectation that the human form be idealized according to a universal standard of beauty helped him to emerge as one of the leading painters in Britain following the Napoleonic Wars. Etty's figures are particular. His Venuses have large breasts and thighs, with girdles of flesh that add irregular curvatures to their silhouettes. A nymph might have conspicuously thick arms, a Grace a distended abdomen. Not one of them is the same.

While Howard's art has Dreaming and Poetic sides, Etty was inescapably a Poet. Although he did not rely on substances such as megilp, like Howard he sought to create striking ocular effects with his paintings. His figures have gleaming, waxy skins that recall figures by Canova, only with more irregular proportions. It was the form of his figures that remained the constant talking point surrounding his work. Even at the apex of his critical acclaim in the late 1830s, a critic blasted a group of his naked sirens as mere "Academy models, whose personal defects the painter has not corrected so completely as to attain the ideal of female beauty."[87] In one of his many takes on *Venus and Cupid*, the goddess stands in contrapposto against an unfinished carmine and russet backdrop (fig. 68). She raises both arms into the air not with the grace of Banks's Thetis but to disclose her breasts in full, their volume emphasized with a soft shadow the color of the ground. One breast appears in profile, the other foreshortened so that its nipple meets the viewer. The painter's earliest biographer notes the dominance of Venus within Etty's *oeuvre*.[88] More often than not, the proportions of his goddesses are so far removed from the conventions of representing the female form that their claim to a mythological identity appears tenuous. Behind

68 William Etty, *Venus and Cupid*, c. 1840, oil on millboard and panel. Russell-Cotes Art Gallery & Museum, Bournemouth.

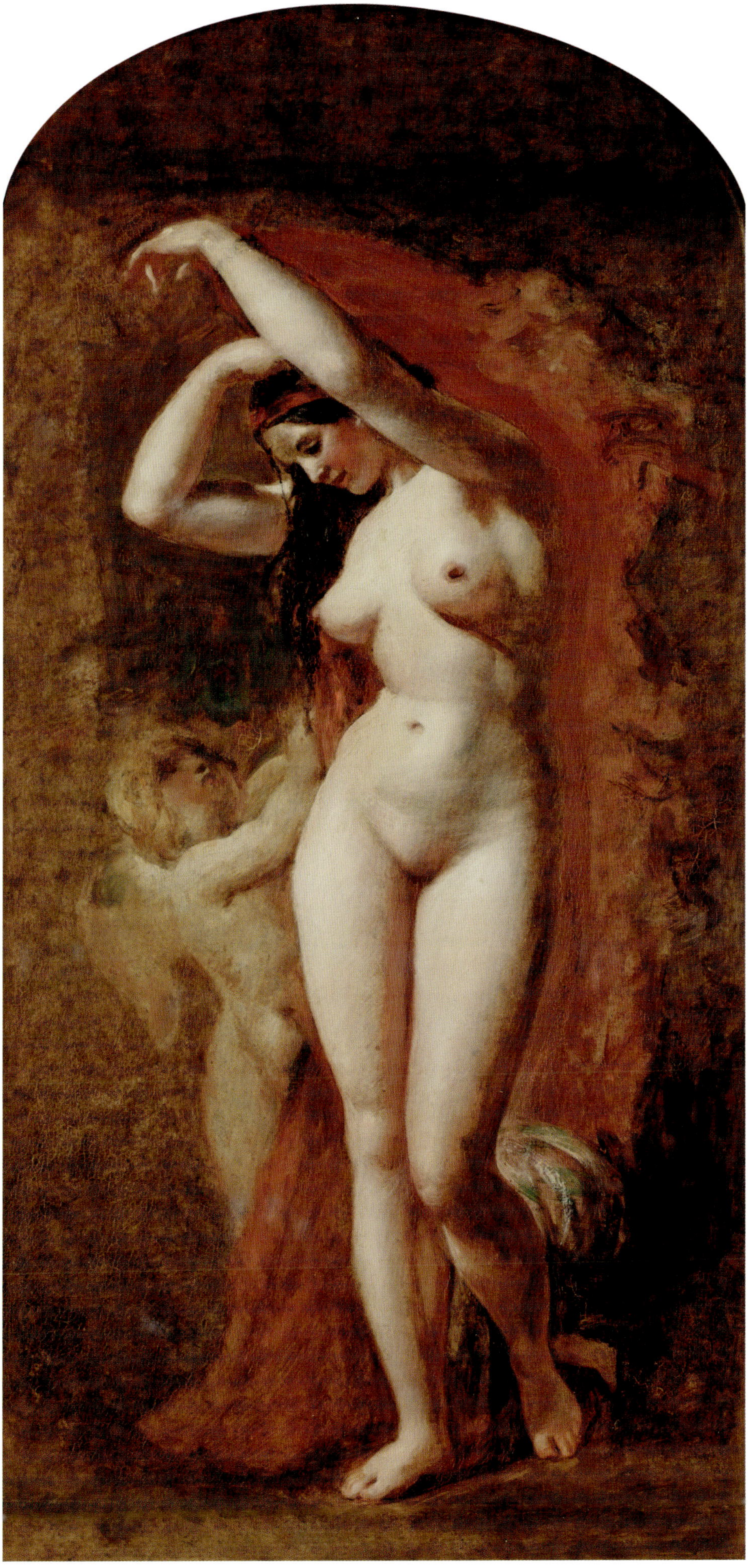

the swell of Venus's hip in this painting, an infant Cupid looks up at his mother. In contrast to the thoughtfully recorded contours of Venus's body, the boy is half-painted and abandoned in a spectral state. Cupid is the only detail affirming that this is, in fact, a Venus: a token gesture to rescue the painting from the limits of propriety.

Etty's abandonment of the antique could be justified with reference to the old masters canonized for their sensuality: the sixteenth-century Venetians, Rubens, even Reynolds, whose late picture *Cymon and Iphigenia* – a work of which Etty began a copy – departs from the strictures of the antique arguably because of the artist's growing awareness of the implication of the classically idealized naked body in radical political discourse.[89] Etty studied these artists intently, but does not adhere to them religiously. Even if other body parts are less uniform, each of the earlier painters portrays naked female figures with breasts that are "small, distinct and delicate" in the vein of sculptures like the *Venus de' Medici*.[90] The typically large breasts we see in Etty's *Venus and Cupid* do away with this norm altogether.

It was precisely the provocative aspect of Etty's work that allowed him to overtake Howard on the track to become Britain's leading painter of the classical body. Far exceeding Howard in terms of financial and critical success, his works came to be eagerly anticipated at Academy exhibitions, making Howard's look meek and uninspired. By the 1830s, Howard was just as susceptible to criticism for his "tame commonplaces" (an indictment paralleling allegations of being too decorative) as Etty for vulgarity.[91] The two could be seen as rivals of a sort, but in their competition Howard was favorable only in the sense that his carefully described forms did not manifest a polarizing eroticism. A critic in *The Times* blasted Etty's contributions to the Academy exhibition of 1822 by comparing him to Howard: "Naked figures, when painted with the purity of Raphael, may be endured; but nakedness without purity is offensive and indecent, and in Mr. Etty's canvasses is mere dirty flesh ... Howard, whose subjects ... require naked figures, never disgusts the eye or mind. Let Mr. Etty strive to a taste equally pure."[92]

Etty's success as a Royal Academician was facilitated by the factor leading to Howard's failure: the separation of painting from sculpture. In contrast to Howard he did not have an aptitude for drawing, tending to paint wet-in-wet and *alla prima*, relying solely on his knack for expressive brushwork. Howard's early success had been guaranteed by the premium placed on delineating three-dimensional figures with finesse – better still, integrating sculptural forms with viscous oil paint. But while classical sculpture held onto its nominal status as the bedrock of all art, British painters were challenging the pedagogic authority of the plaster cast. During one of his stints as visiting professor at the Life Academy, Howard's friend J.M.W. Turner made his students draw from living models placed next to casts of well-known ancient sculptures to gauge the differences between real and idealized flesh.[93] Etty took part in this exercise. In one of his chalk drawings made under Turner's direction, a cast of the *Venus de' Medici* stands next to a living model of roughly the same height, their forms held in direct comparison with one another and hence implicitly on a par (fig. 69). Etty makes sculpture

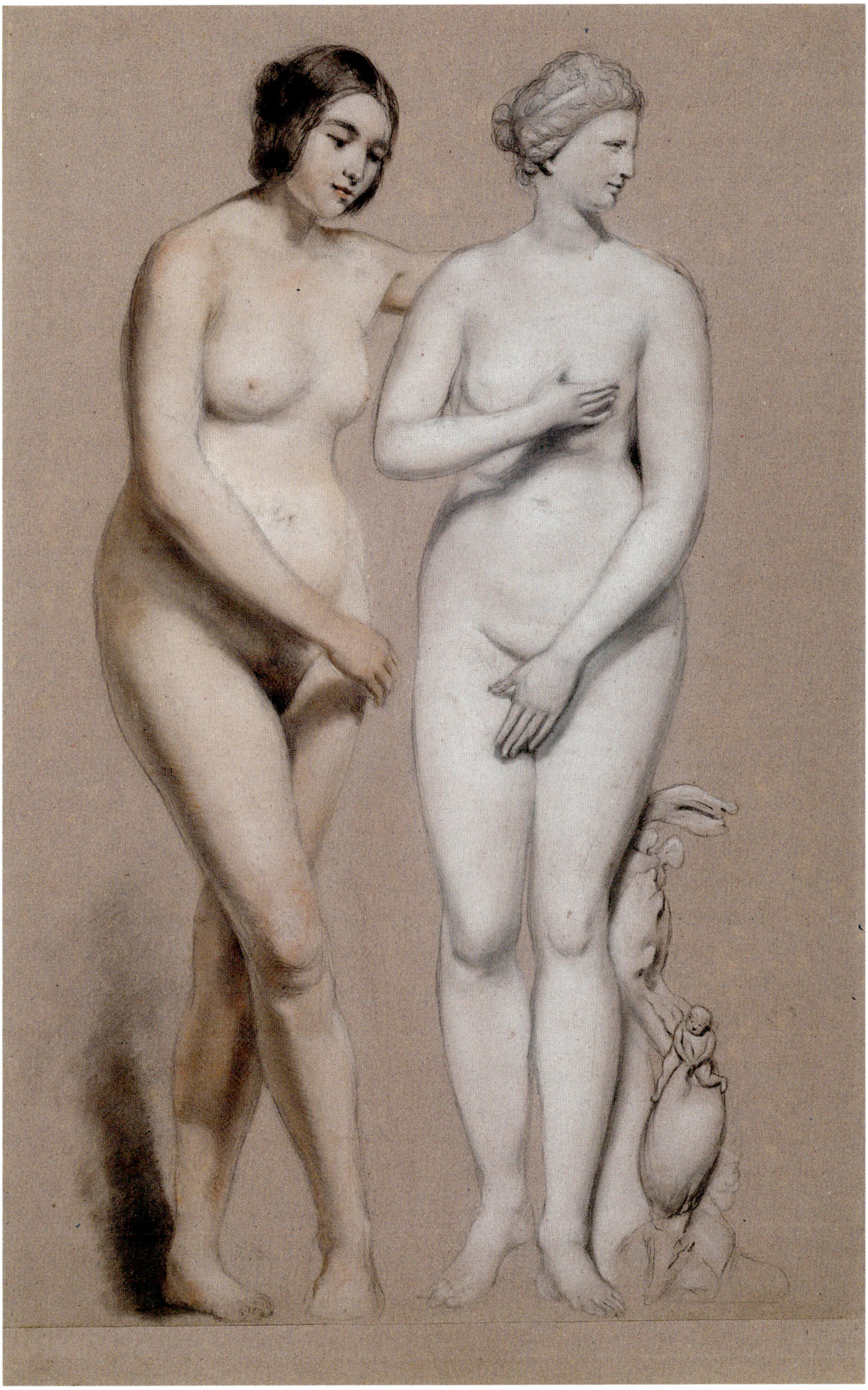

69 William Etty, *A Female Nude with a Cast of the Venus de' Medici*, c. 1835–37, chalk on paper. Courtauld Institute of Art, London.

mimic the model's body rather than the other way around. The arms, hips, and thighs of the cast are swollen, the restored left hand and head consequently looking far too tiny. The model wraps her arm around the cast, suggesting that in the skirmish between the two, living flesh has won. In his own lessons, Etty sought to promote the introduction of unidealized human forms into the highest genres of art. For the sessions he himself organized with life models, he frequented the museum of the Zoological Society to obtain feathers of unusual birds for the wings of his deities, another detail that could give representations of the body a sense of propriety via alignment with the supernatural figures of mythology.[94] Some critics struggled to appreciate the inclusion of scientifically accurate detail in this type of art. Responding to his painting of the *Sirens and Ulysses*, a critic decried that the cluster of "putrid corpses and skeletons" in the foreground was depicted "with loathsome fidelity: the surgeons will be in raptures; indeed, the picture is only fit to adorn a dissecting-room."[95]

Despite their foregrounding of "dirty flesh," Etty's figures are not "naked" in the sense in which I have used the word up until this point. Rather, they are nudes. The very words "nude" and "nudity" only begin to appear in English writings on art during the 1830s when Etty's reputation was at its height. While not necessarily employed to distinguish a certain kind of form, these terms bear a direct correlation with the decline of "the antique" and the growing legitimacy of more lifelike modes of representation. The form of the body is not subject to a process of perfecting in Etty's art, yet the slick rendering of the skin's surface produces an effect which exaggerates the sensual presence of the body, bolstering the erotic charge of the wayward form. In the context of British art, the genre of "the nude" bears connotations of studied eroticism of which Etty's paintings are paradigmatic.

As an emergent genre in Britain, the nude did not have a universal appeal. Etty's art was supported by a particular kind of consumer: the elite, often aristocratic gentleman. When Cumberland and Blake had railed against the biases of the Royal Academy and implicitly the variety of man appointed to the "Committee of Taste," they could not have imagined an artist more indicative of their grievances than Etty. Painterly and devoid of idealizing lines, his achievements self-consciously pandered to patrons like Sir George Beaumont and Edward Bligh, Earl of Darnley, as well as upper-middle-class collectors who aspired to the status of these men. Since the peak of the Grand Tour, aristocratic connoisseurs had coveted works like the *Venus de' Medici* as if they offered a stand-in for the living female body. In 1755, Charles Lennox, Duke of Richmond, wrote from Florence to his friend back in London, "I am in love with the Venus and take great pleasure to stroke her bum and thighs."[96] Etty's goddesses are the consequence of such intersections of libidinal desire and art. Channelling a more voluptuous aesthetic and using mythological subjects to elevate it allowed Etty to chime with a particular crowd.

Coupled with the erotic and sensual qualities of Etty's nudes, their hedonistic appreciation among wealthy men signals the painter's Poetic subjectivity. In his world view, art should "pour out a balm" rather than "vex." In an open letter titled "The Arts in England" published in February 1836 in the *Morning Herald*, he articulates his stance on the role of art in relation to the world around him:

> *Arts on the broad and vulgar world, are like the sight and smell of a freshly-gathered bunch of roses, glittering with dew, in a hot and crowded city. They are an oasis in the desert; something that shows we are not altogether "of the earth, earthly"; a breath from Paradise ... It is our duty, as Artists ... to be the guardians of those Arts, [to prevent] their still, sweet voice from being drowned in the clamour of politics, the din of commerce, or the rattle of railways.*[97]

Etty positions his painting – all art in fact – as immune from technological progress. Art is categorically at odds with "the clamour of politics," "the din of commerce," and "the rattle of railways": in other words, both the radical political Dreams and the Dream of industrial culture. His move to London coincided with the urbanization of his native York, a city comparatively insulated from the ravages of industrialism but still effected by changes to its surrounding landscape. He envisioned his nudes as part of fecund, pre-industrial nature, their bodies organic – that is, the work of God rather than man. He justified his rejection of the antique in religious terms: "I have preferred painting the unsophisticated human form divine," he declared, "in preference to the production of the loom; or in plainer terms preferred painting from the glorious works of God, to draperies, the works of man."[98] Etty did not see his art as a means of preaching the gospel, but rather as demonstrating a pious regard for the living body as a manifestation of God's work. Raised in a strict Methodist family similar to Bacon's, Etty found that denomination to be irreconcilable with the life of an artist, as John Bacon junior discovered for himself. Although he remained devout, Etty took up a more relaxed Christianity than that of his parents, a move that permitted him to separate his religious beliefs from his carnal approach to painting.

In this letter to the *Morning Herald*, Etty's language is sensual; the arts have a "smell," a "breath," a "sweet" voice; they "glitter" like rose petals studded with droplets. Flowers are, of course, not eternal but subject to the continual cycle of growth, bloom, and decay. That he used such earthly terms to invoke art as a lofty sanctuary away from the toil of modern life again points to the capacity of Poetic art to place sensual forms in an untouchable realm apart from mortal concerns. Here lies the distinction between Etty's sensual escapism and the "enchanted ground" of Howard's studio. One is reliant on terrestrial metaphors, the other the sky; whereas the latter compensates for its entrenchment in industrial culture by turning to the last universal element – that is, air – the former accepts and naturalizes social divisions, thereby legitimizing the status of painting and sculpture as luxuries that provide a "balm" for wealthy patrons.

Etty's patrons were drawn to his art because, by embracing the body as a somatic idea, it bore no traces of the political visions contained within representations of the classical body made by artists of the generation before. Etty loathed Dreaming art and did everything he could to distinguish himself from its legacy. Despite his humble birth as the son of a baker, he voiced a low opinion

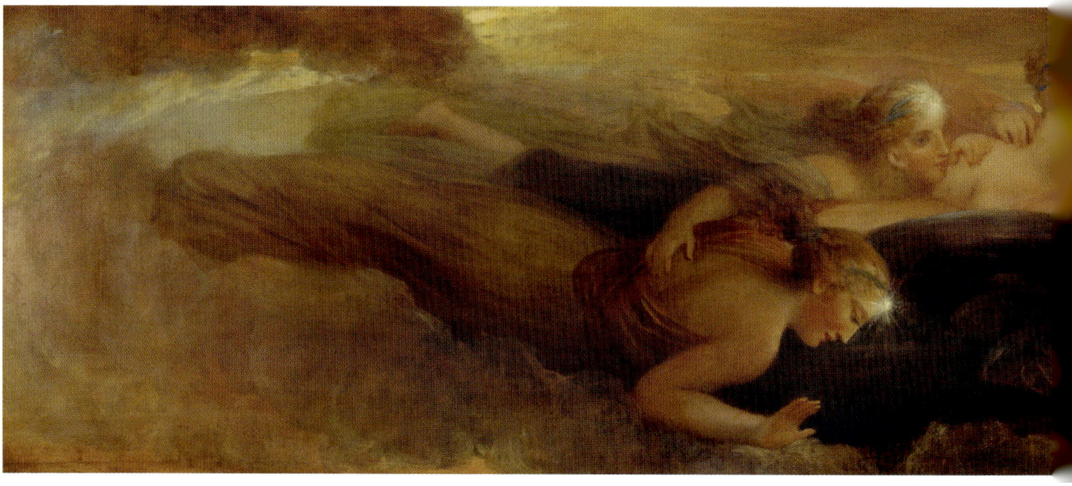

70 Henry Howard, *Night, with the Pleiades*, 1834, oil on panel. Sir John Soane's Museum, London.

of the poor and was vehemently opposed to the Reform Act of 1832. A young child in the 1790s, he happened to be in Paris during the July Revolution, where he was inadvertently caught up in the riots of the Three Glorious Days while on his way to copy the *Pastoral Concert* (initially attributed to Giorgione and now more commonly to Titian) at the Louvre. This experience only strengthened his belief that the fight for liberty and equality was an "evil." [99] His unidealized aesthetic is in harmony with this reaction. In his paintings, the layers torn off by radical classicists are restored in the form of flesh. The Burkean "coat of prejudice" reappears as bodily tissue.[100] The classical body is recorporealized, emptied of Dreams and made into a desirable object. Etty, then, is the inverse of Howard. The latter's female figures are not nudes, per se. They are figurations of the human form that, due to their perceived ornamentality, were marginalized by the very culture of fine art into which Etty's paintings, as definitive nudes, were readily incorporated. As the last vestige of a wilfully accessible classicism, Howard's nymphs and other airborne female figures are technological creatures. They are not fecund but streamlined and efficient, their status as somatic beings undermined by the line that describes them.

In his quest to be accessible, Howard sacrificed his posthumous reputation. A text written on the artist's achievements after his death in 1847 by a prominent Victorian critic suggests that he was born too late:

> *The truth is, Howard ... did not succeed in attaining such a high degree of popularity as would suffice to make his works covetable; he was too high for one class of collectors, not high enough for the other; his subjects are too classical to please the ordinary purchaser ... Had he been born twenty years earlier, his name might have been honourably enrolled among the original founders of the Academy; as it is, however, his works may be regarded as connecting links between the past and the present generation of British artists, partaking of each, yet recognised by neither.*[101]

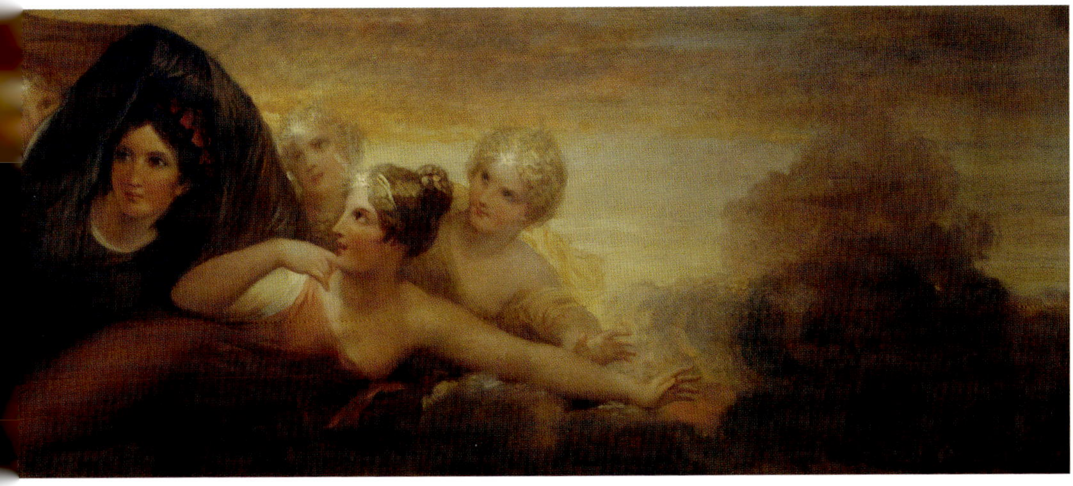

This passage implies that Howard's universal audience did not actually exist; the "ordinary purchaser" is pitted against the "class of collectors" wealthy enough to buy an original painting, a class dominated by the kind of men who lusted after Etty's nudes. Rather than achieving universality, Howard's less discriminating aesthetic, states this author, appeals to no one.

The critic is apt to position Howard as a liminal artist. Scholarship on his friends favors clear-cut identities; Banks is "Britain's first modern sculptor," Flaxman is "master of the purest line."[102] There is no vocabulary with which to recognize the youngest member of their dynasty: a practitioner who, by bridging different worlds, departed from the increasingly precise criteria used to evaluate painting in the context of the Royal Academy. One of his obituaries anticipates his fate, predicting that in the future he will be known only as "Flaxman's friend."[103] The little scholarly literature that does feature his name cites him in relation to Flaxman, Banks (only as the subsequent occupier of his studio), or Fuseli.[104]

One exception is an entry on his work in a volume on decorative painting.[105] Howard was able to make a virtue out of the deteriorating fortunes of his aesthetic by embracing its decorative aspect. In addition to gift books, Howard's art infiltrated homes in the form of large-scale painted schemes on ceilings and walls. Toward the end of his career, he was employed to produce paintings for two very different residential interiors: John Soane's dining room and the southwest drawing room at Lancaster House, residence of George Leveson-Gower, Duke of Sutherland.[106] For Soane he created a series of six panels including a rectangular depiction of *Night, with the Pleiades*, in which the seven stars cluster round the black-robed protagonist like Flaxman's Agnes Cromwell and her angels (fig. 70). Before long, Soane's house would open as a museum, allowing Howard to maintain a degree of visibility among the wider public he wished to reach. Three years later he painted a roundel entitled the *Solar System* onto one of Lancaster House's molded ceilings (fig. 71).[107] At the center of a thread of rainbow, Apollo perches on a cloud, encircled by planets embodied by their

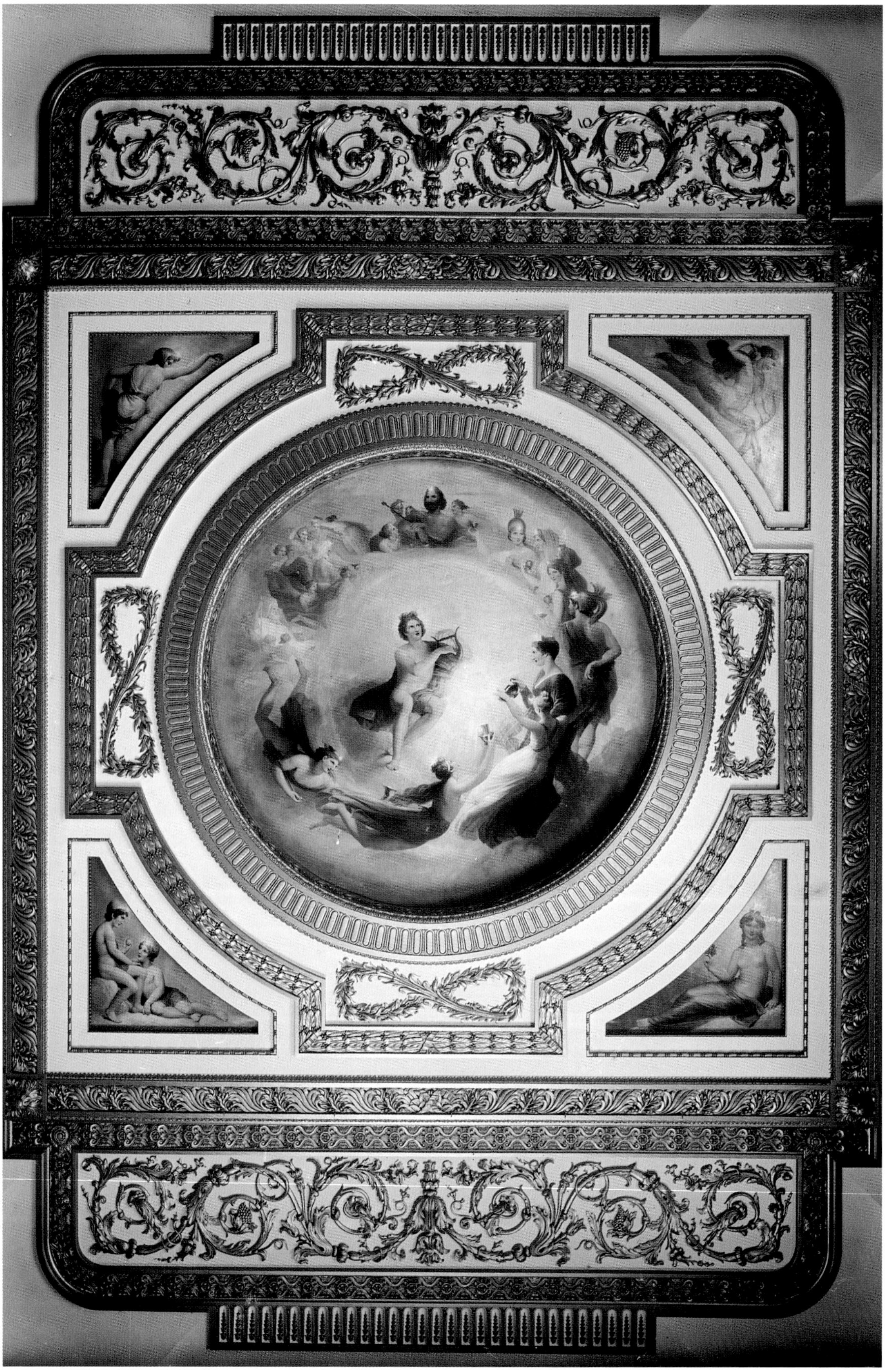

mythological counterparts. Protected from the condemnation of reactionary art critics, male and female forms are integrated, some naked, some draped, their proportions mimicking, as with all figures by Howard, the lineaments of classical statuary. In this exceptional setting, imagery that had proved compatible with mass-produced consumer goods is harmonized with Poetic taste. Leveson-Gower, the duke who paid Howard 800 guineas for the job, was also Etty's patron. Earlier in his career Howard had painted a frieze representing the tale of Cupid and Psyche – the ultimate Poetic subject – in the house of a slave-owning merchant named George Hibbert, for which all designs are untraced. Together with his drawings, paintings, and their print reproductions, all three decorative commissions affirm that in the war between Dreaming and Poetic approaches, Howard never took sides. He was a peacekeeper, a conscientious objector who paid the price for his wish to appease both. His exclusion from the historiography of British art underscores the severity of this war over the classical body. Painters who refused to take part risked disappearing into air.

71 Henry Howard, *Solar System*, 1837, ceiling painting. Lancaster House, London.

72 Edward Hodges Baily,
Eve at the Fountain, 1822 (see fig. 103).

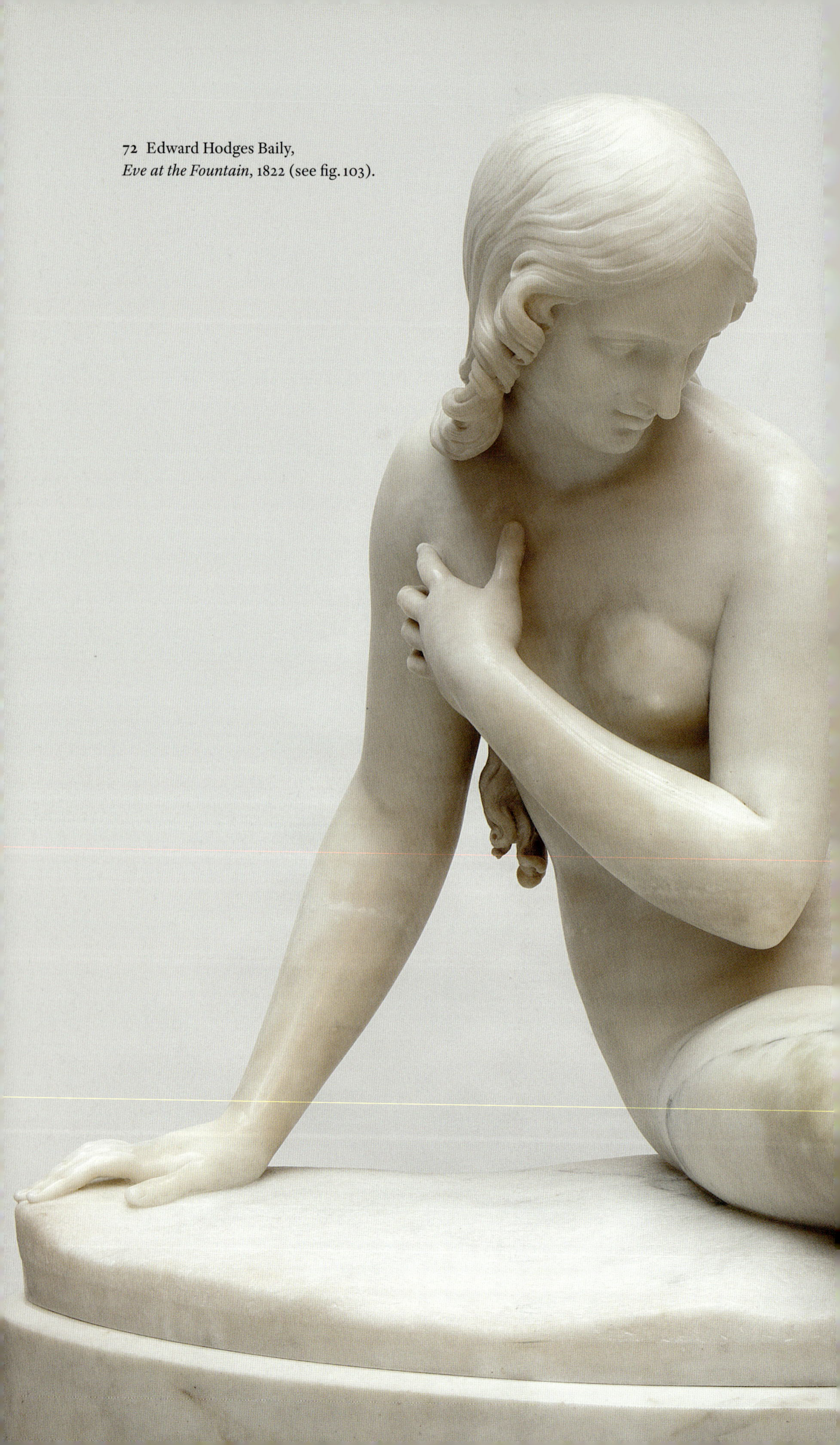

PART II

STONE AND FLESH

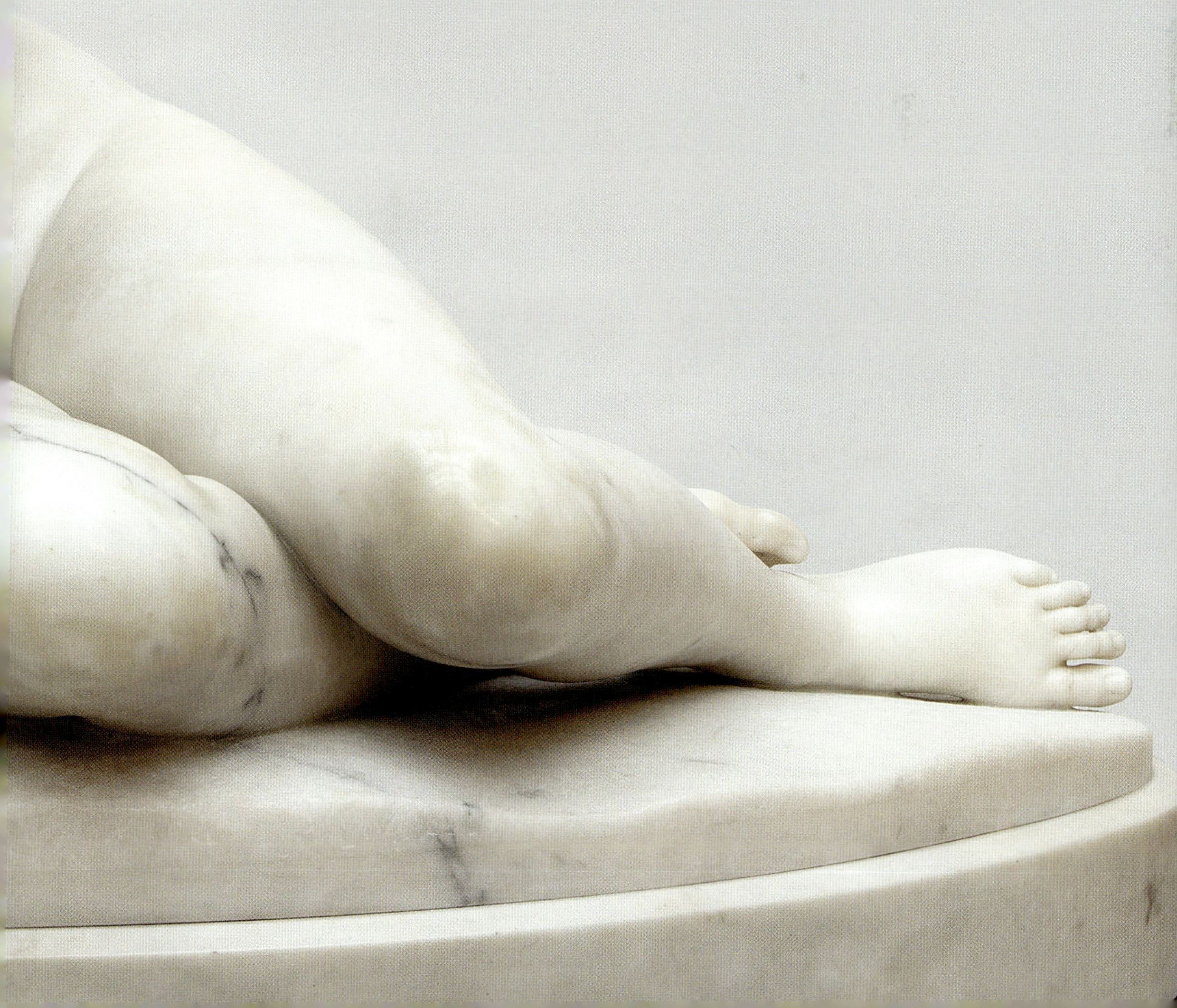

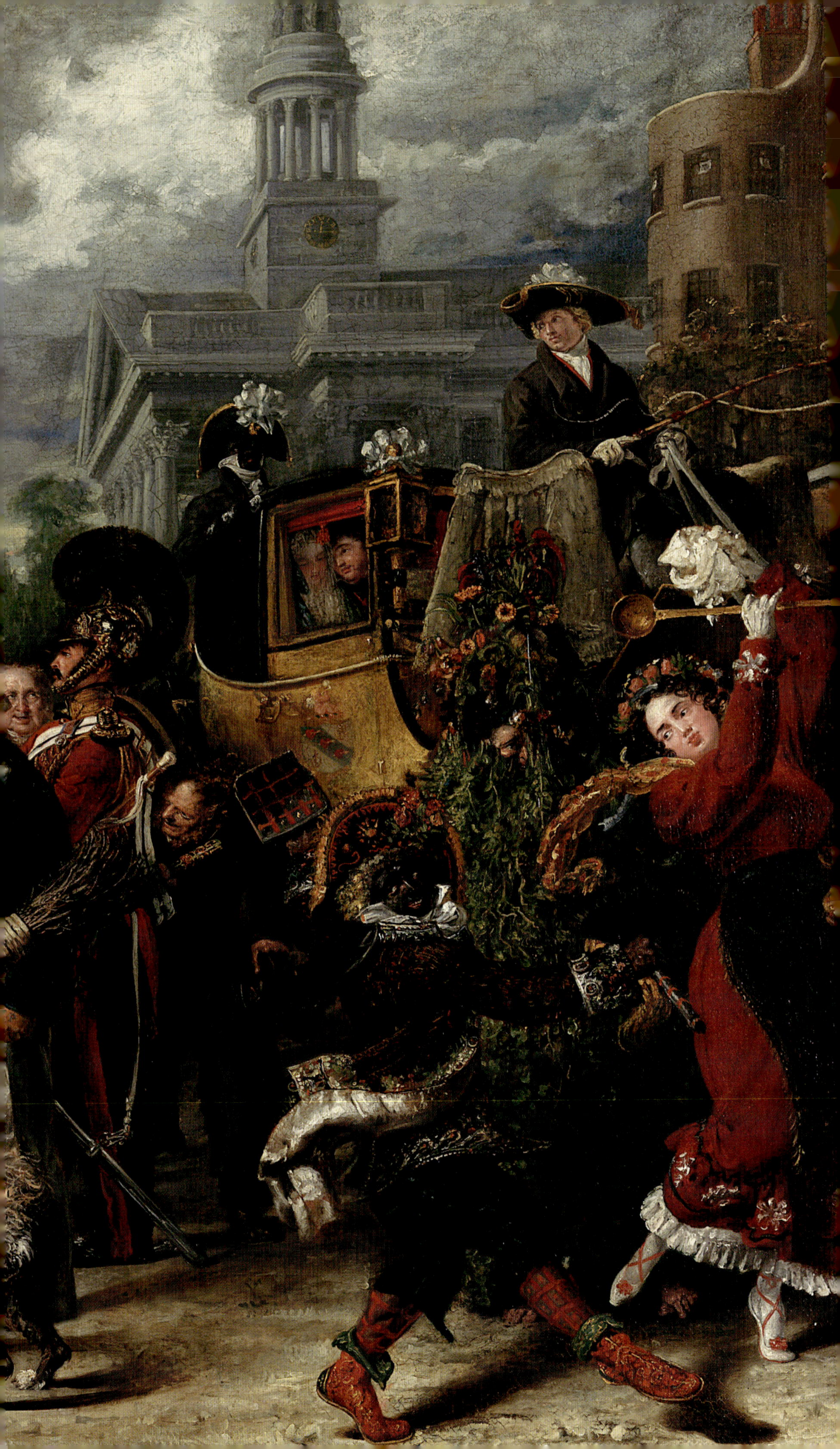

CHAPTER FOUR

LIVING DREAMS AND POEMS

A FEMALE BODY IS on display at a central London venue. Crowds lean in to inspect the contours of her form. She is exposed but not strictly naked, her flesh encased in tight diaphanous fabric. They call her Venus, but like William Etty's figures she is goddess in name only. She too has a body that defies convention, only she is not a richly painted impression of a living model but an actual person. Lamplight suffuses her form as she stares back at a sea of eyes. In 1810 anyone with a spare two shillings could come and look at her.

Much has been said about the public exhibition of Saartjie Baartman at a hall in Piccadilly that year. Brought from the Cape of Good Hope, this Khoisan woman achieved great fame in her lifetime, her image etched into the nation's collective memory for decades to come as the legendary "Hottentot Venus." Flaunted as both natural science exhibit and circus freak, her experience was to some degree unique.[1] Even after her captors were tried at the King's Bench court she continued to be toured across the country, around Ireland and then Paris, having likely been pressured into giving a statement that she was not being abused.[2] But her fate also articulates something significant about evolving approaches to the classical body. She was, after all, touted as a Greco-Roman goddess, her nonconforming form a kind of anti-sculpture in the shadow of the pale marble ideal. A French print from 1815 depicts her in the pose of the *Venus de' Medici,* another body captured and paraded in an alien situation as the "bride" of Napoleon's Louvre (fig. 74). The artist places Baartman on a plinth surrounded by a selection of onlookers – all satirical portrayals of British characters – whose dynamic gestures lay emphasis on her statue-stillness. Compare this image to Thomas Rowlandson's caricature of Emma Hamilton standing naked on a dais in front of her gloating husband and a young man sketching her from life (fig. 75). Hamilton, who in 1786 was shipped off to Naples to become the mistress and then wife of the ambassador, is pictured in the throes of one of her famous "Attitudes": one-woman performances of allegorical personifications or roles from myth, art, literature and history. One of Britain's foremost collectors of vases and other ancient relics, her husband essentially acquired Emma for his hoard, exhibiting her before streams of elite tourists as they passed through southern Italy. The frisson of a living body on display is the subject of both prints, yet these are not Pygmalion-and-Galatea-esque scenes of the vivification of a sculptural form but the reverse: life turned into sculpture. As life turns into sculpture it retains some

73 Detail from Benjamin Robert Haydon, *Punch or May Day* (fig. 85).

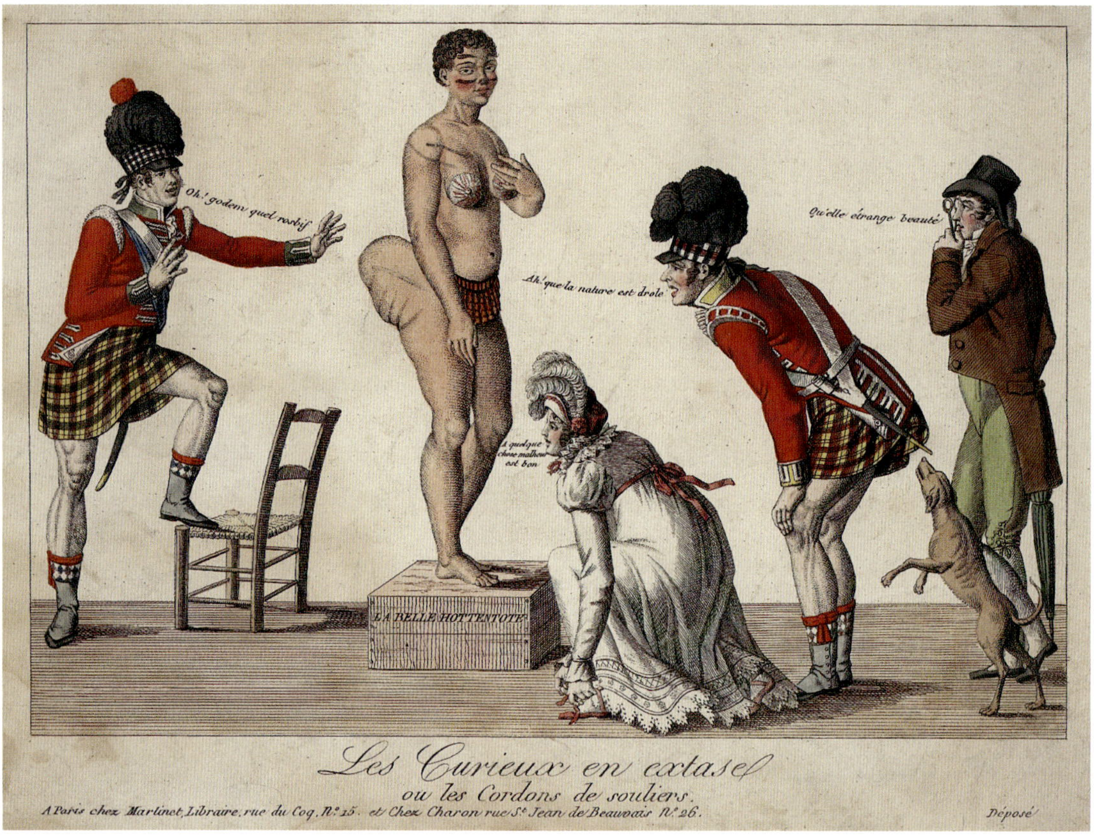

of its unclassical characteristics, preserving them as formal details of the work of art rather than human features; Baartman keeps the silhouette that made her famous, Hamilton her unbound hair, while the hand-coloring of the prints gives the impression of sculpted forms that are tinted with wax and pigment. At the same time as mocking the cult of "the antique," these prints represent the possibility of a new kind of classical body. They indicate a space being opened up for similar deviations from "the antique" – still anchored by the paradigm of the classical – in contemporary art.

In both prints, the conditions for viewing the figure stay exactly the same as for classical statues: a lone, raised form set against multiple clothed spectators, almost all of whom are male. In actual fact, neither Baartman nor Hamilton ever appeared before their audiences in such states of undress.[3] Notice that the single female spectator in the French print crouches down, her presence diminished as the curve of her rear echoes Baartman's. A closer look at the image reveals that this figure is not looking at Baartman at all but at the hidden genitals of the male soldier to the left. Humor is generated from this rerouting of gazes: the

74 Louis François Charon, *Les Curieux en extase ou les cordons de souliers*, 1815, hand-colored etching on paper. British Museum, London.

75 Thomas Rowlandson, *Lady H______ Attitudes*, c. 1800, hand-colored etching and aquatint on paper. Victoria and Albert Museum, London.

absurdity of male nakedness, otherwise covered up, as the object of a woman's curiosity. In both prints, male figures command agency as fighters, proprietors and practitioners. In their migration from living to dead matter, the exposed female forms lose consciousness. Articulated in the face, particularly the eyes which are either closed or fixed away from the audience, their lack of inner life is a prerequisite for the enjoyment of their forms. Needless to say Hamilton was prized for her conventional beauty and Baartman for her errant flesh, the former granted a life of luxury, the latter subject to unspeakable mistreatment. In Rowlandson's print Hamilton uncovers herself, lifting a sheet of drapery to show off her smooth pallor in the manner of the *Callipygian Venus*. Biographically speaking, Hamilton and Baartman present two very different cases. These prints, however, highlight the fact – often taken for granted in analyses of both figures – that the two women became works of classicizing art as soon as they went on

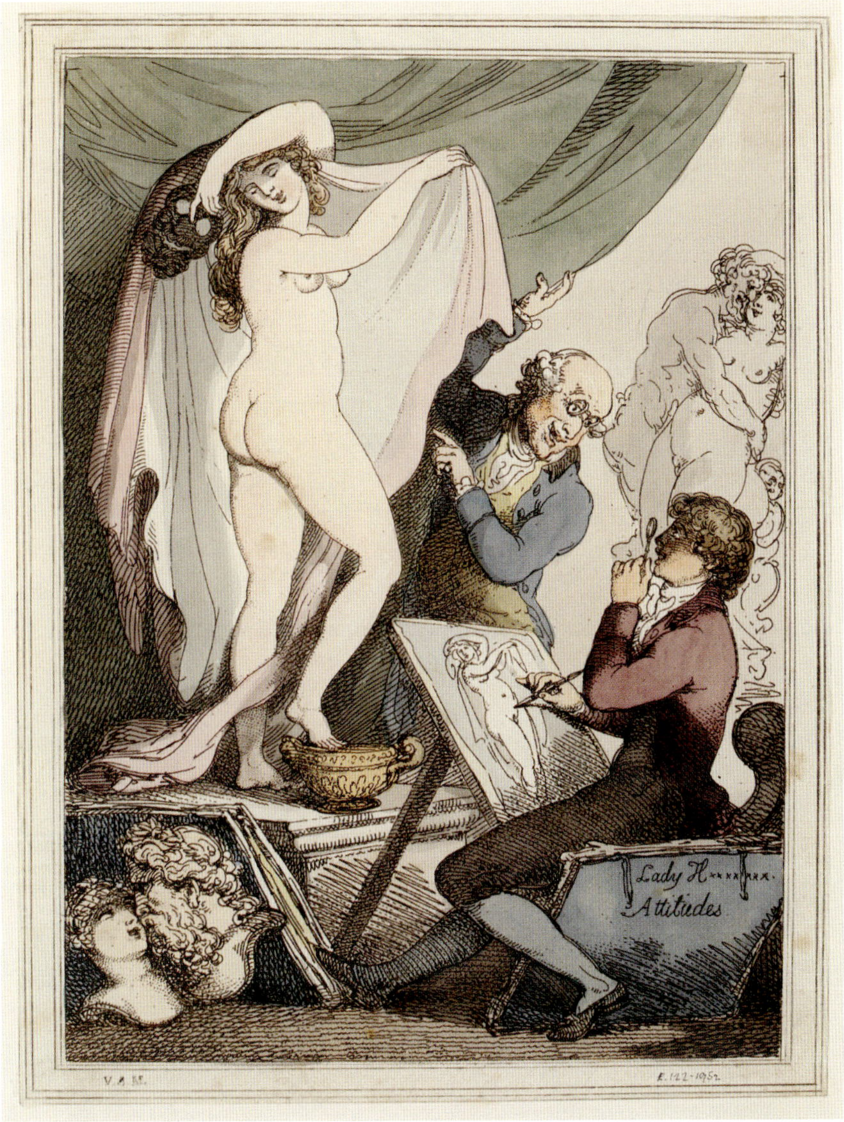

display. Hamilton did not simply provide inspiration for artists such as George Romney and Canova; she was herself a work of art, one that outdid all the others in her husband's collection. When Goethe lavished praise on her performances he did not invoke her as a kind of actress exceptionally capable of conjuring certain roles, but the "acme" of her husband's lifetime of collecting various incarnations of the classical body; in her "beautiful face" and "perfect figure" William Hamilton had "found all the antiquities."[4] As Goethe affirms, Emma Hamilton's allure stemmed from her ability to morph into an array of fantasy figures that would have been familiar to most of her audience. Baartman was cast as a fantasy figure of a more novel kind: the "Hottentot," a derogatory term for Khoisan people. Sander Gilman writes that for the majority of the nineteenth century in both Britain and France, the word "Hottentot" tended to be used exclusively in relation to its female representatives, synonymous with dehumanizing notions of African physiognomy combined with ubiquitous misogyny.[5] Natural scientist Georges Cuvier projected sexual promiscuity onto the anatomy of Khoisan women, using perceived differences in the formation of the genitalia to claim supremacy for white Europeans.[6] Baartman's steatopygia, or relatively large buttocks in relation to her waist, was proclaimed to be main source of fascination among those who paid to view her. This attribute gave her form a sense of erotic mystery that was accentuated by her presentation as a goddess of love. Her body was seen to possess an overabundance of sensuality that guaranteed its success as a spectacle that could titillate or disgust. Indeed, the fact that her image is recorded primarily in satirical prints that purposely distort her body eclipses some of this sensual allure.

In gauging how her image was received, satire remains useful. That her shape conformed to established constructions of the sensual in British culture is confirmed by the correlation between images of Baartman and satirical takes on ladies' clothing from the decades leading up to her display. From the mid-1770s through to the end of the 1780s, it had been the height of elegance for women to wear large pads under their skirts, often stuffed with horsehair or cork, to exaggerate the shape of their rears. A satirical print by R.R. Delin depicts the interior of a Piccadilly boutique – *The Bum Shop* – proffering such wares to clientele of varying sizes (fig. 76). Dated a year later, another print pokes fun at the same trend; *A Modern Venus, or a Lady of the Present Fashion in the State of Nature* portrays a naked woman with exaggerated buttocks and breasts, implying that the padded derrieres and pushed-up cleavages then in vogue imply a body with such proportions (fig. 77). Over two decades before Baartman's arrival, the quintessentially chic British woman could be derided for giving the impression of a body that resembles the later images of steatopygia. One of the broadsheets advertising the spectacle proclaims that "the Female Sex" has a special

76 R. R. Delin, *The Bum Shop*, 1785, hand-colored etching on paper. British Museum, London.

77 Unknown engraver, *A Modern Venus, or a Lady of the Present Fashion in the State of Nature*, 1786, engraving on paper. New York Public Library, New York.

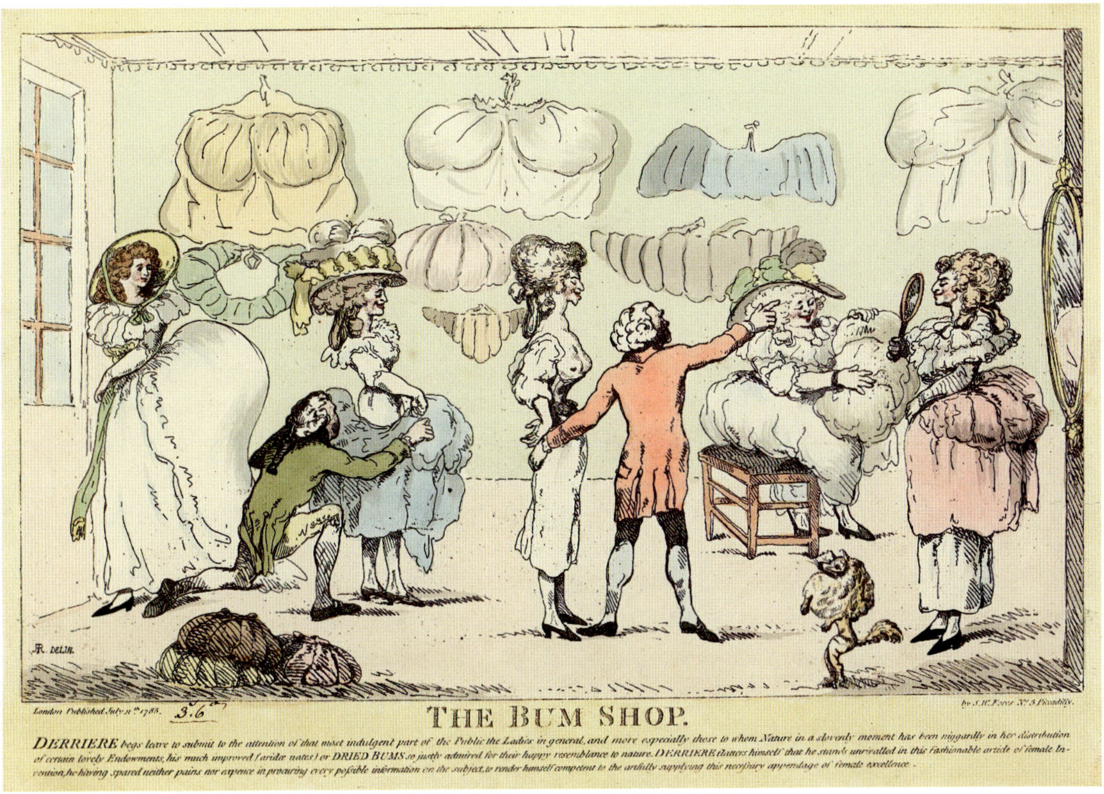
R. DELIN.
London Published July 11th 1785. 3.6
by S.W. Fores No. 3 Piccadilly.
THE BUM SHOP.
DERRIERE begs leave to submit to the attention of that most indulgent part of the Public the Ladies in general, and more especially those to whom Nature in a slovenly moment has been niggardly in her distribution of certain lovely Endowments, his much improved (aridæ nates) or DRIED BUMS so justly admired for their happy resemblance to nature. DERRIERE flatters himself that he stands unrivalled in this fashionable article of female Invention, he having spared neither pains nor expence in procuring every possible information on the subject, to render himself competent to the artfully supplying this necessary appendage of female excellence.

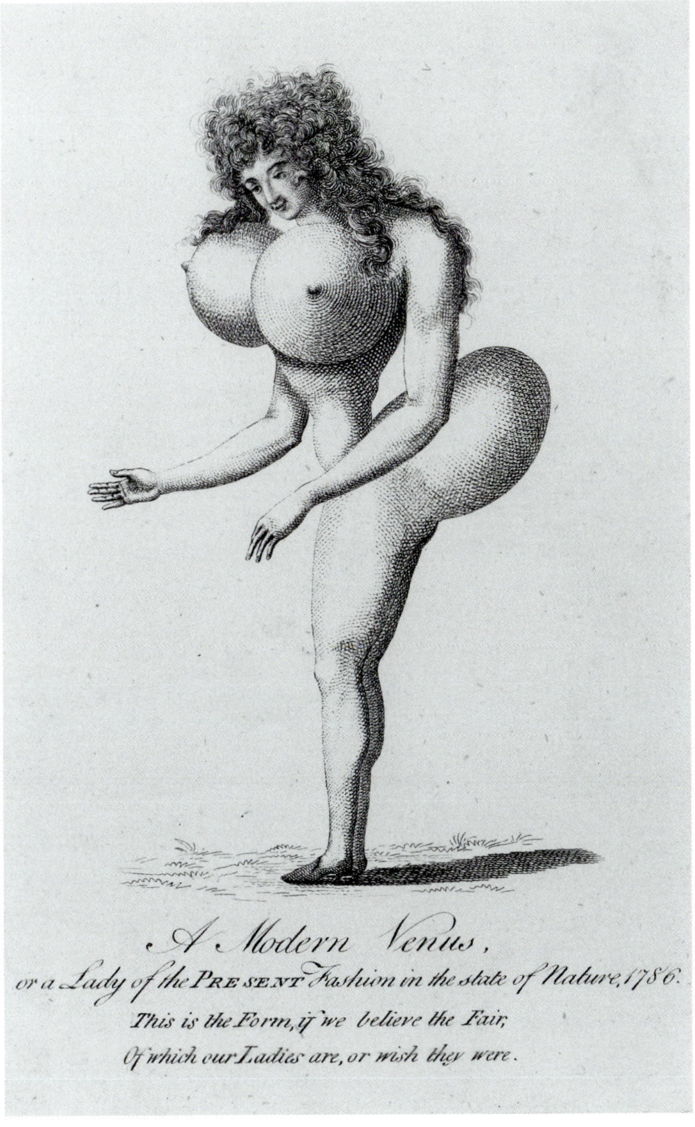
A Modern Venus,
or a Lady of the PRESENT Fashion in the state of Nature, 1786.
This is the Form, if we believe the Fair,
Of which our Ladies are, or wish they were.

relationship to "the Venus" and has "liberally patronized her Exhibition," a qualification that, in trying to compensate for the unavoidable erotic charge of a near naked body on display, ends up strengthening the figure's compatibility with the bodies of women in the audience. Baartman's image is thereby recorporealized, her image distanced from the dehumanizing stereotype.[7] The potential coveting of Baartman's silhouette among British women was ridiculed in an anthology of bawdy verse published after her debut. A ditty entitled "The Hottentot Venus" describes doctors forbidding "ladies going to see her" lest "the Rump-disease be caught by our fair."[8] What motivates these satirical texts is the fact that Baartman's silhouette was not simply an object of ridicule but threatened to be desirable. As a work of art, the "Hottentot Venus" brought together time-honored myths of female sensuality with its manifestations in classical art and in modern ladies' fashion, each amplified by the additional mantle of exotic racial other. Together, these forces bolstered the idea that, in the land of her birth, Baartman might very well embody the epitome of female beauty.[9] It was this layering of fantasies, prototypes and mysteries to forge the "Hottentot Venus" that drove Cuvier and his colleagues to dissect Baartman following her death in 1815. After her silhouette was cut up and her form fragmented, Baartman no longer was a manifestation of Venus but a reference point for the field of comparative anatomy, a means of understanding the variety of species.[10] Fixated on her labia as well as her buttocks, dissection rationalized the sensuality of her form.

In the previous chapter, I acknowledged the way in which idealized outlines of female bodies in painting and sculpture work to rein in the sensuality associated with the female body and delimit its eroticism, hence the controversy generated by Etty's wayward nudes. As much as Baartman's image was sold as an encounter with the "Hottentot," I want to stress that she sat more comfortably within established conceptions of female beauty in Britain than we might assume. Praising the "gently flowing" lines "that compose" the *Venus de' Medici*, William Hogarth concedes in his *Analysis of Beauty* that "winding lines are often the cause of deformity as of grace" and therefore must be monitored by strict attention to design.[11] Design was for Hogarth, however, not the austere and prescriptive linearity of works by Banks, Flaxman, or Howard, but a practice that tolerated a degree of irregularity. The term "steatopygia" is scientific and therefore obscures the sensory and emotional purchase of the form it describes. If the padded derrieres bought on Piccadilly could adhere to Hogarth's cherished "waving line ... being composed of two curves contrasted," then Baartman's body was not far off.[12] Hers was not a body of naked truth but a form targeted toward the imagination.[13]

Both Hogarth's investment in female curves and its corollary in dress are pre-Revolutionary aesthetics. They proffer a conception of the female body that was, for a limited phase in time, challenged by Dreaming art and the universalist image of Greece and of Greek freedom that went with it. As indices of aristocratic decadence, the garments ridiculed in *The Bum Shop* and *A Modern Venus* became the target of radical thinkers like Banks who, as I explored in the first chapter, wished to strip off the copious layers shrouding the human form and allow the body to move freely. *A Modern Venus* naturalizes these garments' "barbarous" – in the words of the Winckelmann-steeped Wollstonecraft – distortion of the female body.[14] If we contrast the "Hottentot Venus" with the heartfelt aspirations of activists to make the classical body a vessel for radical ideas, a case can be made that Baartman's display presented her not just as a work of contemporary sculpture but as an example of the other kind of visual classicism that is this book's concern: Poetic art. In the introduction I argued that, in relation to the temporal limitations of Dreaming images, the evasion of temporal specificity is one of the key characteristics of Poetic works. Not only was Baartman presented as a mystified icon whose flesh was seen to possess a kind of tinted surface as well as a sensual silhouette; as life-turned-to-sculpture she lay outside of history. Hegel voiced an opinion typical of his generation when he declared that Africa "is no historical part of the World; it has no movement or development to exhibit."[15] In addition to her African identity, south African no less, Baartman's legacy further underscores the atemporality embedded into her image. While paradigmatically Dreaming works like Banks's Homeric relief and monument to *Captain Burges* sit in obscurity, references to the "Hottentot Venus" endure beyond the century of her exhibition. In 2016, a rumor emerged that Beyoncé Knowles would be playing Baartman in a biopic, an association that emphasizes both the sensual dimension of the "Hottentot Venus" and the enduring relevance of female bodily display, particularly bodies coveted for their so-called curves. A detail included on the broadsheet marketing Baartman confirms her Poetic status. William Dunlop, the mastermind behind the show, felt it necessary to stress that this Venus was "Remarkably mild and affable in her manners," that is, a "phenomen[on] of pure positivity."[16] She was brandished less as a science exhibit than as a pleasing attraction: a "balm" for the audience.

Banks's concern for the "Oppres'd African" in his letter to George Cumberland following the Treaty of Amiens in 1802 registers the gulf between his Dreaming art and the Poetic spectacle that was Baartman.[17] Near to the fashionable dress shops and not far from Somerset House, the "Hottentot Venus" went on stage as an adaptation of the classical body in stark contrast to his egalitarian mobilization of Greek sculpture. Had Banks been alive he surely would have been one of those objecting to her brutal treatment. But it is hard to conceive of Baartman going on display during the sculptor's lifetime, when the universalist image of Greece and the active connection between Greece and freedom would surely have been obstacles to putting a captured African woman on stage and calling her Venus. If Banks had struggled to come to terms with Napoleon's retrogressive attitude toward slavery in 1802, the political climate had changed even more dramatically by 1810. Although the Piccadilly shops now sold empire-waist gowns with long flowing skirts rather than pads, the promise of bodily liberation brought forth by the Revolution, and by Winckelmann, was now a distant memory. Having lost its capacity to Dream, the kind of classical body perpetuated by Banks persisted in the forcibly remote designs of Flaxman and the paintings of Howard, whom we know only achieved his goal of preserving an accessible classicism by allowing his paintings to be reproduced as steel engravings.

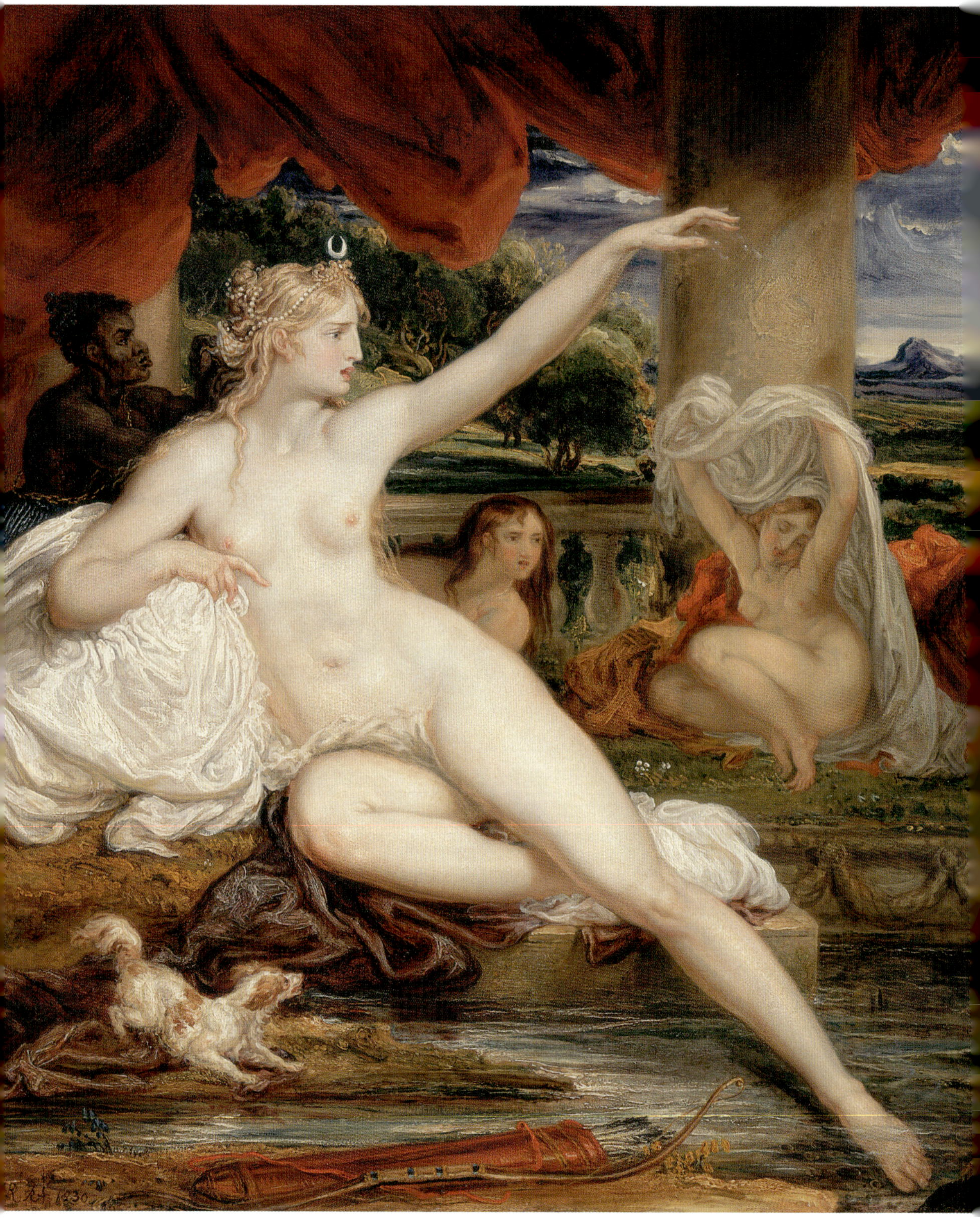

78 James Ward, *Diana at the Bath Disturbed by Actaeon*, 1830, oil on panel. Yale Center for British Art, New Haven.

Reflected in British art criticism, the nationalistic and reactionary turn was one of the factors affecting the reception of classicizing works made in the context of the Royal Academy. Presented as a fleshy incarnation of a classical goddess, Baartman provides insight into the increasing legitimacy of challenging the antique that came to constitute an aesthetic all of its own in Etty's oil paintings. Indeed, her status as Venus indicates a space being opened up that Etty's affront to the pre-eminence of classical sculpture would soon fill. When, in 1830, John Constable dismissed Etty's figures as "lady bums," he ridiculed the infringement of "mere dirty flesh" onto the sanctified world of oil painting.[18] Constable, however, knew that he was not the target audience for this kind of art. He noted that the painting he decried was "bought by an old Marquis" and had been "coveted by the King."[19] Baartman's image was similarly targeted toward the aristocracy and she herself was employed by them in private. The same poster advertising her "mild and affable" nature" boasts that "She has had the Honour of being visited by His Royal Highness the PRINCE REGENT, and several branches of the ROYAL FAMILY, and also the principal NOBILITY." Like Etty's paintings, she moved from public spectacle to guilty pleasure in the homes of aristocrats such as the Duke of Clarence, the future William IV and patron of the Royal Academy, who demanded that she be brought to his mansion to provide entertainment during a party.[20] This is to say that the "Hottentot Venus," like Etty's paintings, was very much the product of a new dawn in British culture in which classicizing art had lost its connection to freedom, and the antique had been outpaced by the exaggerated sensuality of un-Greek bodies.

Both the idea of the "Hottentot Venus" and Etty's nudes present a version of the classical body that encourages the libidinal gaze. The fact that the majority of life models employed by Etty earned money through sex work made Constable all the more disdainful of the thirst for his paintings among the elite. Gilman points out that the idea of the "Hottentot" and the figure of the prostitute were intertwined throughout the nineteenth century, the implied sexual deviance of one providing a vocabulary to condemn the latter.[21] He explores how, in painting, black female figures are sometimes included as adjuncts to white European women in order to heighten the latter's aura of sexual availability.[22] Manet's *Olympia* is a canonized example, but there is an earlier British work that illustrates this same visual code. Painted in 1830, the richly rendered nakedness of James Ward's *Diana at the Bath Disturbed by Actaeon* suggests Etty's influence on his Academic colleagues (fig. 78). The goddess is pictured bathing with some companions, interrupted by Actaeon, who, off-scene, facilitates the glimpse the viewer is granted. It is not so much the fleshiness of the form that ties this work to Etty, but the unusual shape of Diana's pose – two limbs forming a right angle as she turns to face the intruder – and the way it grants the viewer an uncompromised confrontation with the undraped female body for which Etty's paintings set a precedent. Although she possesses "small, distinct and delicate" breasts in the manner of the *Venus de' Medici*, the form of Diana is not the sort of goddess Howard would have painted.[23] Rather, the figure highlights Ward's specialism as an animal painter; there are traces of equine muscularity in her thighs and outstretched haunch that emphasize the somatic status of the body. Behind Diana are the head and upper torso of a stereotypically African female, emerging as if perched on the goddess's shoulder like a demon. This figure's profile is juxtaposed with Diana's so that the former's brutalized physiognomy throws into relief the straight, almost perfectly Greek nose, rosebud lips and tapered jaw of the blonde goddess. In contrast to the unfurled body of Diana, the black figure is in chains: a modernizing aspect of what pretends to be an atemporal mythological tableau. But while the restriction of Ward's black figure conjures still-legal slavery, Gilman's argument indicates that it might also be read as symbolic. Since Diana is the goddess of modesty, her sexuality – represented by the black attendant – is controlled. The attendant magnifies the erotic charge of the goddess's body as it loses this control, unlocking in response to an intrusion. While the sensation around Etty's nudes permitted Ward's foray into this kind of provocative engagement with the female form, the animal painter was also drawing on Titian's version of the subject, in which an African attendant appears as part of Diana's retinue (fig. 79). In the Venetian painting it remains ambiguous whether the attendant is protecting the goddess by covering her nakedness or facilitating her exposure to the voyeur. Either way, the African figure serves as a device for the activation of Diana's sexual allure. When Baartman went on display as the "Hottentot Venus," she was doubly eroticized by her embodiment of both classical goddess and her black foil.

From Canova and Reynolds to Flaxman's outlines to the abject eroticism of the "Hottentot Venus" and Etty's goddesses, Poetic art is diverse. Its unifying characteristics are sensual materiality, atemporality, and its dialectical opposition to the Dreams that filled the classical body with a vision of how society ought to be. Even though I have not stated it plainly, it should already be clear that Poetic art is oriented toward the female body. Using the changing reception of the monument to *Captain Burges* as evidence, I have made the case that, as the idealized male body loses its capacity to represent humanity at large, male figures come to be represented with greater specificity. The division between genders is rigidified by the loss of identity that female forms undergo as a result. Baartman, like Emma Hamilton before her, lost her particularity when she was forced into the template of the "Hottentot." An abstraction capable of taking on a plethora of guises, Hamilton too was a Poetic work, an earlier example of this kind of classicizing art and the "tactile-erotic gazes" that it encouraged.[24] As mortal women selected for their looks, separated from their families and turned into goddesses held at a distance from the rest of humankind, both she and Baartman have more in common with the figure of Psyche than with "vulgar Winckelmannianism" and its version of the classical body.

Following her dissection, Baartman's demystified remains were enlisted on behalf of a different Dream: that of white European supremacy. When she was alive, her powerlessness had been authorized by an implicit understanding that as an African woman she was born inferior to the white majority of British society. This notion only became a Dream once it found expression in the racial-scientific discourse that became prevalent after her death, the claims of which

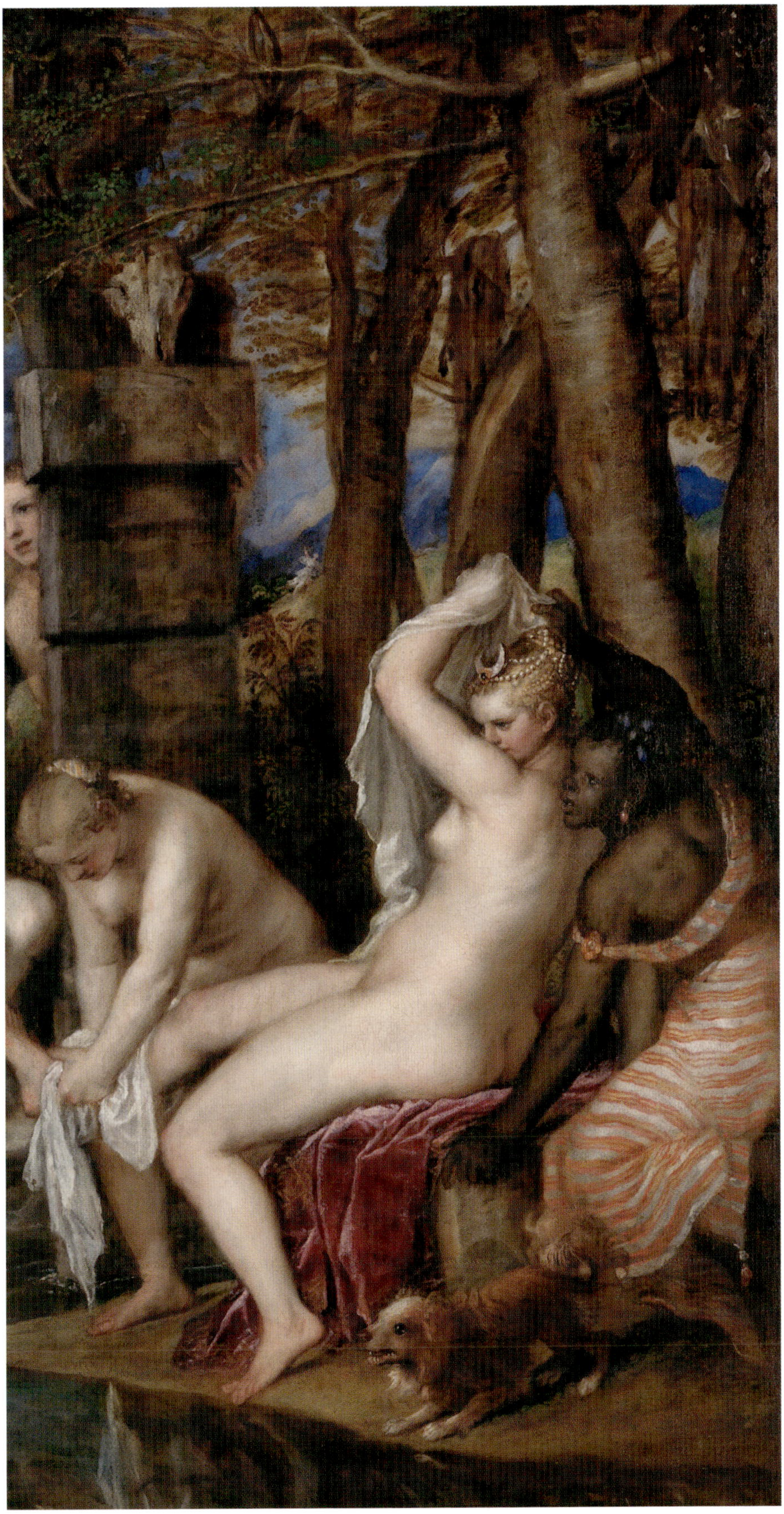

79 Detail from Titian, *Diana and Actaeon*, 1556–9, oil on canvas. National Gallery, London, and Scottish National Gallery, Edinburgh.

gathered speed throughout the century until they changed the way differences between people were commonly understood. In the context of Britain, such theories are documented not just in literature but in the practice of a particular painter: Benjamin Robert Haydon. Wishing to become the leading artist of the day, Haydon found the pervasive nationalism suffusing British culture and the related turn against "the antique" in contemporary art to be complementary with racial-scientific typologies. He incorporated his practice into a new Dream, one whose white supremacist vision was at odds with the Dreams of Banks and other radical activists of the previous generation. The white-supremacist Dream was the driving force behind Haydon's career-long quest to establish himself as a leading artist, one whose Britishness rendered him equal, on racial terms, to the sculptors of Greece.

— THE NEW DREAM —

Haydon came of age as an artist toward the end of the Napoleonic Wars. Had the war against Dreaming art, against the classical body-as-vessel, not been won by this point? Was "the antique" not increasingly downgraded in British artistic practice because of the separation of painting and sculpture, on the one hand, and, on the other, the wider rejection of Greece as a universal idea? Rather than sticking with the image of classical Greek sculpture prevalent in the years around Banks's monument to *Captain Burges*, Haydon positioned himself as the chief advocate of the set of sculpted fragments that had recently been imported to London from Athens: the Parthenon Marbles. In these objects, Haydon found an alternative conception of Hellenic form, one that seemed to prioritize the interior of the body as opposed to the smooth, uninterrupted contours that had been the basis of classical sculpture's appeal up to now. He sought to turn representations of the human body, specifically the male figure, inside out, becoming obsessed with the dynamics of muscles, tendons, ligaments, even the nervous system: the antithesis of Poetic sensuality.

Having begun his career with a marked interest in anatomical science, the timing of the Marbles' arrival was convenient for Haydon. Following his first contact with the fragments in 1808 when he was twenty-two, he enlisted these sculptures as evidence for his burgeoning theory that anatomy was the most important aspect of artistic study. If Phidias, the fifth-century sculptor to whom the Marbles were officially attributed after the Select Committee organized by the government in 1816 sealed their worth (Haydon was convinced from the beginning that they were from the fifth century), possessed an advanced knowledge of anatomy and demonstrated it in his creations, then all aspiring artists must do the same. In the years leading up to the Select Committee, he set out on a mission to draft and disseminate an anatomically grounded revision of the classical body, drawing on a combination of scientific texts, living models, and ancient sculpture.

In order to be taken seriously, Haydon needed to champion the idea that both he and the Marbles were exceptional, and did this by imbibing racial scientific texts that had been published during his childhood. Haydon was all the more drawn to this kind of analysis because he had little time for the rights of humankind, for the pursuit of freedom that had been poured into representations of the classical body. Familiarity with his late painting of the *Anti-Slavery Society Convention* of 1840 might give the erroneous impression that he sided with the likes of Banks and Cumberland.[25] But his extreme views on people of African descent align more with slaveholders than abolitionists. His image of the classical body offered an icon not of humanity at large but of a specific branch of humanity: the white European. Hence when he mobilized the Theseus from the east pediment of the Parthenon as the embodiment of perfection, he did so under the pretext that this figure stood for not just the *aesthetic* supremacy of Greece, but the white European's *genetic* supremacy. As an Englishman, Haydon identified with this racial ideal. In time, he came to view himself as the living equivalent to Phidias, believing that he and the sculptor were biological kin brought together by their whiteness in relation to swarthier others, be they Turkish or "negro." The classical body became a vessel for different contents: racist theories held dear by the artist.

In *Ape to Apollo*, David Bindman navigates the deployment of Greco-Roman sculpture in seventeenth- and eighteenth-century theories of the distinction between various human types, revealing it to be a tendency that long predates Haydon.[26] Aesthetic discourses before the emergence of racial science proper are rife with associative connections between the appearance of the white European man and the *Apollo Belvedere*, which for centuries had been the go-to synecdoche of male corporeal beauty (fig. 80). What racial science did was to convert these connections into a fixed hierarchy informed by polygenetic theories of human origin. Haydon's art and writings are couched in this transition from exterior appearance to interior, that is, genetic difference, only with the *Apollo* exchanged for the Parthenon's Theseus as the principal icon of the masculine ideal. But while racial science flourished throughout the nineteenth century, Haydon's art did not. When the painter took his own life aged sixty, he knew that his mission had failed. His work was too vexing, too laden with overwrought theories of how the body ought to be represented and the principles it needed to uphold. In the end it was Etty, the refuter of the antique, who could legitimately be heralded the savior of classicizing painting in Britain.

Although Haydon remained committed to the antique in contemporary art, he consciously broke with Winckelmann. His rejection of the scholar articulates much about his relationship to the image of the classical body and the extent to which it differs from both Poetic art and the Dreams of Banks and his circle. There is, of course, the fact that the Parthenon Marbles instantly undermined Winckelmann's canon of classical sculpture, a point to which I will return. But Haydon took issue not just with the objects Winckelmann valued, but with the scholar's overall approach. In a letter to William Wordsworth, Haydon rails against Winckelmann for not being exacting enough in his historical account. Winckelmann was, states the painter, evidently "well versed in antiquity, but very superficial in his own conclusions – in everything that required thinking out."[27] These words at once reveal the fall of "vulgar Winckelmannianism" and the rising

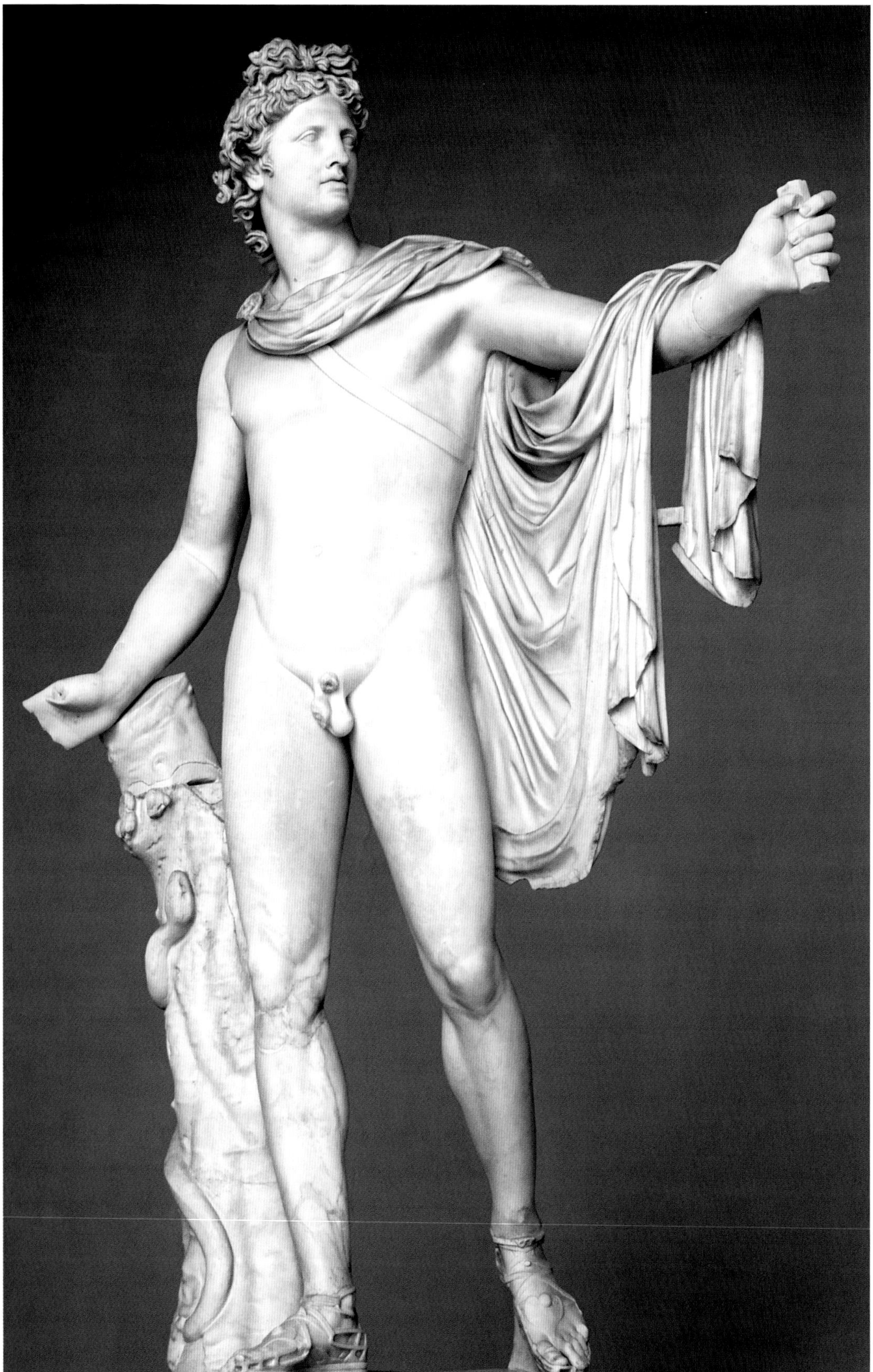

80 After Leochares, *Apollo Belvedere*, first century AD copy of lost Greek sculpture, marble. Vatican Museums, Rome.

need for specificity, literalness and scientific precision, a need that implicated Haydon's favorite subject: the male body. At this juncture, Winckelmann, whom Haydon goes on to describe as a "useless [rhapsodist]," becomes a Poetic figure, an author preoccupied with the external attributes of objects and their sensual enjoyment. Haydon saw his own prioritization of the "raciness of nature" (one of his terms for the anatomically grounded view of the body) as an intervention into the allegedly inauthentic account of Greek sculpture offered by Winckelmann.[28]

His earliest articulation of a racial-scientific interpretation of the Parthenon Marbles did not appear until 1810, two years after his first encounter with the fragments. Yet the seeds of this project had been sown through his eager reading of certain anatomical texts he encountered outside of his training at the Royal Academy Schools, which he began in 1804. The anatomy that compelled Haydon was not of the conventional kind. Since the founding of the Academy in 1768, the science had been a part of the curriculum, first taught by the surgeon William Hunter. In the context of artistic training, anatomy traditionally bore an auxiliary function, useful only as a means of fine-tuning the figure once an understanding of form had been gained from drawing casts and living models. In the previous chapter I looked at how, as the century progressed, the authority of casts after the antique was challenged by Royal Academicians, allowing the unregulated flesh of the life model to invade exhibited works. Another dimension of the defiance of classical sculpture was a new conception of anatomy as the most crucial element of artistic practice.

The Academy, however, took a while to accept this as a viable proposal, and its advocates were forced to take their ideas elsewhere. The main proponent of this prioritized anatomy was Charles Bell, a surgeon and amateur artist. In his major work, the 1806 *Essays on the Anatomy of Expression in Painting*, Bell warns against the "blind and indiscriminate imitation" of either classical statuary or the living model, offering his distinct application of the discipline as a cure for those "errors into which a young artist is most likely to be seduced."[29] According to Bell, the unscientific view of the human body exemplified in the writings of Winckelmann is wholly invalid and ought to be replaced by precise renderings of the effect of various emotions, physical pain, age and other conditions on the muscles of both the body and face. To achieve these renderings, the student must begin with a knowledge of how the body functions from within right down to the workings of the nervous system. If this, what he calls "the anatomy of expression," does not become the very foundation of artistic practice, the "pursuit of ideal beauty" will be ruinous. It is clear that Bell's theories are more applicable to the male body than the female. At various points he reminds his readers that a woman's silhouette is always "soft and undulating," and that in her "attitude and expression, there is nothing irregular, abrupt or harsh."[30] Like infants, women are to have "skin smooth ... limbs round, polished and pyramidal"; the most charming image of all is that of a "lovely woman" complete with a "susceptible mind ... an evanescent illumination of the countenance which words cannot convey."[31] Even in a technical context, female forms are expected to have no individual identities and are reduced to an abstraction. Bell presents the female form as a "phenomen[on] of pure positivity." The anatomist's image of women is Poetic.

Evidently Bell would have preferred Etty to Howard. Because of their persistent use of "the antique" as a corporeal template, Howard's works are against the grain of the *Anatomy of Expression*. Bell's text validates the separation of painting from sculpture that facilitated Etty's overtaking of Howard. The author acknowledges that his theories have more purchase within painting because the sculptor "must exercise his genius on the more ... permanent emotions." Painting, in other words, permits greater spontaneity and specificity, although even sculptors must still be careful not to let their duty to "the antique" collapse their figures into "indifference and insensibility."[32]

The artistic establishment was wary of Bell's theories. Not long after *Anatomy of Expression* was published, the surgeon who would become the Academy's Professor of Anatomy in 1808, Anthony Carlisle, wrote an article blasting the incursion of anatomical knowledge onto painting. The science must maintain its auxiliary role, he argues, and not be deployed to revolutionize the representation of the human form. At present its "utility" is fast becoming "over-rated."[33] Speaking as both surgeon and admirer of classical sculpture, Carlisle is at pains to point out that the Greeks did not possess a sophisticated grasp of anatomy, nor did they need one. Hellenic sculptors, he proclaims, "succeeded in giving soul and sentiment to the imitations of flesh and bones, without exposing the bare mechanism of our animal nature."[34] It was the fact that the naked body was "continually before them" that allowed the Greeks to study, produce, and hone the forms that modern artists have been taught to emulate above all others. Citing Pliny and Galen, Carlisle makes the case that medicine fell into decline during the era separating Homer from Hippocrates, and that this actually fostered rather than prohibited the flourishing of art. All British artists, therefore, are better off drawing after casts and, above all, from conventionally beautiful life models rather than beginning with the interior of the body.

Bell had run against Carlisle for the role of Professor of Anatomy in 1808. A devotee of the *Anatomy of Expression*, Haydon saw Bell's loss to Carlisle as evidence of the Academy's inability to recognize greatness, and he would eventually fall out with the institution as a result of their perceived biases. "The Artists," he wrote in his diary, "will one day know the extent of the loss in selecting him for their professor"; the rejection of a "man so adapted, so delighted with art, ... so anxious to acquire and to communicate what he acquires" is a "Public misfortune to the Art."[35] Before he acquired Bell's *Anatomy of Expression*, Haydon's interest in the science had been peaked by John Bell, Charles's elder brother and fellow surgeon, author, and amateur artist. Published in 1793, John's book of engravings, *The Anatomy of the Bones, Muscles & Joints*, is similarly critical of the devotion to ancient statuary among modern practitioners.[36] Yet, unlike his brother, John praises the "delightful" Greeks as "the most beautiful people; sometimes happy, and always free."[37] He relies on the utopian and universalized conception of Greek civilization similar to that which suffuses radical discourse dating from the same phase in time. For John Bell, it is precisely the ease with which the Greeks lived from day to day that makes their art an unhelpful guide for living artists. He laments that the British do not enjoy the Mediterranean climate and more liberated attitude toward nakedness in public life. He declares unequivocally that no moderns will ever have the luxury of total bodily freedom, and consequently their imitations of Greek forms are sure to be "cold." [38] Therefore, artists should study the mechanisms of the living human body instead of copying casts. Prior to this text, the idea that the cold and wet climate negated the possibility of a thriving artistic culture in Britain had been espoused on the Continent by Winckelmann and others before him.[39]

Still an Academy student at the time, Haydon was probably in the audience when Carlisle gave his first lecture as Professor of Anatomy. Reporting on the event, an author in the *Monthly Magazine* reveals that the surgeon seized the opportunity to rehash the argument he made in his recent anti-anatomy article only in reference to the Parthenon Marbles. To dramatize his point that the representation of the figure ought to be informed by statuary and life models rather than an advanced understanding of the inner workings of the body, Carlisle brought Bob Gregson, a champion pugilist, up onto the stage. The surgeon proceeded to map "geometrical diagrams" onto the athlete's musculature, proclaiming that his body came nearer to the proportions of the Theseus from the Parthenon than any other model.[40] This was no isolated event. Under a year earlier, Carlisle had invited the leading Academicians to his house for breakfast, and when they arrived, they had been greeted by Gregson "stripped naked" and posing like various well-known statues.[41] In contrast to the exhibition of living female bodies I explored at the start of this chapter, Gregson's display was not just for show. Guests were told to get right up close so that they could annotate the fine details of the boxer's body. Joseph Farington reports that "all admired the beauty of His proportions from the Knee or rather from the waist upwards, including His arms, & small head. The Bone of His leg West sd. is too short & His toes are not long enough, & there is something of heaviness abt. the thighs,—Knees, & legs—but on the whole He was allowed to be the finest figure the persons present had seen."[42]

Later that month, Gregson was brought to Lord Elgin's house on Pall Mall, where he was ordered to pose among the Parthenon Marbles to give a side-by-side comparison of his body in relation to the fragments.[43] While the boxer was seen to possess a physique that resembled sculpture, he still embodied a specific idea. As a Lancashire-born prize-fighter, his very existence could defend against the claim that the beautiful body was at odds with British national identity and the cold climate of the British isles. In his anti-anatomy article, Carlisle had conceded that the temperate Greek climate "allowed of a more considerable exposure of the human body than the climate of Northern Europe," yet the surgeon did not see this as an impediment.[44] His employment of Gregson was a way of trying to silence the environmental determinism that made this fact relevant to contemporary British art. In the *Gedanken,* Winckelmann states that the human form was more beautiful in Greece than it is in modern times, an argument echoed by Wollstonecraft in the *Vindication.* At over six feet tall, Gregson provided a nationalistic icon of ideal beauty that could vie with Greek exemplars in spite of his allegedly "too short" leg bone, toes and heavy thighs. The fact that Gregson was no ordinary British man but an exceptional athlete reveals the obsolescence of the political appropriation of Winckelmann's ideas of Greece and freedom. Gregson had worked to achieve his beauty. Beauty was not a birthright as, according to Winckelmann, it had been for the Greeks, or perhaps could be in a liberated Britain, according to the radicals.

Once the Marbles arrived they began to rupture the common understanding of what actually constituted "the antique." It could now be suggested with authority that *Apollo Belvedere* represented a decadent phase of classical sculpture. The visible anatomy of the Parthenon Marbles fed into the growing consensus that not only were the *Apollo* and other sculptures taken by French troops mere copies of Greek originals, but that these "originals" were made in a period of decline rather than bloom.[45] Winckelmann posits the *Apollo* as a representative of the "Beautiful" phase of art in relation to the Phidian "High" style, placing supreme value on the smooth contours of the figure.[46] In the *Apollo*, all is sealed, devoid not only of any outward signs of the internal functions of the body, of veins and organs, but also of an accurate portrayal of the play of muscles through the skin as the body stands in contrapposto. The Marbles included the bulging of bowels through the abdomen, passages of wrinkled flesh, irregular joints and flexing muscles. The contrast between these two manifestations of the classical body was such that they could not be incorporated into the same cyclical narrative. Anything but crude, the Marbles provided a long sought after image of Greek, moreover fifth-century Athenian, authenticity. Their damaged condition only added to their aura of vitality, and the *Apollo* now appeared less like a fulfilment of their promise than a total disappointment of it.

Reliant on objects like the *Apollo*, utopian images of the classical body by Dreaming artists had officially been outpaced. William Hazlitt, Haydon's ally in the defence of the Marbles, quipped: "The Apollo Belvedere is positively bad ... a theatrical coxcomb, and ill-made, compared with the Theseus."[47] In an earlier essay, he plays on the competing temporality of the sculptures: "The Theseus is the age of Theseus: while the Apollo Belvedere is a modern fine gentleman."[48] At first, the dislodging of what previously constituted the ideal male body seemed to work to the advantage of contemporary British art. If London was home to more authentic examples of Greek sculpture than the collection in Paris, then surely art of the Royal Academy would flourish. One of the first to make this case was Reynolds's successor as president of the institution, Benjamin West, an early visitor to the Marbles at Lord Elgin's house on the corner of Piccadilly and Pall Mall. In an open letter to Elgin written in 1809, West declares that

> *unless England establishes the means of cultivating the exalted class of art within herself, she will never be entitled to participate with Greece and Rome in the honour they acquired in the fine arts. Yet I know no people, since the Greeks, so capable, as the inhabitants of this island, of emulating them in art, if rightly directed and patronized – For the British are a scientific and reasoning people in all matters which they undertake to investigate.*[49]

West's invocation of the "island" as a self-contained civilization, one that competes with the ancients rather than modern European nations, betrays the impact of Britain's isolation from the Continent during the Napoleonic Wars. West saw the purchase of the sculptures as the nation's one chance finally to excel in "the exalted class of art." His branding of the national character as "scientific and reasoning" speaks directly to the appearance of the Marbles: their visible anatomy that cast a decadent, feminized light on works like the *Apollo*. Several scholars have acknowledged the mobilization of the Marbles as "emblems of British national identity" during the period.[50] More than just trophies, the very appearance of the sculptures aligned with the nation's self-image as resilient, rugged, and autonomous as well as "scientific and reasoning."[51]

As early as May 1808, West had expressed his belief that the newly arrived sculptures embodied the "perfection of art, where *nature* predominated every where – and was not resolved to be obedient to a system."[52] When called upon to defend the Marbles during the Select Committee of 1816, he returned to the idea of a "systematic" formula: the *Apollo Belvedere*, "the *Torso* [Belvedere], and the *Laocoön* are systematic art; the Theseus and the Illissus [of the Parthenon] stand supreme in art"; in other words, the former sculptures are examples of a prescriptive norm, the latter representations of spontaneous reality.[53] When asked if the "close imitation of nature" that characterizes the Marbles "takes from or adds to their excellence," West answered that the "close imitation of nature visible in these Figures, adds an excellence to them which words are incapable of describing."[54] The sheer passion behind such praise of the Marbles helped to trap Banks's art in time. Quietly couched in extinct Dreams, sculptures like the Homeric relief and Banks's monument to *Captain Burges* re-emerged as examples of the "systematic" approach. It is true that Banks studied corpses, and that in terms of its musculature, his naked captain manifests a slightly more advanced understanding of anatomy than do the classical sculptures that were known to the sculptor. Yet the radical sculptor's investment in anatomical detail was nothing like that conveyed on the surface of the Parthenon Marbles, figures that, in West's words, appear to be captured at the instant "they were converted into marble."[55]

For authorities like West and Carlisle, the Parthenon Marbles made the study of anatomy even less useful, as now there was a Hellenic paradigm that could assume its place, teaching students far more eloquently how the outward play of bones, musculature and organs ought to be portrayed. But while the Academicians were content to stop at the affinity between the Marbles and a figure like Gregson, Haydon sought to go deeper. He went on to forge a conception of the body that drew immovable divisions between what he perceived to be different species of man. He was first given permission to draw the Marbles in the spring of 1808, around the time his elders were comparing the sculptures to the form of the boxer. Having exhibited his early history painting, *The Repose in Egypt*, at Somerset House in 1807, Haydon was already known as a promising young artist with great ambition. By 1812, he had formulated his own terminology for the opposition between two versions of the classical body: what he

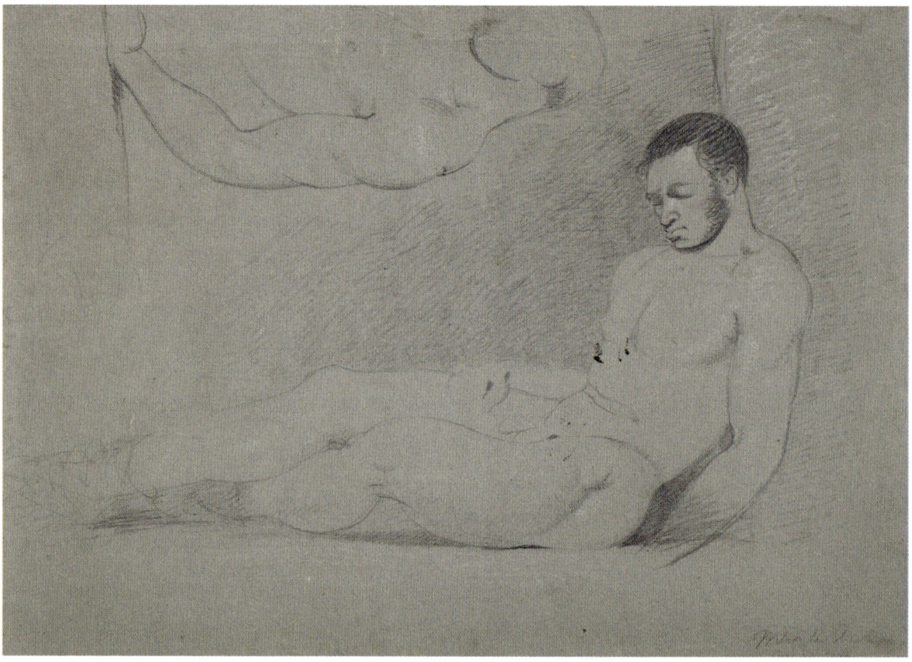

81 Benjamin Robert Haydon, *Wilson the Black*, 1810, chalk on paper. British Museum, London.

designated the "old antique" was synonymous with West's "systematic" category – the *Apollo*, *Venus de' Medici*, the work known as the *Antinous* – everything with minimal or inaccurate traces of anatomical information. The paradoxically older Parthenon Marbles were categorized as "new antique." Haydon contextualized the "new antique" with reference to Charles Bell's *Anatomy of Expression*, cancelling out the author's disavowal of all ancient sculpture and developing a theory of ideal form based on the assertion that Phidias himself had made the interior of the body his point of departure. Recalling one of his long stretches spent sketching the Marbles, Haydon conveys the rapture he felt at the thought of "contemplating what Socrates looked at, and Plato saw"; "I have prayed to God to enlighten my mind to discover the principles of those divine things," he continues, and "I have inward assurances of future glory."[56] These heady encounters with the Marbles led him to align his subject position, and his own body, with Phidias himself.

— THE "GREEK STANDARD OF FIGURE" —

Haydon's interest in racial science was informed not simply by his study of anatomy together with ancient sculpture, but by a chance encounter two years after he first saw the Parthenon Marbles. In August 1810, weeks before Saartjie Baartman went on display as the "Hottentot Venus," Carlisle came across an African-American sailor, newly arrived in London from Boston, with limbs that called classical sculpture to mind. Carlisle was treating the sailor at St. Bartholomew's Hospital for a minor injury when he noticed that his patient's body, like Gregson's, was extraordinarily formed. Excited by what he perceived, Carlisle brought the man, named Wilson, to West and the painter Thomas Lawrence, West's successor as Royal Academy president. The latter is said to have pronounced Wilson "the finest figure he had ever seen, combining the character & perfection of many of the Antique Statues."[57] Joseph Farington reports that Lawrence was enthralled to find that when Wilson's arm was "suspended it appeared like that of the *Antinous*; when contracted for exertion it was like the *Farnese Hercules*."[58]

Word of Wilson got round to Haydon. The artist borrowed £30 from his friend Leigh Hunt to employ the sailor privately for the entire month of September, the very month the show of Baartman opened to the public. The "flexibility and vigour" of Wilson's movements became an indispensable guide for Haydon, helping him advance his knowledge of anatomy and, in turn, the means by and extent to which such knowledge is conveyed on the figures from the Parthenon.[59] In one of his drawings of Wilson, the artist places the figure in the position of the Theseus from the east pediment (fig. 81). Like the sculpture, the model appears in a fragmented state, with no substantial feet or hands. His legs bend and open to the same angle as the sculpture, but with his back against the wall, his figure conveys a sense of exhaustion at odds with the alertness of the Theseus. Although Haydon's drawings of the Marbles were made under different conditions, a comparison between one of his depictions of Theseus and this drawing of Wilson reveals the overlap between these forms in the artist's mind (fig. 82). The sculpture may be viewed from a different angle, but in both images the convex of

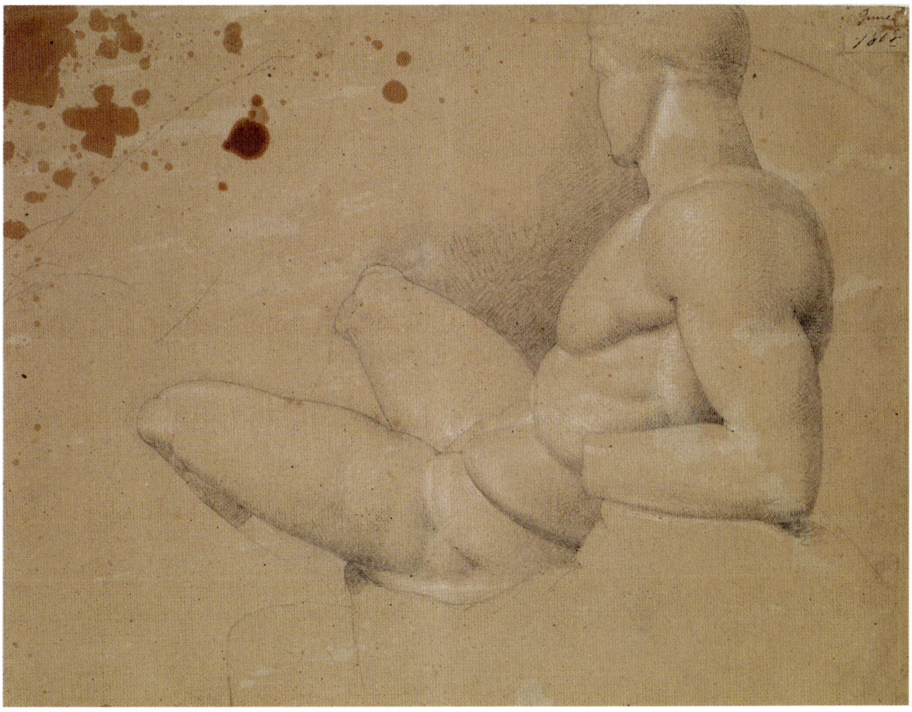

82 Benjamin Robert Haydon, *Theseus*, 1810, chalk on paper. British Museum, London.

certain muscles are heightened by chalk and the contours of the gluteal muscles are pronounced by slight shading in black along the width of their hips and upper thighs. This technique Haydon uses often, but in these two images the integration of light on muscle renders the materiality of flesh and stone interchangeable. Wilson's trunk and legs have the density and gravitational pull of marble, and there is a vitality to Haydon's shading of the sculpture's surface, as well as the relaxed air he affords the sculpture.

In his diary that month, Haydon drew connections between the Marbles, Wilson's body, and Bell's *Anatomy of Expression*. By "Antique" he means the "new antique" or the Parthenon Marbles:

> *the great beauty of the Antique and fine nature is the flexibility of the loins ... Such was [Wilson's] beauty and power that whether in action or relaxation, his forms expressed either more perfectly than I ever before saw them in Nature – the moment he moved, his intentions were evident – this great principle was more strongly than ever impressed upon my mind – that the form of a part depends on the action – he had that perfect suppleness that one felt but never saw – his joints were exquisitely clear – every head of bone, having insertion of tendon – but marked by delicacy and feeling – in repose they became undulating beauties & in action vehicles of energy and refined activity ... I was now convinced from Nature that one great cause of action & strength as I had before observed in the antique was the parts to be moved always to the smaller and depending on the parts moving.*[60]

In Wilson, Haydon saw the Marbles' dynamic manifestation of anatomical knowledge – the "flexibility" of the sculptures – come to life. Charles Bell's influence is relayed via Haydon's insistence that as soon as Wilson moved, "his intentions were evident." In the introduction to his *Essays on the Anatomy of Expression*, the author emphasizes his central tenet that an understanding of the muscles is crucial to "preserving a minuteness of intention" in representations of the body performing any action.[61] What is today called "motor cognition" Bell terms "intention": the brain's activation of the body parts required to carry out a movement, "the muscles and tendons" being "the means by which [man] moves [the bones] as his passions excite him."[62]

In addition to stressing the reciprocity of thought and movement, Bell's text also implies that brain of the "negro" is smaller than that of the white European. Intermittently, the surgeon suggests that the "negro" is inherently brutal, closer to "lower animals" like monkeys and quadrupeds.[63] In a footnote, Bell concedes that "the variety of Africans must be admitted," yet he persists in pitting the white European – possessor of the "common skull" – against the specter of a racial stereotype that is implicitly male. Like the female form, the body of the "negro" is invoked as an abstraction that allows for little or no variation. This was a relatively recent assumption. As Aris Sarafianos explores, earlier observations on black physicality are capable of acknowledging difference from person to person.[64] But with the emergence and growth of racial science, a discipline with which Bell, if not strictly one of its practitioners, was clearly well versed, the singular "negro" evolves into a fantasy figure. With scientific epistemology nominally on its side, this fantasy pretends to contribute to a rational discourse when really it relies on myth and superstition about the bodies of non-whites. Of course, there is no one monolithic African or black physiognomy, nor is there a single European type. In Bell's text, "the negro" is distilled to the same degree as the implicitly white female figure who has "skin smooth" and "limbs round."[65]

In order to establish himself as the artist capable of carrying the classical body into the new age, Haydon needed to convince others of his genius. That his own specific, biological identity placed him above others was one way of achieving this end. He latched, therefore, onto the fantasy of the "negro" contained in Bell's text. One conclusion of the argument that those of African descent are inferior was that Greek and British men are genealogically related, both part of an elite corporeal category at the top of a steep hierarchy. This hierarchy does not take the traditional shape of a pyramid with the smallest group at the apex but rather is shaped like an upside-down pyramid with the distilled, monolithic "negro" at the bottom and the expansive British-European-ancient Greek class of men at the top. Racial scientists deploy another hierarchical model that takes the shape of a chain. With roots in the writings of Plato and Aristotle, the "great chain of being" places God at its supreme station and various minerals at the lowest, with man closer to the divine than animals, then plants. In Haydon's youth, this structure was adapted to theorize racial difference. The white European man was seen to sit closer to God, higher than white women, the implicitly male "negro" and the spectral "negress."[66]

Startling contradictions should already be evident in Haydon's theories. On the one hand, Haydon's time with Wilson – "a perfect Antique figure alive" – appears to have convinced him that people of African descent were on a par, physically at least, with the models employed by Phidias. He describes the sailor as "a perfect model of beauty and activity" and continually praises his form.[67] His drawings of the sailor depict a body barely distinguishable from his sketches of other tall, muscular British-born models. There are certainly no traces of stereotyped physiognomy. Yet Haydon did not employ Wilson as a fellow man, an equal, but as a tool for his private use. The sailor's body helped the artist comprehend what he saw as the foremost aspect of the Parthenon Marbles: their "flexibility" and demonstration of cognitive intention in relation to action. As a tool, Wilson could also be used to elevate the artist's own subject position. While sketching Wilson, he painstakingly searched for "deficiencies" and marks of brutality on his "negro" body. At times he lists these characteristics; concluding that "Blacks in their form approach that of those who are deficient in intellect," he states that his time with Wilson had affirmed the veracity of the kind of racist thinking suggested in Bell's *Anatomy of Expression* and expressed plainly in other, more straightforwardly racial-scientific texts: black peoples' "lobes of ear [are] small, their teeth frequent, lower jaw retreats, the scull is diminished – they have longer bodies, longer fore arms, greater projection of elbows, deficient deltoids."[68] Such passages are sandwiched in between references to the sailor's perfect beauty, which according to him possessed "something of the Discobolus."[69] These contradictions are certainly confusing for the reader, but that is what makes Haydon's output such an invaluable insight into the flimsiness of racial science as an epistemology and way of seeing.

Hugh Honour makes the case that Haydon's racist diatribes are a "ritual gesture, as it were, to current and omnipresent anthropological theories."[70] Other scholars acknowledge Haydon's reading of Charles White, the British obstetrician who wrote the definitive text arguing that all Africans are essentially brutes who will never be capable of civilization or intellectual achievement of any kind due to their position lower down the "immense chain of beings."[71] An adherent of polygenetic theories of racial origin, White was one of the chief agents of the synthesis of beauty and intellect inherent to the discipline of racial science, insisting that the "white European ... being the most removed from the brute creation, may ... be considered as the most beautiful of the human race."[72] Reading White, it becomes clear where Haydon sourced much of his vocabulary: "having the skeleton of a negro amongst others in my museum," writes the obstetrician, "I measured the radius and ulna, and found them nearly an inch longer than in the European skeleton of the same stature."[73] Conscious of the instability of his distillation of the "negro," White claims to have pursued "the comparison with a great number of living subjects, before any fair induction could be obtained" by measuring "the arms of about fifty negroes ... and found the lower arm longer than in Europeans."[74] He goes on to mention an anomalous "negro skeleton" with arms that are "no longer than the medium of Europeans."[75] But while this skeleton forces him to accept that "Africans, as well as Europeans, are liable to some variation," he stresses that "one or two exceptions have no force against the general inference."[76] This skeleton was kept in St. Bartholemew's Hospital, the very site of Wilson's discovery twelve years later.

Like the anomalous skeleton, Wilson could have been the exception to the rule. Indeed, Haydon too was forced to allow for discrepancies, admitting that when it came to the link between anatomy and intelligence there were guaranteed to be persons with the physical characteristics of brutality but without the corresponding mental deficiencies, although "exceptio regulam probat."[77] But, as we know, the artist made it clear that his conclusions on "negro" physiognomy were directly informed by his contact with Wilson. His drawings of the sailor, however, suggest that these claims were not supported by his perception of the figure but indicate another motive. In one of these images the sailor faces the viewer; his limbs, musculature and even genitals appear in harmony, and he has a handsome face. The artist has measured his body in seven heads and three-quarters, the same as the "best-proportioned figures of the ancients" (fig. 83).[78] His forearms do not appear to be longer than his upper arm bones; his skull and deltoids are a normal size. Yet when he recalled his time with Wilson in his autobiography, begun in 1839 and published posthumously in 1853, Haydon still claimed to have found in the sailor all "the positive marks characteristic of brutality. Beautiful as his form was, his calf was high and feeble, his feet flat, and heel projecting, his forearm as long as his arm-bone, his deltoid short, his jaw protrusive, and his forehead receding."[79] His drawings record none of these observations, only an artist mapping out, through the

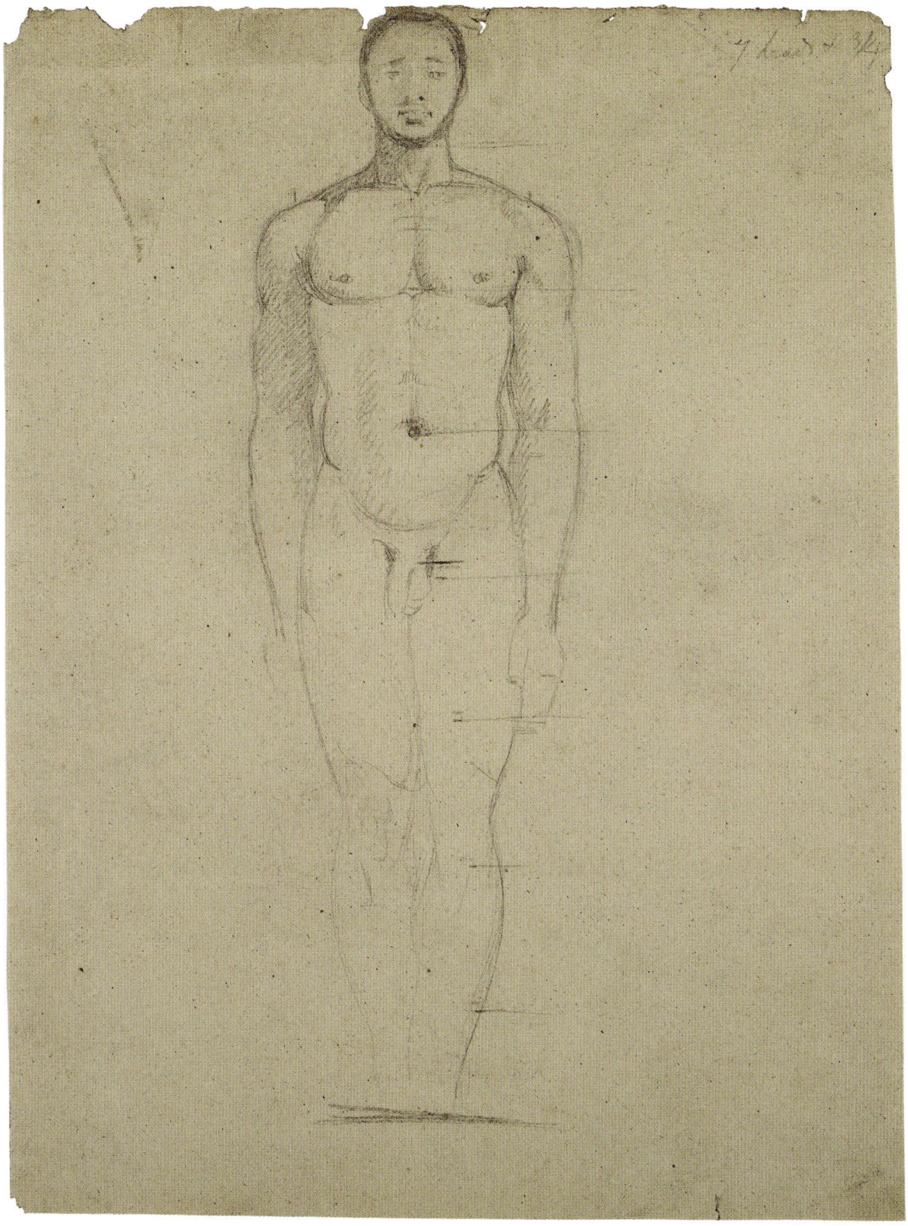

83 Benjamin Robert Haydon, untitled (7 heads & ¾), 1810, chalk on paper. British Museum, London.

careful study of a conventionally beautiful life model, how the classical body could be rehabilitated.

In 1811, exactly a year after his month with Wilson, Haydon went public with his racial-scientific views. Writing under the pseudonym "An English Student," the artist became embroiled in a month-long debate in the *Examiner* over the relationship between different "racial types," in which he argued that white Europeans are superior to all Africans in terms of innate mental and physical formation. His congruent claim that the ancient Greeks are the ancestors of white

Europeans was nothing new. Bindman notes the "growing assumption towards the end of the [eighteenth] century and beyond that ancient Greece at its height represented Europe's Golden Age," while Martin Bernal has explored the "Hellenomania" from the same period that saw ancient Greece as possessors of a northern European bloodline distinct from ancient Egypt.[80] Yet Haydon's incorporation of art, specifically the Parthenon Marbles, as evidence for this claim was unprecedented not simply because the Marbles were recent additions to the canon of ancient sculpture. I agree with David Higgins that Haydon "believed the greatest art to have the same claims to represent objective truth (in ideal form) as modern science."[81] This conviction is one of the factors distinguishing Haydon most starkly from the radical Dreamers. For Haydon, the classical body could represent the "naked truth" in a more literal sense than in the works of Banks. The Parthenon Marbles were not just art, they were an articulation of scientific truth. Again, it is a paradox that the kind of science that encompassed his theories was shrouded in myth and superstition.

The debate in the *Examiner* was sparked by the story of Paul Cuffee, a black man from Massachussetts who had arrived in Liverpool that year after sailing from Philadelphia to Sierra Leone. Cuffee and his all-black crew were embraced by officials in London and managed to raise funds for their mission of social and economic improvement in the British colony at Freetown. The status of black people in England appeared to be rising. That same year, Arthur William Hodge, a British plantation farmer in the Virgin Islands, had been executed for the murder of Prosper, one of his slaves: the first, and last, time a slave owner was sentenced to death for cruelty. Both Hodge's trial and Cuffee's success generated a sense of possibility after the Slave Trade Act of 1807 made illegal the trading of black people in the British Empire. This was the context for Haydon's contrary point of view. The debate began when Hunt, the paper's editor (who had lent Haydon the money to employ Wilson), wrote an article praising Cuffee for his ability to rise above prejudice. Hunt praises Cuffee's "truly interesting" appearance, his "good countenance" and "manly presence," concluding with the suggestion that a monumental sculpture be erected commemorating the Slave Trade Act, an advancement which, while proving the nation's interest in the freedom for all humankind, simultaneously allowed England to assert superiority over Napoleonic France:

> *the Abolition of the Slave Trade – will render our parliament, even in its corruption, more illustrious to posterity than the senators of* BONAPARTE *… False glory has her pillars and her statues without number, and tyrants attempt to look dignified in marble with slaves fettered and writhing at their feet. Why is not a monument erected to our glory, surrounded with freemen and surmounted with the statue of England; it should be as magnificent in size, and as beautiful as art could make it; and that no emblem might be lost, it should be useful as well as glorious, and form a mighty sea-mark for the mariner.*[82]

Here Hunt voices an opinion not unlike that expressed in Banks's censure of Napoleon back in 1802. Recall that, in his letter to Cumberland sent after the

Treaty of Amiens, the sculptor accused the consul of undoing the work that the Jacobins had begun to bring about liberty for slaves.[83] Unfortunately, however, Hunt's idea of a commemoration of England's intervention is overshadowed by a remark earlier in the article: "It is not to be denied," writes Hunt, "that the negro, at present, and as far as we know him, exhibits an inferior animal character to the white man."[84] Haydon did not wade in until a mysterious commentator, writing under the name "Niger," wrote to the paper attacking Hunt's assertion. Niger passionately defended black people against Hunt's racial typology. "It was not because they exhibited an inferior animal character to the Whites that they were made slaves of," writes Niger, "but because they are a most robust and hardy race, that can live and undergo great toils in climates where White men cannot labour, and can hardly live."[85] Haydon wrote to the journal expressing his belief that black people are not only "beings of degraded intellect," of "unintellectual brutality" but that their very physical forms prove their innate "incapabilities."[86] After setting out his "scientifically" informed opinions on the essential characteristics of black people, Haydon promises to prove his convictions "by a reference to the divine works of the inspired ages of Greece."[87]

At various points in the debate, Haydon cites the writings of Charles Bell, the German naturalist Johann Blumenbach, the Dutch anatomist Petrus Camper, and arch-racial scientist Charles White. It was largely due to White that Camper's so-called "facial angle theory" was misappropriated in Britain as an illustration of varying cognitive abilities. Based on the drawings of Albrecht Dürer, the theory presents a spectrum of profiles organized by angle formed by the slant of the forehead as it intercepts the nose and jaw, from a tailed monkey to the head of the *Apollo Belvedere* (fig. 84). Miriam Claude Meijer has explored how Camper's theory, originally designed to assist artists in the portrayal of various faces, was used to further the agenda of racial scientists.[88] From the 1790s onward, it was consistently misinterpreted so that the very name "Camper" became synonymous with racial science. The facial angle theory re-emerged as an illustration of varying cognitive abilities, and an affirmation of the idea that there are different species of human.

By the time of the debate, Haydon had arrived at the opinion that the Parthenon Marbles were "finer ... ten thousand times finer" than the *Apollo*.[89] For now, however, the "old antique" would still have to serve as a paradigm of male beauty and superior intellect. Unrestored, the Theseus is damaged in such a way that his profile is marred into a jagged line, as are the faces of some of the figures in the Parthenon's metopes and friezes. With Haydon's exemplar in a profile-less condition, the painter is not able to revise Camper's facial angle theory with his more authentic ancient head in place of the *Apollo* and its decadent "Roman air."[90] Yet he does manage to forge a link between the Marbles and his racial ideal. To do this he turns not to ancient but to living Greeks:

> *oppression and brutal habits can no more make a Greek a negro, than education can elevate a negro to a Greek; – the great Author of the universe has fixed links, one after the other ... education can no more make a negro a Greek, than a monkey*

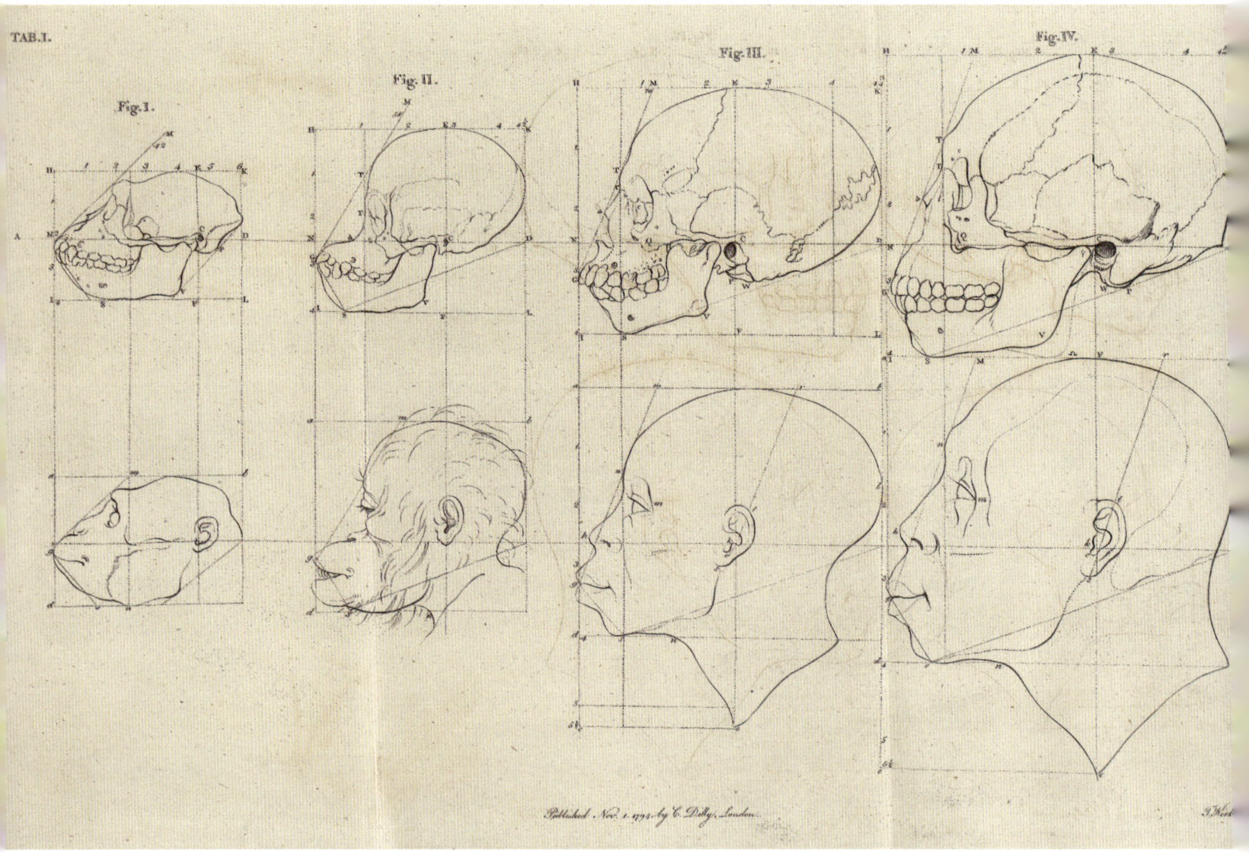

84 Thomas Kirk after Petrus Camper, illustration of the facial angle theory. Printed in *The Works of the Late Professor Camper* (London: C. Dilly, 1794), Table I. Yale Center for British Art, New Haven.

a negro, or a lion a monkey, or a mineral a lion ... a Greek may be a debased Greek, but his nature cannot be totally changed ... But the Greeks are not brutalized or barbarians: there are still men in Athens who relish Homer; who are still refined; who are still sensible to the tyranny they suffer; who, as they wander amid the ruins of the mighty Parthenon, in the twilight of a silvery dawn, or the silence of a golden evening, look back with desponding enthusiasm on the days of their intellectual grandeur.[91]

In spite of their colonization by the "brutal" Turks, modern Greeks, like the British, remain superior in the "chain of being."[92] The fact that the ghostly ruins invoked by Haydon no longer possessed their sculptural ornaments goes unmentioned. During the same month as the debate, Haydon wrote to the *Examiner* criticizing those who dared to accuse Lord Elgin of having "ravaged" the Parthenon. It was God's will that the British save the "exquisite Remains of Grecian Genius" from the "brutal," implicitly swarthy Turks.[93]

By perpetuating the misreading of Camper, Haydon helped the anatomist's theories migrate from artistic practice to the field of racial science. But Haydon goes further, wrenching the "facial angle theory" out of its technical context and into daily life: "Look at the first Negro you meet," he rails, "have him in; compare his face with Camper's drawings" and one will see that they are "mathematical and accurate."[94] But when Haydon had actually met a black person a year earlier and brought him into his home, the results had not yielded anything like the anatomist's drawings. The study of Wilson in which the sailor is placed in the position of the Theseus is the only drawing in which the sailor's face is shown in profile, and in this image there are no traces of a pronounced facial angle. When black people feature in his finished paintings, their appearance is strikingly different. As Higgins notes, the dark-skinned figure at the left of the artist's 1814 *Judgement of Solomon* possesses Camper-esque physiognomy, with a facial angle conspicuously more acute than those around him.[95] Ironically, the muscular, half-naked body of Solomon could be based on Wilson.

In Haydon's later *Punch or May Day*, a genre scene on the scale of a history painting, two black figures appear (fig. 85). The first is a groom standing at the back of a carriage as it navigates the crowded street. The darkness of his skin is brought into relief by the pale gray pillars of the Palladian church behind him and the stiff white collar around his neck. The second figure, some kind of street

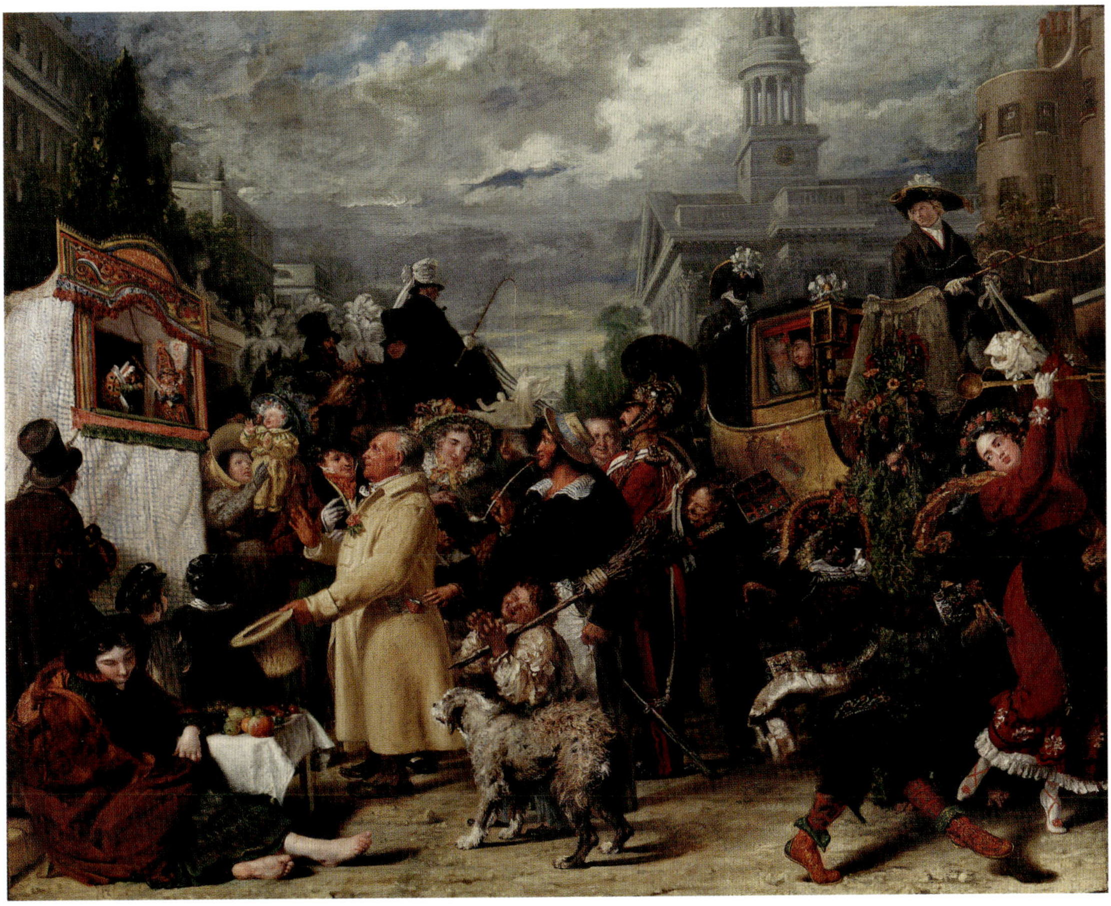

85 Benjamin Robert Haydon, *Punch or May Day*, 1829, oil on canvas. Tate Britain, London.

performer in exotic dress, skips across the right corner of the foreground. This figure seems to be younger and has a delirious smile that contrasts with the groom's buttoned-up mien. There is something strangely synthetic about the latter's features and the unevenness with which his face has been colored. Were it not for his equally sable fist emerging from his brocade cuff, it would appear that the figure is made up in black face. Knowing what we know about Haydon's inconsistent declarations on the "negro," this quality can be explained by the painter's integration of stereotyped physiognomy where he knew it had no bearing on visible reality. Neither of these figure's faces is portrayed in profile, making it impossible to assess their facial angles. Yet they have more in common with the black figures in William Hogarth's genre paintings in that they are caricatures or abstractions. Unlike Hogarth, Haydon was not consciously attempting caricature; the other figures in the painting have studied faces that strive to be anatomically accurate in their expressions and gestures. The discrepancy between the black and white figures in *Punch or May Day* underscores that the increasing specificity with regard to the representation of the human form did not apply to men of African descent. The same rings true for female figures. Each woman in the painting has largely identical features that conform to the artist's own ideal of female beauty seen across his *oeuvre*: milky complexions with pink cheeks, vividly contrasting dark hair and rosebud lips. This is a further indication of the way in which racial science authorized the distillation of female figures as well as black men. In the *Account of the Gradation of Man*, White digresses to praise the "soft features of the beautiful women of Europe" epitomized in the "bosom of the European woman, two such plump and snowy white hemispheres, tipt with vermillion."[96]

Haydon's drawings of Wilson were for private use, but such paintings for public display. The artist's racial scientific declarations, whether written or painted, were always for others to see. Haydon knew that the classical body needed to be rehabilitated if it was to survive the turn against universalist principles. The wielding of scientific "truth" marked him out from his predecessors, including Winckelmann. Drawing contrasts between white Europeans and black Africans fractured the very notion of humanity into disparate pieces.

The *Examiner* debate was a precursor to Haydon's official revelation of his theory on the relationship between Greek sculpture and anatomical science, which he wrote not under a pseudonym but as himself. It was not until the eve of the decision on whether or not the Parthenon Marbles were to become part of the national collection that his conclusions were published. Despite the support of Carlisle, West, Lawrence, and a host of other leading artists (Flaxman among them), others were unsure of the Marbles' worth. The connoisseur Richard Payne Knight, a leading member of the "Committee of Taste" and the Society of Dilettanti, did not believe that they dated from the fifth century. At the Select Committee he stated his belief that some, if not most, of the sculptures were added to the Parthenon in the first century AD, during the reign of Emperor Hadrian.[97] Even though he was not a collector of large-scale sculptures, Payne

Knight had spent too much of his life fixated on the "old antique" to allow his expertise to be overruled. Likely the one responsible for the captions criticizing Howard in *Specimens of Ancient Sculpture,* Payne Knight was prone to mocking the aspirations of British artists.[98] Although Payne Knight did not actively discourage the government from purchasing the Marbles but rather suggested their second-rate status, Haydon was furious about the connoisseur's unwillingness to join the chorus attributing them to the age of Pericles. He decried that the "conceited, vain glance" of the connoisseur was privileged over the "investigating principles & practiced search of the Artist."[99] So, in 1816, before the fragments' purchase had been confirmed, Haydon published an essay entitled "On the Judgment of Connoisseurs being Preferred to that of Professional Men."[100] This was his manifesto imparting the theory he had been formulating since 1808 when he first glimpsed the Marbles. Toward the middle of the article, Haydon segues from bashing the likes of Payne Knight into his definition of "the great Greek standard of figure":

> *First, to select what is peculiarly human in form, feature, and proportion; then to ascertain the great causes of motion; to remember that the opposite contours of a limb can never be the same from inherent formation, nor a trunk if the least inclined from the perpendicular; that the form of a part varies with its action or its repose; and that all action is by the predominance of some of the causes of motion over the others, for if all were equally to act the body would be stationary ... This is the standard of man's figure as a species, and the principle by which to estimate the period of all the works of antiquity.*[101]

Once more, correlations emerge between the language Haydon uses to describe the form of Wilson. So rarely seen in nature, the sailor's combination of "beauty and power" not only facilitated the artist's comprehension of the fragments, but helped him lay claim to the comprehension of how Phidias conceived them. Throughout his career, Haydon referred back to this essay. By the time of its publication, his self-imposed status as an authority on the Parthenon Marbles had been authorized when, a year earlier, he had been given permission to obtain some of their first plaster casts.[102] After the nation agreed to purchase the hoard from Elgin for £35,000, Payne Knight's reputation was ruined, and Haydon's status as the Marbles' chief advocate crystallized in the public eye.

Even in the definitively unidealized *Punch or May Day,* painted over a decade after the Marbles' acquisition, Haydon was not able to put his obsession with the sculptures to rest. Notice at the heart of the work two white statuettes placed on top of a board carried on a man's head (fig. 86). The one on the left is the Theseus, the one on the right is the *Apollo Belvedere,* an allusion to the contrast between the "new" and "old antique." While their presence is hardly conspicuous, the statuettes' central position within the painting emphasizes the importance of Haydon's theories in the construction of his own identity: artistic, professional, genetic. The statuettes are his signature, reminding the viewer of the artist's status as the decoder of the classical body on updated terms.

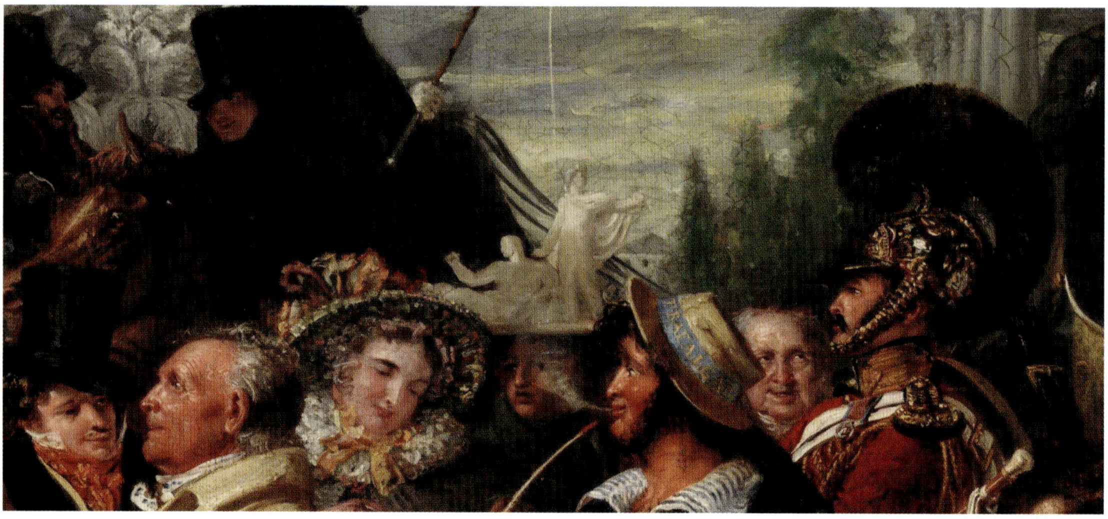

86 Detail from Benjamin Robert Haydon, *Punch or May Day* (fig. 85).

— FASCIST DREAMS, POEMS —

In the little scholarship mentioning Haydon's engagement with racial science, the impact of slavery is not mentioned.[103] Higgins is content to explain Haydon's reading of Charles White in relation to his own desire for greatness, a desire contingent with the quest to renovate British artistic practice. It is certainly the case that Haydon saw himself as "the prophet who was to lead British art out of the wilderness," and that he viewed the Parthenon Marbles as "a sort of miracle which proved that both [he] and Great Britain were blessed by God."[104] But the terms on which he sought validation for this mission can only be grasped when slavery is addressed directly. In their book *Black Personalities in the Era of the Slave Trade*, Paul Edwards and James Walvin do not mention Wilson, and still little is known of the sailor beyond his employment as an artist's model. But these authors do make a point that elucidates why the artist's encounter with the sailor authorized this painter's turn toward racial science: "arguments whether blacks were things or humans were no mere abstractions, debated in the rarefied atmosphere of the courts. Blacks were ... treated as objects in everyday social practice ... as long as slavery continued to survive in the British colonies (as it did until 1838) the view of the black as less than human would persist with the support of the law."[105]

Wilson's form was one of the means by which Haydon pursued his goal of becoming the nation's leading artist. His use of the model's body as a tool – a kind of ruler or protractor – illustrates the tendency that Edwards and Walvin emphasize: that because of Britain's leading role in the slave trade, all people of African descent were readily treated as objects. And if they are correct that "in the late eighteenth century slavery had become synonymous with blackness," then Haydon's sketching of Wilson, championing of a racist agenda, and declaration of his "great Greek standard of figure" can be seen as a tripartite way of sustaining what Agnes Lugo-Ortiz and Angela Rosenthal call the "logic of chattel slavery": the sanctioned brutalization and exploitation of people based on their color and ancestry.[106] So even though Wilson was being paid for his labor, the encounter between the two men was conditioned by both the practice and the ideology of slavery – that is, the false consciousness that allowed for the exploitation and exchange of human beings as if they were inanimate things.[107]

Looking at the drawing in which Wilson is placed in the pose of the Theseus, the model is pacified in order to be objectified. His closed eyes and bowed head convey the inactivity necessary for the technical use of his body. Wilson's complete disengagement from the spectator, in this case the artist, evokes the ritual of power inherent to enslavement. The painter's comment that he had "mastered" Wilson's form confirms this dynamic.[108] That the sailor, in this image, possesses no hands and feet denies him the agency of a free man. At the same time, this detail likens Wilson to the fragmented figure of Theseus while also betraying, I think, the conflict between what Haydon perceived with his eyes (Wilson's "antique" beauty) and the racial scientific theories the artist was imbibing, theories insisting that Wilson's extremities would be grossly out of proportion.

During their month together, Haydon did not just draw and write about Wilson. He also made casts of the sailor's body which he eventually included in a gift to Alexey Olenin, president of the Imperial Academy of Arts in St. Petersburg, along with the early reproductions of the Marbles and some more casts that had been overseen by the sculptor Richard Westmacott. In a letter to Olenin, Haydon explains his decision to include the casts of Wilson, now reduced to "the Negro":

> *In the fragment of the Negro's chest which I sent you, under the left arm-pit you will see the wrinkle of the skin. It is for this reason I cast the Negro, because in the movement of his body he developed the principles of the Elgin Marbles ... what other artist but Phidias would have ventured to put the wrinkle of human skin in the form of a God! ... Phidias knew that, as we could only represent a God by a human form, the finest human form, even if for Jove himself, must have had a heart, liver, and bowels, bones, muscles, and tendons, and a skin to cover all ... Now, Sir, you will find none of these effects of action or repose on the skin of the Apollo, or any other antique figure that we have hitherto admired; and it is this union of the truths and probabilities of common life, joined to elevated and ideal nature, that goes at once to our hearts and sympathies in the Elgin Marbles, and makes them superior to all the works of art hitherto known in the world.*[109]

Here Haydon openly declares what up until now he had only expressed in private: that Wilson's "flexibility" – articulated, among other places, in a wrinkle of skin under the armpit – served as a key by which he unlocked the principles that had governed Phidias. His words confirm that the sailor's body yielded capital for the artist, in this case cultural capital rather than goods such as sugar, tobacco, or cotton. Wilson allowed Haydon to lay claim over the sculptures, synthesizing the painter's subject position and that of the Greek sculptor. Racial science was there to reinforce the idea that Haydon and Phidias were connected by their God-given advantages. As a classical body, Wilson's form became a vessel for this claim.

According to the 1853 autobiography, Haydon had almost killed Wilson while making the casts by suffocating the sailor with plaster. Following several minutes of "senselessness" Wilson recovered, leaving Haydon with "the most beautiful sight on earth ... the impression of his figure [taken] with all the purity of a shell."[110] Whether this actually happened – and we can never be sure with Haydon's retrospective accounts of his earlier life – the anecdote is telling of the artist's motives. As Wilson loses consciousness and becomes an inanimate object, his form is transfigured into a pristinely white container, moreover something that Haydon can use to advance his reputation overseas.

About a century later, the projection of white supremacy onto classical and classicizing art re-emerged in the context of fascism. From Mussolini's Foro Italico to the films of Leni Riefenstahl, Greco-Roman antiquity was appropriated for propagandistic purposes, deployed as an agent of the movement to preserve the perceived purity of the so-called Aryan race. Bernal's *Black Athena* traces the roots of this phenomenon in eighteenth- and nineteenth-century scholarship, exploring how the Greeks were re-envisioned as racially superior.[111] Many of Bernal's protagonists were Haydon's contemporaries, including Wilhelm von Humboldt and Karl Otfried Müller, German historians whose writings paralleled the development of racial science and had complementary aims.[112] Haydon was also close friends with Mary Russell Mitford, cousin of the British historian William Mitford, who, Bernal suggests, is also partly responsible for the bleaching of Hellenic civilization that began during these years. Like the radicals I looked at in the first chapter, these authors were invested in an image of Greece that is utopian in its elevation of the Greeks to an "almost godlike" realm.[113] The vital difference between the radicals' conception of Hellenic civilization and that of the nineteenth-century scholars is the latter's divisive rather than egalitarian agenda.

One only has to glimpse the photo of Mussolini and Hitler admiring Antonio Canova's *Paolina Borghese as Venus Victrix* to gauge how representations of the classical body made by artists under consideration in this book fed directly into fascist ideology (fig. 87).[114] But far more than Canova, it is Haydon who might be considered a forerunner of the sculptor Arno Breker, whose creations combine Phidian anatomy with a masculine rigor coextensive with the racial ideal of Hitler, Breker's patron. Indeed, I have established Canova as a Poet rather than a Dreamer, the appreciation of his sculpture among fascists testament to the atemporality of his works rather than an index of his own subjectivity. Cultivated throughout his career, Haydon's Dream consciously sought to reorder humanity using the Parthenon Marbles as proof of the superiority of white Europeans on the "great chain of being." It is usually Michelangelo who is considered the inspiration behind works such Breker's *Readiness*, a gleaming bronze sculpture of a naked Aryan ideal that Hitler intended to dedicate to Mussolini (fig. 88). During the Third Reich, however, Breker could be compared just as frequently to Phidias.[115] Walter Grasskamp reflects on how the undeniably skilled Breker "sacrificed his artistic identity to the dream that art and state might one day function together."[116] Haydon, like Breker, was a political artist who sought to intervene

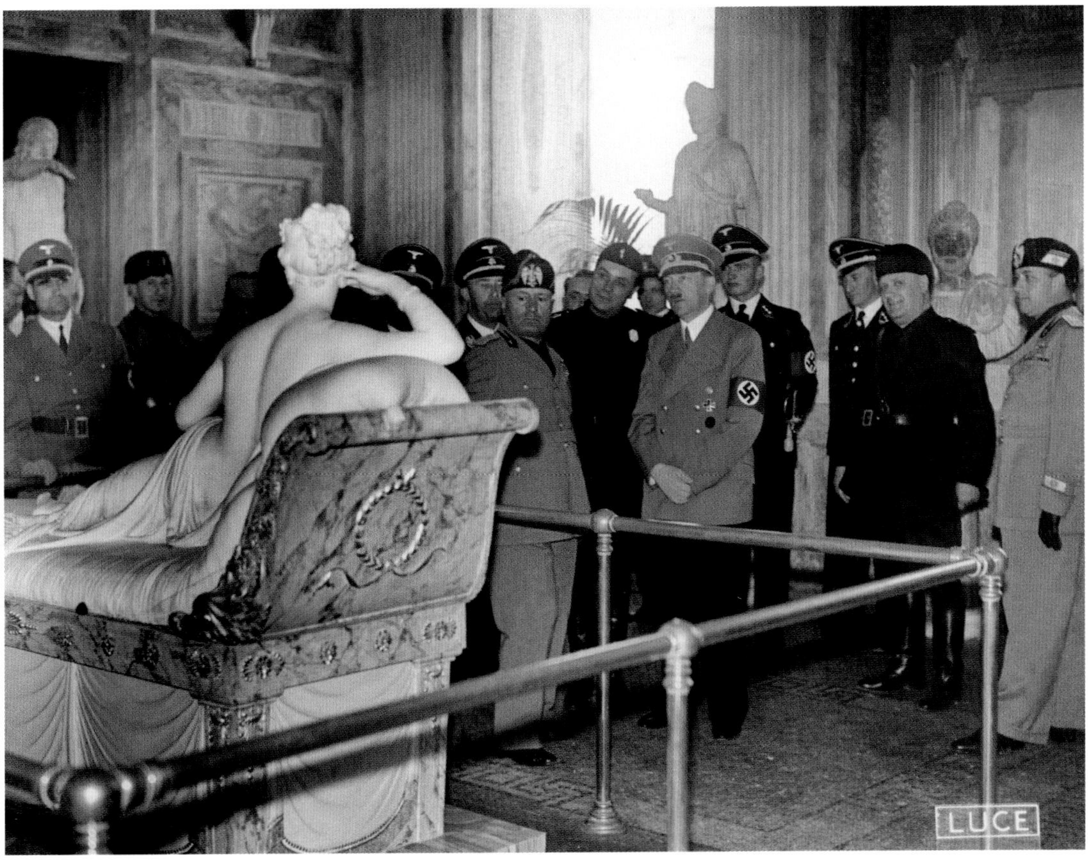

87 Galleria Borghese: Hitler and Mussolini admiring *Paolina Borghese as Venus Vectrix* by Antonio Canova, 1938, photograph. Istituto Luce Cinecittà, Rome.

88 Arno Breker, *Readiness*, 1939, bronze. Private collection.

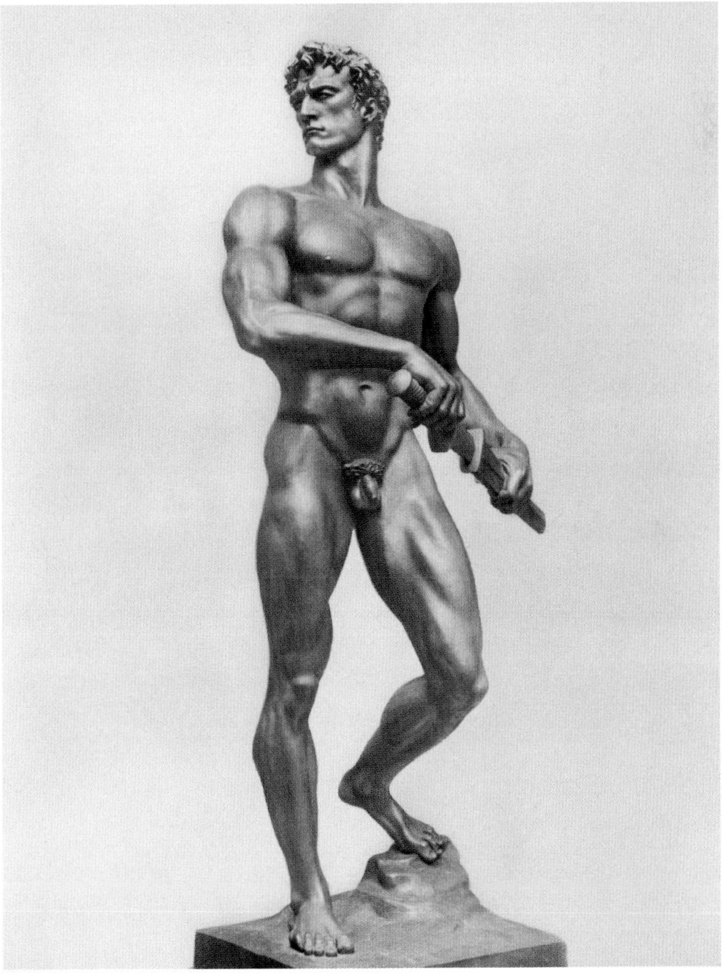

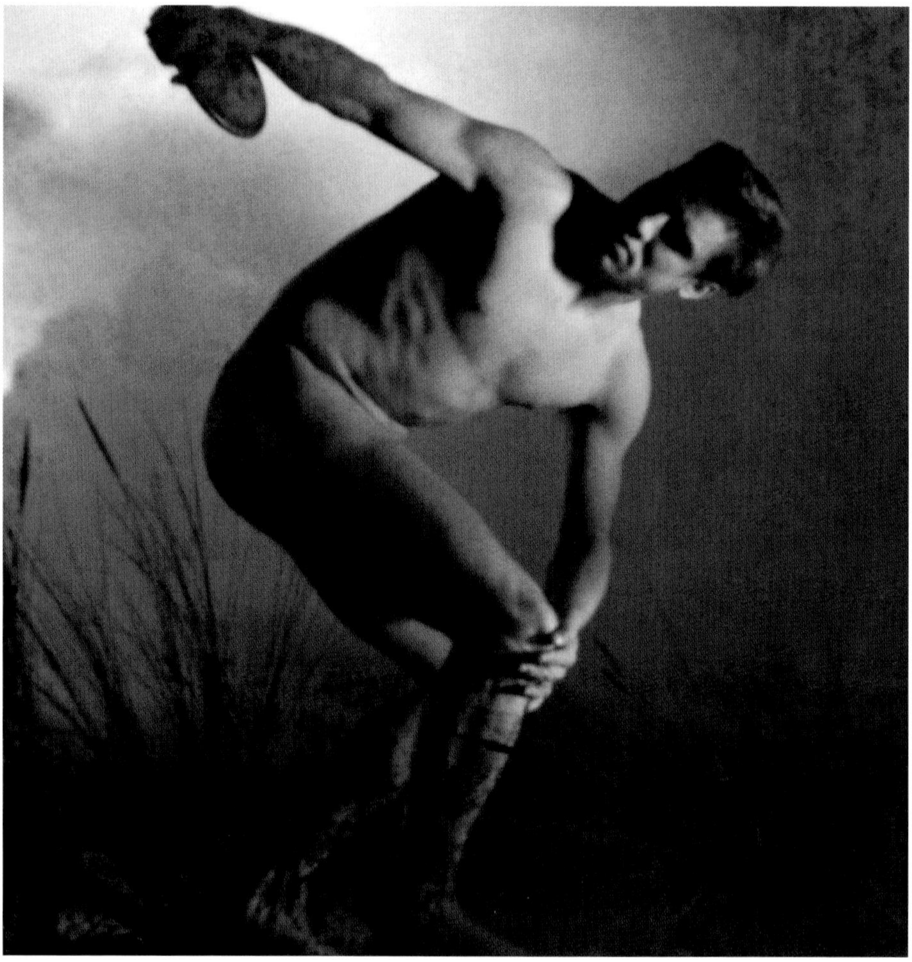

89 Still from Leni Riefenstahl, *Olympia*, 1938.

in the workings of the world rather than "pour out a balm." The Scottish painter David Wilkie applauded him for his participation in the *Examiner* debate as if he were vying for an seat in Parliament: "you had shown a much better acquaintance with the subject, more general learning, and a more philosophical way of reasoning than any of the modern political pamphleteers on the other side."[117] Wilkie is apt to conceive of Haydon as a kind of far-right activist. The painter's comments on black physicality invoke certain passages of *The History of Jamaica* by Edward Long, the plantation owner, defender of the slave trade and proponent of ideas that found legitimacy in racial science.[118]

Susan Sontag posits "the turning of people into things" as one of the defining desires of fascist ideology.[119] This is one of the many common grounds between slavery and fascism. But there are key differences between Haydon and fascist appropriations of Greece. Despite the theoretical value he placed on ancient sculpture, we find that the non-black male figures in his finished paintings are not always general impressions of a white racial ideal but often, as in *Punch or May Day*, particular individuals whose imperfections and bodily and facial expressions are informed by the strain of anatomy pioneered by Charles Bell. Although well-versed in racial scientific texts, Bell would have held the purified idealism of Breker at arm's length precisely because it reduces representations of the human form to an all too "perfect beauty."[120] Idealized bodies, writes the anatomist, "are scarcely ever to be transferred to the representation of the human body; and a modern artist who indiscriminately follows such a model, misapplies the noblest lessons of his art."[121] Likewise, the Parthenon Marbles appealed to Haydon because they are imperfect, their surface intruded upon by veins and wrinkles of flesh under the armpit.

By the time fascists acquired power, a monolithic image of the beautiful white man had been reborn. Depictions of the naked male body by Nazi artists, such as those that filled Munich's Haus der deutschen Kunst, "were forbidden to show any bodily imperfections"; in the words of Sontag, they "look like pictures in male health magazines: pinups which are both sanctimoniously asexual and (in a technical sense) pornographic, for they have the perfection of a fantasy."[122] This fantasy was projected onto living bodies as well works of art. The 1936 Olympic games are the subject of Riefenstahl's *Olympia*, a film whose defining scene consists of the Greek sculpture known as the *Discobolus* (a work that Haydon had likened to Wilson) dissolving into the body of German athlete Erwin Huber (fig. 89).[123] As Sontag suggests, there is lack of eroticism about such images that conforms to my definition of Dreaming art. In addition to the desire "to vex" the world, this aneroticism is what connects Riefenstahl's propaganda to all of the Dreaming works I have looked at so far. But the "fantasy" element identified by Sontag is the factor that distinguishes Nazi art from Haydon's technical attempt to champion white supremacy with reference to Greek sculpture. In order for the Dream of racial purity to take hold, it needed to possess sensual – that is, Poetic – qualities. Breker achieved this via the lustrous patina of his bronzes, Riefenstahl through her consummate cinematography: the aspect of her practice that has salvaged her reputation as a filmmaker from the taint of Nazi ideology. Haydon's refusal to make his forms sensual led to failure. The vessel could no longer hold without spilling out onto the surface.

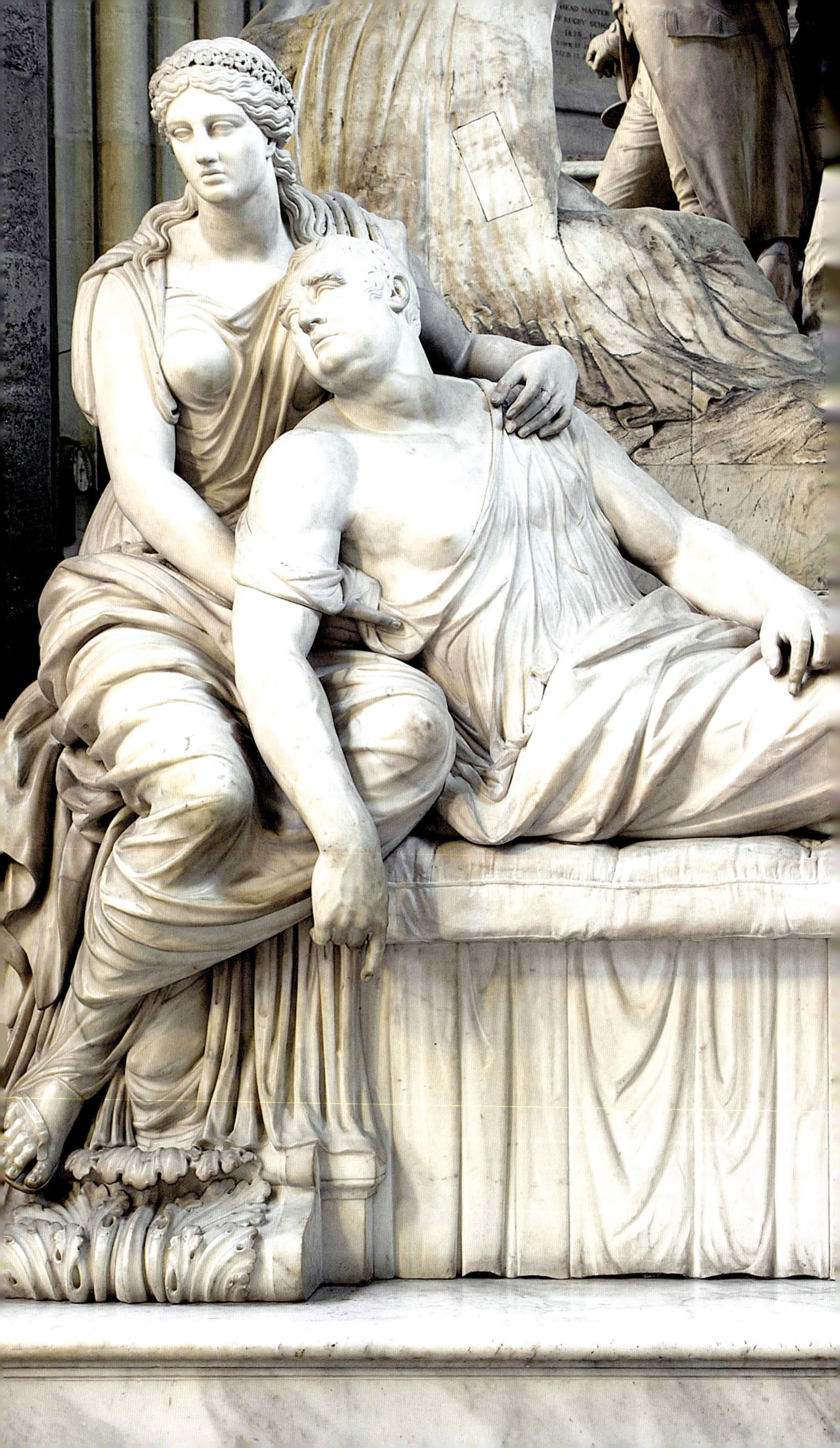
HEAD MASTER

CHAPTER FIVE

POETIC VICTORY

Among his fellow painters, Haydon's fixation on anatomy did not gain traction. Plagued by debt, even imprisoned on two occasions, he failed to earn a living from any cultural capital gained from his attempt to rehabilitate the classical body. As with Howard, the isolation of painting from sculpture had a detrimental effect on his career. Unlike Howard, however, his paintings were not the kind that could be reproduced as engravings within mass-produced periodicals, and after falling out with the Royal Academy in the years around the Parthenon Marbles acquisition, he did not have the option of supporting himself with a professorship. Between 1815 and 1823, Haydon was able run his own private art school based on the study of anatomy and congruent rejection of the "old antique."[1] Several Pre-Raphaelites, the next generation of artists to condemn the Academy's biases, greatly admired him, although less for his theories than for the memory of his rebellious persona.[2]

If Haydon had been a sculptor, he may have had more success. With the Parthenon Marbles as its exemplar, his theory of the primacy of anatomy inevitably had more of an immediate relevance to sculptural practice. Although he cannot take credit for fuelling the various Parthenon-inspired sculptures produced in the wake of the Marbles' acquisition, several are in accordance with his "great Greek standard of figure." At London's Royal Mews, William Theed's tympanum, *Hercules Taming the Thracian Horses*, dates from the year of the Select Committee, and appropriates the metope of a Lapith fighting a Centaur.[3] The veins along the barrel of both horses betray the newfound legitimacy of precise anatomical detail. Designed by the architect Decimus Burton and completed in 1828, the frieze on the entablature of the central arch of the Hyde Park Screen is based on the Parthenon frieze, capturing the sense of spontaneous action that characterizes its reel of overlapping cavalry.[4] Most strikingly, the monument to *Charles James Fox* in Westminster Abbey indicates the sculptor Richard Westmacott's willingness to embrace the Marbles' revision of the classical body (fig. 91). The composition of the group is based on two of the draped females from the east pediment: the figure of Fox assumes the position of the figure reclining in the lap of a seated companion, who in turn becomes a personification of Liberty (fig. 92). The impact of the Marbles' rendering of anatomy is consolidated in the kneeling figure of Africa at the base of the group, a detail acknowledging Fox's instrumental role in passing the Slave Trade Act

90 Detail of Richard Westmacott, *Charles James Fox*, 1816 (fig. 91).

of 1807. This figure manifests an advanced understanding of the interior of the body not previously demonstrated to such an extent in classicizing British art. With its dignified physiognomy, this figure is no caricature, nor is it merely a life-size amplification of the shackled kneeling form on Wedgwood & Co.'s famous cameo, *Am I Not a Man or a Brother?* Every detail of the subdermal structure is attentively carved without exaggeration, especially on the neck and along the arms and the lower leg where the calf presses against the back of the thigh, making Fox's flesh look all the more doughy, the female allegories all the more blank. There is a possibility that this figure may be based on Wilson. Having overseen the production of some of the casts sent to Russia along with "the fragment of the negro's chest," Westmacott was in contact with Haydon while the monument was in its early stages.[5] Given what we know about Haydon's need to broadcast his own expertise, it is likely that the painter would have explained to the sculptor, as he soon would to Alexey Olenin, the continuity he perceived between Wilson and the Marbles. As a black man seen to possess the qualities found in the most revered ancient statues, Wilson offered a template for how to represent an idealized free man in three dimensions. While Haydon's private use of Wilson's body mimics the logic of slavery, the same model's form could feature in a public work of art that supports abolition. But Westmacott – who sculpted more than one monument to a slave-owning plantation owner – was not actively putting forth a counter to Haydon's white-supremacist Dream by mending the Banksian

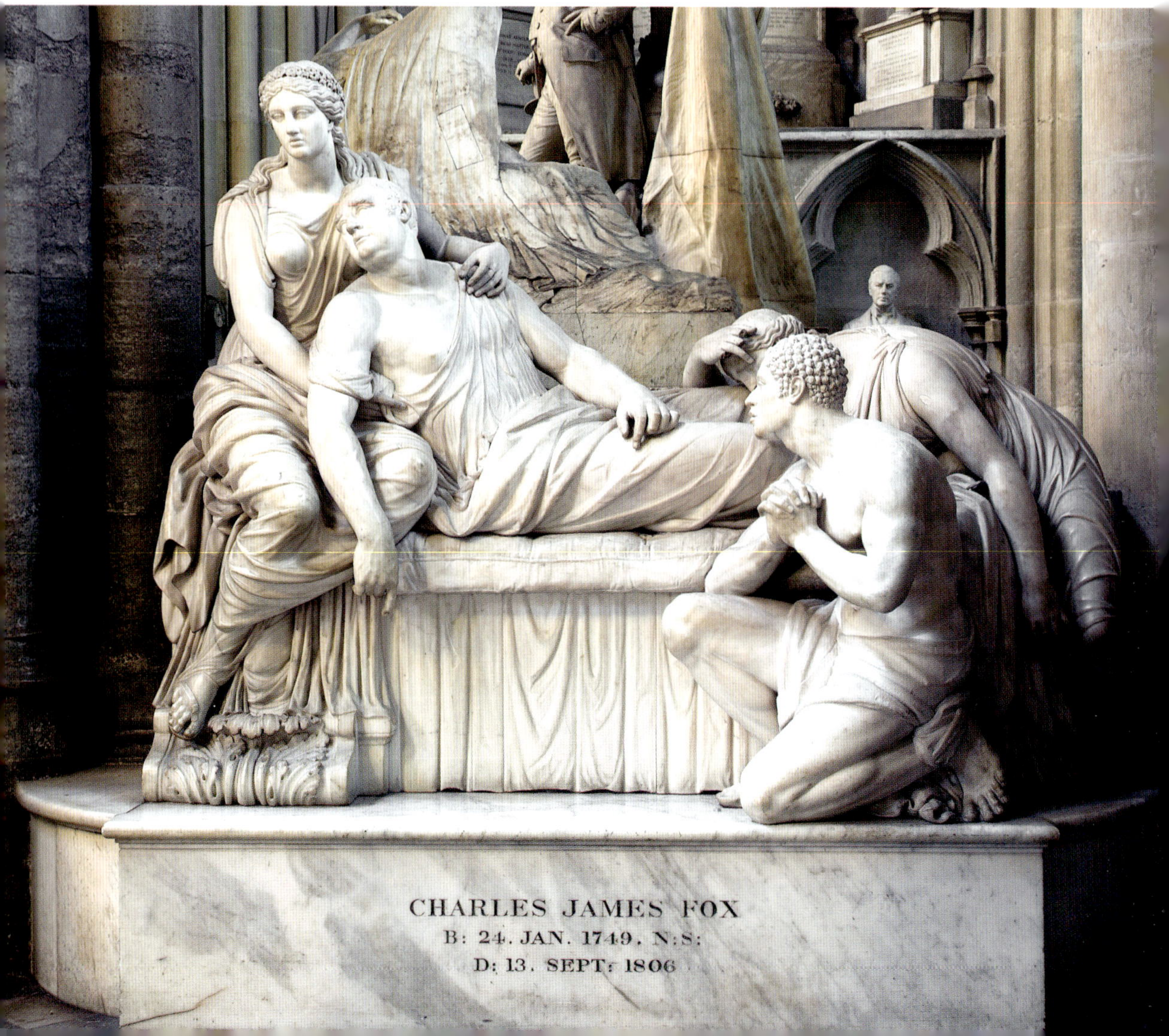

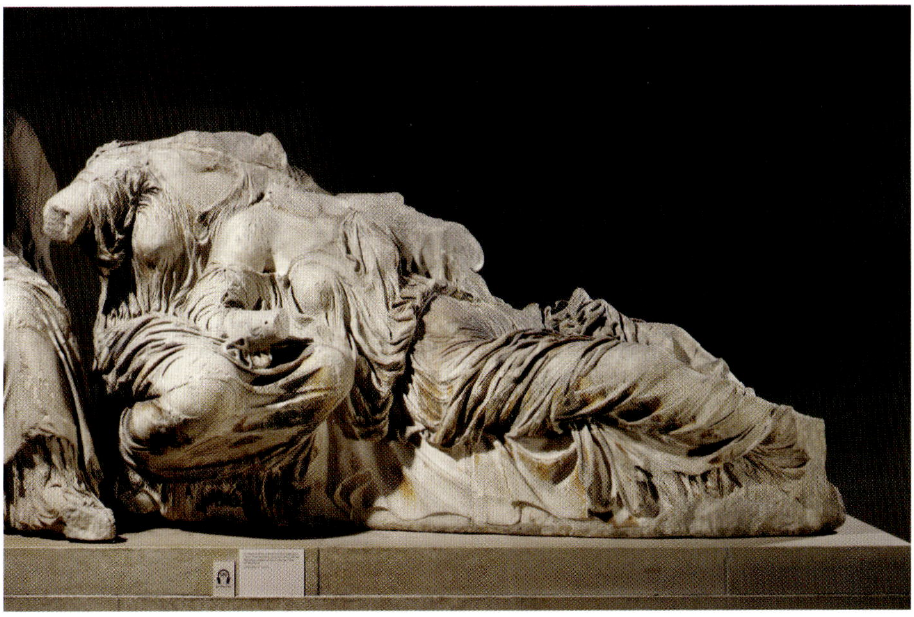

tie between the classical body and freedom via the figure of Africa.[6] Rather, the monument to *Charles James Fox* is similar to John Flaxman's monuments dedicated to Napoleonic war heroes in St. Paul's Cathedral: a straightforward tribute to the deceased subject with no other agenda injected into its forms. Haydon's investment in the Parthenon Marbles may have been more immediately applicable to sculpture, but the politicization of the classical body was as obsolete in sculpture as it was in painting. Apart from the case of Haydon, political Dreams had, by this point, been drained from all manifestations of the classical body.

Sculptors, then, accepted the prioritizing of anatomy but not the Dream that, for Haydon, had accompanied it. Charles Bell insisted that his so-called "anatomy of expression" would have more traction in painting as it was the more progressive art form allowing for a greater scope of bodily and facial expression. In practice, however, the advanced anatomical knowledge promoted by Bell and developed by Haydon was more likely to be appreciated in sculpture because in painting the naked male body was increasingly pushed to the margins. Even Haydon was not forthcoming in introducing naked male forms into his exhibited works, forms that would give him the opportunity to show off his adherence to the *Anatomy of Expression*, the Parthenon Marbles, and his fusion of the two on racial-scientific terms. Likewise, Benjamin West declared that his entire approach to painting had been set on a new course after his exposure to the Marbles, yet the paintings he executed after their arrival leave little room for him to demonstrate such profound influence. West informed the Select Committee that both his *Christ in the Temple* (better known since as *Christ Healing the Sick*) and his

91 Richard Westmacott, *Charles James Fox*, 1816, marble. Westminster Abbey, London.

92 Workshop of Phidias, east pediment of the Parthenon, fifth century BC, marble. British Museum, London.

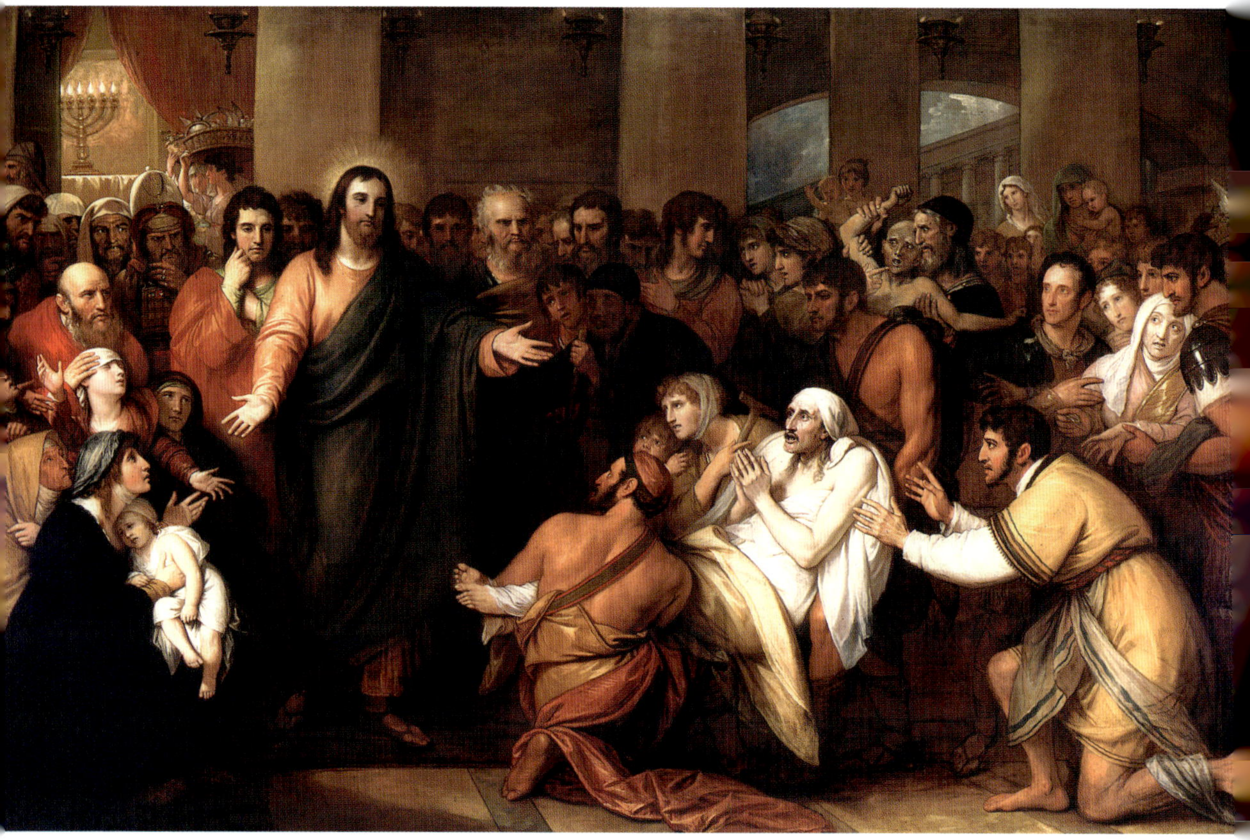

93 Benjamin West, *Christ Healing the Sick in the Temple,* 1811, oil on canvas. University of Pennsylvania Art Collection, Philadelphia, Pennsylvania.

Christ Rejected manifest his deviation from the "systematic" ideal represented by the *Apollo Belvedere* in favor of Phidian spontaneity (fig. 93).[7] Exposed human forms, however, have only a peripheral presence in these paintings. While they do feature male figures with a more intricate anatomy than those in the artist's earlier works, their subjects allow little room for the total revelation of the body one might expect from West's testimony. In spite of their identification of a schism within the canon of Greco-Roman sculpture and their readiness to embrace the Theseus over the *Apollo,* Haydon and West chose biblical subjects that complicated a straightforward emulation of the fragments they so passionately stood up for. Voiced in art criticism, the nationalist turn placed pressure on artists to choose subjects with more of a bearing on life in Britain. For history painters like West and Haydon, this ushered a move toward biblical as opposed to mythological imagery, the exception being the approach shared by Etty and Howard: mythological imagery filtered through Shakespeare, Spencer, and Milton.

When Charles Lock Eastlake, a former pupil of Haydon, placed a naked man front and center in his 1827 *Spartan Isadas,* he signalled a new dawn in the representation of the classical body in British painting (fig. 94). Emptied of the ideological content it once harbored, by now this variety of idealized human figure – here in the vein of Jacques-Louis David and French Revolutionary painting – could be appreciated solely as an expression of a beautiful form. Hence although Eastlake had studied the Parthenon Marbles, he persisted in emulating the "old antique," an approach to the classical body that his own teacher had argued was inauthentic and misguided (unsurprisingly, Haydon was also scathing about David's art).[8] Going on appearance alone, *The Spartan Isadas* could be a work by Howard. Yet the twenty-year age gap between Eastlake and the elder artist separated this particular painting from the taint of Dreaming classicism, and, unlike Howard's neglected paintings, *The Spartan Isadas* was purchased by one of the nation's leading patrons of contemporary sculpture: William Cavendish, Duke of Devonshire. Chatsworth House, the duke's residence, is still known for its collection of marble figures, groups, and reliefs featuring modernizing evocations of the "old antique," most of which postdate the acquisition of the Parthenon Marbles. The orientation of the collection is an eloquent articulation of the afterlife of works in Winckelmann's canon. Now that their "pure" Greekness was exposed as a fantasy, these objects came to possess a different kind of appeal. On a material and ocular level, sculptures like the *Apollo* and the *Borghese Gladiator* (the latter the source for Eastlake's figure) continued to offer an appealing image of the beautiful body, one aligned with the growing preference for sensual surfaces and non-prescriptive stagings of the human figure. David Bindman writes of French critic

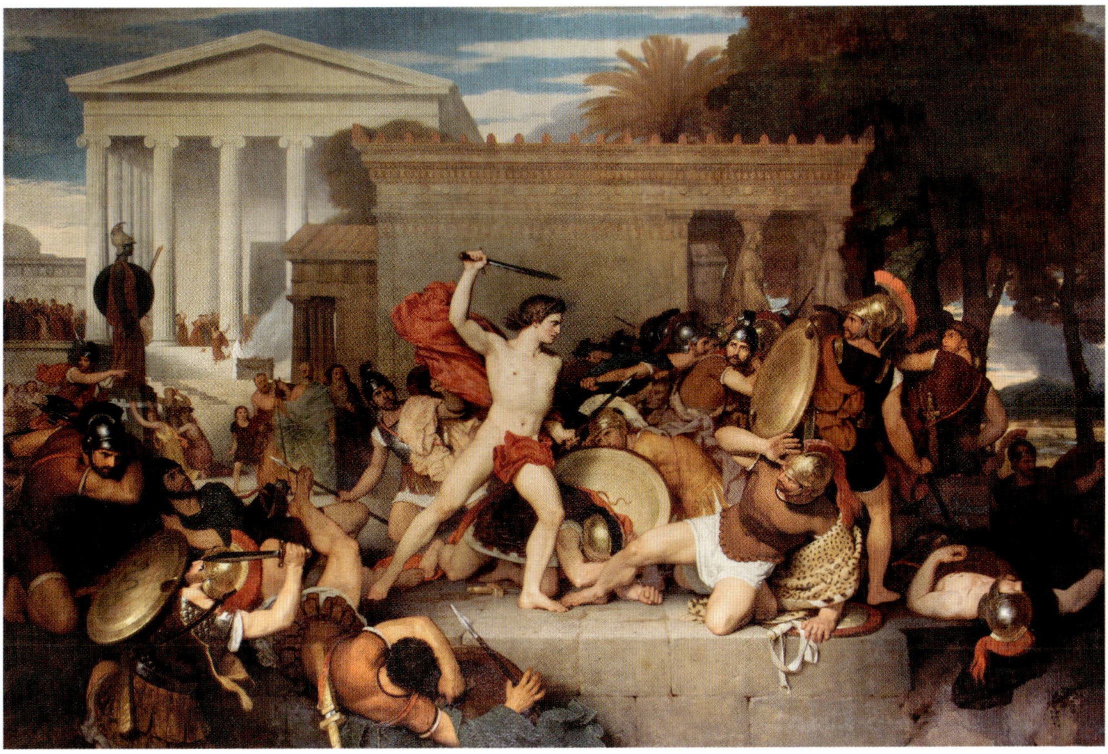

94 Charles Lock Eastlake, *The Spartan Isadas*, 1827, oil on canvas. Chatsworth House, Derbyshire.

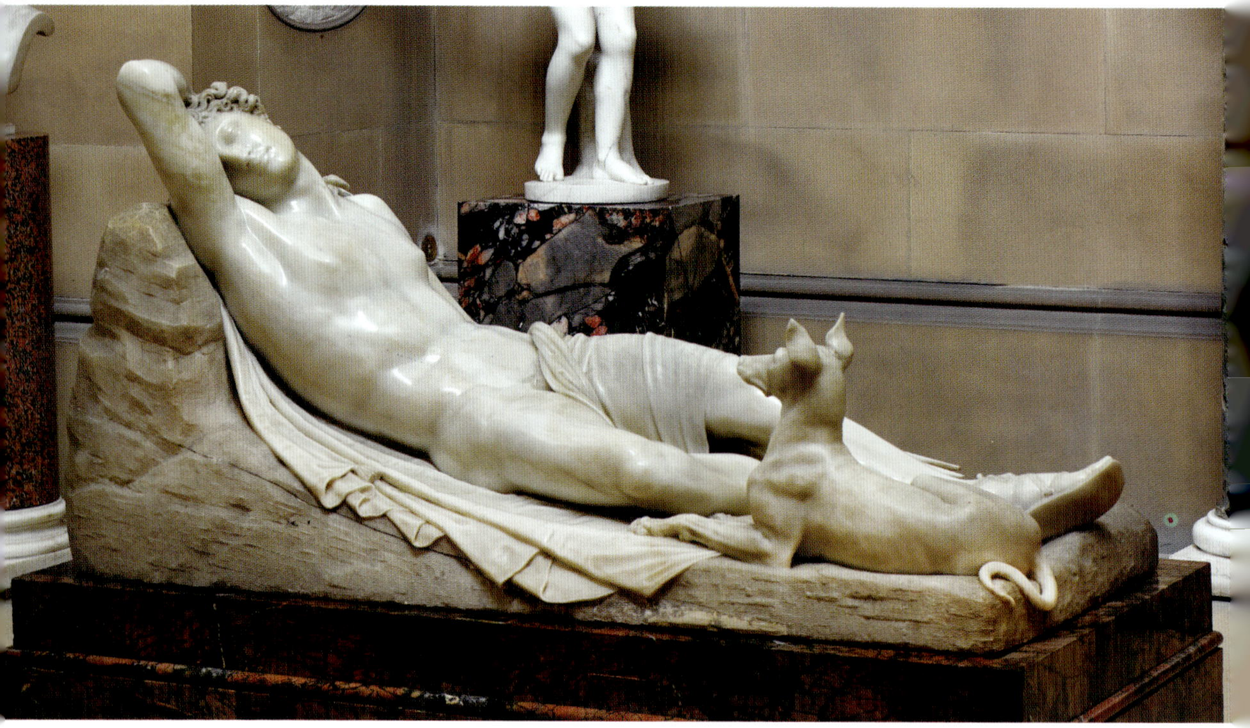

95 Antonio Canova, *Sleeping Endymion*, 1819–22, marble. Chatsworth House, Derbyshire.

Quatremère de Quincy's claim, backed up by ancient commentators, that such latter-day sculptures were originally coated in wax to soften their appearance, enhancing the beauty and fleshiness of the figure and producing forms that are "soothing to the eye" (in other words balm-like).[9] Whether or not this was an actual practice, de Quincy's claim encapsulates the idea that the latter-day classical sculptures, even when restored by modern practitioners and worn by centuries, are inherently pleasing to the senses in the way that the fragments from the Parthenon are not. Twentieth-century scholars of ancient art describe classical sculptures from the fourth century onwards, particularly those in the tradition of Praxiteles (such as the *Venus de' Medici*), as "impressionistic" and "expressionistic."[10] In contrast to the anatomical precision of the Marbles, they seem to value the "impression of visible appearances" over the "knowable form of physical reality."[11] In this context, the word "expression" does not mean the accurate representation of thought and intention as it did for Charles Bell. Rather, because they manifest a superficial rather than scientific view of the human form, such sculptures are held to be relatively "expressionistic" in the twentieth-century sense of the term: subjective and emotionally driven. As I noted, Winckelmann deemed such figures "Beautiful" in relation to the earlier "High" style, believing that the *Apollo* and the *Gladiator* represented the flourishing of Hellenic "perfection."[12] Haydon, West, and Hazlitt came to see them as models of a feminine sculptural aesthetic that did not suit their personal orientations as artists and critics. Haydon used the word "muzzy" in reference to the "old antique" statue known the *Antinous*, an adjective suggesting that his distaste for the figure stemmed from its hazier, softer, more sensual formation.[13]

But precisely for the reasons Haydon, West, and Hazlitt came to reject all ancient sculpture that was not the Parthenon Marbles, many – most, in fact – were unwilling to relinquish the pre-Elgin image of the classical body, the kind copied and imitated by Hellenistic and Roman practitioners. Although Canova lavished endless praise on the fragments after his trip to London in 1815, his own practice did not readily accommodate the straightforward emulation of the Marbles that subsequent scholars argue it displays. Bindman and Satish Padiyar are convinced of the claim made by de Quincy that Canova's *Sleeping Endymion* at Chatsworth sees the sculptor translating his reverence for the fragments into an original work of art (fig. 95).[14] I would argue that, in spite of its more life-like aspects, particularly with respect to the representation of muscles and flesh around the abdomen, Endymion's languid pose neutralizes the anatomical knowledge manifested in the Marbles. When he managed to spend some one-on-one time with Canova in London in 1815, Haydon unquestionably would have stressed his conviction that an advanced degree of anatomical knowledge is represented in both the Illissos – the figure from the west pediment that de Quincy sees as the inspiration behind Canova's *Endymion* – and the Theseus. It may be true that, for Canova, the rendering of anatomy was not the defining characteristic of the Parthenon's figures, but that they had other qualities making them worthy of emulation. Yet, coupled with the complete inertia of the *Endymion* in contrast to the Illissos's dynamically twisting torso, the polished surface of Canova's work suggests the sculptor's unwillingness to give up the pre-Elgin ideal and the soft, "soothing" effects de Quincy had rhapsodized about before the Marbles became known. With its lustrous patina and abstraction of the human figure into a long, molten ember of a form, Canova's work exaggerates the "impressionistic" and "expressionistic" qualities of latter-day classical sculptures to such a degree that a self-consciously inauthentic body is produced. Canova's fidelity to the deauthenticated model of Greek form is only one aspect of the *Endymion*'s atemporality. The patron, too, encouraged the sculpture's break with monolithic exemplars and specific periods in time. When commissioning the work in 1819, Cavendish let Canova have free rein on choosing the subject but did, for guidance, name two earlier works as examples of what he admired most within the sculptor's *oeuvre*. These were not salon sensations such as his celebrated statues of Venus or his *Psyche Revived by a Kiss*, but rather adjunct figures in funerary monuments: the Genius on the tomb of Pope Clement XIII in St. Peter's Basilica and the Genius on the tomb of Maria Christina, Duchess of Teschen, in the Hofburg Palace.[15] With their large wings akin to those in Roman baroque sculpture, these two ephebic Geniuses represent Canova at his least scientific and his least Greek. Their status as adjunct forms on monuments authorizes their limp, planar flesh and lack of subdermal detail. That the Genius in St. Peter's is asleep evidently spurred Canova on to select a subject involving a male body at rest. But there is another work, a horizontal figure, whose striking similarity to Canova's *Endymion* highlights the evasion of authenticity manifested in the figure for the duke. Canova was the first prominent artist of his generation to voice admiration for the mysterious *Veiled Christ* at the Masonic Cappella Sansevero in Naples, completed in 1753 by Giuseppe Sanmartino (fig. 96). To this day in Naples, Canova is rumored to have tried to buy it for his personal collection. Not only does Sanmartino's figure possess a highly reflective surface that sets a precedent for the conspicuous glossiness of the *Endymion*; the corner of drapery that covers the shepherd's pubic area is treated in such a way that it gives the illusion of clinging to the thigh, producing a series of tiny folds that seem to be a direct invocation of Christ's veil. When Cavendish received Canova's finished work, he delighted in the observation that the figure was nothing like the *Apollo Belvedere*, a claim suggesting that he was still anticipating a body in the mold of the "old antique." Rather than the Parthenon Marbles or baroque art, however, in the eyes of the duke Canova's new sculpture called to mind another, very different kind of representation of the human figure. Odd though it may seem, the duke wrote that "the countenance and form" of the *Endymion* was redolent of figures in works by the portrait painter Thomas Lawrence, West's successor as president of the Royal Academy.[16] The duke made this claim in a letter to Lawrence himself and may have wished to flatter the painter, yet to write of a connection between a sleeping, semi-naked stone body and the rosy-cheeked likenesses that make up Lawrence's *oeuvre* was to state that the Greekness of sculpture was not something that the nation's leading patron of contemporary sculpture valued. Instead, a tangible shift in focus away from the fragments' authenticated form made itself visible on the *Endymion*. Canova himself did engage with and take seriously the revision of Greek form embodied by the Marbles, but chose to integrate his study of the newly imported figures with the "old antique," baroque and more recent precedents, producing a work that, through its wrought sensuality and free-floating "spatio-temporal principle," could end up likened to British portraiture in oils.[17]

With its "soothing" effect on the beholder and its refusal to conform to the current understanding of "true" Greek form, Canova's *Endymion* is the ultimate Poetic statement. Despite its connection to objects from various times and places, the figure's appearance testifies to a development that, having occurred in the two decades before its installation in Chatsworth, would help steer the course of British art to come: the victory of Poems over Dreams. At the time of the work's completion, Canova's reputation as Europe's most significant artist continued to go unquestioned. An international star, he alone was credited with having refreshed "the antique" to establish a tradition of classicizing sculpture independent from the historical dynamics that incubated Banks's "vulgar Winckelmannianism." As I noted in the introduction, it was actually Banks who was first to shirk the expectation that practitioners ought to restore and copy antiquities rather than create original works, blazing the trail for what Hugh Honour terms "the empirical approach to the antique."[18] But, just as the deployment of the classical body as a vessel had become a thing of the past, Banks's reputation was beginning to fade away altogether. In 1816, the year of the Select

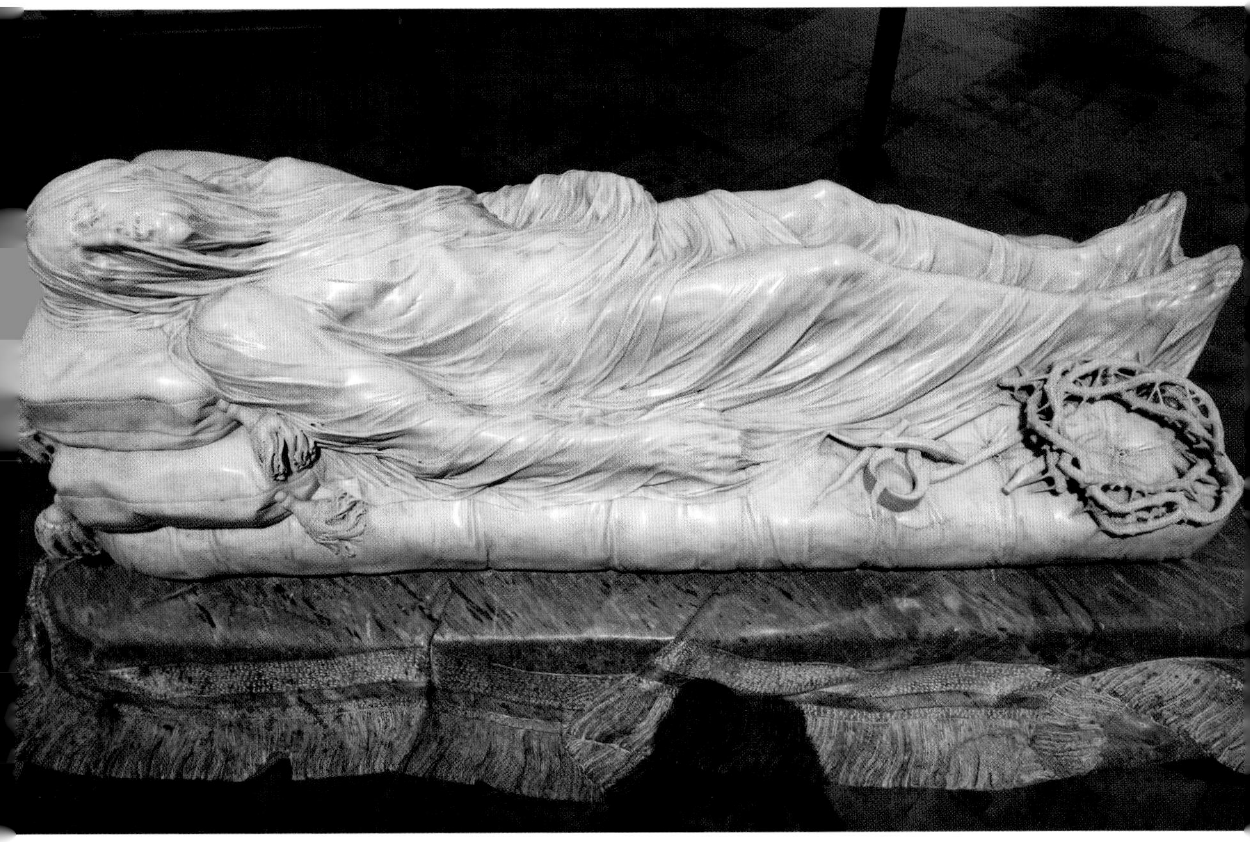

96 Giuseppe Sanmartino, *Veiled Christ*, 1753, marble. Cappella Sansevero, Naples.

Committee, the writer Richard Duppa pronounced Banks a far superior artist to Canova, lamenting that, both at home and abroad, the British sculptor was "neglected when living and is now forgotten."[19] The war between their respective approaches had been won, and Canova's side basked in victory.

If Haydon's failure and Banks's increasing obscurity mark the defeat of Dreams, Canova's *Endymion* is a monument to Poetic art's triumph. Although, as I pointed out in the last chapter, Poetic works tend to be representations of the female or feminine forms, Canova's sleeping shepherd is not an isolated case of fundamentally Poetic characteristics – sensual materiality, atemporality – being united in a male body. Canova's may be a languid figure feminized by its passive pose, yet the musculature and height render this a distinctly masculine body. The idea that the Poetic approach could be reconciled with representations of male forms may jar with my other point that, from the end of the Napoleonic Wars onward, critics demanded that male bodies be represented with a greater specificity and relevance to life in Britain. Canova, a celebrity born and living on the Continent, may have been lauded for producing an abstract adaptation of a mythological subject centered on a naked male protagonist, but ever more negative responses to Banks's monument to *Captain Burges* show that different expectations had arisen for British artists. The need for specificity, however, was not necessarily incompatible with the Poetic qualities I have identified. Indeed, in the decade after the nation's acquisition of the Parthenon Marbles, specific male bodies and the Poetic approach were reconciled. During this phase, the naked male body began to enjoy a revival in contemporary British sculpture. This revival gave way to objects that are at once Poetic and in harmony with the nationalistic turn. And they are Poetic in more subtle ways than Canova's gleaming figure. Unlike the *Endymion*, these emergent sculptures of male bodies do accommodate the recently authenticated model of Greek form embodied by the Parthenon Marbles. Only they do not just reproduce this model in the scientific way Haydon had urged – and here their Poetic status comes into view – but rather reconfigure the study of anatomy so that its demonstration becomes sensual, irrational, and outside of time.

— THE MUSCULAR SURFACE —

As I observed, the "old antique" did not vanish from contemporary British sculpture. Far from it. But this kind of form, with its smooth contours and "soothing" surface, was retained largely for representations of the female body, which remained plentiful at Royal Academy exhibitions, a point to which I will return. Although the Parthenon was not ornamented by male figures alone, the fragments more readily served as models for portraying the bodies of men. In the context of artistic practice, anatomical precision was gendered male, the details of the interior of a woman's body being anathema to the superficial qualities amalgamated in idealized images of the female form. When the draped female figures from the east pediment *are* adapted in sculpture of the period, it is for the representation of a corpulent and unmuscular male body, as in Westmacott's monument to *Charles James Fox*.

But while the idealized female form persisted relatively unchanged in British sculpture, in the decades following the Select Committee there emerged a particular kind of male body whose appearance, while still an index of corporeal beauty, matched the pervasive demand for specificity: that is, figures with particular, precise identities. Along with the rough, imperfect condition of the Parthenon Marbles, their anatomical precision was suited to representations of the athlete, a specific class of male body. This is not an ephebic, youthful type, who, as several scholars have noted with regard to French art, possesses feminine qualities; nor is it the simple, vaguely muscular but not intricately wrought ideal reproduced in Banks's art, a body reliant on the sovereignty of the "old antique."[20] The canonization of the Parthenon Marbles initiated a wave of sculptures of rugged athletic bodies: adaptations of Phidian muscularity into original figures intended to do nothing more than delight the spectator with an "intense muscular display."[21] Although they satisfied the nationalist bent of art criticism by moving away from stock mythological subjects and embracing the nation's most significant acquisition, they are not Dreaming works that uphold an ideological position. Poetic sensuality and anatomical precision are only incompatible in relation to the female form. The rippling muscularity of the athlete functioned to give the carved body an imaginative, even phantasmagorical materiality that generated rapturous responses not unlike those garnered by Canova's polished figures. Although their surfaces are not treated with special ingredients, the forms are layered in muscle in the way that works by the Italian sculptor are layered in wax, or Reynolds's in wax, megilp and other substances. Even when their actions are aggressive and strained, the sculptures of athletes – like all of the Poetic works I have named in this book so far – remain "phenomena of pure positivity," to return to Byung-Chul Han's phrase, an aspect that becomes clear when reading the unanimous praise they garnered.[22]

The artist chiefly responsible for bringing the athletic male body into view during these years was John Graham Lough, a sculptor who had moved to London from Shotley, a lead and coal mining town in Northumberland. In 1827, the penniless artist had been discovered in his humble quarters off the Strand by none other than Haydon, who had heard of a "youthful genius" at work on a nine-foot plaster of the sixth-century Greek wrestler Milo of Croton (fig. 97).[23] After meeting Lough and seeing the sculpture for himself, Haydon was amazed. Since the Greeks, he wrote in his diary with typical hyperbole, "no exception,

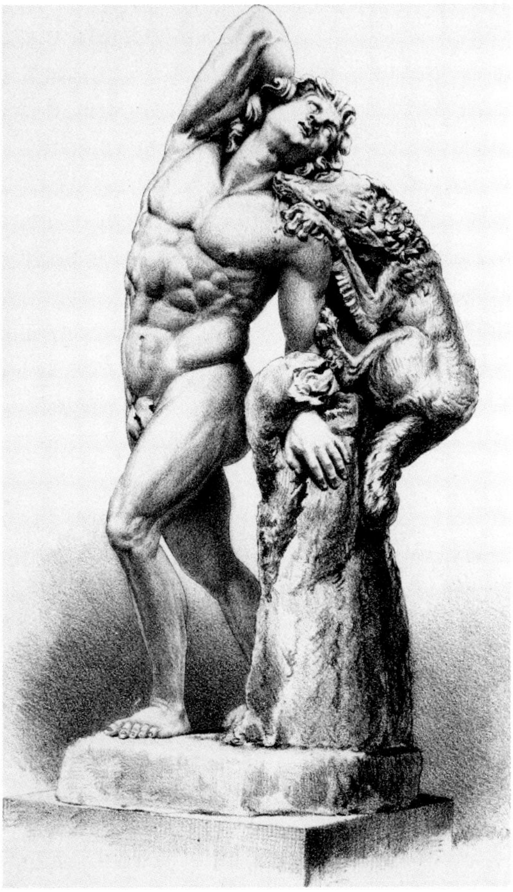

97 Unknown engraver after John Graham Lough, *Milo*, c. 1870, engraving. Printed in Geo Neasham, *North-Country Sketches: Notes, Essays and Reviews* (Durham: Thos. Caldcleugh, 1893).

neither Michael Angelo, Bernini, or Canova, has there been any such a production" as brilliant as Lough's *Milo*.[24] Telepathically, the sculpture seemed to realize the theories the painter had been developing over the course of the past two decades:

> *Under the arm of every human creature the skin folds up in a roll when the arm hangs down in repose ... The first thing I saw in Lough's Milo was this, in his dingy obscure Room. "Why did you put that?" said I, "Because I saw it in life, Sir", he replied ... In as much as this fact proves he knows how to unite Idea & Nature in one part, so does every part of his Milo prove the same. The arm that is up a bit, of flesh is equal to anything in the Elgin Marbles.*[25]

Lough's understanding of anatomy was mediated by encounters with the Parthenon Marbles. Since moving to London in 1825, he had attentively studied the fragments.[26] In 1826, he was accepted as a student at the Academy on the recommendation of John Thomas Smith, Keeper of Prints at the British Museum. Evidently, Lough had spent hours before the Marbles by the time he began the *Milo*. According to an account of his early life informed by his wife, after first arriving in London on a collier from Newcastle, Lough had headed straight to the British Museum.[27] The captain of the collier joined him, and the two men wandered around together until they found the fragments, of which Lough was reportedly in awe. The captain then tried to get the young sculptor to return with him to Newcastle but Lough flatly refused.

Other, less plausible legends surround Lough. One describes the sculptor as a young child making a statuette from clay while his playmate posed naked as the model.[28] Repeated in an array of sources (and even recorded in an 1881 painting by Ralph Hedley), another legend describes the *Milo* piercing the ceiling of the room in which Lough worked, its giant scale at odds with the shabbiness of the sculptor's accommodation.[29] These stories work to individualize Lough, isolating him from Banks, Bacon, and the preceding history of sculpture in Britain. They draw his relationship to the classical body away from the outmoded image of Greece represented in works like the St. Paul's monument and separate his subjectivity from the Dreams of Banks and Bacon both. The subject of *Milo* – a particular individual who had actually lived and died – registers the demand for specificity with regard to the representation of male bodies. Hitherto represented only a few times in art, Milo was not a supernatural being but a mortal man whose achievements are recorded by various ancient commentators. Hence the figure's nakedness was historically specific, literal, and thus acceptable in a way that Banks's naval captain was no longer. Lough does depict a scene from Milo's biography that is likely, at least in part, a fiction: the moment just prior to the wrestler's death. Milo is said to have been devoured by wolves while walking through a forest, an energetic scene that permitted Lough to express the mechanisms of the wrestler's musculature as it erupts and recedes along the outline of the form. As the wrestler reaches back in agony, bending one leg and flexing the other, his arms form a column around which movement rotates centrifugally, highlighting the might of his trunk and each limb in full. Yet this resplendent strength is futile. Milo is no match for the wolf that sinks its jaws into his neck from behind.

Padiyar draws a connection between Haydon's viewing of the Parthenon Marbles and the "licked" surfaces of Canova's works, arguing that the British painter's intense absorption in the musculature of the fragments attests to a space opened up by the Italian sculptor's attention to the surfaces of his own creations.[30] My analysis of the way in which Haydon rationalized this absorption with a racial-scientific agenda suggests that, while he professed to be an ardent fan of Canova, the painter was more concerned with what the Marbles (and his direct contact with Canova in 1815) could mean for his own identity and career rather than how the implicated objects engage with the senses. That being said, Padiyar's point does apply to how Haydon viewed Lough's sculpture. To the painter, the musculature of *Milo* was engrossing in such a way that the figure was readily "imbued with fantasy."[31] One evening, Haydon offered to come and view the figure by candlelight, the same conditions under which Canova finished his works. Inspecting the figure in this way, Haydon was "astonished" by the "beautiful mixture of fleshiness and muscular action, of high style and individual truth." This encounter confirmed that *Milo* was a figure borne from an innate "genius" which "sat on [Lough] night and day like an incubus – goaded, haunted, pressed, worried, drove him into exertion" even though he had no money and little support.[32] Other responses to the sculpture are equally ecstatic. In November 1818, a poem invoking Lough as a "native genius" appeared in the *Gentleman's Magazine*, proclaiming that even "candid critics" are forced to own the enthralling capacity of his works.[33] The pamphlet for his first solo exhibition in 1828 rhapsodizes that "the noble sweep of the whole form" (of the *Milo*) is "not more admirable than the antique beauty of the face, in which the sufferings of the mind appear even more intense than the torment he endures from the relentless fangs of the wolf."[34] As an actual Greek man, the wrestler's "antique beauty" could be seen as literal as opposed to purely derivative. What is more, the musculature of the figure was read less as a register of Lough's scientific knowledge than a superficial adornment that generated unprecedented fascination for a work of British sculpture.

Haydon sought to take Lough under his wing, but the sculptor was not interested in the painter's vexing visions. Although he too was guided by the knowledge of anatomy manifested in the Parthenon Marbles, Lough did not share Haydon's belief that this knowledge would revolutionize artistic practice and, what is more, affirm the supremacy of white Europeans. His *Milo* was an achievement intended to attract interest and establish his name as an artist of great potential. And it worked. Before long, Lough was the talk of London society. His first solo exhibition opened in June 1828 at the Great Rooms, Maddox Street, featuring a cast of *Milo* and a cast of his (untraced, unengraved) *Sampson and the Philistines*. All the fashionable elite flocked to the private view, including the Duke of Wellington and the actress Sarah Siddons. A solo exhibition was a rare opportunity for a living sculptor, one made possible by the separation of painting from sculpture and the newly acquired status of the latter as an autonomous art form requiring certain conditions to appreciate it. With all of its connotations during the Revolutionary era now a distant memory, the naked male body – recently afforded a brawny, anatomically correct form and a specific identity – had been, as it were, rebranded.

Exhibited at the Academy the year of Lough's private view, John Charles Felix Rossi's *The Pugilist* provides another instance of the positive reception of the athletic male body (fig. 98). Carved from a single piece of marble, this life-size sculpture portrays a modern prize fighter with bare fists raised. Initially exhibited as *The Pugilist*, the work became known as *The British Pugilist* after its installation in the sculpture chamber at Petworth House, where it was placed on a plinth with the inscription "Athleta Britannicus." Even before these nationalizing titles were fixed, the work was received on essentialist terms. When it was on display at Somerset House, a critic in the *New Monthly Magazine* wrote that there "is something in this statue perfectly English, something that is applicable to no other country."[35] Another declared that it held out "a fit subject for the display of native talent," showing the glory both of "the manly character of the Briton" and contemporary British art.[36] But these claims were mapped onto the sculpture from outside and say more about the nationalistic climate of the period than this work as a piece of art. The figure was not a vessel for nationalist ideas but rather a fantasy figure whose sensational display of male strength facilitated its reception on jingoistic terms. Like Lough's *Milo*, the boxer is posed in such a way that the fine details of his musculature are allowed to become prominent while still remaining true to living nature, especially around his sinewy knees – slightly bowed – lean calves, and ankles. The work materializes Charles Bell's tenet that in the representation of movement, cognition must sync with action. In harmony with his bodily stance, the boxer's concentrated mien – a slightly furrowed brow and parted lips forming the hint of a competitive snarl – does away with Winckelmannian serenity. On the other hand, the work also represents the approach of Bell's rival Anthony Carlisle, who employed boxers as models in order to downplay the need for anatomical knowledge. Canova had set a precedent for marble boxers with his *pugliatori* in the Pio Clementino: two life-size statues of ancient Greek fighters who, according to Pausanias, engaged in a deathly match.[37] The Italian sculptor affords the victorious fighter Damoxenos a deep frown that exacerbates his unidealized features. Rossi and Canova knew each other from Rome (Rossi described Canova as his "friend" during his testimony at the Select Committee), and the former may have been familiar with the recent engraving of the boxers in outline by Henry Moses.[38] Jason Edwards suggests that Rossi's boxer enters into a competition with Canova's, providing the *pugliatori* an imaginary new opponent.[39] The pose heightens the imaginative play of the work. Raised arms introduce overlying shadows on the torso (which would have been even more intense if viewed by candlelight), and the figure leans back slightly to give a dramatic sense of anticipation. One can almost hear

98 John Charles Felix Rossi, *Athleta Britannicus or The British Pugilist*, 1828, marble. Petworth House, West Sussex.

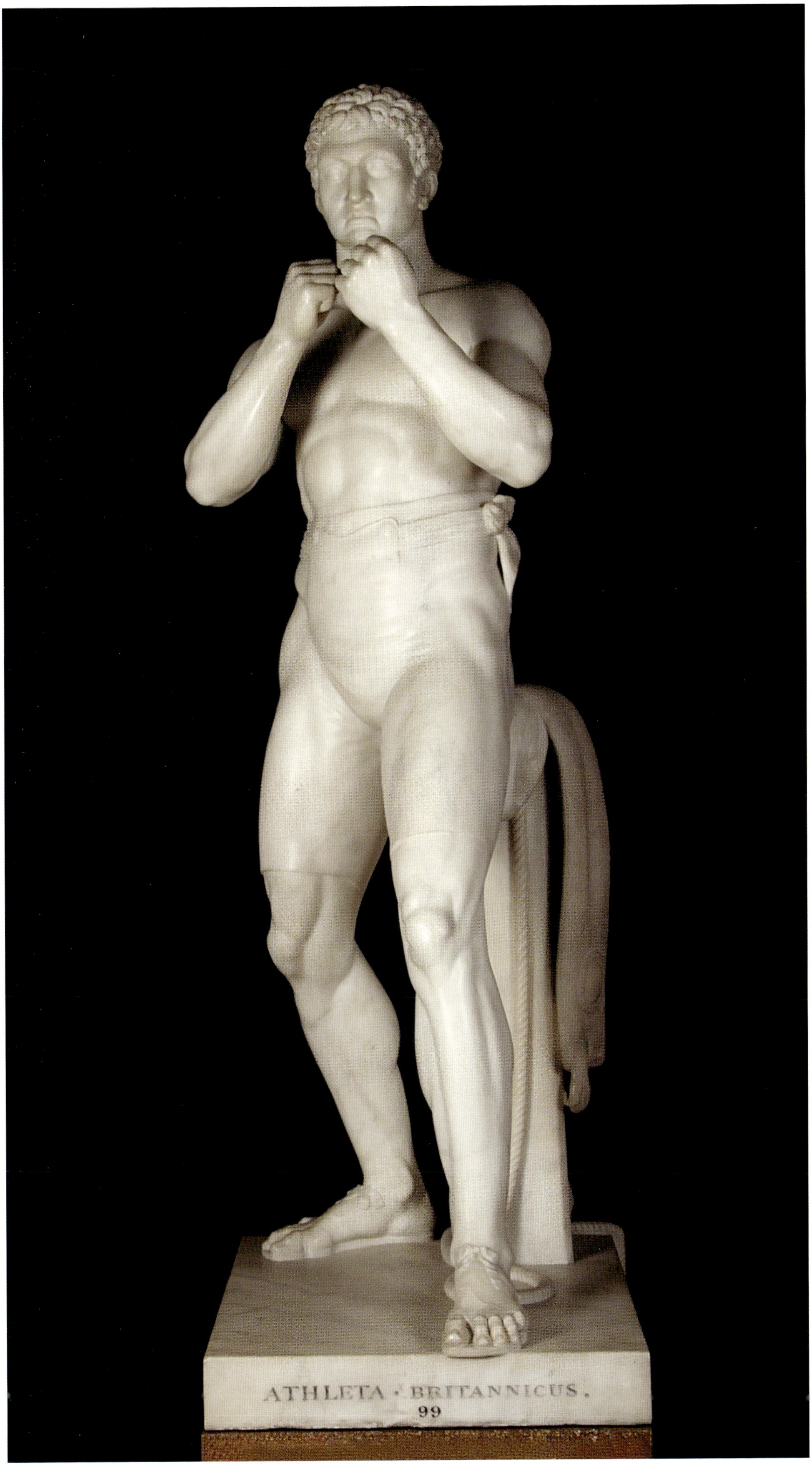
ATHLETA · BRITANNICUS.
99

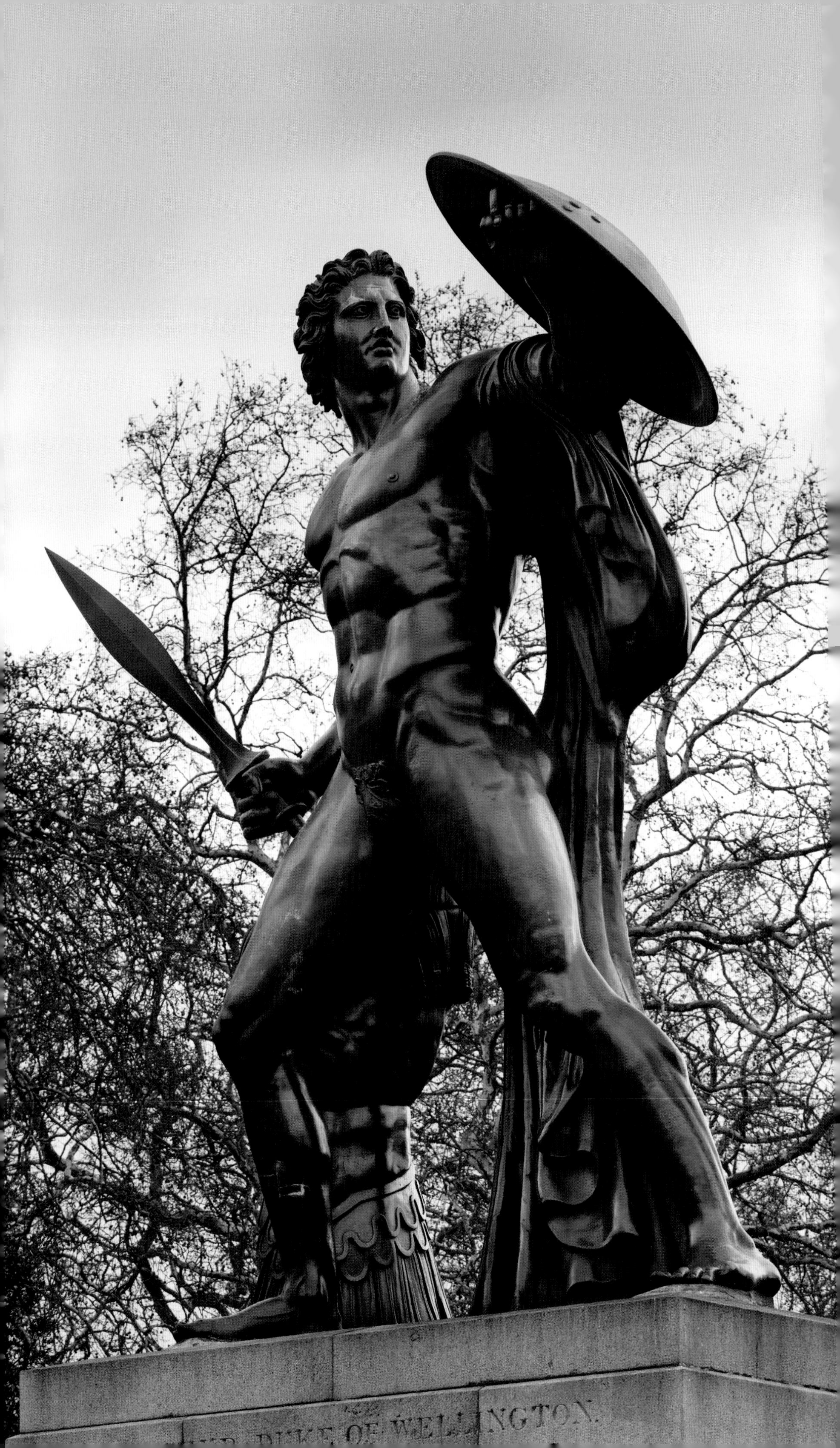

a crowd cheering. With its momentary action, the work stood less as an icon of Britishness than as a specific individual whose spectacular strength was a quality prized by the nation at the time. A contributor to the *Gentleman's Magazine* described the work as "a noble figure of a very fine man," a critic in the *London Literary Gazette* as a "fine specimen of manly strength and just proportion."[40] Possibly modelled on one of the pugilists employed by Carlisle, Rossi's boxer was a case study rather than an abstract type, and thus bears a stronger kinship with the sculptor Francis Chantrey's exacting portrait busts than with classical bodies by Banks. But the connection to Canova, momentary action, and non-specific title turn this individual figure into an atemporal work of art, one with a "spatio-temporal principle" that is impossible to pin down. The artist himself was not interested in putting forward a historically specific version of the classical body. When called on to testify at the Select Committee, Rossi made it clear that the splitting of Greco-Roman antiquity into different phases based on their supposed authenticity was not something that concerned, or had ever concerned, him. He considered the Marbles the "finest" sculptures he had ever seen, but did not care about their status as "true" Greek.[41]

As alternative images of the naked or partially naked male body, one might expect the figures by Lough and Rossi to rediscover some of the eroticism that was purged from the classical body when it became a vessel for vexing ideas, but this is not the case. Though these forms possess a spectacular corporeality that excited their first audiences, their intensive gendering as male via the rippling musculature de-eroticizes them so that they end up as sexless as the Dreaming figures made in a bygone era. Michael Hatt writes of a similar process inflecting images of the male body in British art of the late nineteenth century, when upholders of physical culture pursued a "masculinisation of the body, a gendering that aims to purify the male form of unhealthy desire."[42] By this time, concerns around homosexuality had entered British cultural discourse, meaning that the sexlessness of muscular male bodies was consciously cultivated in order to stave off homoerotic gazes. Not surprisingly it is Haydon, with his theories of racial purity, that gives us an embryonic articulation of this sentiment when he praises Lough for not having gone to Italy in his youth: "What becomes of those that go and doze in the Vatican? They come back castrated."[43]

Hatt suggests that images of the muscular male body became part of a Dream later on in the century, when fears around sexual and racial "degeneration" pervaded British artistic discourse. In the years around Lough and Rossi's sculptures, however, such bodies were allowed to be Poems. Sensual fantasy figures, they were intended for contemplation in specially arranged exhibitions or private galleries. When it came to public monuments, the muscular, exposed male figure did not give audiences the same pleasure. After the erection, in 1822, of Westmacott's statue of the Duke of Wellington as a bronze Achilles in Hyde Park, the response could not have been more different to the feting of Lough and Rossi just a few years later (fig. 99). Standing at thirty-six feet on its Dartmoor

99 Richard Westmacott, *Wellington Monument*, 1822, bronze. Hyde Park Corner, London.

granite pedestal near one of London's busiest corners, this jet-black colossus was not a sensual appropriation of the classical body but a stark intervention in the landscape of the city, and the outcry it caused was one of virulent hostility. First, there was the fact that the sculpture had been paid for by donations from British women, a circumstance that worked to eroticize a figure which, in order to be accepted as a public work of art, needed to appear sexually sanitized. Some commentators were able to discern that these "Ladies" had nothing to do with the design, but for many the notion that the brazen display of nakedness was the result of women's influence enhanced the scandal.[44] One author in the *English Chronicle* wrote:

> *The Lady Patronesses of this statue have ... tried to cheat us into a good opinion of it, by the semblance of classical taste, and of patriotic spirit, but the people of England cannot be so deceived. They cannot, by such an artifice, be made to fall down and worship the brazen image which the Ladies of England have set up. In a gigantic naked Statue, they will see nothing that reflects the honour of a military Commander, nothing that tells the glory of his followers, but they will find in it, that which will bring a rude stare into the gaze of the forward, and a blush into the cheek of the modest.*[45]

The *Worcester Journal* reported that since "the exposure of this unmeaning memorial, the promenade near it has been deserted."[46] The word "unmeaning" accuses the work of being arbitrary, so offensive in its distance from British custom and national character.[47] This brings up the second issue with the sculpture, which was that it represented an actual person, a living war hero at that, not as an idealized version of how he looked in the flesh, but pressed into a foreign, anachronistic mold. The literate public were informed that the sculpture was based on the statues flanking the obelisk on Rome's Piazza Quirinale: a set of two symmetrical groups known during the period as the "horse tamers." At the time, these were thought to be authentically Greek and designed by Phidias no less. In 1816, while the Select Committee met to debate the Marbles, casts after them had been exhibited at the Royal Mews.[48] But what relation did they bear to the British field marshal? In an era preoccupied with specificity, to replicate a naked ancient horseman only to rename it both Achilles and Wellington now seemed ridiculous. As we know, the status of the Greeks as the "human universal" had long been out of fashion.[49] The meaning of the sculpture persisted only through its material; the sculpture had been cast from bronze mixed with twelve "24 pounder" long gun cannons taken from the battles of Salamanca, Vitoria, Toulouse, and Waterloo, the conflicts that mythologized Wellington's military leadership. But this subtext was not plainly visible on the surface of the figure, and hence did not guarantee the work's success as a work of art. The monument became known as "the naked unknown," "that unhappy bronze," "a lasting reproach to the persons who chose it" with "no analogy to England, to Wellington, to the army, to the arts, or the customs" of the times.[50] Meanwhile across the road, Canova's statue of *Napoleon as Mars the Peacemaker* had recently been installed at Apsley House, Wellington's own residence (see fig. 7).

Purchased for 66,000 francs by the government as a token of victory for the duke, the figure embodied what were essentially the same set of conventions as Westmacott's figure: a living military leader represented in a mythological guise, naked. But as controversy raged around the bronze monument, Canova's *Napoleon* acquired the status of a gallery sculpture and could be enjoyed like the *Endymion* at Chatsworth. Now that its function as a monument (always tenuous given Napoleon's unease with the work) had been officially deactivated, the Poetic nature of Canova's figure was allowed to come to the fore, sealing the work's value as an object to be contemplated in private. Forced into the open air, the Wellington monument was painfully out of touch: an empty vessel brandished as if it still held ideas that would resonate.

— RECORPOREALIZATION —

Like the works of Lough and Rossi, Canova's *Napoleon* turns the muscular contours of the male body into a sensual Poetic surface. Despite Napoleon's complaints, however, that the statue is "too athletic," this work does not possess the teeming strength of the later British figures, and hence manifests an eroticism that is anathema to the sexlessness of *Milo* and the pugilist.[51] Where the statue's genre dictates that it ought to be active and authoritative, Canova's figure favors the feminine qualities of softness and acquiescence. It was made before Canova's exposure to the Parthenon Marbles, and is a straightforward emulation of the "old antique." Over the course of subsequent decades, the "old antique" – the model of the classical body now rendered latter-day – persisted in works centered on the female and feminine forms.

I have stated that, around the time of the Marbles' acquisition, anatomical precision was gendered male in the context of British artistic practice. Even before, in Bell's *Anatomy of Expression*, the rendering of muscles, veins, tendons, and ligaments and the reciprocity between cognition and action are invoked solely in relation to the representation of adult male figures. Among the Marbles' most passionate defenders, however, attempts were made to scrutinize representations of the female body on the same terms and to the same degree as their male counterparts. If the *Venus de' Medici*, they wondered, is a specimen of the "old antique," then what might a naked female body in the allegedly more authentic Greek mold look like? William Hazlitt accused the *Venus* of being no more than an "exquisite marble doll," a "beautiful toy" with "no expression of mental refinement."[52] Viewing the sculpture at the Uffizi where it had recently been returned from Paris, he complained that the work is essentially too ideal, manifesting a "great softness, sweetness, symmetry, and timid grace – a faultless tameness, a negative perfection."[53] But when the same author dismissed the *Apollo* on similar grounds, he could offer the Parthenon Marbles as an alternative. In contrast to the *Apollo*'s perceived foppishness, the Theseus seemed the epitome of rugged masculinity. Headless and shrouded in fabric, the female figures from the east pediment offered no such antidote. With regard to the carved female body, what would constitute an image of perfection in the manner of the anatomically accurate but still ideal male bodies of the Parthenon? Hazlitt does mention Phidias's long lost gold-embellished ivory Venus as a hypothetical replacement.[54] Elsewhere, however, he rails against decoration in sculpture. In a review of Flaxman's *Lectures on Sculpture* he proclaims that because a "statue is the utmost possible development of form," it ought, "by the laws of intellectual creation, to stand alone in that simplicity and unsullied nakedness in which it has been wrought."[55] He also criticizes the more ornate achievements of Canova, such as the gold-amphora and cup-wielding *Hebe*, for being "worked up to a high pitch of perfection" when they "might just as well have been left alone."[56] There simply was no ancient representation of a female figure that matched both the author's fixation on anatomy and his belief that sculptural forms ought to be as simple as possible. Hazlitt further contradicts himself when, having complained that the *Venus de' Medici* is too widely admired to be appreciated with fresh eyes, he goes on to declare that she is "not the statue Pygmalion fell in love with; nor did any man ever wish or fancy his mistress to be like it."[57] Efforts to force the female form into the same light in which male figures were now being examined led to striking inconsistencies. The very idea of female bodily beauty belied Hazlitt's "scientific and reasoning" approach.

Haydon too attempted to dethrone the *Venus de' Medici* by viewing her through the same lens he used to appraise images of the male body. In exchange for the shipment of casts to St. Petersburg, Alexey Olenin sent three casts from

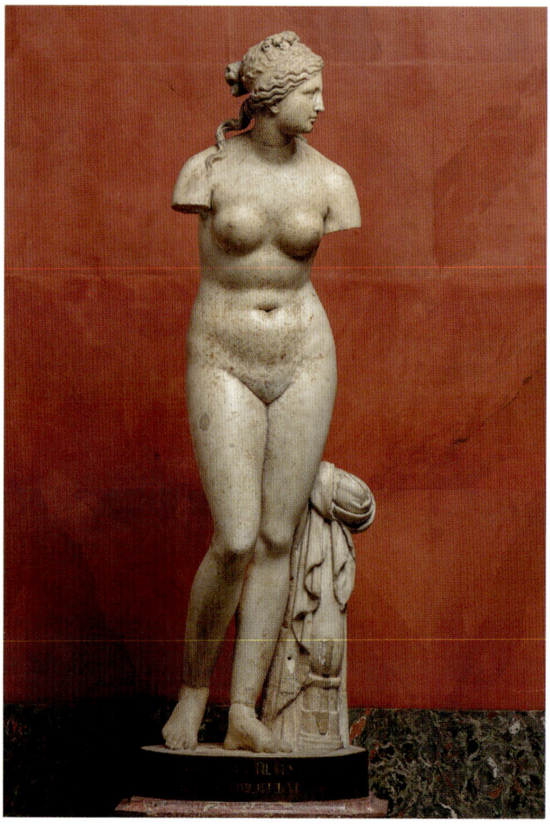

100 *Venus Tauride*, third century BC, marble. Hermitage, St. Petersburg.

the Imperial Academy, including a *Venus* on a similar scale to the *Venus de' Medici*, most likely a reproduction of the sculpture known as the *Venus Tauride*: the first ever Greco-Roman statue to arrive in Russia (fig. 100). In a letter thanking Olenin, Haydon judges the gifts and describes them in relation to his theories. When it comes to the female body, he cannot make the distinction between artistic merit in terms of anatomical precision and artistic merit in terms of beauty:

> *With respect to the Venus the trunk is singularly beautiful; the legs, feet, and head, I think very inferior; but the trunk is superior certainly to the Venus de Medicis, and, being of a younger age, has a more agreeable character. The lower part of the trunk of the Venus de Medicis has skin wrinkled ... all proofs of great truth and knowledge of nature in the sculptor. In the Venus which you have done me the honour to send ... the skin is tight &c &c. It is, indeed, a most beautiful statue, and has all the air of a fresh and pure Virgin, young, elastic, and lovely, uninjured by the passions of our nature, and without having suffered from the anxieties of life.*[58]

According to Haydon, because they chose to include the supposed flaws of a post-pregnancy body – in this case, wrinkles around the abdomen equivalent to the wrinkles in the armpit of the Theseus or the roll of flesh on the arm of Lough's *Milo* – the artist behind the *Venus de' Medici* is lauded for their "great truth and knowledge." Yet it is precisely this "defect" that makes the sculpture second-rate in relation to the Russian *Venus*. That the ancient artist knew and suggested the effects of age on the surface of the form makes the *Venus de' Medici* less attractive because it demotes the figure from the heights of virginal freshness. As a woman, the figure is undesirable, but as a work of art it demonstrates "great truth." But it is the status of the *Venus* as an image of woman that ultimately determines the object's worth.

Contemporary sculpture exposes this same tension between anatomy and female beauty. After seeing Richard James Wyatt's *A Nymph at the Bath* at the Royal Academy exhibition of 1837, a critic declared that "in aiming at ideal beauty, the artist has sacrificed truth; the nymph has no blade bones – her shoulders are cushions"; this did not, however, prevent the work from being deemed "the most graceful figure in the room" (fig. 101).[59] What use was anatomical precision on representations of the female form if its exclusion did nothing to lessen the figure's beauty? Describing Westmacott's *Euphrosyne* at the same exhibition, the critic affirms that the representation of subdermal structures on contemporary sculpture is still a relatively recent expectation: "If the ideal be the unnatural, or, as it was defined to us by a sculptor, consist in showing the form in motion without muscular action, then this is ideal; though, by the by, some appearance of muscle was recognized as essential by this definition, and in this figure there are none."[60] This author confirms that the revision of the classical body brought forth by the Parthenon Marbles introduced the necessity of "some appearance of muscle" in sculpture. Female bodies could be criticized for their inability to conform to this development, yet if their anatomy was realistically represented they risked losing their claim to any beauty at all, as in Haydon's assessment of the past-her-prime *Venus*. By stark contrast, when it came to

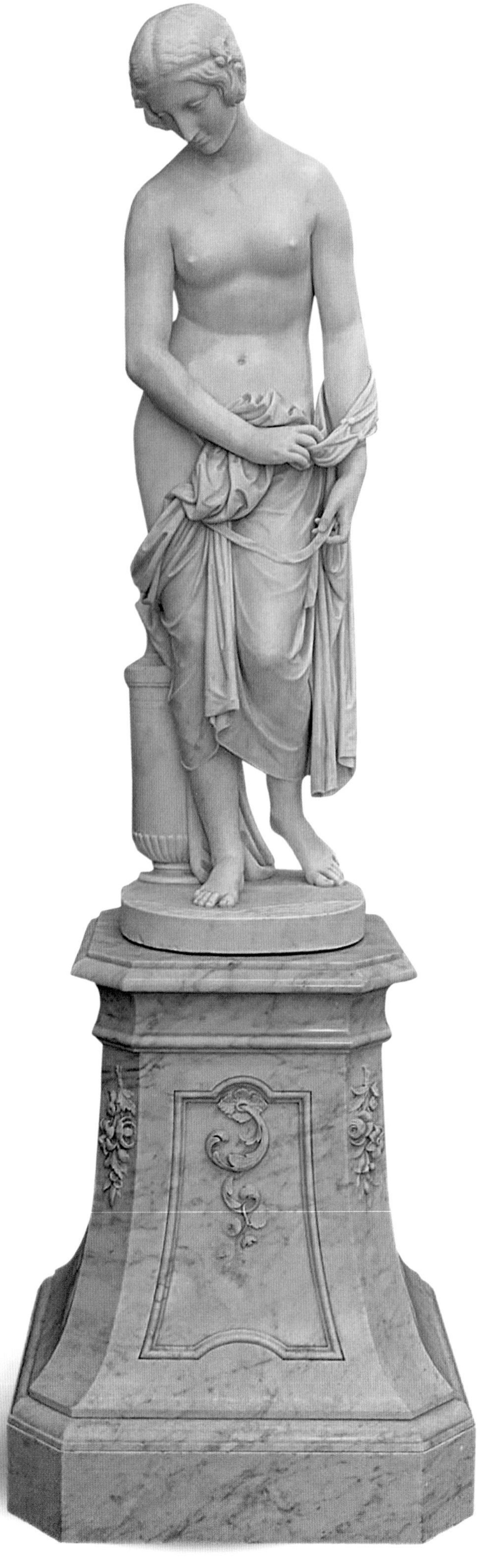

the portrayal of male figures, anatomical precision and sensual appeal did not conflict. One of the other sculptures in Olenin's shipment was a figure of which Haydon approved unreservedly. The "protrusion of the bowels from the action of leaning, the pressure of the muscles of the left arm and shoulder, as well as the hanging over of the pectoral muscles from the skin being filled out with fat," he writes, "has so much the character of a fat man."[61] Such details add character to the form, enhancing a specific corporeal quality (fatness) that is wholly denied to three-dimensional female figures.

Haydon was not the first to have suggested that the *Venus de' Medici* bears the stamp of sexual maturity. Frederick Hervey, the Irish earl-bishop and Banks's unreliable patron, declared in a letter to Canova that the sculpture has "l'attitude d'une Coquette, ou d'une Putain."[62] Howard conveys a preference for the *Venus Braschi*, a statue he describes as "more delicate and youthful" than "the Medicean."[63] Flaxman dismisses the *Venus de Medici* as "insinuating," while James Barry declares that "something of the mother was perceivable about the breasts and abdomen" of the sculpture.[64] Each of these judgments challenge the claim made by Winckelmann that the *Venus de' Medici* resembles "a rose that after a beautiful dawn, unfolds at sunrise," her body of "the age that, like fruit not fully ripened, is hard and slightly tart."[65] Yet even he, who implies that the sculpture represents an adolescent rather than a fully grown woman, felt it necessary to suggest that the *Venus* has an air of erotic awakening: "her breasts ... already more developed than those of tender maidens."[66] That the sculpture was readily perceived, in various terms, to be sexually open indicates a lack of consensus surrounding what actually constituted the ideal female body to begin with. At what point did the softness and roundness tied to female beauty become a postnatal signifier, overly voluptuous, or sexually enticing? Not long after he wrote to Olenin, Haydon glimpsed a work that realized his vision of a toned and "elastic" female ideal even more directly than the cast from Russia: Canova's *Venere Italica*, the sculpture conceived as a substitute of the *Venus de' Medici* after the work's looting by the French (fig. 102).[67] This figure is slightly taller than her ancient counterpart and noticeably slimmer, with elongated limbs and an up-to-date coiffure.[68]

While they profess a deep understanding of the body, the responses of Hazlitt, Haydon, and the critic reviewing the exhibition confine the female form to the realm of the abstract. When it came down to it, the interior of the actual female body was far too mysterious and perplexing to be analyzed using art-theoretical terms generated by encounters with the Parthenon Marbles. Yet representations of the female body in British sculpture proliferate at this time. In the wake of the Marbles' acquisition and while muscular male bodies are bursting onto the scene, sculptures with the opposite kind of form – soft bodies emphatically gendered female – dominate at the Academy. This gendering is carried out by way of building on the characteristics associated with the "old antique": the

101 Richard James Wyatt, *A Nymph at the Bath*, c. 1837, marble. Wrest Park, Bedfordshire.

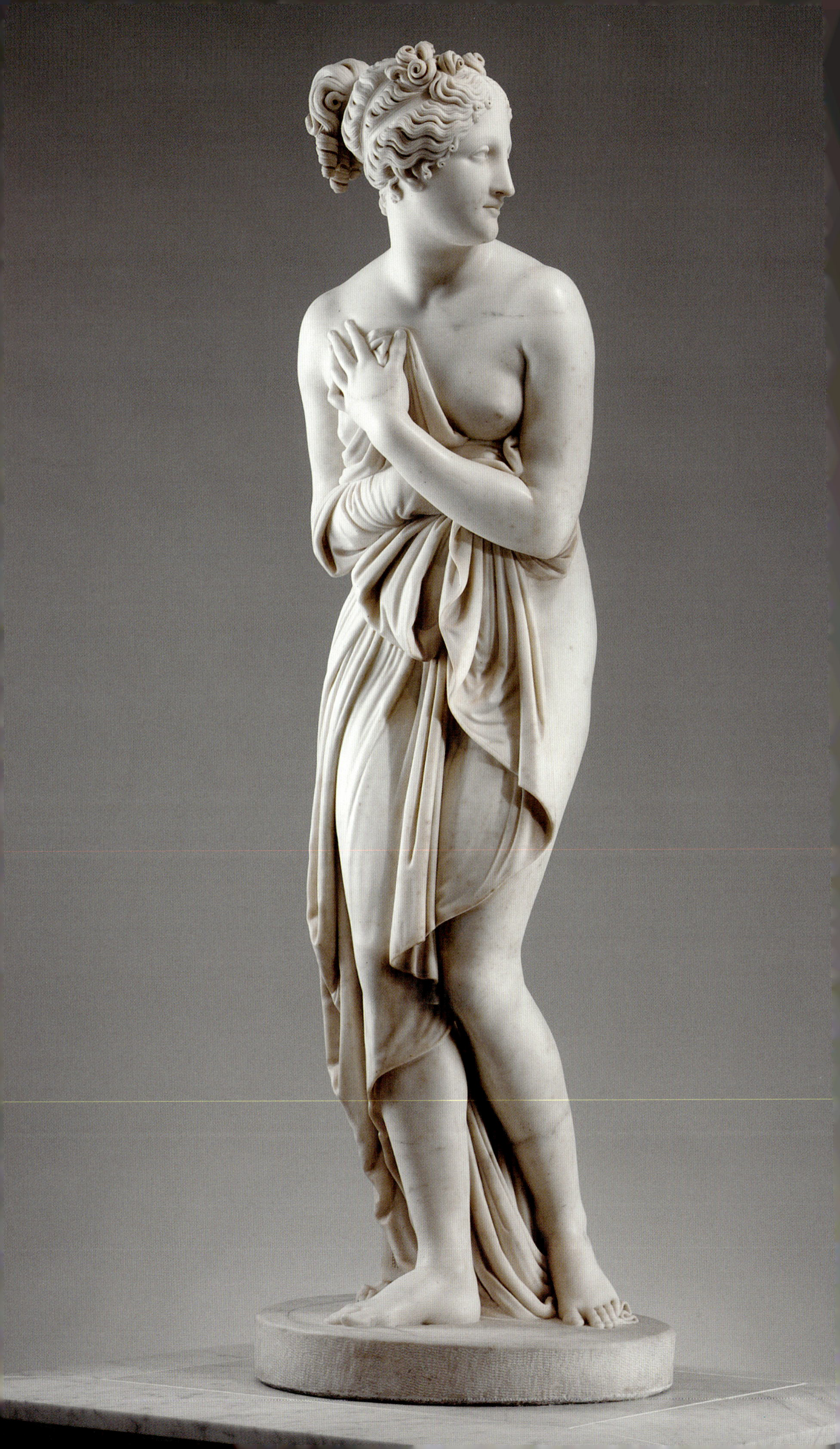

absence of anatomical precision and the smooth sensuality of contour and surface, qualities Haydon describes as "muzzy" and what later scholars have termed "expressionistic."

With her "cushion"-like shoulders, Wyatt's *Nymph at the Bath* is a paradigmatic case of the endurance of the "old antique" as an exemplar to be built on and exaggerated. Another is Edward Hodges Baily's *Eve at the Fountain*, a sculpture that would go on to become one of the most familiar art objects in Victorian Britain, repeated in various formats and materials (fig. 103). It had taken the public some time to appreciate this sculpture. When first exhibited at the Academy in 1822, "the *largeness* of the thighs" was flagged as an issue, a complaint testifying to the confinement of the female body within a slippery but narrow image of ideal beauty.[69] Sources suggest that, rather than a reworking of an ancient form, Baily's *Eve* is based on a cast of a particular life model.[70] But

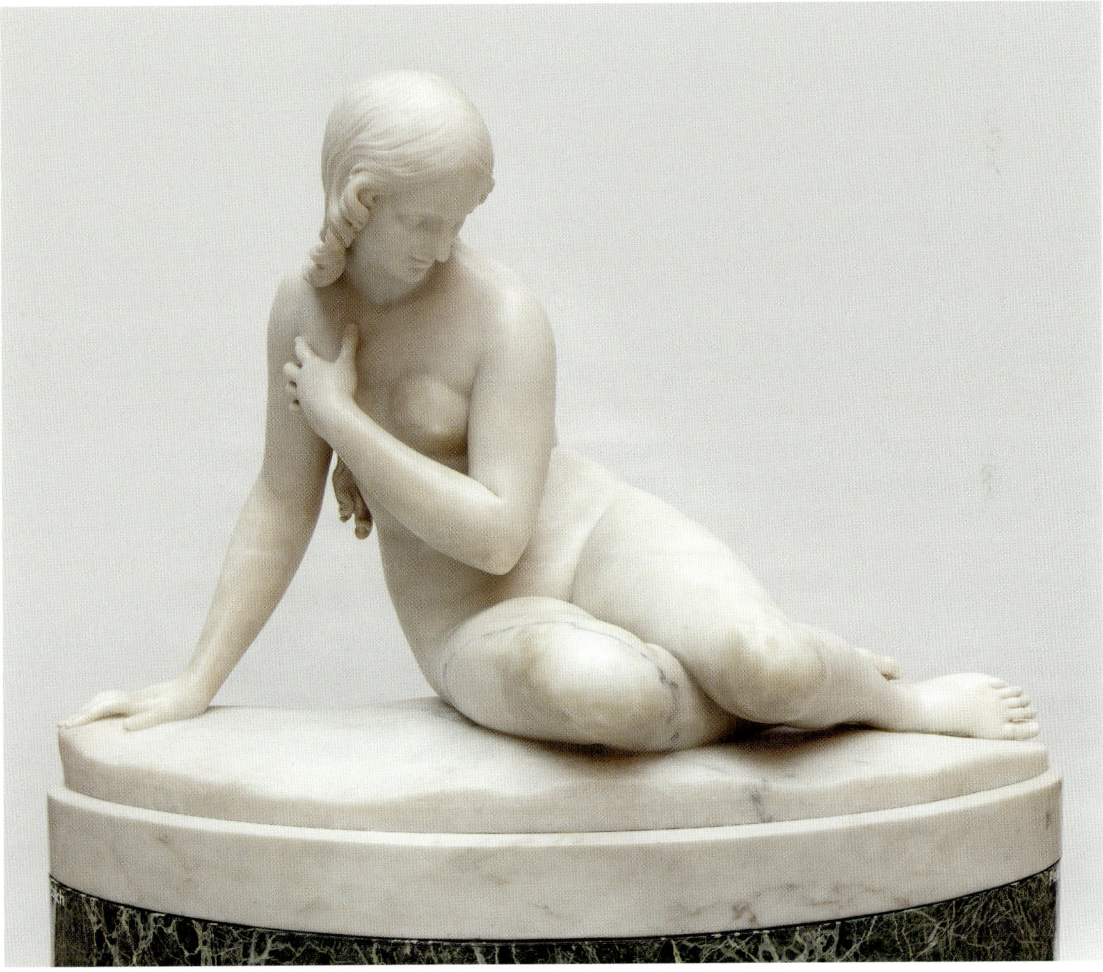

102 Workshop of Antonio Canova, *Venere Italica*, c. 1820, marble. Metropolitan Museum of Art, New York.

103 Edward Hodges Baily, *Eve at the Fountain*, 1822, marble. Bristol Museum and Art Gallery, Bristol.

although there are aspects of the sculpture that hint this could be one element of its genesis, the form is marked by an unnatural roundness that smooths out all anatomical mechanisms, even on the arm that supports the weight of the figure's upper body. *Eve*'s interior is denied outward expression, her body parts a series of interconnecting ovals that make some of Etty's goddesses look like *écorchées*. In spite of tepid early responses, Baily's sculpture was soon heralded as a legitimate contender for the quintessential embodiment of the ideal female form, one that adhered to contemporary standards of female beauty and the desire for sensual surfaces that went with it. By 1826, a critic could point out that Baily been "charged with seducing away the worshippers of the Venus de Medicis, and getting them to transfer their admiration to Eve at the Fountain."[71] The biblical subject safeguarded the work against allegations that the figure's form was sexually mature. Naked, this was Eve before the fall. What is more, the work was understood to be Eve from *Paradise Lost*, making the exposure of the flesh not only literal but a British appropriation, like Howard's Miltonic nymphs.

Not that it mattered, of course. The female form did not need to be granted a national identity in order to be accepted. In fact, non-specific subjects, such as Patrick Macdowell's *Girl Reading* and Canova's unnamed dancers, increased during these years.[72] A particularly striking manifestation of, on the one hand, the emphatic gendering of female bodies via the illusion of softness and the lack of anatomical detail and, on the other, the tolerance of non-specific figures consists in the mother and child group. This was a recurring subject in Royal Academic sculpture from the early 1820s and throughout the next decade until its popularity dwindled around 1840. In 1830, a critic could complain about the sheer volume of "stone mothers" on show at Somerset House: "an excess of 'mother and child'."[73] This particular subject highlighted the vulnerability of marble as a material: its tiny skin-like pores and capacity, if treated in a certain way, to conjure soft tissue. Exhibited in 1837, the marble version of Baily's *Maternal Affection* centers on a generic mother amusing her infant son (fig. 104). Loosely draped from the waist down, she leans forward as he crawls along the length of her back, his lips reaching for hers as she cranes her head toward him. Flawless pale stone is finished to a lactic sheen that heightens the sentimentality of the subject. From 1823, Baily completed six mother and child groups, as well as several reliefs on the same theme.[74] By 1837, the number of such groups had lessened, yet two variations were included in that year's exhibition: *Maternal Playfulness* by Edward Physick and *Mother and Children* by Frederick Thrupp.[75]

The allure of the post-Napoleonic mother and child group was the legitimacy of its sensuality and exaggeration of qualities associated with the female body. The combination of the subject's innocence – the sacred bond between a mother and her infant – and invocations of the perceived softness of actual maternal bodies was guaranteed to chime at this point in time, when fleshier female figures lay open to denigration as "mere dirty flesh" yet were simultaneously sought after as viable rivals to "the antique."[76] Such groups rein in the disorderly reputation of the living postnatal body, its association with leaking fluids and hormonal fluctuations. As Marina Warner notes, the body "of a woman, when used

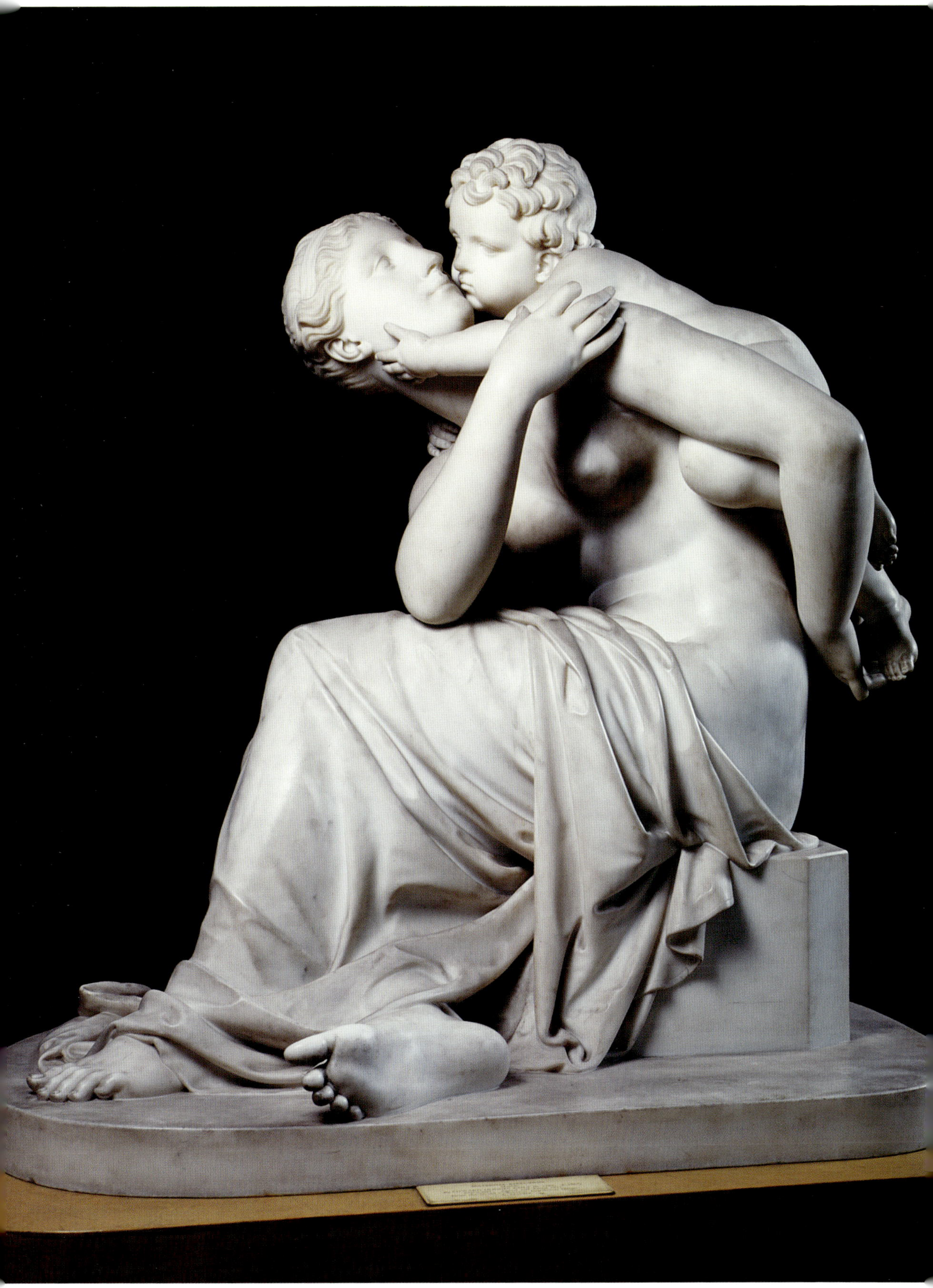

104 Edward Hodges Baily, *Maternal Affection*, c. 1825–37, marble.
Victoria and Albert Museum, London.

to represent generalized concepts that strain at absolute definition" – including and especially the maternal prototype – "must have its surfaces reinforced."[77] In marble sculptures like Baily's *Maternal Affection*, the boundary of the object is secured by an "emphasis on contour": the flow of one curvilinear form upon the other, infant limb, folds of fabric, and every inch of flesh from the cheeks and undulating hair to the polished soles of feet.[78] Hatt also writes of the way in which contour can be "deployed to limit the amount of bodily matter and to retain a sense of beautiful form rather than gross materiality."[79] Instead of delimiting the eroticism of the figure, the lyrical contours of the mother and child groups permit the maternal body to retain an erotic allure by containing it with the template of the conventional bodily ideals of classical sculpture.

As idealized representations of the unquestionably post-virginal body, the mother and child groups quelled anxieties that ancient figures such as the *Venus de' Medici* portray a body scarred by childbirth. The drapery in *Maternal Affection* calls to mind another ancient sculpture, the *Venus de Milo*, unearthed in 1820, of which the sculptor Francis Chantrey brought back a cast from Paris.[80] When it comes to the representation of breasts, the mother and child groups are not permitted to deviate from the "small, distinct, delicate" mold set by the Greco-Roman Venuses, despite the fact that the enlargement of the breasts is a definitive aspect of the maternal duties they portray.[81] From the title alone of Thrupp's lost *A Mother Bending over her Sleeping Infant*, an untraced work exhibited in 1835, we can assume a clear and visible friction between the visceral connotations of nursing a baby and the basic prototype of female corporeal beauty embodied in the ancient Venuses.[82] Considered in relation to the orb-like breasts of Etty's contemporaneous Venuses on canvas, the widening gulf between painting and sculpture again comes into view.

From Westmacott's nymph to the mother and child groups, the loyalty to the "old antique" demonstrated in these representations of the female form consists in their materiality as well as their form. Such works give the opportunity to treat the surface of the work so as to enhance the sense of softness that is a positive connotation of both female beauty and the "old antique." When on the Continent in 1826, the painter David Wilkie observed that "the working of the material" in sculptures from the Borghese Collection in Naples – all specimens of the "old antique" – reminded him "of what we call surface in a picture, such a perfect-knowledge of the effect of light and shadow on that surface, that the hard stone is made to indicate sharpness and softness with as much ease as we see it done in a picture by Correggio."[83] Ever since Vasari, the overarching contribution of the Emilian old master Correggio was considered the skill with which he portrayed subtle gradations of light through the elimination of hard lines, creating a sense of softness: *morbidezza*.[84] By comparing the marble sculptures with the most painterly of painters, Wilkie embraces the "expressionistic" qualities of the "old antique" rather than positing such relics, like his friend Haydon did, as symptoms of decline. Through polish, the careful selection of the marble, and, later on, tinting with wax and pigment, the British sculptures of female and feminine forms amplify the qualities Wilkie, and de Quincy before him, perceived in works falling under the umbrella of "old antique."[85] Earlier sculptors did not care for the material in this way. As we know, Bacon was not skilled in carving or finishing stone, nor did he need to be, as his monuments were mostly intended to be viewed at a distance. Banks washed his marble in a coffee-based solution to give his figures an aged appearance that helped them function as Dreaming vessels rooted in a utopian conception of Greece.[86] In his *Thoughts on Outline*, his fellow radical activist George Cumberland remarks that bestowing too much attention on the quality of the material in sculpture "is very capricious and childish … and is a mark of little discernment in the art."[87] Motivated by piety rather than politics, Flaxman did not devote himself to the illusory finish of his sculptures lest their wrought materiality cancel out their Poetic remoteness (I have argued, however, that his outline illustrations possess a "sweet" sensuality that might be seen as a forerunner of the later emphasis on surface in sculpture). Alan Cunningham could look back on Flaxman's works in marble and complain that "his female forms … want finished luxuriance."[88] But the subsequent generation of sculptors had a marked investment in the appearance of the material. The vehicle for this investment was female and feminine forms. This turn, of course, indicates Canova's influence, the tender, Poetic surfaces of the Italian sculptor's figures being, as we know, his signature touch, so much so that he was christened "the Correggio of sculpture."[89] Canova's biographer Melchior Missirini also informs us that Canova, in a confirmation of Wilkie's observation, "noticed a preparation on the surface of some antique works that had given a greater harmony to their lineaments, tempering their harshness and sweetening the contours of the form."[90] Missirini condemns rumors that, in order to replicate this softness and sweetness, the Italian sculptor augmented his figures with painterly "nostrums" including *ombra di minio*, an ingredient similar to the litharge (lead oxide) used by Reynolds, Howard, and other British oil painters.[91] For both Reynolds and Howard, Correggio was a central point of reference in the pursuit of such effects. Likewise, Canova admired Correggio, so much that he set out to sculpt his bust and produced several oil paintings that draw on the master's style.[92] When it came to ancient art, then, the rift between painting and sculpture was ameliorated by the recurring observation that Greco-Roman sculptures belonging to Haydon's category of the "old antique" possess, or had once possessed, a materiality similar to a particular kind of painting. As with the Duke of Devonshire's reference to the work of Thomas Lawrence in his account of Canova's *Endymion*, this aspect served to render appropriations of the "old antique" atemporal; it did not matter that their form had recently been outed as latter-day by the Parthenon Marbles, because they had their own, indispensable claim to beauty.

John Gibson, Canova's mentee in Rome, was the first major British sculptor to tint his creations in the manner of Canova, transcending the experiments of the elder artist by working up his 1862 *Venus* so that the goddess has blue irises and flaxen hair (see fig. 5). Prior to this watershed, British sculptors demonstrated a newfound attentiveness to the materiality of marble through attempts to find stone with a uniform color, that is, without any "flaws." When, in 1819, the chemist Humphry Davy made it his mission to "determine if the spots in Carrara marble are iron oxide, and if they can be obliterated," he sought to aid British sculptors in their quest to create figures of unblemished "purity."[93] Canova's British patrons tried to deter him from adding rouge to the figures they had ordered.[94] The ubiquitous desire for "pure" stone did not signify the wish to establish aesthetic conditions akin to the white cube galleries of today. Rather, the pursuit of spotless, untinted marble over Canovian artifice reflects the implication of sculpted figures in the standards to which living women were being judged. "Pure" marble was aligned with ideals of female modesty to the extent that sculpted figures did not need to be given blonde hair and blue eyes in order to stand as icons of perfection in life as well as art. First published in 1836, Alexander Walker's *Beauty: Illustrated chiefly by an analysis and classification of beauty in women* cites the pallor of marble as possessing essentially the same hue

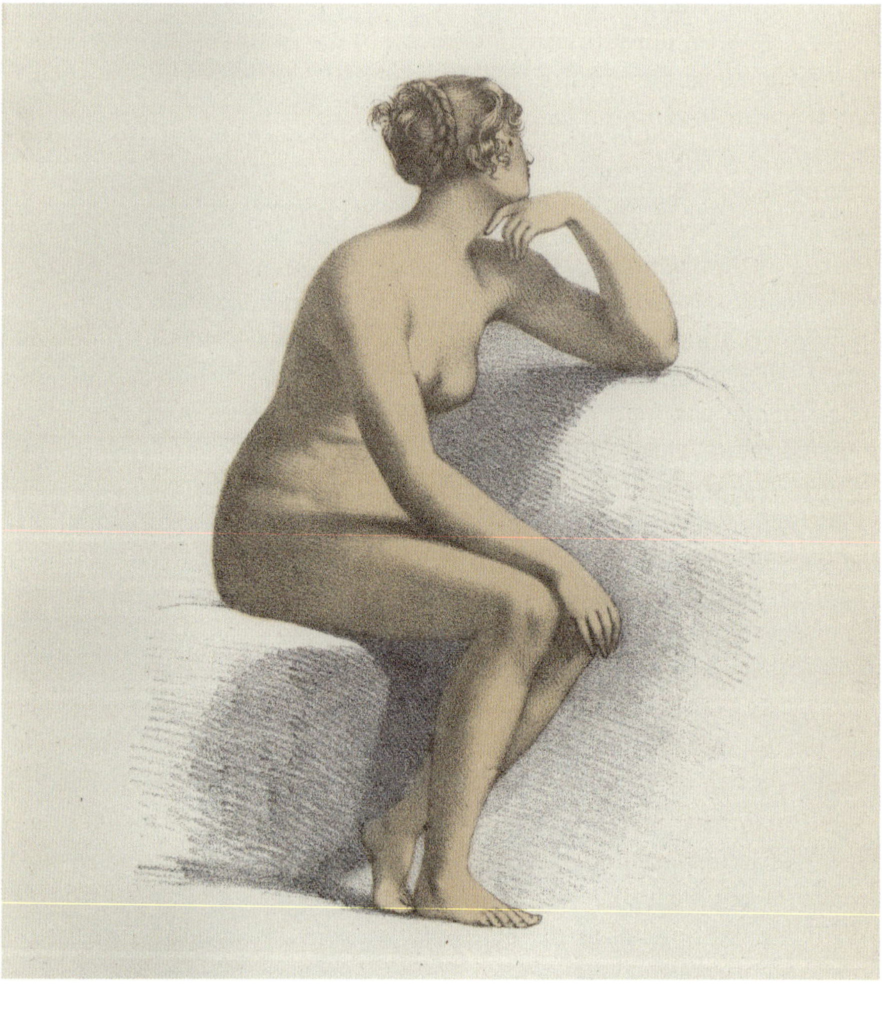

105 Unknown artist after Henry Howard, life drawing, c. 1799, lithograph. Printed in Alexander Walker, *Beauty: Illustrated chiefly by an analysis and classification of beauty in women* (London: Henry G. Bohn, 1846), pl. XXII. Yale Center for British Art, New Haven.

as "the most delicate skin of the fairest damsel of the frigid zone."[95] The author continually presents living women and the figures of art as interchangeable, particularly works of Greco-Roman sculpture. In attractive maidens, the "circulating vessels," Walker writes, "bestow upon the skin a whiteness, a transparency, and a complexion, which are necessary to beauty ... The ancients regarded whiteness, in particular, as the distinctive character of beauty; and they estimated that character so highly, that the name of Venus, from the Celtic *ven*, *ben*, or *ban*, signifies white, or whiteness."[96] Walker was a physician, and his text purports to examine the topic of female beauty through a rigorously scientific lens. He writes often of the interior of the body, making it clear that there was now a language that could reconcile sensual surfaces with an advanced understanding of how the body operates on the inside. Women will be less beautiful, he writes, "if the ligaments and the articulations they form, be not proportionally small ... in woman, this portion of the locomotive system ought also to be completely subordinate to the vital."[97] Clearly, Walker's version of science, like Bell's and Haydon's before him, is reliant on myth, superstition, and spurious claims, etymological, physiological, and otherwise. Throughout the book, life drawings made by Howard during his years as an Academy student appear in the form of lithographs, each representing a naked model whose proportions match a particular point the author wishes to make. Plate XXII, for example, is an illustration intended to show what happens when "former plumpness" leaves "the previously filled cellular tissue and expanded integuments enfeebled" (fig. 105).[98] Walker cites Howard as "an artist who inherits so much of the spirit of the ancients"; even when supposed "plumpness" is illustrated, it needs to be idealized by an artist who made his name drawing from "the antique."

Although anatomy was gendered male in British artistic practice, the interior of the female body had long been alluded to in British art. In particular, numerous painted portraits of women feature sensitively rendered contrasts between the idealized pallor of the sitter's skin and the natural flush of the cheeks, precisely the same dependency of "circulating vessels" and whiteness mentioned by Walker and exploited by Canova's artificial rouge. Angela Rosenthal explores how, long before Walker, the skin of an archetypally beautiful British woman could be invoked as having the "semi-translucent surface of marble," a quality valued because it allowed emotional responses to become visible through blushing.[99] Considered the preserve of white Europeans, the blush only heightened the beautiful woman's allure by marking her out from those of a darker complexion. To conjure this productive tension between cool pallor and vital warmth, Canova and Gibson tinted their works. Untinted objects could too, thanks to their cultivated purity, smooth contours and studied softness of surface, give audiences the impression of a living female body capable of responding to external stimuli. Faced with Westmacott's *Psyche*, exhibited at the Academy in 1822, a critic wrote that the "polished roundness of those limbs seems to warrant pressure" (fig. 106).[100] Coupled with allegations that ancient sculptures of Venus represent a post-pregnancy body, and the mother and child groups, this response renders the female body pliant, sensitive, and tactile, turning it back

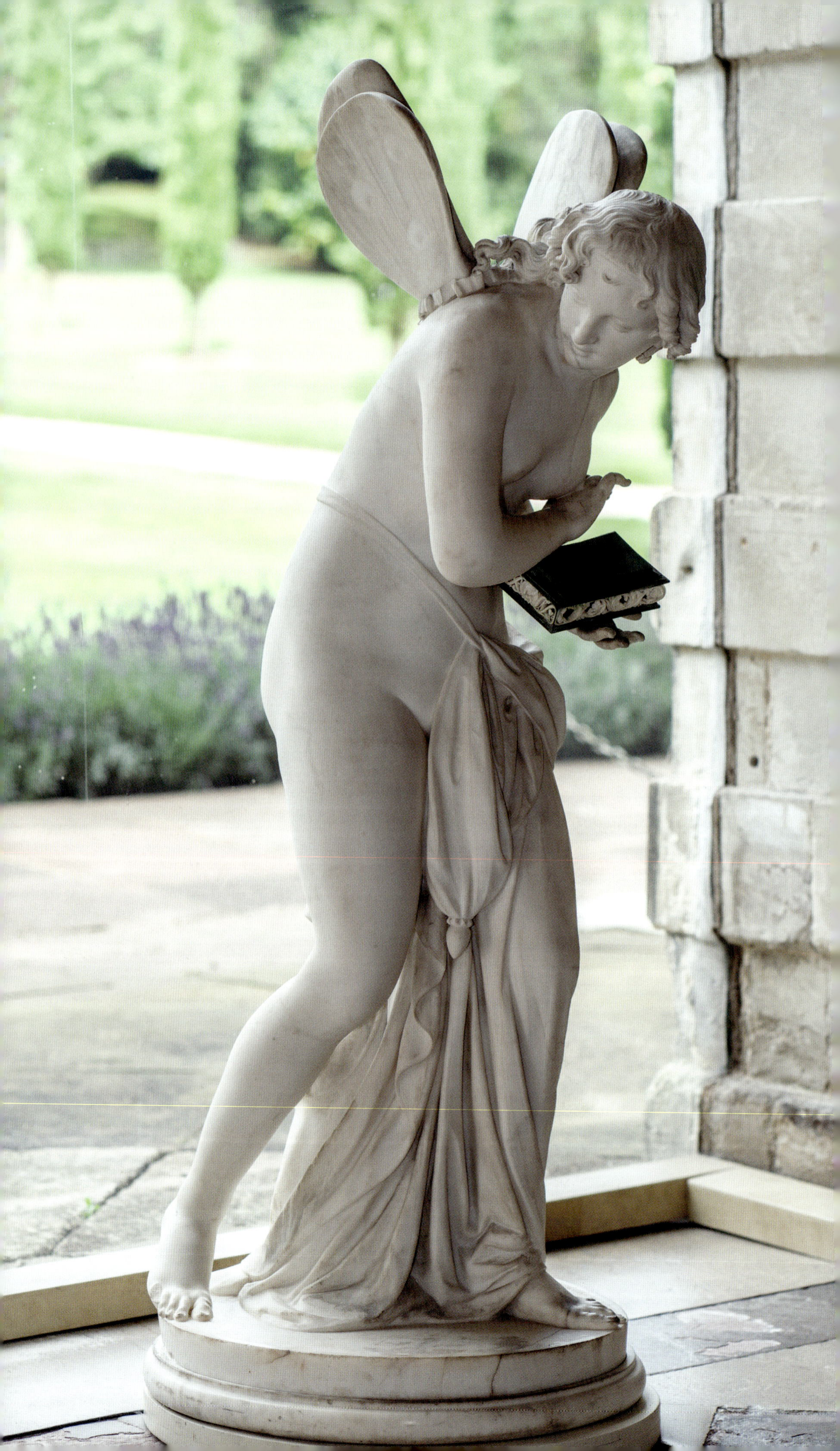

into a somatic entity. Such representations of the female body are reliant on the human form having been emptied of the Dreams that made the idealized human figure a vessel for notions beyond its form. Somatic contents – veins, for example, or the stifled allusions to lactation in the mother and child groups – replace these Dreams.[101] This is the process of recorporealization I have identified as a characteristic of Poetic art. Of course, it was primarily the male body that had been mobilized as such. But such focus on the compatibility between marble and organic matter indicates the growing preference for bodies that halt the injection of political agendas into representations of the conventionally beautiful human form. Emphatically gendered forms censor the Dreams that had infused the classical body in an earlier age.

— OLD FORMS, YOUNG BODIES —

Although sculptures of female bodies were not expected to answer the same need for specificity as their masculine counterparts, the established pantheon of Greco-Roman subjects was falling out of favor in British sculpture. A desire for novelty and a congruent wish for figures that complemented the nation's "scientific and reasoning" self-image mark the reception of these works. In spite of their generalized titles and "old antique" form, even the mother and child groups were read on nationalistic terms. A volume of engravings after contemporary British art states that such groups prove that "the English mother fondling her young child is ... a fit subject for the chisel."[102] It was in reference to a mother and child group that a critic wrote in 1832 that "subjects found in our own land are most to our liking."[103] But although they were readily enlisted to bolster nationalist rhetoric, these sculptures – like Rossi's boxer – are not inherently politicized but categorically Poetic. Co-dependent, their content and form function as a balm in direct opposition to vexing ideas. Together with their obvious allusions to Christian art, their departure from Greco-Roman subject matter was the factor allowing the mother and child groups to be interpreted as English/British. Rarely were they presented as a Venus and Cupid. If they did bear mythological titles they tended to be atypical, such as Wyatt's *Ino and the Infant Bacchus* (fig. 107). Traditional Greco-Roman subjects remained visible in Etty's contemporaneous *oeuvre*, but in sculpture they were pushed to the margins. If the form of female figures had to remain wedded to the "old antique" in order to be deemed beautiful, then the subjects needed to be refreshed to compensate for the inflexibility of the corporeal template. One exception to the displacement of mythological subjects is the increase in representations of Psyche, a Greco-Roman figure whose latter-day identity agreed with the evolving priorities of both practitioners and audiences.

In his published conversations with the painter James Northcote from the early 1820s, Hazlitt spoke on behalf of the nation at large when he cited Northcote declaring that "We are tired of the Antique; yet, at any rate, it is better than the

106 Richard Westmacott, *Psyche*, 1822, marble and mixed media. Woburn Abbey, Bedfordshire.

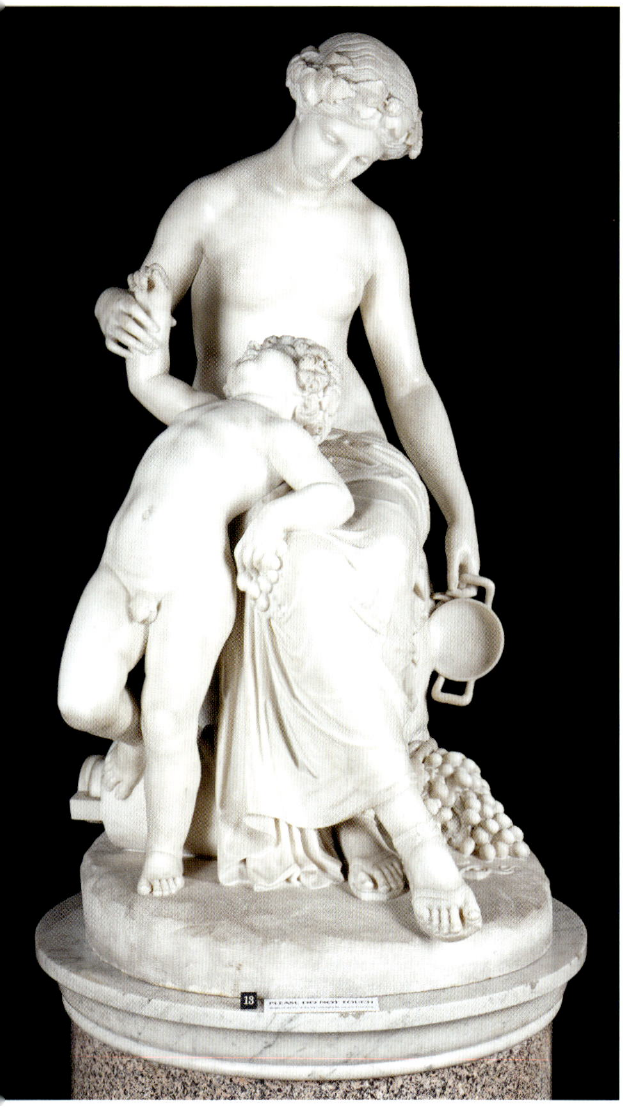

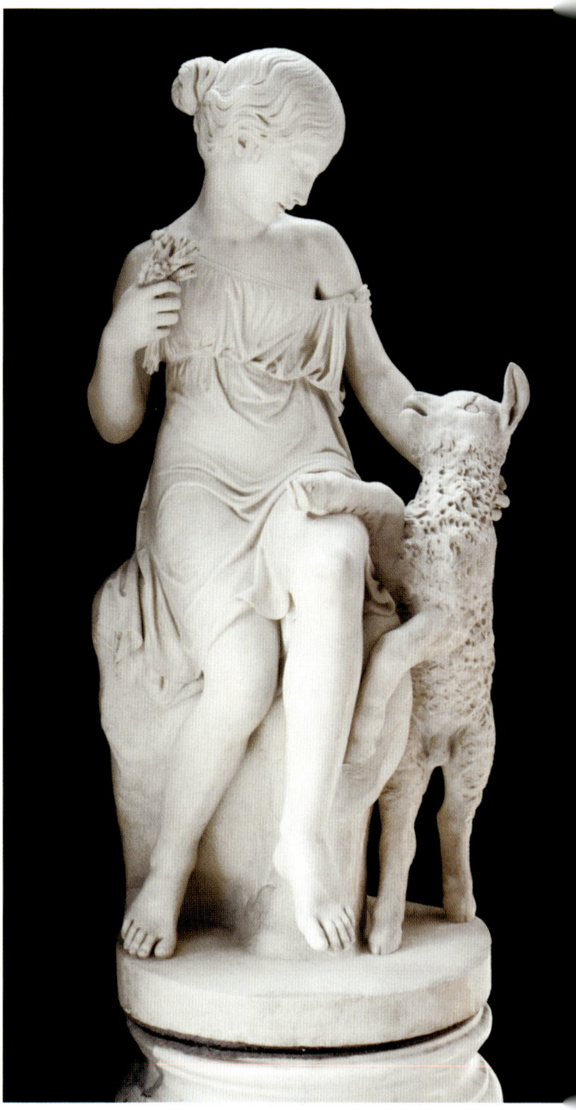

107 Richard James Wyatt, *Ino and the Infant Bacchus*, c. 1834–36, marble. Fitzwilliam Museum, Cambridge.

108 Richard James Wyatt, *Shepherdess*, c. 1840, marble. Essie Persian Carpets, London.

vapid imitation of it. The world wants something new, and will have it. No matter whether it is better or worse, if there is but an infusion of new life and spirit, it will go down to posterity."[104] Lough, Baily, and other sculptors were responding to this exact sentiment – voiced more and more in British criticism – that the imitation of "the antique" no longer satisfied in three dimensions. This, however, meant in terms of subject rather than form. The idea that the thighs of Baily's *Eve* were too large indicates how little room there was for a complete paradigm shift, despite consistent lip service to "new life and spirit." About a decade after Hazlitt's conversation with Northcote was published, the *Athenaeum* informed readers that fatigue with stock mythological subjects had not abated: "We cannot say that we are at all partial to heathen gods and goddesses: they have had their day, and we long for something new."[105] Another critic argued that the lack of religious faith in Greco-Roman deities made the reproduction of such figures ridiculous in the present day: "Can we imagine Phidias carving the gods of Egypt or Syria? Should Shakespeare have written 'Hamlet' in Latin? (He ought to have written it in Danish). ... I confess it is very difficult to think of Nollekens's Venus, Canova's Venus, Gibson's Venus, everybody's Venus with due decorum."[106] The need for specificity was obsessive, but when it came to representations of female figures, it affected only the name of the sculpture and perhaps a few details, not the shape of the body itself.

One variety of figure that could reinvigorate the template of the "old antique" while maintaining its logic was the young girl. As with the mother and child groups, the prepubescent female form was less ambiguous than that of the nubile woman. But it was a body that still needed to be sensually rendered, made smooth and soft. Finished about two decades after the sculptor's permanent relocation to Rome to study under Canova, Wyatt's life-size marble *Shepherdess* registers the ability of the young girl's body to satisfy an array of demands (fig. 108). Sitting on the tree-stump support conventional in sculptures belonging to the "old antique," the figure cannot be more than ten years old and feasibly younger. She stares straight into the eyes of a lamb – a symbol of innocence – whose lightly textured wool makes the velvety pallor of her skin appear all the more tender, its surface characteristic of the finishing technique Wyatt learned from the Monégasque sculptor François Bosio, with whom he studied on his way to Rome. While the pastoral subject was not necessarily novel, earlier portrayals of shepherds and shepherdesses tended to be statuettes or in relief. As a potter in Southwark, Bacon began his career "forming shepherds, and shepherdesses, and such like small ornamental pieces" in porcelain.[107] Pastoral figurines dating from the pre-Revolutionary period are executed in the so-called "modern" sculptural aesthetic practiced by Bacon even after the cleaner lines of "the antique" had displaced it.[108] Wyatt's group breaks with "modern" pastoral imagery, representing the type of classical body Banks had based his practice on, the type designated "old antique" by Haydon. The lineaments of the latter-day sculptures are refracted through a child's body. The girl's simple drapery, an above-the-knee chiton slipped to reveal her shoulder, is also ancient rather than "modern." There is a variance, then, between form and content, as in the ancient world and until fairly recently a shepherdess, and such a young female figure more generally, would never have been rendered life-size, free standing, and in marble.[109] The integration of pastoral subject, loyalty to the "old antique," and relatively large scale made the work adhere to the demand for "something new."

Marina Warner writes that because "eroticism is a condition of the depicted female body, a semi-naked figure, who is no longer constrained by it, becomes free."[110] In Wyatt's sculpture we see this doubled: the young age of the shepherdess gives her soft, exposed female flesh an extra layer of insulation against libidinal interpretations. But the proximity between the shepherdess and the eroticism projected onto nubile female figures is uncomfortably close. This becomes clear when we view a similar sculpture by Wyatt's Italian contemporary Giovanni Maria Benzoni, *Innocence Protected by Fidelity*, executed roughly a decade later (fig. 109). Benzoni depicts a girl of the same age in a similar position, accompanied by a spaniel the same size as Wyatt's lamb. Benzoni's allegorical title underscores the sentimental pitch of Wyatt's earlier work; both groups represent an abstract and artificial type – the innocent rustic child – that lends itself especially well to representations of young girls (similar figures appear in paintings by Reynolds and Thomas Gainsborough). Such figures have a unique "spatio-temporal principle." Both are neither infants nor adolescents, and thus are poised on the precipice of physical changes associated with sexual awakening.

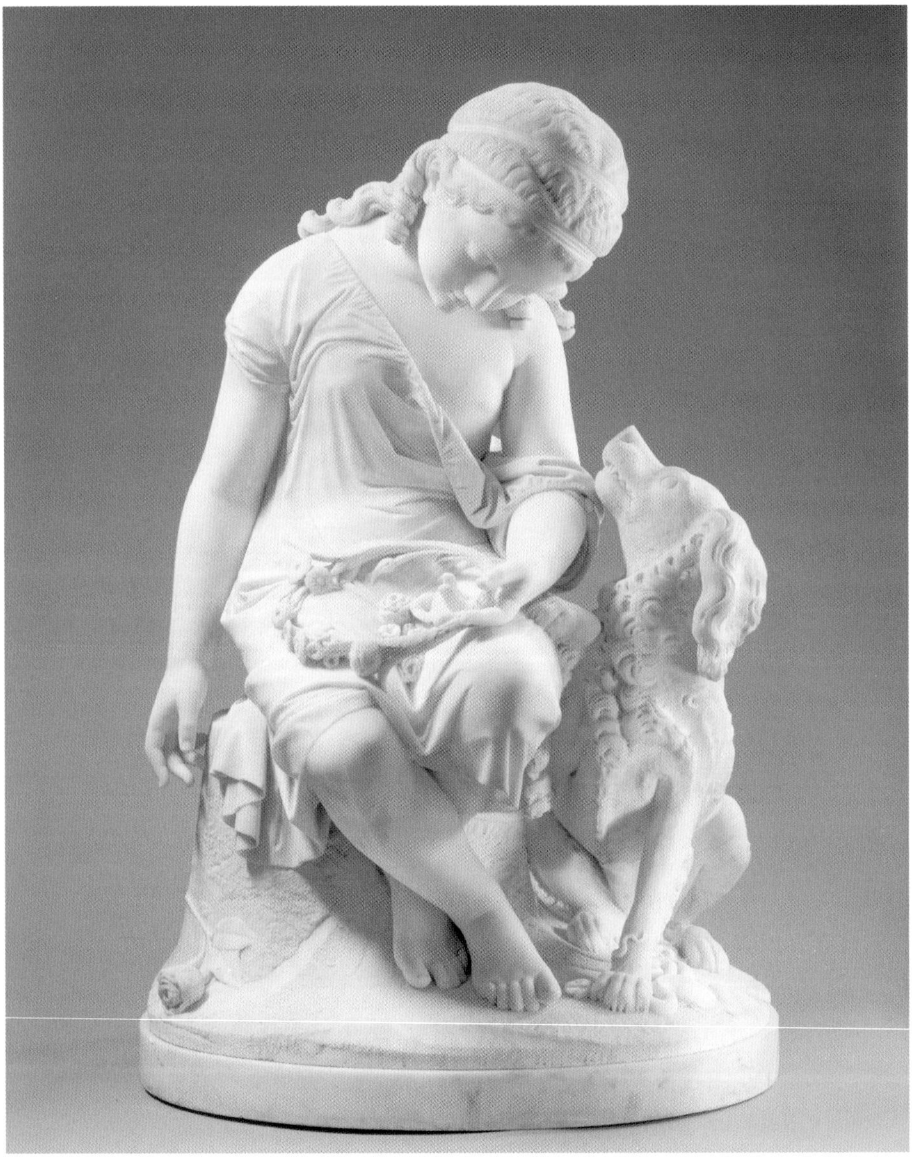

109 Giovanni Maria Benzoni, *Innocence Protected by Fidelity*, 1852, marble. Metropolitan Museum of Art, New York.

We know from responses to the *Venus de' Medici* that, more often than not, these were terms on which carved female bodies were received. Marble traps these innocent beings before they pass from childhood into the phase described by Winckelmann in his interpretation of the *Venus de' Medici*.[111] They are representations of impending flux. Wyatt substitutes the breast usually bared by the slipped chiton with a delicate naked shoulder. Benzoni is bolder, exposing the girl's nipple, her breast no more than a mound. The particular charm of a female figure approaching sexual availability was expressed in criticism of contemporary sculpture. Responding to Henry Weekes's *Bust of a Young Lady*, exhibited in 1832, a critic urged the sculptor to "try his hand on the fact of a lady about to be married who is very beautiful, and not unaware of it, and he will find he has a quick silvery sort of subject."[112]

Assessing Wyatt's *oeuvre*, you would not know that his career began at a time in which the received image of Greek form had been reconceived as a result of the Parthenon Marbles acquisition. His works bear nothing of the anatomical understanding demonstrated in the fragments, nor the rugged muscularity that gave new form to this knowledge in Lough's muscular figures. Age twenty-one and an Academy student during the Select Committee, Wyatt would have been surrounded by talk of the Marbles from the very start of his career, especially as he came from a family of practitioners and was apprenticed in Rossi's studio before his move to Rome. But he avoided the Marbles' impact by focusing almost exclusively on female forms that require an especially soft treatment. Even though casts after the fragments were kept at the Accademia di San Luca, part of the appeal of Rome was the enduring ascendancy of the "old antique" in the city, hence Haydon's remark about the castrating effects of a Roman training. A mutual friend of Wyatt and Benzoni, the Irish sculptor John Hogan made explicit his aversion to Phidias's figures after stopping in London on his way to Rome in 1823. The Marbles do not "deserve so much praise as is bestowed upon them by the English," he declared; if they were in his "possession [he] should throw half of them into the Thames."[113] In 1825, Hogan took over a part of Canova's old studio. His first completed work in Rome, *Italian Shepherd Boy*, was inspired by the *Endymion*.[114] Hogan's antipathy toward the Marbles supports my contention that, in spite of de Quincy's insistence that the Illissos is the central inspiration for the figure at Chatsworth, Canova's practice, too, was thought to be immune from Phidian authenticity.

Also in Rome was Joseph Gott, a Leeds-born sculptor who permanently relocated to the Continent with his wife and daughters in 1822, a year after Wyatt. In his youth Gott studied at the Royal Academy and was apprenticed to Flaxman. He too saw Rome as a means of breaking away from the "scientific and reasoning" current of British art to embrace the atemporal allure of the "old antique." Though he never gained the title of Royal Academician, his works in marble, mostly of female figures, children, and animals, were regularly shown at the annual exhibitions. Slightly larger than a conventional porcelain figurine, his *Little Red Riding Hood* shows Gott's proficiency with clay, an intrinsically soft and sensual material (fig. 110). A young girl stands with a basket slipped over her

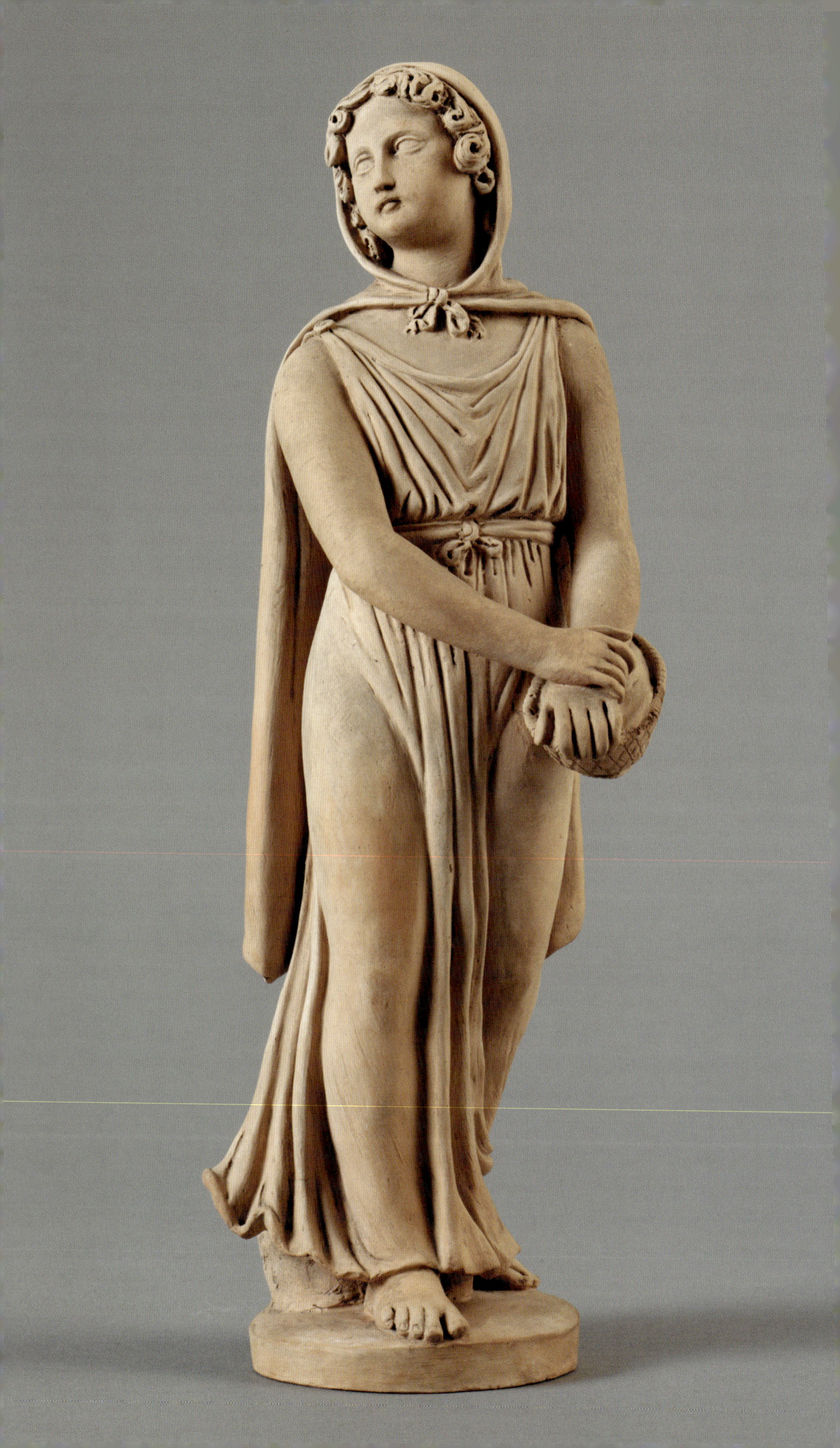

wrist as she gazes out into space, her face framed by clusters of rose-like ringlets. The hooded cape falls back to reveal her naked arms, while her legs emerge from within a diaphanous drapery that is markedly classical. Immature rather than fecund, Gott's figure brandishes the same protean innocence as the figures by Wyatt and Benzoni. Like the marble works, *Little Red Riding Hood* contains a tension between content and form. Remove the cape and this is an "old antique" figure. And while terracotta may appear to be a material that pulls the figure toward the "modern" end of the spectrum, pottery bore associations with the ancient world that rendered it just as much of a legitimate substance as marble, one that, in this instance, testifies to newfound attentiveness to the question of material in sculpture.[115] Gott's statuette does not appear to be a rehearsal for a larger figure but rather a work in its own right.[116] The sculptor did execute a four-foot version of *Little Red Riding Hood* in marble quite different to the terracotta, in which one of the child's nascent breasts is exposed (fig. 111).

For the novel subject, Gott was following a precedent recently set by his benefactor Thomas Lawrence, the portrait painter whose works the Duke of

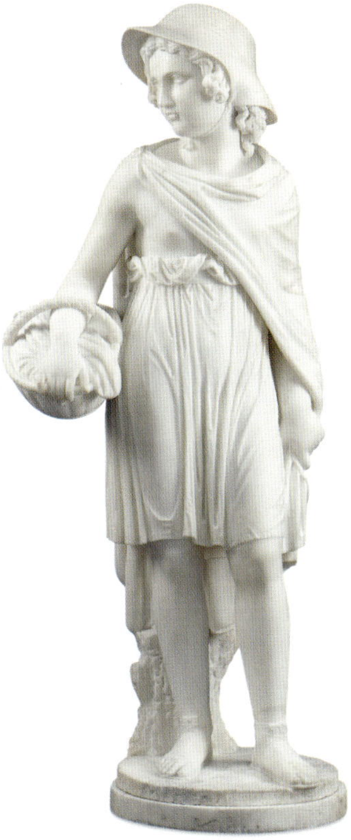

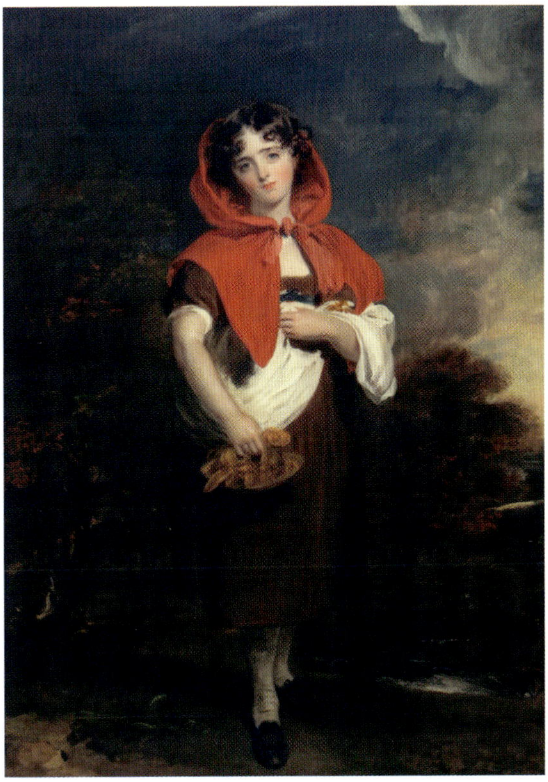

110 Joseph Gott, *Little Red Riding Hood*, 1827, terracotta. Victoria and Albert Museum, London.

111 Joseph Gott, *Little Red Riding Hood*, 1827–32, marble. M. S. Rau Antiques, New Orleans.

112 Thomas Lawrence, *Emily Anderson as Little Red Riding Hood*, 1821, oil on canvas. Huntington European Art Gallery, San Marino, Calif.

Devonshire likened to Canova's *Endymion*. In 1821, Lawrence had portrayed a young English girl, Emily Anderson, in the guise of Little Red Riding Hood (fig. 112). That a contemporary portrait could inform the appearance of sculpted figures which – cast in the mold of the "old antique" – ought to shirk the particularity of portraiture returns us to the evasion of authenticity that characterizes these works. It also suggests that the affinity identified by the duke was not merely an attempt to flatter Lawrence, and that there was something profound yoking the painter's glossy impressions of actual individuals to this kind of sculpture. Richard Brilliant proclaims that portraiture "challenges the transiency or irrelevancy of human existence"; these sculptures do the same, not by giving a "visible identity sign by which someone can be known, possibly forever," but by freeing an image of the classical body from its mooring in a fixed image of Greece, immortalizing, at the same time, the otherwise transient qualities of youth and softness seen in Lawrence's paintings.[117]

Of all the practitioners who emerged in the decade following the end of the Napoleonic Wars and the acquisition of the Parthenon Marbles, Gibson – by far the most successful – strayed the least from Greco-Roman subjects. He still favored, however, representations of female or feminized forms – whether nymphs, goddesses, and graces or infant and youthful male bodies – that do away with the need for anatomical precision that was projected onto adult male figures. Gibson did express reverence for the Marbles, flaunting his grasp of anatomy in *Mars Restrained by Cupid* of 1825; the adult god in this group, however, is feminized by an acquiescent pose that loosens the musculature.[118] Gibson was prolific, and when one takes into account his copious drawings as well as his sculptures, it becomes clear that his favorite of all subjects was the definitively feminine, sensual, and atemporal figure of Psyche. In addition to his numerous reliefs depicting moments from Apuleius's fable and his group *Psyche Borne Aloft by the Zephyrs* (see fig. 6), he produced a series of Flaxmanesque outline drawings illustrating scenes from *The Story of Psyche*, published in a single volume toward the end of his life.[119] From the very start of his career, Psyche had been with Gibson. When he was still living with his family in Liverpool, he modelled a life-size version of the goddess admiring a butterfly. His first contribution to a Royal Academy exhibition was a bas-relief of Psyche carried by the Zephyrs, which he went on to reconfigure for the three-dimensional group with the encouragement of Canova in Rome. Elizabeth Eastlake, the author of Gibson's biography who knew the sculptor well, writes that Psyche was "equally real" to the artist as his closest friend Margaret Sandbach.[120] Writing to Sandbach during a holiday in Switzerland, Gibson was eager to tell her that he used the same pen to communicate with her as he used to draw the goddess.[121] Psyche and Sandbach were, according to the sculptor, his most steadfast companions. In plaster, marble, chalk, pen, pencil, wash, and even flesh, images of Psyche preoccupied Gibson for over five decades.

Gibson professed that what he liked most about Apuleius's fable is that it "presents so many varied pictures."[122] There was more, however, so much more driving his passion for this one particular subject than its wealth of imagery. For a Greco-Roman icon, Psyche lacks agency. She is no Venus, who, as Caroline Arscott observes, often appears as an overbearing and mature maternal figure in Gibson's *oeuvre*.[123] Psyche's manipulation by forces greater than herself resonated with the sculptor's mystical view of his own destiny and, in turn, his aversion to art that attempted to intervene in the fortunes of humanity. Born into a strict religious family, he was forced, like Bacon junior and Etty, to give up his parents' degree of piety in order to be an artist focused on the classical body. He still describes the trajectory of his life in providential terms that, if not Christian, possess the perfumed sensuality of Apuleius's story. In a passage of memoir included in Eastlake's biography, Gibson tells his mother of a dream that he has had of an eagle carrying him up into the celestial realm before depositing him in Rome. Although it is his strictly Christian mother who assures him that this is a sign that he will definitely journey to Rome one day, the dream itself is pagan, resembling Psyche's encounter with an eagle after she is ordered by Venus to complete the arduous tasks. Later, while living in Rome, Gibson describes another vision, this time of Cupid visiting him in the night, as the same god did to Psyche when their marriage was consummated in the dark. This time, the god allows himself to be seen. Entering into an imaginary dialogue with Cupid, Gibson is in awe of the god's features: his "celestial countenance" and "ambrosial locks which wave luxuriantly around [his] feminine shoulders": equal parts young boy and young girl. Cupid urges Gibson to enhance the surface of his recent work *Love Disguised as a Shepherd*, reminding him that Praxiteles had called on the painter Nicias (famed for his embellishments to carved figures) to give the "last finish" to his own statue of the god (fig. 113). Here, the cherished sensuality of the "old antique" is represented in terms that are at once rational (there was a growing conversation around the claim that Greek sculptors had colored their works) and completely irrational, in that this conversation takes place in the form of a night-time reverie. With Gibson's memoirs as the meat of her biography, Eastlake chose to omit the second dream because it is "too marvellous," in other words, gives too much weight to fantasy and the imagination.[124] Just as much as any work of art, Gibson's recounting of the dream dramatizes the artist's willful distance from Dreams: those collective and rational rather than private and irrational visions. Identified by Giorgio Agamben and discussed at the start of this book, the imagination's loss of authority in Enlightenment discourse is restored by Gibson in this moment.[125]

Although they consider their agenda of universal significance, Dreamers are destined to be wedded to a specific chapter in history. By contrast, Gibson's vision is atemporal in that it takes place outside of linear time and therefore is pushed to the fringes of the historical record, belonging, like Psyche herself, to "poetic and erotic time, the time of the amorous body."[126] Eastlake's choice to omit the scene from her biography is testament to the dream's wayward "spatio-temporal principle." As with images of Psyche by Reynolds and Canova, Gibson's reverie encapsulates an artistic subjectivity at war with politicized deployments of the classical body. The difference is that Gibson offers his image long after their side had won.

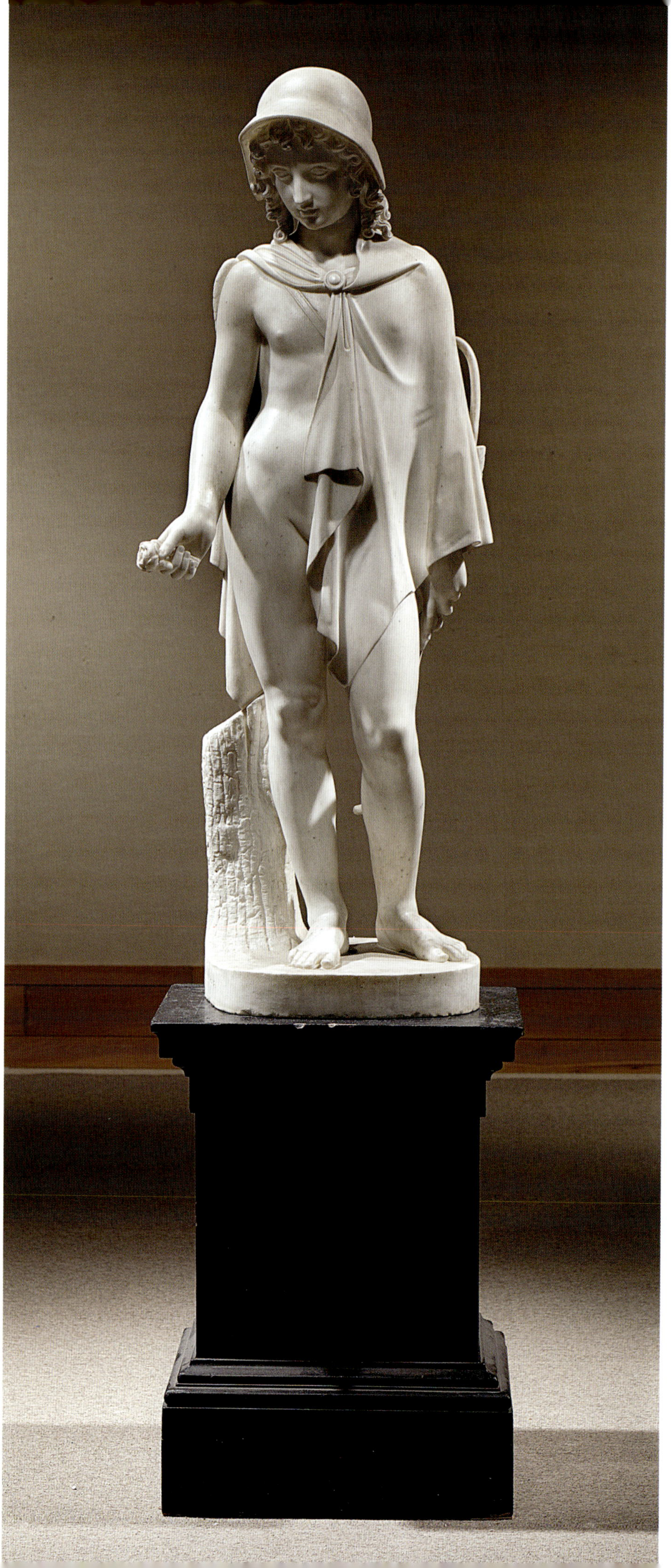

Centering on the "sweetened" materiality of sculpture, Gibson's dream is, like all of his works, Poetic. Its undeniable erotic frisson points to the mystification and recorporealization of classical and classicizing sculpture, processes that underpinned his practice. In his memoirs, the sculptor revels, like Winckelmann, in other androgynous male bodies.[127] Indeed, when Gibson cites the German scholar, it is a wholly different Winckelmann from the one on whose writings Banks based his politically radical notions of freedom. Rather than emphasizing the discrepancy between Greco-Roman antiquity and contemporary life that gives "vulgar Winkelmannianism" its charge, Gibson's Winckelmann is a strictly sensual figure who brings the classical body closer. The sculptor credits the scholar with the observation that "now and then there springs up at Rome a face *equal* to the antique"; Gibson also defers to Winckelmann's authority on one of his favorite works in Rome: the relief of Antinous kept in the Villa Albani, an inescapably pederastic object in that it portrays Emperor Hadrian's lover.[128]

The patently homoerotic aspect of Gibson's dream and of his reception of Winckelmann is less valuable for what it says about the sculptor's sexuality than for the way it distinguishes his practice from the sexless monuments centered on naked male figures. Gibson was well aware of the disaster that was the bronze Wellington-as-Achilles in Hyde Park. The sculptor was convinced that the failure of this work stemmed from the fact that not a single member of the committee overseeing the design was an artist.[129] This was a veiled way of saying that the work is flawed because it forces the classical body to carry ideas belonging to a sphere outside that of artistic practice. Instead of using art to harbor a world view attached but ultimately separable from ancient Greece, artists ought to engage with the human form in order to cultivate, in Eastlake's words in her assessment of Gibson's *oeuvre*, "Art for her own sake only."[130] And it was the figure of Psyche who, even after the twilight of mythological subjects in British sculpture, was poised to receive this command. Psyche's dominion may be the soul, but she is the figure that turns the classical body back into a body. She is not a vessel but a girl whose beauty grants her immortality: a life outside of time. Lough, Baily, Gott, Wyatt, and Benzoni all produced their own representations of the belated goddess, as did countless other sculptors, and painters, of their generation and beyond.

113 John Gibson, *Love Disguised as a Shepherd*, c. 1836, marble. Yale Center for British Art, New Haven.

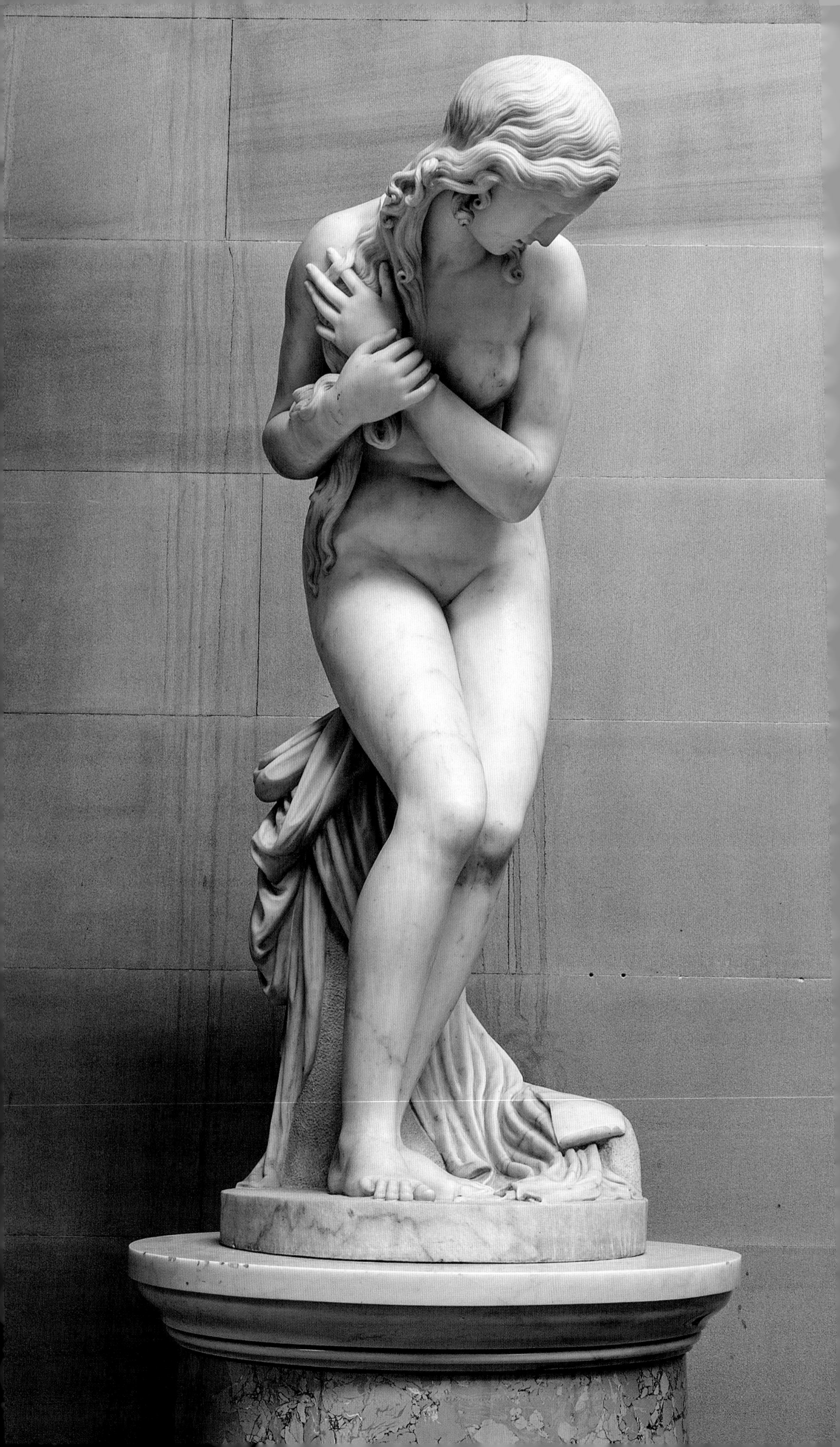

PSYCHE'S TRIUMPH
Poetic Sculpture

Keats arrived in Rome toward the end of 1820. At the very start of this book I mentioned Richard Monkton Milnes's account of the poet's intention to visit Canova's studio. This detail may be factually inaccurate; yet it manages to identify the kinship between poet and sculptor, a bond representative of an entire movement within the reception of Greco-Roman antiquity in the context of British art, and a pivotal one at that. For a time, Rome was the capital of this movement. When Keats arrived, Gibson had been living there for several years. Wyatt relocated in 1821, Gott in 1822, and Lough for a shorter stint in 1834. Many others were based in Rome over the course of these years. After Keats's death in the winter of 1821 his friend Joseph Severn, the actual recipient of the letter of introduction to Canova, reflected that the poet would have delighted in Gott's sculptures: a body of work dominated by forms that, whether in polished Carrara marble or tactile clay, are smooth, softly rendered, and emphatically feminine.[1] Poetic subjectivity finds expression in such works. Severn's suggestion of a thread binding Keats to Gott's art is as eloquent as Milnes's account of the missed encounter between the poet and Canova.

Indeed, while Keats had Dreaming tendencies, he was immortalized, in Rome, as a Poet: an artist withdrawn from the desire to change the world. Although this has since been contested, Severn claimed that Keats's final work was "Bright star, would that I were steadfast as thou art," a sonnet in which events on "earth's human shores" are dwarfed by the "unchangeable" workings of a "priestlike" Nature whose dominion spans water, mountains, and moors as well as the sky.[2] Like Coleridge's clouds and Flaxman's Swedenborgian view of the heavens, Keats's star diminishes mortal agency. And like works by Canova, Reynolds, Flaxman, Etty, and Gibson, the poem casts a celestial light on sensual imagery. The speaker covets the star's fixity while he touches his lover's body, surrendering to the "soft fall and swell" of a "ripening breast" that could belong to a figure by the hand of any one of these artists. Restored to a position of power, fantasy and the imagination are the forces that transfigure sensuality into a sacred experience. Fantasy and the imagination recover the somatic status of the represented body and re-envelop it – whether painted, drawn, modelled, cast, carved, or conjured through words – in mystery. One word given to this mystery is "sweetness," a term that recurs in relation to Poetic achievements. In "Bright star," Keats presents celestial sensuality as a feeling of "sweet unrest."

114 Joseph Gott, *Musidora,* 1827, marble. Chatsworth House, Derbyshire.

Instead of cementing his affinity with the likes of Flaxman and Etty, this line betrays that Keats was not a fully fledged Poet like these visual artists. Rather than a purely positive phenomenon, sweetness, according to the speaker of this sonnet at least, brings forth a modicum of discomfort, of restlessness. While Keats died a Poet in Rome, he maintained an awareness that there was another side to the image of the body, that art could, and perhaps should, do more than "pour out a balm."

Keats's Rome was not the Rome that Banks, or Flaxman and Howard for that matter, had trained in during the decades leading up to French Revolution and the outbreak of the Napoleonic Wars. Haydon and Hazlitt expressed disapproval of those choosing to move to Rome in the post-Napoleonic period because, rather than energizing artists and encouraging them to experiment, the postwar city seemed to have a pacifying effect.[3] Despite the threat of cholera and street violence, Rome, as Poetic capital, was itself a balm, a literal comfort zone for artists. There, in the "Eternal City," the ascendency of the "old antique" went mostly unquestioned, sensuality was encouraged in all areas of life from love to art to food, and, most significantly, artists could create Poetic works with less financial strain. Baily, the sculptor who helped to cultivate the British mother and child group, never went to Rome. In 1831, he went bankrupt and, six years later, was imprisoned for debt mere months after the display of his *Maternal Affection* at the Royal Academy. His fate is a far cry from that of Bacon senior, whose decision not to go to Rome worked in his favor and nurtured his use of the classical body as a vessel. In the battle against Dreams, Poetic art may ultimately have been triumphant. Only in Rome, however, could Poetic sculpture flourish.

At some point during the interval between the cessation of the Napoleonic Wars and the widespread relocation of artists to Rome from Britain, works by Canova, Gibson, Wyatt, Lough, Gott, and Baily came actually to be known as "poetic sculpture." This is the point at which the period's official vocabulary intersects with the dialectic, sourced from Keats, that I have deployed in the preceding chapters. For a sculpted form to be classed "poetic," it had to represent some kind of fictional or remotely historical figure. Historians that touch on the emergence of "poetic sculpture" interpret the category as an index of the literary underpinning of these works: their correlation with passages from particular texts.[4] Often, however, figures were not lifted from a literary source, as with Wyatt's *Shepherdess* or the corpus of anonymous nymphs by the same sculptor. What made these sculptures "poetic" was a factor more abstract than literal. The very notion of the "poetic" stood for a retreat into fantasy and the imagination, into a space forcibly separate from all the social and civic concerns that the classical body had, at one point, harbored. By 1835, a critic could describe a specific audience for such objects as "a visitor who, amid the heavier realities of life, is in a quest of the fanciful or the poetic."[5]

In the years after his death, Banks's political activism was blotted out from his legacy. This meant that the radical sculptor who, as we know, pioneered the creation of original works in the mold of the antique could be cast as the grandfather of poetic sculpture in the burgeoning historiography of British art.[6] Bringing his political commitment back into view and, moreover, the co-dependency of his activism and the classical body, alters this claim. In fact, it was the downfall of the variety of visual classicism practiced by Banks that led to the blossoming of poetic sculpture among the next generation. William Calder Marshall, a leading sculptor of the Victorian period who, in his youth, trained under Gibson's guidance in Rome, recoiled at the mere thought of radical politics. Writing to his mother, he scoffed at the legacy of French Revolutionary ideals, dismissing them as "absurd."[7] Gott's tenant for a while on the Via Pontifici, Calder Marshall too specialized in soft, sensual portrayals of feminine forms. His *oeuvre* includes at least four versions of Psyche, one of which was made in Rome with Gibson's supervision.[8] Inadvertently, his confession of contempt for radical discourse reignites the war that raged between the two types of art I have charted in this book. It points to a dormant feature of what came to be called "poetic sculpture": its hostility, articulated predominantly in the materiality and temporality of the art object, toward politicized classicism.

Despite the fact that, when it comes to sculpture, the period's own vocabulary converges so neatly with the parlance of this book, it was painting that provided more fertile ground for the development and enrichment of Poetic subjectivity as the nineteenth century progressed. Edward Burne-Jones, a leading contributor to the Aesthetic movement that crystallized after the deaths of even the youngest artists who feature in this book, was fixated on the figure of Psyche. For him, representing the belated goddess offered a means of synthesizing an array of art-historical influences, thereby transcending them all to produce autotelic objects capable of driving contemporary art in new directions. Psyche's atemporality allowed Burne-Jones's representations of Apuleius's tale happily to accommodate elements taken from Greek and Greco-Roman sculpture (increasingly divisible), medieval, fifteenth- and early sixteenth-century paintings.[9] Such a reconciliation in the name of art that, in the words of Elizabeth Prettejohn, "refuses subservience to 'reality' in the form of either visual realism or social and political engagement" was the aim of the Aesthetic movement at large.[10] Another definitive aspect of Aesthetic paintings is that, through rich color, gilding, and embellished textures, they "systematically interpose a process of artificialisation between the work and 'nature.'"[11] Artists like Reynolds, Canova, and Gibson possessed values that are antithetical to the more avant-garde leanings of Burne-Jones, who was anti-establishment and suspicious of the Royal Academy. Yet the eccentric material practices of the three elder artists – as well as their overall attention to the materiality of their objects – set a precedent for the Aesthetic "process of artificialisation." Canova especially anticipates the Aesthetic movement. The sculptor's birth in the Veneto gave him a self-conscious relationship to painting of the Venetian Renaissance, a branch of art that he not only emulated (along with paintings by Correggio) in his own paintings on canvas, but was used by critics to justify the exaggerated sensuality of his marble figures: their carnal tints and waxy finishes that somehow manage to bring them closer to "reality" in spite of their artifice.[12] Venetian painting was a predominant influence on the Aesthetic movement, and was the context for Walter Pater's proclamation on art and music.

That the closing decades of the nineteenth century see the Poetic mission appreciated in painting, poetry, and prose and less so sculpture is an index of the division between media that grew during the period under consideration in this book. Marginalized at Royal Academy exhibitions and essentially exiled to Rome, sensual, emphatically gendered sculptures that actively evade the "heavier realities of life" – otherwise known as "poetic sculpture" – were resistant to the innovations and integrations that comprised Aestheticism in other media.

This is not to say that sculpture as an art form did not thrive. The works christened "New Sculpture" by Edmund Gosse in the 1890s signal a new chapter, a break not only with the classical body-as-vessel, but the classical body-as-balm, too. Rejected by Gosse, both conceptions of the human form rely heavily on the corporeal template of the antique: its Winckelmannian connection to freedom, on the one hand, and its equally Winckelmannian sensuality and erotic charge, on the other. By 1883, Gosse could criticize both Banks and Calder Marshall for their "bondage to tradition."[13] In sculpture, innovation meant doing away with that template altogether in favor of a momentary naturalism beyond even the anatomical veracity – still idealized – of the Parthenon Marbles. Frederic Leighton's sculpture of *An Athlete Wrestling with a Python* is a very different statement to his painting of the *Bath of Psyche*, the latter a work that, although exhibited almost two decades after the artist's "new" sculpture, extends and safeguards the Poetic tradition. With limbs slightly longer than the *Callipygian Venus* but faithful to the classical sculpture's logic, Leighton's goddess could be a wax-coated figure by Canova (fig. 115).

Poetic sculpture proper was gradually phased out, its sweetness dismissed as mawkish: the very embodiment of what Clement Greenberg would eventually designate "kitsch."[14] Some of its last vestiges are the mass-produced Parianware statuettes of figures by Gibson and those he worked alongside: objects that found their way, just like steel engravings in gift books, into the homes of middle-class consumers. Gibson was a savvy businessman who acquired great wealth by allowing his work to be reproduced in this way. Although an arch-Poet, his commercial sensibility casts his desire to "pour out a balm" in a more mechanical, even a more alienated light than the mission of his mentor Canova.

The destiny of Poetic sculpture, or "poetic sculpture," exposes the fact that, only in the context of three-dimensional art was the classical body incompatible with the desire for novelty. Novelty in sculpture leads ultimately to the renovation of form, and while surface and subject – materiality and temporality – were adaptable, "poetic" bodies are inexorably tied to an earlier age, an earlier conflict. The objects themselves register the pressures exerted on sculpture from both sides of history. A common characteristic of works by Gibson, his peers, and followers is the way that the classical body is contracted into a quiet pose that shuts out the world around it. Of the sculptures I have already named, Wyatt's *Shepherdess* and Baily's *Eve at the Fountain* are two instances of this folding

115 Frederic Leighton, *Bath of Psyche*, exhibited 1890, oil on canvas.
Tate Britain, London.

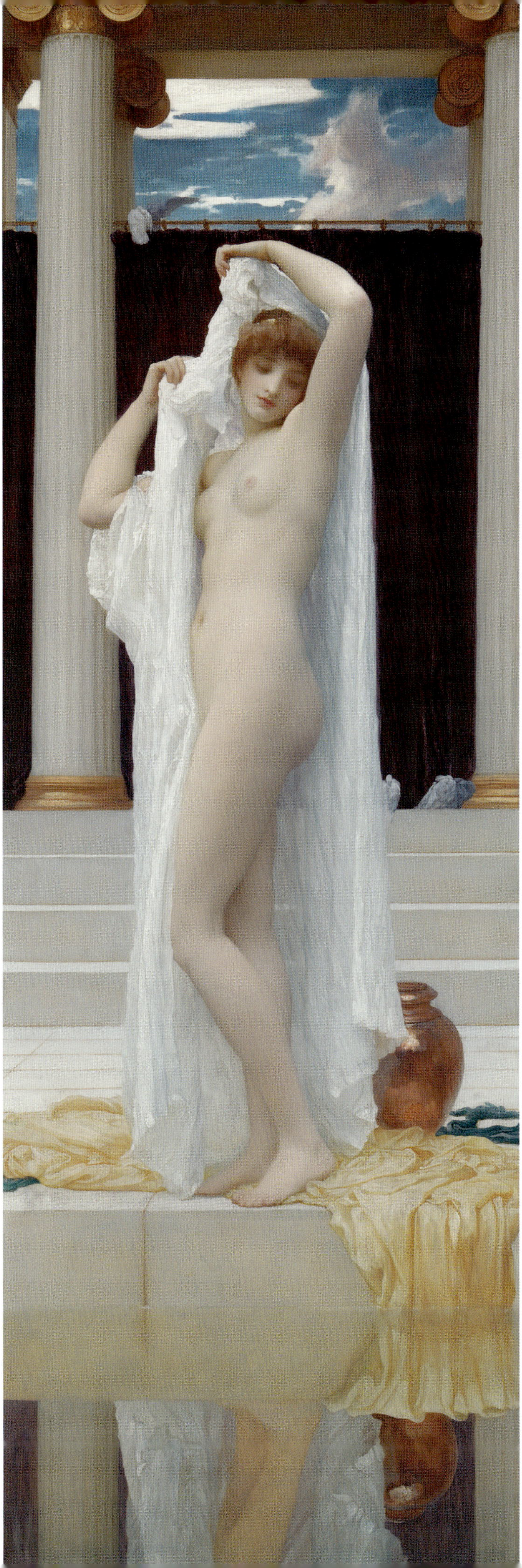

inwards to a space that is not shared with the viewer (see figs. 108 and 103). In such works, the self-containment paradigmatic of statues like the *Venus de' Medici* is redoubled.[15] Other striking cases abound: a *Wounded Amazon* by Gibson is absorbed by a trickle of blood on her upper thigh; Gott's *Ruth* is engrossed in the act of gleaning, her back an arch of polished stone; the same artist's *Musidora* at Chatsworth stoops, crossing her arms over her chest not in response to an outside disturbance but to stay fixed within a secret realm which only our imaginations – if we honor their power – are able to enter (figs. 117, 116, and see fig. 114). There are countless others in this vein. In each, the classical body is pushed to its limits *as a form* without crossing over into a "new" paradigm.[16] But this is only half the story. Simultaneously, these works embody the once urgent need to wrest the human body from the "heavier realities of life," a phrase that encompasses the injustices radical activists fought against. These figures appear busy. It is as if they are blocking out memories of the war that shaped them.

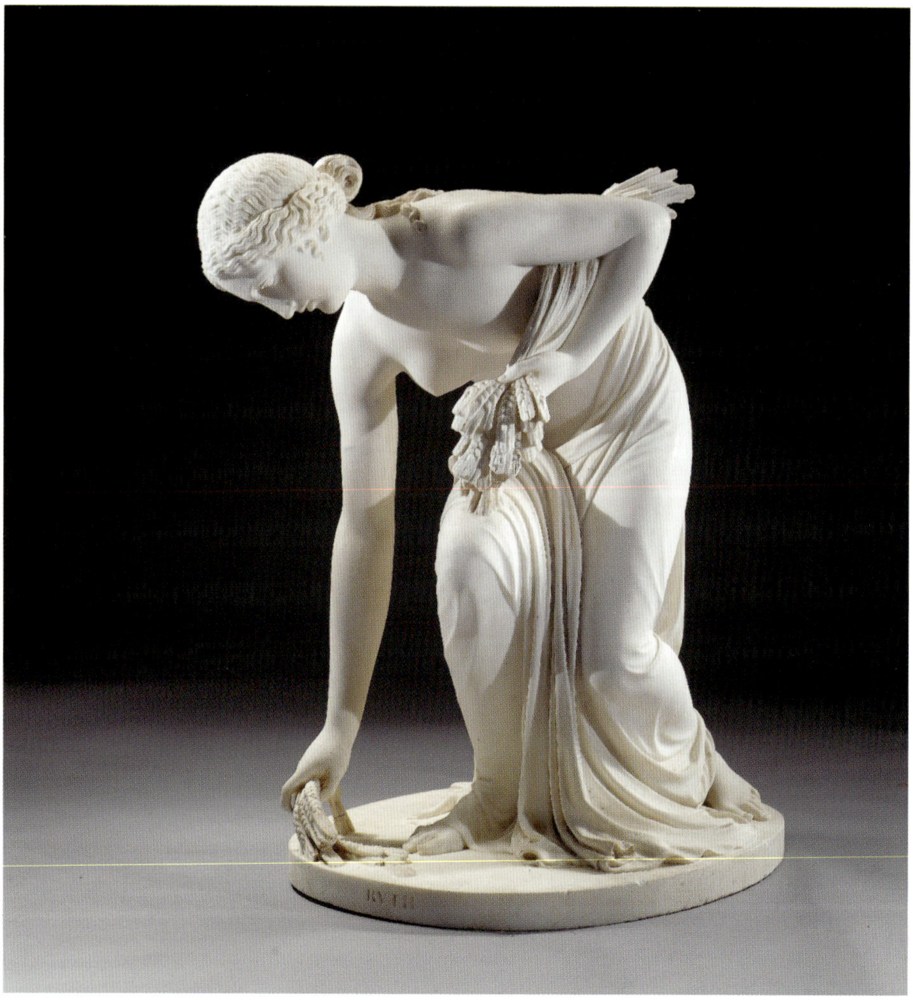

116 Joseph Gott, *Ruth*, c. 1830, marble. Collection of Richard H. Driehaus, Chicago.

117 John Gibson, *Wounded Amazon*, c. 1840–53, marble. National Museum Wales, Cardiff.

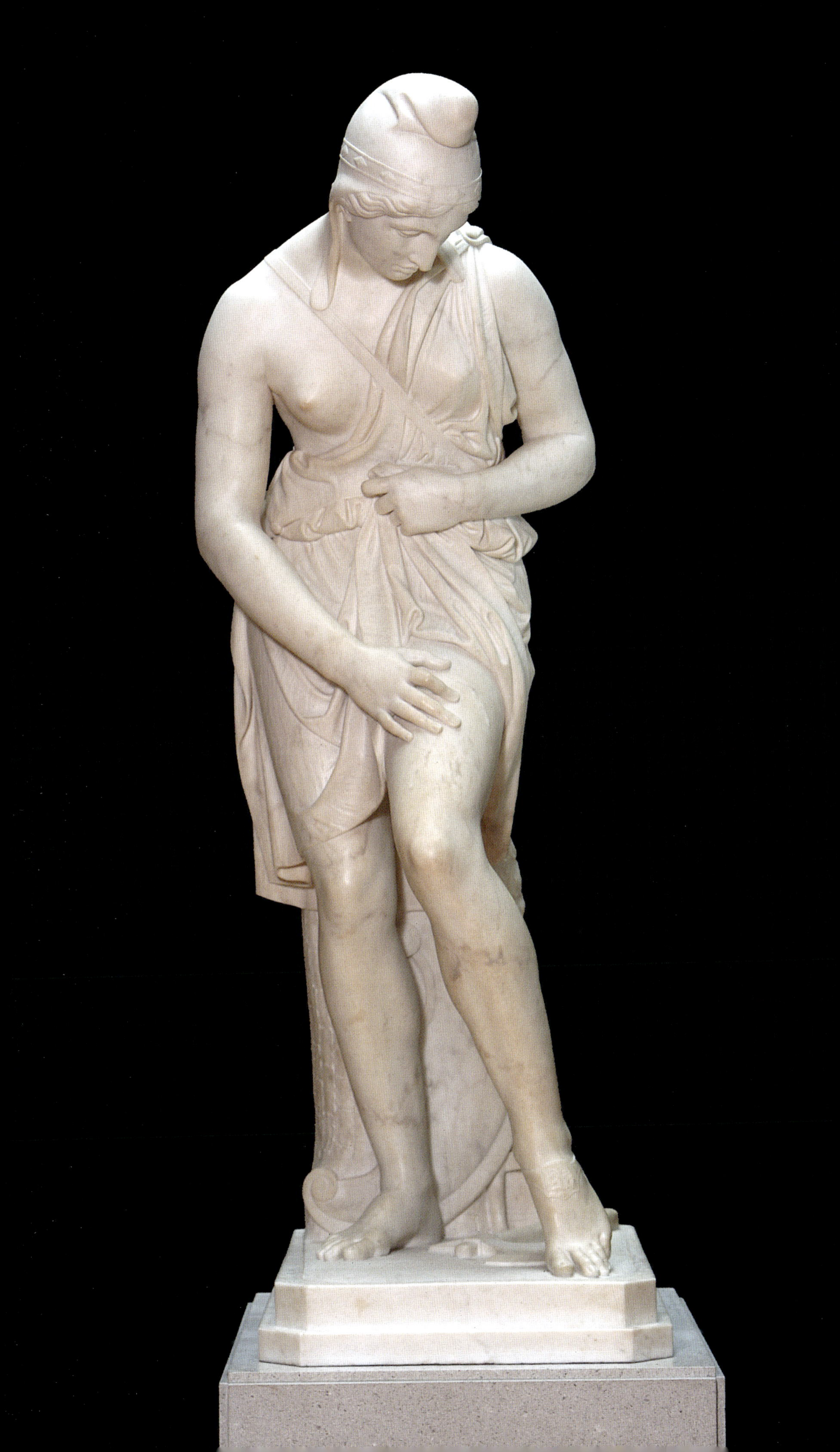

Preface *pages xi–xiii*

1. Richard Monkton Milnes, *Life, Letters and Literary Remains of John Keats*, vol. 2 (London: Edward Moxton, 1848), 81.

2. See the entry on "smooth" in Michael G. Becker, Robert J. Dilligan, and Todd K. Bender (eds.), *A Concordance to the Poems of John Keats* (London and New York: Routledge, 2016), 482.

3. Quoted in Alexander Gilchrist, *Life of William Etty, RA*, 2 vols. (London: David Bogue, 1855), vol. 2, 42–3.

Introduction *pages 1–27*

1. A paradigmatic instance of the usage of this phrase is found in John Dryden's appendix to the English translation of Charles Alphonse du Fresnoy's *Art of Painting*. See C. A. du Fresnoy, *Art of Painting, with annotations by Joshua Reynolds*, trans. William Mason (York: A. Ward, 1783), 165.

2. Joshua Reynolds's concept of "ancient taste" bears close correlations with the concept of the "classical," referring to both the sculpture of Greco-Roman antiquity and old master painting. This all-encompassing phrase is used throughout his writings, acquiring a special charge in his "Ironical Discourse": a late text unpublished during his lifetime. The "Ironical Discourse" is featured in Frederick W. Hilles (ed.), *Portraits by Sir Joshua Reynolds* (London: Heinemann, 1952), 127–44.

3. William Holman Hunt, *Pre-Raphaelitism and the Pre-Raphaelite Brotherhood*, vol. 1 (New York and London: Macmillan & Co., 1905), 84.

4. Reflecting on the previous generation of Royal Academicians, the painter Benjamin Robert Haydon, for example, wrote that "Never were four men so essentially different as West, Fuzeli, Flaxman and Stothard." B. R. Haydon, *Lectures on Painting and Design* (London: Longman, Brown, Green, and Longmans, 1846), 33.

5. Martin Myrone, *Bodybuilding: Reforming Masculinities in British Art* (New Haven and London: Yale University Press, 2005).

6. See, for example, Viccy Coltman, *Fabricating the Antique: Neoclassicism in Britain, 1760–1800* (Chicago: University of Chicago Press, 2006).

7. For insight into Winckelmann's approximation of Greek art, see Elizabeth Prettejohn, *The Modernity of Ancient Sculpture: Greek Sculpture and Modern Art from Winckelmann to Picasso* (London and New York: I. B. Tauris, 2012), 23–5.

8. Printed in *Lettere di pittori e scrittori Italiani* (from the collection of the Countess of Cigonara) (Venice: G. Passeri Bragadin, 1844), no. 5 (unpaginated).

9. Hugh Honour, "Antonio Canova and the Anglo-Romans: Part 1: The First Visit to Rome," *Connoisseur* 143 (1959a), 244.

10. Julius Bryant, *Thomas Banks: Britain's First Modern Sculptor* (London: Sir John Soane's Museum, 2005); Julius Bryant, "Eccentric Pioneers? Patrons of Modern Sculpture for Britain," in Diana Dethloff, Tessa Murdoch, and Kim Sloan, with Caroline Elam (eds.), *Burning Bright: Essays in Honour of David Bindman* (London: UCL Press, 2015), 66–76.

11. Honour, "Canova and the Anglo-Romans: 1," 243. Bryant, "Eccentric Pioneers," 68.

12. Honour, "Canova and the Anglo-Romans: 1," 243.

13. In his discussion of Banks's colleague and collaborator Henry Fuseli, Myrone writes that "new subjects served to distinguish [the painter] from his contemporaries simply by virtue of his novelty." This appears in a discussion of the thriving artistic communities in Rome during these years and Fuseli's own

innovative take on Greco-Roman models. See Myrone, *Bodybuilding*, 178–9.

14. Johann Joachim Winckelmann, *Geschichte der Kunst des Alterthums* (Dresden: in der Waltherischen Hof-Buchandlung, 1764).

15. Johann Joachim Winckelmann, *History of the Art of Antiquity*, trans. Harry Francis Mallgrave (Los Angeles: Getty Research Institute, 2006), 121. The complexities and inconsistencies of this model are discussed at length in Alex Potts, *Flesh and the Ideal: Winckelmann and the Origins of Art History* (New Haven and London: Yale University Press, 1994).

16. Though he posits Periclean democracy as the apogee of Greek freedom, Winckelmann sees the freedom of the Greeks as a fundamental condition that existed even in the context of monarchic rule: "With regard to the constitution and government of Greece, freedom was the chief reason for their art's superiority. Freedom always had its seat in Greece, even beside the thrones of kings, who ruled paternally before the enlightenment of reason allowed people to taste ... full freedom [during the age of Pericles]" (Winckelmann, *History of the Art of Antiquity*, 187). Potts writes that Winckelmann's conception of freedom is as a precondition of beauty rather than a reflection of beauty: "Freedom marks the prelude to an artistic flowering for which it prepares the way, but with which it can never be identical" (Potts, *Flesh and the Ideal*, 53).

17. See Katherine Harloe, "Pausanias as Historian in Winckelmann's History," *Classical Receptions Journal* 2/2 (2010), 174–96. For a discussion of Winckelmann's reception of Whig theorist Anthony Ashley-Cooper, 3rd Earl of Shaftesbury, see David Irwin (ed.), *Winckelmann: Writings on Art* (New York: Phaidon, 1972), 38–41.

18. See Potts's discussion of Jacques-Louis David in *Flesh and the Ideal*, 222–38. Earlier in the book, Potts notes that "Winckelmann's understanding of freedom has little of the civic public dimension already evident in the more progressive writings of his immediate French contemporaries, who held up antiquity as the model for an art based on republican liberty" (55). This did not stop his writings from being incorporated into radical discourse around the time of the French Revolution; Padiyar describes a "liberating Winckelmannian aesthetic," Satish Padiyar, *Chains: David, Canova, and the Fall of the Public Hero in Postrevolutionary France* (University Park, Pennsylvania State University Press, 2007), 93.

19. Whitney Davis, *Queer Beauty: Sexuality and Aesthetics from Winckelmann to Freud and Beyond* (New York: Columbia University Press, 2010), 33.

20. David Bindman, *Warm Flesh, Cold Marble: Canova, Thorvaldsen and their Critics* (New Haven and London, Yale University Press, 2014), 1–2; Michael Baxandall, *Patterns of Intention* (New Haven and London: Yale University Press, 1988), 76–7.

21. When a version of Winckelmann's text was first published in London, it bore the title: *The History of Ancient Art Among the Greeks*. A year earlier, an edition of the same translation had been published in Boston, entitled *The History of Ancient Art*, but this title was thought to be too general since the translator, G. Henry Lodge, had omitted sections of the work that concentrate on the art of other civilizations. Johann Joachim Winckelmann, *The History of Ancient Art Among the Greeks*, trans. G. Henry Lodge (London: John Chapman, 1850).

22. An entry in Joseph Farington's diary reveals that Banks was involved with controversial political activities in Rome. According to Banks's friend John Flaxman (whose words are summarized by Farington), Banks's "indiscretion in that respect both in Italy and England had hurt his interest." Kenneth Garlick and Angus Macintyre (eds.), *The Diary of Joseph Farington*, vol. 1 (New Haven and London: Yale University Press, 1979), 161.

23. Johann Joachim Winckelmann, *Reflections on the Painting and Sculpture of the Greeks*, trans. Henry Fuseli (London: printed for the translator, 1765).

24. Ibid., 4–5.

25. Hugh Honour, "Canova and David," *Apollo* 96 (1972), 312; Mario Praz describes the "escapist" conception of Canova as a "commonplace" surrounding the artist. See M. Praz, "Canova: Ice and Eros," *Art News Annual* 29 (1964), 125.

26. In the context of painting and sculpture made on the Continent during the same period (particularly but not exclusively in France), Satish Padiyar identifies a binary between two types of classical body that is similar to the split I identify within British art:

the "socratic body" versus the "anacreontic body." For Padiyar, "socratic" representations of the human figure are oriented toward bourgeois conceptions of virtue and self-denial, whereas their "anacreontic" counterparts manifest an aristocratic tolerance for leisure, indulgence, and excess. The form of the body is fundamentally the same in both incarnations, that is, the body remains idealized according to the principles of Greco-Roman sculpture. Yet the context for that form, and the spirit in which that form is portrayed, are antithetical. Canova is one of the artists whose achievements Padiyar describes as paradigmatically "anacreontic"; in the context of Britain, Canova's approach appealed to the burgeoning middle classes and to the aristocracy alike (the division between the two less self-evident than in France). Banks's art was couched in a network of radical activists from various backgrounds, and his works – commissioned by the state, the middle class (one of his patrons was the MP and farmer Thomas Johnes), and the aristocracy – are aimed at a universal idea of the human subject that transcends class distinctions while validating the "common man." Furthermore, Padiyar's distinction is less stable in the context of Britain because the legacy of Socrates was irrelevant to an artist like Banks, who did not know Greek or Latin. The classical body was a vessel for the sculptor's own politically radical ideas rather than virtues drawing directly on ancient philosophy. That being said, William Etty, an artist whose work has much in common with Padiyar's "anacreontic" model, did target aristocratic patrons, as I shall discuss in Chapters 3 and 4. See Padiyar, *Chains*, 57.

27. MSS Canoviani VII.835/4428, Museo Civico, Bassano del Grappa. Quoted in Hugh Honour, "Antonio Canova and the Anglo-Romans: Part 2: The First Years in Rome," *Connoisseur* 144 (1959b), 229.

28. See Stanley Plumly, "The Odes for their Own Sake," *Kenyon Review* 33/4 (2011), 163–4; Alan J. Bewell, "The Political Implication of Keats's Classicist Aesthetics," *Studies in Romanticism* 25/2 (1986), 220.

29. Praz writes, "If one wishes to be aware of the poetic atmosphere underlying Canova's Venuses, Graces, Psyches and Lovers (and when I say poetic atmosphere it should be understood that I consider it fully expressed in plastic form), one should read certain lines of *Ode on a Grecian Urn* by Keats, another artist of refined and inexperienced sensuality" ("Canova: Ice and Eros," 155–6); Ian Jack describes Canova as "the sculptor whose taste has such a kinship with that of Keats." Ian Jack, *Keats and the Mirror of Art* (Oxford: Clarendon Press, 1967), 211.

30. In a letter to his siblings, Keats declares that the Revolution "had an unlucky termination. It put a stop to the rapid progress of free sentiments in England." Hyder Edward Rollins (ed.), *The Letters of John Keats 1814–1821* (Cambridge: Cambridge University Press, 1958), vol. 1, 193. See also Henry Stead, "Swinish Classics; or a Conservative Clash with Cockney Culture," in Henry Stead and Edith Hall (eds.), *Greek and Roman Classics in the British Struggle for Social Reform* (London: Bloomsbury, 2015), 55–78.

31. For an enlightening discussion of Keats's reception as a "cockney," see Jeffrey N. Cox, *Poetry and Politics in the Cockney School: Keats, Shelley, Hunt and their Circle* (Cambridge: Cambridge University Press, 1998).

32. Reynolds is quoted in Allan Cunningham, *The Lives of the Most Eminent British Painters and Sculptors*, vol. 3 (London: John Murray, 1830), 87; the quote about Keats appears in Stephen A. Larrabee, *English Bards and Grecian Marbles: The Relationship between Sculpture and Poetry especially in the Romantic Period* (Port Washington: Kennikat Press, 1964), 205.

33. For a thorough discussion of Canova's standing in Britain, see Christopher M. S. Johns, *Antonio Canova and the Politics of Patronage in Revolutionary and Napoleonic Europe* (Berkeley, Los Angeles, and London: University of California Press, 1998), 145–95.

34. Martin Aske, *Keats and Hellenism: An Essay* (Cambridge: Cambridge University Press, 2004), 6.

35. This aspect of Banks's practice is noted in Bryant, *Modern Sculptor*, 35, 51.

36. Edmund Burke, *Reflections on the Revolution in France* (London: J. Dodsley, 1791), 114.

37. Giorgio Agamben, *Infancy and History: The Destruction of Experience*, trans. Liz Heron (London and New York: Verso, 1993), 25–8.

38. In terms of ancient literature, a particularly striking example of the mediating role of the imagination consists in the discussion of love and the perception of the loved one's beauty in

Plato's *Phaedrus*. Here, Socrates describes the experience of being in love as the soul growing wings. Plato, *Phaedrus*, trans. R. Hackforth (Cambridge: Cambridge University Press, 1997), 96–8. This ancient text anticipates the later reception of the figure of Psyche as an icon of the mystifying powers of the imagination and of sensuality as well as the soul.

39. For a discussion of the "discovery," that is, rationalization, of the imagination in Enlightenment texts, see George S. Rousseau, *Nervous Acts: Essays on Literature, Culture and Sensibility* (London: Palgrave Macmillan, 2004), 83–112.

40. Sexual scientific literature from the period sees the imagination as the force behind a dangerously unbridled erotic desire. See D. T. Bienville, *Nymphomania! or, a Dissertation concerning the furor uterinus, etc.*, trans. Edward Sloane Wilmot (London, J. Bew, 1775). See also Rousseau, *Nervous Acts*, 185–210.

41. Roberto Calasso, *Tiepolo Pink*, trans. Alistair McEwen (London: Bodley Head, 2010), 9.

42. Ibid., 65.

43. See A. R. Mengs, *The Works of Antony Raphael Mengs* (London: R. Faulder, 1796), 205.

44. See, for instance, Barrell's claim that "No artist before Flaxman ... had succeeded in depicting the classical body so thoroughly eviscerated and drained, and no earlier theorist of painting had attempted to dematerialise the human figure to the same degree as Joshua Reynolds ... the emptier the space enclosed by the classical body's outline, the more it was enabled to represent the classical body in general, the classical body of the public" (John Barrell, *The Birth of Pandora and the Division of Knowledge* (Basingstoke: Macmillan, 1982, 150)). This statement is complicated by late works such as *Cupid and Psyche* and *Cymon and Iphigenia*, in which the representation of the classical body actively shirks such values and, in the case of the latter, presents a more naturalistic corporeality. The second painting is in the Royal Collection, London. Due to cleaning it lacks the luster it would have possessed in the artist's lifetime, like so many of his works.

45. Reynolds was once the owner of a drawing of the *Holy Family* by Tiepolo now in the collection of the Morgan Library and Museum, New York. The artist also made a drawing of Tiepolo's *Meeting of Antony and Cleopatra* at the Palazzo Labia, Venice, in 1752 during a stint on the Continent. This drawing is in the collection of the British Museum, London.

46. Robert R. Wark (ed.), *Discourses on Art: Sir Joshua Reynolds* (London: Paul Mellon Centre for Studies in British Art, 1997), 230.

47. Ibid., 233.

48. Ibid., 151.

49. Winckelmann perceived "simplicity" of contour to be essential to beauty in art. In Fuseli's translation of the *Gedanken*, which Reynolds would have known, Winckelmann's formula for the particular allure of Greek statuary – "edle einfalt stille größe" – is translated into "noble simplicity and sedate grandeur"; throughout the *Geschichte*, the author refers to simplicity as a positive characteristic. See Winckelmann, *Reflections*, 181; Winckelmann, *History of the Art of Antiquity*, 11, 196.

50. In the "Ironical Discourse," Reynolds ridicules the artist who seeks to destroy "ancient taste" by tearing down the fabric of artistic decorum. Although (somewhat confusingly) Reynolds conceives of this artist as one who favors modern dress as opposed to strictly classicizing aesthetics, one can easily deduce that his real target is republican classicism, which shirks the modern masters Reynolds adored (particularly Michelangelo) in favour of Greek art and its attendant associations with freedom. Hilles suggests that Reynolds had in mind James Barry, the Greco-Roman sculpture obsessed painter whose radical views would see him ejected from the Royal Academy in 1798. See Hilles, *Portraits*, 122.

51. See also Reynolds's painting *Cymon and Iphigenia*, a scene from Boccaccio's *Decameron* that, in terms of both form and subject matter, privileges the sensuality of the classical body rather than its Greek idealism. The work is in the Royal Collection, housed at Buckingham Palace, London.

52. Wark, *Discourses*, 170.

53. This aspect of Reynolds's art is discussed in Lucy Davis and Mark Hallett (eds.), *Joshua Reynolds: Experiments in Paint* (London: Paul Holberton, 2015); M. Kirby Talley, Jr., "'All good pictures crack': Sir Joshua Reynolds's Practice and Studio," in Nicholas Penny (ed.), *Reynolds* (New York: Abrams, 1986), 55–70; with regard to Canova's reticence to expose

the secrecy of his finishing technique, Padiyar describes how "the object was removed to Canova's private sanctuary, a reverential secrecy surrounded the final stage" (*Chains*, 131).

54. Thomas Love Peacock, *Headlong Hall* (London: T. Hookham, Jun. and Co., 1816), 36.

55. W. E. Frye, *After Waterloo: Reminiscences of European Travel 1815–1819* (London: William Heinemann, 1908), 289.

56. For a discussion of Canova's art in relation to the figure of the supermodel, see Cora Gilroy-Ware, "Antonio Canova and the Whatever Body," *Open Library of Humanities* 3/1 (2017), 2.

57. Jack, *Mirror of Art*, 201.

58. John Keats, *Lamia, Isabella, The Eve of St. Agnes and Other Poems* (London: Taylor and Hessey, 1820), 120.

59. Aske, *Keats and Hellenism*, 6.

60. In reference to Fuseli's circle, Myrone writes that the "political freedom represented in the classical world" was related "to the erotic freedom of the male individual" (*Bodybuilding*, 176).

61. Potts, *Flesh and the Ideal*, 222–38.

62. Padiyar contrasts David's "socratic" aesthetic against an "anacreontic" approach to the body that embraces sexual pleasure (*Chains*, 57).

63. Kenneth Clark, *The Nude* (Harmondsworth: Penguin, 1964), 6.

64. *Civilisation*, "Heroic Materialism" (episode 13), directed by Michael Gill, performance by Kenneth Clark (BBC, 1969, video file).

65. Clark, *The Nude*, 62.

66. Davis, *Queer Beauty*, 26–9.

67. John Barrell examines a host of potential reasons why the marginalization of eroticism from representations of the classical body is a particularly English tendency: "Whatever is imagined as or projected as the nature of the classical body – its cleanliness, its impermeability, its emptiness, the distance it keeps, its refusal to acknowledge its sexual character, its 'finished' quality, its entirely abstract nature – all that seems to be somehow *especially* true of the form taken by the neo-classical body in late eighteenth century Britain. It is not hard to think of reasons why this should have been so: the very late, and so very academic attempt to establish the British school as one of the great European schools of art; the discourse of civic self-denial in which that attempt was conceived; the traditional protestant suspicion, which survived even in the Anglican church, of artistic representation" (Barrell, *Birth of Pandora*, 150).

68. Michael Hatt, "Physical Culture: The Male Nude and Sculpture in Late Victorian Britain," in Elizabeth Prettejohn (ed.), *After the Pre-Raphaelites: Art and Aestheticism in Victorian England* (Manchester: Manchester University Press, 1999), 240–56; Jason Edwards, *Alfred Gilbert's Aestheticism: Gilbert amongst Whistler, Wilde, Leighton, Pater and Burne-Jones* (London: Routledge, 2016).

69. Martin Bernal, *Black Athena: The Afroasiatic Roots of Classical Civilization*, vol. 1 (London: Random House, 2012), 288.

70. Percy B. Shelley, *Hellas: A Lyrical Drama* (London: Charles and James Ollier Vere Street, 1822), viii.

71. Whitney Davis, "Eternal Moment: Pater on the Temporality of the Classical Ideal in Art," in Charles Martindale, Stefano Evangelista, and Elizabeth Prettejohn (eds.), *Pater the Classicist: Classical Scholarship, Reception and Aestheticism* (Oxford: Oxford University Press, 2017), 81.

72. *Spectator* (June 10, 1837), 548.

73. *Art Union* (June 1844), 170.

74. Elizabeth Prettejohn, *Modern Painters, Old Masters: The Art of Imitation from the Pre-Raphaelites to the First World War* (New Haven and London: Paul Mellon Centre for Studies in British Art by Yale University Press, 2017), 55–7.

75. Among many texts on nineteenth-century historicism, see the influential book by Stephen Bann, *The Clothing of Clio* (Cambridge: Cambridge University Press, 1984), 6. In another article, Bann discusses the changing display of ancient sculpture during these years. What he describes as the "ahistorical zone of neoclassical perfection" that was displaced by an archaeological and scientific view of objects is preserved, I am suggesting, in contemporary sculpture. Stephen Bann, "Image, Text and Object in the Formation of Historical Consciousness," in H. Aram Veeser (ed.), *The New Historicism* (London and New York: Routledge, 1989), 105.

76. Apuleius, *Metamorphoses (The Golden Ass)*, vol. 1, trans. J. Arthur Hanson (Cambridge,

Mass. and London: Harvard University Press, 1989).

77. Keats, *Lamia, Isabella*, 118.

78. Rollins, *Letters*, 106.

79. Psyche's status as a fundamentally modern goddess was cemented from the cinquecento onwards when various scenes from Apuleius's version were represented in such schemes as Giulio Romano's frescoes at the Palazzo Te in Mantua and Raphael's in the loggia of the Villa Farnesia, Rome. See Sonia Cavicchioli, *The Tale of Cupid and Psyche: An Illustrated History* (New York: George Brazillier, 2002).

80. In Chapter 1 I discuss one of these artists, John Bacon, at length.

81. Thomas Taylor, *The Fable of Cupid and Psyche* (London: printed for the author, 1795). Taylor's *Vindication of the Rights of Brutes* was a spoof on Wollstonecraft's *Vindication of the Rights of Woman* and Thomas Paine's *Rights of Man*. See Thomas Taylor (published anonymously), *A Vindication of the Rights of Brutes* (London: printed for the author, 1792).

82. My use of the word "sexlessness" does not mean androgynous as it means for Walter Pater when he describes "the beauty of Greek statues" as a "sexless beauty," but rather prudish and anerotic, as Thomas Hardy uses the word in *Jude the Obscure*. An exasperated Jude accuses his cousin/partner Sue Bridehead of being "the most ethereal, least sensual woman ... to exist without inhuman sexlessness." Walter Pater, *The Renaissance: Studies in Art and Poetry* [1893 text] (Berkeley, Los Angeles, and London: University of California Press, 1980), 176; Thomas Hardy, *Jude the Obscure* (London: Macmillan & Co., 1951), 451.

83. Michel Maffesoli, *The Shadow of Dionysus: A Contribution to the Sociology of the Orgy*, trans. Cindy Linse and Mary Kristina Palmquist (Albany: State University of New York Press, 1993), 31.

84. For a discussion of the Choice of Hercules in relation to Enlightenment thought, see Karen Valhora, *Austen's Oughts: Judgement after Locke and Shaftesbury* (Newark: University of Delaware Press, 2010), 235–7.

85. Keats, *Lamia, Isabella*, 180.

86. Bewell, "Political Implication," 221.

87. Potts explores how, in its original articulation, Winckelmann's notion of Greek freedom is not necessarily applicable to contemporary political debates. See *Flesh and the Ideal*, 54–60.

88. Prettejohn examines the temporal and material characteristics that bind together aesthetic writing and visual art. These characteristics have something vital in common with the earlier works of sensual classicism I have discussed so far: Elizabeth Prettejohn, "Walter Pater and Aesthetic Painting," in Prettejohn, *After the Pre-Raphaelites*, 36–58; Prettejohn, *Modern Painters*, 54–7, 219–37.

89. Charles Martindale, Stefano Evangelista, and Elizabeth Prettejohn (eds.), *Pater the Classicist: Classical Scholarship, Reception and Aestheticism* (Oxford: Oxford University Press, 2017).

90. Elizabeth (Lady) Eastlake, *Life of John Gibson, R.A., Sculptor* (London: Longmans, Green and Co., 1870), 10. For an analysis of Gibson's complex relationship with the modern, see Jason Edwards, "By Abstraction Brings Forth Ideal Beauty? The 'Real Academy' and John Gibson's Anglo-Roman Modernity," in Sarah Monks, John Barrell, and Mark Hallett (eds.), *Living with the Royal Academy: Artistic Ideals and Experiences in England, 1768–1848* (Farnham: Ashgate, 2013), 195–220.

91. Gibson's reaction to monuments of this kind is discussed in the final part of Chapter 5.

92. See, for example, Humphrey Hopper's monument to *Major General Andrew Hay*, which shows the dead subject expiring into the arms of a naked figure of Valor, whose streamlined limbs clash against the hero's uniformed corpse, the silhouette of marching infantry in the background, and the mournful soldier at the left of the group leaning on a bayonet. Likewise, Josephus Kendrick's tablets honoring Sir William Myers and General Robert Ross include a naked Hercules and another naked Valor respectively.

93. "The Fall of Hyperion" was abandoned in an unfinished state and was revised by subsequent critics. In order to stay as close to Keats's intentions, I will reference the "transliteration" of the original manuscript. John Keats, *Hyperion: A Facsimile of Keats's Autograph Manuscript with a Transliteration of the Manuscript of The Fall of Hyperion, a Dream* (Oxford: Clarendon Press, 1905), 33–50.

94. Varying discussions of this distinction can be found in, for example, Keith D. White, *John Keats and the Loss of Romantic Innocence*

(Amsterdam and Atlanta: Rodopi, 1996), 170; Małgorzata Łuczyńska-Hołdys, *Soft-Shed Kisses: Re-visioning the Femme Fatale in English Poetry of the 19th Century* (Cambridge: Cambridge Scholars Publishing, 2013), 73–7; Thomas Macfarland, *The Masks of Keats: The Endeavour of a Poet* (Oxford: Oxford University Press, 2000), 115–18.

95. Burke, *Reflections*, 114.

96. The critic Melchior Missirini uses the Italian words "dolce" and "dolcezza" in relation to Canova's treatment of the marble in his *Della vita di Antonio Canova*, vol. 1 (Milan: Nicolò Bettoni, 1824), 119. For further insight into Canova's working of the material, see Christina Ferando, "'Plasmati dalle sue mani': Canova's Touch and the Gipsoteca of Possagno," in Andrew Graciano (ed.), *Exhibiting Outside the Academy, Salon and Biennial, 1775–1999: Alternative Venues for Display* (Farnham: Ashgate, 2015), 111–30; Bindman, *Warm Flesh*, 90, 121; Mark Norman and Richard Cook, "'Just a tiny bit of rouge upon the lips and cheeks': Canova, Colour and the Classical Ideal," in Katharine Eustace (ed.), *Antonio Canova: Ideal Heads* (Oxford: Ashmolean Museum, 1997), 47–58.

97. Davis, 'Eternal Moment', 84.

98. Thomas Crow, review of *Chains: David, Canova, and the Fall of the Public Hero in Postrevolutionary France*, by Satish Padiyar, *Journal of Modern History* 81/3 (2009), 686.

1 · Hidden Dreams *pages 31–67*

1. Quoted in Marina Warner, *Monuments and Maidens: The Allegory of the Female Form* (Berkeley: University of California Press, 1985), 21–2.

2. Whitney Davis, "Eternal Moment: Pater on the Temporality of the Classical Ideal in Art," in Charles Martindale, Stefano Evangelista, and Elizabeth Prettejohn (eds.), *Pater the Classicist: Classical Scholarship, Reception and Aestheticism* (Oxford: Oxford University Press, 2017), 81.

3. The monument I am referring to here is John Charles Felix Rossi's *Captain Robert Faulknor*, the central group of which resembles figures found in history paintings of the 1770s and 1780s, particularly works by Gavin Hamilton (a leading advocate of "the antique") such as his *Juno and Jupiter* in the collection at Holkham Hall, Norfolk. The work also contains "modern" or "rococo" elements, such as the Bernini-esque fish emerging from between the legs of the figure of Neptune.

4. When a group of painters, including Joshua Reynolds and Angelica Kauffman, made a plea in 1773 to decorate St. Paul's with a cycle of biblical paintings, the lead bishops had gruffly turned them down on the grounds that all religious imagery reeked of Catholic influence. See James Northcote, *The Life of Sir Joshua Reynolds*, vol. 1 (London: Henry Colburn, 1819), 307–9.

5. Alaric A. Watts (ed.), *The New Year's Gift and Juvenile Souvenir* (London: Longman, Rees, Orme, Brown, and Green, 1830), 32.

6. Sarah Burnage, "Introduction: The British School of Sculpture – A Case Study," in Jason Edwards and Sarah Burnage (eds.), *The British School of Sculpture c. 1760–1832* (London and New York: Routledge, 2017), 21.

7. For insight into the process of getting these monuments made, see ibid., 26.

8. Matthew Craske, "Model Making and Anti-Competitive Practices in the Late Eighteenth-Century London Sculpure Trade," *RIHA Journal* 87 (2014): http://www.riha-journal.org/articles/2014/2014-jan-mar/special-issue-art-design-history/craske-model-making (accessed March 21, 2019).

9. Richard Cecil, *Memoirs of John Bacon* (London: F. and C. Rivington, 1801).

10. *Gentleman's Magazine* (September 1799), 809–10.

11. G. M. Ditchfield writes: "According to a widely circulated anecdote, George III deplored an anti-Methodist commotion with the words 'The Methodists are a quiet, good kind of people, and will disturb nobody'; according to another, possibly better informed, source, the king reinstated a labourer at Windsor who had been dismissed for his Methodist allegiance and declared: 'If I were to change my religion I should turn Methodist too!'" *George III: An Essay on Monarchy* (Basingstoke: Palgrave Macmillan, 2002), 105; the latter quote appears in Thomas Baxter Aveling, *Memorials of the Clayton Family* (London: Jackson, Walford, and Hopper, 1867), 147.

12. Élie Halévy, *England in 1815* (London: Ernest Benn, 1949), 347–485. See also E. J.

Hobsbawm, *The Labouring Men: Studies in the History of Labour* (London: Weidenfeld and Nicolson, 1964), 23–33.

13. See Cecil, *Bacon*, 54.

14. See E. P. Thompson, "Time, Work-Discipline, and Industrial Capitalism," *Past & Present* 38 (1967), 55–97.

15. See Cecil, *Bacon*, 52.

16. See entry on Bacon in the Katherine Ada Esdaile Sculpture Archive, Huntington Library, Pasadena, California.

17. See Thompson, "Time, Work-Discipline," 55–97.

18. Cecil, *Bacon*, 57.

19. See Anon., *Methodism Vindicated, from the charge of ignorance and enthusiasm ... by a member of the Church of England* (Margate: J. Parsons, 1795).

20. Josiah Pratt (ed.), *The Works of Richard Cecil*, vol. 1 (London: L. B. Seeley, 1816), 161.

21. Cecil, *Bacon*, 42.

22. See Craske, "Model Making."

23. Gosse's essay on modern British sculpture is featured as the introduction to J. T. Smith's biography of the sculptor Joseph Nollekens. J. T. Smith, *Nollekens and his Times* (London: Richard Bentley and Son, 1895), 11.

24. Ibid., 61.

25. Ibid., 94.

26. Cecil, *Bacon*, 42.

27. Craske, "Model Making."

28. See Eveline G. Bouwers, *Public Pantheons in Revolutionary Europe: Comparing Cultures of Remembrance c. 1790–1840* (Basingstoke: Palgrave Macmillan, 2011), 58.

29. See, for example, the central figure in John Wilton's monument to *General Wolfe*, Westminster Abbey, London.

30. Cecil, *Bacon*, 61.

31. Thomas Walsh, "The Whole Armour of God: A Sermon," *Magazine of the Wesleyan Methodist Church* (August 1799), 427.

32. Richard Cecil, *Short Hints to a Soldier, in a letter from his friend* (London: J. Tibling, 1810), 2.

33. Ibid., 6.

34. Ibid., 7.

35. Ibid., 6.

36. Ibid.

37. *Monthly Magazine* (April 1806), 255.

38. Phyllis Mack, *Heart Religion in the British Enlightenment: Gender and Emotion in Early Methodism* (Cambridge: Cambridge University Press, 2008), 26.

39. See Gareth Lloyd, "Repression and Resistance: Wesleyan Female Public Ministry in the Generation after 1791," *Proceedings of the Wesley Historical Society* 55/3 (2005), 101–14.

40. Cecil, *Bacon*, 62.

41. Edmund Burke, *Reflections on the Revolution in France* (London: J. Dodsley, 1791), 250.

42. Ibid., 114.

43. Ibid., 130, 114.

44. Bacon claimed to have invented the "pointing machine" used by Houdon. Cecil, *Bacon*, 7. Their meeting is mentioned in Katharine Ada Esdaile, *English Monumental Sculpture since the Renaissance* (New York: Hyperion Press, 1979), 22. Bacon's self-fashioning as a distinctly English sculptor is discussed in Sarah Burnage, "'Delighting the Common People': John Bacon's Monuments to the Earl of Chatham (1778–1784)" in Edwards and Burnage, *British School of Sculpture*, 79–102.

45. See James Dallaway, *Anecdotes of the Arts in England* (London: T. Cadell & W. Davies, 1800), 403.

46. Cecil, *Bacon*, 95.

47. See Burnage, "Introduction," 26.

48. Ibid.

49. Robert R. Wark (ed.), *Discourses on Art: Sir Joshua Reynolds* (London: Paul Mellon Centre for Studies in British Art, 1997), 182.

50. Ibid., 177.

51. See R. Wittkower, "Bernini Studies – I: The Group of Neptune and Triton," *Burlington Magazine* 94 (1952), 68–76.

52. This statuette is in the Victoria and Albert Museum, London.

53. *Monthly Mirror* (October 1796), 346. For fascinating insight into the younger Bacon's take on the style of British war monuments, see Burnage, "Introduction," 28–9. It is intriguing to note that the sculptor saw the prioritization of ancient art as the index of aristocratic taste rather than a political vision. This shows the compatibility between the style of Banks's

sculpture and the taste of the elite, as well as the fact that "the antique" belonged to both everyone and nobody in particular.

54. For an account of Bacon's retirement in order to "[devote] himself entirely to Bible meetings and religious exercises," see Gertrude Bacon, *The Record of an Aeronaut, Being the Life of John Bacon* (London: John Long, 1907), 21.

55. For insight into the tension between images of the female body and evangelicism, see Alison Smith, *The Victorian Nude: Sexuality, Morality and Art* (Manchester: Manchester University Press, 1996), 62–77, 216–21.

56. Antje Matthews, "John Russell's Mysterious Moon," *Proceedings of the Wesley Historical Society* 55/6 (2006), 258. Another example is the painter William Etty, whom I look at in Chapter 3, an artist raised by Methodists of the same generation as Bacon senior but, in order to pursue a career as a classicizing artist, forced to cast aside the denomination in favor of a more relaxed Christianity.

57. Rob Humphreys, "The City/St. Paul's Cathedral," in *The Rough Guide to London* (Rough Guides, e-book, 2012), unpaginated.

58. Ibid.

59. Julius Bryant, "The Church Memorials of Thomas Banks," *Church Monuments: Journal of the Church Monuments Society* 1 (1985), 49.

60. Holger Hoock, *Empires of the Imagination: Politics, War and the Arts in the British World* (London: Profile Books, 2010), 165.

61. Margaret Whinney, *Sculpture in Britain 1530–1830* (New Haven and London: Yale University Press, 1992), 332.

62. Margaret Whinney, *English Sculpture 1720–1830* (London: Victoria and Albert Museum, 1971), 127.

63. John Wilkes (ed.), *Encyclopaedia Londoninesis*, vol. 8 (London: J. Alard, 1815), 409.

64. See John Barrell, "Thomas Banks and the Society for Constitutional Information," in Sarah Monks, John Barrell, and Mark Hallett (eds.), *Living with the Royal Academy: Artistic Ideals and Experiences in England, 1768–1848* (Farnham: Ashgate, 2013), 131–52.

65. Banks is presented as such in the Soane Museum's 2005 exhibition on the sculptor. See Julius Bryant, *Thomas Banks: Britain's First Modern Sculptor* (London: Sir John Soane's Museum, 2005).

66. Julius Bryant, "The Royal Academy's 'Violent Democrat': Thomas Banks," *British Art Journal* 6/3 (2005), 51–8; Barrell, "Thomas Banks," 145.

67. British Library, Add. MSS 36499, fol. 89. Quoted in Charles Francis Bell, *Annals of Thomas Banks* (Cambridge: Cambridge University Press, 1938), 149.

68. British Library, Add. MSS 36498, fol. 229. Quoted in Bell, *Annals*, 118.

69. Mary Favret, "The Necessity of Violence: The Suicide and the Soldier," a keynote lecture for Contested Views: Visual Culture and the Revolutionary and Napoleonic Wars, a two-day conference held at Tate Britain, London, Thursday, July 12, 2012. Quoted with permission from the author.

70. British Library, Add. MSS 36499, fol. 26. Quoted in Bell, *Annals*, 142.

71. Winckelmann implies that a specific combination of factors – democracy, warm climate, genetics ("blood"), the liberation of children, sport – made the Greeks and their art beautiful. Johann Joachim Winckelmann, *Reflections on the Painting and Sculpture of the Greeks*, trans. Henry Fuseli (London: printed for the translator, 1765), 1–22.

72. The mask is untraced. It was included in the inventory of Banks's works at the posthumous sale on Wednesday, May 22, 1805. See Bell, *Annals*, 193.

73. Wollstonecraft had an intense relationship with Henry Fuseli, the first translator of Winckelmann's *Gedanken* into English. For insight into their connection, see Miriam Brody, *Mary Wollstonecraft: Mother of Women's Rights* (Oxford: Oxford University Press, 2000), 85–7.

74. Mary Wollstonecraft, *A Vindication of the Rights of Woman with Strictures on Political and Moral Subjects* (Dublin: J. Stockdale, 1793), 225.

75. Quoted in Allan Cunningham, *The Lives of the Most Eminent British Painters and Sculptors*, vol. 3 (London: John Murray, 1830), 92.

76. Wollstonecraft, *Vindication*, 225.

77. See Warner, *Monuments and Maidens*, 313–15.

78. William Godwin (ed.), *Memoirs and Posthumous Works of Mary Wollstonecraft Godwin* (London: Joseph Johnson, 1798).

79. This is discussed in the next chapter. See Bell, *Annals*, 185–6.

80. That she herself was interested in activism is supported by the portrait painted of her in republican costume, illustrated in Bryant, *Modern Sculptor*, 58. Later in the decade, the poet Samuel Rogers alluded to her as "the girl with the silver voice." See R. Ellis Roberts, *Samuel Rogers and his Circle* (London: Methuen & Co., 1910), 40–41.

81. Andrew Tooke, *The Pantheon, Representing the Fabulous Histories of the Heathen Gods and Most Illustrious Heroes* (London: Charles Harper, 1709); Joseph Spence, *Polymetis* (London: J. Dodsley, 1774); John Lemprière, *Classical Dictionary* (Dublin: William M'Kenzie, 1792).

82. William Godwin (writing as Edward Baldwin), *The Pantheon, or Ancient History of the Gods of Greece and Rome* (London: M. J. Godwin, 1809), 3.

83. William Godwin, *Enquiry Concerning Political Justice*, vol. 2 (London: G. G. & J. Robinson, 1798), 102.

84. Anon., *Buff, or a dissertation on nakedness: A parody on Paine's Rights of Man* (London: Matthew, 1792).

85. Thomas Paine, *Rights of Man: Part the Second* (London: J. S. Jordan, 1792), 4. Anon., *Buff*, 7 (original italics).

86. Wollstonecraft, *Vindication*, 183.

87. David Erdman (ed.), *The Complete Poetry and Prose of William Blake* (Berkeley, Los Angeles, and London: University of California Press, 2008), 544.

88. See David Erdman, *Blake: Prophet Against Empire* (New York: Dover Publications, 2013), 42.

89. Ibid., 2.

90. John Horne Tooke, *Diversions of Purley*, part 1, 2nd edn (London: Joseph Johnson, 1798). Cumberland's attempt to convince Tooke to employ Blake is quoted in G. E. Bentley, Jr., *A Bibliography of George Cumberland (1754–1848)* (New York: Garland Publishing, 1975), 92.

91. Sharp's obituary states that he "engraved the figure of Mercury putting on his sandal wings, after a model or drawing by Banks for 'The Diversions of Purley'." Anon., "William Sharp Esq: Honorary Member of the Imperial and Bavarian Academies," in *The Annual Biography and Obituary for the Year*, vol. 9 (London: Longman, Hurst, Rees, Orme, Brown, and Green, 1825), 224–5.

92. Tooke, *Diversions*, 27.

93. George Cumberland, *The Captive of the Castle of Sennaar* (London: Egerton, 1798), 83.

94. Ibid., 95.

95. In relation to an earlier sculpture by Banks, evidence survives of Cumberland's direct input on the appearance of the work. Of the small painted plaster known as the *Hindu Deity Camadeva with his Mistress on a Crocodile* (Sir John Soane's Museum, London), Bell writes that Banks's correspondence with Cumberland on the work shows "that Cumberland assisted Banks in giving the subject a correct oriental flavour." *Annals*, 142.

96. Kenneth Garlick and Angus Macintyre (eds.), *The Diary of Joseph Farington*, vol. 1 (New Haven and London: Yale University Press, 1979), 144.

97. Hoock, *Empires*, 134–5.

98. See Rolf Reichardt and Hubertus Kohle, *Visualizing the Revolution: Politics and Pictorial Arts in Late Eighteenth-Century France* (London: Reaktion, 2008), 175–6.

99. Linda Colley, *Britons: Forging the Nation 1707–1837* (New Haven and London: Yale University Press, 1992), 318.

100. Karl Marx, "Der 18te Brumiare des Louis Napoleon," *Die Revolution* (1852), in Karl Marx and Friedrich Engels, *Werke*, vol. 8 (Berlin: Dietz Verlag, 1960), 115. Quoted in Susan Buck-Morss, *The Dialectics of Seeing: Walter Benjamin and the Arcades Project* (Cambridge, Mass., and London: MIT Press, 1991), 122.

101. J. Richardson (ed.), *The Works of Jonathan Richardson* (Twickenham: Strawberry Hill, 1792), 94.

102. See Hugh Honour, "English Patrons and Italian Sculptors in the First Half of the Eighteenth Century," *Connoisseur* 141 (1958), 220–26.

103. Banks's support for Barry's belief in the "excellence of every thing of Greek & Roman Art in this way to any thing Modern" is conveyed in a letter to Cumberland on July 27,

1798. British Library, Add. MSS 36498, fol. 235. Quoted in Bell, *Annals*, 121.

104. The painter praises "the generous exertion of David and his noble fellow-labourers ... wishing [him] a long and prosperous" career. James Barry, *A Letter to the Dilettanti Society* (London: J. Walker, 1798), 26.

105. Lynn Hunt, *Politics, Culture, Class in the French Revolution* (Berkeley, Los Angeles, and London: University of California Press, 2004), 27.

106. See Linda Walsh, "'Crushing Infamy': The Revolutionary Sculpture of Joseph Chinard," *Journal for Eighteenth-Century Studies*, 26/1 (2003), 109–28.

107. Bryant, "Violent Democrat," 56.

108. Smith, *Nollekens*, 13.

109. For insight into the nationalist and royalist orientation of St. Paul's at the time, see Nigel Aston, "St. Paul's and the Public Culture of Eighteenth Century Britain," in Derek Keene, Arthur Burns, and Andrew Saint (eds.), *St. Paul's: The Cathedral Church of London 604–2004* (New Haven and London: Yale University Press, 2004), 363–71.

110. This sculpture is in the collection of the Louvre Museum, Paris.

111. The relationship between the aesthetic of Banks's work and his behavior is discussed in Martin Myrone, *Bodybuilding: Reforming Masculinities in British Art* (New Haven and London: Yale University Press, 2005), 177.

112. Smith, *Nollekens*, 10.

113. See *Blackwood's Edinburgh Magazine* 6 (October 1819), 77.

2 · Poetic Departures *pages 69–113*

1. British Library, Add. MSS 36499, fol. 89. Quoted in Charles Francis Bell, *Annals of Thomas Banks* (Cambridge: Cambridge University Press, 1938), 149.

2. Eleanor Hughes, "Smoke and Marble: Thomas Banks's Monument to Captain George Blagdon Westcott," in Jason Edwards and Sarah Burnage (eds.), *The British School of Sculpture, c. 1760–1832* (London and New York: Routledge, 2017), 163–87.

3. As far as I know, the practice of collective viewing of sculptures by candlelight (as was common when these objects were in their former locations) was phased out during these years, only to return after the cessation of the Napoleonic Wars.

4. See A. Zobi, *Storia civile della Toscana dal MDCCXXVII al MDCCCXLVIII*, vol. 3 (Florence: Luigi Molini, 1851), 518–22.

5. See Hugh Honour, "Canova's Statues of Venus", *Burlington Magazine* 114/835 (1972), 658.

6. F.B. Goodrich describes the procession as "the most wonderful spectacle that the world has ever seen. Twenty-nine huge chariots laden with marble and pictorial trophies marched in procession over the Boulevards." *The Court of Napoleon* (New York: Derby & Jackson, 1857), 309.

7. Lynn Hunt, *Politics, Culture, Class in the French Revolution* (Berkeley, Los Angeles, and London: University of California Press, 2004), 27.

8. David Bindman, *Warm Flesh, Cold Marble: Canova, Thorvaldsen and their Critics* (New Haven and London: Yale University Press, 2014).

9. Napoleon's response to the sculpture is featured in a letter included in Marie-Anne Dupuy, Isabelle Le Masne de Chermont, and Elaine Williamson (eds.), *Vivant Denon, Directeur des Musées sous le Consulat et l'Empire: Correspondance (1802–1815)*, vol. 1 (Paris: Éd. de la Réunion des musées nationaux, 1999), 713. Also quoted in Christopher M.S. Johns, *Antonio Canova and the Politics of Patronage in Revolutionary and Napoleonic Europe* (Berkeley, Los Angeles, and London: University of California Press, 1998), 100–01.

10. Allan Cunningham, *The Lives of the Most Eminent British Painters and Sculptors*, vol. 3 (London: John Murray, 1830), 107.

11. Ibid., 115.

12. *European Magazine and London Review* 44 (July 1803), 28.

13. Kenneth Garlick and Angus Macintyre (eds.), *The Diary of Joseph Farington*, vol. 7 (New Haven and London: Yale University Press, 1979), 2761.

14. Elizabeth Prettejohn, *Modern Painters, Old Masters: The Art of Imitation from the Pre-Raphaelites to the First World War* (New Haven and London: Paul Mellon Centre for

Studies in British Art by Yale University Press, 2017), 5–6.

15. Quoted in Bell, *Annals*, 121–5.

16. Of Flaxman, Craske writes that "the rise to virtue through taste was a process of Christian salvation. A Swedenborgian evangelical, he reformed sculpture to make it an instrument of God." Matthew Craske, "Reviving the School of Phidias: The Invention of a National School of Sculpture in Britain (1780–1830)," *Visual Culture in Britain* 7/2 (2006), 29.

17. John Flaxman, *Lectures on Sculpture*, 2nd edn. (London: Henry G. Bohn, 1838), 264.

18. Ibid.

19. Ibid., 15.

20. Satish Padiyar, "Crisis? What Crisis?," *Art History* 21/2 (1998), 275.

21. This drawing is in the collection of the British Museum, London (1965,1211.33).

22. Flaxman, *Lectures on Sculpture*, 279, 290. Carl Ludwig Fernow, *Über den Bildhauer Canova und dessen Werke* (Zurich: Heinrich Gessner, 1806), 14. Quoted in Bindman, *Warm Flesh*, 35.

23. Julius Bryant, "The Royal Academy's 'Violent Democrat': Thomas Banks," *British Art Journal* 6/3 (2005), 52.

24. Private collection, illustrated in Bryant, "Violent Democrat," 57.

25. Quoted in Bell, *Annals*, 186.

26. Ibid., 170.

27. Ibid.

28. Ibid., 77

29. Coleridge's "France: An Ode" was originally titled "The Recantation." The poem was first published in the *Morning Post*, Monday, April 16, 1798.

30. The eroticism of the ancient narrative and its portrayals by artists of the period is discussed in Carol Ockman, *Ingres's Eroticized Bodies: Retracing the Serpentine Line* (New Haven and London: Yale University Press, 1995), 22–7.

31. Farington reveals that Flaxman was convinced that Banks's "indiscretion in that respect both in Italy and England had hurt his interest." Garlick and Macintyre, *Farington*, vol. 1, 161.

32. Julius Byrant, "Eccentric Pioneers? Patrons of Modern Sculpture for Britain," in Diana Dethloff, Tessa Murdoch, and Kim Sloan, with Caroline Elam (eds.), *Burning Bright: Essays in Honour of David Bindman* (London: UCL Press, 2015), 68.

33. In 1796, the MP John B. S. Morritt described Hervey as "a drunkard and an atheist though a bishop." See George Eden Marindin (ed.), *The Letters of John B. S. Morritt of Rokeby: Descriptive Journeys in Europe and Asia Minor in the Years 1794–1796* (Cambridge: Cambridge University Press, 2012), 289.

34. See Graham Gargett, *Voltaire and Protestantism* (Oxford: Voltaire Foudation at the Taylor Institution, 1980), 496.

35. Martin Sherlock, *Letters from an English Traveller*, vol. 2 (London: J. Nichols, T. Cadell, P. Elmsley, H. Payne, and N. Conant, 1781), 37, 190–91.

36. Hugh Honour, *Neo-classicism: Style and Civilization* (Harmondsworth: Penguin, 1968), 62.

37. Johann Joachim Winckelmann, *History of the Art of Antiquity*, trans. Harry Francis Mallgrave (Los Angeles: Getty Research Institute, 2006), 233.

38. See Byrant, "Eccentric pioneers," 68.

39. See James David Draper et al., *Playing with Fire: European Terracotta Models, 1740–1840* (New Haven and London: Yale University Press, 2003), 211.

40. Cunningham, *Lives*, vol. 3, 109.

41. Quoted in G. E. Bentley, Jr., *A Bibliography of George Cumberland (1754–1848)* (New York: Garland Publishing, 1975), 92.

42. Alice Oswald, *Memorial* (London: Faber & Faber, 2011).

43. John Flaxman, *The Classical Compositions of John Flaxman, R.A.* (London: Bell and Daldy, 1870), *Homer's Iliad*, pl. 27; Alexander Pope, *The Iliad of Homer*, vol. 6 (London: H. Baldwin, 1796), 186.

44. Flaxman quotes Homer (possibly his own translation) in relation to the sculpture: *Lectures on Sculpture*, 292. For insight into the metaphor of mist in relation to Homeric figures, see Marina Warner, *Monuments and Maidens: The Allegory of the Female Form* (Berkeley: University of California Press, 1985), 89.

45. Flaxman, *Lectures on Sculpture*, 292.

46. Banks's sketches after Ghiberti are in the collection of Leeds Museums and Galleries. See Julius Bryant, *Thomas Banks: Britain's First Modern Sculptor* (London: Sir John Soane's Museum, 2005), 57.

47. In his lecture on modern sculpture, Flaxman quotes Reynolds's judgment of the *Gates*: "The criticism of Sir Joshua Reynolds was one indisputable proof of that great man's judgment in the sister arts. His observation amounted to this, that Ghiberti's 'landscape and buildings occupied so large a portion of the compartments, that the figures remained but secondary objects, entirely contrary to the principle of the ancients.'" Flaxman, *Lectures on Sculpture*, 248.

48. Ibid., 245.

49. Victor Chan, *Rubens to Picasso: Four Centuries of Master Drawings* (Edmonton: University of Alberta Press, 1995), 52.

50. Dora Panofsky and Erwin Panofsky, *Pandora's Box: The Changing Aspects of a Mythical Symbol*, 2nd edn (New York: Harper & Row, 1965), 91.

51. See Julia Sarah Symmons, *Flaxman and Europe: The Outline Illustrations and their Influence* (New York and London: Garland Publishing, 1984), 119.

52. See Martin Myrone, *Bodybuilding: Reforming Masculinities in British Art* (New Haven and London: Yale University Press, 2005), 75–90.

53. George Cumberland, *Thoughts on Outline, Sculpture, and the System that Guided the Ancient Artists in Composing Their Figures and Groupes* (London: W. Wilson, 1796), 40.

54. Letter to George Cumberland, December 23, 1796. See David Erdman (ed.), *The Complete Poetry and Prose of William Blake* (Berkeley, Los Angeles, and London: University of California Press, 2008), 700.

55. Ibid., 584.

56. Myrone, *Bodybuilding*, 288.

57. Benjamin Robert Haydon, *Lectures on Painting and Design* (London: Longman, Brown, Green, and Longmans, 1846), 463.

58. J. Jouse, *Jouse's Pocket Dictionary of Italian, French and English Musical Terms* (London: D'Alaime & Co., 1837), 28.

59. For a discussion of Flaxman's influence on early twentieth-century artists, see Robert Rosenblum, *Transformations in Late Eighteenth Century Art* (Princeton: Princeton University Press, 1970), 90–95.

60. See Edmund Husserl, *The Phenomenology of Internal Time-Consciousness*, trans. James Churchill (London and Bloomington: Indiana University Press, 1964); Theodor Adorno, *Aesthetic Theory*, trans. Robert Hullot-Kentor (Minneapolis: University of Minnesota Press, 1998).

61. Adorno, *Aesthetic Theory*, 137.

62. Walter Pater, *The Renaissance: Studies in Art and Poetry* [1893 text] (Berkeley, Los Angeles, and London: University of California Press, 1980), 106.

63. Ibid., 190. Pater writes that Keats and Giorgione offer the same "sensuous gift" to humanity (270). In his essay on Michelangelo's poetry, Pater describes the master's "sweetness and strength" (57). With regard to Simeon Solomon, Pater mentions the painter's work in his 1876 "Essay on Dionysus," digressing to write a short ekphrasis on Solomon's painting of the ancient deity, labelling him the god of "things too sweet." Walter Pater, *Greek Studies: A Series of Essays* (Honolulu: University of the Pacific, 2002), 37.

64. Edmund Burke, *A Philosophical Enquiry into the Origin of Our Ideas of the Sublime and Beautiful* (London: J. Dodsley, 1767), 292.

65. Byung-Chul Han, *Saving Beauty* (Cambridge: Polity Press, 2018), 16–18.

66. Myrone, *Bodybuilding*, 181.

67. *New York Quarterly* (January 1853), 567.

68. Flaxman, *Classical Compositions, Works and Days of Hesiod*, pl. 19.

69. Aby Warburg, *The Renewal of Pagan Antiquity*, trans. David Britt (Los Angeles: Getty Research Institute, 1999), 598.

70. See "Fragment on the Ninfa," in Ernst Hans Gombrich, *Aby Warburg: An Intellectual Biography* (London: Phaidon, 1986), 107–8.

71. Margaret Whinney, "Flaxman and the Eighteenth Century: A Commemorative Lecture," *Journal of the Warburg and Courtauld Institutes* 19/3–4 (1956), 279.

72. Flaxman's instructions for how to depict "progressive movement" and its undulating effects on drapery refers to the "bacchanalian" nymphs, for which there is an illustration of "One of the Menades [*sic*]." See Flaxman,

Lectures on Sculpture, 247, pl. 45. The illustration is not by Flaxman but by Thomas Fairchild.

73. Bryant, *Modern Sculptor*, 30.

74. Myrone, *Bodybuilding*, 181.

75. Flaxman, *Classical Compositions, The Tragedies of Aeschylus*, pl. 5.

76. Ibid., pl. 6.

77. Ibid., pl. 7.

78. Jane E. Everson, "From Dante to Dante Sonata," in Antonella Braida and Luisa Calé (eds.), *Dante on View: The Reception of Dante in the Visual and Performing Arts* (Aldershot: Ashgate, 2007), 53–64.

79. Ibid., 56.

80. For insight into Ashton's activities during the war, see Alistair Macaulay, "Spring: Ashton's Symphonic Variations in America," in Alexandra Carter, Jens Giersdorf, and Yutian Wong (eds.), *The Routledge Dance Studies Reader* (London: Routledge, 1998), 114.

81. Everson, "Dante Sonata," 55.

82. *Illustrated London News* 8 (February 21, 1846), 133.

83. Ibid.

84. Ibid., 132. This quote was originally printed in an entry on Banks in *The Penny Cyclopedia*, vol. 3 (London: Charles Knight, 1835), 405.

85. The maenadic quality of Ghiberti's relief is discussed in Maurizio Ghelardi, "Lo sviluppo del pittorico nei rilievi di Ghiberti: Un seminario inedito di Aby Warburg," in Klaus Bergdolt and Giorgio Bonsanti (eds.), *Opere e giorni: Studi su mille anni di arte europea dedicati a Max Seidel* (Venice: Marsilio, 2007), 741–8.

86. Jill Bennett, *Practical Aesthetics: Events, Affect and Art After 9/11* (London and New York: I. B. Tauris, 2012), 101.

87. For insight into Coleridge's religious identity, see Jeffrey W. Barbeau, *Coleridge, the Bible, and Religion* (Basingstoke: Palgrave Macmillan, 2008).

88. Lawrence H. Simon (ed.), *Karl Marx: Selected Writings* (Cambridge and Indianapolis: Hackett Publishing, 1994), 28.

89. Cunningham, *Lives*, vol. 3, 325.

90. Alex Potts, *Flesh and the Ideal: Winckelmann and the Origins of Art History* (New Haven and London: Yale University Press, 1994), 53.

91. These sculptures are at Ickworth House, Suffolk, and Petworth House, West Sussex, respectively.

92. Philip McEvansoneya, "Lord Egremont and Flaxman's 'St Michael Overcoming Satan'", *Burlington Magazine* 143/1179 (2001), 351.

93. Susan Buck-Morss, *The Dialectics of Seeing: Walter Benjamin and the Arcades Project* (Cambridge, Mass., and London: MIT Press, 1991), 93.

94. David Bindman, *European Sculpture from Bernini to Rodin* (London: Studio Vista, 1970), 106.

95. "The Funeral," *Littell's Living Age* (January 1853), 51.

3 · Industrial Dreams, Consumer Poems *pages 115–153*

1. See two articles by Dwight E. Robinson: "Ode on a 'New Etrurian' Urn," *Keats-Shelley Journal* 7 (1963), 11–35; "A Question of the Imprint of Wedgwood in the Longer Poems of Keats," *Keats-Shelley Journal* 16 (1967), 22–8.

2. *Art Union* (April 1847), 120.

3. Susan Buck-Morss, *The Dialectics of Seeing: Walter Benjamin and the Arcades Project* (Cambridge, Mass., and London: MIT Press, 1991), 86–7.

4. Ibid., 85.

5. Susan Buck-Morss, *Dreamworld and Catastrophe: The Passing of Mass Utopia in East and West* (Cambridge, Mass., and London: MIT Press, 2002), ix.

6. See Cara Denison et al., *From Mantegna to Picasso: Drawings from the Thaw Collection at the Pierpont Morgan Library, New York* (London: Royal Academy, 1997), 84.

7. For an account of Banks and Fuseli in Rome, see Martin Myrone, *Bodybuilding: Reforming Masculinities in British Art* (New Haven and London: Yale University Press, 2005), 163–90.

8. See John Barrell, *The Political Theory of Painting from Reynolds to Hazlitt* (New Haven and London: Yale University Press, 1995), 259.

9. See Fuseli's eleventh lecture delivered at the Royal Academy during his tenure as Professor of Painting: John Knowles (ed.), *The Life and*

Writings of Henry Fuseli, vol. 3 (London: Henry Colburn and Richard Bentley, 1831), 8.

10. Nicola Bown, *Fairies in Nineteenth-Century Art and Literature* (Cambridge: Cambridge University Press, 2001), 28.

11. Andrei Pop, *Antiquity, Theatre, and the Painting of Henry Fuseli* (Oxford: Oxford University Press, 2015).

12. Thomas Sadler (ed.), *Diary, Reminiscences and Correspondence of Henry Crabb Robinson* (Boston: Houghton, Mifflin & Co., 1869), 205.

13. See, for example, Fuseli's criticism of Correggio, an old master painter he perceives to be overly ornamental and "no more than a Machinist." See Ralph N. Wornum (ed.), *Lectures on Painting by the Royal Academicians Barry, Opie and Fuseli* (London: Henry G. Bohn, 1848), 461–2.

14. Martin Myrone mentions Howard as one of several 'Fuseliesque' painters attached to the Royal Academy in *Henry Fuseli* (London: Tate Publishing, 2001), 66.

15. *La Belle Assemblée* 11 (January–June 1830), 275.

16. George Walter Thornbury, *The Life of J.M.W. Turner*, vol. 2 (London: Hurst and Blackett, 1862), 76; *Star Chamber* 1 (May 24, 1826), 124.

17. *Examiner* (May 15, 1814), 317. In 1839, a critic complained that the public are all too "familiar with the classical elegance of Mr Howard's celestial groups." *Bell's Weekly Messenger* (May 18, 1839), 6.

18. The painting and these drawings are untraced. They are mentioned in Henry Howard, *A Course of Lectures on Painting delivered at the Royal Academy of Arts* (London: Henry G. Bohn, 1848), lxii, lxiv.

19. Both of these paintings belong to the National Portrait Gallery, London.

20. This painting is untraced. See Julius Bryant, *Thomas Banks: Britain's First Modern Sculptor* (London: Sir John Soane's Museum, 2005), 58.

21. Bryant notes that, while the marble was being finished, the plaster that would become Soane's was kept at Newman Street. See Ibid., 31.

22. Howard, *Lectures*, 215.

23. "Henry Howard, Esq., R.A.," *Gentleman's Magazine* 182 (1847), 646.

24. John Flaxman, *Compositions from the Tragedies of Aeschylus* (London: Seeley, Jackson, & Halliday, 1879).

25. Howard, *Lectures*, 4.

26. Ibid., 145.

27. Thornbury, *Turner*, vol. 2, 76.

28. One of the most striking documents of this reaction is an essay by William Thackeray on French art, first published in 1839. See "On the French School of Painting," *Fraser's Magazine* 20 (December 1839), 686.

29. Howard, *Lectures*, lxxx.

30. Ibid., 16.

31. Walter Benjamin, *Illuminations*, trans. Harry Zohn (New York: Schocken Books, 2007), 224.

32. Like so many of Howard's original works, these drawings are at present untraced. They are mentioned in Howard, *Lectures*, lxi.

33. Howard's drawings of sculpture in Rome are mentioned in William Hayley, *An Essay on Sculpture: In a series of epistles to John Flaxman, Esq.* RA (London: T. Cadell, 1800), 251.

34. Howard, *Lectures*, lxi.

35. James Northcote, *The Life of Sir Joshua Reynolds*, vol. 2 (London: Henry Colburn, 1819), 273.

36. Girodet and Flaxman's correspondence is discussed in Edward Morris, *French Art in Nineteenth-Century Britain* (New Haven and London: Paul Mellon Centre for Studies in British Art by Yale University Press, 2005), 18–19.

37. Satish Padiyar, "Crisis? What Crisis?," *Art History* 21/2 (1998), 275.

38. Hayley, *Essay*, 251.

39. Richard Payne Knight, *Specimens of Ancient Sculpture, Ægyptian, Etruscan, Greek, and Roman: Selected from Different Collections in Great Britain* (London: T. Bensley, 1809).

40. See the condemnation of James Barry's history paintings by Richard Payne Knight (anonymously): "The Works and Life of James Barry," *Edinburgh Review: Or Critical Journal* 16 (August 1810), 293–326.

41. Knight, *Specimens*, pl. VI.

42. George Cumberland, *Thoughts on Outline, Sculpture, and the System that Guided the Ancient Artists in Composing Their Figures and Groupes* (London: W. Wilson, 1796), 4.

43. William Vaughan, "'David's Brickdust' and the Rise of the British School," in Alison Yarrington and Kelvin Everest (eds.), *Reflections of Revolution: Images of Romanticism* (London and New York: Routledge, 1993), 141. Vaughan is referring to a painting by Benjamin West possessing a similar aesthetic to Howard's.

44. See Trimmer's account of Howard in Thornbury, *Turner*, vol. 2, 78.

45. See M. Kirby Talley, Jr., "'All good pictures crack': Sir Joshua Reynolds's Practice and Studio," in Nicholas Penny (ed.), *Reynolds* (New York: Abrams, 1986), 55–70; this aspect of Reynolds's practice was explored in the Wallace Collection's exhibition *Joshua Reynolds: Experiments in Paint* and accompanying catalog: Lucy Davis and Mark Hallett (eds.), *Joshua Reynolds: Experiments in Paint* (London: Paul Holberton, 2015).

46. Barry's condemnation of "magilphs and other mysteries" is conveyed in a letter to Edmund Burke sent while the painter was living in Rome. See Edward Fryer (ed.), *The Works of James Barry*, 2 vols. (London: T. Cadell & W. Davies, 1809), vol. 1, 70.

47. Benjamin Bates to Anne Denman Flaxman, January 4, 1787, British Library, Add. MSS 39, 781, fols. 362–3. Quoted in Myrone, *Bodybuilding*, 288.

48. *Morning Post* (May 18, 1839), 3.

49. See Rosie Dias, "Colour, Effect and the Formation of an English School of Painting," in Peter Humphrey (ed.), *The Reception of Titian in Britain: From Reynolds to Ruskin* (Turnhout: Brepols, 2013); Rosie Dias, "Venetian Secrets: Benjamin West and the Contexts of Colour at the Royal Academy," in Sarah Monks, John Barrell, and Mark Hallett (eds.), *Living with the Royal Academy: Artistic Ideals and Experiences in England, 1768–1848* (Farnham: Ashgate, 2013), 111–30.

50. See Fryer, *Works,* vol. 1, 85.

51. See Shelley M. Bennett, *Thomas Stothard and the Mechanisms of Art Patronage in England c. 1800* (Columbia: University of Missouri Press, 1988).

52. See Sarah Burnage, "Introduction," in Jason Edwards and Sarah Burnage (eds.), *The British School of Sculpture, c. 1760–1832* (London and New York: Routledge, 2017), 23–4.

53. Martin Bernal, *Black Athena: The Afroasiatic Roots of Classical Civilization*, vol. 1 (London: Random House, 2012), 288.

54. *Monthly Mirror* (May 1796), 151.

55. Ibid., 152.

56. A colored lithograph after Howard's painting of *Hylas and the Nymphs* was published in Paris as *Hylas enlevé par les Nymphes*, engraved by Achille Devéria c. 1840.

57. See Kathryn Ledbetter, *Tennyson and Victorian Periodicals: Commodities in Context* (London: Routledge, 2016).

58. See Kathryn Ledbetter, *British Victorian Women's Periodicals: Beauty, Civilization, and Poetry* (Basingstoke: Palgrave Macmillan, 2009).

59. See Basil Hunnisett, *Steel-Engraved Book Illustration in England* (Boston: David R. Godine, 1980).

60. Alaric A. Watts (ed.), *Lyrics of the Heart, with Other Poems* (London: Longman, Brown, Green, and Longmans, 1851), 77; Katherine Haskins, *The Art Journal and Fine Art Publishing in Victorian England* (Abingdon: Taylor & Francis, 2016), 49–51.

61. *Literary Gazette* (May 18, 1833), 314.

62. Alaric A. Watts (ed.), *The Cabinet of Modern Art and Literary Souvenir*, vol. 2 (London: Whittaker & Co., 1836), xviii.

63. Alaric A. Watts (ed.), *The Cabinet of Modern Art and Literary Souvenir*, vol. 1 (London: Whittaker & Co., 1835), 20–21.

64. See the account given by Henry Scott Trimmer in Thornbury, *Turner*, vol. 1, 172.

65. John Wilkes (ed.), *Encyclopaedia Londinensis*, vol. 8 (London: J. Alard, 1815), 409.

66. "Application and Intent of the various Styles of Architecture," *Quarterly Review* 27 (July 1822), 324.

67. See Linda Colley, *Britons: Forging the Nation 1707–1837* (New Haven and London: Yale University Press, 1992), 147–76.

68. *Blackwood's Edinburgh Magazine* 6 (October 1819), 77.

69. See the review of John Opie's *Lectures on Painting* in the *Anti-Jacobin Review and Protestant Advocate* (October 1809), 123; the same sentiment characterizes the review of Benjamin West's painting *The Harmony of*

Affection in the *Edinburgh Annual Register* (1808); see also Thackeray, "On the French School of Painting," 679–88.

70. See William Godwin, *History of Greece: From the earliest records of that country to the time in which it was reduced to a Roman province* (London: Baldwin & Craddock, 1828).

71. Edward Wedlake Brayley, *London and Middlesex; Or, an Historical, Commercial & Descriptive Survey of the Metropolis of Great Britain*, vol. 2 (London: J. Harris, 1814), 285.

72. This is how Howard describes Banks's nymphs in his Academy lecture on composition (*Lectures*, 215).

73. The painting was exhibited as *A Chaldean Shepherd Contemplating the Heavenly Bodies: The Supposed Origin of Poetical Astronomy.* Although it does not name it directly, the painting seems to allude to Canto III of Byron's *Childe Harold's Pilgrimage*:

> *Like the Chaldean, he could watch the stars,*
> *Till he had peopled them with beings bright*
> *As their own beams; and earth,*
> *and earth-born jars,*
> *And human frailties, were forgotten quite.*

See Thomas Moore (ed.), *Lord Byron: Childe Harold's Pilgrimage* (Philadelphia: Henry Carey Baird, 1854), 123. Howard also included some of his own poetry in the Academy exhibition catalogue:

> *And fancy rapt, sees in the fleecy clouds*
> *Celestial shapes that wait upon the moon,*
> *In her swift course, or rise from Ocean lap,*
> *Continuous.*

Quoted in Howard, *Lectures*, lxxiv.

74. Marina Warner, *Monuments and Maidens: The Allegory of the Female Form* (Berkeley: University of California Press, 1985), 12.

75. The Englishwoman's supremacy in this regard is discussed in Klaus Theweleit, *Male Fantasies*, vol. 1 (Minneapolis: University of Minnesota Press, 2003), 339.

76. Farington writes that on September 1, 1802, he, John Opie, Benjamin West, and other British artists discussed the beauty of women in Paris, with Opie claiming he "had seen more handsome Woemen in walking from Berners-street to the end of Oxford street than in all Paris in the fortnight He has been here." The next day they resumed this conversation: "We talked of the beauty of French Woemen, or rather what pretensions they had to it. All seemed to agree that they are in this respect inferior to the English Woemen." On September 12, the architect Robert Smirke is quoted confessing his opinion that "the Parissian Woemen [are] generally much thinner than the English Woemen and that He saw but few such complexions as are common in England, and much less beauty." A week later, after attending a large public gathering at the Jardin de Tivoli, Farington states his conclusion that "beauty among Woemen is much more rarer than it is in England in large Assemblies, but in form, and more particularly in carriage, the French Woemen cannot be looked upon without much interest." Kenneth Garlick and Angus Macintyre (eds.), *The Diary of Joseph Farington*, vol. 5 (New Haven and London: Yale University Press, 1979), 1820, 1823, 1851.

77. See Joyce Outshoorn, Radka Dudová, Ana Prata, and Lenita Freidenvall, "Women's Movements and Bodily Integrity," in Joyce Outshoorn (ed.), *European Women's Movements and Body Politics: The Struggle for Autonomy* (Basingstoke: Palgrave Macmillan, 2016), 153–177.

78. Theweleit, *Male Fantasies*, vol. 1, 339.

79. Wollstonecraft urges women to aspire to the beauty of Greek sculptures. See *A Vindication of the Rights of Woman with Strictures on Political and Moral Subjects* (Dublin: J. Stockdale, 1793), 225.

80. Cumberland, *Thoughts*, 33–4.

81. Warner, *Monuments and Maidens*, 12–13.

82. These volumes have multiple editions. See Marguerite Gardiner (Countess of Blessington) (ed.), *Heath's Book of Beauty* (London: J. Moyes, 1835); William Finden, *Finden's Gallery of the Graces* (London: Charles Tilt, 1834). *Heath's Book of Beauty* was edited by both Marguerite Gardiner, Countess of Blessington, and Letitia Elizabeth Landon, a prolific poet of the period.

83. Anon., "Application and Intent," 324. As M. G. Sullivan notes, Cunningham was the author of an important article on British sculpture also in the *Quarterly Review*. For insight into Cunningham's nationalistic art criticism, see M. G. Sullivan, "Cunningham, Chantrey, and the British School of Sculpture," in Jason Edwards and Sarah Burnage (eds.), *The British School of*

Sculpture, c. 1760–1832 (London and New York: Routledge, 2017), 218–20.

84. Alaric A. Watts (ed.), *The Cabinet of Modern Art and Literary Souvenir*, vol. 3 (London: Whittaker & Co., 1837), 209.

85. Carol Ockman, *Ingres's Eroticized Bodies: Retracing the Serpentine Line* (New Haven and London: Yale University Press, 1995).

86. See Martin Myrone, "'Something Too Academical': The Problem with Etty," in Sarah Burnage, Mark Hallett, and Laura Turner (eds.), *William Etty: Art & Controversy* (London: Philip Wilson in association with York Museums Trust, 2011), 47–59; Martin Myrone, "William Etty: 'A Child of the Royal Academy,'" in Monks, Barrell, and Hallett, *Living with the Royal Academy*, 171–94.

87. *Spectator* (May 20, 1837), 475.

88. Alexander Gilchrist, *Life of William Etty, RA*, 2 vols. (London: David Bogue, 1855), vol. 1, 98.

89. Reynolds's *Cymon and Iphigenia* is in the Royal Collection, hung at Buckingham Palace. Etty's (unfinished) copy of the painting is in the collection of York Art Gallery.

90. This is how Joseph Spence describes the *Venus de' Medici*'s breasts. See Joseph Spence, *Polymetis* (London: J. Dodsley, 1774), 68.

91. See Royal Academy Critiques for 1837, Royal Academy Library and Archive, London.

92. *The Times* (January 29, 1822), quoted in Dennis Farr, *William Etty* (London: Routledge & Kegan Paul, 1958), 31.

93. See Cora Gilroy-Ware, "William Etty's Female Nude with a Cast of the *Venus de' Medici*: Corporeal Possibilities beyond the 'Graceful Bend,'" in Joanna Selbourne (ed.), *Life, Legend, Landscape: Victorian Drawings and Watercolors* (London: Paul Holberton Books, 2011).

94. This practice is mentioned in the *London Reviewer* (February 5, 1835), 5.

95. *Spectator* (May 20, 1837), 475.

96. Quoted in Joan Coutu, *Then and Now: Collecting and Classicism in Eighteenth-Century England* (Montreal and Kingston: McGill-Queen's University Press, 2015), 67.

97. Etty wrote this letter as a plea to the government to purchase Thomas Lawrence's collection of old master drawings on behalf of the nation. The letter is quoted in Gilchrist, *Life*, vol. 2, 42–3.

98. This quote appears in Etty's obituary in the *Gentleman's Magazine* (January 1850), 98.

99. In a letter to his friend George Bulmer, Etty writes that "the two great evils of the day" are cholera and reform. Quoted in Gilchrist, *Life*, vol. 2, 346. See also the book's section, "A Painter's Politics," 346–7.

100. Edmund Burke, *Reflections on the Revolution in France* (London: J. Dodsley, 1791), 130.

101. Anon., "The Flower-Girl," in Samuel Carter Hall (ed.), *The Vernon Gallery of British Art*, vol. 2 (London: George Virtue, 1851), unpaginated.

102. Bryant, *Modern Sculptor*; David Bindman (ed.), *John Flaxman 1755–1826: Master of the Purest Line* (London: Sir John Soane's Museum, 2003).

103. *Athenaeum* (October 9, 1847), 1060.

104. For other fleeting references to Howard, see Marcia Pointon, *Milton & English Art: A Study in the Pictorial Artist's Use of a Literary Source* (Manchester: Manchester University Press, 1970), 199–201; Myrone, *Fuseli*, 66.

105. Edward Croft-Murray, *Decorative Painting in England 1537–1837*, vol. 2 (London: Country Life, 1970), 224.

106. See James Yorke, *Lancaster House: London's Greatest Town House* (London: Merrell, 2001), 37.

107. Frank Howard's memoir suggests a different chronology to Yorke's. "In 1834 he was engaged ... on the adaptation of the 'Solar System' to a circle twelve feet in diameter, for the ceiling of the boudoir of the Duchess of Sutherland ... In 1835 he was engaged upon the pictures for the ceiling in Sir John Soane's Museum.' Howard, *Lectures*, lxxv.

4 · Living Dreams and Poems
pages 157–193

1. Roughly two decades after Baartman's exhibition, another woman was employed as the "Hottentot Venus" at a salon held by Marie-Caroline de Bourbon-Sicile, Duchess of Berry. The episode is recorded in a watercolor by Sebastien Coure from c. 1830 (private collection).

2. The trial is discussed in Gillian Whitlock, *Postcolonial Life Narratives: Testimonial Transactions* (Oxford: Oxford University Press, 2015), 38–9.

3. It is worth noting that the line between real and marble flesh is even more ambiguous in the uncolored editions of Rowlandson's print.

4. Johann Wolfgang von Goethe, *Italian Journey (1786–1788)*, trans. W. H. Auden and Elizabeth Mayer (Harmondsworth: Penguin, 1970), 208.

5. Sander Gilman, "Black Bodies, White Bodies: Toward an Iconography of Female Sexuality in Late Nineteenth Century Art, Medicine and Literature," *Critical Inquiry* 12/1 (1985), 206.

6. See ibid., 213.

7. The broadsheet is discussed in Clifton Crais and Pamela Scully, *Sara Baartman and the Hottentot Venus: A Ghost Story and a Biography* (Princeton and Oxford: Princeton University Press, 2010), 111.

8. Thomas Tegg, *Tegg's Prime Song Book, Bang up to the Mark!* (London: printed for the author, 1810), 36.

9. In an article written in the *Idler*, Joshua Reynolds articulates the strain of discourse that ideals of beauty were variable and specific to different places. Though he refers to "Ethopians" rather than "Hottentots," he taps into the period's construction of difference between Europeans and a widespread conception of pan-African physiognomy: "I suppose no body will doubt, if [an Ethopian painter] was to paint the Goddess of Beauty, but that he would represent her black, with thick lips, flat nose, and woolly hair." See *The Works of Sir Joshua Reynolds, Knight*, vol. 2 (London: T. Cadell, junior, and W. Davis, 1798), 240.

10. See Gilman, "Black Bodies," 216–18.

11. William Hogarth, *The Analysis of Beauty: Written with a view of fixing the fluctuating ideas of taste* (London: W. Strahan, 1772), viii.

12. Ibid., 38.

13. For a brilliant discussion of Hogarth's references to female fashion in his *Analysis of Beauty*, and the role of the imagination with regard to the image of the female body, see Kathleen Lubey, *Excitable Imaginations: Eroticism and Reading in Britain, 1660–1760* (Lewisburg, Penn.: Bucknell University Press, 2012), 199–201.

14. Mary Wollstonecraft, *A Vindication of the Rights of Woman with Strictures on Political and Moral Subjects* (Dublin: J. Stockdale, 1793), 225.

15. Georg Wilhelm Friedrich Hegel, *The Philosophy of History*, trans. J. Sibree (New York: Dover Publications, 1956), 99.

16. The copy of the broadsheet is in the collection of the Wellcome Institute, London.

17. British Library, Add. MSS 36499, fol. 89. Quoted in Charles Francis Bell, *Annals of Thomas Banks* (Cambridge: Cambridge University Press, 1938), 149.

18. R. B. Beckett (ed.), *John Constable's Correspondence*, vol. 6 (Woodbridge: Boydell and Brewer, 1968), 236. See the criticism of Etty's works in *The Times* (January 29, 1822).

19. Beckett, *Constable's Correspondence*, vol. 6, 236.

20. This episode is mentioned in Crais and Scully, *Sara Baartman*, 95.

21. Gilman, "Black Bodies," 221.

22. Ibid.

23. Joseph Spence, *Polymetis* (London: J. Dodsley, 1774), 68.

24. For a discussion of Hamilton as a "visceral" spectacle, see Angela Rosenthal, "Visceral Culture: Blushing and the Legibility of Whiteness in Eighteenth Century British Portraiture," *Art History* 27/4 (2004), 567.

25. This painting is in the collection of the National Portrait Gallery, London. For insight into the complexities of this painting, see David Higgins, "Art, Genius, and Racial Theory in the Early Nineteenth Century: Benjamin Robert Haydon," *History Workshop Journal* 58 (2004), 24–5.

26. David Bindman, *Ape to Apollo: Aesthetics and the Idea of Race in the 18th Century* (London: Reaktion, 2002).

27. Benjamin Robert Haydon, *Correspondence and Table-Talk*, vol. 2 (London: Chatto and Windus, 1876), 22.

28. Ibid.

29. Charles Bell, *Essays on the Anatomy of Expression in Painting* (London: Longman, Hurst, Rees, and Orme, 1806), 3.

30. Ibid., 173.

31. Ibid., 167.

32. Ibid., 6.

33. Anthony Carlisle, "On the Connexion between Anatomy and the Arts of Design," *Artist*, no. 17 (July 4, 1807), 2.

34. Ibid.

35. William Bissell Pope (ed.), *The Diary of Benjamin Robert Haydon*, vol. 1 (Cambridge, Mass.: Harvard University Press, 1960), 130.

36. John Bell, *The Anatomy of the Bones, Muscles & Joints* (Edinburgh: John Paterson, 1793), xiii–xiv.

37. Ibid.

38. Ibid., xiv.

39. For insight into the climate debate, see Aris Sarafianos, "Hyporborean Meterologies of Culture: Art's Progress and Medical Environmentalism in Arbuthnot, Burke and Barry," in Koen Vemeir and Michael Funk Deckard (eds.), *The Science of Sensibility: Reading Burke's Philosophical Enquiry* (London and New York: Springer Dordrecht Heidelberg, 2012), 69–90.

40. *New Monthly Magazine* (March 1, 1809), 179.

41. Kenneth Garlick and Angus Macintyre (eds.), *The Diary of Joseph Farington*, 16 vols. (New Haven and London: Yale University Press, 1979), vol. 9, 3300–01.

42. Ibid.

43. Ibid., 3306.

44. Carlisle, "Connexion," 6.

45. See Elizabeth Prettejohn, *The Modernity of Ancient Sculpture: Greek Sculpture and Modern Art from Winckelmann to Picasso* (London and New York: I. B. Tauris, 2012), 7–27.

46. Johann Joachim Winckelmann, *History of the Art of Antiquity*, trans. Harry Francis Malgrave (Los Angeles: Getty Research Institute, 2006), 198.

47. William Hazlitt, *Notes of a Journey through France and Italy* (London: Hunt and Clarke, 1826), 260.

48. William Hazlitt, *Sketches of the Principal Picture-Galleries in England* (London: Taylor and Hessey, 1824), 55.

49. West's letter is featured in William Richard Hamilton, *Memorandum on the Subject of the Earl of Elgin's Pursuits in Greece* (London: William Miller, 1811), 56.

50. See Debbie Challis, "The Parthenon Sculptures: Emblems of British National Identity," *British Art Journal* 7/1 (2006), 33–9.

51. See David Bindman, *Inventing Britain: British Art and National Identity* (London: Tate Publishing, 2004), 2.

52. Garlick and Macintyre, *Farington*, vol. 9, 3282.

53. Anon., *Report from the Select Committee of the House of Commons on the Earl of Elgin's Collection of Sculptured Marbles* (London: John Murray, 1816), 151.

54. Ibid., 152.

55. Hamilton, *Memorandum*, 55.

56. Tom Taylor (ed.), *Life of Benjamin Robert Haydon, historical painter, from his Autobiography and Journals*, vol. 1 (New York: Harper & Brothers, 1853), 88.

57. Garlick and Macintyre, *Farington*, vol. 10, 3713. The sculpture known as the *Farnese Hercules*, now in the National Archaeological Museum in Naples, provides an interesting case study. This figure possesses an intricate musculature that gives of the form an imposing multifaceted surface. Critics during the period argued that the sculpture does present an accurate understanding of the interior of the body but an exaggerated and artificial anatomy. See E. Bulwer, *Literary Remains of the Late William Hazlitt*, vol. 2 (London: Saunders and Otley, 1836), 122.

58. Garlick and Macintyre, *Farington*, vol. 10, 3713.

59. Pope, *Haydon*, vol. 1, 183–5.

60. Ibid.

61. Bell, *Expression*, 14.

62. Benjamin Robert Haydon, *Lectures on Painting and Design* (London: Longman, Brown, Green, and Longmans, 1846), 234.

63. Bell, *Expression*, 14.

64. Aris Sarafianos, "B. R. Haydon and Racial Science: The Politics of the Human Figure and the Art Profession in the Early Nineteenth Century," *Visual Culture in Britain* 7/1 (2006), 79–106.

65. For insight into the relationship between the representation of black figures and idealized images of white women, see Rosenthal, "Visceral Culture," 566–86.

66. See Charles White, *An Account of the Regular Gradation in Man, and in Different Animals and Vegetables* (London: C. Dilly, 1799).

67. Pope, *Haydon*, vol. 1, 183–5.

68. Ibid., 188.

69. Pope, *Diary*, vol. 1, 182, 183.

70. Hugh Honour, *The Image of the Black in Western Art*, vol. 4 (Cambridge, Mass.: Harvard University Press, 1989), 26.

71. White, *An Account*, 1.

72. Ibid., 135.

73. Ibid., 42.

74. Ibid., 52.

75. Ibid., 53.

76. Ibid.

77. Pope, *Haydon*, vol. 1, 189.

78. This is how the proportions of ideal beauty are laid out in the entry on "Drawing" in an encyclopaedia published the year Haydon employed Wilson; see *Encyclopaedia Britannica*, vol. 7 (Edinburgh: Andrew Bell, 1829), 318.

79. Taylor, *Haydon*, vol. 1, 134.

80. Bindman, *Ape*, 25; Martin Bernal, *Black Athena: The Afroasiatic Roots of Classical Civilization*, vol. 1 (London: Random House, 2012), 317–30.

81. Higgins, "Art, Genius," 28.

82. *Examiner* (August 4, 1811), 492.

83. British Library, Add. MSS 36499, fol. 89. Quoted in Bell, *Annals*, 149.

84. *Examiner* (August 4, 1811), 491.

85. Ibid. (September 1, 1811), 566.

86. Ibid., 567–8.

87. Ibid., 580.

88. Miriam Claude Meijer, *Race and Aesthetics in the Anthropology of Petrus Camper (1772–1789)* (Amsterdam and Atlanta: Rodopi, 1999). See also Bindman, *Ape*, 201–55; Winthrop Jordan, *White Over Black: American Attitudes toward the Negro* (Chapel Hill: University of North Carolina Press, 1968), 225–30.

89. Pope, *Haydon*, vol. 1, 117.

90. Ibid.

91. *Examiner* (September 22, 1811), 612.

92. Haydon refers to the Turks as a "brutal people," ibid. (December 1, 1811), 773.

93. Ibid.

94. Ibid. (September 1, 1811), 567.

95. Higgins, "Art, Genius," 19.

96. White, *An Account*, 135. Angela Rosenthal writes of the currency of flushed cheeks within the period's poetics of female beauty. See "Visceral Culture," 566.

97. See Knight's testimony in Anon., *Report from the Select Committee*, 92–104.

98. See the condemnation of James Barry's history paintings by Richard Payne Knight (anonymously): "The Works and Life of James Barry," *Edinburgh Review: or Critical Journal* 16 (August 1810), 293–326.

99. Pope, *Haydon*, vol. 1, 434.

100. The manifesto was first printed in the *Examiner* (March 17, 1816).

101. Haydon, *Lectures*, 235.

102. See Taylor, *Haydon*, vol. 1, 282–3.

103. See Higgins, "Art, Genius," 17–40; Sarafianos, "B. R. Haydon and Racial Science," 79–106. Sarafianos does not mention Wilson and the hypocrisy at work in Haydon's turn to racial science.

104. Higgins, "Art, Genius," 30.

105. Paul Edwards and James Walvin, *Black Personalities in the Era of the Slave Trade* (London and Basingstoke: Macmillan Press, 1983), 44.

106. Agnes Lugo-Ortiz and Angela Rosenthal, "Introduction: Envisioning Slave Portraiture," in Agnes Lugo-Ortiz and Angela Rosenthal (eds.), *Slave Portraiture in the Atlantic World* (New York and Cambridge: Cambridge University Press, 2013), 6.

107. The idea that blackness and slavery were coextensive in Haydon's lifetime is reinforced by the black attendant in James Ward's *Diana at the Bath* (see fig. 78). Although this figure's captivity can be read as symbolic, it simultaneously points to the coextension of captivity and black corporeality in Britain during the period.

108. Taylor, *Haydon*, vol. 1, 134.

109. Haydon, *Correspondence*, 329.

110. Taylor, *Haydon*, vol. 1, 135.

111. Bernal, *Black Athena*, vol. 1.

112. The German anthropologist Johann Friedrich Blumenbach is central to this overlap.

See Bindman, *Ape*, 160–62; Bernal, *Black Athena*, vol. 1, 220–21.

113. Bernal, *Black Athena*, vol. 1, 287.

114. For insight into the appropriation of Bertel Thorvaldsen's art in Nazi Germany, see David Bindman, *Warm Flesh, Cold Marble: Canova, Thorvaldsen and their Critics* (New Haven and London: Yale University Press, 2014), 10, 135–6.

115. See Alex Scobie, *Hitler's State Architecture: The Impact of Classical Antiquity* (University Park and London: Pennsylvania State University Press, 1990), 15. The connection between Michelangelo and the sculpture's intended dedication to Mussolini are discussed in Walter Grasskamp, "The De-Nazification of Nazi Art: Arno Breker and Albert Speer Today," in Brandon Taylor and Wilfred van der Will (eds.), *The Nazification of Art: Art, Design, Music, Architecture and Film in the Third Reich* (Winchester: Winchester Press, 1990), 241, 243.

116. Grasskamp, "De-Nazification," 243.

117. Haydon, *Correspondence*, vol. 1, 262.

118. Compare Long's statement that Africans "are void of any genius, and seem almost incapable of making any progress in the civility of science" with Haydon's that "Men of genius are always born with views beyond their time ... But [negroes have] never given birth to great lawgivers ... never produced astronomers from contemplating the heavens." Edward Long, *The History of Jamaica, or, General Survey of the Antient and Modern State of that Island*, vol. 2 (London: T. Lowndes, 1774), 353; *Examiner* (September 1, 1811), 568.

119. Susan Sontag, "Fascinating Fascism," *New York Times* (February 6, 1975), http://www.nybooks.com/articles/1975/02/06/fascinating-fascism/ (accessed May 20, 2019).

120. Bell, *Expression*, 5.

121. Ibid., 4.

122. Sontag, "Fascinating Fascism."

123. See Graham Mcfee and Alan Tomlinson, "Riefenstahl's Olympia: Ideology and Aesthetics in the Shaping of the Aryan Athletic Body," *International Journal of the History of Sport* 16/2 (1999), 86–106.

5 · Poetic Victory *pages 195–237*

1. See Frederick Cummings, "B. R. Haydon and his School," *Journal of the Warburg and Courtauld Institutes* 26/3–4 (1963), 367–80.

2. William Holman Hunt calls Haydon "the bravest yet the most unfortunate" artist of the post-Napoleonic period. See William Holman Hunt, *Pre-Raphaelitism and the Pre-Raphaelite Brotherhood*, vol. 1 (New York and London: Macmillan & Co., 1905), 46–7.

3. See Nikolaus Pevsner, *London: The Cities of London and Westminster* (London: Penguin, 1962), 266.

4. See Dana Arnold, *Rural Urbanism: London Landscapes in the Early Nineteenth Century* (Manchester and New York: Manchester University Press, 2005), 143–4.

5. Benjamin Robert Haydon, *Correspondence and Table-Talk*, vol. 1 (London: Chatto and Windus, 1876), 326.

6. Westmacott's patronage by slave owners is discussed in Madge Dresser, "Set in Stone? Statues and Slavery in London," *History Workshop Journal* 64/1 (2007), 162–99.

7. Anon., *Report from the Select Committee of the House of Commons on the Earl of Elgin's Collection of Sculptured Marbles* (London: John Murray, 1816), 152.

8. For Haydon's passing reference to the "brickdust" of David's coloring, see Tom Taylor (ed.), *Life of Benjamin Robert Haydon, historical painter, from his Autobiography and Journals*, vol. 2 (New York: Harper & Brothers, 1853), 171.

9. Quoted in David Bindman, *Warm Flesh, Cold Marble: Canova, Thorvaldsen and their Critics* (New Haven and London: Yale University Press, 2014), 126.

10. William A. P. Childs, "The Classic as Realism in Greek Art," *Art Journal* 47/1 (1988), 12.

11. Ibid.

12. Johann Joachim Winckelmann, *History of the Art of Antiquity*, trans. Harry Francis Malgrave (Los Angeles: Getty Research Institute, 2006), 232–9.

13. William Bissell Pope (ed.), *The Diary of Benjamin Robert Haydon*, 5 vols. (Cambridge, Mass.: Harvard University Press, 1960), vol. 1, 247.

14. Bindman, *Warm Flesh*, 138–9; Satish Padiyar, *Chains: David, Canova, and the Fall of the Public Hero in Postrevolutionary France* (University Park: Pennsylvania State University Press, 2007), 139–40.

15. Extracts from Canova's correspondence with the duke are included in John Kenworthy-Browne, "A Ducal Patron of Sculpture," *Apollo* 105 (1977), 323.

16. Ibid.

17. Whitney Davis, "Eternal Moment: Pater on the Temporality of the Classical Ideal in Art," in Charles Martindale, Stefano Evangelista, and Elizabeth Prettejohn (eds.), *Pater the Classicist: Classical Scholarship, Reception and Aestheticism* (Oxford: Oxford University Press, 2017), 81.

18. Hugh Honour, "Antonio Canova and the Anglo-Romans, Part 1: The First Visit to Rome," *Connoisseur* 143 (1959a), 243.

19. Richard Duppa, *The Life of Michael Angelo Buonaroti* (London: Longman, Hurst, Rees, Orme, and Brown, 1816), 263–6 (n. 3).

20. For a discussion of the femininity of the ephebic male figure, see Carol Ockman, *Ingres's Eroticized Bodies: Retracing the Serpentine Line* (New Haven and London: Yale University Press, 1995), 11–33; Abigail Solomon-Godeau, *Male Trouble: A Crisis in Representation* (London: Thames and Hudson, 1997).

21. See the article on the work of sculptor John Graham Lough in *Art Journal* 25 (1863), 322.

22. Byung-Chul Han, *Saving Beauty* (Cambridge: Polity Press, 2018), 18.

23. The plaster sculpture is untraced. See John Lough and Elizabeth Merson, *John Graham Lough: A Northumbrian Sculptor* (Woodbridge and Wolfeboro: Boydell Press, 1987), 9.

24. Pope, *Haydon*, vol. 3, 199.

25. Ibid., 204.

26. See Lough, *Northumbrian Sculptor*, 8.

27. Geo Neasham, *North-Country Sketches: Notes, Essays and Reviews* (Durham: Thos. Caldcleugh, 1893), 10.

28. See Lough, *Northumbrian Sculptor*, 4.

29. This painting is in the collection of the Laing Art Gallery, Newcastle.

30. Padiyar, *Chains*, 124–5.

31. Ibid., 128.

32. Pope, *Haydon*, vol. 3, 199.

33. *Gentleman's Magazine* 144 (part 2) (November 1818), 457.

34. Anon., *Statues of John Graham Lough: Somnus and Iris, Musidora, Milo, and Sampson* (London: Thomas Davison, 1828), 13–14.

35. *New Monthly Magazine* (June 1, 1828), 256–7.

36. *Bell's Life in London and Sporting Chronicle* (June 1, 1828), 2.

37. See Bindman, *Warm Flesh*, 51.

38. Anon., *Select Committee*, 88.

39. See Jason Edwards, "Introduction," in Jason Edwards and Sarah Burnage (eds.), *The British School of Sculpture, c. 1760–1832* (London and New York: Routledge, 2017), 6; John Kenworthy-Browne, "The Third Earl of Egremont and Neoclassical Sculpture," *Apollo* 105 (1977), 367–75; Max Egremont, "The 3rd Earl of Egremont and his Friends," *Apollo* 122 (1985), 280–87.

40. *Gentleman's Magazine* (June 1828), 623; *London Literary Gazette* (June 14, 1828), 380.

41. Anon., *Select Committee*, 88. It is worth noting that, along with Bacon and Banks, Rossi was one of the sculptors to be commissioned for a St. Paul's war monument, and that his was the only out of the three not to Dream. Long before his theatrical boxer was conceived, Rossi laid the groundwork for the Poetic turn with his reclining figure of *Eve*, exhibited at the Academy in 1796, a work (now untraced) lauded for its sensuality. The atemporality of this sculpture – the way in which its subject was simultaneously biblical and Miltonic but its form "antique" – is an indication of which side Rossi adhered to in the war that was still occurring when *Eve* was created. This sculpture is discussed in Caroline Patricia Jordan, "Edward Hodges Baily (1788–1867) and the Notion of Poetic Sculpture c. 1800–1845" (PhD thesis, University of Leeds, 2007), 17, 82.

42. Michael Hatt, "Physical Culture: The Male Nude and Sculpture in Late Victorian Britain," in Elizabeth Prettejohn (ed.), *After the Pre-Raphaelites: Art and Aestheticism in Victorian England* (Manchester: Manchester University Press, 1999), 240.

43. Pope, *Haydon*, vol. 3, 199.

44. Among other disparaging nicknames, Westmacott's sculpture came to be known as the "Ladies' Statue." See George Cleghorn,

Remarks on Ancient and Modern (London: T. Cadell, 1824), 94.

45. *English Chronicle* quoted in *Worcester Journal* (August 1, 1822).

46. Ibid.

47. William Richard Hamilton, *Memorandum on the Subject of the Earl of Elgin's Pursuits in Greece* (London: William Miller, 1811), 56.

48. See Anon., *Royal Mews Gallery: Exhibition of the celebrated heroic equestrian group of Monte Cavallo at Rome* (London: W. Bulmer & Co., 1816).

49. Martin Bernal, *Black Athena: The Afroasiatic Roots of Classical Civilization*, vol. 1 (London: Random House, 2012), 288.

50. See the entry on "Sculpture" in *Encyclopaedia Londinensis*, vol. 22 (London: G. Jones, 1827), 880; *Quarterly Review* 32, 347; John Britton, *The Original Picture of London: Enlarged and Improved* (London: Longman, Rees, Orme, Brown, and Green, 1826), 195.

51. See Chapter 2, n. 9 on p. 257.

52. William Hazlitt, *Notes of a Journey through France and Italy* (London: Hunt and Clarke, 1826), 260–61.

53. Ibid., 260.

54. Ibid., 261.

55. William Hazlitt, *Criticisms on Art* (London: John Templeman, 1843), 333.

56. E. Bulwer, *Literary Remains of the Late William Hazlitt*, vol. 2 (London: Saunders and Otley, 1836), 438.

57. Ibid.

58. Haydon, *Correspondence*, vol. 1, 330.

59. *Spectator* (June 10, 1837), 548.

60. Ibid.

61. Haydon, *Correspondence*, vol. 1, 330.

62. Hugh Honour, "Antonio Canova and the Anglo-Romans, Part 2: The First Years in Rome," *Connoisseur* 144 (1959b), 230.

63. Howard and Flaxman's consensus on the superiority of this sculpture is mentioned in Henry Howard, *A Course of Lectures on Painting delivered at the Royal Academy of Arts* (London: Henry G. Bohn, 1848), lxxix.

64. John Flaxman, *Lectures on Sculpture*, 2nd edn. (London: Henry G. Bohn, 1838), 25; Edward Fryer (ed.), *The Works of James Barry*, vol. 2 (London: T. Cadell & W. Davies, 1809), 146.

65. Winckelmann, *History*, 203.

66. Ibid.

67. A version of the *Venere Italica* was at Landsdowne House, which Haydon reports visiting in 1825. Taylor, *Haydon*, vol. 1, 460.

68. For insight into the differences between this sculpture and the *Venus de' Medici*, see Hugh Honour, "Canova's Statues of Venus," *Burlington Magazine* 114/835 (1972), 658–71.

69. *London Journal of Arts and Sciences* (June 1822), 321.

70. *Fraser's Magazine* (February 1845), 172.

71. *Spirit of the Times* (February 18, 1826), 294.

72. Macdowell's work is in the collection of the Royal Society, Dublin, in Leinster, Ireland.

73. *Athenaeum* (June 12, 1830), 365.

74. See Jordan, "Baily," 105.

75. These works are untraced.

76. See the response to Etty in *The Times* (January 29, 1822), quoted in Dennis Farr, *William Etty* (London: Routledge & Kegan Paul, 1958), 31.

77. Marina Warner, *Monuments and Maidens: The Allegory of the Female Form* (Berkeley: University of California Press, 1985), 258. The author also notes that in certain medieval texts, "the materiality of women's bodies increases with fertility and parturition, since pregnancy opens the container and lets out the dangerous contents" (251–2).

78. Ibid., 260.

79. Hatt, "Physical Culture," 251.

80. See Chantrey's letter to the President and Council of the Royal Academy, March 8, 1822, Royal Academy of Arts Library and Archive, London, LAW/4/6.

81. Joseph Spence, *Polymetis* (London: J. Dodsley, 1774), 68.

82. This work is untraced. For insight into breastfeeding in relation to such works, see Jordan, "Baily," 133–4.

83. Allan Cunningham, *The Life of Sir David Wilkie*, vol. 2 (London: John Murray, 1843), 269.

84. Giorgio Vasari, *Le Vite de' piu eccellenti pittori scultori ed architettori*, vol. 4 (Florence: G. C. Sansoni, 1879), 115.

85. The notion that marble could be softened in the hands of a skilled practitioner was nothing new. Italian contemporaries of Flemish sculptor François Duquesnoy set a precedent when they describe the flesh of his infant putti as akin to "animated flesh" or "milk rather than hard stone." See Joris van Gastel, *Il Marmo Spirante: Sculpture and Experience in Seventeenth Century Rome* (Leiden: Leiden University Press, 2012), 145–6. Sculptors of the new wave of mother and child groups, however, were reacting to their British predecessors rather than continental models. It was this aspect which John Gibson was referring to when, after returning to London from his adopted homeland of Rome, he complained that sculpture of his native land had been polluted by "a soft, smooth treatment" more appropriate for painting. He was an admirer of Canovian coatings as opposed to the transformation of the raw material alone, taking them to new heights with his polychrome sculptures. Paradoxically, this technique is more straightforwardly pictorial than the plain but treated marble. See Elizabeth Eastlake, *Life of John Gibson, R.A., Sculptor* (London: Longmans, Green and Co., 1870), 35.

86. See Julius Bryant, *Thomas Banks: Britain's First Modern Sculptor* (London: Sir John Soane's Museum, 2005), 51.

87. George Cumberland, *Thoughts on Outline, Sculpture, and the System that Guided the Ancient Artists in Composing Their Figures and Groupes* (London: W. Wilson, 1796), 8–9.

88. Allan Cunningham, *The Lives of the Most Eminent British Painters and Sculptors*, vol. 3 (London: John Murray, 1830), 311–12.

89. Pietro Martini, *Studi intorno il Correggio* (Parma: F. Carmignani, 1865), 12.

90. Quoted in Bindman, *Warm Flesh*, 121.

91. Melchior Missirini, *Della vita di Antonio Canova*, vol. 1 (Milan: Nicolò Bettoni, 1824), 119.

92. For an exploration of these paintings, see Ottorino Stefani, *Canova pittore* (Milan: Electa, 1992), 30–43.

93. John Davy (ed.), *Fragmentary Remains, literary and scientific, of Sir Humphry Davy, Bart.* (London: John Churchill, 1858), 227.

94. See Mark Norman and Richard Cook, "'Just a tiny bit of rouge upon the lips and cheeks': Canova, Colour and the Classical Ideal," in Katharine Eustace (ed.), *Antonio Canova: Ideal Heads* (Oxford: Ashmolean Museum, 1997), 47–58.

95. Alexander Walker, *Beauty: Illustrated chiefly by an analysis and classification of beauty in women* (London: Henry G. Bohn, 1846), 187.

96. Ibid., 212.

97. Ibid., 372.

98. Ibid., 380.

99. Angela Rosenthal, "Visceral Culture: Blushing and the Legibility of Whiteness in Eighteenth Century British Portraiture," *Art History* 27/4 (2004), 572.

100. *London Literary Gazette* (June 22, 1822), 393.

101. Following on from claims made in Elizabeth Grosz's *Volatile Bodies*, Rosenthal describes the reception of the female body as a "vessel": a leaky container whose physiological status is in dialectical opposition to the sealed, impermeable image of ideal man. This is a different use of the word "vessel" to the one on which my argument rests; the body's capacity to function as a vessel is dependent on transcending the body, whether male or female, as a physiological or somatic entity. In order to serve as a container, the body must stop functioning as a body. See Rosenthal, "Visceral Culture," 578; Elizabeth Grosz, *Volatile Bodies: Toward a Corporeal Feminism* (Bloomington and Indianapolis: Indiana University Press, 1994), 196–203. As Grosz notes, the metaphor of the body as a vessel is also discussed in Mary Douglas, *Purity and Pleasure* (London: Routledge & Kegan Paul, 1980), 126.

102. Anon., *The National Gallery of British Pictures and of Modern Sculpture presented to the nation by Robert Vernon* (London: Virtue, 1852), unpaginated.

103. *Athenaeum* (June 30, 1832), 410.

104. William Hazlitt, *Conversations of James Northcote, Esq., RA* (London: Henry Colburn and Richard Bentley, 1830), 52.

105. *Athenaeum* (June 30, 1832), 419.

106. Francis Turner Palgrave, *Descriptive Handbook to the Fine Art Collections in the International Exhibition of 1862* (London and Cambridge: Macmillan & Co., 1862), 89.

107. *Gentleman's Magazine* (September 1799), 808.

108. See, for example, the relief of a shepherd and shepherdess, attributed to Henry Cheere

and William Collins, Victoria and Albert Museum, London.

109. See Malcolm Baker, *Figured in Marble: The Making and Viewing of Eighteenth Century Sculpture* (London: Victoria and Albert Museum, 2000), 164–6.

110. Warner, *Monuments and Maidens*, 277.

111. Winckelmann, *History*, 203.

112. *Athenaeum* (June 30, 1832), 415.

113. Quoted in John Turpin, *John Hogan: Irish Neoclassical Sculptor in Rome, 1800–1858* (Leinster: Irish Academic Press, 1982), 40.

114. This sculpture is untraced.

115. Winckelmann writes that clay is an authoritative material for sculpture because it was the first substance used to create three-dimensional forms. See Winckelmann, *History*, 114–15.

116. See Diane Bilbey and Marjorie Trusted, *British Sculpture 1470–2000: A Concise Catalogue of the Collection at the Victoria and Albert Museum* (London: Victoria and Albert Museum, 2002), 288–9.

117. Richard Brilliant, *Portraiture* (London: Reaktion, 2013), 14.

118. This sculpture is at Chatsworth House.

119. Gibson's lifelong commitment to Psyche is discussed in Anna Frasca Rath and Annette Wickham, *John Gibson: A British Sculptor in Rome* (London: Royal Academy of Arts, 2016), 37.

120. Elizabeth Eastlake, *Gibson*, 104.

121. Ibid., 105.

122. Ibid., 106.

123. Caroline Arscott, "Venus as Dominatrix: Nineteenth-Century Artists and their Creations," in Caroline Arscott and Katie Scott (eds.), *Manifestations of Venus: Art and Sexuality* (Manchester and New York: Manchester University Press, 2000), 109–25.

124. An account of this dream is included in a later biography of Gibson: T. Matthews, *The Biography of John Gibson, R.A., Sculptor, Rome* (London: William Heinemann, 1911), 76–8.

125. Giorgio Agamben, *Infancy and History: The Destruction of Experience*, trans. Liz Heron (London and New York: Verso, 1993), 25–8.

126. Michel Maffesoli, *The Shadow of Dionysus: A Contribution to the Sociology of the Orgy*, trans. Cindy Linse and Mary Kristina Palmquist (Albany: State University of New York Press, 1993), 31.

127. Eastlake, *Gibson*, 195.

128. Ibid., 93.

129. Ibid., 203.

130. Ibid., 10.

Conclusion *pages 239–244*

1. For an account of Severn and Canova in Rome, see Sue Brown, *Joseph Severn, a Life: The Rewards of Friendship* (Oxford: Oxford University Press, 2009), 86–107; for information about Gott and his *oeuvre*, see Terry Friedman and Timothy Stevens (eds.), *Joseph Gott, 1786–1860, Sculptor* (Leeds and Liverpool: Lund Humphries, 1972).

2. This poem was first printed in the *Plymouth and Devonport Weekly Journal* on October 4, 1838. Other publications followed, including the *Leicester Chronicle*, which printed it on September 21, 1839. Severn claimed that the poem was Keats's last in a letter to Charles Armitage Brown sent on September 19, 1821. See William Sharp, *The Life and Letters of Joseph Severn* (London: Sampson, Low, Marston & Company, 1892), 110.

3. First published in 1826, Hazlitt's essay "English Students at Rome" argues that Rome's surfeit of art makes for an unproductive environment. William Hazlitt, *Criticisms on Art*, second series (London: C. Templeman, 1844), 203–22. See also Haydon's comment on the castrating effects of a Roman training: William Bissell Pope (ed.), *The Diary of Benjamin Robert Haydon*, vol. 3 (Cambridge, Mass.: Harvard University Press, 1960), 199.

4. See Alison Yarrington and Nigel Wood, "Ut Sculptura Poesis: English Romantic Poetry and Sculptural Form," in Thomas Frangenberg (ed.), *Poetry on Art: Renaissance to Romanticism* (Donington: Schaun Tyas, 2003), 215–35; Alison Yarrington, "The Poetics of Sculpture: Pedestal, Verse and Inscription," in Alexandra Gerstein (ed.), *Display and Displacement: Sculpture and the Pedestal from Renaissance to Post-Modern* (London: Paul Holberton, 2007), 73–96.

5. *Athenaeum* (May 23, 1835), 395.

6. Cunningham makes a passing reference to Banks's politics only to belittle it, presenting

Banks as the definitive "poetic" artist. After declaring that it "is pleasing to turn from the agony of politics to the repose of sculpture," he writes that "Banks had long desired to introduce a more poetic style of art into our national monuments." Allan Cunningham, *The Lives of the Most Eminent British Painters and Sculptors*, vol. 3 (London: John Murray, 1830), 109, 113.

7. See Calder Marshall correspondence, Royal Academy of Arts Library and Archive, London, MAR/3/13/6.

8. Calder Marshall's versions of Psyche include *Psyche Kneeling with a Butterfly* (1854, Hospitalfield House, Abroath, Scotland), *Psyche Feeling Cupid's Arrows* (1868, untraced), *Psyche Opening the Box of Cosmetics* (1842, untraced), and a medallion of *Psyche Borne by Zephyrs* (1855, untraced). A Psyche made in Rome c. 1837 is mentioned in his correspondence in the Royal Academy archives: MAR/3/5/8.

9. See, for example, his painting of *Pan and Psyche* (1872–74, Fogg Art Museum, Cambridge, Mass.). In this work, the landscape background and coloring betray the influence of sixteenth-century Venetian painting, while the staging of the figures has a medieval immediacy; Psyche is depicted in the style of a Hellenistic or Roman marble figure while Pan's musculature recalls the intricate anatomy of the Parthenon Marbles.

10. Elizabeth Prettejohn, "Walter Pater and Aesthetic Painting," in Elizabeth Prettejohn (ed.), *After the Pre-Raphaelites: Art and Aestheticism in Victorian England* (Manchester: Manchester University Press, 1999), 38.

11. Ibid., 48.

12. See Ottorino Stefani, *Canova pittore* (Milan: Electa, 1992), 30–43.

13. In an 1883 essay on living sculptors, Gosse writes that "Calder Marshall has never become entirely free from this bondage to tradition. He still thinks that sculpture only moves with safety when it walks closely and demurely in the traces of Greek art, and of Greek art not as by analogy we may judge it to have been, but as by existing relics we know it to be." This is similar to his pronouncements on Banks: "In all Banks's poetic figures we see the reconstituted ideal made up of recollected fragments of antique statuary, and it is dangerous to praise his work without being certain where he obtained the beauty of it." *Century Illustrated Monthly Magazine* 26 (June 1883), 175; J. T. Smith, *Nollekens and his Times* (London: Richard Bentley and Son, 1895), 15.

14. Clement Greenberg, "The Avant-Garde and the Kitsch," in Gillo Dorfles (ed.), *Kitsch: An Anthology of Bad Taste* (Milan: Gabriele Mazzotta, 1968), 116–26.

15. See Alex Potts's discussion of the *Venus de' Medici* and Canova's sculpture in Alex Potts, *The Sculptural Imagination: Figurative, Modernist, Minimalist* (New Haven and London: Yale University Press, 2000), 39–42.

16. Other such works include *Girl with a Carrier Pigeon*, exhibited in 1835, by Lawrence Macdonald, a Scottish artist who joined Gibson and the rest in Rome. This sculpture is in the collection of the Russell-Coates Gallery, Bournemouth. A later example is Henry Weekes's *Young Naturalist*, exhibited in 1854, in the collection of Lotherton Hall, Leeds.

BIBLIOGRAPHY

ADORNO, Theodor, *Aesthetic Theory*, trans. Robert Hullot-Kentor (Minneapolis: University of Minnesota Press, 1998).

AGAMBEN, Giorgio, *Infancy and History: The Destruction of Experience*, trans. Liz Heron (London and New York: Verso, 1993).

ANON., *Buff, or a dissertation on nakedness: A parody on Paine's Rights of Man* (London: Matthew, 1792).

ANON., "The Flower-Girl," in Samuel Carter Hall (ed.), *The Vernon Gallery of British Art*, vol. 2 (London: George Virtue, 1851).

ANON., *Methodism Vindicated, from the charge of ignorance and enthusiasm ... by a member of the Church of England* (Margate: J. Parsons, 1795).

ANON., *The National Gallery of British Pictures and of Modern Sculpture presented to the nation by Robert Vernon* (London: Virtue, 1852).

ANON., *Report from the Select Committee of the House of Commons on the Earl of Elgin's Collection of Sculptured Marbles* (London: John Murray, 1816).

ANON., *Royal Mews Gallery: Exhibition of the celebrated heroic equestrian group of Monte Cavallo at Rome* (London: W. Bulmer & Co., 1816).

ANON., *Statues of John Graham Lough: Somnus and Iris, Musidora, Milo, and Sampson* (London: Thomas Davison, 1828).

ANON., "William Sharp Esq: Honorary Member of the Imperial and Bavarian Academies," in *The Annual Biography and Obituary for the Year*, vol. 9 (London: Longman, Hurst, Rees, Orme, Brown, and Green, 1825).

ANON. [RICHARD PAYNE KNIGHT], "The Works and Life of James Barry," *Edinburgh Review: or Critical Journal* 16 (August 1810), 293–326.

APULEIUS, *Metamorphoses (The Golden Ass)*, vol. 1, trans. J. Arthur Hanson (Cambridge, Mass., and London: Harvard University Press, 1989).

ARNOLD, Dana, *Rural Urbanism: London Landscapes in the Early Nineteenth Century* (Manchester and New York: Manchester University Press, 2005).

ARSCOTT, Caroline, "Venus as Dominatrix: Nineteenth-Century Artists and their Creations," in Caroline Arscott and Katie Scott (eds.), *Manifestations of Venus: Art and Sexuality* (Manchester and New York: Manchester University Press, 2000), 109–25.

A.S., "Hogan, the Sculptor," *Irish Monthly* 2 (1874), 383–400.

ASKE, Martin, *Keats and Hellenism: An Essay* (Cambridge: Cambridge University Press, 2004).

ASTON, Nigel, "St. Paul's and the Public Culture of Eighteenth Century Britain," in Derek Keene, Arthur Burns, and Andrew Saint (eds.), *St. Paul's: The Cathedral Church of London 604–2004* (New Haven and London: Yale University Press, 2004), 363–71.

AVELING, Thomas Baxter, *Memorials of the Clayton Family* (London: Jackson, Walford, and Hopper, 1867).

BACON, Gertrude, *The Record of an Aeronaut, Being the Life of John Bacon* (London: John Long, 1907).

BAKER, Malcolm, *Figured in Marble: The Making and Viewing of Eighteenth Century Sculpture* (London: Victoria and Albert Museum, 2000).

BAKHTIN, Mikhail, *Rabelais and his World*, trans. Helene Iswolsky (Bloomington: Indiana University Press, 1984).

BALDWIN, Edward (William Godwin), *The Pantheon, or Ancient History of the Gods of*

Greece and Rome (London: M. J. Godwin, 1809).

Bann, Stephen, *The Clothing of Clio: A Study of the Representation of History in Britain and in France* (Cambridge: Cambridge University Press, 1984).

——, "Image, Text and Object in the Formation of Historical Consciousness," in H. Aram Veeser (ed.), *The New Historicism* (London and New York: Routledge, 1989).

Barbeau, Jeffrey W., *Coleridge, the Bible, and Religion* (Basingstoke: Palgrave Macmillan, 2008).

Barrell, John, *The Birth of Pandora and the Division of Knowledge* (Basingstoke: Macmillan, 1982).

——, "'The Dangerous Goddess': Masculinity, Prestige, and the Aesthetic in Early Eighteenth-Century Britain," *Cultural Critique* 12 (1989), 101–31.

——, *The Political Theory of Painting from Reynolds to Hazlitt* (New Haven and London: Yale University Press, 1995).

——, "Thomas Banks and the Society for Constitutional Information," in Sarah Monks, John Barrell, and Mark Hallett (eds.), *Living with the Royal Academy: Artistic Ideals and Experiences in England, 1768–1848* (Farnham: Ashgate, 2013), 131–52.

Barry, James, *A Letter to the Dilettanti Society* (London: J. Walker, 1798).

Baxandall, Michael, *Patterns of Intention* (New Haven and London: Yale University Press, 1988).

Becker, Michael G., Robert J. Dilligan, and Todd K. Bender (eds.), *A Concordance to the Poems of John Keats* (London and New York: Routledge, 2016).

Beckett, R. B. (ed.), *John Constable's Correspondence*, vol. 6 (Woodbridge: Boydell and Brewer, 1968).

Bell, Charles, *Essays on the Anatomy of Expression in Painting* (London: Longman, Hurst, Rees, and Orme, 1806).

Bell, Charles Francis, *Annals of Thomas Banks* (Cambridge: Cambridge University Press, 1938).

Bell, John, *The Anatomy of the Bones, Muscles & Joints* (Edinburgh: John Paterson, 1793).

Benjamin, Walter, *The Arcades Project*, trans. Howard Eiland and Kevin McLaughlin (Cambridge, Mass., and London: Belknap Press by Harvard University Press, 1999).

——, *Illuminations*, trans. Harry Zohn (New York: Schocken Books, 2007).

Bennett, Jill, *Practical Aesthetics: Events, Affect and Art After 9/11* (London and New York: I. B. Tauris, 2012).

Bennett, Shelley M., *Thomas Stothard and the Mechanisms of Art Patronage in England c. 1800* (Columbia: University of Missouri Press, 1988).

Bentley, G. E., Jr., *A Bibliography of George Cumberland (1754–1848)* (New York: Garland Publishing, 1975).

——, "The Suppression of George Cumberland's Captive of the Castle of Sennaar (1798) Liberty vs. Commerce," *Yale University Library Gazette*, 71/3–4 (1997), 155–8.

Bernal, Martin, *Black Athena: The Afroasiatic Roots of Classical Civilization*, vol. 1 (London: Random House, 2012).

Bewell, Alan J., "The Political Implication of Keats's Classicist Aesthetics," *Studies in Romanticism* 25/2 (1986), 220–29.

Bienville, D. T., *Nymphomania! or, a Dissertation concerning the furor uterinus, etc.*, trans. Edward Sloane Wilmot (London, J. Bew, 1775).

Bignamini, Ilaria, and Martin Postle, *The Artist's Model: Its Role in British Art from Lely to Etty* (Nottingham: Nottingham University Art Gallery, 1991).

Bilbey, Diane, and Marjorie Trusted, *British Sculpture 1470–2000: A Concise Catalogue of the Collection at the Victoria and Albert Museum* (London: Victoria and Albert Museum, 2002).

Bindman, David, *Ape to Apollo: Aesthetics and the Idea of Race in the 18th Century* (London: Reaktion, 2002).

——, *European Sculpture from Bernini to Rodin* (London: Studio Vista, 1970).

——, *Inventing Britain: British Art and National Identity* (London: Tate Publishing, 2004).

—— (ed.), *John Flaxman 1755–1826: Master of the Purest Line* (London: Sir John Soane's Museum, 2003).

——, *Warm Flesh, Cold Marble: Canova, Thorvaldsen and their Critics* (New Haven and London: Yale University Press, 2014).

Boddy, Kasia, *Boxing: A Cultural History* (London: Reaktion, 2008).

Bouwers, Eveline G., *Public Pantheons in Revolutionary Europe: Comparing Cultures of Remembrance c. 1790–1840* (Basingstoke: Palgrave Macmillan, 2011).

Bown, Nicola, *Fairies in Nineteenth-Century Art and Literature* (Cambridge: Cambridge University Press, 2001).

Brayley, Edward Wedlake, *London and Middlesex; Or, an Historical, Commercial & Descriptive Survey of the Metropolis of Great Britain*, vol. 2 (London: J. Harris, 1814).

Brilliant, Richard, *Portraiture* (London: Reaktion, 2013).

Britton, John, *The Original Picture of London: Enlarged and Improved* (London: Longman, Rees, Orme, Brown, and Green, 1826).

Brody, Miriam, *Mary Wollstonecraft: Mother of Women's Rights* (Oxford: Oxford University Press, 2000).

Brown, Sue, *Joseph Severn, a Life: The Rewards of Friendship* (Oxford: Oxford University Press, 2009).

Bryant, Julius, "The Church Memorials of Thomas Banks," *Church Monuments: Journal of the Church Monuments Society* 1 (1985), 49–64.

——, "Eccentric Pioneers? Patrons of Modern Sculpture for Britain," in Diana Dethloff, Tessa Murdoch, and Kim Sloan, with Caroline Elam (eds.), *Burning Bright: Essays in Honour of David Bindman* (London: UCL Press, 2015).

——, "The Royal Academy's 'Violent Democrat': Thomas Banks," *British Art Journal* 6/3 (2005), 51–8.

——, *Thomas Banks: Britain's First Modern Sculptor* (London: Sir John Soane's Museum, 2005).

Buchhart, Dieter, "The Endless Political Line," in Dieter Buchhart (ed.), *Keith Haring: The Political Line* (Munich, London, and New York: Delmonico Books, 2014).

Buck-Morss, Susan, *The Dialectics of Seeing: Walter Benjamin and the Arcades Project* (Cambridge, Mass., and London: MIT Press, 1991).

——, *Dreamworld and Catastrophe: The Passing of Mass Utopia in East and West* (Cambridge, Mass., and London: MIT Press, 2002).

Bulwer, E., *Literary Remains of the Late William Hazlitt*, vol. 2 (London: Saunders and Otley, 1836).

Burke, Edmund, *A Philosophical Enquiry into the Origin of Our Ideas of the Sublime and Beautiful* (London: J. Dodsley, 1767).

——, *Reflections on the Revolution in France* (London: J. Dodsley, 1791).

Burnage, Sarah, "'Delighting the Common People': John Bacon's Monuments to the Earl of Chatham (1778–1784)," in Jason Edwards and Sarah Burnage (eds.), *The British School of Sculpture, c. 1760–1832* (London and New York: Routledge, 2017), 79–102.

——, "Introduction: The British School of Sculpture – A Case Study," in Jason Edwards and Sarah Burnage (eds.), *The British School of Sculpture, c. 1760–1832* (London and New York: Routledge, 2017), 21–34.

——, 'Painting the Nude and "Inflicting Divine Vengeance on the Wicked,"' in Sarah Burnage, Mark Hallett, and Laura Turner (eds.), *William Etty: Art & Controversy* (London: Philip Wilson in association with York Museums Trust, 2011), 39–44.

Busco, Marie, "'The Houseless Traveller' and Related Sculptures by Richard Westmacott," *Notes on the History of Art* 11/3–4 (1992), 3–10.

Calasso, Roberto, *Tiepolo Pink*, trans. Alistair McEwen (London: Bodley Head, 2010).

Carey, William, *The National Obstacle to the National Public Style Considered: Observations on the Probable Decline or Extinction of British Historical Painting* (London: Howlett & Brimmer, 1825).

Carlisle, Anthony, "On the Connexion between Anatomy and the Arts of Design," *Artist*, no. 17 (July 4, 1807), 2.

Cavicchioli, Sonia, *The Tale of Cupid and Psyche: An Illustrated History* (New York: George Brazillier, 2002).

Cavina, Anna Ottani, *Geometries of Silence: Three Approaches to Neoclassical Art*, trans. Alistair McEwen (New York: Columbia University Press, 2004).

Cecil, Richard, *Memoirs of John Bacon* (London: F. and C. Rivington, 1801).

——, *Short Hints to a Soldier, in a letter from his friend* (London: J. Tibling, 1810).

Challis, Debbie, "The Parthenon Sculptures: Emblems of British National Identity," *British Art Journal* 7/1 (2006), 33–9.

Chan, Victor, *Rubens to Picasso: Four Centuries of Master Drawings* (Edmonton: University of Alberta Press, 1995).

Childs, William A. P., "The Classic as Realism in Greek Art," *Art Journal* 47/1 (1988), 10–14.

Clark, Kenneth, *The Nude* (Harmondsworth: Penguin, 1964).

Cleghorn, George, *Remarks on Ancient and Modern* (London: T. Cadell, 1824).

Colley, Linda, *Britons: Forging the Nation 1707–1837* (New Haven and London: Yale University Press, 1992).

Coltman, Viccy, *Fabricating the Antique: Neoclassicism in Britain, 1760–1800* (Chicago: University of Chicago Press, 2006).

Cooper, Anthony Ashley, *Characteristicks of men, manners, opinions, times*, vol. 3 (London: J. Darby, 1723).

Coutu, Joan, *Then and Now: Collecting and Classicism in Eighteenth-Century England* (Montreal and Kingston: McGill-Queen's University Press, 2015).

Cox, Jeffrey N., *Poetry and Politics in the Cockney School: Keats, Shelley, Hunt and their Circle* (Cambridge: Cambridge University Press, 1998).

Crais, Clifton, and Pamela Scully, *Sara Baartman and the Hottentot Venus: A Ghost Story and a Biography* (Princeton and Oxford: Princeton University Press, 2010).

Craske, Matthew, *Art in Europe 1700–1830: A History of the Visual Arts in an Era of Unprecedented Economic Growth* (Oxford: Oxford University Press, 1997).

——, "Model Making and Anti-Competitive Practices in the Late Eighteenth-Century London Sculpure Trade," riha *Journal* 87 (2014): http://www.riha-journal.org/articles/2014/2014-jan-mar/special-issue-art-design-history/craske-model-making.

——, "Reviving the School of Phidias: The Invention of a National School of Sculpture in Britain (1780–1830)," *Visual Culture in Britain* 7/2 (2006), 24–46.

Croft-Murray, Edward, *Decorative Painting in England 1537–1837*, vol. 2 (London: Country Life, 1970).

Crow, Thomas, review of *Chains: David, Canova, and the Fall of the Public Hero in Postrevolutionary France*, by Satish Padiyar, *Journal of Modern History* 81/3 (2009), 686.

Cumberland, George, *The Captive of the Castle of Sennaar* (London: Egerton, 1798).

——, *Thoughts on Outline, Sculpture, and the System that Guided the Ancient Artists in Composing Their Figures and Groupes* (London: W. Wilson, 1796).

Cummings, Frederick, "B. R. Haydon and his School," *Journal of the Warburg and Courtauld Institutes* 26/3–4 (1963), 367–80.

Cunningham, Allan, *The Life of Sir David Wilkie*, vol. 2 (London: John Murray, 1843).

——, *The Lives of the Most Eminent British Painters and Sculptors*, vol. 3 (London: John Murray, 1830).

Dallaway, James, *Anecdotes of the Arts in England* (London: T. Cadell & W. Davies, 1800).

Davis, Lucy, and Mark Hallett (eds.), *Joshua Reynolds: Experiments in Paint* (London: Paul Holberton, 2015).

Davis, Whitney, "Eternal Moment: Pater on the Temporality of the Classical Ideal in Art," in Charles Martindale, Stefano Evangelista, and Elizabeth Prettejohn (eds.), *Pater the Classicist: Classical Scholarship, Reception and Aestheticism* (Oxford: Oxford University Press, 2017), 81–100.

——, *Queer Beauty: Sexuality and Aesthetics from Winckelmann to Freud and Beyond* (New York: Columbia University Press, 2010).

Davy, John (ed.), *Fragmentary Remains, literary and scientific, of Sir Humphry Davy, Bart.* (London: John Churchill, 1858).

Dempsey, Charles, *The Early Renaissance and Vernacular Culture* (Cambridge, Mass.: Harvard University Press, 2012).

Denison, Cara, et al., *From Mantegna to Picasso: Drawings from the Thaw Collection at the Pierpont Morgan Library, New York* (London: Royal Academy, 1997).

Dias, Rosie, "Colour, Effect and the Formation of an English School of Painting," in Peter Humphrey (ed.), *The Reception of Titian in Britain: From Reynolds to Ruskin* (Turnhout: Brepols, 2013).

——, "Venetian Secrets: Benjamin West and the Contexts of Colour at the Royal Academy," in Sarah Monks, John Barrell, and Mark Hallett (eds.), *Living with the Royal Academy: Artistic

Ideals and Experiences in England, 1768–1848 (Farnham: Ashgate, 2013), 111–30.

DIJKSTRA, Bram, *Idols of Perversity: Fantasies of Feminine Evil in Fin-de-Siècle Culture* (New York and Oxford: Oxford University Press, 1986).

DITCHFIELD, G. M., *George III: An Essay on Monarchy* (Basingstoke: Palgrave Macmillan, 2002).

DOUGLAS, Mary, *Purity and Pleasure* (London: Routledge & Kegan Paul, 1980).

DRAPER, James David, et al., *Playing with Fire: European Terracotta Models, 1740–1840* (New Haven and London: Yale University Press, 2003).

DRESSER, Madge, "Set in Stone? Statues and Slavery in London," *History Workshop Journal* 64/1 (2007), 162–99.

DU FRESNOY, Charles Alphonse, *Art of Painting, with annotations by Joshua Reynolds*, trans. William Mason (York: A. Ward, 1783).

DUPPA, Richard, *The Life of Michael Angelo Buonaroti* (London: Longman, Hurst, Rees, Orme, and Brown, 1816).

DUPUY, Marie-Anne, Isabelle Le Masne de Chermont, and Elaine Williamson (eds.), *Vivant Denon, Directeur des Musées sous le Consulat et l'Empire: Correspondance (1802–1815)*, vol. 1 (Paris: Éd. de la Réunion des musées nationaux, 1999).

EASTLAKE, Elizabeth, *Life of John Gibson, R.A., Sculptor* (London: Longmans, Green and Co., 1870).

EBENSTEIN, Joanna, "Ode to an Anatomical Venus," *Women's Studies Quarterly* 40/3–4 (2012), 346–52.

EDWARDS, Jason, *Alfred Gilbert's Aestheticism: Gilbert amongst Whistler, Wilde, Leighton, Pater and Burne-Jones* (London: Routledge, 2016).

——, "By Abstraction Brings Forth Ideal Beauty? The 'Real Academy' and John Gibson's Anglo-Roman Modernity," in Sarah Monks, John Barrell, and Mark Hallett (eds.), *Living with the Royal Academy: Artistic Ideals and Experiences in England, 1768–1848* (Farnham: Ashgate, 2013), 195–220.

——, "Introduction: Sculpture Victorious? The British School and the Problems of Periodisation," in Jason Edwards and Sarah Burnage (eds.), *The British School of Sculpture, c. 1760–1832* (London and New York: Routledge, 2017), 1–20.

——, "John Charles Felix Rossi's Cornwallis monument (1807–11) and the Colonial-Cosmopolitanism of the British School," in Jason Edwards and Sarah Burnage (eds.), *The British School of Sculpture, c. 1760–1832* (London and New York: Routledge, 2017), 188–209.

EDWARDS, Paul, and James Walvin, *Black Personalities in the Era of the Slave Trade* (London and Basingstoke: Macmillan Press, 1983).

EGREMONT, Max, "The 3rd Earl of Egremont and his Friends," *Apollo* 122 (1985), 280–87.

ERDMAN, David, *Blake: Prophet Against Empire* (New York: Dover Publications, 2013).

—— (ed.), *The Complete Poetry and Prose of William Blake* (Berkeley, Los Angeles, and London: University of California Press, 2008).

ESDAILE, Katharine Ada, *English Monumental Sculpture since the Renaissance* (New York: Hyperion Press, 1979).

EVANGELISTA, Stefano, *British Aestheticism and Ancient Greece* (Basingstoke: Palgrave Macmillan, 2009).

EVERSON, Jane E., "From Dante to Dante Sonata," in Antonella Braida and Luisa Calé (eds.), *Dante on View: The Reception of Dante in the Visual and Performing Arts* (Aldershot: Ashgate, 2007).

FARR, Dennis, *William Etty* (London: Routledge & Kegan Paul, 1958).

FERANDO, Christina, "'Plasmati dalle sue mani': Canova's Touch and the Gipsoteca of Possagno," in Andrew Graciano (ed.), *Exhibiting Outside the Academy, Salon and Biennial, 1775–1999: Alternative Venues for Display* (Farnham: Ashgate, 2015), 111–30.

FERNOW, Karl Ludwig, *Über den Bildhauer Canova und dessen Werke* (Zurich: Heinrich Gessner, 1806).

FERRARO, Robert, "Before Rome: John Gibson and the British School of Art," in Jason Edwards and Sarah Burnage (eds.), *The British School of Sculpture, c. 1760–1832* (London and New York: Routledge, 2017), 126–45.

FINDEN, William, *Finden's Gallery of the Graces* (London: Charles Tilt, 1834).

FLAXMAN, John, *The Classical Compositions of John Flaxman, R.A.* (London: Bell and Daldy, 1870).

——, *Compositions from the Tragedies of Aeschylus* (London: Seeley, Jackson, & Halliday, 1879).

——, *Lectures on Sculpture*, 2nd edn. (London: Henry G. Bohn, 1838).

Foot, M.R.D., *The Gladstone Diaries*, vol. 1 (Oxford: Clarendon Press, 1968).

Frasca Rath, Anna, and Annette Wickham, *John Gibson: A British Sculptor in Rome* (London: Royal Academy of Arts, 2016).

Friedman, Terry, and Timothy Stevens (eds.), *Joseph Gott, 1786–1860, Sculptor* (Leeds and Liverpool: Lund Humphries, 1972).

Frye, W. E., *After Waterloo: Reminiscences of European Travel 1815–1819* (London: William Heinemann, 1908).

Fryer, Edward (ed.), *The Works of James Barry*, 2 vols. (London: T. Cadell & W. Davies, 1809).

Gard, Greta, "Toward a Queer Ecofeminism," in Bonnie Kime Scott, Susan E. Cayleff, Anne Donadey, and Irene Lara (eds.), *Women in Culture: An Intersectional Anthology for Gender and Women's Studies* (Chichester: Wiley Blackwell, 2017), 323–34.

Gardiner, Marguerite (Countess of Blessington) (ed.), *Heath's Book of Beauty* (London: J. Moyes, 1835).

Gargett, Graham, *Voltaire and Protestantism* (Oxford: Voltaire Foudation at the Taylor Institution, 1980).

Garlick, Kenneth, and Angus Macintyre (eds.), *The Diary of Joseph Farington*, 16 vols. (New Haven and London: Yale University Press, 1979).

Gastel, Joris van, *Il Marmo Spirante: Sculpture and Experience in Seventeenth Century Rome* (Leiden: Leiden University Press, 2012).

Ghelardi, Maurizio, "Lo sviluppo del pittorico nei rilievi di Ghiberti: Un seminario inedito di Aby Warburg," in Klaus Bergdolt and Giorgio Bonsanti (eds.), *Opere e giorni: Studi su mille anni di arte europea dedicati a Max Seidel* (Venice: Marsilio, 2007), 741–8.

Gilchrist, Alexander, *Life of William Blake* (London: Macmillan & Co., 1863).

——, *Life of William Etty, RA*, 2 vols. (London: David Bogue, 1855).

Gilman, Sander, "Black Bodies, White Bodies: Toward an Iconography of Female Sexuality in Late Nineteenth Century Art, Medicine and Literature," *Critical Inquiry* 12/1 (1985), 204–42.

Gilroy-Ware, Cora, "Antonio Canova and the Whatever Body," *Open Library of Humanities* 3/1 (2017), 2.

——, "William Etty's Female Nude with a Cast of the *Venus de' Medici*: Corporeal Possibilities beyond the 'Graceful Bend,'" in Joanna Selbourne (ed.), *Life, Legend, Landscape: Victorian Drawings and Watercolors* (London: Paul Holberton Books, 2011).

Godwin, William, *Enquiry Concerning Political Justice*, vol. 2 (London: G. G. & J. Robinson, 1798).

——, *History of Greece: From the earliest records of that country to the time in which it was reduced to a Roman province* (London: Baldwin & Craddock, 1828).

—— (ed.), *Memoirs and Posthumous Works of Mary Wollstonecraft Godwin* (London: Joseph Johnson, 1798).

——, [writing as Edward Baldwin], *The Pantheon, or Ancient History of the Gods of Greece and Rome* (London: M. J. Godwin, 1809).

Goellnicht, Donald C., *The Poet-Physician: Keats and Medical Science* (Pittsburgh: University of Pittsburgh Press, 1984).

Goethe, Johann Wolfgang von, *Italian Journey (1786–1788)*, trans. W. H. Auden and Elizabeth Mayer (Harmondsworth: Penguin, 1970).

Gombrich, Ernst Hans, *Aby Warburg: An Intellectual Biography* (London: Phaidon, 1986).

Goodrich, F. B., *The Court of Napoleon* (New York: Derby & Jackson, 1857).

Grasskamp, Walter, "The De-Nazification of Nazi Art: Arno Breker and Albert Speer Today," in Brandon Taylor and Wilfred van der Will (eds.), *The Nazification of Art: Art, Design, Music, Architecture and Film in the Third Reich* (Winchester: Winchester Press, 1990).

Greenberg, Clement, "The Avant-Garde and the Kitsch," in Gillo Dorfles (ed.), *Kitsch: An Anthology of Bad Taste* (Milan: Gabriele Mazzotta, 1968), 116–26.

Grigsby, Darcy Grimaldo, "Nudity à la grecque in 1799," *Art Bulletin* 80/2 (1998), 311–35.

Groseclose, Barbara, *British Sculpture and the Company Raj: Church Monuments and Public Statuary in Madras, Calcutta, and Bombay to 1858* (London: Associated University Press, 1995).

Grosz, Elizabeth, *Volatile Bodies: Toward a Corporeal Feminism* (Bloomington and Indianapolis: Indiana University Press, 1994).

Halévy, Élie, *England in 1815* (London: Ernest Benn, 1949).

Hamilton, William Richard, *Memorandum on the Subject of the Earl of Elgin's Pursuits in Greece* (London: William Miller, 1811).

Han, Byung-Chul, *Saving Beauty* (Cambridge: Polity Press, 2018).

Hardy, Thomas, *Jude the Obscure* (London: Macmillan & Co., 1951).

Harloe, Katherine, "Pausanias as Historian in Winckelmann's History," *Classical Receptions Journal* 2/2 (2010), 174–96.

——, *Winckelmann and the Invention of Antiquity: History and Aesthetics in the Age of Altertumswissenschaft* (Oxford: Oxford University Press, 2013).

Haskins, Katherine, *The Art Journal and Fine Art Publishing in Victorian England* (Abingdon: Taylor & Francis, 2016).

Hatt, Michael, "Physical Culture: The Male Nude and Sculpture in Late Victorian Britain," in Elizabeth Prettejohn (ed.), *After the Pre-Raphaelites: Art and Aestheticism in Victorian England* (Manchester: Manchester University Press, 1999), 240–56.

Haydon, Benjamin Robert, *Correspondence and Table-Talk*, 2 vols. (London: Chatto and Windus, 1876).

——, *Lectures on Painting and Design* (London: Longman, Brown, Green, and Longmans, 1846).

Hayley, William, *An Essay on Sculpture: In a series of epistles to John Flaxman, Esq.* RA (London: T. Cadell, 1800).

Hazlitt, William, *Conversations of James Northcote, Esq.*, RA (London: Henry Colburn and Richard Bentley, 1830).

——, *Criticisms on Art* (London: John Templeman, 1843).

——, *Criticisms on Art*, second series (London: C. Templeman, 1844).

——, *Notes of a Journey through France and Italy* (London: Hunt and Clarke, 1826).

——, *Sketches of the Principal Picture-Galleries in England* (London: Taylor and Hessey, 1824).

Hegel, Georg Wilhelm Friedrich, *The Philosophy of History*, trans. J. Sibree (New York: Dover Publications, 1956).

Higgins, David, "Art, Genius, and Racial Theory in the Early Nineteenth Century: Benjamin Robert Haydon," *History Workshop Journal* 58 (2004), 24–5.

Hilles, Frederick W. (ed.), *Portraits by Sir Joshua Reynolds* (London: Heinemann, 1952).

Hobsbawm, E. J., *The Labouring Men: Studies in the History of Labour* (London: Weidenfeld and Nicolson, 1964).

Hogarth, William, *The Analysis of Beauty: Written with a view of fixing the fluctuating ideas of taste* (London: W. Strahan, 1772).

Holman Hunt, William, *Pre-Raphaelitism and the Pre-Raphaelite Brotherhood*, vol. 1 (New York and London: Macmillan & Co., 1905).

Honour, Hugh, "Antonio Canova and the Anglo-Romans, Part 1: The First Visit to Rome," *Connoisseur* 143 (1959a), 241–5.

——, "Antonio Canova and the Anglo-Romans, Part 2: The First Years in Rome," *Connoisseur* 144 (1959b), 225–3.

——, "Canova and David," *Apollo* 96 (1972), 312–17.

——, "Canova's Statues of Venus," *Burlington Magazine* 114/835 (1972), 658–71.

——, "English Patrons and Italian Sculptors in the First Half of the Eighteenth Century," *Connoisseur* 141 (1958), 220–26.

——, *The Image of the Black in Western Art*, vol. 4 (Cambridge, Mass.: Harvard University Press, 1989).

——, *Neo-classicism: Style and Civilization* (Harmondsworth: Penguin, 1968).

Hoock, Holger, *Empires of the Imagination: Politics, War and the Arts in the British World* (London: Profile Books, 2010).

Horne, Richard, *A New Spirit of the Age*, vol. 1 (New York: Harper & Brothers, 1844).

Howard, Henry, *A Course of Lectures on Painting delivered at the Royal Academy of Arts* (London: Henry G. Bohn, 1848).

Hughes, Eleanor, "Smoke and Marble: Thomas Banks's Monument to Captain George Blagdon Westcott," in Jason Edwards and Sarah Burnage (eds.), *The British School of Sculpture, c. 1760–1832* (London and New York: Routledge, 2017), 163–87.

HUMPHREYS, Rob, "The City/St. Paul's Cathedral," in *The Rough Guide to London* (Rough Guides, e-book, 2012).

HUNNISETT, Basil, *Steel-Engraved Book Illustration in England* (Boston: David R. Godine, 1980).

HUNT, Leigh, *The Autobiography of Leigh Hunt*, vol.2 (London: Smith, Elder & Co., 1870).

HUNT, Lynn, *Politics, Culture, Class in the French Revolution* (Berkeley, Los Angeles, and London: University of California Press, 2004).

HUSSERL, Edmund, *The Phenomenology of Internal Time-Consciousness*, trans. James Churchill (London and Bloomington: Indiana University Press, 1964).

IRWIN, David, *Neoclassicism* (London: Phaidon, 1997).

—— (ed.), *Winckelmann: Writings on Art* (New York: Phaidon, 1972).

JACK, Ian, *Keats and the Mirror of Art* (Oxford: Clarendon Press, 1967).

JAMESON, Anna, *Handbook to the Public Galleries of Art in and Near London* (London: J. Murray, 1842).

JOHNS, Christopher M. S., *Antonio Canova and the Politics of Patronage in Revolutionary and Napoleonic Europe* (Berkeley, Los Angeles, and London: University of California Press, 1998).

JORDAN, Caroline Patricia, "Edward Hodges Baily (1788–1867) and the Notion of Poetic Sculpture c. 1800–1845" (PhD thesis, University of Leeds, 2007).

JORDAN, Winthrop, *White Over Black: American Attitudes toward the Negro* (Chapel Hill: University of North Carolina Press, 1968).

JORDANOVA, Ludmilla, *Sexual Visions: Images of Gender in Science and Medicine between the Eighteenth and Twentieth Centuries* (Madison: University of Wisconsin Press, 1989).

JOUSE, J., *Jouse's Pocket Dictionary of Italian, French and English Musical Terms* (London: D'Alaime & Co., 1837).

KEATS, John, *Hyperion: A Facsimile of Keats's Autograph Manuscript with a Transliteration of the Manuscript of The Fall of Hyperion, a Dream* (Oxford: Clarendon Press, 1905).

——, *Lamia, Isabella, the Eve of St. Agnes and Other Poems* (London: Taylor and Hessey, 1820).

KENWORTHY-BROWNE, John, "A Ducal Patron of Sculpture," *Apollo* 105 (1977), 322–31.

——, "The Third Earl of Egremond and Neoclassical Sculpture," *Apollo* 105 (1977), 367–75.

KNIGHT, Richard Payne, *Specimens of Ancient Sculpture, Ægyptian, Etruscan, Greek, and Roman: Selected from Different Collections in Great Britain* (London: T. Bensley, 1809).

KNOWLES, John (ed.), *The Life and Writings of Henry Fuseli*, vol. 3 (London: Henry Colburn and Richard Bentley, 1831).

KURTZ, Donna, *The Reception of Classical Art in Britain: An Oxford Story of Plaster Casts from the Antique* (Oxford: Archaeopress, 2000).

KWASNY, Melissa (ed.), *Toward the Open Field: Poets on the Art of Poetry 1800–1950* (Middletown: Weslyan University Press, 2004).

LANDOR, Walter Savage, *The Last Fruit off an Old Tree* (London: Edward Moxon, 1853).

LANGE-BERNDT, Petra, "Introduction: How to be Complicit with Materials," in Petra Lange-Berndt (ed.), *Materiality* (Cambridge, Mass.: MIT Press, 2015), 12–20.

LARRABEE, Stephen A., *English Bards and Grecian Marbles: The Relationship between Sculpture and Poetry especially in the Romantic Period* (Port Washington: Kennikat Press, 1964).

LEDBETTER, Kathryn, *British Victorian Women's Periodicals: Beauty, Civilization, and Poetry* (Basingstoke: Palgrave Macmillan, 2009).

——, *Tennyson and Victorian Periodicals: Commodities in Context* (London: Routledge, 2016).

LEMPRIÈRE, John, *Classical Dictionary* (Dublin: William M'Kenzie, 1792).

Lettere di pittori e scrittori Italiani (from the collection of the Countess of Cigonara) (Venice: G. Passeri Bragadin, 1844).

LEVI-STRAUSS, Claude, *The Savage Mind* (Chicago: University of Chicago Press, 1966).

LLOYD, Gareth, "Repression and Resistance: Wesleyan Female Public Ministry in the Generation after 1791," *Proceedings of the Wesley Historical Society* 55/3 (2005), 101–14.

LOH, Maria, *Titian Remade: Repetition and the Transformation of Early Modern Italian Art* (Los Angeles: Getty Research Institute, 2007).

LONG, Edward, *The History of Jamaica, or, General Survey of the Antient and Modern State of that Island*, vol. 2 (London: T. Lowndes, 1774).

LOUGH, John, and Elizabeth Merson, *John Graham Lough: A Northumbrian Sculptor* (Woodbridge and Wolfeboro: Boydell Press, 1987).

LUBEY, Kathleen, *Excitable Imaginations: Eroticism and Reading in Britain, 1660–1760* (Lewisburg, Penn.: Bucknell University Press, 2012).

ŁUCZYŃSKA-HOŁDYS, Małgorzata, *Soft-Shed Kisses: Re-visioning the Femme Fatale in English Poetry of the 19th Century* (Cambridge: Cambridge Scholars Publishing, 2013).

LUGO-ORTIZ, Agnes, and Angela Rosenthal, "Introduction: Envisioning Slave Portraiture," in Agnes Lugo-Ortiz and Angela Rosenthal (eds.), *Slave Portraiture in the Atlantic World* (New York and Cambridge: Cambridge University Press, 2013), 1–40.

MACAULAY, Alistair, "Spring: Ashton's Symphonic Variations in America," in Alexandra Carter, Jens Giersdorf, and Yutian Wong (eds.), *The Routledge Dance Studies Reader* (London: Routledge, 1998), 113–18.

MCEVANSONEYA, Philip, "Lord Egremont and Flaxman's 'St Michael Overcoming Satan,'" *Burlington Magazine* 143/1179 (2001), 351–9.

MACFARLAND, Thomas, *The Masks of Keats: The Endeavour of a Poet* (Oxford: Oxford University Press, 2000).

MCFEE, Graham, and Alan Tomlinson, "Riefenstahl's Olympia: Ideology and Aesthetics in the Shaping of the Aryan Athletic Body," *International Journal of the History of Sport* 16/2 (1999), 86–106.

MACK, Phyllis, *Heart Religion in the British Enlightenment: Gender and Emotion in Early Methodism* (Cambridge: Cambridge University Press, 2008).

MACSOTAY, Tomas, "Autonomy and Marginality in Foreign Artists' Circles in Rome," in Frank O'Gorman and Lia Guerra (eds.), *The Centre and the Margins in Eighteenth-Century British and Italian Cultures* (Newcastle: Cambridge Scholars Publishing, 2013), 155–72.

MAFFESOLI, Michel, *The Shadow of Dionysus: A Contribution to the Sociology of the Orgy*, trans. Cindy Linse and Mary Kristina Palmquist (Albany: State University of New York Press, 1993).

MARINDIN, George Eden (ed.), *The Letters of John B. S. Morritt of Rokeby: Descriptive Journeys in Europe and Asia Minor in the Years 1794–1796* (Cambridge: Cambridge University Press, 2012).

MARTINDALE, Charles, Stefano Evangelista, and Elizabeth Prettejohn (eds.), *Pater the Classicist: Classical Scholarship, Reception and Aestheticism* (Oxford: Oxford University Press, 2017).

MARTINI, Pietro, *Studi intorno il Correggio* (Parma: F. Carmignani, 1865).

MARX, Karl, "Der 18te Brumiare des Louis Napoleon," *Die Revolution* (1852), in Karl Marx and Friedrich Engels, *Werke*, vol. 8 (Berlin: Dietz Verlag, 1960).

MATTHEWS, Antje, "John Russell's Mysterious Moon," *Proceedings of the Wesley Historical Society*" 55/6 (2006), 252–8.

MATTHEWS, T., *The Biography of John Gibson, R.A., Sculptor, Rome* (London: William Heinemann, 1911).

MEIJER, Miriam Claude, *Race and Aesthetics in the Anthropology of Petrus Camper (1772–1789)* (Amsterdam and Atlanta: Rodopi, 1999).

MENGS, Anton Raphael, *The Works of Antony Raphael Mengs* (London: R. Faulder, 1796).

MESSENGER, Michael Frederick, *Coalport 1795–1926: An Introduction to the History and Porcelains of John Rose and Company* (Woodbridge: Antique Collectors Club, 1995).

MILNES, Richard Monkton, *Life, Letters and Literary Remains of John Keats*, vol. 2 (London: Edward Moxton, 1848).

MISSIRINI, Melchior, *Della vita di Antonio Canova*, vol. 1 (Milan: Nicolò Bettoni, 1824).

MOORE, Thomas (ed.), *Lord Byron: Childe Harold's Pilgrimage* (Philadelphia: Henry Carey Baird, 1854).

MORRIS, Edward, *French Art in Nineteenth-Century Britain* (New Haven and London: Paul Mellon Centre for Studies in British Art by Yale University Press, 2005).

MYRONE, Martin, *Bodybuilding: Reforming Masculinities in British Art* (New Haven and London: Yale University Press, 2005).

——, *Henry Fuseli* (London: Tate Publishing, 2001).

——, "'Something Too Academical': The Problem with Etty," in Sarah Burnage, Mark Hallett, and Laura Turner (eds.), *William Etty: Art & Controversy* (London: Philip Wilson in association with York Museums Trust, 2011), 47–59.

——, "William Etty: 'A Child of the Royal Academy,'" in Sarah Monks, John Barrell, and Mark Hallett (eds.), *Living with the Royal Academy: Artistic Ideals and Experiences in England, 1768–1848* (Farnham: Ashgate, 2013), 171–94.

Napoleon and Canova: Eight Conversations Held at the Chateau of the Tuileries, in 1810 (London: Treuttel and Wurtz, Treuttel, jun., and Richter, 1825).

Neasham, Geo, *North-Country Sketches: Notes, Essays and Reviews* (Durham: Thos. Caldcleugh, 1893).

Neer, Richard, *The Emergence of the Classical Style in Greek Sculpture* (Chicago and London: University of Chicago Press, 2010).

Norman, Mark, and Richard Cook, "'Just a tiny bit of rouge upon the lips and cheeks': Canova, Colour and the Classical Ideal," in Katharine Eustace (ed.), *Antonio Canova: Ideal Heads* (Oxford: Ashmolean Museum, 1997).

Northcote, James *The Life of Sir Joshua Reynolds*, 2 vols. (London, Henry Colburn, 1819).

Ockman, Carol, *Ingres's Eroticized Bodies: Retracing the Serpentine Line* (New Haven and London: Yale University Press, 1995).

Oswald, Alice, *Memorial* (London: Faber & Faber, 2011).

Outshoorn, Joyce, Radka Dudová, Ana Prata, and Lenita Freidenvall, "Women's Movements and Bodily Integrity," in Joyce Outshoorn (ed.), *European Women's Movements and Body Politics: The Struggle for Autonomy* (Basingstoke: Palgrave Macmillan, 2016), 153–77.

Padiyar, Satish, *Chains: David, Canova, and the Fall of the Public Hero in Postrevolutionary France* (University Park: Pennsylvania State University Press, 2007).

——, "Crisis? What Crisis?," *Art History* 21/2 (1998), 272–8.

Paine, Thomas, *Rights of Man: Part the Second* (London: J. S. Jordan, 1792).

Palgrave, Francis Turner, *Descriptive Handbook to the Fine Art Collections in the International Exhibition of 1862* (London and Cambridge: Macmillan & Co., 1862).

Panofsky, Dora, and Erwin Panofsky, *Pandora's Box: The Changing Aspects of a Mythical Symbol*, 2nd edn. (New York: Harper & Row, 1965).

Pater, Walter, *Greek Studies: A Series of Essays* (Honolulu: University of the Pacific, 2002).

——, *The Renaissance: Studies in Art and Poetry* [1893 text] (Berkeley, Los Angeles, and London: University of California Press, 1980).

Peacock, Thomas Love, *Headlong Hall* (London: T. Hookham, Jun. and Co., 1816).

The Penny Cyclopedia, vol. 3 (London: Charles Knight, 1835).

Pevsner, Nikolaus, *London: The Cities of London and Westminster* (London: Penguin, 1962).

Plato, *Phaedrus*, trans. R. Hackforth (Cambridge: Cambridge University Press, 1997).

Plumly, Stanley, "The Odes for their Own Sake," *Kenyon Review* 33/4 (2011), 161–6.

Pointon, Marcia, *Milton & English Art: A Study in the Pictorial Artist's Use of a Literary Source* (Manchester: Manchester University Press, 1970).

——, *Portrayal and the Search for Identity* (London: Reaktion, 2013).

Pop, Andrei, *Antiquity, Theatre, and the Painting of Henry Fuseli* (Oxford: Oxford University Press, 2015).

Pope, Alexander, *The Iliad of Homer*, vol. 6 (London: H. Baldwin, 1796).

Pope, William Bissell (ed.), *The Diary of Benjamin Robert Haydon*, 5 vols. (Cambridge, Mass.: Harvard University Press, 1960).

Postle, Martin (ed.), *Model and Supermodel: The Artist's Model in British Art and Culture* (Manchester: Manchester University Press, 2007).

Potts, Alex, *Flesh and the Ideal: Winckelmann and the Origins of Art History* (New Haven and London: Yale University Press, 1994).

——, "Greek Sculpture and Roman Copies I: Anton Raphael Mengs and the Eighteenth Century," *Journal of the Warburg and Courtauld Institutes* 43 (1980), 150–73.

——, *The Sculptural Imagination: Figurative, Modernist, Minimalist* (New Haven and London: Yale University Press, 2000).

Pratt, Josiah (ed.), *The Works of Richard Cecil*, vol. 1 (London: L. B. Seeley, 1816).

Praz, Mario, "Canova: Ice and Eros," *Art News Annual* 29 (1964), 122–8, 154–7.

——, *On Neoclassicism*, trans. Angus Davidson (London: Thames and Hudson, 1969).

Prettejohn, Elizabeth, *Modern Painters, Old Masters: The Art of Imitation from the Pre-Raphaelites to the First World War* (New Haven and London: Paul Mellon Centre for Studies in British Art by Yale University Press, 2017).

——, *The Modernity of Ancient Sculpture: Greek Sculpture and Modern Art from Winckelmann to Picasso* (London and New York: I. B. Tauris, 2012).

——, "Walter Pater and Aesthetic Painting," in Elizabeth Prettejohn (ed.), *After the Pre-Raphaelites: Art and Aestheticism in Victorian England* (Manchester: Manchester University Press, 1999), 36–58.

Raynor, Vivien, "The Best of the 'Pompiers' at the Atheneum," *New York Times*, November 4, 1984: http://www.nytimes.com/1984/11/04/nyregion/art-best-of-the-pompiers-at-the-atheneum.html.

Reichardt, Rolf, and Hubertus Kohle, *Visualizing the Revolution: Politics and Pictorial Arts in Late Eighteenth-Century France* (London: Reaktion, 2008).

Reynolds, Joshua, *The Works of Sir Joshua Reynolds, Knight*, vol. 2 (London: T. Cadell, junior, and W. Davis, 1798).

Richardson, J. (ed.), *The Works of Jonathan Richardson* (Twickenham: Strawberry Hill, 1792).

Roberts, R. Ellis, *Samuel Rogers and his Circle* (London: Methuen & Co., 1910).

Robinson, Dwight E., "Ode on a 'New Etrurian' Urn," *Keats-Shelley Journal* 7 (1963), 11–35.

——, "A Question of the Imprint of Wedgwood in the Longer Poems of Keats," *Keats-Shelley Journal* 16 (1967), 22–8.

Robinson, Leonard, *William Etty: The Life and Art* (Jefferson and London: Macfarland & Company, 2007).

Rollins, Hyder Edward (ed.), *The Letters of John Keats 1814–1821*, 2 vols (Cambridge: Cambridge University Press, 1958).

Rosenblum, Robert, *Transformations in Late Eighteenth Century Art* (Princeton: Princeton University Press, 1970).

Rosenthal, Angela, "Visceral Culture: Blushing and the Legibility of Whiteness in Eighteenth Century British Portraiture," *Art History* 27/4 (2004), 563–92.

Rousseau, George S., *Nervous Acts: Essays on Literature, Culture and Sensibility* (London: Palgrave Macmillan, 2004).

Sadler, Thomas (ed.), *Diary, Reminiscences and Correspondence of Henry Crabb Robinson* (Boston: Houghton, Mifflin & Co., 1869).

Sarafianos, Aris, "B. R. Haydon and Racial Science: The Politics of the Human Figure and the Art Profession in the Early Nineteenth Century," *Visual Culture in Britain* 7/1 (2006), 79–106.

——, "Hyporborean Meterologies of Culture: Art's Progress and Medical Environmentalism in Arbuthnot, Burke and Barry," in Koen Vemeir and Michael Funk Deckard (eds.), *The Science of Sensibility: Reading Burke's Philosophical Enquiry* (London and New York: Springer Dordrecht Heidelberg, 2012), 69–90.

Scholz, Susanne, *Body Narratives: Writing the Nation and Fashioning the Subject in Early Modern England* (Basingstoke: Palgrave Macmillan, 2000).

Scobie, Alex, *Hitler's State Architecture: The Impact of Classical Antiquity* (University Park and London: Pennsylvania State University Press, 1990).

Sennett, Richard, *Flesh and Stone: The Body and the City in Western Civilization* (New York and London: W. W. Norton & Company, 1994).

Sharp, William, *The Life and Letters of Joseph Severn* (London: Sampson, Low, Marston & Company, 1892).

Shelley, Percy B., *Hellas: A Lyrical Drama* (London: Charles and James Ollier Vere Street, 1822).

Sherlock, Martin, *Letters from an English Traveller*, vol. 2 (London: J. Nichols, T. Cadell, P. Elmsley, H. Payne, and N. Conant, 1781).

Sicca, Cinzia, and Alison Yarrington, *The Lustrous Trade: Material Culture and the History of Sculpture in England and Italy c. 1700–c. 1860*

(London and New York: Leicester University Press, 2000).

SIDOROV, Alexei, "An Art that Promotes Friendship," *News: A Review of World Events* 17/52 (1953), 28–9.

SIMON, Lawrence H. (ed.), *Karl Marx: Selected Writings* (Cambridge and Indianapolis: Hackett Publishing, 1994).

SMITH, Alison, *The Victorian Nude: Sexuality, Morality and Art* (Manchester: Manchester University Press, 1996).

SMITH, J. T., *Nollekens and his Times* (London: Richard Bentley and Son, 1895).

SOLOMON-GODEAU, Abigail, *Male Trouble: A Crisis in Representation* (London: Thames and Hudson, 1997).

SONTAG, Susan, "Fascinating Fascism," *New York Times* (February 6, 1975): http://www.nybooks.com/articles/1975/02/06/fascinating-fascism/.

SPENCE, Joseph, *Polymetis* (London: J. Dodsley, 1774).

STEAD, Henry, "Swinish Classics; or a Conservative Clash with Cockney Culture," in Henry Stead and Edith Hall (eds.), *Greek and Roman Classics in the British Struggle for Social Reform* (London: Bloomsbury, 2015), 55–78.

STEFANI, Ottorino, *Canova pittore* (Milan: Electa, 1992).

STUART, James, and Nicholas Revett, *The Antiquities of Athens and Other Monuments of Greece* (London: Henry G. Bohn, 1858).

SULLIVAN, M. G., "Cunningham, Chantrey, and the British School of Sculpture," in Jason Edwards and Sarah Burnage (eds.), *The British School of Sculpture, c. 1760–1832* (London and New York: Routledge, 2017), 210–32.

SYMMONS, Julia Sarah, *Flaxman and Europe: The Outline Illustrations and their Influence* (New York and London: Garland Publishing, 1984).

TALLEY, M. Kirby, Jr., "'All good pictures crack': Sir Joshua Reynolds's Practice and Studio," in Nicholas Penny (ed.), *Reynolds* (New York: Abrams, 1986), 55–70.

TAYLOR, Thomas, *The Fable of Cupid and Psyche* (London: printed for the author, 1795).

—— (published anonymously), *A Vindication of the Rights of Brutes* (London: printed for the author, 1792).

TAYLOR, Tom (ed.), *Life of Benjamin Robert Haydon, historical painter, from his Autobiography and Journals*, 2 vols. (New York: Harper & Brothers, 1853).

TEGG, Thomas, *Tegg's Prime Song Book, Bang up to the Mark!* (London: printed for the author, 1810).

THEWELEIT, Klaus, *Male Fantasies*, vol. 1 (Minneapolis: University of Minnesota Press, 2003).

THOMPSON, E. P., "Time, Work-Discipline, and Industrial Capitalism," *Past & Present* 38 (1967), 55–97.

THORNBURY, George Walter, *The Life of J.M.W. Turner*, 2 vols. (London: Hurst and Blackett, 1862).

TOOKE, Andrew, *The Pantheon, Representing the Fabulous Histories of the Heathen Gods and Most Illustrious Heroes* (London: Charles Harper, 1709).

TOOKE, John Horne, *Diversions of Purley*, part 1, 2nd edn. (London: Joseph Johnson, 1798).

TURPIN, John, *John Hogan: Irish Neoclassical Sculptor in Rome, 1800–1858* (Leinster: Irish Academic Press, 1982).

UPHAM, Thomas Cogswell, *Elements of Mental Philosophy, embracing the two departments of the Intellect and the Sensibilities*, vol. 2 (Portland: William Hyde, 1839).

VALHORA, Karen, *Austen's Oughts: Judgement after Locke and Shaftesbury* (Newark: University of Delaware Press, 2010).

VASARI, Giorgio, *Le Vite de' piu eccellenti pittori scultori ed architettori*, vol. 4 (Florence: G. C. Sansoni, 1879).

VAUGHAN, William, "'David's Brickdust' and the Rise of the British School," in Alison Yarrington and Kelvin Everest (eds.), *Reflections of Revolution: Images of Romanticism* (London and New York: Routledge, 1993), 134–58.

WALKER, Alexander, *Beauty: Illustrated chiefly by an analysis and classification of beauty in women* (London: Henry G. Bohn, 1846).

WALSH, Linda, "'Crushing Infamy': The Revolutionary Sculpture of Joseph Chinard," *Journal for Eighteenth-Century Studies* 26/1 (2003), 109–28.

WALSH, Thomas, "The Whole Armour of God: A Sermon," *Magazine of the Wesleyan Methodist Church* (August 1799), 427.

Warburg, Aby, *The Renewal of Pagan Antiquity*, trans. David Britt (Los Angeles: Getty Research Institute, 1999).

Wark, Robert R. (ed.), *Discourses on Art: Sir Joshua Reynolds* (London: Paul Mellon Centre for Studies in British Art, 1997).

Warner, Marina, *Monuments and Maidens: The Allegory of the Female Form* (Berkeley: University of California Press, 1985).

Watts, Alaric A. (ed.), *The Cabinet of Modern Art and Literary Souvenir*, vol. 1 (London: Whittaker & Co., 1835).

——, *The Cabinet of Modern Art and Literary Souvenir*, vol. 2 (London: Whittaker & Co., 1836).

——, *The Cabinet of Modern Art and Literary Souvenir*, vol. 3 (London: Whittaker & Co., 1837).

——, *Lyrics of the Heart, with Other Poems* (London: Longman, Brown, Green, and Longmans, 1851).

——, *The New Year's Gift and Juvenile Souvenir* (London: Longman, Rees, Orme, Brown, and Green, 1830).

—— (ed.), *Londiniana: Or Reminiscences of the British Metropolis*, vol. 3 (London, Hurst, Chance, and Co., 1828).

Whinney, Margaret, *English Sculpture 1720–1830* (London: Victoria and Albert Museum, 1971).

——, "Flaxman and the Eighteenth Century: A Commemorative Lecture," *Journal of the Warburg and Courtauld Institutes* 19/3–4 (1956), 269–82.

——, *Sculpture in Britain 1530–1830* (New Haven and London: Yale University Press, 1992).

White, Charles, *An Account of the Regular Gradation in Man, and in Different Animals and Vegetables* (London: C. Dilly, 1799).

White, Keith D., *John Keats and the Loss of Romantic Innocence* (Amsterdam and Atlanta: Rodopi, 1996).

Whitlock, Gillian, *Postcolonial Life Narratives: Testimonial Transactions* (Oxford: Oxford University Press, 2015).

Wilkes, John (ed.), *Encyclopaedia Londinensis*, vol. 8 (London: J. Alard, 1815).

Winckelmann, Johann Joachim, *Geschichte der Kunst des Alterthums* (Dresden: in der Waltherischen Hof-Buchandlung, 1764).

——, *The History of Ancient Art Among the Greeks*, trans. G. Henry Lodge (London: John Chapman, 1850).

——, *History of the Art of Antiquity*, trans. Harry Francis Mallgrave (Los Angeles: Getty Research Institute, 2006).

——, *Reflections on the Painting and Sculpture of the Greeks*, trans. Henry Fuseli (London: printed for the translator, 1765).

Wittkower, R., "Bernini Studies – I: The Group of Neptune and Triton," *Burlington Magazine* 94 (1952), 68–76.

Wollstonecraft, Mary, *A Vindication of the Rights of Woman with Strictures on Political and Moral Subjects* (Dublin: J. Stockdale, 1793).

Wornum, Ralph N. (ed.), *Lectures on Painting by the Royal Academicians Barry, Opie and Fuseli* (London: Henry G. Bohn, 1848).

Wright, Alison E., "In the Spirit: Flaxman and Swedenborg," in David Bindman (ed.), *John Flaxman 1755–1826: Master of the Purest Line* (London: Sir John Soane's Museum and University College, 2003), 17–24.

Yarrington, Alison, "Art in the Dark: Viewing and Exhibiting Sculpture at Somerset House," in David H. Solkin (ed.), *Art On the Line: The Royal Academy Exhibitions at Somerset House 1780–1836* (New Haven and London: Yale University Press, 2001).

——, *The Commemoration of the Hero, 1800–1864: Monuments to the British Victors of the Napoleonic Wars* (New York: Garland, 1988).

——, "The Poetics of Sculpture: Pedestal, Verse and Inscription," in Alexandra Gerstein (ed.), *Display and Displacement: Sculpture and the Pedestal from Renaissance to Post-Modern* (London: Paul Holberton, 2007), 73–96.

Yarrington, Alison, and Nigel Wood, "Ut Sculptura Poesis: English Romantic Poetry and Sculptural Form," in Thomas Frangenberg (ed.), *Poetry on Art: Renaissance to Romanticism* (Donington: Shaun Tyas, 2003), 215–35.

Yorke, James, *Lancaster House: London's Greatest Town House* (London: Merrell, 2001).

Zobi, A., *Storia civile della Toscana dal MDCCXXVII al MDCCCXLVIII*, vol. 3 (Florence: Luigi Molini, 1851).

PHOTOGRAPH CREDITS

© The Samuel Courtauld Trust, the Courtauld Gallery, London: 1, 3, 69.

© Victoria and Albert Museum, London: 2, 32, 33, 61, 104, 110.

© Francis Ware courtesy of St. Paul's Cathedral: 4, 9, 10, 11, 12, 13, 15, 17, 27, 51, 52.

© Regan Vercruysse: 5.

© Galerie Nazionali di Arte Antica: 6.

© Historic England Archive: 7, 71.

© British Library, London: 8, 30, 44, 53, 60.

© National Archives, Kew: 14, 24.

© Royal Academy of Arts, London: 16, 26, 34, 36, 37, 38, 39, 40, 41, 45, 46, 49, 63.

© Getty Images: 18, 47, 67, 80, 89, 96.

© Tate, London 2019: 19, 73, 85, 86, 115.

© The Trustees of the British Museum, London: 20, 28, 31, 35, 43, 50, 58, 62, 64, 65, 74, 75, 76, 81, 82, 83, 92.

© Irène Andréani/Musée Carnavalet/Roger-Viollet: 21, 22.

© Musée Carnavalet/Roger-Viollet: 23.

© National Portrait Gallery, London: 25, 29.

© Conway Library, Courtauld Institute of Art: 42.

© Warburg Institute, University of London: 48.

© Fredrik Nilsen courtesy of the Huntington Art Collections, San Marino, California: 54.

© The Morgan Library & Museum, New York: 55.

© Lytham St Annes Art Collection, Fylde Borough Council: 56.

© Lewis Bush / Sir John Soane's Museum, London: 57.

© Francis Ware courtesy of Petworth House: 59.

© Galleria Bazzanti Florence: 66.

© Russell-Cotes Art Gallery & Museum: 68.

© Andy Johnson / Sir John Soane's Museum, London: 70.

© Bristol Culture (Bristol Museum and Art Gallery): 72, 103.

© New York Public Library: 77.

© Yale Center for British Art: 78, 84, 105, 113.

© National Gallery, London: 79.

© Istituto Luce Cinecittà: 87.

© DACS 2019: 88.

© Dean and Chapter of Westminster: 90, 91.

© University of Pennsylvania Art Collection, Philadelphia, Pennsylvania: 93.

© The Devonshire Collections, Chatsworth: 94, 95, 114.

© Andrew Featherston / National Trust: 98.

© Dennis Gilbert / Bridgeman Images: 99.

© Alexander Lavrentyev / The State Hermitage Museum: 100.

© Alamy Limited: 101.

© Metropolitan Museum of Art: 102, 109.

© Woburn Abbey: 106.

© Fitzwilliam Museum, Cambridge: 107.

© Essie Sakhai: 108.

© M. S. Rau Antiques, New Orleans: 111.

© The Huntington Art Collections, San Marino, California: 112.

© Sotheby's Inc. 2012: 116.

© Amgueddfa Cymru: 117

INDEX

Page numbers in *italics* indicate illustrations